Financial and Monetary Integration
in the New Europe

To Max Fry

Financial and Monetary Integration in the New Europe

Convergence between the EU and Central and Eastern Europe

Edited by

David G. Dickinson

Director of Money, Banking and Finance and Senior Lecturer, Department of Economics, University of Birmingham, UK

and

Andrew W. Mullineux

Professor of Money and Banking, University of Birmingham, UK

Edward Elgar
Cheltenham, UK • Northampton, MA, USA

Published by
Edward Elgar Publishing Limited
Glensanda House
Montpellier Parade
Cheltenham
Glos GL50 1UA
UK

Edward Elgar Publishing, Inc.
136 West Street
Suite 202
Northampton
Massachusetts 01060
USA

A catalogue record for this book
is available from the British Library

Library of Congress Cataloguing in Publication Data

Financial and monetary integration in the new Europe: convergence between the
EU and Central and Eastern Europe/edited by David G. Dickinson and
Andrew W. Mullineux.
        p. cm.
    Papers from a workshop held in Jurmala, Latvia (July 1998) and a conference
    in Bordeaux, France (April 1999)
    Includes index.
    1. Finance—Europe, Eastern—Congresses. 2. Monetary policy—Europe,
    Eastern—Congresses. 3. Foreign exchange—Europe, Eastern—Congresses.
    4. European Union—Europe, Eastern—Congresses. 5. Europe—Economic
    integration—Congresses. I. Dickinson, David G. II. Mullineux, A.W.

HG186.E82 F565 2001
337.1'42—dc21   00–067341

ISBN 1 84064 2467

Typeset by Cambrian Typesetters, Frimley, Surrey
Printed and bound in Great Britain by MPG Books Ltd, Bodmin, Cornwall

Contents

Figures

Tables

Contributors

Dr Juda Agung   Central Bank of Indonesia and Department of Economics, University of Birmingham, UK.

Jean-Baptiste Desquilbet   GDR, Economié Monétaire et Financier, Université d'Orleans, France.

Dr David G. Dickinson   Department of Economics, University of Birmingham, UK.

Professor Maxwell J. Fry   Business School, University of Birmingham, UK.

Professor Eric Girardin   CEDERS, Université de la Méditerranée, Aix-Marseille 2, France.

Céline Gondat-Larralde   Financial Services Authority and Department of Economics, University of Birmingham, UK.

Daniel Goyeau   GRIEF, Université de Poitiers, France.

Boguslaw Grabowski   Institute of Economics, University of Lodż, Poland.

Nicholas Horsewood   Department of Economics, University of Birmingham, UK.

Tatiana Houbenova   Institute of Economics, Sofia, Bulgaria.

Miroslav Hrnčíř   Council of Advisors, Czech National Bank, Prague, Czech Republic.

Salomėja Jasinskaitė   New Economy Institute, Vilnius, Lithuania.

Laetitia Lepetit   CRMM, Université de Limoges, France.

Roman Matoušek   Institute of Economics, Czech National Bank, Prague, Czech Republic.

Rasa Melnikienė   New Economy Institute, Vilnius, Lithuania.

Professor Andrew W. Mullineux   Department of Economics, University of Birmingham, UK.

Professor Victor Murinde   Department of Accounting and Finance, University of Birmingham, UK, and IDPM, University of Manchester, UK.

Dr Jerzy Pruski   Institute of Economics, University of Lodž, Poland.

Dr Andrzej Raczko   Institute of Economics, University of Lodž, Poland.

Professor Alain Sauviat   CRMM, Université de Limoges, France.

Dr Kateřina Šmídková   Council of Advisors, Czech National Bank, Prague, Czech Republic.

Professor Inna Šteinbuka   International Monetary Fund and University of Latvia, Latvia.

Dr Douglas Sutherland   Organization for Economic Cooperation and Development, Paris, France.

Professor Amine Tarazi   CRMM, Université de Limoges, France.

Dalia Vidickienė   New Economy Institute, Vilnius, Lithuania.

Preface and acknowledgements

This book contains chapters written by a team of researchers working on Project Number P96-6159-R sponsored by the European Commission's PHARE (ACE) programme. We are very grateful to the European Union for the financial support provided.

The team was led by Professor Maxwell J. Fry (Business School, University of Birmingham), who, due to severe illness, was unable to join us at the workshop in Jurmala, Latvia (July 1998) or the Conference in Bordeaux (April 1999) at which the papers were presented. Energetic as ever, however, Max was able to make a substantial contribution to this volume.

The workshop was excellently organized by Inna Šteinbuka (Department of Economics, University of Latvia).

The conference was a great success, for which we thank the organizers, Sandrine Robert (Department of Economics, University of Montesquieu, Bordeaux) and Eric Girardin (ex Bordeaux, now CEDERS, Université de la Méditerranée, Aix-Marseille 2).

Finally, thanks are due to Jo Quarry, Samantha McCauley and Margaret Ball (Department of Economics Office, University of Birmingham) who helped at various stages to prepare the typescript for submission, and to the invaluable assistance provided by the editors and the rest of the team at the publishers, Edward Elgar.

Regretfully, Max did not live long enough to see this volume in print. We dedicate this volume to his memory.

1. Financial integration between the EU and the economies of Central and Eastern Europe: an overview

David G. Dickinson and Andrew W. Mullineux

INTRODUCTION

The development of the financial sector and its implications for economic growth and the conduct of macroeconomic policy is an issue of major concern for the Central and Eastern European (CEE) countries as they negotiate the terms of their membership of the European Union (EU). This introduction reports work carried out by a team of researchers in both the EU and Central and Eastern Europe which forms the basis for the remaining chapters. It contains analysis of a number of key issues related to the financial sector. The broad themes addressed are: the conduct of monetary policy and the exchange rate regime during a period of financial liberalization; and the impact of increasing convergence of the financial systems of the CEE countries with those in the EU.

BACKGROUND

This section briefly reviews the economic and policy-making background from which CEE countries are moving on towards EU membership. Overall the transition economies of Central and Eastern Europe have made great strides in their economic transformation towards market-based economies. Following the early stage transition recessions, most have experienced significant economic growth, although at least some of this will come from the quality and range of goods on offer rather than from increased production. As reported by Šteinbuka (Chapter 6, Table 6.2) we may observe, for example, that during the 1993–97 period, the Czech Republic experienced growth in GDP per capita (at current prices and exchange rates) of about 65 per cent, in Poland above 60 per cent and Latvia over 180 per cent. Hungary, as the most developed economy at the start of the transition has grown more modestly while Bulgaria experienced the problems associated with its failure to stabilize the financial sector and the economy until 1997. There is clear evidence of catching-up taking place in the transition economies. Despite this the gap between EU and CEE economies in terms of GDP per capita is still very large, as reported in Šteinbuka (Table 6.1) where we may observe that the Czech Republic (which is the richest of the transition economies) is still below 50 per cent of the EU average, while Hungary and Poland are below 40 per cent of that average. Perhaps more useful is to compare the CEE economies with economies like Portugal or Greece. Here the catching-up required is much more achievable and potentially can take place quite rapidly.

The dynamic behaviour of the CEE economies during their transition process has varied across the different countries although the basic features have been quite similar. In particular we have seen an output fall at the start of the transition followed by rapid growth. For example, Lithuania (see Jasinskaitė et al., Chapter 7, Table 7.1) saw a drop in output of 16.2 per cent in 1993 and a further decline of 9.8 per cent in 1994 but during the 1995–98 period, growth has been positive and recently strong. Alternatively Poland (Grabowski and Pruski, Chapter 9, Table 9.1) had its large output falls in 1990 and 1991 and since then has been growing and is now the strongest performer of all the transition economies. The Czech Republic, however, has fallen from its position of being the most successful of the transition economies (see Šmídková, Chapter 4, Table 4.1). An issue we shall take up later is the reason for this and what it tells us about the future.

As we have noted, all the transition economies studied in the project had to adopt stabilization packages at the start of their economic reform process. The Czech Republic has been consistently the most stable in terms of inflation performance although, as noted, this reputation has recently been somewhat undermined following the collapse of the fixed exchange rate in 1997 (Šmídková, Table 4.1). Poland has experienced the reverse case with persistent moderate inflation although declining now to low double-digit levels (Grabowski and Pruski, Table 9.1). The situation for the Baltic states, as reported by Šteinbuka, shows a similar decline over time with maintenance of single-digit inflation for Latvia and Lithuania in 1997 and 1998. Hence there is a degree of macroeconomic stability which may be associated with improved real economic performance (although the structural reforms which have taken place are also crucial). In this regard, the experience of Bulgaria, which took several years to attempt a proper stabilization package and has moved rather slowly on structural reforms, has been a further example of the latter's importance (see Houbenova, Chapter 8 for commentary on this). Thus we have a current period in which the transition economies are in relatively robust economic health (their emergence relatively unscathed from the various financial crises around the world, including that of

Russia in 1998, is evidence of this) and where structural reforms have brought dividends to the real economy.

This study considers the impact of closer integration of financial sectors in CEE countries and those of the EU. Thus we shall now briefly review the developments which have taken place in the financial sector to provide the background to our later analysis. The financial sector of the transition economies can be characterized as bank dominated. This is despite mass privatization programmes and the resulting establishment of stock markets, and reflects in part the underdevelopment of capital markets and of non-bank financial intermediaries, particularly investments and investors. The creation of private health and pension schemes will provide an alternative, more market-based mechanism for channelling funds from savers to borrowers. Poland has the most ambitious pension reform programme to date. The actual structure of the banking sector has been quite variable over time. The picture painted by Matoušek (Chapter 16, Table 16.1) for the Czech Republic is one of increasing consolidation and concentration of power (see Matoušek, Table 16.2). While this is a reflection of financial problems within the sector, it is also a trend observed in other more developed banking systems. It is also worth noting that generally the CEE countries have opened their banking sector fully to foreign competition. While this is partly a response to the lack of well-functioning domestic banks, it also indicates a recognition that banking is fast becoming a global market. In the case of Poland, Raczko (Chapter 15) provides detailed discussion of the development of the foreign bank sector. Recent take-overs, and large participations acquired through privatizations of state-owned commercial banks, of domestic banks by foreign banks have furthered the trend towards increasing the penetration of the foreign banks into the Polish market. One important aspect of Poland's approach to foreign banks has been to avoid unnecessary regulation to stifle product innovation. This, of course, is a major welfare gain from allowing foreign banks into the domestic market; along with the transfer of skills, and know-how and enhancement of capital and governance through strategic foreign bank investment.

One feature of the banking sector during transition has been a continuing bad-loan problem. This is perhaps a natural consequence of the learning process which banks needed to operate successfully in the market economy, as well as a reflection of the riskiness of business in a rapidly changing environment. From a policy maker's point of view it did imply that it was important to get bank regulation right. Although the transition economies have made great strides in this respect there is still more work to be done (as we shall discuss later). In addition, the performance of the banking sector, particularly in respect of bad loans, has placed considerable strains on the supervisory authorities and reduced confidence.

The importance of the banking sector has, to some extent, reflected the inability of capital markets to provide effective competition. Stock markets have been noted for their volatility, lack of liquidity and transparency, and their failure to become an important source of funds for investment. As has been indicated, this situation is now changing for the better. But the experience of the transition economies shows that it takes time for savers and borrowers to become used to new institutional environments and that institutional evolution naturally takes time. Furthermore, the relative lack of experience has created some institutional anomalies. For example, we may observe that the concentration of power in the hand of 'mutual funds' in the Czech Republic, which then had a close relationship with banks, created circumstances under which the corporate governance role of financial markets was seriously compromised.

To summarize, we have a situation where policy-makers have generally been able to stabilize the economy through various mechanisms while failing to deal fully with limitations in the financial sector. It is this environment which the transition economies bring into the future. There are still significant policy choices to be made and much institution building is still to be carried out. These are the issues which have been explored in the research for this project and to which we now turn.

MONETARY AND EXCHANGE RATE POLICY

This section considers a number of interrelated issues. We shall examine the possible monetary policy strategies which the transition economies could follow in the immediate future as they continue on their path to EU membership, particularly in the context of the Maastricht criteria. One issue of particular interest is financial convergence (in the sense of increasing integration of transition economies' financial sectors with those of the EU) and the impact this has on capital flows into and out of the transition economies. The implications for monetary policy choices is of special concern. We also look further into the future and examine the possibilities for membership of the European Monetary Union (EMU).

To begin, however, we shall first discuss broadly the impact of monetary policy choices on economic development in the transition economies. Fry (Chapter 2) has considered this aspect in some detail. In particular he highlights the importance of institutional features such as central bank independence and its effect on the reaction of the economy to monetary policy. For many developing countries the issue is one of avoiding monetary creation in the financing of the fiscal deficit. Although the CEE transition economies have not been particularly guilty in this respect (Fry observes that CEE economies have modelled the legal status of their central banks along the lines of the

Bundesbank), the credibility associated with central bank independence, allied to a strong nominal anchor, such as an exchange rate peg, has been a successful institutional framework for achieving macroeconomic stability. Fry argues that the most successful central banks (in terms of maintaining monetary control) are those which exist in economies where fiscal discipline is maintained. In economies where fiscal deficits are excessively large, it is impossible for monetary policy to be independent. He also points out that there is a tension between the central bank and the government in that the more transparent monetary policy is (through, say, a monetary policy committee), the greater the possibility of running a stable monetary policy and maintaining fiscal discipline. To summarize therefore, we should expect that appropriate monetary policy requires a clear delineation between the responsibilities of the central bank and government. The more transparent are the relationships and the clearer is the policy-making process, the more credible the policy will be.

It is interesting to interpret these observations in the context of the conduct of monetary policy in the Czech Republic, which is the focus of chapters by Šmídková (Chapter 4), Hrnčíř and Šmídková (Chapter 3) and Girardin and Horsewood (Chapter 5). We have already observed in the previous section that the Czech Republic has been notable for its running of monetary policy, even though there have been significant recent difficulties following the destabilization of its exchange rate in 1997. Hrnčíř and Šmídková discuss the outcome of the currency crisis which hit the Czech Republic in 1997. This led to a move from exchange rate targeting to inflation targeting. Prior to the currency crisis, monetary policy was guided by an exchange rate peg with a secondary target of a band for monetary growth. This policy was remarkably successful in the early stages of the transition process, even though Czechoslovakia split into two countries. Hrnčíř and Šmídková acknowledge that the two intermediate targets created some confusion, but it seems that the exchange rate peg was paramount. Certainly a monetary target is unreliable in times of major structural change and financial reform such as that being experienced by the transition economies. Hence the problems with monetary policy when the peg collapsed under a speculative attack. We shall refer back to the problems of a pegged exchange rate for small open economies at a later stage. For now we shall consider why the Czech Republic's switch to inflation targeting has been relatively successful.

First, it is clear that the Czech National Bank rapidly developed a considerable reputation for managing monetary policy very effectively. Second, they took the decision to be as transparent as possible in operating the new regime. It is interesting to note that the lack of a nominal anchor during the immediate post-crisis period did create a rise in inflationary expectations and wages settlements negotiated, as evidenced by a rise in inflation in early 1998. Once the inflation target was established, it gained credibility quickly. As is well known, an advantage of the inflation target is the flexibility it allows to respond to recessionary forces in contrast to an exchange rate target. Consequently other transition economies may wish to consider inflation as an alternative to their current monetary policy targets. The experience of the Czech Republic has been that a high reputation is not lost if the process of switching policy is conducted as transparently as possible. Note also that Hrnčíř and Šmídková point out the importance of fiscal discipline, which has been holding in the Czech Republic despite various political crises. Furthermore, they highlight that in setting the inflation target they have opted for short- and medium-run targets, the former to bring inflationary expectations down quickly, and the latter to ensure that they stay down.

In a companion study (Chapter 4), Šmídková uses the fundamental equilibrium exchange rate (FEER) methodology and applies it to the pre- and post-currency crisis periods. She recognizes that defining the FEER for a transition economy is not straightforward since it will be affected by structural changes. Of course one can use purchasing power parity (PPP), but this ignores the possibility that a country may be prepared to experience a trade imbalance if it is sustainable. However, the danger then is that the FEER is a function of a policy target which is not well defined. For both PPP and FEER approaches she finds significant overvaluation of the Czech koruna prior to the onset of the currency crisis. A further issue raised relates to the impact of privatization proceeds on individual wealth and the pattern of aggregate demand. This is an issue which other transition economies need to recognize in setting targets for exchange rates as a monetary policy objective. Finally, it is pointed out that external shocks can have a major impact on the sustainability of an exchange rate target.

The chapter by Girardin and Horsewood (Chapter 5) is somewhat more speculative in that it considers empirical evidence as to how the Czech economy has responded to the shift from an exchange rate to an inflation target. They point out the difficulty of finding a nominal anchor when an economy is undergoing major structural changes. Their analysis of the switch from exchange rate to monetary targeting is consistent with the discussion in Hrnčíř and Šmídková. Girardin and Horsewood find that there is evidence that the exchange rate target was less of a blunt instrument than is normally assumed since it took the form of a band which allowed a more flexible response to output and trade shifts than would be the case in a pure pegged regime. However, they do not find any significant effect of the widening of bands in 1996; in other words the policy of widening the bands was to deal with foreign exchange market turbulence rather than to give the monetary authorities more flexibility. Their (preliminary) analysis of the post-crisis inflation target period indicates that the adoption of the inflation target did influence wage/price expectations and the new regime appears to be operating in a reasonably predictable way. Hence they regard the Czech case as an example of a smooth transition from one policy regime to another, although, as noted in the previous section, output growth has been depressed in the attempt to re-establish monetary control. The growth recession in the Czech case may, however, reflect the impact of inadequate structural reform, to which we return later.

Beyond the recent experience of the Czech Republic, a second set of studies report, in part, the experience of other transition economies (Poland, Bulgaria, Latvia and Lithuania) with regard to monetary policy and the impact of capital flows. It is important to note at the outset that these economies have mainly adopted a liberalized capital account so that capital can flow freely into and out of domestic financial markets. Policy towards the exchange rate regime has been variable, however. Thus Latvia has maintained a pegged exchange rate (against the Deutschmark (DM), Lithuania has adopted a currency board (although, as we shall discuss below, the current issue is how to exit from this arrangement) while Bulgaria has also adopted a currency board in a successful but belated effort to achieve macroeconomic stability, and Poland has operated a crawling peg system (against a basket of currencies) for most of its transition.

Šteinbuka (Chapter 6) notes that Latvia has been experiencing increasing current account deficits as a result of an investment boom (financed mainly by foreign-direct investment (FDI) inflows). As long as this investment is productive, then the position may be sustainable. The exchange rate regime is also crucial to the sustainability of the situation. If there are significant capital inflows, a deteriorating current account position and a failure of investment to deliver real growth, then the exchange rate will ultimately have to adjust to correct the situation. Another issue is the extent to which the capital inflows will continue. As Šteinbuka points out, the privatization process may be a significant factor in encouraging these capital inflows. In this case they may be a short-run phenomena and Latvia would therefore expect some slow-down or even a reversal in the future. In this case, again, there may come a point where the exchange rate will have to adjust. Hence there is the potential for the current pegged exchange rate regime to come under pressure. However, it is comforting to note that Latvia has emerged relatively unscathed, in terms of speculative attacks on its currency, from the Russian crisis and hence there may be time to adjust to shocks which may cause sudden reversals of the current capital inflows (for example, an upward movement in world interest rates). But, as Šteinbuka also notes, it is important to ensure that there is a balance between monetary and fiscal policy since monetary policy actions are restricted by the fiscal policy stance (for example, requiring interest rates to be higher than would otherwise be desirable where fiscal deficits are large). If this imbalance persists for any length of time strains are likely to appear which may threaten the maintenance of the exchange rate regime.

Šteinbuka also points out the importance of maintaining an economic climate which is attractive to foreign portfolios and/or direct investors. She envisages a switch to portfolio investment and within this category she sees a growing role for debt-type capital inflows into Latvia. This may well create a more volatile basis for capital flows which will need to be carefully monitored and for pre-emptive policy action to be taken if developments are unfavourable. Šteinbuka indicates that one way of reducing volatility of capital flows is to ensure a stable growth path for the economy. It is also important to maintain and improve regulation of the financial sector. A third aspect highlighted is to encourage the development of a greater level of domestic savings to reduce reliance on capital inflows (although she notes that this does not mean that capital inflows will not take place). These last two aspects are issues which are taken up in the next section.

It is interesting to compare the situation in Latvia with that in Lithuania. Jasinskaitė et al. (Chapter 7) provide an analysis of recent monetary policy actions in Lithuania as well as a look ahead to the prospects for the pre-EU accession period. Lithuania switched to a currency board in 1994 following unsuccessful attempts to stabilize the economy under flexible exchange rates at the start of the transition period. As is the case for other countries which have adopted this policy, a currency board has been successful in achieving monetary control and the consequent reduction in inflation. Jasinskaitė et al. provide a detailed analysis of the way in which the currency board provided a solid basis on which to achieve stabilization.

However, the existence of a currency board in Lithuania raises a series of issues about future policy choices and, indeed, the possible need to exit from a currency board arrangement at some stage in the near future. As Jasinskaitė et al. discuss, the other transition economies using a currency board (Bulgaria and Estonia) may view matters differently, but a number of issues arise which need consideration. Thus it would appear that a currency board with the exchange rate pegged against the DM (or the euro) is one possible strategy which transition economies could follow. Currently, Estonia and Bulgaria have this in place. However, the current policy in Lithuania is to abandon the currency board arrangement. This may be because the Lithuanian currency is pegged to the US dollar, which is clearly not consistent with its membership of EMU. An alternative strategy which could be followed in Lithuania is to maintain the currency board but convert to a DM peg. Jasinskaitė et al. provide reasons why this is not the chosen policy.

Membership of EMU requires countries to have properly functioning central banks with appropriate market-based methods of monetary control. Since membership of the EU may require some commitment to EMU then these policy options must be available. In addition, there are a number of disadvantages of the currency board arrangement: the difficulty of dealing with banking crises through lender-of-last-resort interventions; the lack of flexibility of a currency board in the face of adverse real shocks; the difficulty of dealing with volatile capital inflows; the impact of capital inflows on current account deficits; and the issue of the sustainability of such deficits (Although it is notable that Lithuania has done rather poorly in respect of FDI, flows have, however, increased in the recent past, ironically during a time when the policy has become one of dismantling the currency board system).

Thus the central bank of Lithuania has announced a phased withdrawal from the currency board arrangement. How this is to be done practically is not clear at this time and the confusion over the exact procedure highlights the potential problems of introducing a currency board in the first place. We have already noted the importance of making monetary policy transparent, and this also applies to major structural changes. While a currency board may facilitate stabilization of the macroeconomy, a great deal of uncertainty may be created following a decision to abandon it. Jasinskaitė et al. summarize the need to develop a proper monetary policy with clearly defined targets and goals, and appropriate policy instruments. As is indicated, one possible strategy is to switch from a pure currency board system to a pegged exchange rate and for the central bank to be given the necessary, market-based, control over interest rates. Note that the central bank has already achieved influence through repo operations and Lombard rates. However, there is the danger that the abandonment of the currency board will be seen as reducing the credibility of the pegged exchange rate and consequently the main impact will be to leave the central bank with a currency crisis. These are thus issues which need to be considered in determining the exact timing and nature of the process of abandoning a currency board. However, one possible bulwark which the central bank can use to make the procedure more open is the need to meet Maastricht criteria. Hence the overall stance of monetary policy could be set in terms of meeting the exchange rate stability, inflation, fiscal deficit and government debt criteria within a particular time frame and tying the move towards a more flexible monetary policy arrangement.

The experience of Bulgaria with its currency board is documented in Houbenova (Chapter 8). This is an economy which illustrates the benefits of adopting a currency board system. Prior to the onset of the banking and foreign exchange crisis in late 1996, the Bulgarian economy lacked any semblance of macroeconomic stability. As a result its real economy has suffered. The only way to correct an institutional environment in which bank enterprises and government were inextricably linked was to take monetary control outside of the domestic economy. Thus the currency board regime was implemented. It should be recognized that, in addition to its stabilization properties, the currency board also requires a sound banking and financial system.

Hence the improvement in regulation of the banking system which Houbenova points to is a crucial part of the success of the current strategy.

Houbenova discusses particularly the sustainability of the currency board system. She presents detailed discussion of the operation of the currency board system in Bulgaria. Note that there is no single model for a currency board and Bulgaria has adopted one which is restrictive in terms of the flexibility given to the monetary authorities. Hence the issue of sustainability involves two considerations. First, does the operation of the system provide enough discretion for the path of money supply to promote continued economic growth? Second, is there a necessity to consider replacement of the current system with something more flexible at some stage in the future? In answering the first question, Houbenova argues that the current situation is sustainable in that monetary growth is consistent with the overall economic climate, both in terms of ensuring real economic growth and having flexibility to deal with any problems which may occur in the banking sector. However, she suggests that possible instability in the demand for money, which is a product of structural reform, may create difficulties in the medium term. Further critical issues which will affect the stability of the currency board are: the fiscal stance and the ability of the government to finance its deficit through monetary creation; the impact of the currency board on the stability of the banking system; and the overall development of the financial system. Houbenova considers each of these issues in detail. With regard to the first issue, there is some doubt whether fiscal policy has an impact on monetary creation. For the banking system, it may be observed that confidence in it is still low even though its overall condition has improved. Finally, development of non-bank financial institutions and markets is a positive aspect, but does create problems in the context of generating instability in the demand for money.

Overall, Bulgaria has found that adoption of a currency board has been an important part of their new economic strategy. The necessary structural reforms are now taking place and the maintenance of fiscal discipline is also regarded as crucial. However, the experience of Lithuania shows that difficult choices will have to be made in the future once it is recognized that a more flexible method of monetary policy operation is required, for example, to deal with external developments (such as increased capital inflows) which have detrimental impacts on Bulgaria's trading position.

The long-term viability of pegged exchange rates and their currency board incarnations in transition and emerging market economies is thus questionable. The alternatives appear to be flexible exchange rate policies or participating in a monetary union. The latter, that is, membership of EMU, is some way off for the countries considered in this project, and so alternatives such as Poland's wide band crawling peg, need to be carefully considered once pegs or currency boards are abandoned.

Poland has become the most successful transition economy in Central and Eastern Europe. However, as pointed out by Grabowski and Pruski (Chapter 9), there are still policy dilemmas which need to be resolved. The particular one which forms the basis of their chapter is the effects of international capital movements in a situation where a transition economy is moving towards EU membership. The basic argument is that as Poland and other CEE transition economies achieve the sort of macroeconomic conditions associated with the Maastricht criteria they will become increasingly attractive for global (portfolio) investors. The impact of this has already been discussed in the case of the Czech Republic. The question is whether these experiences are likely to be repeated across the region, with the consequent instability and deteriorating real economic performance. In addition, it is likely that policy makers will face other dilemmas. In particular, the need for structural reform will inevitably require increasing government expenditure with the possibility of a rising fiscal deficit, possibly in contravention of one of the basic Maastricht criteria. Even if fiscal prudence is maintained there is a need to achieve a reduction in inflation, which may imply increased interest rates and consequent higher inflows of capital into domestic debt instruments. These factors work together to create a set of policy choices which ultimately will depend upon how quickly countries wish to join EMU, although membership of EMU may mitigate some of the effects of increased capital inflows. The recent experience in Poland has been similar to the earlier experiences of the Czech Republic and Latvia, namely an investment boom which has fuelled economic growth, partly financed by inflows of FDI. As a result there has been a significant and growing current account deficit covered by capital inflows, mainly from FDI with foreign portfolio investment being much more volatile. A tightening of monetary policy in 1997 has increased real interest rates significantly. However this has not had a major effect on demand growth. In response there was a tightening of fiscal policy. Allied to relatively weak world markets this encouraged a further significant inflow of capital. Grabowski and Pruski document how monetary policy has been redesigned around an inflation target with widening bands within which the exchange rate is allowed to fluctuate, and a reduction in the rate at which devaluation can take place through the crawling peg mechanism. Hence we have seen within the space of a year the adoption of a new monetary policy along the lines of the Czech Republic. As a result of these measures, interest rates have been brought down from 24 per cent to 13 per cent. Longer-term yields have followed suit, indicating that the new policy structure has credibility. Indeed, capital inflows during 1998 continued with further appreciation of the zloty. Although there has been a fall in aggregate demand growth, the current account deficit has stayed at high levels.

Grabowski and Pruski go on to consider further the effects of moving towards the EMU criteria. In terms of inflation rate, Poland has a significant way to go until the rate is reduced to EU levels. However, its government deficit is much closer to conforming with the EU's Stability Pact. But the process of meeting other (for example, social) EU requirements is likely to increase the fiscal deficit, so there may be conflicting policy options in the near future. In particular, Grabowski and Pruski point towards an imbalance between relatively loose fiscal policy and tight monetary policy pushing interest rates up, generating excessive capital inflows, and the real appreciation of the domestic currency. Their chapter also considers the other aspects of EU membership. Overall government debt is rather low and hence does not represent a problem. The need to follow ERM2 on accession (with bands of ±15 per cent) is not inconsistent with current policy and the bands are sufficiently wide to allow some flexible policy response to problems such as increased capital inflows. Finally, there is clearly a significant way to go before Poland can move to the average level of nominal interest rates in the EU. However, a significant reduction in real interest rates is likely to be one of the main outcomes of EU membership and hence the current position may be a very poor guide to the future.

Throughout their analysis, Grabowski and Pruski emphasize the potential destabilizing effects of international capital inflows. This is an issue which lies at the heart of an analysis of financial integration between EU and CEE economies. The Asian financial crisis provides a case study of how economies with relatively underdeveloped financial sectors can be affected by international capital flows. The chapter by Dickinson and Mullineux (Chapter 10) draws lessons from the Asian crisis for CEE economies. It argues that it was the inadequacies of the domestic financial structure which caused the problems. Hence the Asian financial crisis does not require CEE economies to be cautious about opening up their economies, and specifically their financial markets, to global competition, but rather to ensure that proper regulation of financial markets and institutions is in place. This is, of course, a message which has been registered previously. However, Dickinson and Mullineux emphasize the corporate governance aspects of financial markets as being crucial. Thus they argue that investment booms which the Asian economies experienced during the 1990s were, at least partly, the result of a failure of financial markets and institutions to exert appropriate control over firms' decisions. Consequently, excessive risks were taken and also objectives other than value maximization, such as sales growth, were inadvisably used to guide investment decisions. Thus the investment boom was unsustainable in the sense that it was never going to produce the returns necessary for it to be justifiable. When this is taken together with the fact that significant parts of the investment were financed with short-term bank loans denominated in foreign currency, then the makings of a financial crisis were clear.

What then are the lessons for CEE economies? Dickinson and Mullineux highlight the need to have proper financial sector regulation and suggest a number of features which would characterize a suitable system (note that the next section discusses regulation in much greater detail). In addition, they emphasize the importance of ensuring that financial markets fulfil their important governance role. This implies instituting policies which have recently gained greater prominence in developed economies. Examples are increasing the power of non-executive directors, promoting salary structures which encourage managers to maximize value rather than some other measure of performance, promoting widespread ownership of shares by protecting small shareholders while encouraging them and institutional shareholders to make their views known. Once again these issues will be considered in the next section. A clear lesson of the Asian financial sector crisis has been the difficulty of operating a pegged exchange rate regime when the domestic financial market is open to foreign capital flows. This is something which seems to have been taken on board by a number of CEE economies. We have highlighted the case of Poland and the Czech Republic. Clearly other countries will need to be aware of the difficulties which potentially lie ahead.

While much of the discussion so far has been in the context of the choices for monetary policy as CEE economies converge with the EU prior to accession to membership, a longer-term issue is the decision to join EMU. We have already highlighted some issues with regard to monetary policy operation during this pre-accession process. However, we can also consider the specific issue of membership of EMU. Grabowski and Pruski have pointed out the potentially long period of time which will be needed before countries like Poland will be able to consider joining the eurozone. Jasinskaitė et al. (Chapter 7) have also considered how exiting from a currency board may be a necessary precursor to such a decision. Dickinson and Desquilbet (Chapter 11) analyse the decision to join EMU by viewing it as an irreversible investment and argue that, by doing so, some new insights can be gained into this key decision.

The basic framework which Dickinson and Desquilbet use is as follows. The benefits of joining the EU come from increased trade opportunities and more importantly, from a reduction in real interest rates which will have important growth effects and hence in the long run will be much more significant. Membership of the EU will imply not only a higher growth rate, but also that output will follow a different stochastic process. The gains to be had from membership of EMU will be the present value of (long-run) output gains. The costs of membership will be the (short-run) output losses which will result from the need to bring the CEE economy into line with the criteria for joining the eurozone. These latter costs are essentially sunk-costs. In other words, once a country has started on the process of meeting the criteria the output losses are incurred and cannot be recovered. Viewing the decision in this way implies that the intuition of the irreversible investment literature is applicable. Thus if there is great uncertainty about the future stochastic benefits which will accrue (for example, because of macroeconomic shocks or because the financial sector is relatively underdeveloped) then it may be better for the policy makers to delay the decision to join. Dickinson and Desquilbet then argue that the current level of instability in the economy can be used as an indicator of the benefits and costs of membership of EMU. They argue that there are a number of alternative possibilities and as a result show that the decision to join is not clear-cut in the sense that the option value of waiting always dominates. As a consequence some low-volatility countries may prefer to stay out, while high-volatility countries will wish to join. Dickinson and Desquilbet then use these ideas to assess the current state of the argument in a number of the CEE accession countries.

To conclude this section we draw together the main lessons from the chapters discussed. There are three areas which have been considered:

1. the conduct of monetary policy within the CEE economies and current developments;
2. the future path of monetary policy, particularly with regard to choice of exchange rate regime; and
3. the decision which CEE economies will have to face at some stage about the adoption of the euro.

We shall take each of these in turn. There have been some significant shifts in monetary policy through the transition process. In the early stages, these have taken the form of searching for methods of achieving macro stability. In extreme cases this has involved adoption of currency boards. However, more recently stability has brought its own problems with surging levels of aggregate demand, an investment boom and increasing current account deficits financed by inflows of (possibly short-term) capital. Such a scenario led to abandonment of the (until then) successful Czech experiment with pegged exchange rates. As a result the Czech National Bank has now adopted inflation targeting with some success. Other economies have had different experiences. Thus Poland has also moved voluntarily towards an inflation target without any major currency crisis. Latvia maintains its pegged exchange rate regime, although it is now experiencing some of the symptoms previously displayed by the Czech Republic. Lithuania has announced that it is moving towards an exit from its currency board arrangement. Hence we seem to be moving to a rather mobile picture as the transition economies continue their preparations for membership of the EU. This is perhaps a natural consequence of the process since each economy has the same target but is coming to it from a very different situation. There is no reason to suppose that there is a single optimal way ('turnpike') of achieving the necessary conditions to qualify for membership of the EU, but it is natural that there will be an incentive to adopt more flexible policies so as to be able to react to the shocks which may occur.

The danger of excessive capital inflows destabilizing the economy (as in the extreme case of the South-East Asian economies) is a further incentive to keep policy adaptable for the foreseeable future. The experience of the previously highly successful South-East Asian economies also provides some pointers towards what the future may hold for policy. Continued use of a pegged exchange rate seems to fly in the face of the South-East Asian experience. The desire for a flexible policy, which will assist in the response to shocks which will inevitably occur in the future, is also inconsistent with a fixed exchange rate regime. Of course it can be argued that the only credible pegged exchange rate system is a currency board, but, as we have argued, this presents its own dangers in terms of its lack of flexibility. If the Czech and Polish experiments with inflation targeting continue to be successful, it should provide a good model for other transition economies to consider seriously.

A decision which lies someway ahead of the need to achieve the necessary conditions for membership of EU, is membership of the EMU. However, if it is true that the significant benefits from EU membership are partly tied to adoption of the euro, then we have a potential policy conflict. The previous discussion has indicated the desirability of giving policy flexibility in order to avoid the type of problems which have afflicted other parts of the world. However, if many of those problems were the consequence of poor regulation, then the picture becomes somewhat more encouraging. The decision to join the single European currency will require the exchange rate to be targeted against the euro, though initially with wide bands (±15 per cent) during the ERM2 phase. Consequently, participating countries would lose a great deal of their flexibility in monetary policy operation. One way of thinking about this issue is to view the decision to join as an irreversible investment. Thus increasing uncertainty about the future path of transition economy output under EMU would mean that the decision should be delayed. However, the analysis of a number of transition economies suggests that there is a lot of ground to be made up to get near the likely conditions for membership of the euro, and hence too much uncertainty at the moment for the decision to be made in the near future. Nevertheless, it is important to retain the option for this decision to be made.

FINANCIAL SECTOR DEVELOPMENT

The analysis of the previous section has highlighted that a problem with monetary policy operation is the impact of financial sector development. Hence a complementary analysis involves considering what sort of developments are taking place, and what their effects will be, on the financial systems of CEE economies as they converge with financial sector conditions in the EU. This is the issue to which we now turn.

Two chapters tackle issues relating to financial sector development from a broad perspective. Fry (Chapter 12) considers an issue which is very important in financial sector development. This is the preservation of financial stability. He points out that the early stages of transition were difficult periods for maintaining stability since there was a lack of appropriate expertise in regulation and bank management. Despite major improvements in this, some of the transition economies have performed better than others and there are still significant problems. Hence financial stability is a crucial issue during the process of liberalization which will accompany convergence of CEE economies to EU standards. Fry emphasizes how broadening the basis of the financial system to include a wide range of financial markets and institutions is one way of increasing the ability of the system to absorb shocks. The market for government debt is often a focus in the early stages of development. This is partly a method for moving away from the banking system as a source of funding of fiscal deficits. However, it is also important to promote the development of private sector usage of financial markets by, for example, privatizing funded pension provision and encouraging a greater degree of private insurance provision. The existence of such long-term saving institutions will also assist in the development of an efficient stock market. Once these markets and institutions are operating properly there will be the benefit in terms of competition to the banking sector. Hence there are spillover effects from development in one sector to another.

A second feature which Fry identifies is the problem of having inefficient regulation during a process of financial liberalization. Hence we may find that, rather than creating a more efficient allocation of capital, freeing up interest rates has the perverse effect of forcing borrowers who are already in financial distress to borrow even more to service their existing debts. The failure of banks to act against this trend reflects a lack of proper control over their actions. Ultimately, it indicates a failure of supervisory regulations. In an increasingly global financial marketplace the problems of supervision are growing. The recent experience of South-East Asia (see Dickinson and Mullineux, Chapter 10) has indicated that CEE economies need to be aware of the effects of increased debt inflows to finance domestic investment. However, these debt flows are more a symptom than a cause, which is rather the failure of regulation, supervision and corporate governance. Hence preserving financial stability requires these functions to be carried out effectively, and the updating of the regulatory system must keep pace with private sector innovation. It is also a matter of educating investors to recognize that markets go up as well as down. More sophisticated regulatory techniques using such concepts as 'value at risk' may also need to be adopted in order to preserve competitiveness of the domestic financial system in the face of global competition. In other words, the key issue is flexibility of regulatory policy in the face of financial sector evolution.

A further issue which is identified by Fry (Chapter 13) is that of the stability and efficiency of payments systems. This has been rather neglected in the analysis of the role of central banks. The experience of the CEE economies, in the early stages of their transition process, has been one where payments systems did not work very effectively. However, these problems have, in the main, been resolved. Nevertheless, it has become increasingly important for central banks to ensure that payments systems are stable and efficient. As Fry points out, this is necessary to ensure that growth in the economy is not interrupted. One way in which central banks intervene is in the avoidance of systemic risk where a large payer defaults. Fry analyses a number of pertinent aspects. Thus a real time gross settlement (RTGS) system can provide a method of avoiding this risk. However, it does involve a potential conflict with monetary policy since additional liquidity is required to operate it. For the CEE transition economies, the increasing financial sector development and the further opening of financial markets may create structural changes within the payments system which generate greater risks of failure. Hence there may need to be greater supervision of payments systems by central banks during the next few years. By maintaining confidence in the system, central banks will contribute to the process of financial and consequent economic development.

The next four chapters relate some of the general issues raised above to the specific cases of selected CEE economies. Vidickienė et al. (Chapter 14) examine how transition countries can raise savings ratios on the grounds that increased reliance on foreign capital to finance domestic investment opens the economy to risks that that flows of funds can be turned off as easily as they are turned on. Generally we have observed declining savings rates in transition economies. Vidickienė et al. attribute this trend to increased uncertainty during the early stages of the transition process, although much of the decline was the result of the demise of forced savings which characterized the planned economy. It must surely also be true that a lack of savings instruments, particularly ones which protected wealth against the ravages of inflation, was a major disincentive to making greater wealth-accumulating commitments. This may have been compounded by a perception that the government sector was responsible for welfare provision and pensions for the elderly. Recent trends towards more private provision (for example, of pensions in Poland) will correct this latter factor. In addition, rising levels of confidence, assisted by the process of convergence of the financial sector to EU standards and the increased presence of foreign financial institutions in the domestic markets, have contributed positively to an improved climate for savings. Note also that increased liberalization will have encouraged the repatriation of flight capital, which was a problem in the early stages of transition. Thus the situation has stabilized and there is the prospect that more positive trends will now appear. It is also important to remember that financial sector development will be important not only for promoting domestic savings but also to open up the possibility of increased and stable inflows of capital, particularly from the EU. Recall the point made by Fry that financial sector stability is assisted by a range of fully operating markets and institutions that are now emerging.

Two further chapters, by Raczko (Chapter 15, for Poland) and Matoušek (Chapter 16, for the Czech Republic) concentrate on the banking sector. We have already noted that the Czech economy has slipped from its position as top-performing transition economy. As Matoušek illustrates, this is explained in part by shortcomings in the banking sector and the consequent need for its restructuring. One can, with the benefit of hindsight, regard the banking sector problems as a case of missed opportunities. Despite having the resources to restructure the system at the outset of the reform process, the job was only half done (resulting in moral hazard problems) in the Czech Republic. As a result, and aided by a liberal policy towards issuing banking licensing, there were increasing bad-loans problems. These were partly a reflection of the riskiness of the economy, but also were a consequence of the lack of expertise in the banks themselves as well as in regulation. Indeed, Matoušek indicates that some of the problems of small banks are due to criminal activity. In any event a restructuring programme has been ongoing, with the government taking over responsibility for non-performing loans. Allied to this is a privatization programme which has resulted in most major domestic banks ending up in foreign hands. If the consequence of this is to improve bank management, this can only be a positive development.

Raczko reviews the development of the Polish banking sector and the convergence of regulations to EU standards. He highlights a number of features which describe the development of the Polish banking sector. The increasing involvement of foreign banks is notable. Essentially this was to ensure that the principle of no discrimination was applied to foreign banks operating in Poland. This was an important element of EU policy towards the single market. As a result an increased presence of foreign banks has been seen in Poland, through the opening of branches and, increasingly through take-overs of, or participations in, domestic banks. The general principle that the involvement of foreign banks improves the operation and efficiency of the domestic system seems to have been borne out in the case of Poland. A second feature of the development of the Polish banking sector is the way in which prudential regulation has been refined. Essentially there has been a move towards adopting the EU regulatory structure, which conforms to the Basle

Accord. Raczko documents a number of key changes which have taken place. First, we may note the adoption of the risk-related capital adequacy ratio. This required proper assessment of bank exposure to loan defaults and also created a pressing need for bank recapitalization. In addition, Raczko notes that it was important to improve the organization of bank supervision. This was achieved through the adoption of a set of directives based on the EU regulatory structure, such as bank accounting, exposure and disclosure rules.

Beyond this current implementation, Poland has announced a programme to move within seven years to full compliance with EU regulations. As a result, the Polish banking sector will be fully integrated into the single EU market. This presents threats as well as opportunities. The strategy of foreign banks is a key feature. It has already been noted that foreign banks can provide considerable expertise in terms of new product creation which will assist the development of the domestic market. Furthermore, they can bring much needed expertise into such areas as risk management. However, there is the possibility that certain sectors of activity will be effectively taken over by foreign banks. If, at the same time, the main base of operations is kept geographically outside of the country, then the market may develop to serve the consumers', rather than the domestic banks', interests. However, given that the trend is towards increasing consolidation of the banking and financial services market in the EU, then this may be an inevitable consequence. If Polish banks can adapt to the new market and regulatory environment then they can survive and grow. Certainly the way in which this will happen is through consolidation across the sector. If not, then the domestic market will be serviced increasingly by foreign providers. In any case the consumer will benefit from having a more efficient service.

Beyond the banking sector there is the potential for further gains to be had from expanding the use of other financial markets. However, the behaviour of stock markets in the region, with their high levels of volatility and the suspicion that the markets, which lack liquidity, are controlled and manipulated by large investors, has inhibited their development. Horsewood and Sutherland (Chapter 17) provide an analysis of the efficiency of several stock markets in the region and also examine the possible transmission of changes across different markets. In order to test for efficiency, they attempt to find evidence of cointegration, which suggests that market movements are predictable. They use daily data on stock indices for Russia, Poland, Hungary and the Czech Republic. After testing for non-stationarity (which confirms that a time series of an individual index cannot be predicted by looking solely at its own past behaviour) they conduct a multivariate cointegration analysis. Perhaps rather surprisingly, their findings support the view that these four markets are efficient. However, with daily data and relatively illiquid markets, there is the suspicion that transaction costs are driving this result.

In addition to looking for cointegration they use causality tests to investigate whether the short-run changes in indices transmit from one market to another. This transmission mechanism would then be regarded as evidence of contagion effects. They conduct bilateral tests and find evidence for transmission across selected markets, including from the London market to the others. Hence there appears to be contagion effects. Overall we may conclude that the results from the Horsewood and Sutherland study are indicative that equity markets in CEE countries may be better functioning than previously thought. Hence, they could well be a useful focus for development of the financial market as a whole.

The final three chapters provide empirical evidence on the efficiency of the banking sector in CEE economies and its convergence on those of the EU. Goyeau et al. (Chapter 18), provide analysis of the relationship between risk and profitability of commercial banks in Central and Eastern Europe. They develop a model of bank interest margins which takes account of both credit and interest rate risks. This can be formulated into an empirically testable form. They then estimate the model using annual data for nine CEE economies from 1992 to 1996. Generally their results are supportive of their model and suggest that banks are taking risk into account when setting interest rates. However, other factors which should be important such as operating costs and maturity risk are not found to be significant. Thus there is some evidence that banking sectors of the CEE economies are using modern management methods when pricing the risks they face but they also continue to ignore important aspects of their business. One aspect of their study which suggests that not all factors are properly captured by their model is that quantity and pricing decisions do not seem to be fully consistent with each other. In other words banks may be pricing risks properly but then over- or under-lending at the chosen interest rates.

The chapter by Gondat-Larralde and Lepetit (Chapter 19) attempts to analyse whether market power is a significant determinant of bank behaviour and hence of the performance of the market. The chapter provides evidence which suggests that the banking market in CEE economies is quite concentrated. Thus, in general, the three largest banks have a market share greater than 60 per cent, although the figure is less than 50 per cent for Poland and Latvia. The main element of their chapter is an empirical analysis of the structure–conduct–performance model of the banking market. The results of this analysis is that market share does seem to have an influence on bank profitability. Hence the chapter concludes that there is a tendency in these markets for mergers to take place on efficiency grounds. Until the market is fully open to foreign competition this may well allow exploitation of market power. However, this may also imply that domestic banks will be able to build enough financial muscle to compete successfully with the competition from abroad, particularly the EU.

These two chapters indicate that convergence of CEE economies' banking systems with the EU is likely to alter the performance of the domestic banking market radically. The final chapter in this area by Murinde et al. (Chapter 20) considers whether there is much evidence of convergence. As a consequence, we have further background against which to assess the impact of opening the financial sector to EU competition. Murinde et al. recognize that the development of the banking sector in the CEE transition economies has been to some extent influenced by the level of bad loans and the way the problem has been solved. We have already alluded to this in the discussions of Poland and the Czech Republic. The way in which they test for convergence is to consider the literature on convergence of real economies, but to respecify the model in terms of bank output, rather than the total output of the countries studied. It is a natural extension of the idea, although there are many aspects of banking sector convergence relating to convergence of banking efficiency which could have been used. The data period used is 1993–97, a time during which major strides have been made to reform banking systems in transition economies. Murinde et al. look for convergence both across transition economies as well as between transition economies and EU economies. The results of their analysis of convergence across transition economies are mixed: they find that there is convergence in terms of lending to the government sector; however, the evidence for convergence in lending to public sector enterprises is less strong. These results may well reflect the different pace of restructuring which has taken place in the countries of the data set. However, when attention is turned to lending to private sector enterprises, the convergence hypothesis seems again to hold. Alternatively one can view deposits as output. Using this measure Murinde et al. find that for demand deposits there is evidence of convergence, but not for time or savings deposits. We have noted before that inflation has a major impact on savings and hence the different inflation performance across the transition economies during the time period studied may have had an influence on time and savings deposits.

Murinde et al. then turn to convergence between the transition economies and the EU. Here, when defining output in terms of loans, they find that there does appear to be convergence for private sector lending. Hence the trends observed in the EU are to some extent replicated in the transition economies. For the deposits measure of output, there is no evidence of convergence. Once again this may reflect the very different inflation performances across the two sets of countries. Hence the chapter finds that there is some evidence of convergence, both across the transition economies as well as between the transition economies and the EU. This convergence can be regarded as taking place in banking product markets, rather than in terms of banking performance. The methodology used, though, could also be applied in a more general context to investigate the convergence of the wider financial sector.

This section has summarized the chapters which have considered the issue of financial sector development within the CEE transition economies. We end the section with an overview of the results. It is widely accepted that financial sector restructuring is an important issue in overall economic development. The transition economies have accorded a higher priority to financial sector reform as they have moved towards membership of the EU. This is essential if an underperforming financial sector can retard the growth of the real economy. The negative impact of the financial sector on growth may be due to financial instability and repression, as discussed by Fry (Chapters 2 and 12). This implies that it is important to promote both financial deepening, which itself can assist in generating stability, and to ensure that proper regulation and supervision is in place. This is a challenge faced by all financial systems, not just in transition or developing countries. Fry (Chapter 13) also illustrates these ideas by pointing out the need to develop and maintain an efficient and sound payments system. In a highly dynamic environment there is always the risk of failure which can create a systemic crisis and regulators must guard against these risks.

Studies of the CEE economies have reinforced these general messages about the need to promote financial sector development while avoiding financial instability. Vidickienė et al. (Chapter 14) have discussed the issue of savings mobilization. While it is possible to finance domestic investment mainly through global capital markets (and indeed this may become the norm) this can lead to a lack of growth of the domestic financial sector. This is unlikely to be a desirable situation and hence mobilization of domestic savings is an important component in the overall development of the financial sector. Stabilization of the economy and promotion of private insurance and pensions schemes are two important prerequisites for domestic savings to increase. Raczko (Chapter 15) and Matoušek (Chapter 16) consider specific issues with regard to the banking sector. Raczko views the development of the regulatory system as being a crucial component in the strengthening of the Polish banking sector, while Matoušek concentrates on the bad-loan problems which have dogged the Czech Republic banking sector over the whole of the transition period. The message of both chapters is that banks must be given freedom to act competitively, but that there must be a well-specified regulatory environment in which they operate that affords adequate protection to depositors and taxpayers. This must include a proper expectation on the part of bank management that they and the bank's shareholders and bondholders will not be bailed out by the government should their decisions prove to be bad ones. In any event, by following these general principles, policy makers will ensure that their domestic banking system is operating efficiently and is in a position to provide the required level of service to the real economy.

The chapter by Horsewood and Sutherland (Chapter 17) allows for the discussion to move into other areas of the financial sector. They find that, while there may be contagion effects across transition economies (and from developed to transition economies), there is not significant evidence of market inefficiency in the sense that movement in one market can be used to predict changes in another. While this is encouraging for the transition economies, it does not mean that there is not a great deal of work to be done to bring capital markets to a standard consistent with global standards. The same sort of considerations of regulation and maintenance of stability which were discussed in relation to the banking sector apply to stock markets and any other financial institutions.

The empirical chapters by Goyeau et al. (Chapter 18), Gondat-Larralde and Lepetit (Chapter 19) and Murinde et al. (Chapter 20) provide further background analysis suggesting that the banking sectors of the transition economies have some way to go before they can converge to the standards in the EU. There are, of course, many ways in which this can be achieved, but, given the increasing consolidation of the banking market within the EU, it seems that the strategy of allowing more foreign penetration into the banking sector will be a prominent method of achieving this objective. It is the one which is being increasingly adopted and one which has the potential benefit of moving the transition economies towards convergence with the EU at a faster pace.

CONCLUSIONS

The chapters in this book have considered a wide-ranging set of issues within the general context of closer integration between the monetary and financial sectors in the transition economies of Central and Eastern Europe and those in the EU. They highlight that monetary policy needs to be conducted flexibly in a way which allows the ongoing convergence to be handled successfully and hence argue for a relatively flexible policy stance, particularly with respect to exchange rates. It has been noted that two of the most advanced countries of the region have adopted an inflation target which has the advantage of giving more flexibility to monetary policy than, say, a pegged exchange rate. However, the possibility of future adoption of the euro will also influence the policy choices taken now. Thus it is important for policy to be operated in a way which is not inconsistent with future membership of the single European currency.

It is hoped that one of the key aspects of membership of the EU will be the development of a more efficient financial sector. If this does not happen, then the anticipated (dynamic) benefits of membership may not be achieved. The studies reported here have emphasized the importance of developing a regulatory and supervisory structure that assures both financial stability and effective corporate governance, while promoting competition. This is no easy task, and it is one which is facing the developed economies as well as transition and other emerging market countries. As they prepare for EU entry, the transition economies will need to adopt best-practice procedures which are evolving over time, both out of the experience of the developed economies and from their own experience.

This book inevitably poses almost as many questions as it tries to answer. There is clearly scope for further research on the appropriate paths of monetary and financial sector policies, taking into account the need to hit targets for EU membership which may be similar, but not identical, to those for joining EMU. The respective role of domestic and foreign institutions in the transitions economies' financial sectors and the need to bring their efficiency up to international standards as quickly as possible, is also worthy of further analysis. Finally, more work on the development of a regulatory structure which is both suitable for the transition economies as they are currently structured, but which will also facilitate convergence on the rapidly evolving EU financial structure, is clearly also needed.

PART I

Monetary and Exchange Rate Policy

2. Monetary policy and economic development in transitional economies

Maxwell J. Fry

INTRODUCTION

The extent to which a central bank can choose and implement appropriate monetary, financial stability and payment system policies varies considerably across countries. In the transitional economies, expertise formed one serious constraint in the early years (Knight 1997). Not only was expertise scarce in the central bank but also within the financial sector as a whole. Rapid transformation from a monobanking system into a two-tier banking system faced not only lack of expertise and experience but also little understanding of fundamental economic concepts such as opportunity cost and time value of money. Many gaps existed in the financial landscape in terms of institutions and markets that typically constitute financial sectors in the industrial countries. Central bankers also faced uncompetitive and uncooperative commercial banking systems.

Much has changed over the past decade in the transitional economies. But some transitional economies have adapted to their new environments more quickly and successfully than others. So there is perhaps more diversity now than there was at the outset. Nevertheless, there are several common features of the process of financial liberalization and financial development. For example, whatever legal independence is assigned, central banks in transitional economies have been constrained by their countries' fiscal situation and exchange rate regime (Fry and Nuti 1992; Koch 1997). Since good monetary policy contributes to economic development, in this chapter I shall examine some constraints to implementing stabilizing monetary policy that exist in transitional and developing countries.

INFLATION GROWTH RELATIONSHIPS

In the 1960s, much of the economics profession accepted the finding that a trade-off existed between inflation and growth: higher growth could be achieved at the cost of higher inflation. In the 1970s, more sophisticated expectations-augmented Phillips curves became popular. Ironically, David Hume provided one of the clearest expositions of the expectations-augmented Phillips curve in 1752:

> Accordingly we find, that in every kingdom, into which money begins to flow in greater abundance than formerly, every thing takes a new face; labour and industry gain life; the merchant becomes more enterprizing; the manufacturer more diligent and skillful; and even the farmer follows his plough with greater alacrity and attention. . . . To account, then, for this phænomenon, we must consider, that tho' the high price of commodities be a necessary consequence of the encrease of gold and silver, yet it follows not immediately upon that encrease; but some time is requir'd before the money circulate thro' the whole state, and make its effects be felt on all ranks of people. At first, no alteration is perceiv'd; by degrees, the price rises, first of one commodity, then of another, till the whole at last reaches a just proportion, with the new quantity of specie, which is in the kingdom. In my opinion, 'tis only in this interval or intermediate situation, betwixt the acquisition of money and rise of prices, that the encreasing quantity of gold and silver is favourable to industry. (Hume 1752, pp. 46–7)

In fact, simple bivariate cross-section and pooled time-series regressions produce *negative* relationships between inflation and growth for various country groups in both long and short runs. Negative-sloping long-run expectations-augmented Phillips curve relationships between inflation and growth have also been found, particularly in developing countries (Fry 1995, ch. 10).

Far from there being any exploitable trade-off in the medium and longer terms between inflation and higher output levels, the accepted view now is that in the longer term this relationship is negative, that is, more inflation is associated with lower growth (Barro 1995; De Gregorio 1994; Fischer 1994). While the deleterious effects of hyperinflation on growth, with the dislocations caused to saving patterns and to the monetary and pricing mechanisms, are fairly obvious, inflation has, so it is claimed, a negative effect on growth even at low or moderate levels. In part, this latter effect may be because a higher level of inflation is generally associated with a greater variability of inflation and hence a greater riskiness of longer-term unindexed contracts. As John Locke (1695, p. 189) wrote:

> I see no reason to think, that a little bigger or less size of the pieces coined is of any moment, one way or the other. . . . The harm comes by the change, which unreasonably and unjustly gives away and transfers men's properties, disorders trade, puzzles accounts, and needs a new arithmetic to cast up reckonings, and keep accounts in; besides a thousand other inconveniences.

There are a wide variety of potential channels for both negative and positive effects running from inflation to growth and vice versa. In developing countries, fixed nominal interest and exchange rates may have been particularly harmful (Fry 1995, ch. 8). As inflation rises, lower real interest rates resulting from fixed nominal rates reduce credit availability and distort resource allocation, while a fixed exchange rate prices exports out of world markets. Both effects are growth reducing.

All financial systems in market economies, whether they are industrial, developing or transitional, perform two basic functions: (a) administering the country's payment mechanisms; and (b) intermediating between savers and investors. On the first function, there is little disagreement that high inflation impairs the domestic currency's attributes not only of a store of value but also of a means of payment. As James Tobin (1992, p. 772) states: 'A society's money is necessarily a store of value. Otherwise it could not be an acceptable means of payment'. So financial systems are impeded in performing both of their basic functions under high inflation. Society turns to substitute means of payment (foreign currencies or barter trade), thereby bypassing the domestic financial system. This substitution is one manifestation of the law of demand. As the opportunity cost of holding money rises, the demand for money expressed at constant prices or in real terms falls.

In the simplest balance sheet of the banking system, commercial banks hold loans L and reserves R as their assets and deposits D as their liabilities:

Assets		Liabilities	
Reserves	R	Deposits	D
Loans	L		

The balance sheet identity implies $R + L = D$. Naturally, this balance sheet identity is still preserved if one divides both assets and liabilities by nominal GNP Y:

Assets		Liabilities	
Reserves	R/Y	Deposits	D/Y
Loans	L/Y		

Ceteris paribus, the ratio D/Y falls as inflation accelerates because households and firms choose to hold smaller money balances in relation to their expenditure levels due to the rising cost of holding money. Therefore, the ratio $(R + L)/Y$ must also fall.[1] If the ratio R/L remains roughly constant, then both R/Y and L/Y fall as D/Y falls. Since L/Y is the ratio of bank loans to the nominal value of output, business firms find themselves facing a credit squeeze as inflation rises. Unable to obtain the necessary loans to cover the costs of their working capital, some firms may be unable to stay in business. The aggregate level of output in real terms would then fall. In this case, therefore, the deterioration of money reduces the extents to which the banking system administers the country's payment mechanism and intermediates between savers and investors; performance in both functions is related. Perhaps the former effect reduces income levels while the latter effect reduces income growth.

FISCAL DOMINANCE

Fiscal difficulties frequently lie behind many features and problems of financial systems in developing and transitional countries. Many developing and transitional country governments find it virtually impossible to satisfy their intertemporal budget constraint with conventional tax revenue. Hence, they rely on revenue from the inflation tax and they reduce their interest costs through financial repression (Agénor and Montiel 1996 p. 156; Brock 1989, p. 116; Fry 1997, ch. 3; Giovannini and de Melo 1993). Both the theoretical and empirical findings reviewed in this chapter suggest that financial repression is a particularly damaging quasi-tax from the perspective of economic growth.

Governments can finance their deficits in four major ways.[2]

1. Monetizing the deficit by borrowing at zero cost from the central bank.
2. Borrowing at below-market interest rates by thrusting debt down the throats of captive buyers, primarily commercial banks.
3. Borrowing abroad in foreign currency.
4. Borrowing at market interest rates from voluntary lenders in domestic currency markets.

The typical Organization for Economic Cooperation and Development (OECD) country finances about 50 per cent of its deficit in voluntary domestic currency markets, while the typical developing country finances only about 8 per cent of its deficit from this source.

Why this matters is that, for any given persistent government deficit, greater use of the first three sources is associated with higher inflation rates, lower saving ratios and lower rates of economic growth (Fry 1997). Government recourse to the central bank inevitably leads to inflation. Indeed, such inflationary finance can be considered a source of tax revenue in that inflation imposes a tax on moneyholders.

Financial repression, the second way of financing the government deficit, is also taxlike in that it involves forcing captive buyers to hold government debt at interest rates below market yields. By reducing its interest costs, this method reduces the government's recorded deficit. Foreign borrowing, which for all developing and virtually all transitional countries implies borrowing and repaying foreign rather than domestic currency, constitutes the third method of financing a deficit. Elsewhere, I demonstrate that excessive reliance on these three ways of financing government deficits impedes economic development (Fry 1997).

All this conflicts with the views of Robert Barro (1974, 1989) and James Buchanan (1976) on Ricardian equivalence. Barro (1989, p. 39) states that the Ricardian equivalence theorem, proposed only to be dismissed by David Ricardo (1817, pp. 336–8) himself, holds that:

> The substitution of a budget deficit for current taxes (or any other rearrangement of the timing of taxes) has no impact on the aggregate demand for goods. In this sense, budget deficits and taxation have equivalent effects on the economy – hence the term 'Ricardian equivalence theorem'. To put the equivalence result another way, a decrease in the government's saving (that is, a current budget deficit) leads to an offsetting increase in desired private saving, and hence to no change in desired national saving.

It also follows that Ricardian equivalence implies that the method of financing government deficits has no impact on the macroeconomy.

While Barro (1989, p. 52) interprets the empirical evidence to provide general support for the Ricardian equivalence theorem, the evidence cited is drawn largely from the United States where the assumptions of the theorem are perhaps most likely to hold. As Pierre-Richard Agénor and Peter Montiel (1996, p. 127) suggest:

> In developing countries where financial systems are underdeveloped, capital markets are highly distorted or subject to financial repression, and private agents are subject to considerable uncertainty regarding the incidence of taxes, many of the considerations necessary for debt neutrality to hold are unlikely to be valid.

Hence, the assumptions on which Ricardian equivalence rests (Barro 1989, pp. 39–48) are almost bound to be violated sufficiently to negate the theorem in these countries. Indeed, Agénor and Montiel (1996, p. 127) conclude: 'the empirical evidence [from developing countries] has indeed failed to provide much support for the Ricardian equivalence proposition'. The empirical evidence presented in Fry (1997, Part II) confirms the Agénor–Montiel position.

The negative effect of deficit finance on growth is typically demonstrated by estimating a relationship between inflation and economic growth; here inflation *INF* is measured by the continuously compounded rate of change in the consumer price index and growth by the continuously compounded rate of change in GDP measured at constant prices *YG*. To confront the problem that inflation has been far more variable (heteroscedastic) in some countries than in others, I estimate the relationship between economic growth and inflation here using iterative three-stage least squares on a system of equations with the same slope parameters but different intercepts for each country. Furthermore,

I deal with the problem of simultaneity by treating inflation as an endogenous variable. Initial tests for non-linearities indicated that the inclusion of both squared and cubed inflation (INF^2 and INF^3) as explanatory variables for economic growth produced better results than the level ($INFG$). The estimate (with *t* values in brackets) for a sample of 41 developing countries for 1971–94 period (860 observations), is:[3]

$$YG = -0.056 \; \widehat{INF}^2 + 0.015 \; \widehat{INF}^3.$$
$$(-13.648) \qquad (10.346) \qquad\qquad (2.1)$$
$$\bar{R}^2 = 0.154$$

Figure 2.1 illustrates this estimated growth inflation relationship. I estimate a similar relationship for a sample of 20 transitional economies chosen for this study.[4] Prakash Loungani and Nathan Sheets (1997) also find a strong and robust negative relationships between inflation and subsequent economic growth in a sample of 25 transitional economies. Glenn Hoggarth (1997, p. 33) observes that 'a sustained recovery of output has only occurred once inflation has been brought down to relatively low rates, say below 50 per cent per annum'.

The problem I have with equation (2.1) and similar estimates is its size. *Ceteris paribus*, could a rise in inflation from zero to 225 per cent, the range

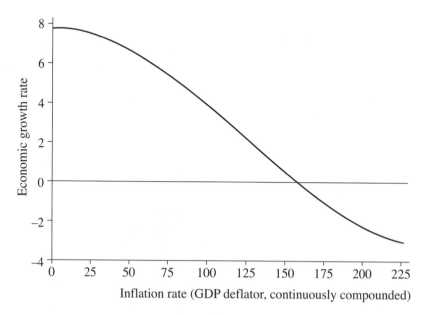

Figure 2.1   Non-linear relationship between economic growth and inflation

*Table 2.1.   Fiscal attributes in high- and low-growth developing countries,
1972–1995 (average annual percentages)*

Fiscal attribute	Low growth	High growth	Low fiscal	High fiscal
Government deficit/GNP	9.5	1.4	–1.6	12.8
Δ Reserve money/GNP	4.1	1.4	0.7	6.6
Reserve/deposits	29.2	12.5	6.6	46.9
Growth	0.6	8.1	7.0	3.2
Inflation	40.1	8.2	9.4	27.0

covering virtually all the observations, really reduce growth by 10 percentage points? Since the magnitude of this estimated effect seems unreasonable to me, I suggest that at least not all of this relationship is causal. Rather, I suggest that both economic growth and inflation are affected in opposite directions by fiscal variables.

To examine the relationship between deficit finance and economic growth more carefully, I obtained data for 70 developing countries for the 1972–95 period and the sample of 20 transitional economies for the 1980–97 period.[5] The first sample includes all developing countries with a reasonable number of observations for the relevant fiscal variables. My first examination of the data involves ranking these 70 countries on the basis of various potential discriminating variables. I then select the ten countries with the highest average values of the discriminating variable and the ten countries with the lowest average values of this discriminating variable during the 1972–95 period.

Table 2.1 shows some of the relationships between developing countries' fiscal attributes and their inflation and growth performance. The table compares the mean values of the fiscal variables when countries are selected on growth rates with their mean values when countries are selected on the fiscal variables themselves. The numbers represent means of all annual values for the country group. In the columns labelled 'Low fiscal' and 'High fiscal', the countries differ for each fiscal factor. So the ten lowest-deficit countries averaged surpluses of 1.6 per cent (that is, deficits of –1.6 per cent), compared with average deficits of 12.8 per cent in the ten highest-deficit countries. Annual changes in reserve money in the ten countries with lowest reserve-money growth averaged 0.7 per cent of GDP compared with 6.6 per cent in the ten countries with highest reserve-money growth.[6] Finally, the ratio of bank reserves to bank deposits averaged 6.6 per cent in the ten countries with the lowest ratios compared with 46.9 per cent in the ten countries with the highest ratios.

In the columns labelled 'Low growth' and 'High growth' the data relate to the same group of countries. So in the ten lowest-growing countries, government deficits averaged 9.5 per cent of GDP, reserve money growth averaged 4.1 per cent of GDP and bank reserves averaged 29.2 per cent of bank deposits. In the ten highest-growing countries, government deficits averaged 1.4 per cent of GDP, reserve money growth averaged 1.4 per cent of GDP and bank reserves averaged 12.5 per cent of bank deposits. Inflation and growth rates reported in the last two rows are averages for the ten lowest-growth, highest-growth, lowest-deficit and highest-deficit countries.

All the differences between high- and low-growth countries are highly significant. In all cases, high-growth countries exhibit low averages for fiscal variables, that is, low deficits, low reserve-money growth, and low reserve/deposit ratios. In other words, countries with good fiscal characteristics perform better economically with higher growth and lower inflation than those with poor fiscal characteristics. I conjecture that these fiscal characteristics explain much of the negative association observed between inflation and growth. After conducting formal causality tests, Stanley Fischer (1993, p. 510) concludes that 'small deficits are good for growth'.

Table 2.2 provides some comparable statistics for the 20 transitional economies. In this table, the column labelled 'Low' shows the average values of each variable for the ten lowest countries in each category. So the ten transitional countries with the lowest government deficits posted deficits averaging 0.5 per cent of GDP over the 1993–97 period. Similarly, the ten countries

Table 2.2   Fiscal attributes in 20 transitional countries 1993–1997, (average annual percentages)

Fiscal attribute	Low	High	Average*
Government deficit/GNP	0.5	5.7	2.9
Δ Reserve money/GNP	2.3	7.1	4.7
Reserves/deposits	15.0	34.4	24.2
DCGR	4.1	40.8	22.4
Growth	−10.8	5.3	−2.7
Inflation	22.6	628.4	325.5

Note: *No data are available for the reserve deposit ratio for Kazakhstan. No data on government deficits are available for Armenia, Azerbaijan, Belarus, Moldova, the Russian Federation, the Slovak Republic and Ukraine. So for the reserve/deposit ratio, figures are for the lowest ten and highest nine countries. For the government deficits, the averages are for the lowest seven and highest six countries.

Source: These data were extracted from *International Financial Statistics*, March 1998, CD-ROM, and *World Development Indicators* 1997, CD-ROM.

with the highest reserve/deposit ratios produce an average of 34.4 per cent for 1993–97. The row labelled '*DCGR*' gives the ratio of net domestic credit to the central government as a percentage of aggregate domestic credit. The ten lowest countries averaged 4.1 per cent compared with the ten highest countries that averaged 40.8 per cent. The final column gives the simple average for all 20 countries. In the ten lowest-growth transitional economies, inflation averaged 451 per cent compared with 200 per cent in the ten highest-growth economies. The negative relationship between inflation and growth holds for this country group, just as it does for many other country samples.

However, the fiscal variables exhibit far weaker relationships in the transitional economies than they do in the sample of 70 developing countries. This may well be due to large public sectors in some transitional economies. In China, for example, quasi-fiscal activities of the People's Bank of China and the state-owned banks in the form of subsidies to state-owned enterprises explain why a modest government deficit is found alongside a high reserve/deposit ratio (Fry 1998b).

Elsewhere, I suggest that poor fiscal policy is likely to be accompanied by accommodating or inflationary monetary policy (Fry 1998a). To examine the relationship between fiscal and monetary policies, I estimate monetary policy reaction functions for groups of countries selected on their fiscal characteristics, drawn from the sample of 70 developing countries used in Table 2.1. The results suggest that, far from offsetting expansionary fiscal policy, monetary policy tends to compound any inflationary fiscal stance in these countries. Larger deficits and greater reliance by governments on the domestic banking system are associated not only with less monetary policy neutralization (that is, changes in government borrowing from the domestic banking system are not countered by equal and opposite changes in credit to the private sector), but also with less sterilization of increases in foreign exchange reserves. In other words, more inflationary fiscal policies are accompanied by more accommodating and so more inflationary monetary policies.

INFLATION AND CENTRAL BANK INDEPENDENCE

Abel et al. (1998, ch. 9) point out that new central banking laws in Central European transitional economies have been modeled along the lines of the Deutsche Bundesbank's statutes. Ironically, this implies that legal independence is rather modest. By law, the Bundesbank is required to support the government's economic policy. Loungani and Sheets (1997) find a negative relationship between central bank independence and inflation across 12 transitional economies. However, legal independence provides no predictive power whatsoever in terms of inflationary outcomes in developing countries (Fry 1998a).

I suggest that measures of central bank independence constructed and used by Loungani and Sheets and others are endogenous variables. The most important necessary condition for de facto central bank independence is fiscal discipline. In other words, central bank independence is a luxury that governments in dire fiscal plights cannot afford. Fiscal discipline is not a sufficient condition for central bank independence because central bank independence is gained in large part through the central bank's competence and the ability to demonstrate it. Alex Cukierman (1992, pp. 393–4) makes the point that:

> A governor who is backed by an absolutely and relatively strong research department carries more weight *vis-à-vis* the Treasury and other branches of government. The reason is probably that the governor is perceived as a relatively impartial provider of reliable information about the economy. A possible indicator of the quality of a bank's research department is the quality of the annual report it produces.

Closer and more regular contact with government can provide the central bank with the means to demonstrate its competence, as well as to educate its government in what can and cannot be achieved by the central bank. Specifically, the establishment of a monetary policy committee consisting of, among others, the minister of finance and the central bank governor may enable the central bank to achieve greater influence over the thrust of monetary policy.

The Mauritian experiment with such an arrangement since June 1994 appeared to increase central bank independence quite considerably, despite the fact that no other change in personalities or legal powers occurred. The monthly Monetary Policy Committee meetings enabled the Bank of Mauritius not only to set the agenda for the debate between it and the government on possible conflicting objectives of monetary policy but also to explain to the government in analytical fashion matters pertaining to monetary policy. The results were both considerably more harmonious relations between government and central bank as well as, more importantly, more effective and successful monetary policy implementation.

This experiment also demonstrated the value of a well-staffed central bank research department. In the Mauritian case, it was given the opportunity to communicate on a regular basis with the minister of finance and other government officials through a briefing paper modelled along the lines of the Bank of England's *Inflation Report*. Since briefing papers for these meetings were prepared by the research staff of the central bank, this provided the central bank with a forum for explaining what it believed to be appropriate policy and what consequences would follow from pursuing alternative policies. In this light, expertise within the central bank and an opportunity for regular demonstration of such expertise may well be the keys to independence, regardless of any statutory provisions.

A second key ingredient of central bank independence in practice lies in an understanding by the government of the macroeconomic effects of its funding activities. Acknowledging the benefits to the economy of competing with other borrowers on a level playing field is the first step to producing marketable government debt. This, in turn, is a prerequisite both for monetary policy to be separated from fiscal policy and for a central bank to implement monetary policy through open market operations. Perhaps most important is the fact that, once the government accepts the case against financial repression for raising funds at below-market interest rates, the central bank can assume the responsibility of funding the government by auctioning treasury bills.

Again, Mauritius provides an example. After the government accepted the level playing-field principle, monetary policy was divorced from fiscal policy and the Bank of Mauritius was able to conduct treasury bill auctions independently from fiscal concerns. By ensuring that the government was not directly affected financially by how its deficit was financed, the Bank of Mauritius could offer the appropriate volume of treasury bills for auction each week without regard to the precise weekly or monthly financing requirements of the government. When sales exceeded the government financing requirement, the balance was placed in a special treasury bill management account at the Bank of Mauritius that earned interest equal to the auction yield. When sales fell short of the government financing requirement, the Bank of Mauritius lent to the government at a rate equal to the auction yield. In this way, the Bank of Mauritius could determine the appropriate volume of treasury bills to offer without consulting the ministry of finance over the financing implications (Fry and Basant Roi 1995).

Cukierman (1992, p. 395) makes a related point in a situation in which the government had not accepted the benefits of marketable debt (which necessitates level playing-field government borrowing): 'The ability of the Bank of Israel to conduct open market operations is seriously restricted despite the fact that it holds a large amount of government securities. The reason is that these securities are not tradable and the Israeli Treasury has consistently refused to make them tradable'.

All this suggests, I think, that a move away from inflationary finance, financial repression and excessive reliance on foreign currency borrowing towards developing voluntary domestic markets for government debt offers benefits in terms of lower inflation and higher saving and economic growth rates. High growth, in turn, alleviates the deficit. There is, therefore, some hint of a virtuous circle in which less financial repression and greater use of voluntary domestic markets lowers inflation and raises growth, both of which reduce the government's deficit. In general, developing and transitional countries make too little use of voluntary leaders in domestic currency markets.

Given fiscal discipline, removing existing distortions and resisting the imposition of new distortions on financial markets constitute growth-enhancing government policies. Undistorted domestic financial markets promote economic growth by enhancing both the quality and the quantity of investment. Well-functioning domestic financial markets facilitate the allocation of capital inflows from abroad to their most productive uses; they also deter capital flight. Central banks can play key roles in fostering these changes in their financial sectors.

Nevertheless, increased vigilance is imperative because of the potential for increased financial system fragility that accompanies the global trend towards market-based financial structures. The convergence hypothesis argues that state- and bank-based financial systems are becoming increasingly uncompetitive in the global environment (Peréz 1997; Vitols 1997, pp. 221–55). The new financial institution is a lightly regulated financial supermarket offering a range of financial products to a mobile pool of consumers seeking short-term relationships on the basis of price competition. The development of direct financial markets, particularly secondary markets for government securities and corporate paper, is increasingly important for the competitive survival of financial systems in this age of globalization.

While the market-based financial structure may dominate international finance at the end of the twentieth century, it tends to substitute efficiency for stability and short-term profit for long-term relationships aimed at sustained productivity gains. Globalization introduces new problems for national financial regulators in terms of surges in international capital flows that can be, and have been in several countries, highly destabilizing. Given the belief that financial structures may well be converging on the market-based model, we must now focus on aspects of the liberalization and globalization process that may confront transitional economies over the next decade as their central banks introduce further domestic and international financial liberalization.

CONCLUSION

One common prerequisite for monetary stability is a level playing field. In my opinion, central banks in the transitional economies could usefully promote development of a secondary market for government debt; the government should certainly compete with other borrowers on a level playing field. This enables monetary policy to be separated from fiscal policy. With this prerequisite satisfied, central banks in transitional economies can concentrate on building their own expertise with which to implement monetary policy.

NOTES

1. Even a competitive banking system cannot raise deposit rates of interest in step with inflation when subject to non-interest-bearing reserve requirements. The reserve requirement tax burden which increases with inflation is passed on to depositors or lenders.

2. Under cash-based budgets, arrears and other deferred payment arrangements together with unfunded future liabilities such as state pensions constitute additional techniques of disguising the true magnitude of a deficit.
3. The instruments are lagged inflation, lagged money and output growth rates, oil inflation and the OECD growth rate. The estimation procedure, which is asymptotically full-information maximum likelihood, automatically corrects for heteroscedasticity across equations and therefore, in this case, across countries (Johnston 1984, pp. 486–90).
4. Albania, Armenia, Azerbaijan, Belarus, China, Croatia, the Czech Republic, Estonia, Hungary, Kazakhstan, Latvia, Lithuania, Moldova, Mongolia, Poland, Romania, The Russian Federation, The Slovak Republic. Slovenia and Ukraine.
5. Details of the developing country sample and the data definitions are presented in Fry (1997).
6. If reserve money represented 10 per cent of GDP, this 6.6 per cent would correspond to an annual average rate of growth in reserve money of 66 per cent.

REFERENCES

Ábel, István, Pierre L. Siklos and István P. Székely (1998), *Money and Finance in the Transition to a Market Economy*, Cheltenham, UK and Northampton, MA, USA: Edward Elgar.
Agénor, Pierre-Richard and Peter J. Montiel (1996), *Development Macroeconomics*, Princeton, NJ: Princeton University Press.
Barro, Robert J. (1974), 'Are government bonds net wealth?', *Journal of Political Economy*, **82** (6), November/December, 1095–117.
Barro, Robert J. (1989), 'The Ricardian approach to budget deficits', *Journal of Economic Perspectives*, **3** (2), Spring, 37–54.
Barro, Robert J. (1995), 'Inflation and economic growth', *Bank of England Quarterly Bulletin*, **35** (2), May, 166–76.
Brock, Philip L. (1989), 'Reserve requirements and the inflation tax', *Journal of Money, Credit and Banking*, **21** (1), February, 106–21.
Buchanan, James M. (1976), 'Barro on the Ricardian equivalence theorem', *Journal of Political Economy*, **84** (2), April, 337–42.
Cukierman, Alex (1992), *Central Bank Strategy, Credibility, and Independence*, Cambridge, MA: MIT Press.
De Gregorio, José (1994), 'Inflation, growth and central banks: theory and evidence', Washington, DC: International Monetary Fund, May.
Fischer, Stanley (1993), 'The role of macroeconomic factors in growth', *Journal of Monetary Economics*, **32** (3), December, 485–512.
Fischer, Stanley (1994), 'Modern central banking', in Forrest Capie, Charles Goodhart, Stanley Fischer and Norbert Schnadt (eds), *The Future of Central Banking: The Tercentenary Symposium of the Bank of England*, Cambridge: Cambridge University Press, pp. 262–308.
Fry, Maxwell J. (1995), *Money, Interest, and Banking in Economic Development*, 2nd edn, Baltimore, MD: Johns Hopkins University Press.
Fry, Maxwell J. (1997), *Emancipating the Banking System and Developing Markets for Government Debt*, London: Routledge.
Fry, Maxwell J. (1998a), 'Assessing central bank independence in developing countries: do actions speak louder than words?', *Oxford Economic Papers*, **50**, 512–29.
Fry, Maxwell J. (1998b), 'Can seigniorage revenue keep China's financial system afloat?', in Donald J.S. Brean (ed.), *Taxation in Modern China*, New York: Routledge, pp. 93–123.

Fry, Maxwell J. and D. Mario Nuti (1992), 'Monetary and exchange rate policies during Eastern Europe's transition: lessons from further east', *Oxford Review of Economic Policy*, **8** (1), Spring, 27–43.

Fry, Maxwell J. and Ramesh Basant Roi (1995), 'Monetary policy-making in Mauritius', *Bank of Mauritius Quarterly Bulletin*, **35**, January–March, 11–16.

Giovannini, Alberto and Martha de Melo (1993), 'Government revenue from financial repression', *American Economic Review*, **83** (4), September, 953–63.

Hoggarth, Glenn (1997), 'Monetary policy in transition – the case of Central Europe', *Central Banking*, **8** (1), Summer, 32–43.

Hume, David (1752), 'Of money', in *Political Discourses*, 2nd edn, Edinburgh: Kincaid & Donaldson, pp. 41–59.

Johnston, Jack (1984), *Econometric Methods*, 3rd edn, New York: McGraw-Hill.

Knight, Malcolm (1997), 'Central bank reforms in the Baltics, Russia, and the other countries of the former Soviet Union', Washington, DC: International Monetary Fund, Occasional Paper 157, December.

Koch, Elmar B. (1997), 'Exchange rates and monetary policy in Central Europe: a survey of some issues', Vienna: Oesterreichische Nationalbank, Working Paper no. 24, September.

Locke, John (1695), *Further Considerations Concerning Raising the Value of Money*, 2nd edn, London: A. & J. Churchill.

Loungani, Prakash and Nathan Sheets (1997), 'Central bank independence, inflation, and growth in transition economies', *Journal of Money, Credit and Banking*, **29** (3), August, 381–99.

Peréz, Sofía A. (1997), '"Strong" states and "Cheap" credit: economic policy strategy and financial regulation France and Spain', in Douglas J. Forsyth and Ton Notermans (eds), *Regimes Changes: Macroeconomic Policy and Financial Regulation in Europe from the 1930s to the 1990s*, Providence, RI: Berghahn Books, pp. 169–220.

Ricardo, David (1817), *On the Principles of Political Economy and Taxation*, London: John Murray.

Tobin, James (1992), 'Money', in Peter Newman, Murray Milgate and John Eatwell (eds), *The New Palgrave Dictionary of Money and Finance*, Vol. 2, London: Macmillan, pp. 770–78.

Vitols Sigurt (1997), 'Financial systems and industrial policy in Germany and Great Britain: the limits of convergence', in Douglas J. Forsyth and Ton Notermans (eds), *Regimes Changes: Macroeconomic Policy and Financial Regulation in Europe from the 1930s to the 1990s*, Providence, RI: Berghahn Books, pp. 221–55.

3. The Czech approach to inflation targeting

Miroslav Hrnčíř and Kateřina Šmídková[*]

INTRODUCING INFLATION TARGETING

In December 1997, the Czech National Bank (CNB) announced that it would switch to inflation targeting. After eight years of relying on intermediate targets, this represented a historic change in the strategy of monetary policy. It is worth noting that price stability has always been the ultimate target of Czech monetary policy.

However, there were different strategies applied to reaching this long-term target. In the framework of inflation targeting, the inflation targets have been explicitly specified in terms of *net inflation* derived from consumer price index (CPI) inflation for two time horizons: net inflation to be 6 per cent ±0.5 per cent by the end of 1998 and 4.5 per cent ±1 per cent by the end of the year 2000. (See Figure 3.1.)

A Short History

The stability of the Czech koruna has been the ultimate monetary policy target of the CNB according to bank law since the very beginning of the bank's existence.[1] In 1993, the Czech Republic had reached the halfway mark in both the transitional process and the process of disinflation. As a consequence, it was necessary to derive the strategy of monetary policy from some concept of medium-term stability. During 1993–97, before switching to inflation targeting, the CNB had used three strategies. All three were based on working with intermediate targets and were to a significant extent affected by the transitional process. For example, instruments were being changed quite often as financial markets progressed from an embryonic stage of development to more advanced stages.

The first strategy was used in 1993–95. The koruna was pegged to a basket of currencies, and the money supply was used as a complementary intermediate target. Each year, the targeted interval was announced for money-supply

* This chapter was prepared for the ACE project conference in April 1999. The views expressed are those of the authors and do not necessarily represent those of the Czech National Bank.

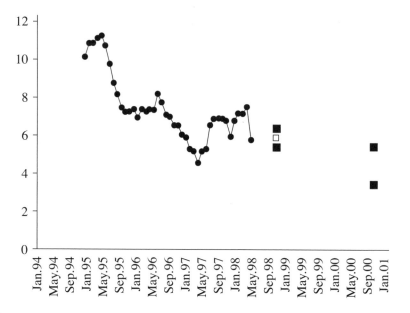

Note: The historical series of net inflation was calculated backwards in 1997 for the purposes of inflation targeting by the Czech Statistical Office for the 1995–97 period. The CNB expects that net inflation will be close to the lower edge of the targeted interval by the end of 1998.

Figure 3.1   Inflation targets announced in 1997

annual growth together with a forecast of CPI inflation that was projected in accordance with both intermediate targets. Table 3.1 shows that in these years, the CNB was aiming at slow disinflation.

In the first years of transition, the pegged exchange rate provided a nominal anchor for the Czech economy and was a key intermediate target for the CNB. Due to the low degree of koruna convertibility, it was possible to work with the money supply as well. This complementary intermediate target was important since, because of embryonic financial markets, the only available operational targets were quantitative ones. Also, the target for money supply had its important signalling role, because the credit limits were characteristic features of the previous stages of transition.

In the 1993–95 period, two operational targets were used simultaneously (monetary base, free reserves), and these targets were compatible with money-supply targeting. The main reason for working with volume targets was that the financial markets were in an embryonic stage of development and were too thin to give reliable information on prices. In 1995, when markets became more advanced, the combined operational target was used for free reserves

Table 3.1   Targets and inflation forecasts, 1993–1997

	Forecast of CPI inflation (%)	Intermediate target: money supply growth (%)	Intermediate target: exchange rate peg	Operational targets/ instruments
1993	15 (18)	Complementary 16 ±1 (21)	1992 peg, band 0.5%	Monetary base
1994	10 (10)	Complementary 13.5 ±1.5 (22)	1992 peg, band 0.5%	Free reserves
1995	9 (9)	Complementary 15.5 ±1.5 (19)	1992 peg, band 0.75%	Free reserves with overwriting rule
1996	9 (9)	15 ±2 (8)	1992 peg, band 7.5%	Short-term rates Repo rate
1997	8 (9)	10 ±2 (10)	1992 peg, band 7.5% May: koruna floats	Short-term rates Repo rate

Note: The overview of intermediate, operational targets/instruments and inflation forecasts is based on Annual Reports by the CNB and the annual monetary documents prepared for each year in December of the previous year. Although some targets were modified during the year, we do not report the modifications here for the sake of simplicity. For example, in 1994 due to capital inflow, the target for money supply growth was modified upwards, but the growth exceeded the upper limit. The actual values of respective variables are in parentheses. The actual CPI inflation deviated from the forecast in two periods when monetary policy decisions were subject to transitional uncertainty. In 1993, the VAT reform was an exogenous shock with the impact on CPI inflation higher than anticipated. In 1997, exchange rate turbulence and subsequent exchange rate depreciation were the causes of deviation.

with the overwriting rule for maximum value of the short-term money market rate. The strategy of monetary policy was changed for the first time in 1996. As a response to large capital inflows, financial market developments and liberalization of capital account transactions, the relative importance of intermediate targets was altered. The koruna was still pegged to a basket, but bands were much wider, and intervention on the foreign exchange market became rare. The target for money-supply growth gained significance due to increased autonomy. Figures 3.2 and 3.3 demonstrate the switch in importance of the two intermediate targets.

The general framework of monetary policy remained the same. For each year, the targeted interval was announced for money-supply annual growth together with a forecast of CPI inflation that was projected in accordance with both intermediate targets (see Table 3.1). Similar to the 1993–95 period, the choice of operational targets was determined mainly by the stage of financial market development. In 1996, the short-term rates became an operational target of monetary policy with the repo rate being the instrument.

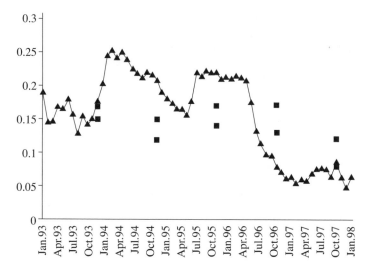

Note: Annual growth of M2 (in %) is compared to announced intervals for the end of each year in 1993–97.

Figure 3.2   Intermediate targets: money supply

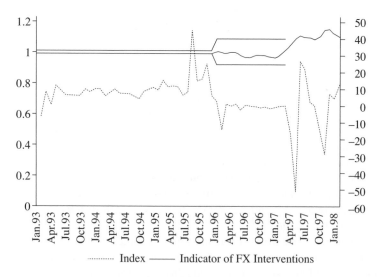

.... Index ——— Indicator of FX Interventions

Note: On the left axis, the exchange rate bands and index are scaled. The bands were abandoned in May 1997. The indicator of foreign exchange rate intervention is scaled on the right axis (billion koruna).

Figure 3.3   Intermediate targets: exchange rate

The second change in the strategy of monetary policy before introducing inflation targeting came in May 1997. After exchange rate turbulence,[2] the CNB let the koruna float. Hence, the second half of 1997 was a period of 'pure' monetary targeting since the target for growth of M2 was not modified and had been reached by the end of the year (see Figure 3.2). The short-term rates remained the operational target for monetary policy although three months after the attack on the koruna, interest rate levels were predetermined by the strategy of landing.

Reasons for Introducing the New Strategy

The CNB Board's decision to switch to inflation targeting, announced on 21 December 1997, was the result of an intensive programme of studies and discussions within the bank. This programme was launched with the aim of overcoming ambiguity in the focus of monetary policy since the discontinuation of the pegged exchange rate regime and the shift to managed floating at the end of May 1997 left the central bank without a transparent nominal anchor for its policy. Arguments in favour of the adopted decision are explained in the following paragraphs.

First, the key issue has become the challenge of securing effective control over the formation of inflation expectations. Although the Czech Republic was the first transition economy in the region to achieve one-digit inflation in terms of CPI in 1994, some inflation inertia prevailed, and CPI inflation has fluctuated around 9–10 per cent since then. Moreover, in late 1997 a new inflation episode had begun to develop. The outlook for the first months of 1998 signalled the acceleration of inflation well above one-digit levels for the first time since 1994.

In the aftermath of exchange rate turbulence, not only did the economy lose its nominal exchange rate anchor of the past eight years, but the experience suggested that the previous strategies were not effective enough to reduce inflation expectations in the changing conditions of the successive transitional stages. In particular, the wage negotiations continued to be based on a double-digit assumption[3] despite the fact that the koruna was pegged to the basket of Deutschmarks and US dollars with no change in central parity up until May 1997. The parallel intermediary target, the money supply in terms of M2, was also met in 1997. The conclusion followed that those frameworks were neither capable nor credible enough to affect the expectations, and therefore could not secure the continuation of the disinflation process.

The strategy of inflation targeting offered an attractive alternative. Unlike previous non-binding annual forecasts, inflation targeting implies the unambiguous declaration of the disinflationary path and explicit quantitative targets of the disinflation process as a public commitment of the CNB. Disinflation became not only a prime objective, but also a direct objective of monetary policy. Accordingly, economic agents were provided with a new medium-term nominal anchor on which they could base their expectations and decision-making processes. This new nominal anchor also supplied economic agents with a longer time horizon than annual forecasts. Moreover, given the solid reputation of the CNB and its independence, this anchor was likely to be more credible than the previous forecasts.

Second, the intermediary targets, that is the pegged exchange rate and monetary aggregates, showed increased inconsistency with the underlying conditions of an advanced stage of financial openness. In its relatively flexible version of a horizontal band of ±7.5 per cent, though, the pegged exchange rate regime proved to be non-sustainable and lost credibility during the exchange rate turbulence in May 1997. The option to reintroduce this peg seemed therefore entirely unfeasible, especially due to two features: (i) the open capital account and liberalized financial markets made massive capital flows possible (both inflows and outflows) which started to dominate exchange rate developments especially in the short run, and (ii) the process of relative price adjustments especially in the segment of still-administered prices, such as energy prices for households, rents, transport tariffs and utility prices, was targeted to continue in the forthcoming period.

Accordingly, the option of importing low inflation from abroad via the pegged exchange rate regime could not be expected to be sustainable. The risk of large external imbalances parallel to the developments of 1996 and 1997 would be rather high. The managed float alternative, on the other hand, provided for the flexibility of timely, smooth corrections. In the case of increasing major imbalances, the exchange rate movements would signal inconsistency in the policies. The flexible character of the exchange rate arrangement was necessary in a regime of inflation targeting.

As for monetary aggregates and the monetary transmission mechanism, the previous experience had revealed some limitations and weaknesses. The links between money supply (M2) and price developments (CPI inflation) as well as between the intermediate target (M2) and controlled interest rates (repo rates) did not prove to be predictable or sufficiently stable. In addition to the constraints observed elsewhere, the conditions of an economy in transition made their application even less reliable.

This was due, in particular, to (i) a sequence of price shocks related to transition (corrections of administered prices, tax reforms) which distorted the link between the money supply and price developments; (ii) the institutional features of financial markets going through profound changes within a relatively short time span. This refers also to the operational targets and instruments of monetary policy. In principle, monetary transmission switched from quantities to prices; and (iii) the emergence of new financial assets, as well as new types of transactions and new market players making the demand for money function very unstable. The behaviour of commercial banks, for example, was subject to far-reaching changes in their regulation, in the impact of privatization as well as in the macroeconomic environment.

Consequently, monetary targeting itself could hardly secure a reliable basis for the medium-term disinflation strategy. Inflation targeting, on the other hand, provided a framework integrating a number of relevant economic indicators (including money supply as an important one). The common focus and the organizing criterion for their assessment contributed to the final goal of disinflation.

Third, inflation targeting has provided a scheme for filtering out exogenous price shocks from 'standard' inflationary pressures. The adopted concept of net inflation excluded regulated or administered prices as well as the effects of indirect taxes on the prices of the remaining goods and services. Accordingly, net inflation allowed monetary policy to accommodate the primary inflation impulses of transitional shocks such as corrections of administered prices. On the other hand, this framework allowed the central bank to react to their secondary inflationary effects and to prevent a spillover to price-level increases.

Implementation

In December 1997, the CNB defined its inflation targets in terms of *net inflation* with the aim of excluding transitional price shocks such as price corrections (sometimes also called price deregulation) and changes in taxes. The net inflation index was calculated backwards by the Czech Statistical Office for the purposes of inflation targeting. The consumer basket defined for the purposes of the CPI was adjusted for items with regulated prices and prices affected by other administrative measures. According to this definition, the net inflation index represents approximately 82 per cent of the consumer price index (it covers 663 of the 754 price items).

The list of items excluded from the total consumer price index was as follows: (i) prices regulated by the ministry of finance (for example, electricity) and prices regulated by local authorities (for example, taxis) – weight in CPI, 7.4 per cent, (ii) items with semi-regulated prices (for example, postal service) – weight in CPI, 6 per cent; and (iii) fees (for example, TV and radio fees) – weight in CPI, 4.4 per cent. It is worth noting that the index of net inflation can change from year to year due to this definition if there is a change in government strategy. For example, in 1997 taxis became a sector regulated by local authorities. Hence, the price of taxis was excluded from the net inflation index.

In the next step, the growth rate was calculated for this reduced index and

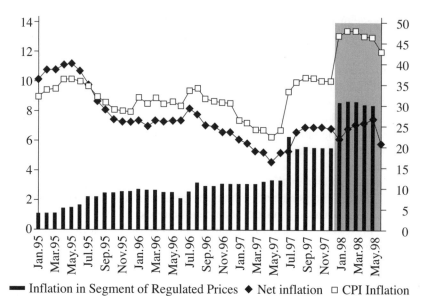

— Inflation in Segment of Regulated Prices   ◆ Net inflation   □ CPI Inflation

Note: Net inflation and CPI inflation are scaled on the left axis (%). Inflation in the segment of regulated prices is a complementary indicator to net inflation with respect to CPI inflation. This is scaled on the right axis. The shaded area shows information which was not available at the time of introducing inflation targeting.

Figure 3.4   Inflation indicators, January 1995 to July 1998

the inflation rate was modified in order to exclude the impact of changes in indirect taxes (for example, tobacco tax) or the impact of changes in subsidies. This means that items whose prices change due to tax changes remained a part of the net inflation index, however, the influence of tax changes was eliminated from net inflation. Figure 3.4 shows the values of three inflation indicators – net inflation, CPI inflation and inflation in the segment of regulated prices. Data for the 1995–97 period were available at the time of introducing inflation targeting. It is interesting to note that the pattern of dynamics had changed quite dramatically over time. In 1995, net inflation exceeded CPI inflation due to nearly zero price corrections. On the contrary, the weight of price corrections in CPI inflation was exceptional in the second half of 1997, by causing CPI inflation to exceed net inflation.

When introducing inflation targeting, the CNB worked with two time horizons. It was not possible to announce a target only in the form of the defined price stability (for example, 2 per cent inflation with 1 per cent bands) since the economy was on its disinflationary path. Hence, the 'key' target was announced for the medium term: net inflation 3.5–5.5 per cent by the end of

2000. The centre of the targeted interval was specified to guarantee the conver-gence of net inflation to European inflation before the Czech Republic's entry into the EU. The three-year horizon reflected time lags in monetary transmis-sion. The short-term target was announced for the end of 1998: net inflation 5.5–6.5 per cent. This was declared as an 'orientation target' that was derived from the medium-term disinflation trajectory. It provided a nominal anchor for economic contracts, the horizon of which usually did not exceed one year. These contracts were linked to previously published annual inflation forecasts.

During the first months of inflation targeting, the CNB explained the strat-egy of its decision-making process at several press conferences and also via press releases. It has been declared that achieving the net inflation targets will be the ultimate criterion for monetary policy decisions. Decisions will be taken on an *ex ante* basis when analysing the conditional inflation outlooks and comparing them to targeted intervals. The methods of obtaining inflation outlooks have been described. The CNB would evaluate both sets of economic indicators[4] as well as rely on model simulations. The following decision scheme was specified: should the inflation outlook deviate from the inflation target, an adjustment of the operational target (repo rate) will be considered.

Inflation targeting has been reflected in the CNB's approach to the general public. In order to increase transparency, the CNB has started publicizing the minutes of the board meetings on the internet two weeks after a meeting is held, with a fairly detailed description of the discussion as well as the reason-ing behind monetary policy decisions. At the end of the quarter, the CNB started producing inflation reports that focus on price and monetary develop-ments, inform about real economy and external sector developments and include an inflation outlook together with an explanation of monetary measures.

THE DECISION-MAKING PROCESS: JANUARY–JULY 1998

Let us now describe the decision-making process in the first seven months of inflation targeting in the Czech Republic. Following this, we shall summarize some important features of the process. Our source of information has been the Minutes of the Board Meetings on monetary policy issues. The minutes are officially publicized each month, two weeks after the meeting is held.

In January 1998, the repo rate was left unchanged. During the first month of inflation targeting, the most of the available information was from December. Despite many uncertainties, the inflation outlook was in compliance with the inflation target for the end of 1998. However, a high trade deficit in December and the consequences of the Asian crisis were viewed as a potential impulse for weakening the exchange rate. Also, the January price deregulation together with the expected consequences of regular January re-pricing increased the probability that the inflation outlook would be closer to the upper limit of the targeted interval. It was evident that in the first months of 1998, net inflation would increase due to past developments.

In February, the repo rate was again unchanged. However, this time there were two alternatives considered (the other being to raise the REPO rate). On the one hand, in this month, the inflation outlook started signalling that net inflation would be in the upper part of the targeted interval by the end of 1998. On the other, an agreement was reached that the decision on raising the repo rate should not be based on the unexpectedly high month-on-month increase in prices. The inflation outlook was modified upwards due to the previously underestimated scope of both the January re-pricing effect and the impact of deregulation on net inflation. An implication for future monetary policy decisions was that inflation expectations should be considered as a very important transmission channel and that there could be increased probability of their acceleration.

In March, by a majority vote, the repo rate was increased by 0.25 per cent to 15 per cent. The newly available February data on inflation confirmed that the risks of higher inflation in the future might outweigh the favourable trends in the economy. Various price indices signalled that without an adequate policy response, net inflation might exceed the upper limit of the targeted interval in December 1998. Moreover, the available CPI forecasts for the end of 1998 (announced by various institutions) suggested that targeted net inflation should be in the middle of this interval rather than approaching its upper band, in order to compensate for the higher than expected CPI inflation. The hypothesis of the potential for accelerating expectations formulated during a previous meeting was confirmed by the upward slope of the interest yield curve. According to the slope, inflation expectations exceeded the targeted values. It was said during the discussion that, although the observed exchange rate development supported a gradual reduction in inflation, it would not be desirable to shift the weight of the monetary transmission mechanism from an interest rate to an exchange rate channel. Consequently, the modest repo rate increase was mainly designed to affect the economy via the expectation channel.

In April, the repo rate remained unchanged. The inflation outlook for net inflation at the end of 1998 had moved back to the targeted interval. There was new information on the reduction of annualized trade and current account deficits as well as the closing of the gap between productivity and wage increases that was accompanied by the appreciation of the koruna. Also, imported deflation of input prices was reflected in domestic inflation development. At the same time, inflation expectations started decelerating.

In May, the repo rate had again remained unchanged. As in the previous month, the newly available information was favourable. The inflation outlook was in accordance with the targeted interval for the end of 1998. However, it was agreed that to some extent this was the result of external factors. First, the part of slower inflation was imported via input prices (mainly raw materials) that were purely exogenous. Second, the situation on both domestic and international financial markets caused the koruna to appreciate. On the one hand, this was partially an endogenous process linked to improving the domestic economic fundamentals. On the other hand, it was a consequence of exogenous factors since crises on some emerging markets made the koruna relatively more attractive to foreign investors. Since the above-listed external factors were viewed as temporary, this exogenous slow-down in inflation was called 'borrowed disinflation'.

In July, the repo rate was cut from 15 per cent to 14.5 per cent. According to the inflation outlook, net inflation was likely to be close to the lower band of the targeted interval by the end of 1998. The newly set repo rate was consistent with the medium-term target for 2000. It was stressed that the latest koruna appreciation was not a reason for cutting rates and that the exchange rate would not be directly affected by this monetary policy decision. The economic situation was characterized by a lower risk premium and a fall in inflation expectations. These were likely to slowly decelerate because of 'borrowed disinflation'. Also, one of the main factors – the impact of price deregulation – would have a different impact in July from the one in January since the composition of prices that were subject to changes was different and the impact on net inflation would be smaller due to an income effect.

After describing the decision-making process, the main features can be summarized. First, all decisions were discussed strictly in the framework of inflation targeting. There was no conflict of targets revealed during the discussions. The repo rate's level was clearly linked to the inflation target and the inflation outlook. When the inflation outlook signalled a deviation of net inflation from the targeted interval at the end of 1998, the repo rate was changed. It is interesting to note that decisions were symmetrical since the repo rate was increased when the outlook signalled overshooting of the targeted interval and cut when the outlook signalled undershooting.

Second, three periods of the introduction of inflation targeting can be identified. Until March, although the economic fundamentals such as the trade deficit or consumption improved, inflation expectations were not in line with the disinflationary path due to the backward-looking approach as well as to the re-pricing effect, the secondary impact of deregulation and increased exchange rate uncertainty. Until July, the situation stabilized as expectations were formed more by economic fundamentals. Since July, expectations have been on a disinflationary path to some extent due to the impact of external factors.

Third, it is important to note that the time horizon of the decision-making process did not change, because the weight of the targeted interval for the medium term had increased gradually. At the same time, the uncertainty linked with external factors forming inflation increased. The problem of 'borrowed disinflation' that helped in forming inflation expectations gained importance since external factors could be reversed in the medium-term and destabilize expectations once again.

IS A TRANSITIONAL COUNTRY A 'GOOD' INFLATION TARGETER?

The Czech Republic was the first economy in transition to adopt a regime of inflation targeting as the explicit framework for its monetary policy. Two important questions therefore arise. First, in the Czech case, do underlying conditions which still have specific features of transition allow for the effective implementation of inflation targeting? Second, what are the possible reactions to some transitional challenges within the framework of inflation targeting?

The Necessary Conditions for Effective Implementation

The first important issue is the emphasis that society puts on price and currency stability. If the priority of stability is high, the central bank's strategy as a whole is supported. The Czech experience suggests that the koruna has enjoyed remarkable stability in the course of past developments. After the First World War, the currency of the newly formed Czechoslovak Republic was the only one in the region which had avoided hyperinflation. The relatively modest monetary overhang was also a favourable feature of the macroeconomic situation in the post-Second World War era. And again, since the start of transition, unlike most other countries in the region which sooner or later adjusted their framework to the requirements of external balance and external competitiveness,[5] the priority attached to domestic price stability has remained a distinguishing feature of the Czech transitional strategy.[6]

The conclusion follows that price and currency stability are highly respected and supported by society, and therefore have been 'built into' Czech economic development and policies. This seems to be the underlying factor that is of utmost importance for the feasibility and sustainability of the inflation targeting regime in the Czech case. In situations where acceleration of economic activity and the disinflation process are discussed in terms of a short-run trade-off issue, the arguments of price stability can find public support.

The second important factor is the institutional and economic preconditions of the inflation targeting regime. The first institutional requirement to be satisfied was evidently the capability of the central bank to conduct its monetary policy with a fairly high degree of independence. This precondition for the adoption of inflation targeting was, without a doubt, in place. According to the Constitution and central bank law, the CNB is independent of the government and has sole responsibility for the conduct of monetary policy. And even more importantly, in the course of the entire transition, this independence was put into practice and demonstrated in the domain of both instruments and goals.

The second prerequisite, related to the real independence of the central bank, was fiscal discipline. With extensive public borrowing from the banking system (involving substantial increases in public debt, with shallow financial markets not being able to absorb the placement of debt instruments and high dependence on revenues from seigniorage), monetary policy would not be in a position to secure the meeting of disinflation targets. In this type of situation, inflationary pressures of a fiscal origin would develop, the effectiveness of policies for attaining nominal targets would be undermined, and the central bank would be forced to follow an increasingly accommodative monetary policy. In the case of the Czech economy, the principle of a balanced budget policy was followed throughout the past period, and the public sector borrowing requirement remained moderate. Nevertheless, the revealed 'hidden debt' of transformation institutions inflated the previous officially declared debt level.

There are other institutional factors that relate to the issue of inflation targeting. Specifically, a certain level in the development of financial markets is required. With a floating exchange rate, there is a need for a well-developed foreign exchange market that is complex enough to cushion the short-term volatility of capital flows. Also, instruments reducing exchange rate uncertainty should be available to economic agents. Moreover, if inflation targeting is introduced before major changes on financial markets take place, extensive structural breaks would make it difficult to create inflation forecasts or outlooks. Last but not least, it is very important that at the initial stage of introducing the strategy, external factors such as import prices do not damage the credibility of the new framework via significant shocks. In the Czech case, the external factors sent favourable impulses and helped set inflation expectations on the disinflationary path.

Inflation Targeting As a Disinflation Strategy

The Czech approach to inflation targeting has been influenced by the necessity of distinguishing between the long-term objective in the form of price stability and the medium-term target of disinflation. Obviously, no threshold inflation rate could be defined as a prerequisite for a viable shift to inflation targeting.

Nevertheless, the experience from other countries suggested that this regime had not been introduced in times of high or moderate inflation. Moreover, most countries switched to inflation targeting only after inflation was under control and on a decreasing path. As a rule, the CPI index had one-digit values and in the majority of cases, the central bank was faced with the problem of reducing inflation fluctuations rather than the problem of disinflation.

In the Czech case, the inflation level fluctuated around 10 per cent[7] with some inertia for several consecutive years. This level, though moderate, was higher than in other countries when shifting to inflation targeting. Moreover, an acceleration of the inflation rate was envisaged for the first months of 1998, and market expectations for the future rate of inflation seemed quite unstable with little confidence from the public that the disinflation process would be reinstituted in the foreseeable future.

Under these circumstances, despite an unfavourable outlook or rather, because of that outlook, the CNB Board did not want to wait to take a clear stand on price stability as the main objective of monetary policy. The public commitment to the explicit disinflation target and the related resolute policy stance were aimed at reversing expectations and reassuring the markets and the public. Given the situation of increased political uncertainty, highlighted by the resignation of the government, the independent central bank commitment to sound, transparent long-term goals seemed to be of utmost importance, irrespective of the potential swings in political power.

The design of inflation targets has reflected the above-analysed problems. In December 1998, the public announcement of switching to inflation targeting reassured the public that monetary policy is devoted to providing price stability. By specifying the two targets for the short- and medium-term horizons, the CNB also declared that monetary policy would aim at disinflation in a horizon that is relevant for negotiated contracts. This made the objective of price stability more realistic, since previous strategies did not declare any time horizon for reaching the European level of inflation. Hence, the channel of inflation expectations through which monetary policy affects economic decisions has become more efficient. Moreover, the new strategy probably also changed the mode in which expectations are formed, from an adaptive mode to one that was more forward looking. This has been a very important achievement. Should wages be negotiated under a strictly backward-looking mode of expectations, the costs of disinflation would be much higher and the risk of reappearance of the external imbalance would increase.

Transitional Challenges

The Czech experience in the first eight months of inflation targeting revealed two important challenges for policy makers. It has been necessary to deal with transitional shocks to prices and the consequences of having an emerging financial market. Let us describe the problem of price shocks first, since it enters both the decision-making process as well as the process of target specification. Countries that are inflation targeters usually deal with the problem of price shocks by modifying the CPI index or by declaring 'caveats'. Central banks do not commit themselves to influencing CPI inflation as a whole. Both methods are used to distinguish inflation from primary exogenous shocks to prices in order to avoid a counterproductive reaction of monetary policy.

During transition, this problem is more complex since this reform carries with it a sequence of exogenous price shocks such as tax reform or the so-called 'deregulation scheme' in which relative prices in previously regulated sectors are gradually corrected. As a result, there is a trade-off for policy makers. On the one hand, if the CPI index is modified in order to minimize the risk of a counterproductive reaction of monetary policy or the risk of missing the target, it is necessary to add to standard caveats the expected transitional shocks during transition. In this case, the new index used for specification of the target could become irrelevant to economic decisions since the share of excluded categories is high and CPI inflation might diverge from the targeted inflation.[8] Consequently, the transmission channel through expectations is weakened significantly.

On the other hand, if only standard caveats are used, the targeted inflation is more likely to converge to CPI inflation and contracts would be linked to the target. However, during transition the excluded shocks would be quite significant, as shown in Figure 3.4. Consequently, there would be three possible reactions of monetary policy: (i) to compromise on the slope of the disinflationary path and derive its slope from a deregulation scheme with all the disadvantages (for example, large fluctuations around the disinflation trend caused by changes in government strategy); (ii) to compromise on the credibility of the target itself and allow for missing it in the case of large-scale deregulation; and (iii) to rely on the substitution effect between regulated and non-regulated price segments and to accept the costs of non-accommodated supply price shocks.

In the Czech case, the first alternative has been evaluated as less costly. However, the CNB did not use many caveats explicitly when defining net inflation, because net inflation filters out some standard shocks such as the impact of indirect taxes. The majority of excluded items are those in the segment of regulated prices. Hence, one can classify net inflation as a 'transitional' concept, and it is likely that in the medium term, after major deregulation steps are completed, the two inflation rates would converge. Not only is the existence of a deregulation scheme and implied uncertainty a limiting factor when defining the target, it has consequences for the decision-making process as well. As the summary of the minutes of the meeting shows, it has been very difficult to predict the spillover effect from the segment of regulated prices to net inflation due to the unavailability of historical data as well as structural breaks.

The second important challenge for policy makers has been the problem of the existence of emerging financial markets. It is important to note that in the Czech case, the pegged exchange rate played the role of a nominal anchor for the entire period from 1990 to 1997. In May 1997, the peg was discontinued, and a more flexible regime in the form of managed floating was introduced. This shift was consistent with the requirements of the inflation targeting regime since it is feasible to target domestic inflation only in the context of a flexible exchange rate, otherwise conflicts of commitments to different targeted variables are likely to arise and the effectiveness of inflation targeting is undermined.

The shift to a floating exchange rate notwithstanding, the policy approach to the role of the exchange rate in the new setting remained an issue. Given the small size and the significant openness of the Czech economy, the exchange rate has had a remarkably large and direct impact on the CPI. At the same time, capital flows, much larger and more volatile than trade flows, have increasingly dominated short-term exchange rate developments. Moreover, in a transition economy with still relatively thin markets, wide interest rate differentials and a volatile risk premium, the exchange rate response to various shocks, new economic and political data and to changing perceptions of investors, is much more volatile and occasionally even erratic in nature. In the given circumstances, some issues related to the exchange rate within the framework of inflation targeting required clarification – for example, policy stance.

On the one hand, the level of the exchange rate can be neither an explicit nor implicit objective of monetary policy. This is because the control of the exchange rate level is neither feasible in the existing conditions nor consistent with the inflation targeting framework. Accordingly, problems of external imbalances must be coped with within a broader framework of macroeconomic policies and their combination. The foreign exchange interventions aim at smoothing the moves from one exchange rate level to another and at reducing the volatility and erratic responses in the exposed but still relatively thin koruna foreign exchange market. On the other hand, for a small, open economy, movements in the exchange rate are a significant factor that enters the decision-making process of the central bank. Subsequently, foreign investors tend to guess the reaction function of the central bank and use the implicit bands to reduce foreign exchange risk when speculating on the foreign exchange market.

Transparency Gain

An important advantage of the shift to inflation targeting was related to the increased transparency of monetary policy. Transparency, in fact, has improved in both specifying the target and decision making. As far as target specification is concerned, the adoption of an inflation targeting regime introduced a clear-cut focus for monetary policy. It has been a move from ambiguous specification of the disinflationary path to explicit specification of the slope of the path as well as the time horizons.

Moreover, in comparison to the previous situation with two parallel intermediary targets and non-binding inflation forecasts, the potential conflict of criteria that could emerge as a result of various imbalances has been removed. For example, when using two parallel intermediate targets in periods of capital inflow, it was not easy to determine which target should gain more importance in the decision-making process. Excessive monetary growth and an excessive current account deficit put monetary policy into a position in which only one parallel target could be achieved. With the inflation target, the importance of various indicators has been unambiguously (although implicitly) determined by their weight in the transmission scheme from interest rate to inflation outlook.

The second important improvement has been an increase in the transparency of the decision-making process itself. The policy steps of the central bank have become smoother and more predictable since, with a clearly defined scheme of targets and instruments, the policy rule was now unambiguous. Also, the decision-making process was made transparent due to publicizing the minutes of the meetings. By the same token, this process is more exposed to the reactions of professional economists and the general public.

This gained transparency and accountability of monetary policy proved to be beneficial. It has had a positive impact on staff efforts and performance within the bank. It has contributed as well to a better understanding of the problem and to increased and more diversified public involvement. Also, it provided a clear framework for discussions about monetary policy since the target has been defined clearly and the commitment to ensuring disinflation has been explicit. There has been no conflict with other targets such as the external balance. One of the most important benefits has been the successful formation of expectations that have reduced the costs of the disinflation process. Also, an increase in the credibility of monetary policy has reduced the costs of external financing due to lowered risk premium.

Many foreign institutions have looked upon the new strategy as a real achievement. For example, the OECD report states:

> Globally, monetary policy has successfully negotiated a very difficult period. The decision to abandon the fixed-exchange rate regime was made before too many reserves had been spent and the Central Bank has managed to use the subsequent period to partially restock them. Although subject to volatility emanating from the developments in Asia, there have been no precipitous falls in the currency since the Spring 1997 crisis and the depreciation observed in recent months appears to be in

line with economic fundamentals. Appropriately, given the still large trade and current account deficits, monetary policy has remained restrictive, while the announcement of a new inflation-targeting framework brought a welcome end to a period of uncertainty as to the main focus of policy.[9]

NOTES

1. The Czech National Bank was established on 1 January 1993 after the dissolution of Czechoslovakia, and became a successor to the State Bank of Czechoslovakia.
2. For more information on the May exchange rate turbulence, see Kateřina Šmídková, with *Jiri Behounek, Tibor Hledik, Josef Jilek, Miroslav Kostel, Ivana Matalikova, Dana Rottova and Jana Stankova,* 'Koruna exchange rate turbulence in May 1997', CNB Working Paper no. 2, 1998. We can mention briefly here the main reasons for the turbulence. There were growing internal and external imbalances. Although monetary restriction in mid-1996 was quite significant, it was not sufficiently backed by corresponding fiscal and wage policies. In May, various impulses such as the Asian crisis and domestic political instability triggered an attack on the koruna that was followed by resident panic. After a few days of defending the bands, the CNB and the government let the koruna float.
3. In 1993, growth of average nominal wage was 25 per cent, in 1994 17 per cent, 1995 18 per cent, 1996 14 per cent and 1997 12 per cent.
4. A set of indicators is formulated in such a way as to cover the main components of inflationary influences, that is, demand and cost factors, as well as factors related to inflation expectations. The set of indicators includes: specific consumer price indices which cover various items of inflation and indicate inflation expectations; producer price indices indicating cost-related inflationary pressure; exchange rate indices; a complex of indicators characterizing monetary development, specifically monetary aggregates and interest rates; a group of indicators expressing the mutual relationship between supply and demand (from which it will be possible to derive demand pressures); indicators of labour market and wage development.
5. For example, Hungary and Poland used crawling-peg regimes. Under this scheme, the objective of monetary policy is not unambiguous since the process of disinflation can conflict with the external balance.
6. Two types of nominal anchors were drawn upon in the course of the transition years in order to affect domestic stability. In the initial stages, this was the exchange rate nominal anchor. Despite persistent real appreciation, the koruna peg to the basket was maintained with unchanged central parity and the horizontal band over the whole period from January 1991 to May 1997. In the aftermath of exchange rate turbulence, the priority of domestic stability continued via the adoption of inflation targeting.
7. There were three detectable inflation episodes. In 1993, the inflation impulse was created by the VAT reform. In 1995, the impact of capital inflow on demand started to affect inflation. In 1997, the exchange rate turbulence and the consequent depreciation of the koruna was a significant factor in the development of inflation.
8. As was shown in Figure 3.4, two types of divergence are possible. During a period of small-scale deregulation, in which inflation in the segment of regulated prices was lower than inflation in the remaining price segments, net inflation exceeded CPI inflation. Large-scale deregulation caused the CPI to exceed net inflation. Since the scheme of deregulation was usually announced on an annual basis and was conditioned by political stability, there has been uncertainty for both the scope and the direction of the divergence. Moreover, the index of net inflation itself is subject to uncertainty since the government can theoretically redefine the segment of regulated prices significantly.
9. OECD, *Economic Survey Czech Republic 1999/2000,* Paris: OECD, 2000.

4. The link between FEER and fiscal policy in a transitional period: the case of the Czech economy

Kateřina Šmídková[*]

INTRODUCTION

In 1996, the Czech Republic had already been through four successful years of transition. The Czech transitional strategy was based on rapid trade and financial liberalization, the voucher privatization scheme and a stabilization programme for which a pegged exchange rate provided a nominal anchor with the support of a balanced budget. During 1993–96, these transitional steps led to relatively low inflation, the increasing role of the private sector, economic growth and rapid financial market development.

As a consequence of these characteristics, the Czech Republic has experienced the benefits as well as the costs of capital inflow when foreign investors started showing interest in its emerging financial market. Similar to other countries in this group, the Czech economy was hit by currency turbulence[1] after a period of inflows that was followed by a reversal in capital flows. In 1997, the koruna exchange rate regime was abolished, and the koruna was allowed to float. The sustainability of the exchange rate regime became a topical issue, and the question had arisen whether there was a problem of exchange rate mismanagement.

The basic macro indicators give a general overview of the situation. Table 4.1 shows that the country's inflation and growth records were satisfactory. Specifically, in 1994–96 after shocks from both the price liberalization as well as Czechoslovakia's separation had been absorbed, the growth rate was high, and inflation was reduced to one-digit levels. However, inflation remained higher than in the countries whose currencies served as basket currencies. In 1997, the growth rate slowed down to a mere one per cent.

During the analysed transitional years, the saving ratio was high. However,

* This chapter was prepared for the ACE Conference in April 1999. The views expressed are those of the author, and do not necessarily represent those of the CNB. The author would like to thank Ray Barrell, Eric Girardin and Jan Klacek for their useful comments and suggestions.

Monetary and exchange rate policy

Table 4.1   Basic macroeconomic indicators

	y	p	s	ca	budget	deficit	m
1992	−6.40	11.00	27.45	−1.09	–	–	–
1993	−0.67	20.80	20.23	0.37	0.1	2.3	19.8
1994	2.62	10.00	20.11	−0.14	0.9	0.5	19.9
1995	6.40	9.10	22.76	−2.98	0.5	0.2	19.8
1996	3.90	8.80	22.74	−8.57	−0.1	−1.4	9.2
1997	1.00	8.50	26.60	−6.06	−1.0	−1.7	10.1

Note: The indicators are defined as follows: y = growth rate (GDP), p = inflation (CPI), s = (GDP – C – G)/GDP in current prices, ca = a ratio of current balance to GDP in current prices, *budget* = balance of the central budget (% of GDP), *deficit* = public sector deficit (% of GDP), m = money-supply growth.

Sources: Czech National Bank (CNB), Czech Statistical Office (CSU).

there was a persistent gap between domestic savings and the investment needs of the economy that resulted in a current account deficit. The external imbalance reached its peak in 1996. This was also the year in which both the central and general budgets were in deficit for the first time, although there had been a tendency towards deterioration of balance between government revenues and spending. Moreover, fiscal expansion was probably much higher than signalled with these indicators, since the 'hidden debt' was estimated to be approximately the size of the official government debt (20 per cent of GDP) in 1998.

In the 1993–95 period, during which capital flowed into the country under the pegged rate system, money supply grew significantly. Since 1996, after broadening the exchange rate bands, growth of money supply was much lower. It is worth noting that the fixed exchange rate regime was not the sole reason for capital inflows in 1993–95. Figure 4.1. describes the structure of net foreign assets (NFA) by category of capital flows. The short-term flows were not among the most important categories while the flows linked with various government privatisation schemes, such as foreign direct investment (FDI) or portfolio investments, contributed significantly to NFA dynamics.

Capital inflows reached their peak in 1995 when surplus on the capital account was 18 per cent of GDP. As a policy response to large inflows, the koruna exchange rate regime was changed in 1996. The bands around central parity were broadened from 0.5 to 7.5 per cent. Figure 4.2 shows nominal appreciation of the koruna that followed this modification of the bands. The trend reverted in the last quarter of 1996. Since then the koruna has depreciated and went outside the bands after the turbulence in May when the exchange rate regime was changed to a managed float.

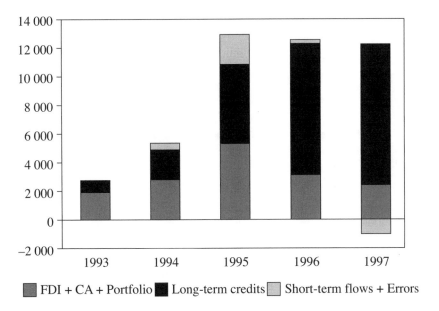

■ FDI + CA + Portfolio ■ Long-term credits □ Short-term flows + Errors

Note: The categories of capital flows are defined as follows (all in millions of dollars): FDI + CA + portfolio = cumulative sum of current account balance, FDI and portfolio investment flows, long-term credits = cumulative sum of long-term investment flows (in form of net credits), short-term flows + errors = cumulative sum of speculative flows, errors and omissions.

Sources: Czech National Bank (CNB).

Figure 4.1 Structure of net foreign assets by category of capital flows

Figure 4.3 allows us to compare nominal developments of the exchange rate to real developments. The indicator derived from the producer price index suggests that after a large nominal devaluation in 1990, the koruna returned to its pre-transitional level in real terms in 1993. There was a tendency towards real appreciation of the koruna over the whole period, disrupted only with the May turbulence in 1997. Until 1996, this tendency was a consequence of the cumulative inflation differential as well as nominal appreciation. In 1997, the inflation differential was the cause of real appreciation.

The general overview given by the indicators summarized above suggests that although in 1996 there was not a problem either of unsustainable foreign indebtedness or of solvency, there was a problem of external imbalance, which helped trigger the turbulence in May 1997. Due to a very large current imbalance, the Czech economy was placed in the group of economies having the highest deficits in the world in 1996.[2] Moreover, some simple indicators of

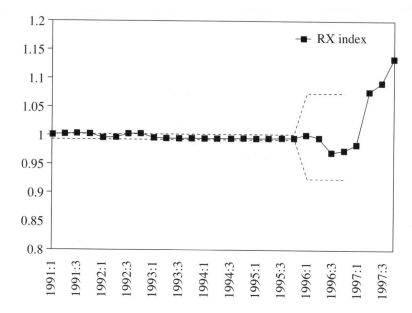

Note: The RX index is the nominal exchange rate index of the koruna *vis-à-vis* its basket currencies (with approximate weights of 65 per cent for Deutschmarks and 35 per cent for US dollars.
The dotted lines show exchange rate bands.

Sources: Czech National Bank (CNB).

Figure 4.2   Changes in the koruna exchange rate regime

competitiveness that were watched by markets (such as those presented in
Figure 4.3) signalled that the koruna had been overvalued in 1993–95.

Several studies using different criteria have tried to answer the question of
whether the koruna was overvalued in 1996. However, they did not give an
unambiguous answer, nor did they attempt to explain the causes of possible
exchange rate misalignment.[3] In this chapter, a specific model framework is
employed in order to analyse the issues of sustainability of the koruna
exchange rate regime in 1997. The FEER (fundamental equilibrium exchange
rate) model framework applied here has been developed in order to indicate a
need for a change in the economic policy package.

The FEER methodology has been suggested in Clark et al. (1994) and
Williamson (1994) as a superior approach to methods based on the purchasing
power parity (PPP) indicators if real exchange rate issues are a matter of
concern to policy makers. The FEER approach was outlined in Barrell and
Wren-Lewis (1989) and further extended in Artis and Taylor (1995) and

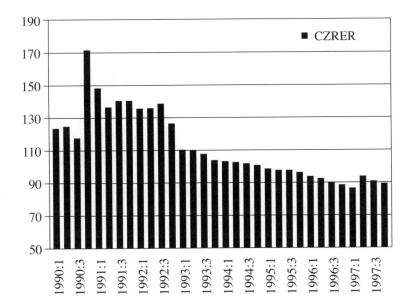

Note: The CZRER indicator is an index of competitiveness derived as a real exchange rate using producer indices.

Sources: Czech National Bank (CNB), Czech Statistical Office (CSU), International Financial Statistics (IMF).

Figure 4.3   Loss of competiveness: the PPP indicator

Barrell and Sefton (1997).[4] Similarly, we use a Mundell–Fleming framework in which the internal balance is defined as a medium-term concept consistent with sustainable output growth, and the external balance requires trade balance plus structural flows to be consistent with the target set by the authorities. FEER is derived as the real exchange rate that ensures that this external balance is reached. Thus, the FEER indicator is partially normative, since whether or not a currency is overvalued depends in part on how the authorities set their target in the model. However, sensitivity analysis can be used to reduce this problem.

The FEER model is used in this chapter in order to evaluate to what extent the koruna was overvalued before the 1997 turbulence and what were the links between FEER developments and variables approximating the stance of fiscal policy during transition in the Czech economy. The FEER framework has several relevant features. To some extent, the FEER approach helps avoid the problem of assuming that the economy starts from an equilibrium position since it has a forward-looking dimension. The model defines the equilibrium with respect to the future desired level of foreign indebtedness.

The FEER approach also aids in interpreting a suitable equilibrium for a transitional country[5] going through a period of medium-term imbalances in order to catch up with the developed world without losing the prospect of a medium-run external balance. FEER can also identify other sources of real exchange rate appreciation that are not a threat to the external stability of a domestic economy. Specifically, if a country goes through a period of significant productivity growth or changes in their portfolio, the exchange rate regime can be sustainable even with a tendency towards real appreciation of the domestic currency.

The next section of this chapter presents the underlying FEER model for the Czech economy. In the third section, the impact of fiscal policy on FEER in the model is explained, together with a short description of the specific features of fiscal policy in transition. The fourth section summarizes what the FEER simulations suggest about the sustainability of Czech external developments. The last section presents conclusions and remarks.

THE FEER MODEL

The structure of the FEER model can be summarized in the following way:[6] the model works with four trade equations (export of goods, export of services, import of goods, import of services) that are modelled in a standard way. Exports increase with foreign demand and with real exchange rate depreciation. Imports increase with domestic demand and real exchange rate appreciation:

$$MG = \sigma_1 \cdot D^{\sigma_2} \cdot \left(\frac{E \cdot Pm^*}{P} \right)^{\pm \sigma_3}, \tag{4.1}$$

where MG is import of goods in volumes, D is final expenditures, E is Koruna dollar exchange rate, P is domestic price (CPI), and Pm^* is price of imports defined as the effective index of prices of exports of trading partners,

$$MS = \delta_1 \cdot D^{\delta_2} \cdot \left(\frac{E \cdot Pm^*}{P} \right)^{\pm \delta_3}, \tag{4.2}$$

where MS is import of services in volumes,

$$XG = \chi_1 \cdot (Sg^*)^{\chi_2} \cdot \left(\frac{E \cdot Px^*}{P} \right)^{\chi_3}, \tag{4.3}$$

where *XG* is export of goods in volumes, *Sg** is foreign demand for goods (effective index), and *Px** is price of exports defined as the effective index from the CPIs of trading partners,

$$XS = \varsigma_1 \cdot (S^*) \cdot \left(\frac{E \cdot Px^*}{P} \right)^{\varsigma_3 + 1}, \tag{4.4}$$

where *XS* is export of services in volumes and *S** is foreign demand for services.

The trade balance, together with factor payments on net foreign assets, gives us the current account equation. The model captures well the dynamics of the debt problem. In each period, a change in net foreign assets is derived from current account and structural flows. With a high current deficit, net foreign assets are reduced. As a result, the external imbalance is, *ceteris paribus*, worsened further due to reduced factor income:

$$\frac{CA}{E \cdot Px^*} = \varsigma_1 \cdot S^* \cdot \left(\frac{E \cdot Px^*}{P} \right)^{\varsigma_3 + 1} + \chi_1 \cdot Sg^{*\chi_2} \cdot \left(\frac{E \cdot Px^*}{P} \right)^{\chi_3}$$
$$\pm \sigma_1 \cdot D^{\sigma_2} \cdot \left(\frac{E \cdot Pm^*}{P} \right)^{\pm \sigma_3} \cdot \frac{Pm^*}{Px^*} \tag{4.5}$$
$$\pm \delta_1 \cdot D^{\delta_2} \cdot \left(\frac{E \cdot Pm^*}{P} \right)^{\pm \delta_3} \cdot \frac{Pm^*}{Px^*} + \frac{r^* \cdot F_{\pm 1}}{E \cdot Px^*},$$

where *CA* is current account balance, *r** is foreign real interest rate, and F_{-1} is net foreign assets at the end of the previous period,

$$F = CA + F_{-1} + FDI, \tag{4.6}$$

where *F* is net foreign assets at the end of the current period, and *FDI* is exogenous structural inflow defined as foreign direct investment.

Final expenditures that enter the import equations as an activity variable consist of private demand, government demand and demand by the foreign sector for domestic goods. It is worth noting that private demand is driven by higher output (defined in a standard way) as well as higher real financial wealth held by the private sector. The wealth channel is very important in modelling the link between the real exchange rate and fiscal policy. There are two policy variables in this equation: government expenditures and financial wealth of the private sector. We shall come to the interpretation of the wealth variable in the next section.

$$D = \beta_0 \cdot Y^{\beta_1} \cdot RW^{\beta_2} + G + XG + XS, \qquad (4.7)$$

where D is final expenditures (private demand plus government consumption plus foreign demand), Y is output, RW ($= NW/P$) is real financial wealth of the private sector, NW is financial wealth, including both government debt as well as narrow money, P is the domestic price level and G is government consumption.

$$Y = D - MG - MS, \qquad (4.8)$$

where Y is output, D is final expenditures and MG and MS are imports of goods and services.

The internal balance is defined with a price equation that captures both external as well as internal pressures. On the external side, the price level increases if there is exchange rate depreciation or an increase in the foreign price level. On the internal side, the price level increases if the wage increase exceeds the sustainable rate of wage growth that is derived from the projected path for productivity growth:

$$P = \pi_0 \cdot (W/T)^{\pi_1} \cdot (Px^* \cdot E)^{\pi_2}, \qquad (4.9)$$

where P is domestic price, W is nominal wage and T is the projected path of productivity.

FEER is obtained when solving the system of ten equations for the real exchange rate ($Px^* \cdot E/P$), which is compatible with the target set by the authorities for the external balance. The target t is set in the form of a ratio of a sum of the current account deficit and structural flows with respect to nominal GDP:

$$t = \frac{CA(FEER) + FDI}{Y \cdot P}, \qquad (4.10)$$

where t is a ratio targeted by the authorities, and Y is output.

To sum up, there are eleven endogenous variables in the model: XG, XS, MG, MS, CA, F, D, Y, P, RW and $FEER$. There are three categories of exogenous variables: (i) foreign variables (r^*, FDI, Pm^*, Px^*, S^*, Sg^*), (ii) domestic variables that are projected according to their medium-run trends (W, T) and (iii) domestic variables that represent the policy scenario (G, NW, t). The link between FEER and the third-category variables is the subject of the analysis presented in this chapter. The coefficients are defined in Table 4.2.

There are two remarks worth making. First, a path of simulated FEER

Table 4.2   Long-Run Elasticities

Coefficient	Elasticity	Value
σ_2	Import of goods to final expenditures	1.47
σ_3	Import of goods to real exchange rate	0.45
δ_2	Import of services to final expenditures	1.08
δ_3	Import of services to real exchange rate	0.68
χ_2	Export of goods to foreign demand	1.00*
χ_3	Export of goods to real exchange rate	0.81
ξ_2	Export of services to foreign demand	1.54
ξ_{3+1}	Export of services to real exchange rate	0.90
β_1	Private demand to output	0.79
β_2	Private demand to real financial wealth	0.21*
π_1	Domestic prices to W/T	0.65
π_2	Domestic prices to $Px^*.E$	0.35*

Note: The values of the coefficients labelled with (*) have been imposed during estimations. Exports, imports and foreign demand are defined in volumes.

values is a normative result since it depends on what the authorities in the model consider to be a sustainable current account deficit. The stricter the target, *ceteris paribus*, the more overvalued the domestic currency is since the FEER values get higher. There is no simple answer to the question of medium-term sustainability. In this exercise, we use the commonly quoted rules of thumb that are considered important because of their attractiveness to foreign investors. The underlying story is that, although a deficit may be sustainable from the point of view of solvency constraint, once foreign investors decide that a deficit is excessive (for example, due to high risk in the region), and they start leaving the country, the currency is overvalued – even though the solvency constraint was not binding. Hence, the authorities in this model are assumed to stay on the safe side.

Second, the path is formed by exogenous variables and important elasticities in export, import, consumption functions and the price equation. Also, the initial stock of net foreign assets determines the path of the solution. Specifically, the domestic currency becomes overvalued as FEER values become higher if (*ceteris paribus*): (i) financial wealth increases or (ii) the structural inflow is reduced. As a result, there is a clear link in the model simulations between the FEER values and policy scenarios that capture fiscal and monetary policy actions.

FISCAL POLICY IN THE FEER MODEL

For the purposes of the FEER model, we need to find a definition of the private sector's financial wealth that would have an empirical counterpart. Barrell et al. (1992) define wealth of the private sector as a sum of the stock of money and government bonds and equities in the hands of the private sector in order to analyse problems of exchange-rate misalignment in European monetary union. The bonds are introduced under the assumption that full Ricardian equivalence does not hold up. The wealth effect adds an important mechanism to the model since a rise in wealth causes consumption and subsequently the current account deficit to increase.[7] It follows that in this framework FEER is co-determined by way of financing the fiscal deficit.

In the FEER model for the Czech economy, we define financial wealth analogously as a sum of narrow money, government bonds in the hands of the private sector, and voucher shares that have been transferred to the hands of the private sector during voucher privatization:[8]

$$NW = F + NDA + B + V \cdot PS, \tag{4.11}$$

where NW is financial wealth of the private sector, $M = F + NDA$ is narrow money (a stock of non-interest-bearing monetary assets), F is net foreign assets as defined by equation (4.6), NDA is net domestic asset, B is stock of government bonds, V is stock of shares held by the private sector and PS is a share price index.

This definition helps us to clarify the concept of fiscal expansion in transition. There are more actions that the authorities can take that have an impact on the real exchange rate misalignment than in standard market economies. In the initial stage of transition, the government is the owner of equities (though they do not exist yet in a materialized form) and the private sector has its own stock of monetary savings. Financial markets are non-existent, including the one with government bonds. As transition proceeds, markets develop, and the government starts issuing bonds if there is a fiscal deficit.

In addition to this standard form of increasing the private sector's wealth, the authorities employ various privatization schemes which may increase the private sector's wealth as well. For example, during voucher privatization, households were given vouchers to bid for equities. Other privatization schemes attract foreign investors, and consequently allow for a country to have a higher current account deficit since, as a result of structural inflows, foreign debt does not increase. It is worth noting that in the first case, it is not likely that the government will reduce its spending accordingly. In the second case, privatization allows for 'hidden' fiscal expansion since it is possible to

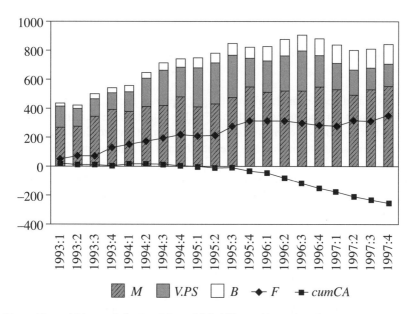

Note: The variables are defined as follows (all in billions of koruna): *M* is narrow money, *V* is voucher shares transferred to the hands of households, *PS* is market price approximated with the PSE index (Prague stock exchange index), *B* is stock of government bonds, *F* is net foreign assets, *cumCA* is the cumulative sum of current account deficits.

Figure 4.4   Financial wealth: approximation of the structures

postpone some cuts in spending due to temporary privatization revenues and finance consolidation of 'old bad' debts.

Summing up, one can say that FEER is co-determined not only by fiscal discipline and financing means, but also by temporary transitional fiscal tools linked with privatization and subsequent transfers of wealth. Figure 4.4 compares the impact of transitional tools with the impact of bond deficit financing in the case of the Czech economy. We work with an approximation of the private sector's wealth since there is a lack of data on the flow of funds between sectors in the economy. Figure 4.4 shows that the stock of bonds issued by the government during transitional years is relatively low in comparison to other sources of financial wealth.

The most dynamic part of financial wealth is the stock of equities held by households. In 1992, households held no equities. Then in two waves of voucher privatization, a significant portion of state wealth was transferred to the hands of households. This increase in wealth was reduced by a lack of liquidity on the domestic market, which caused prices to fall on the Prague stock exchange. Narrow money grew steadily over the observed period. The main source of growth was capital inflow attracted by both the interest rate differential under the fixed exchange rate regime as well as privatization schemes. In 1993, NFA covered 20 per cent of narrow money. In 1997, it covered 76 per cent of narrow money even after the May attack on the koruna.

As stated above, financial wealth of the private sector is approximated in this chapter for the purposes of the FEER simulations. Since the impact of wealth redistribution during transition on consumption decisions was high, it was not possible to neglect the wealth channel in simulations, although the approximation is far from ideal. Two important factors are not captured with our variable NW. First, a portion of bonds as well as voucher shares was traded between residents and foreign investors. Second, the hidden fiscal expansion is not described at all. The first factor would reduce wealth, and the second one would increase it. Hence, it is difficult to say what kind of bias our approximation has.

Despite possible biases, our variable describes well one important feature of the transitional process. In 1994–95, as a consequence of the privatization strategy, the private sector's wealth increased significantly. At the same time, this strategy together with other institutional reforms (such as the introduction of the convertibility of the koruna or the emergence of financial markets) attracted capital inflows. Under the fixed exchange rate regime, it was not possible for the nominal exchange rate to accommodate these dramatic changes. As a result, in subsequent years, the wealth channel described at the beginning of this section helped accommodate them.

In order to simulate the FEER values for 1993–97, we make several assumptions that correspond to the above-described feature when selecting policy variables in the model. We assume that defending the koruna exchange rate regime was a priority for monetary policy. We assume that financial wealth is a policy variable for fiscal authority in the model. It is exogenous to the private sector, which is a driving force of the model via its consumption, for the following reasons. The privatization strategy and institutional reforms determine the stock of equities held by the private sector and their prices. Similarly, to a large extent these two factors govern the scope of capital inflows to which the central bank responds with narrow money creation (and partial sterilization).

With this definition of policy variables in the model, the exchange rate misalignment, defined by deviation of the real exchange rate from the FEER values, can have two causes: (i) a significant external shock such as a fall in foreign demand or a fall in foreign prices, and (ii) inconsistency of the nominal exchange rate and financial wealth – the two key policy variables in the model. In the latter case, the FEER simulation does not give an answer to which policy variable should have been changed.

MODEL SIMULATIONS

The model simulations have been run for the 1993–97 period (four quarters out of the estimation sample) in order to detect whether FEER started diverging significantly from the corridor implied by the koruna exchange rate regime. The simulations were carried out for 12 policy scenarios, all having the same paths for productivity and wage growth which approximate internal inflation pressure on domestic prices: these were derived from average annual wage growth rates over the 1991–96 period and the assumption that sustainable output growth in this period was about 1 per cent.[9]

As far as exogenous policy variables are concerned, the 12 scenarios differ in the assumptions about the value of the target t for the external balance and the assumptions on the level of structural inflows (FDI) and on the path of nominal financial wealth. As stated above, the path for financial wealth has been subject to policy analysis while the other two assumptions are used to test how the simulation results are sensitive to model assumptions.

There have been three alternative targets considered as definitions of a sustainable current deficit: (i) 'zero' target ($t = 0$ per cent) in which authorities strictly define the target as a balance – this scenario implies constant foreign indebtedness; (ii) 'ambitious' target ($t = -4$ per cent) in which authorities assume that a country will be able to repay a higher stock of debt – this scenario implies a relatively fast increase in foreign indebtedness; and (iii) 'realistic' target ($t = -2.04$ per cent) in which authorities allow for a low deficit – this scenario implies a slower increase in foreign indebtedness.

There have been two alternative assumptions for the structural flows: (i) a 'low-inflow' assumption takes the average value of FDI inflows from the whole 1991–96 period; and (ii) an 'average-inflow' assumption works with the average value of FDI inflows in 1993–96. The latter assumption is more optimistic since it considers only the period of relatively high structural inflows attracted to a significant extent by various privatisation schemes.[10]

For the purposes of policy simulations, two alternative paths for nominal financial wealth have been used: (i) a 'restrictive' path has been derived from the actual values of financial wealth in 1993–97; and (ii) an 'expansive' path has been defined for the 1996–97 period by the average growth rate of financial wealth in 1993–95. Table 4.3 compares the 12 scenarios with the simulation scenarios described above.

The 12 paths of FEER obtained from the simulations under alternative scenarios described in Table 4.3 have been used in order to construct the FEER corridor. It captures some of the uncertainty linked with the assumptions that were necessary for model solution. In order to relate the FEER corridor to the limits of the exchange rate regime, the real exchange rate corridor has been constructed for the koruna, which shows the maximum possible exchange rate

Table 4.3   Twelve Simulation Scenarios

Scenario	Real financial wealth	Value of t (%)	FDI
	Policy variable	Sensitivity analysis	
1	Restrictive	0.00	Average
2	Restrictive	−4.00	Average
3	Restrictive	−4.00	Low
4	Restrictive	−2.04	Average
5	Restrictive	0.00	Low
6	Restrictive	−2.04	Low
7	Expansive	0.00	Average
8	Expansive	−4.00	Average
9	Expansive	−4.00	Low
10	Expansive	−2.04	Average
11	Expansive	0.00	Low
12	Expansive	−2.04	Low

Note: The value of t is a target for the current account, real financial wealth is a policy variable determined by a mix of monetary and fiscal policies as well as the privatisation strategy, FDI is structural inflow (foreign direct investment).

movements implied by the bands. Figures 4.5 and 4.6 compare the simulation results for the two categories of solutions. Figure 4.5 shows the FEER corridor for restrictive scenarios 1–6 from Table 4.3. Figure 4.6 presents the FEER corridor based on scenarios 7–12 from Table 4.3.

Given the definition of policy scenarios, the FEER paths (or centre values of both corridors) differ due to the policy scenario for nominal financial wealth. The bands of the FEER corridors are in both cases determined by a sensitivity of solutions to assumptions about the scope of structural flows and the target for t. Both restrictive as well as expansive scenarios start indicating the overvaluation of the koruna since 1996, when for both categories of scenarios the real exchange rate left the FEER corridor.

However, the two categories of solutions differ in the scale of overvaluation implied. First, under restrictive scenarios, the currency turbulence in May 1997 and subsequent depreciation moved the observed values of the koruna real exchange rate back to the FEER corridor. Should both fiscal expansions in 1996 and 1997 continue at a rate similar to previous years, the wealth channel in the model would make the problem of overvaluation much worse. As a result, the depreciation observed in May 1997 would not be enough to correct for external imbalance.

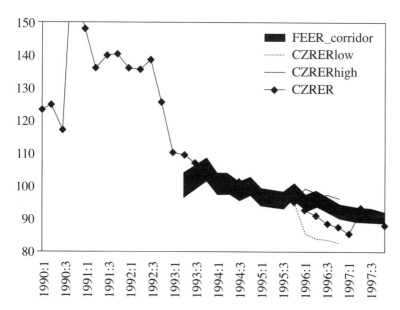

Note: CZRER is the real effective exchange rate of the koruna. The FEER_corridor has been constructed around the average value of the FEER solutions of scenarios 1–6 (Table 4.3) under the assumption of actual economic policies. The bands (CZRERlow, CZRERhigh) show the limits of the koruna exchange rate regime (abolished in May 1997).

Figure 4.5 '*Restrictive' scenarios*

Second, it is interesting to note that even in 1997 the restrictive scenarios did not imply that the koruna exchange rate regime was not sustainable. The FEER corridor did not diverge from the bands implied by the exchange rate regime. This is not true for the expansive scenarios. Some of them were not consistent with the bands implied by the koruna exchange rate regime since the upper band is in the middle of the FEER corridor.

CONCLUSIONS

We saw in the introductory section that many approaches did not give an unambiguous answer to whether the koruna was overvalued in May 1997 or to whether the exchange rate regime was unsustainable. On one hand, due to a very low level of foreign indebtedness,[11] even a quite large current account deficit was sustainable in the medium term. On the other hand, indicators based on the PPP signalled that there had been a problem of overvaluation

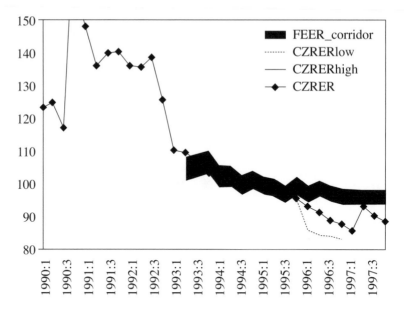

Note: CZRER is the real effective exchange rate of the koruna. The FEER_corridor has been constructed around the average value of the FEER solutions of scenarios 7–12 (Table 4.3) under the assumption of expansive growth in nominal financial wealth. The bands (CZRERlow, CZRERhigh) show the limits of the koruna exchange rate regime (abolished in May 1997).

Figure 4.6 'Expansive' scenarios

since 1993. The FEER simulations allow us to try to interpret this issue in the structural model framework.

According to the FEER model, the koruna became overvalued in 1996. This result is consistent with our intuition that the simple PPP indicators, which do not take into account some important factors, tend to exaggerate the problem of exchange rate misalignment. The simulations suggest that a correction of misalignment was possible within relatively broad exchange rate bands. Hence, under certain conditions the regime was sustainable. In the FEER model, these conditions would be met if players on financial markets understood that the impact of fiscal restrictions accepted in 1997 together with completion of various temporary fiscal transitional actions would reduce demand pressure significantly.

The FEER simulations suggest that if expectations of those players were formed on past experience with the impact of fiscal actions on the domestic economy, the exchange rate regime would not appear to be sustainable. Moreover, under this assumption, depreciation of the koruna in May 1997 was not enough to correct the exchange rate misalignment. One important conclusion follows.

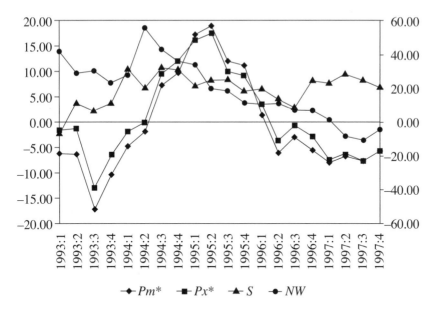

$$\rightarrow Pm^* \quad \rightarrow Px^* \quad \rightarrow S \quad \rightarrow NW$$

Note: The variables are defined as follows S = weighted average of foreign activity variables (S = 0.8 · Sg^* + 0.2 · S^*), Pm^* = price of imports (effective index, prices of exports of trading partners), Px^* = price of exports (effective index, CPIs of trading partners), NW = financial wealth of the private sector (secondary axis).

Figure 4.7   Exogenous factors: policy versus external variables (%)

Policy makers as well as the players on financial markets should understand the role of wealth redistribution in the economy and that fiscal actions are as transparent as possible. The second important conclusion suggested by the results of the FEER simulations is that the problem of exchange rate misalignment may also arise due to 'bad luck' if external factors worsen the current account imbalance. Figure 4.7 compares the path of our policy variable with the ones of external variables.

As far as exogenous variables in the model are concerned, there was a time coincidence of several events. Financial wealth continued to increase until the end of 1996, although at a decelerating rate since 1994. Foreign demand continued to increase at an accelerating rate only until 1995. The decelerating trend was reversed at the end of 1996. Since 1994, foreign prices of both Czech exporters as well as importers continued to increase at an accelerating rate until 1995. Since the second half of 1995, foreign prices were increasing at a decelerating rate. They started falling in the second half of 1996.

In the FEER framework, one can interpret these observations as follows. Our wealth policy variable contributed to divergence of the real exchange rate from FEER in the period from 1993 to 1996. In 1997, the domestic wealth channel helped reduce the external imbalance. The dynamics of foreign demand improved the external balance in the period from 1993 to 1995 and in 1997, but caused the exchange rate to diverge in 1996. Developments in foreign prices worsened the problem of the external imbalance in the period from 1996 to 1997.

Summing up, according to the FEER model, the koruna became overvalued in 1996 due to a coincidence of three events: continuing growth in financial wealth, a slow-down in foreign demand and a decline in foreign prices. Indicated exchange rate misalignment had both domestic as well as external causes. It is possible to extend this conclusion further and say that in May 1997, the attack on the koruna emerged because of the inconsistency of three factors: the fixed exchange rate regime, the overestimated scope of ongoing fiscal expansion and unfavourable external developments. This result demonstrates well the possibilities of the FEER methodology. It helps in detecting the problem of exchange rate misalignment. However, it cannot suggest the solution for policy makers since the signalled misalignment should be viewed as a consequence of the mix of events rather than of an inappropriate exchange-rate policy alone.[12]

NOTES

1. For a description of the koruna turbulence in May 1997, see Šmídková et al. (1998).
2. See, for example, *Emerging Markets Biweekly*, Issue No. 97/10 by Goldman Sachs which compared various indicators for 26 emerging markets in Africa, Eastern Europe, Latin America, the Middle East and Asia. In this report, in 1996 the Czech Republic had the highest current account deficit (% per cent of GDP), and the recommendation for foreign investors was to stay short in their koruna positions.
3. Lazarova and Kreidl (1997) estimated the equilibrium exchange rate for the Czech economy. The results suggested quite strong nominal overvaluation of the koruna at the end of 1996. Their conclusion relied on partial analysis with only two trade equations included in the model under the implicit assumption that the exchange rate was in equilibrium in 1990. Halpern and Wyplosz (1996) estimated the equilibrium exchange rates for several transitional economies using the international comparison of dollar wages. For the Czech Republic, they argued that the initial undervaluation of the koruna was not completely reversed by the end of 1996, due to a change in national characteristics such as the size of the government sector, GDP per worker, school enrolment and the ratio of agriculture to industry.
4. There are other concepts of the equilibrium exchange rate. For example, see Edwards (1989) and Stein and Allen (1995).
5. The approach has been used for other Asian developing countries in Barrell et al. (1996).
6. In order to apply the FEER methodology to the Czech case, it was necessary to find the parameters for the presented model framework. For this purpose, the Czech model presented in Šmídková (1998) has been slightly modified. Values of long-run elasticities presented in the Table 4.2 stay the same.
7. Barrell et al. (1992) also demonstrate the dynamics of the problem. Over a longer time horizon, there is an integral control mechanism in the model. With a high current account deficit,

it is likely that nominal financial wealth would be reduced via a fall in net foreign assets. Moreover, the price level accommodates inflationary pressures of increased consumption. Hence, the real wealth is reduced further. Since both mechanisms can be very protracted, the real exchange rate can deviate from FEER for a considerable time period during which a currency crisis occurs.

8. See Allen and Šmídková (1997) for a description of the voucher privatization scheme and an analysis of the impact of voucher privatization on the private sector's demand for goods and financial assets.
9. This assumption was subject to the sensitivity analysis presented in Šmídková (1998).
10. See Lansbury et al. (1996) for an analysis of determinants of the FDI inflows in Central and Eastern Europe.
11. In 1993, the ratio of foreign debt netted against foreign exchange reserves to GDP was 15 per cent. In 1997, it was approximately 25 per cent.
12. The ambiguity of the concept of the real equilibrium exchange rate is recognized by Breuer (in Williamson 1994), who exposes the problem of whether the desired exchange rate system should ensure internal and external stability or whether policies should be designed to create the internal and external conditions under which the desired equilibrium emerges naturally. The conflict between tools and targets is also explained in Williamson (1994). If a target zone is the selected exchange rate regime, fiscal policy becomes a tool for defending the zone, and cannot be designed according to another fiscal rule. Adding to the difficulties, there is no agreement on which policy tool (whether fiscal or monetary policy) should be assigned to the exchange rate target.

REFERENCES

Allen, Ch. and K. Šmídková. (1997), 'Voucher privatization, households' demand for consumption goods and financial assets and implications for monetary policy', Institute of Economics, Working Paper no. 70.

Artis, M.J. and M.P. Taylor (1995), 'Misalignment, debt accumulation and fundamental equilibrium exchange rates', *National Institute Economic Review*, August, 61–83.

Barrell R., B. Anderton, M. Lansbury and J. Sefton (1996) 'Exchange rate policies and development strategies in Taiwan, Korea, Singapore and Thailand', National Institute of Economic and Social Research, London, mimeo.

Barrell R., J.W. In't Welt and A. Gurney (1992) 'The real exchange rate, fiscal policy and the role of wealth', *Journal of Forecasting*, **11**, 361–88.

Barrell, R. and J. Sefton (1997), 'Fiscal policy, real exchange rates and monetary union', National Institute of Economic and Social Research, London, mimeo.

Barrell, R. and S. Wren-Lewis (1989) 'Fundamental equilibrium exchange rates for the G-7', Centre for Economic Policy Research Discussion Paper no. 323, June.

Clark, P., L. Bartolini, T. Bayoumi and S. Symansky (1994), 'Exchange rates and economic fundamentals: a framework for analysis', International Monetary Fund Occasional Paper no. 115.

Edwards, S. (1989), *Real Exchange Rates, Devaluation, and Adjustment: Exchange Rate Policy in Developing Countries*, Cambridge, MA and London: MIT Press.

Halpern, L. and Ch. Wyplosz (1996), 'Equilibrium exchange rates in transition economies', International Monetary Fund Working Paper no. 125.

Lansbury, M., N. Pain and K. Šmídková (1996), 'Foreign direct investment in Central Europe since 1990: an economic study', *National Institute Economic Review*, no. 156, May.

Lazarova, Stepana and Vladimir Kreidl (1997), 'Rovnovazny Kurz', CNB Working Paper no. 75.

Šmídková K. (1998), 'Estimating the FEER for the Czech economy, Institute of Economics, Czech National Bank, Working Paper no. 87.

Šmídková K., with Jiri Behounek, Tibor Hledik, Josef Jilek, Miroslav Kostel, Ivana Matalikova, Dana Rottova and Jana Stankova (1998), 'Koruna exchange-rate turbulence in May 1997', Czech National Bank, Working Paper no. 2.

Stein, J.L. and P.R. Allen (1995), *Fundamental Determinants of Exchange Rates*, New York and Oxford: Oxford University Press, Clarendon Press.

Williamson J. (1994), *Estimating Equilibrium Exchange Rates*, Washington, DC: Institute for International Economics.

5. Interest rate policy and inflation behaviour in the Czech Republic: from exchange rate to inflation targeting

Eric Girardin and Nicholas Horsewood

INTRODUCTION

After the speculative attacks which hit the Czech koruna in spring 1997, the Czech monetary authorities abandoned exchange rate targeting in favour of inflation targeting towards the end of 1997. Given the change of focus of economic policy, it is useful to try to isolate the arguments of the interest rate reaction function of the Czech monetary authorities in the former period and determine to what extent they changed in the subsequent period.

One needs to evaluate the success of the inflation targeting strategy by examining its impact on inflation forecasts and on the dynamics of the inflation process. Previous work, which examined the experience of inflation targeting in the Czech Republic (Mahadeva and Šmídková 1998), relied on a calibrated model. We rather favour here an econometric approach that may look somewhat tentative given the short span of data available. However, we manage to partially side step this limitation by using monthly data, with the key series displaying considerable variability.

In the next section of this chapter we review briefly the experience of the Czech Republic with the search for a nominal anchor, relying initially on exchange rate targeting and switching to inflation targeting some time after the collapse of the target zone. The following section provides estimates of the interest rate reaction function of the Czech National Bank (CNB) over the two regimes. Then, we offer a first assessment of inflation targeting based on an analysis of the change in inflation behaviour and on the quality of inflation forecasts provided by a Phillips curve. The final section concludes.

THE SEARCH FOR A NOMINAL ANCHOR

From Exchange Rate to Inflation Targeting

The tradition of valuing price stability is an ancient one in the former Czechoslovakia. In the 1920s it avoided the hyperinflation that plagued its neighbours, and the post-velvet revolution inherited stable public finances testifying that the tradition was jealously kept.

The Czech economy has followed in the footsteps of the Czechoslovakia of the early 1990s, and chosen an exchange rate anchor as a means of achieving price stability (see Bordes and Girardin 1998). This choice was motivated (Tosovsky 1996) by two factors. First, the difficulty in predicting the speed and extent of the changes in the velocity of money during the early stages of transition. Second, the high degree of openness of the Czech economy (some 40 per cent of GDP for the average share of imports and exports) made the reduction of exchange rate uncertainty a major policy goal if international trade was to be stabilized during the transition process. Furthermore, the high visibility of the exchange rate to the general public made it easier for the population to assess the seriousness of the commitment of monetary authorities, which had no track record to back their credibility.

The policy officially followed by the CNB since the split of the former Czechoslovakia has been characterized, except for more than a quarter in 1997, by the adherence to nominal anchors. This consistency aimed at ensuring a gradual fall in inflation. From early 1993 to mid-1997, the authorities favoured an exchange rate target with a peg to a basket composed of the Deutschmark and the US dollar, accompanied by some target range for the growth in money supply.

However, inflation remained persistently higher than in trading partners, and the current account deteriorated very substantially. All the more so that the 'impossible trilogy' implied that capital inflows took advantage of the high interest rate differential and the expected stability of the exchange rate, leading to the sustained growth in money supply, which the central bank could not really sterilize (Girardin and Klacek 1999). Efforts by the authorities to reduce domestic demand and dampen inflationary pressures were thus unsuccessful. The collapse of the target zone in late May 1997, in spite of a wise pre-emptive (but insufficient) widening of the band in late February 1996, led to a 10 per cent depreciation in the koruna *vis-à-vis* its basket of currencies and the switch to a floating regime.

The period after the collapse of the target zone up to the end of 1997 is generally considered (for instance OECD 1998) to represent a period of 'uncertainty' with respect to the strategy that the authorities would follow. The authorities reintroduced a nominal anchor only at the end of December 1997

with the adoption of an inflation target. This aimed at committing the authorities to a well-defined medium-term strategy in an attempt to anchor expectations. The target is defined in terms of 'net inflation', excluding from the
consumer price index (CPI) measure both administered prices and increases in
indirect taxes. The objective was to reduce this preferred measure of inflation
to 6 per cent by the end of 1998 with a 0.5 per cent band for freedom, and to
4.5 per cent by the end of 2000 with a 1 per cent band. It is noteworthy,
however, that in its early inflation reports, the Czech National Bank emphasized that 'the introduction of a new monetary policy strategy does not imply
a change in its target as such, but only in the way the monetary policy is implemented' (Czech National Bank Inflation Report 1999, p. 6).

Recent literature has stressed that inflation targeting should not be taken
as representing a rule-based monetary policy. Such a strategy does not
prevent some policy activism. 'It provides a framework which allows for the
pursuit of other objectives than price stability in a more disciplined and
consistent manner' (Bernanke et al. 1998, p. 21). Within the constraints
imposed by their medium- to long-term inflation targets, inflation targeting
confers a considerable degree of discretion to policy makers, who can thus
respond in the short run to changes in economic activity or movements in
exchange rates. Inflation targeting is thus a policy of 'constrained discretion'
(Bernanke et al. 1998).

It is well known that exchange rate target zones with reasonably wide bands
(such as the one adopted by the Czech monetary authorities in 1996) can also
offer the authorities some margin for manoeuvre in the short run, what
Svensson (1994) dubbed 'monetary independence in spite of fixed exchange
rates'.

The Czech case offers yet another opportunity, akin to the Swedish one, to
reflect on the basic strengths and weaknesses of exchange rate versus inflation
targeting. The lesson from theoretical work (Canzoneri et al. 1997) is that
inflation targeting works best in an environment where political pressures are
not too strong, where shocks causing the stabilization problem are primarily
asymmetric and where the foreign central bank (the currency of which is used
as an anchor) is pursuing very different policy goals. By contrast, a target zone
is to be preferred when domestic political pressures are strong, shocks are
symmetric and policy preferences are similar. Moreover, the two approaches
differ in the penalty mechanisms involved. Indeed, the exchange rate, as an
asset price, provides an immediate 'verdict' on the effectiveness of present as
well as expected future policies. By contrast, in the case of inflation targeting
there is a delay of at least a year between 'action and punishment'. 'The
exchange rate mechanism may therefore be thought to be more credible, but it
is also open to self-fulfilling speculative attacks' (Canzoneri et al. 1997, p. 59).
As a result inflation targeting seems able to survive under conditions which

would not allow the survival of an exchange rate target zone. This certainly corresponds to the Czech experience since 1997.

The Movements in the Main Macroeconomic Variables

The database we use below is from the Institute of Economics of the Czech National Bank,[1] with updates from OECD Main Economic Indicators. The variable we take as representing the stance of Czech monetary policy is the three-month interest rate (pribor). The other variables we shall be considering are the exchange rate of the koruna *vis-à-vis* the mark and the dollar. We also take into account a measure of inflation, either the rate of change of the CPI or the 'net inflation' series and an indicator of capacity utilisation: the output gap.

Two features of the movements in PRIBOR are particularly striking. First, during the second half of 1994 the rise in US interest rates seems to have been paralleled in an amplified way, while German interest rates were falling (Figure 5.1). Second, there was a sharp drop in the Czech interest rate in January 1995. The stability of market rates from late 1994, within a corridor of 10 to 13 per cent, until the eve of the speculative attack in May 1997 is also remarkable. Before the crisis, the authorities had tightened monetary policy

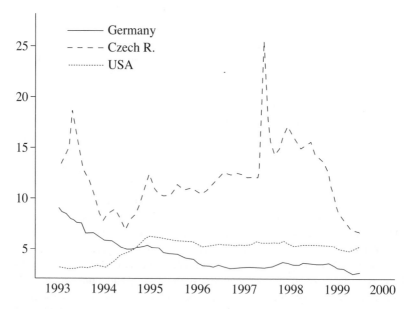

Figure 5.1   Three-month interest rates: the Czech Republic, Germany and the USA

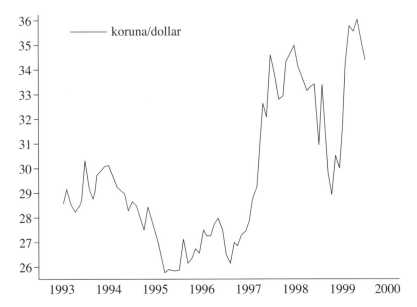

Figure 5.2   Dollar per koruna

with a 100 basis point increase in the discount rate (reaching 10.5 per cent) leading to a rise in the market rates. At the time of the crisis the latter when up to 26 per cent with the Lombard rate reaching double this figure. The subsequent decrease in the Lombard rate was only very gradual with a fall to 23 per cent in June 1997 and to 19 per cent in January 1998. Market rates displayed some inertia and went down to 15 per cent in early autumn 1997 before increasing again later in the year to 17 per cent due to renewed pressures on international currency markets and domestic political difficulties. The restrictive stance during 1997 aimed initially at preventing an 'excessive' depreciation of the koruna, and later at cooling down domestic demand and moderating the inflationary impact of the depreciation. Over the period from early 1998 up to June 1999, market rates fell continually, reaching below 7 per cent by the end of the period.

The depreciation of the koruna *vis-à-vis* the Deutschmark in 1997 occurred in two stages with the first wave linked to the speculative attack in May and a second one associated with spillovers from currency crises in East Asia in the autumn. However, the koruna appreciated again in 1998 (Figures 5.2 and 5.3).

In order to compute the output gap for industrial production, we use a standard technique, for instance as commonly implemented by the OECD. We estimate the trend with a Hodrick–Prescott (1997) filter (with $\lambda = 126\ 400$, given that we use monthly data) and generate the gap as the difference

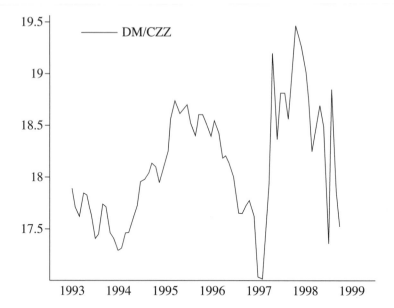

Figure 5.3   Koruna per Deutschmark

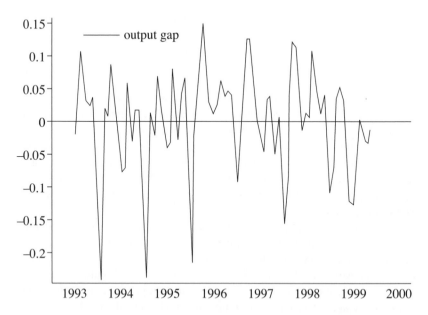

Figure 5.4   Output-gap (actual industrial output minus Hodrick–Prescott trend)

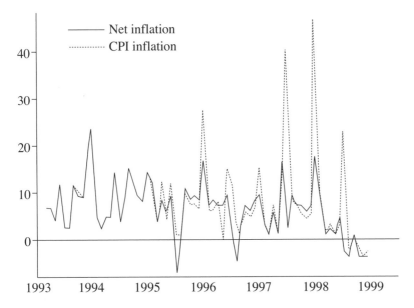

Figure 5.5   Official CPI and net inflation (annual rate, %)

between the actual log of industrial production and the calculated trend. The series we obtain is graphed on Figure 5.4.

Net inflation, as used by the CNB, excludes movements in administered or controlled prices (including health and general insurance) as well as the impact of changes in indirect taxes on the prices of other goods. In other words, net inflation excludes the bulk of non-traded goods and services, to the effect that in the net inflation basket, 85 per cent of goods are traded ones as against 66 per cent in the CPI. This implies that net inflation is more sensitive (by about 30 per cent) to exchange rate movements than CPI inflation. Broadly speaking (Figure 5.5), the two measures of inflation diverged in January and July every year since mid-1995. Net inflation was computed back to early 1995 by the Czech National Bank.

In order to assess the extent of success of disinflation under inflation targeting, we computed the inflation rate with respect to the same month of the previous year expressed as an annual percentage. Figure 5.6 shows that by late 1998 the CPI inflation rate had fallen back to its early 1997 level, on the eve of the speculative attack against the koruna.

There is, of course, the cautionary note that disinflation in the Czech Republic could have simply mirrored the general disinflation experienced in industrial countries over the recent period. To put aside such an easy explanation, it is enough to observe that disinflation in the Czech Republic was particularly

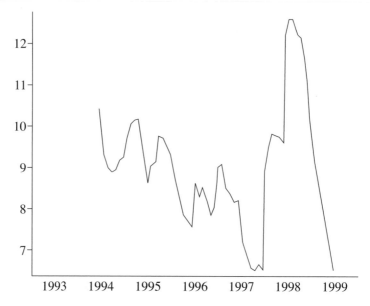

Figure 5.6   Smoothed CPI inflation (change in CPI with respect to same month of previous year)

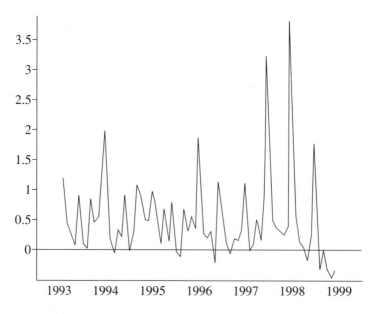

Figure 5.7   Czech inflation differential with the USA

remarkable, as illustrated by the decline in the Czech inflation differential with the USA, as plotted on Figure 5.7.

The causality of the target and the outcome needs to be questioned: did the timing of the adoption of inflation targets simply coincide with a period when the Czech Republic was most likely to meet those targets? Indeed, given that it took place right after a burst of inflation, it is not clear that the primary concern would have been as in the British, Australian and Canadian experiences 'to lock in previous reduction in inflation in the face of a one-time price level rise (here from the devaluation)' (Bernanke et al. 1998, p. 148). The Czech case may have been closer to the British one, where the situation was more urgent than in the case of the other two pioneers (see also Leiderman and Svensson 1995).

THE CENTRAL BANK REACTION FUNCTION

We shall use monthly data on the period[2] from mid-1993 to mid-1999 to examine the determinants of interest rate policy in the Czech Republic and investigate the stability of such a policy.

The central bank reaction function is estimated over the period from July 1993 to July 1999 and is presented in Table 5.1, where *t*-statistics are given in parentheses. In the long run the Czech interest rate (PRIBOR) is linked to the arithmetic average of the US interest rate, denoted iUS, and the German interest rate, represented by iG. This indicates that when setting

Table 5.1   Interest rate reaction function, July 1993 to July 1999

$\Delta PRIBOR_t = 2.01 + 1.39 \, \Delta_4 iG_{t-1} + 3.53 \, M_{13}[GAP_t] - 0.107 \, \Delta_3 PRIBOR_{t-2} + 6.96 \, \Delta_3 lnIND_{t-1}$
        (4.13)   (8.15)   (5.02)   (7.96)   (2.94)
        $-0.208 \, [PRIBOR - 0.5(iG + iUS)]_{t-1} + 0.46 \, M_{13}[NETINF_t] + 7.19 \, D97m5$
        (−7.25)   (7.96)   (13.9)
        $+ 6.99 \, D97m6 - 5.78 \, D97m7 + seasonals$
        (11.8)   (−9.11)

$R^2 = 0.95$	$F(20,52) = 52.9 \, [0.0]$	$\sigma = 0.444349$	DW = 1.77
AR 1– 1 F(1, 51) = 0.61 [0.43]		ARCH 1 F(1, 50) = 0.061 [0.80]	
Normality $\chi^2(2) = 3.16$ [0.20]		RESET F(1, 51) = 0.35 [0.55]	

Legend
$M_{ij}(X_t)$	Moving average of X_{t-i} to X_{t-j}
AR	LM test for autocorrelated residuals
ARCH	LM test for autocorrelated squared residuals
Normality $\chi^2(2)$	Jarque–Bera normality test
RESET	Regression specification test.

interest rates the Czech National Bank is influenced by world financial developments, proxied by the USA, as well as by those in Europe. The constraint of a 0.5 coefficient is imposed on interest rates but is a valid restriction. The equilibrium correction coefficient implies a mean lag of four months, which is consistent with the speed of policy response. Domestic concerns influence the Czech National Bank as the authorities raise the interest rate whenever net inflation rises in the previous months, with a one-half spillover effect. The estimated reaction function of the Czech National Bank displays plausible dynamic features. The Czech interest rate also rises when the Bundesbank lifts its interest rate over the previous four months (with an amplifying effect: from one to 1.7) and when there is an acceleration in the change of the US interest rate over the previous quarter. The Czech interest rate is also raised whenever the koruna depreciates *vis-à-vis* the basket of the US dollar and the German mark, denoted IND, and captures short-run exchange rate considerations. Monetary policy is also used for output stabilization since a rise in the output gap (GAP), measured as actual output over trend output, over the previous quarter leads to an increase in the Czech interest rate. The effects of the currency crisis in May 1997 are partialled out by dummies, where DXmY represents a dummy for year X and month Y.

Since the estimation period covers the fixed exchange rate regime, prior to May 1997, there is evidence that the Czech National Bank seems to have enjoyed some 'monetary independence in spite of fixed exchange rates' (Svensson 1994, p. 158). Interest rate decisions were determined by the output gap and net inflation, denoted NETINF.

Historical episodes of monetary policy suggest three potential break points for the interest rate reaction function of the Czech National Bank. First, there was the widening of the currency band (from 0.75 to 7.5 per cent) in February 1996. Second, the exchange rate crisis of May 1997, with the abandonment of fixed exchange rates and the adoption of floating regime, may have led to an instability of the interest rate reaction function. The final possible timing of a structural break was the official switch to inflation targeting with effect from early 1998. In order to test for the presence of any such break point in the reaction function, we estimate it recursively and implement the usual stability tests (Figure 5.10). There is no evidence of instability at any of these dates. In other words, there is no evidence of a change in the regime of monetary policy over the period from 1993 to 1999. The goodness of fit can be gleaned from Figures 5.8 and 5.9.

In order to check that the switch to inflation targeting did not lead to a change in the interest rate reaction function of the Czech National Bank, we forecast changes in PRIBOR after January 1998 with the reaction function estimated over the period prior to that date (Figure 5.11). The conclusion

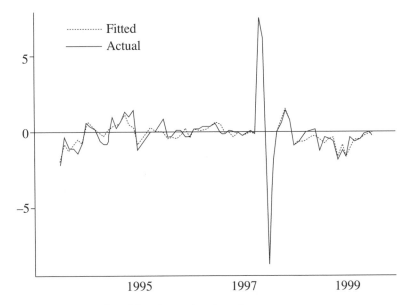

Figure 5.8   Actual and fitted reaction function

about the lack of instability is confirmed by the lack of significance of individual forecast errors over the post-January 1998 period (Appendix Table 5A.1). The reaction function estimated over the exchange rate targeting period performs reasonably in out-of-sample forecasting with insignificant forecast errors.

ASSESSING INFLATION TARGETING

Since the adoption of inflation targeting is a very recent phenomenon in the Czech Republic, any attempt to identify the determinants of inflation and to assess such a policy strategy must be provisional. The problem is compounded by the fact that the adoption of the policy followed closely after a period of upheavals sparked by the speculative attack on the koruna. The analysis is thus especially difficult since one may end up attributing some structural changes to the new monetary policy regime, when in fact one may have simply identified a series of outliers linked to the period of upheavals. Keeping in mind this note of caution, we shall provide some tentative assessment of the new developments.

In order to discover to what extent targeting inflation enabled the Czech monetary authorities to reduce inflation more than macroeconomic conditions

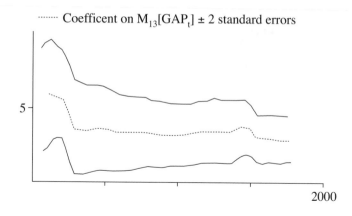

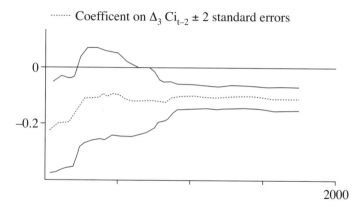

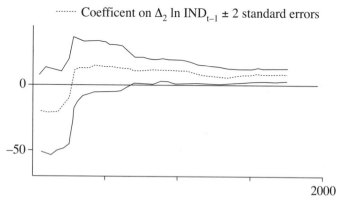

Figure 5.9   Recursive coefficients

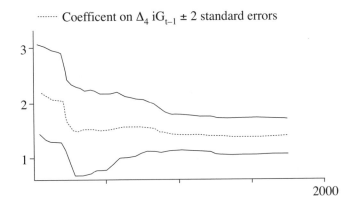

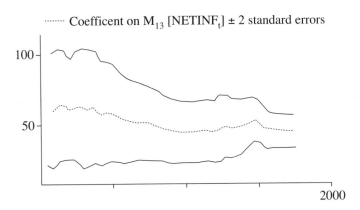

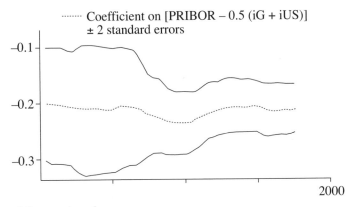

Figure 5.9 continued

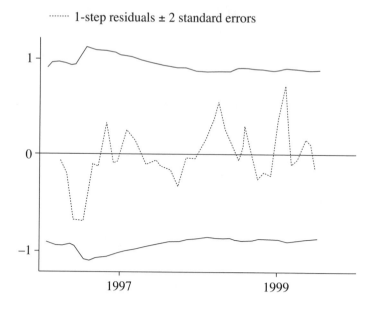

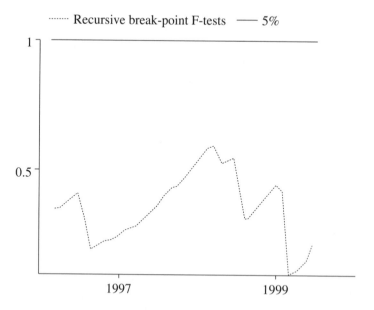

Figure 5.10   Recursive residuals and break-point Chow tests

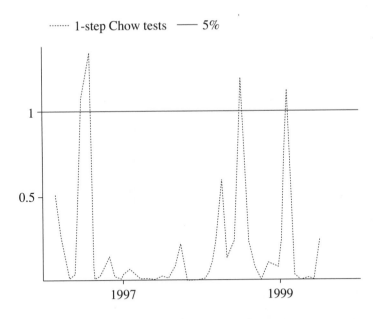

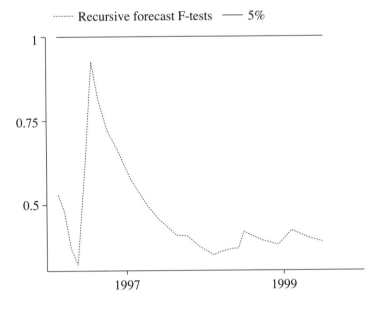

Figure 5.10 continued

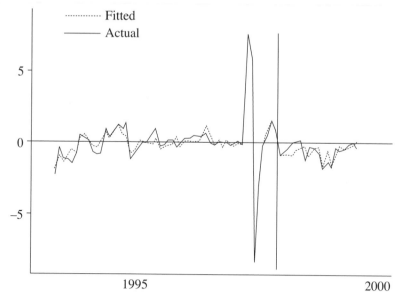

Notes
Model estimated over the July 1993–December 1997 period.
Tests of parameter constancy over Jan. 1998–July 1999.
Forecast $\chi^2(19) = 25.12$ (0.15);   Chow $F(19, 33) = 0.87$ (0.61).

Figure 5.11   Forecasting performance after the adoption of inflation, post-December 1997

would have predicted, we use the methodology suggested by Gordon (1985) and by Fuhrer (1995) and applied to inflation targeting countries by Bernanke et al. (1998). This consists in forecasting inflation during the targeting regime from a Phillips curve estimated over the period before the implementation of inflation targeting. Such a procedure is helpful on two fronts. First, it will enable us to investigate whether inflation, during the inflation-targeting period, dropped by more than could be attributed to normal domestic and international cyclical factors. Second, it will highlight to what extent changes in price and wage setting were generated by the change in the monetary policy regime.

Previous work (Mahadeva and Šmídková 1998) on a calibrated model of the Czech economy emphasized the importance of the value of the coefficient of the output gap in a Phillips curve equation. This work also stressed that such a coefficient is expected to fall during the process of transition with a reduction in the frequency and size of productivity shocks as well as the rise in nominal rigidities. However, these assumptions were not validated by

Table 5.2   A Phillips curve for the Czech Republic, November 1993 to March 1999

$$\text{NETINF}_t = -0.0091 + 0.53 \text{ NETINF}_{t-1} + 0.706 \, \Delta_3 \text{IND}_{t-1} + 0.16 \, M_{49}[\text{NETINF}_t]$$
$$\phantom{\text{NETINF}_t = }(-0.51) \quad (5.68) \qquad\qquad (5.37) \qquad\qquad\qquad (4.54)$$
$$\phantom{\text{NETINF}_t = }+ 0.304 \text{ GAP}_{t-9} + 0.12 \, \Delta^2 \text{lnPoil}_{t-3} - 0.432 \, \Delta_2 \text{PROD}_{t-1} + \text{seasonals}$$
$$\phantom{\text{NETINF}_t = }(2.65) \qquad\qquad (2.93) \qquad\qquad (-1.64)$$

$R^2 = 0.84$	$F(17,47) = 14.9 \, [0.0]$	$\sigma = 0.002$	$DW = 2.17$
AR 1– 1 $F(1, 46) = 0.58 \, [0.44]$		ARCH 1 $F(1, 45) = 0.51 \, [0.47]$	
Normality $\chi 2(2) = 0.31 \, [0.85]$		RESET $F(1, 46) = 0.061 \, [0.80]$	

econometric tests. The following estimates will bring some new light on these two issues.

Table 5.2 presents a modified Phillips curve for the Czech Republic esti-mated from November 1993 to March 1999. The output gap nine months earlier impacts significantly and positively on the annual rate of inflation while the change in the exchange rate index over the previous quarter has a positive impact. The parameter on the exchange rate is more than twice as large as the coefficient on the output gap, reflecting the high degree of open-ness of the Czech economy. Thus a 1% depreciation in the koruna *vis-à-vis* the basket index leads to a 0.71 per cent rise in inflation, while the latter rises only by 0.3% when the output gap rises by 1 per cent. Such sensitivity with respect to the output gap is on the lower side of the range of estimates avail-able for industrial countries, ranging from 0.2 in France to 0.5 in the UK according to Britton and Whitley (1997). It is also on the low side of the values used by Mahadeva and Šmídková (1998) in their simulations of a cali-brated model for the Czech economy. The influence of a supply-side shock can be identified; a 1 percentage point acceleration in the koruna price of oil, $\Delta^2 \text{lnPoil}$, leads to a 0.12 percentage point increase in Czech net inflation. Finally, there is some evidence that changes in labour productivity, $\Delta_2 \text{PROD}$, moderates net inflation.

We are here mainly interested in the potential changes in the Phillips curve. To get information on this, we estimate the regression over the period from 1993 to 1999 and test for parameter instability. If the adoption of inflation targets led to a shift in the Phillips curve we should observe parameter insta-bility after the change of monetary policy regime in January 1998 or sometime after. Both the recursive residuals and the break-point Chow test show that there was no break over this period (Figure 5.12).

In order to check the timing of the movement in parameters, we plot the value of the recursively estimated parameters (Figure 5.13). The downward fall in the parameter of the output gap was gradual after early 1996, before the adoption of inflation targeting (Figure 5.13). However, such a fall is not a

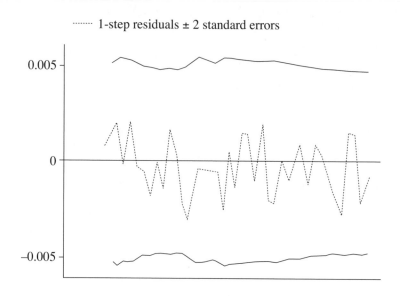

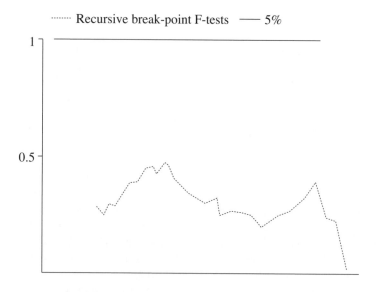

Figure 5.12   Recursive residuals and break-point Chow tests

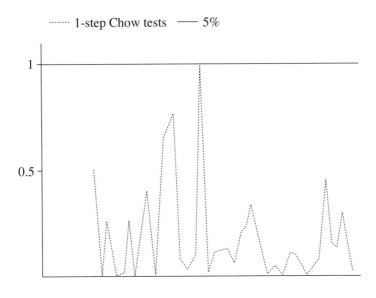

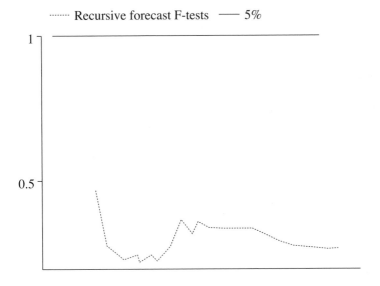

Figure 5.12   continued

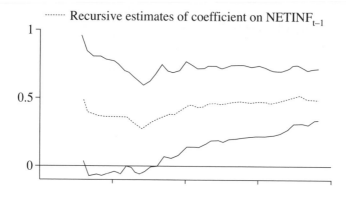

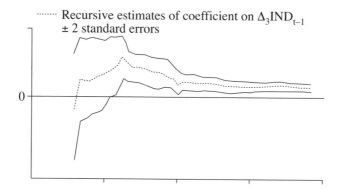

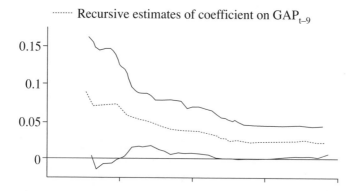

Figure 5.13   Recursive coefficients

source of instability of the net inflation equation. These results do not unambiguously vindicate the expectation by Mahadeva and Šmídková (1998) that
the value of the coefficient of the output gap in the Phillips curve is expected
to fall during the process of transition[3] with a reduction in the frequency and
size of productivity shocks as well as the rise in nominal rigidities. The graphs
of the recursively estimated coefficients display a narrowing of confidence
intervals as the estimation period proceeds, consistent with the accrual of
information.

This evidence of parameter stability has to be checked for its robustness.
We thus try to compare whether during the inflation targeting regime inflation was below the values predicted by the Phillips curve estimated over the
initial policy regime. We thus perform out-of-sample forecasts over the
period from January 1998 to March 1999. We only run one-step ahead forecasts since if static forecasts prove unreliable, then there will be clear
evidence of instability. Indeed we use here actual lagged values of all variables including inflation itself. The quality of the forecasts from the net inflation equation (Figure 5.14) appear good since forecast errors are never
significant (Appendix Table 5A.2).

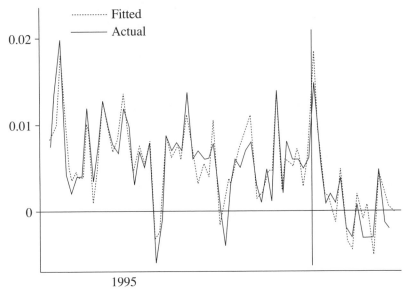

Notes
Tests of parameter constancy over January 1998–March 1999.
Forecast $\chi^2(15) = 11.4$ (0.72);   Chow $F(15, 32) = 0.48$ (0.93).

Figure 5.14   Phillips curve: out of sample forecasting performance

With such a lack of evidence in favour of a shift in the behaviour of inflation after the switch to inflation targeting, the Czech case is in line with the experience of most countries studied by Bernanke et al. (1998) using similar instability tests and out-of-sample forecasting exercises.

CONCLUSION

When examining the determinants of the interest rate reaction function of the Czech National Bank and of inflation in the Czech Republic over the 1993–99 period, this chapter reached three results. The first finding is that the widening of the band in February 1996, or the switch to a floating exchange rate in May 1997, or the adoption of inflation targeting in January 1998 do not seem to have led to a change in the interest rate reaction function of the Czech monetary authorities. It is thus remarkable that under the veil of (officially) different monetary policy regimes – fixed exchange rates with narrow and with wide bands, a floating exchange rate without any official nominal anchor, and inflation targeting – the same variables with stable weights have determined the interest rate decisions of the Czech National Bank. This implies that that the 'uncertainty' (OECD 1998) over the strategy to be followed by the authorities between May and December 1997 was only an appearance, and that the Czech National Bank was right to emphasize in early 1998 that 'the introduction of a new monetary policy strategy [did] not imply a change in its target as such, but only in the way the monetary policy is implemented'.

A second result is that prior to the collapse of the fixed exchange rate regime, the Czech monetary authorities exploited the monetary independence that target zones offer, since the reaction function does include net inflation and the output gap among the explanatory variables.

The third result has two components. First, the coefficient of the output gap in the Phillips curve equation seems on the low side of comparable estimates for major European Union countries. It has not been characterized by a significant downward shift, in contrast with expectations of such a development during the process of transition. This may imply that the expected reductions in the frequency and size of productivity shocks, as well as nominal rigidities, have not yet taken place. Second, there is no evidence of instability in the Phillips curve equation. This lack of substantial change indicates that the switch in the official Czech monetary policy regime, especially the introduction of inflation targeting, did not lead to a substantial shift in price and/or wage-setting behaviour. The Czech experience does not seem any different on this front from most available experiences of countries that adopted inflation targeting.

The limited sample period available at the time of the conference prevented us from splitting the 1990s into two sub-periods around the crisis of May 1997. Such a split would have led us to test competing models for the interest rate reaction function for each sub-period, including forward looking inflation variables, using the now standard errors-in-variables approach and GMM estimation, along the lines pioneered by Clarida, Gali and Gertler (1997). By so doing we would determine to what extent Czech interest rate decisions, after the introduction of inflation targeting, have ceased to be determined by external factors in favour of domestic ones (see Adam, Cobham and Girardin 2001 for an application to the UK). Similarly the estimation of the inflation equation would include the introduction of forward inflation terms, as recently documented by empirical work on the so-called 'new Phillips curve'. Work along these lines for the Czech case is currently being carried out by the present authors.

NOTES

1. We thank Katerina Šmídková for kindly providing us with this database.
2. Our starting point can be justified by the observation that '*around the middle of 1993 the Czech economy entered a new economic landscape* . . . [since] *the wheels of a market-based economy started to turn round more and more smoothly. The national economy climbed out of the transformation recession and showed the first sign of a robust recovery.*' (Tosovsky 1996, p. 152).
3. Actually in their econometric work these authors did not find significant coefficients for the output gap in the Phillips curve equation.

REFERENCES

Bernanke, B.S., T. Laubach, F.S. Mishkin and A.S. Prosen (1998), *Inflation Targeting: Lessons from the International Experience*, Princeton, NJ: Princeton University Press.

Bordes, C. and E. Girardin (1998), 'Estimation of a central bank reaction function for the Czech Republic and Slovakia', ACE–PHARE Network: The design of a monetary policy strategy for Central European countries in transition, June.

Britton, E. and J. Whitley (1997), 'Comparing the monetary transmission mechanism in France, Germany and the United Kingdom: some issues and results', *Bank of England Quarterly Bulletin*.

Canzoneri, M.B., C. Nolan and A. Yeates (1997), 'Mechanisms for achieving monetary stability: inflation targeting versus the ERM', *Journal of Money, Credit and Banking*, **29**(1), February, 46–60.

Fuhrer, J. (1995), 'Forward-looking behavior and the stability of a conventional monetary policy rule', *Journal of Money, Credit and Banking*, Part 1.

Girardin, E. and J. Klacek (1999), 'Sterilization of capital inflows in transition economies: an econometric investigation of the Czech and Polish cases', in A. Mullineux and C.J. Green (eds), *Economic Performance and Financial Sector Reform* in *Central and Eastern Europe: Capital Flows, Bank and Enterprise Restructuring*, Cheltenham, UK, Northampton, MA, USA: Edward Elgar, pp. 256–74.

Gordon, R. (1985), 'Understanding inflation in the 1980s', *Brookings Papers on Economic Activity*, **16**(1), 263–99.

Hodrick, R.J. and E.C. Prescott (1997), 'Post-war U.S. business cycles: an empirical investigation', *Journal of Money, Credit and Banking*, **29**(1), February, 1–17.

Leiderman, L. and L. Svensson (eds) (1995), *Inflation Targets*, London: Centre for Economic Policy Research.

Mahadeva, L. and K. Šmídková (1998), 'Inflation targeting in the Czech Republic: questions, model simulations, preliminary answers', Working Paper, Czech National Bank, November.

Organization for Economic Cooperation and Development (OECD) (1998), *Czech Republic*, Country Studies, Paris: OECD.

Svensson, L.E.O. (1994), 'Why exchange rate bands: monetary independence in spite of fixed exchange rates', *Journal of Monetary Economics*, **33**, 157–99.

Tosovsky, J. (1996), 'Disinflation in the Czech Republic: looking forward and backward', in *Achieving Price Stability*, Kansas: Federal Bank of Kansas City.

APPENDIX 5A   FORECASTING PERFORMANCES OF THE INTEREST RATE REACTION FUNCTION AND THE PHILLIPS CURVE

Table 5A.1   Forecasting performances of the interest rate reaction function (one step forecasts)

Date		Actual	Forecast	Forecast error	*t*-value
1998	1	–0.90	–0.907	0.0070	0.0120
1998	2	–0.70	–0.868	0.1680	0.3120
1998	3	–0.40	–0.811	0.4110	0.7500
1998	4	0.00	–0.883	0.8830	1.4370
1998	5	0.10	–0.472	0.5720	0.9920
1998	6	0.20	–0.403	0.6030	1.0700
1998	7	–1.30	–0.246	–1.0530	–1.9300
1998	8	–0.30	–1.010	0.7150	1.0780
1998	9	–0.40	–0.386	–0.0130	–0.0250
1998	10	–0.60	–0.210	–0.3890	–0.7360
1998	11	–1.90	–1.903	0.0033	0.0040
1998	12	–1.20	–0.590	–0.6090	–0.9790
1999	1	–1.60	–1.597	–0.0020	–0.0032
1999	2	–0.30	–1.047	–0.7470	0.9290
1999	3	–0.60	–0.226	–0.3730	–0.4000
1999	4	–0.50	–0.350	–0.1490	–0.2030
1999	5	–0.10	–0.313	0.2130	0.3470
1999	6	0.00	–0.216	0.2160	0.3590
1999	7	–0.40	0.367	–0.7670	–1.2480

Note: The model is estimated over the July 1993–December 1997 period, and forecasts are made over the January 1998–July 1999 period.

Table 5A.2   Forecasting performances of the Phillips curve (one-step forecasts)

Date		Actual	Forecast	Forecast error	*t*-value
1998	1	0.015	0.0190	−0.0041	−1.230
1998	2	−0.007	0.0069	0.0000	0.027
1998	3	0.001	0.0019	−0.0009	−0.330
1998	4	0.002	0.0015	0.0004	0.160
1998	5	0.001	−0.0012	0.0022	0.710
1998	6	0.004	0.0049	−0.0009	−0.300
1998	7	−0.002	−0.0030	0.0010	0.320
1998	8	−0.003	−0.0040	0.0010	0.380
1998	9	0.001	0.0020	−0.0010	−0.370
1998	10	−0.003	−0.0008	−0.0020	−0.630
1998	11	−0.003	0.0009	−0.0030	−1.190
1998	12	−0.003	−0.0050	0.0020	0.570
1999	1	0.005	0.0038	0.0011	0.320
1999	2	−0.001	0.0028	−0.0038	−1.080
1999	3	−0.002	−0.0005	−0.0020	−0.680

Note: The model is estimated over the July 1993–December 1997 period, and forecasts are made over the January 1998–July 1999 period.

6. Latvia on the way to the European Union: economic policy convergence

Inna Šteinbuka

INTRODUCTION

Full economic transformation is directly linked to European integration. The potential economic advantages of closer integration with the high-income, large EU market are:

- increasing EU–Latvian trade and investments;
- strengthening the legal framework and institution-building in the process of gradual harmonization of Latvian legislation with EU standards; and
- promoting Latvia's macroeconomic and structural convergence towards the average level of the EU member states as a result of access to the structural funds of the EU.

The Copenhagen Summit criteria provide a very broad guiding principle in several areas for the accession of the Central and Eastern European (CEE) countries to the EU. The Latvian adoption of the 'Medium-term economic strategy in the context of accession to the European Union' (Ministry of Finance . . . 1998) and signing of the 'Joint assessment of the economic policy priorities of Latvia' (Ministry of Finance 1998; IMF 1999a) clearly demonstrates a strong determination to stick to the integration approach.

The concept of distance from the EU is multidimensional. While the political, legal and institutional criteria cannot be overestimated, we focus more on the economic aspect. Thus, the focus of this chapter lies more in distance in terms of economic space.

To approach the average level of EU living standards and to ensure sustainable economic development, Latvia has to pay special attention to evaluating its competitive capacity. The question of how long it will take Latvia to close the income gap with EU countries depends on the competitiveness of the economy in the international market, particularly the EU market. The problem of Latvian competitiveness recently became more sensitive in the wake of the large current account deficit, the Russian crisis, and especially the depreciation of the ruble. This is why the question of economic competitiveness has been addressed in this chapter.

The spirit of this chapter was influenced only marginally by the positive message from the Helsinki Summit in mid-December 1999. The EU decision to open negotiations with Latvia was announced shortly before the chapter was completed.

MACROECONOMIC CONVERGENCE

Relative to countries already in the EU, Riga is geographically not far from Brussels; it is even closer than Helsinki, Lisbon and Athens. By this standard, Latvia conforms with EU norms. Geographical factors or physical distance from Brussels have been indicated by Fischer et al. (1998). Geographical factors may be regarded as trivial, but in reality they are not. In particular, they relate to non-trade elements of the EU, such as common foreign and security policy, and cooperation on internal factors, as well as the flow of labour (Csaba 1997).

For this section, however, the distances in which we are most interested are of an economic nature. Therefore three issues of economic distance from the EU are presented:

- the income gap and the challenges for real convergence (how and when it is possible to close the income gap);
- macroeconomic performance and prospects for nominal (fiscal and monetary) convergence; and
- implementing a market-based economic system and progress in structural convergence.

Real Convergence

The achievement of real convergence through the acceleration of economic development and increased competitiveness is the most difficult task Latvia has to face on the way to the European Union.

GDP, particularly as expressed per inhabitant, is one of the main indicators used for measurement of real convergence, involving comparisons over time and between regions. For international comparisons, GDP expressed in a common currency does not always give a good indication of the actual volume of component goods and services. In order to resolve this problem, the GDP for each country is expressed in an artificial currency known as the 'purchasing power standard', which eliminates the effects of different price levels from one country to another.

*Table 6.1   The European Union and Eastern Europe: per capita income,
1995 (USD, PPP based)*

European Union		Central and Eastern Europe	
Belgium	19 928	Czech Republic	8 173
Netherlands	19 376	Slovenia	6 342
Luxembourg	30 063	Slovak Republic	6 671
France	20 829	Croatia	4 142
Germany	18 988	Hungary	6 211
UK	18 857	Poland	6 364
Denmark	20 737	*Latvia*	*5 002*
Ireland	15 611	Lithuania	3 035
Austria	19 922	Albania	538
Italy	19 745	Estonia	7 203
Sweden	18 712	Macedonia	1 628
Spain	14 408	Bulgaria	5 132
Finland	17 433	Romania	3 542
Portugal	11 935		
Greece	8 727		

Source: Fischer et al. 1998.

GDP per capita in Latvia, as shown in Table 6.1, is very low compared to other European countries. Bearing in mind the severe banking crisis Latvia faced in 1995, one can argue that this particular year is not very suitable for any comparisons. However, more recent figures are not very impressive either. As part of the preparations for the next round of EU enlargement, Eurostat has provided the Commission with a new set of comparable output data on the candidate countries (CC). This report describes the development of GDP, as well as per capita figures in comparison with those of the EU (Table 6.2). According to these official statistics, GDP per capita in Latvia at purchasing power parity is ten times lower than the EU average, and three to four times lower than in the least-developed EU countries (Eurostat 1998/28).

It is very difficult methodologically to evaluate to what extent Latvia has dropped behind. Official output statistics in transition economies are subject to several deficiencies. In Latvia these deficiencies are due not to the weakness of statistical methods used for drawing up the national accounts, but rather to the large informal sector in the economy. The result is an underestimation in the level of GDP and certainly in the level of well-being of the population. Other factors which add to the underestimation include primarily tax avoidance and a lack of accounting standards. Therefore, the official data

Table 6.2   GDP per capita at current prices and exchange rates

	Ecu					EU-15 = 100				
	1993	1994	1995	1996	1997	1993	1994	1995	1996	1997
Bulgaria	1 100	1 000	1 300	900	1 100	7	6	8	5	6
Cyprus	8 900	9 800	10 400	10 700	11 400	56	59	60	59	60
Czech Rep.	2 800	3 200	3 800	4 300	4 500	18	19	22	24	23
Estonia	900	1 300	1 800	2 300	2 800	6	8	11	13	15
Hungary	3 200	3 400	3 300	3 500	3 900	20	20	19	19	21
Latvia	*700*	*1 200*	*1 400*	*1 600*	*2 000*	*4*	*7*	*8*	*9*	*10*
Lithuania	600	1 000	1 200	1 700	2 300	4	6	7	9	12
Poland	1 900	2 000	2 400	2 700	3 100	12	12	14	15	16
Romania	1 000	1 100	1 200	1 200	1 400	6	7	7	7	7
Slovak Rep.	1 900	2 200	2 500	2 800	3 200	12	13	14	15	17
Slovenia	5 400	6 100	7 200	7 500	8 100	34	36	42	41	43
Total CC	1 900	2 100	2 300	2 600	2 900	12	12	14	14	15

Source: Eurostat (1998/28).

are underestimated, and may exaggerate decline, understate growth, and show recovery later than it occurred (see Bloem et al. 1996).

However, even taking into account the underestimation of GDP, it would be very difficult to close the large income gap between Latvia and the EU.

We now ask how long it would take for Latvia to catch up with the EU. This question is related to another one: how to accelerate growth by promoting growth-driving forces.

According to *endogenous growth theory* the main factor behind growth is expansion of capital, augmented by exogenous technological progress. The explanation of technical progress is based on increasing returns, R&D and imperfect competition, human capital and government policies. Macroeconomic stability, liberalization and other macro policies are important in this process, but so too are such policies as property rights, the rule of law, institution-building and prevention of corruption. For transition economies, the impact of these factors depends on the stage of transition the country has reached.

Macroeconomic stabilization and general progress on market-orientated reforms were the main determinants of recovery in Latvia at the beginning of transition. According to the IMF, 'There is a strong consensus that good economic policy (macroeconomic stability and nondistortive interventions) has a strong effect on growth' (IMF 1998). The medium-term economic strategy for Latvia states that sustained growth requires sustained disinflation (Ministry of Finance . . . 1998). In spite of rapid progress in Latvia in macroeconomic stabilization, liberalization and restructuring, it is absolutely clear that stabilization along with structural reforms are necessary but not sufficient preconditions for growth.

As for investment, there is little disagreement among Latvian decision makers that it is a major engine of growth in the medium to long terms. The share of investment has increased considerably, reaching 23 per cent of GDP in 1998.[1] Both private (foreign and domestic) as well as public investments have contributed to this increase.

We can think now in the framework of *conditional convergence* (Fischer et al. 1998) assuming that because of the combination of different policies and factors, income in poorer countries is growing more rapidly than in richer countries. In transition economies this would mean that in the first stage, the growth process is driven by the transition itself, and only in the long run can investment and export-driven growth be identified.

In line with conditional convergence theory, the actual GDP growth in Latvia in 1996–98 was stronger than in the EU member states. Latvia recorded higher growth rates than the EU average for 1996 (Latvia: 3.3 per cent; EU: 1.7 per cent) and 1997 (Latvia: 8.6 per cent; EU: 2.6 per cent; CC: 3.6 per cent). GDP growth slowed considerably in 1998 as a result of the Russian crisis, which has impacted the Latvian economy through both direct and indirect channels. However, even in 1998 annual economic growth still remained higher than that of the EU (Latvia: 3.6 per cent; EU: 2.7 per cent). In 1999, only marginal real growth (0.1 per cent) was observed in Latvia. Growth projections for 2000 have been revised dowwards. However, economic activity has picked up faster than expected and in Latvia the growth rate (6.6 per cent) outpaced that in the EU in 2000. According to the various scenarios, economic growth in Latvia should accelerate over the medium term and reach a higher annual rate (about 5–7 per cent) than that expected in the EU.

Evaluating possible GDP growth in the medium term, one has to conclude that the income gap between Latvia and the EU will still be larger than desirable at the moment of joining the EU. Problems might arise in areas such as the EU budget, labour mobility and capital flows. Thus, approaching real convergence is not only a precondition, but also an outcome, of membership in the EU.

Latvia is similar to Portugal, Spain and Greece in the sense that their level of development is much lower than the EU average. For membership of the EU to proceed successfully, there are two main objectives to be achieved. First, in a transition period of harmonization of the legal and institutional frameworks, Latvia should meet the standards of the common market. Second, the Latvian government consequently needs to realize a set of policies (paying special attention to such areas as rule of law and prevention of corruption) that would promote growth, thus ensuring a decrease in the income gap between the present EU member states and Latvia.

Nominal Convergence

With no specific guidelines on economic performance for CEE membership in the EU, Fischer at al. (1998) choose to use the Maastricht criteria as a guiding principle for determining policy convergence. The Maastricht criteria specify measures of macroeconomic convergence required for European Monetary Union (EMU) membership. The criteria relate to inflation, long-term interest rates, the general government budget deficit, gross government debt and exchange rates.

It is instructive to note that there is as yet no clear agreement between the EU member states about what level of monetary and fiscal convergence should be exercised by the EU applicant countries. Moreover, the Maastricht criteria are known to be neither necessary nor sufficient conditions for establishing a single currency in Europe. There is no background for using these criteria to assess the EU maturity of Central European would-be members. Referring to Csaba (1997), it is hardly by chance that Commission officials never interpreted the convergence criteria in this way. However, generally one should agree that all of the countries joining the EU must reach the level of nominal convergence (to meet the fiscal and monetary convergence criteria) in a relatively short period of time after joining the EU.

Of course, the convergence criteria form only one group of parameters that could influence the process of joining the EU; however, they should not be underestimated. Independent of joining the EU, application of the convergence criteria is a good policy in forming a stable and predictable business environment, setting strict limitations for the fiscal deficit and debt, and eliminating the pressure of inflation.

A close look at the actual state of Latvian convergence with the Maastricht criteria, shows that the Bank of Latvia and the government of Latvia have fulfilled the basic requirements to meet the criteria. Latvia has made significant progress towards macroeconomic stability. The inflation rate has entered single-digit territory, the fiscal deficit has declined and public debt is very low. The last two criteria – interest rates and exchange rates – are more difficult to evaluate. The interest rate criterion is hard to apply for CEE countries since markets for long-term debt are not well developed. The criterion on exchange rates is, strictly speaking, not applicable for CEE countries since they do not share a regional exchange rate arrangement.

However, Latvia has achieved stability of its exchange rate. The Latvian national currency was introduced in 1993, and since then, the Bank of Latvia has maintained a restrained monetary policy. Since 1994 the lats has been pegged to the special drawing right (SDR) currency basket, and monetary policy, including interest rate policy, has been geared towards maintaining the exchange rate peg.

According to its medium-term strategy, Latvia should not have any medium-term problems with continuing to move towards convergence.

Inflation

Inflation has been an economic as well as a social problem in Latvia from the early 1990s. For the average Latvian, inflation was an unjust way of taxing personal financial wealth, something that has been associated with the emergence of great income inequalities and, for many people, with a fall below the poverty line. For most people, the concept of inflation is synonymous with the rise in the cost of living and, as the prices with inelastic demand have increased more than the average, something against which they could not easily defend themselves. About one-quarter of the Latvian population are pensioners whose pensions are only partially indexed and for whom high and even moderate inflation has been a most painful experience.

As in other transition economies, inflation in Latvia surged in the early stage of transition (1991–92) and reached some 960 per cent (12-month basis). This surge was caused by the elimination of an initial monetary overhang and price liberalization.

Once these factors had worked themselves out, helped by nominal exchange rate appreciation and financial policy restraint, a very rapid decline in inflation took place, from an annual rate of 960 per cent in 1992 to just over 100 per cent in 1993 and further to 35 per cent in 1994. The pace at which inflation was reduced during late 1993 and early 1994 reflected the fact that the lats was allowed to appreciate substantially in nominal terms as the central bank sought to control monetary growth. (Since February 1994, however, the lats has been pegged to the SDR.) Inflation proved to be relatively stubborn during 1995–96, and by the end of 1996 was close to 18 per cent. In 1997 inflation declined sharply from double digit to single digit; the 12-month inflation rate has fallen to 8.4 per cent. The lowest price increase were recorded in 1998 (2.8 per cent) and 1999 (3.2 per cent).

What were the main factors behind inflation? Neither wage nor incomes policies and capital inflow played an important role. Only in 1995 was inflation reflected to a certain extent by a surge in liquidity (stemming from balance-of-payments surpluses in late 1994) and public sector wage increases. Latvia has had very small budget deficits. Therefore fiscal policy did not influence inflation either.

The main reasons behind inflation in 1994–96 were (a) an initial undervaluation of the currency relative to its medium-term equilibrium value; (b) a process of domestic relative price adjustment, particularly the adjustment of administered prices; (c) an adjustment in excise taxes; (d) the differential productivity growth between the traded and non-traded goods sectors; and (e) quasi-fiscal activities by the banking system in the early stages of reform, later reflected in problems in the banking system – a severe banking crisis was experienced by Latvia in 1995.

In 1994 the price level in Latvia was substantially below its equilibrium. A price survey conducted in May 1994 suggests that the prices of a wide range of goods and services were about 30 per cent of Swedish prices. Auer (1995) estimated that the Latvian price level was about 26 per cent of the Austrian level in 1993. Based on OECD price-level data for that year, this corresponds to about 30 per cent of the US price level.

Continued tight monetary policy and weakening domestic demand due to the Russian crisis have contributed to the rapid fall in inflation in 1998–99. Inflation impedes growth. Relatively high inflation has been seen as the primary reason for the underdevelopment of long-term capital markets, the cautious attitude of banks towards long-term lending, and the reluctance of private enterprises to undertake as much long-term investment as one would think the country's potential would allow for. Thus, the reduction of inflation is a prerequisite for achieving sustainable growth. Therefore price stability has become an explicit objective of Latvian economic and monetary policy as witnessed by the adoption of ambitious inflation targets in the government declarations. It is expected that following rapid initial disinflation, in the period since the lats was pegged to the SDR, the process of disinflation will slow down, although it will still continue at a considerable pace. Within this scenario, it is assumed that strict monetary policy, a stable exchange rate and a controlled money supply will continue to prevail, along with strict fiscal policies.

There is broad agreement that in Latvia, when currency exchange rates were set, the local currency was undervalued, and there are some signs that the price level adjustment process is continuing. The reason for inflation has been and continues to be adjustment to international price levels. According to IMF estimates (IMF 1996), the price level in Latvia in 1996 was about 60 per cent of the price level in the United States. Room for an adjustment of prices continues to exist in the non-tradables sector, particularly in transport services, housing and energy.

At this stage, prices have been largely liberalized. Only a few administered prices remain, relating to transportation, energy and housing rents. The process of convergence of Latvian prices to Western levels may still not be completed by the year 2002, suggesting that inflation may continue above Western European levels for several years to come.

The level of inflation in Latvia is relatively low (see Tables 6.3 and 6.4, below). In 1999 and 2000 the consumer prize index inflation (2.4 and 2.6 per cent) was about the level required by the Maastricht criteria. The main issue of concern is sustainability of the trend. Curbing inflation to the level which meets the Maastricht criteria (that is, about 2.5 per cent) over the medium to long terms will require additional time and effort. A rapid achievement of this objective exclusively through tough deflationary measures would seriously restrict the country's growth rate and have a negative effect on employment levels.

Fiscal policies
Any problems that Latvia has experienced with its fiscal deficit can be linked to the banking crisis, which occurred in 1995, and to the Russian crisis in 1998.

The essential precondition for the implementation of the economic transformation in Latvia was fiscal and budgetary reform. In the context of macroeconomic stabilization, the achievement of sustainable fiscal policy is crucial. Ideally, the budget of a transition economy should promote economic recovery and serve to establish favourable conditions for the development of private entrepreneurship, while at the same time providing adequate social security. The realization of these tasks, however, is constrained by the need to maintain a budget consistent with macroeconomic stability.

The implementation of tax reform in Latvia has taken place under very difficult circumstances (Pautola 1997; Šteinbuka and Kazacs 1996), as tax revenue has decreased (to a certain extent) with the collapse of reported production at the same time as huge demands have emerged for social benefits and the build-up of infrastructure. Nevertheless, Latvia has moved quite rapidly in transforming its fiscal system, and according to the *World Economic Outlook* (IMF 1996), overall fiscal reform has started well and has made rapid progress.

Indeed, the general government fiscal balance[2] recorded a surplus of 0.6 per cent of GDP in 1993. Fiscal policy turned expansionary in 1994, with the fiscal balance moving to a deficit of 4.4 per cent of GDP, reflecting increases in net lending. In 1995, the fiscal problems were exacerbated by the banking crisis, which had both a direct and indirect effect on revenue collection. Total revenue fell by about 1 percentage point of GDP in 1995. Nevertheless, as a result of a major compression of net lending, the overall fiscal deficit was reduced to 3.9 per cent of GDP in 1995.

Fiscal policy was tighter than programmed in 1996. The general government fiscal deficit was reduced to 1.7 per cent of GDP through a major revenue mobilization effort combined with expenditure restraints. Commitment to fiscal discipline is reflected in the fact that the consolidated government budget for year 1997 had a financial surplus amounting to 0.1 per cent of GDP.

The Russian crisis led to a large and unexpected external shock for Latvia. Economic growth has slowed considerably in the second half of 1998. Nevertheless, the overall fiscal performance for 1998 remained positive, with the consolidated general government ending the year with 0.8 per cent deficit (when privatization receipts are treated as financing).

The 1999 budget in Latvia was drafted before the Russian crisis in mid-1998 and therefore was based on unrealistic revenue projections. The impending parliamentary elections made agreement on revised budget projections (in response to the expected economic slowdown) difficult and the budgets were approved with only minor changes related to the composition rather than the level of revenues and expenditures. As a result, the deficit of the consolidated government widened sharply in the first half of 1999. The negative supplementary budget has been approved by parliament to contain the deficit to about 3.9 per cent of GDP.

In early December 1999, the Latvian parliament approved the national budget for the year 2000 in the final reading with a planned fiscal deficit of 1.9 per cent of GDP. However, underperformance of revenues, primarily because of the weak euro and rocketed oil prices, coupled with the need to comply with the identified political priorities, have led to overshooting the original fiscal target. As under a currency board or fixed peg regime the fiscal system is the main line of defence against a negative external shock, fiscal policy should be prudent and needs to be tightened over the medium term. The government plans a return to near fiscal balance over the medium term.

Latvia has made good progress in establishing the institutions needed for fiscal management in a market economy; important among these are a well-functioning treasury system that has been set up for central government operations, and a tax system geared towards the needs of a market-based economy. Over the last few years, the major changes introduced in the tax system were aimed at complying with market economy principles and were consistent with Latvia's plans to join the European Union.

The standard value added tax (VAT) rate at 18 per cent of the taxable value of supplies of goods and services has been introduced. Corporate and personal income taxes are fixed at a reasonable level of 25 per cent.

Social tax has been introduced to ensure a strong Social Insurance Fund that can meet its future pension liabilities. The transitional regulations of the law on the social tax which were adopted in 1995, specify that through 2001, the total social tax rate is to decline from 36 to 33 per cent. In order to balance the proportions between the employer-paid social tax and the employee-paid social tax, it is envisaged that the employer's tax burden will be reduced, and the employee's burden will be increased.

Simultaneously with the year 2000 budget, the Latvian parliament adopted amendments to a number of tax laws, primarily on the real estate tax and excise taxes, aimed at strengthening budget revenues, increasing economic activity in the country, and conforming to EU norms.

In the light of the relatively high tax rates already in place, the revenue effort will continue to focus on tax administration. Budgetary pressures arising during fiscal reform due to deficiencies of tax administration have taken two forms: tax avoidance and tax arrears.

Collecting the budget revenues poses serious problems in Latvia. This is explained by the appearance of the underground economy, which did not exist or was insignificant under the administrative economy. Tax avoidance, although difficult to quantify because of its invisible nature, is evidenced by falling corporate income tax revenues and custom revenues in an environment of booming imports.

Tax administration is at the heart of fiscal reform as it is the only way to provide the government with resources without increasing the tax burden and encouraging greater tax evasion, and hence, faster growth of the underground economy. Taxes have to become the next 'inevitable thing after death'.

The expenditure side of the budget is dominated by current spending, of which wages and salaries and transfers to households are important components. Investment spending was fairly low (about 2 per cent of GDP) and increased somewhat in the last two years (3.9 and 4.0 per cent of GDP, respectively, in 1998 and 1999). The budget 2000 has established education and the hoped-for accession to the North Atlantic Treaty Organization (NATO) as priority areas.

Discussions on fiscal policy are an important aspect of political debate in Latvia. One distinctive feature of the current discussions is that Latvian policy makers are analysing not only economic (utilitarian) approaches but have expanded the discussion to include issues involving political philosophy. In other words, current analyses and discussions begin by constructing a philosophical base upon which a tax system can be built, and then the ways in which such a system can be structured are examined.

The first philosophical issue is the theory of voluntary taxation. Almost all counterparts conclude that taxation is coercive in nature, not voluntary. Evasion is a problem in any country that has a tax system, but it is an especially serious problem in a transition economy, since the collection mechanism is not yet firmly in place.

The second philosophical issue has to do with two competing views of taxation, the cost–benefit view and the ability-to-pay view. The cost–benefit view begins with the premise that the government provides services and the taxpayers should pay for those services. There is some connection between what is received and what is paid. The ability-to-pay view takes the position that individuals should pay taxes based on their ability to pay without regard to the benefits they receive from government. Usually the disputants conclude that the cost–benefit approach is philosophically superior because it is not based on exploitation. However, the ability-to-pay approach is only a precondition for tight fiscal policy.

The third philosophical issue which is usually accepted by all political parties and interest groups is whether government should support or discourage certain activities through the tax system. All sides conclude that the tax system must be used as a punishment tool for certain kinds of behaviour such as smoking and drinking.

The fourth very important philosophical aspect discussed is the role of the state. Should government limit itself to the role of a night-watchman state – or should it be active in the redistribution of income as well? Should the public finance system be used solely to raise the funds necessary for essential government services, or should the system also be used as a tool of *industrial* policy?

Latvia's leading coalition trusts the solution of economic problems to market forces and certain aspects of competition policy and dismisses all other forms of state intervention except fiscal deficit and macroeconomic balances. Centre-right politicians argue that interventionist government policy is ineffective and must be limited in scope and duration. They have concluded that attempts to use the fiscal system as a tool of industrial policy usually result in supporting inefficient industries at the expense of everyone else, which results in the misallocation of resources.

At the same time there is some scepticism in society, for both theoretical and empirical reasons, towards unregulated market forces and trade liberalization as means of obtaining benefits for all parties involved. Those opposed to shock therapy argue that restoration of government activity, particularly in relation to public expenditure, is crucial for future development. Focusing mainly on negative aspects of the Latvian economy, they state that the policy options available within the strict budget are very narrow.

A very common viewpoint within the opposition is that all too often the solution to fiscal problems is higher taxes. At the same time, the state is reducing its support for social, educational, cultural, health and other needs.

An *anti-capitalism mentality* so far is typical of old people who have been educated to believe that self-interest and private property are evil. The social-orientated parties have also incorporated these views into the statements about taxation: those who have more should be forced to pay more.

The *welfare state mentality*, the view that government should be the provider of a wide range of services, also exists in Latvia to a certain extent. This presents a special problem because a large percentage of the people think that government should provide a large basket of services, which is impossible under current budget constraints.

The main conclusion, which has been reached by the opposition, is that low tax rates are better than high tax rates and a large basket of government services is better than a small one.

The *future challenge* for economic policy in Latvia is to ensure the availability of the resources necessary to *integrate social and fiscal responsibility*. In this respect, fiscal policy must aim at eliminating deficits, while at the same time providing the necessary financing for social objectives and social safety nets. Further, fiscal policy should encourage savings, because savings form the base for financing the high levels of investment required for sustained growth and economic wealth.

Given these challenges of fiscal policy in ensuring adequate social protection, raising savings and maintaining economic growth, there are several concrete actions and changes to be made in the future. These changes focus both on the expenditure as well as on the revenue side:

- Eligibility and benefits standards governing the distribution of social benefits must be reformed.
- Tax collection efficiency must be improved.
- Budgetary expenditure discipline must be strengthened and the efficiency of public expenditure and social welfare protection programmes should be increased.
- Effective targeting mechanisms for the provision of benefits must be incorporated.
- Tax policy should focus on improving the effectiveness of taxes on the traditional sectors. Higher tax revenues are likely to be achieved by a further broadening of the tax bases and the removal of various exemptions.
- Tax rates should be gradually rationalized as revenue collection improves.
- Tax administration could be improved by better organization of auditing, registration, taxpayer information, returns processing and so on. In particular, new taxpayers in emerging sectors must be meticulously identified and registered.

Taxpayers also need to be aware that if they fail to pay their taxes according to the tax laws, they will be punished.

We have every reason to expect that Latvia will continue on its current path towards a Western fiscal system. This, in turn, should give greater confidence to both domestic and foreign investors, whose inputs play a crucial role in maintaining economic growth in Latvia.

Public debt in Latvia has remained at a reasonably low level. Although the EU does not yet require the accession candidates to fulfil the Maastricht criteria, nevertheless, Latvia comfortably satisfied the public debt criteria. Latvia's *government debt* at the end of 1997 amounted to 12.0 per cent of GDP and at the end of 2000 it was 13.2 per cent. Compared to a number of EU member states, these are encouraging figures (see Tables 6.3 and 6.4). In the medium-term strategy for Latvia, it is envisaged that government debt will be maintained at a reasonably low level.

Table 6.3   Convergence criteria: EU and the Baltics

	Consumer price index			General government balance/GDP			Gross government debt/GDP		
	1996	1997	1998	1996	1997	1998	1996	1997	1998
Germany	1.5	1.8	0.9	−3.4	−2.6	−2.0	60.8	61.5	61.1
France	2.0	1.2	0.7	−4.2	−3.0	−2.7	55.4	57.8	58.2
Italy	3.9	1.7	1.8	−7.0	−2.8	−2.7	122.5	120.1	118.7
UK	2.9	2.8	2.7	−4.4	−2.1	0.3	64.8	65.8	65.8
Total EU	2.5	1.9	1.5	−4.2	−2.4	−1.5	74.3	76.4	71.8
Latvia	17.6	8.4	4.7	−1.7	0.1	−0.8	14.4	12.0	9.9
Lithuania	24.7	8.8	5.1	−4.5	−1.8	−5.8	23.4	21.1	22.5
Estonia	23.1	11.2	8.2	−1.5	2.0	−0.3	6.9	6.0	7.4

Source: IMF, World Economic Outlook (1999).

Table 6.4   Convergence criteria: CEE countries and the Baltics

	Consumer price index			General government balance*/GDP			Gross government debt/GDP		
	1996	1997	1998	1996	1997	1998	1996	1997	1998
Albania	12.7	32.1	20.9	−11.7	−12.6	−10.4	59.9	71.3	59.4
Bulgaria	123.0	1082.2	22.3	−12.9	−5.7	−0.8	105.8	104.4	84.3
Croatia	3.5	3.6	5.7	−1.8	−2.1	−1.5	27.6	26.5	24.5
Czech Rep.	8.8	8.4	10.7	−2.3	−2.3	−1.6	9.9	10.3	10.7
Hungary	23.5	18.3	14.3	−11.5	−19.3	−6.4	71.5	62.9	60.4
Poland	19.9	15.1	12.0	−4.3	−4.5	−4.6	54.6	46.5	43.8
Romania	38.8	154.8	59.1	−4.0	−4.6	−5.5	22.7	27.3	28.4
Slovak Rep.	5.8	6.1	6.7	−3.1	−7.7	−7.9	24.8	27.1	30.6
Slovenia	9.9	8.4	8.0	na	na	na	18.7	22.8	23.2
Estonia	23.1	11.2	8.2	−1.7	0.1	−0.8	14.4	12.0	9.9
Latvia	17.6	8.4	4.7	−4.5	−1.8	−5.8	23.4	21.1	22.5
Lithuania	24.7	8.8	5.1	−1.5	2.0	−0.3	6.9	6.0	7.4

Source: IMF, World Economic Outlook (1999); IMF materials.

Note: * Balance excluding privatization receipts.

Structural Policy Convergence

Latvia has made impressive progress in putting market mechanisms in place. This section presents a brief description of structural policy reform, emphasizing policies in three areas (Fischer et al. 1998):

- liberalization and competition;
- trade and foreign exchange regime; and
- privatization and banking reform.

Latvia liberalized her economy very quickly; the formerly centrally settled prices (and quantities) were set free at the very beginning of transition. The economy was opened fully to the world, allowing not only goods and services to flow freely over the borders, but also capital, implying full currency convertibility, for most current and capital account transactions.

The privatization scheme was less impressive at the start. There are at least two reasons why the privatization of large enterprises was relatively slow (Yndgaard 1998). First, the manufacturing sector of the Latvian economy has been dominated by large producers of special goods to the former Soviet Union (FSU) (electronics, for example). It is more difficult to privatize large companies than small to medium-size firms. Second, the tight fiscal policy represented a serious impediment to privatization: restructuring would imply a fiscally costly lay-off of redundant labour.

Table 6.5 presents measures of structural policy reform for the CEE countries. In principle, the indices could range from zero for a country in which no reform has taken place, to one for a country that has reformed completely. The remarkable aspect of the data is the extent of structural policy reform in Latvia as compared with another CEE countries in 1995. With regard to price liberalization and competition, Latvia was on the top even in 1995. The trade and foreign exchange regime has an index value of one. Because of delays in privatization and the severe banking crisis in 1995, the index reflecting privatization and banking reform was estimated at 0.6. Because of the negative impact of the privatization scheme and slow bank restructuring, the aggregate index shows that in 1995 Latvia had completed 81 per cent of reforms (generally speaking, even this range was not too low, as only four countries – the Czech Republic, Estonia, Hungary and Poland – had a score of 89 per cent or higher). Let us stress again that these relate to 1995, but since then, major progress has been achieved in privatization and banking reform.

Currently almost all large companies have been privatized. In statistical terms this means that about two-thirds of GDP is now produced by the private sector.

Table 6.5   Central and Eastern Europe: economic liberalization indices, 1995

	Weighted economic liberalization index (weights)	Price liberalization and competition (0.3)	Trade and foreign exchange regime (0.3)	Privatization and banking reform (0.4)
Czech Republic	0.93	0.9	1.0	0.9
Slovenia	0.85	0.9	1.0	0.7
Slovak Republic	0.86	0.9	0.9	0.8
Croatia	0.85	0.9	1.0	0.7
Hungary	0.93	0.9	1.0	0.9
Poland	0.89	0.9	1.0	0.8
Latvia	0.81	0.9	1.0	0.6
Lithuania	0.86	0.8	1.0	0.8
Albania	0.74	0.9	0.9	0.5
Estonia	0.93	0.9	1.0	0.9
Macedonia	0.78	0.9	0.9	0.6
Bulgaria	0.61	0.7	0.8	0.4
Romania	0.71	0.8	0.9	0.5

Source: De Melo et al. (1995).

Since the banking crisis in 1995, Latvia has managed to implement some of the most stringent banking regulations in Eastern Europe and a sound and profitable banking sector is now emerging.

THE COMPETITIVENESS OF THE ECONOMY

In the European Commission's 1997 report, a decisive argument against Latvia's accession was that: 'Latvia would face serious difficulties to cope with *competitive pressure and market forces* within the Union in the medium term. The Latvian economy is relatively open and labour costs are low. However, exports consist mainly of low value-added goods. Industrial restructuring, as well as enterprise restructuring, is still needed' (European Commission 1997/98, section C, italics added). According to Yndgaard (1998) this statement means

- first, in the absence of competitiveness in Latvia, there will be a call for protective measures, which would undermine the single market; and

- second, a sustained record of implementation of economic reforms reduces the risk that Latvia will be unable to maintain its commitment to the economic obligations.

This section argues that the margins for competitiveness of Latvian exports still exist and refutes the view that Latvia would not be capable of resisting interest-group pressures. The range of factors that determine competitiveness is very wide. Competitiveness is constantly affected by a broad range of economic policy instruments, such as fiscal policy, monetary policy and so on. There are economic indicators that help to evaluate competitiveness. These evaluation procedures are extremely important, but also extremely complicated, due to methodological problems. Based upon the dynamics of the exchange rate, exports, FDI, wage level and productivity, the evaluation of competitiveness that follows shows that Latvia's economic potential is rather high.

Factors Working to Increase or to Limit Latvia's Competitiveness

The competitiveness of the Latvian economy is primarily determined by:

- geographic location;
- well-developed infrastructure, ports, transportation gateway between West and East;
- recent experience in market economy;
- rapid and consequent reform pace;
- liberal, market-orientated policies;
- well-educated and relatively inexpensive labour force;
- stock of mineral substances (gypsum, clay, sand); and
- high-quality natural resources (soil, fish and timber resources).

Meanwhile, several factors so far working to limit Latvia's competitiveness have to be identified. Among them are:

- small domestic market;
- lack of energy resources;
- lack of resources other than those listed above; and
- incomplete structural reforms.

Besides clearly positive and clearly negative factors, there are those with an unclear impact on competitiveness. One of the most controversial of these factors is comparative advantage in core industrial sectors.

Section 2.1 of Agenda 2000 states: 'Relatively large and sophisticated industries were established in Latvia, because of its comparatively well-developed infrastructure ... Under the Soviet regime the main areas were machine building, electronics, and light industries' (European Commission 1997/98). Notwithstanding the Commission's negative interpretation of the Soviet 'post-industrial' legacy, we would argue that the above-cited statement could be interpreted in a positive sense as well. The country possesses comparative advantages not only in traditional wood and light industries, but also in electronics, machine building and the chemical industry *in the form of human capital*. Yndgaard comments that

> [I]n a comparative advantage context, Latvia is in possession of a large fund of know-how within the above-mentioned large-scale industrial sectors; in the short to medium term the scarcest resources of all, human capital, alias skilled workers, are on hand within these branches, ready to exploit the economies of scale ... If modern capital equipment and management were introduced, a rapid recovery of a substantial part of the Latvian economy could result (1998).

Exchange Rate

The exchange rate is a substantial factor in the scope of external competitiveness. Overvaluation of the exchange rate negatively influences exports and can cause sharp decreases in the pace of exports growth. It is extremely hard to estimate correctly the value of the exchange rate in developed countries. It is even harder to trace this process in transition economies, where the programmes of macroeconomic stabilization start with undervaluation of the exchange rate, and a sharp increase in productivity due to reforms and structural changes.

Several indicators are used to estimate the dynamics of the currency value, of which *the real effective exchange rate* (REER) is among the most important. The REER of the lats is calculated in the Bank of Latvia in terms of different indices. Consumer price index (CPI)-based exchange rate indicators are the most frequently used indicators of external competitiveness.

However, REER indicators suffer from a number of conceptual shortcomings as measures of competitiveness in the context of transition economies (IMF 1999c). The IMF analysts argued that

- REER could not directly answer the question of whether an exchange rate is 'too high' or 'too low';
- an appreciation as measured by the price-based REER does not necessarily provide evidence of loss of competitiveness;
- given the initial undervaluation, increases in REERs could reflect a movement towards the equilibrium exchange rate, rather than a competitiveness problem;

- price-based REER indicators are distorted by the fact that the CPI reflects changes in prices of both traded and non-traded goods that are very different in nature; and
- price-based REER indicators do not capture price developments for intermediate goods, which dominate international trade.

The fixing of the lats to the SDR has brought an exceptionally successful reduction of inflation and interest rates to levels comparable to the West.

The CPI-based REER of the lats has appreciated by about 325 per cent since the beginning of 1992. Two phases of appreciation are noticeable. The first phase was during the period from 1992 to 1994 when Latvia's inflation was well above the EU level. During this period, the lats appreciated by about 260 per cent in real effective terms. After a few years of relative stability in the REER, it entered into a second phase of appreciation with the collapse of the Russian ruble and other Commonwealth of Independent States (CIS) currencies, starting in mid-1998. This appreciation has been much smaller, however, and amounted to about 13 per cent.

According to the IMF (1999c) the producer price index (PPI)-based REERs suggest a much smaller appreciation during 1994–99 as compared with the CPI-based REERs. *Vis-à-vis* Germany, as a proxy for the EU, appreciation was estimated at about 36 per cent.

The different REER indices and can be seen in Table 6.6. An increase in the index indicates real appreciation. The figures clearly show an effective depreciation of the lats towards the East, indicating a fall in relative prices of Latvian goods in Eastern markets. Although the real value of the lats increased in Western markets in 1995, since then it has been fairly stable.

Because of ineffective restructuring, the recession of the Latvian economy was inevitable. There is no statistical evidence proving the link between the real exchange rate of the lats and the size of exports, thus it is very hard to estimate

Table 6.6   Real effective exchange rate of the lats, December 1994 to March 1998

	1994:12	1995:12	1996:12	1997:12	1998:3
CPI index	121.6	114.2	122.5	130.1	132.5
Vs West	121.3	138.0	155.0	172.2	177.8
Vs East	121.8	96.7	99.7	95.4	95.7
PPI index	104.3	87.3	90.3	97.8	–
Wage earnings index	134.9	114.7	129.0	124.3 (Oct.)	–

Source: World Bank (1998).

the impact of its appreciation on foreign trade. The weak trade communication network could explain slow growth of Latvian exports at the beginning of the transition process. However, the development of new markets and improvements of quality standards of Latvian goods increased the pace of export growth noticeably (World Bank 1998).

The Bank of Latvia argues that the lats is still undervalued. The nominal exchange rate of the lats is estimated to be about 1.8 times lower than in developed countries, using the purchasing power parity rate. However, in order to prevent potential distortion of competitiveness, Latvia cannot neutralize domestic excess inflation by revaluing its currency.

Export Development

As part of the USSR, the Latvian economy was completely closed to international markets. The Soviet currency was not convertible, and internal prices were not suitable for external trade agreements, so all transactions were dependent upon decisions by Soviet authorities. Because of political incompatibility, trade with Western countries hardly existed. Even in 1991, the share of non-Soviet countries in Latvian exports was just a few per cent, while the exchange of goods among the republics was promoted artificially, with no economic underpinning, leading to severe distortions in economic structures in the various republics.

In the starting stage of the reforms in Latvia, GDP and exports tended to decrease because of the conflicting trade relations with the CIS countries. The fall in exports was, in fact, even bigger than the decrease in GDP. As a result, the share of exports in GDP decreased considerably. After the initial breakdown, having partially adjusted to the factors of a market economy, exports started to increase again.

Stable growth in exports of goods and services and their proportion in the markets of the EU member countries are the main indicators of Latvia's foreign competitiveness. Table 6.7 shows robust exports growth during the period from 1994 to 1998. To a certain extent, the dynamics of exports indicates an increase in the competitiveness of Latvia's economy.

Export growth slowed considerably after the Russian crisis from 22 per cent in 1997 to 10 per cent in 1998. This slowdown was primarily due to a contraction in CIS markets, to which exports fell by 29 per cent. This decline was dominated by a 41 per cent drop in exports to Russia, with Latvian exports to other CIS countries contracting by only 2 per cent over the year. In the first quarter of 1999, total exports were down 13 per cent year-on-year, while exports to the CIS remained more than 60 per cent lower than one year earlier.

After the collapse of the communist regime, Latvia began to reorientate its trade flows away from CIS markets. Rapid stabilization, price and trade

*Table 6.7   Selected indicators of merchandise export performance, January
1994 to February 1998 (%)*

	1994	1995	1996	1997	1998
Exports/GDP	27.1	30.7	29.0	32.6	31.5
Share of non-CIS markets in exports	57.3	61.7	64.2	70.5	na
Growth of exports (in lats)*	–	24.4	15.5	22.2	10.0
Of which to non-CIS	–	34.0	20.2	34.2	24.6
Of which to CIS	–	11.5	8.0	0.7	–29.4

Note: *Growth rates relative to same period of the previous year.

Sources: IMF; Latvian authorities.

reform, and the initial undervaluation of exchange rates all helped to create
incentives for a successful reorientation of trade to Western markets. As a
result, the *destination of exports* changed as the share of exports to CIS countries in total exports declined, and the share of exports to the EU increased.
Over just a few years, the EU became the major trading partner for Latvia.
This shift was facilitated by quality improvements as well as by an increase in
the marketing capability brought about in large part by accumulated foreign
direct investment. This was possible also because of liberalization of foreign
trade, as well as progress in economic and political diplomacy with the EU.

Exports to Western countries grew considerably faster than to the markets
in the East. Theoretically, taking into consideration the dynamics of the
exchange rate, the situation should have been radically different; export
expansion should rather have been in Eastern markets. Such a paradoxical
outcome, on the one hand, reveals the complex nature of the evaluation of the
transition economies' competitiveness. On the other hand, export growth to
Western markets could be interpreted as the result of Latvia's foreign trade
policy, and the ability to adopt the requirements of the market economy and
quality standards quickly and comprehensively. (World Bank 1998)

In the immediate aftermath of independence, trade with the EU was typically of an inter-industry nature. Latvia exchanged raw materials (domestic
materials such as wood or re-export materials such as petrol and metals) for
machinery and consumer goods. In 1995, resource-based goods (specifically
wood) continued to dominate Latvia's exports to the EU. Some intra-industry
trade, such as processing of textiles from EU raw materials has emerged in
Latvia. Latvia is also becoming an exporter of foodstuffs to the CIS countries,
exploiting past market links and experience gained as processed food producers under the system of centralized planning. Entrance to the EU markets is

still highly complicated because of tough quality standards and certification. Regional trade agreements contributed significantly to the development of intra-industry trade in textiles and machinery with Latvia and helped the transition by demanding a rapid approximation of laws to Western standards.

The *structure of exports* exhibited a clear transformation between 1993 and 1998 with the shares of wood products and textiles in total exports increasing significantly from 10 per cent and 13 per cent to 37 per cent and 16 per cent, respectively. On the other hand, food products, machinery and chemicals, and vehicles fell, reflecting a reorientation towards Latvia's comparative advantages.

The share of Latvia's export structure differs over the group of trade partners. The dominant export to the EU in 1997 was wood and wood products. In 1997, the wood industry accounted for 19 per cent of total manufacturing output, with 90 per cent being exported and representing 30 per cent of Latvia's total merchandise exports. About 90 per cent of wood sector exports were destined for the EU, and less than 1 per cent to Russia. Therefore the downturn in Russia had only a minor impact on exports in this sector. Total exports in this category expanded by 24 per cent in 1998.

The second-largest export category is textile (16 per cent of total exports). Textiles accounted for 12 per cent of manufacturing in 1997 with about 68 per cent of its output being exported, of which 60 per cent went to the EU and 26 per cent to the CIS (16 per cent to Russia). During 1998, textile exports to the CIS fell by 30 per cent (28 per cent decline to Russia), while exports to the EU rose by 14 per cent.

The largest sector within manufacturing (39 per cent of total output) and the third-largest item in exports with a share of 10 per cent is food products and beverages. The food-processing industry has a competitive advantage only in the CIS markets (in 1997 about three-quarters of exports went to the CIS, of which 51 per cent went to Russia). In 1998, total exports in this category fell by 27 per cent, including a 47 per cent drop to the CIS (51 per cent drop in exports to Russia). These developments indicate that Latvian food exporters could lose their competitiveness.

In recent years, some positive tendencies have been observed in the structure of exports: the share of medium- to low-value exports has increased. For example, the share of sawn timber in the total volume of wood product exports increased from 54.3 per cent in 1996 to 57.8 per cent in 1997. Furniture exports increased rapidly in recent years, growing at an average rate of 20 per cent since 1994. The share of textile clothes in the category of textile products increased from 32.8 to 39.6 per cent over the year 1997.

In spite of these positive tendencies, the European Commission was correct in pointing to the fact that Latvian exports to Western markets at present rely mainly on low value-added goods, although the country has an advantage in labour-intensive goods (the labour force in Latvia is relatively cheap, but highly qualified). However, we share Yndgaard's position: 'what is relevant here is not the unit value-added contribution, but total value-added ... If the quantity produced and exported is high enough, there is no problem here' (1998).

The most direct export-related measure of competitiveness is *market share*. According to an IMF staff assessment (IMF 1999a), Latvia's market share in goods has been growing at about 10 per cent over the last two years. The share of Latvia's exports of goods and services has been growing at an average rate of about 8 per cent over the last three years. According to the IMF staff assessment, Latvian exports have been particularly successful in penetrating new markets in important EU economies, including Germany and the Scandinavian countries, in which Latvia's market share has been growing steadily over the last three years (Tables 6.8 and 6.9).

*Table 6.8 Latvia: analysis of global export market share, 1993–1998
(% change)*

	1993	1994	1995	1996	1997	1998
Goods and services						
Market growth	4.8	5.5	10.0	11.3	9.4	3.3
Growth of Latvia's exports	37.0	–0.6	7.2	26.3	13.5	10.7
Change in Latvia's market share	30.7	–5.8	–2.5	13.5	3.7	7.2
Goods						
Market growth	6.3	6.2	10.4	10.8	8.8	1.7
Growth of Latvia's exports	9.5	–28.9	6.8	8.9	20.2	11.3
Change in Latvia's market share	3.0	–33.1	–3.3	–1.7	10.5	9.4

Source: IMF (199a).

*Table 6.9 Latvia's export market share in selected EU countries,
1996–1998 (%)*

	1996	1997	1998
Germany	0.036	0.041	0.047
Finland	0.097	0.070	0.095
Sweden	0.113	0.167	0.217
Denmark	0.100	0.115	0.161
UK	0.045	0.061	0.059

Source: IMF (1999a).

Productivity, Wages and Unit Labour Costs

Yndgaard (1998) states that, the question of maintaining a sufficient competitiveness reduces to the following question: is Latvia able to keep the inflation rate lower than (or equal to) that of foreign competitors? If Latvia fails to do so, then under free trade conditions, imported goods will supplant domestic tradable goods. The competitiveness of the economy reveals the competitiveness of companies: under excess inflation, domestic companies will be unable to export their own products.

It has been argued above that Latvia cannot neutralize domestic excess inflation stemming from further price adjustment in the non-tradables sector. However, prices in a market economy originate primarily from two sources: wage rates and productivity. Therefore, the dynamic aspect of competitiveness essentially becomes a question of the possibilities of increasing labour productivity fast enough as compared to wage increases. This means that the competitiveness of companies is influenced by two factors, the level and dynamics of real wages and productivity. If the increase in productivity is faster than the growth in real wages, competitiveness increases. According to a World Bank study (1998) there were some positive trends in the Latvian economy in 1996–97 (see Table 6.10).

As can be seen, the real product wage decreased in 1996, while productivity increased. The following year, the pace of growth for real wages was higher than that of productivity, indicating a decrease in competitiveness. Two years of data is not enough to draw definitive conclusions about trends, especially when the relative movement of the wages/productivity ratio is opposite in the two years. None the less, over the two years, there was clearly a net gain in competitiveness.

The latest IMF assessment corresponds only partly with this conclusion. Cumulative labour productivity in manufacturing (IMF 1999a)[3] in the period from 1994 to 1997 has ranked in the top tier in transition economies.[4] However, wages in the sector have been growing even faster than productivity, resulting in a positive growth in unit labour cost in this sector (Table 6.11).

Accurate calculations of unit labour cost as one of the preferred indicators

Table 6.10   Real product wage and productivity (%)

	1996	1997	Cumulative 1996–97
Real after-tax product wages	−5.7	7.9	1.6
Growth in average labour productivity	6.2	4.8	11.1

Source: World Bank (1998).

Table 6.11   Productivity and unit labour cost in manufacturing, 1993–1996

	1993	1994	1995	1996	1997	1998
Average nominal wages in lats	46.2	73.7	91.8	104.3	127.4	134.2
Average nominal wage (percent change)	–	59.7	24.6	13.6	22.2	5.3
Labour productivity (annual percentage change)	–	5.1	1.7	8.2	15.1	4.2
Unit labour costs (annual percentage change)	–	52.0	22.5	5.0	7.9	1.1

Source: IMF (1990a).

of competitiveness are not available. According to the IMF staff estimates, the unit labour cost index in Latvia has not changed much over the last few years. However, Latvia's competitiveness measured by unit labour cost deteriorated somewhat. On the other hand, it is noted by the IMF that this measure indicates more the relative change in the level of competitiveness rather than whether the country is competitive or not in absolute terms.

The Size of Foreign Direct Investment

The amount of foreign direct investment (FDI) in Latvia during recent years has increased considerably (Table 6.12). Compared to other countries of Central and Eastern Europe, only Hungary, the Czech Republic, Estonia and Slovenia have higher FDI per capita. The ratio of inward FDI to the current account deficit was about 180 per cent in 1996 and 1997. However, this ratio declined to 45 per cent in 1998 due to the less favourable international sentiments in the wake of the Asian and Russian crises.

Notwithstanding these negative signals, the general improvement of the investment climate in Latvia has been reflected in the increasing international ratings granted by Standard & Poor's and Moody's. An ability to bring in FDI is also indicative of the attractiveness, stability and competitiveness of a country.

Table 6.12   Foreign direct investment in Latvia, 1995–1998

	1995	1996	1997	1998
FDI (net, USDm)	244.6	378.6	515.0	219.6
FDI stock (% of GDP)	12.4	15.4	13.0	15.0

Source: IMF (1999a).

CONCLUSIONS

1. The concept of distance from the EU is multidimensional. With regard to economic space, three issues are of primary importance:
    *   income gap and the challenges for real convergence (how and when is it possible to close the income gap);
    *   macroeconomic performance and prospects for nominal (fiscal and monetary) convergence; and
    *   progress in adopting a market-based system or structural convergence.

2. GDP per capita in Latvia is very low, compared to European countries. It is very hard methodologically to evaluate whether Latvia has dropped behind. Official output statistics in transition economies are subject to several deficiencies. In Latvia these deficiencies are not due to a weakness of statistical methods used for drawing up the national accounts, but to the large informal sector of the economy. This informal sector is very large compared to the EU member countries; therefore, the difference in the real GDP figures is smaller than in the official ones.

3. To close the large income gap between Latvia and the EU it is necessary to promote investments as a major engine of growth in the medium to long terms. Macroeconomic stabilization and general progress on market-orientated reforms are dominant determinants of recovery in Latvia at the beginning of transition. Stabilization along with structural reforms are necessary but not sufficient preconditions for growth. Special attention should be paid to the policies in such areas as rule of law and prevention of corruption.

4. In line with conditional convergence theory, because of the combination of different policies and factors, income in poorer countries is growing more rapidly than in richer countries. Both the actual and predicted GDP growth in Latvia is more rapid than in the EU member states.

5. Real convergence is not a precondition, but an outcome, of membership in EU.

6. Important preconditions for integration into the EU are the prospects for nominal convergence. Even though the convergence (Maastricht) criteria do not capture all the aspects of the development, and even though they are too strict to be used as mandatory conditions for joining the EU, convergence criteria are important. All of the countries joining the EU have to be able to reach the level of nominal convergence (to meet the fiscal and monetary convergence criteria) in a relatively short period of time after joining the EU.

7. The accomplishment of nominal convergence standards should be set as the goal of medium- and long-term economic stability. Latvia has made

significant progress toward macroeconomic stability. The exchange rate is stable, the inflation rate has entered single-digit territory, and the fiscal deficit and public debt are low.

8. Latvia has made impressive progress in promoting structural convergence. With regard to price liberalization and competition, Latvia was on the top even in 1995. Since then major progress has been achieved in privatization and banking reform. Currently almost all large companies have been privatized. In statistical terms this means that about two-thirds of GDP is produced by the private sector. Since the banking crisis in 1995, Latvia has managed to implement some of the most stringent banking regulations in Eastern Europe and a sound and profitable banking sector is now emerging.

9. The question of how long it will take Latvia to close the income gap with EU countries depends on the competitiveness of the economy in the international market, particularly the EU market, the dynamics of the exchange rate, exports, FDI, the wage level and productivity. The evaluation of competitiveness as of now shows that Latvia's competitive capacity is fairly high.

10. To overcome the reversal of economic fortunes in response to the external shock, the prudent economic policy aimed at further integrating the country with the EU and world economy must be continued.

NOTES

1. Because of the Russian crisis the share of investment has decreased somewhat and according to the IMF estimates was about 20 per cent of GDP in 1999. A gradual increase of the share of investment is expected over the medium term; however, the 1998 level could be reached only in 2002.
2. The fiscal balance presentation in this chapter differs from official national data because privatization receipts are not treated as general government revenues but as financing.
3. Detailed productivity data are available only for the manufacturing sector.
4. According to the European Bank for Reconstruction and Development, Latvia came second in a group of 12 transition economies.

BIBLIOGRAPHY

Auer, Josef (1995), 'Report on the Central and Eastern European comparison', Paper presented to the Conference of European Statisticians.

Bloem, Adriaan M., Pait Cotterell and Terry Gigantes (1996), 'National accounts in transition countries: distortions and biases', International Monetary Fund Working Paper no. 96/130, Washington, DC: IMF.

Csaba, Laslo (1997), 'Comment on Stanley Fischer, Ratna Sahau and Carlos A. Vegh "How far is Eastern Europe from Brussels?" ', Kiel, 'Quo Vadis Europe?'.

de Melo, Martha, Cevdet Denizer and Alan Gelb (1995), 'From plan to market: patterns of transition', unpublished, Washington, DC: World Bank.

European Commission (1997/98), *Agenda 2000*, Commission Opinion on Latvia's Application for Membership of the European Union, Brussels.

Eurostat (1998/28), 'The GDP of the candidate countries of Central and Eastern Europe and Cyprus – initial figures for 1997 and new calculations in real terms', Statistics in Focus. Economy and Finance.

Fischer, Stanley, Ratha Sahay and Carlos A. Vegh (1998), 'How far is Eastern Europe from Brussels?', International Monetary Fund Working Paper, Washington, DC: IMF, April.

International Monetary Fund (IMF) (1996), *World Economic Outlook*, Washington, DC: IMF, May.

International Monetary Fund (IMF) (1998), 'Growth experience in transition economies', unpublished, Washington, DC: IMF, September.

International Monetary Fund (IMF) (1999a), *Republic of Latvia – Selected Issues and Statistical Appendix*, Washington, DC: IMF, July.

International Monetary Fund (IMF) (1999b), *Republic of Latvia – Request for Stand-By Arrangement*, Washington, DC: IMF, November.

International Monetary Fund (IMF) (1999c), *The Baltics – Exchange Rate Regimes and External Sustainability*, Washington, DC: IMF, November.

Ministry of Finance (1998), *The Joint Assessment of the Government of Latvia and the European Commission on Economic Policy Priorities*, Riga.

Ministry of Finance, Ministry of Economy and Bank of Latvia (1998), 'Medium-term economic strategy in the context of accession to the European Union', Riga.

Pautola, Niina (1997) 'Fiscal transition in the Baltics', *Review of Economies in Transition*, no. 2, Bank of Finland, Helsinki.

Šteinbuka, Inna and Martins Kazaks (1996), 'Fiscal adjustment in Latvia under transition', Centre for Economic Policy Research (CEPR) Discussion Paper no. 96/1, Heriot-Watt University, Edinburgh.

World Bank (1998), 'Latvia – Macroeconomic and financial sector vulnerability review', unpublished, Washington and Riga.

Yndgaard, Ebbe (1998), 'EU enlargement – Latvia is ready', Department of Economics Working paper no. 1998–13, University of Aarhus, Denmark.

7. Monetary policy prospects and Maastricht criteria in Lithuania before accession to the EU

Salomėja Jasinskaitė, Dalia Vidickienė and Rasa Melnikienė

INTRODUCTION

Lithuania, like most of other Central and Eastern European (CEE) countries, is striving for membership in the European Union (EU) and regards this aspiration as its most important economic and political goal. In 1993, the European Council in Copenhagen set certain economic requirements for countries seeking EU membership. Alongside such conditions as a functioning market economy and the ability to cope with competitive pressure within the EU, CEE countries must be capable of taking on obligations of membership, including participation in the European Economic and Monetary Union (EMU). Therefore, the applicant countries are challenged by new tasks in the sphere of monetary and exchange rate policy. This is especially characteristic of the countries that have introduced a currency board arrangement (CBA), whose operating mechanism differs in principle from the monetary policy pursued by EU countries.

Many economists acknowledge that the operation of a CBA made an impact on financial stabilization in both Lithuania and Estonia. However, apart from the fact that the CBA is entirely inconsistent with standards of EU central banking (Krzak 1997), this regime is a factor that restricts the pursuit of an active monetary policy. Therefore, taking into account Lithuania's declared wish to join the EU and participate in EMU, the principles of the monetary policy model in Lithuania must be evaluated and self-determination concerning the further functioning of the CBA and the exchange rate regime must be embraced.

REASONS AND CONDITIONS FOR ABANDONING THE CBA

Currently, among the countries that aspire to become members of the EU, three countries – Lithuania, Estonia and Bulgaria – base their monetary policy on a CBA, and recently another transition economy, Bosnia–Herzegovina, also consolidated a CBA. So far, neither Estonia nor Bulgaria have planned to replace the CBA with another monetary policy arrangement.

Bulgaria, which has only recently started basing its monetary policy on a CBA (since mid-1997) has not yet attained the set goals of achieving monetary and financial stabilization. Further policy in Bulgaria is focused on strengthening the medium-term sustainability of the currency board regime, so that for the next few years at least, the CBA should serve as a monetary framework contributing to macroeconomic stabilization and the implementation of extensive structural reforms. Therefore, consideration to substituting an alternative system for the CBA is still premature in Bulgaria.

It is most likely that Estonia, which had introduced a CBA earlier (June 1992) and which evaluates the impact of this arrangement on economic development of the country very positively, will lay emphasis on the stability factor of monetary policy and preserve the CBA. The 1998 economic policy programme of the Estonian government and the Bank of Estonia confirms this presumption; it is planned that the fixed exchange rate of the Estonian kroon against the Deutschmark, and the CBA, will continue to be the main monetary policy framework. It was decided that after 1 January 1999, the Deutschmark, the anchor currency of the Estonian kroon, would be replaced by the euro according to the conversion rate of the Deutschmark to the euro.[1] The International Monetary Fund (IMF) approves Estonia's decision, although it also makes negative comments about changes in the monetary policy of transition countries.

Lithuania still remains the only country in transition planning to abandon the CBA, which has been functioning since April 1994, and to restore most of the functions of the central bank. The latter is provided for in the monetary policy programme up to 2000, announced by the Bank of Lithuania.[2]

Differences in future prospects of monetary policy may be partially explained by disparities between the CBAs of Lithuania and Estonia as well as that of Bulgaria. The Lithuanian national currency was pegged to the US dollar, while the national currencies of Estonia and Bulgaria were pegged to the Deutschmark. As the EU member state national currency has been selected as the base currency, this will enable them to pass over to another anchor currency – the euro – more easily.

What are the main conditions and reasons that have predetermined the decision to modify the institutional structure of monetary policy in Lithuania? One can distinguish both internal and external conditions that influence such a decision.

The integration into the EU determines the external factors that are instrumental in the desire to change the CBA in Lithuania and approximate the monetary policy framework to those functioning in the EU countries, that is, to restore to the Bank of Lithuania all the usual functions of a central bank.

In this respect two factors can be emphasized, both related to the official requirement for EU membership: to abide by the aims of economic and monetary union. First, the basic features of the CBA actually make it impossible for Lithuania to participate fully in institutionalized monetary and exchange rate policy cooperation within the EU. Monetary policy cooperation implies the use of market-based monetary policy instruments, most of which cannot be used under the CBA. This means that Lithuania can take an active part in the process of EU monetary policy harmonization only if it returns to the modern central bank model. Complications also arise concerning the requirement to participate in an exchange rate mechanism (ERM) after joining the EU, largely because under the CBA the Bank of Lithuania has no instruments for regulating interest rates. Monetary operations are restricted under the CBA, so changes in foreign exchange reserves are automatically reflected in domestic money liquidity and interest rates. Consequently, the unsustainability of joining the ERM will be the main obstacle to entering the eurozone, which is the next prescribed step after joining the EU. So, to meet one of the EU membership criteria – to participate in EMU – it is necessary to change the current monetary policy arrangement.

Second, the European Central Bank (ECB), using a set of discrete monetary policy instruments, will be the central actor of monetary union. It is expected that any national bank operating as a component part of the European central banking system, will be capable of implementing monetary policy decisions taken by the ECB. Readiness to fulfil this task will take some time even for EU member countries, because each country maintains a more or less different monetary policy. It is especially true for countries with a CBA, since their central banks have no or very little experience of how to use open market operations and other monetary policy instruments. Moreover, continuing to operate a CBA will slow down the learning process. This implies that a gradual extension of the set of monetary policy instruments available to the central bank will be necessary, which amounts to the gradual abandonment of the CBA.

However, the decision to abandon the CBA was preconditioned not only by and due to external conditions, that is, the need to introduce an appropriate monetary policy arrangement for joining the EU and eventual participation in the eurozone, but also by the conditions within Lithuania.

The CBA was introduced in Lithuania to achieve macroeconomic stabilization by supporting an economic reform programme that would ensure stability of the national currency, and in such a way as would build up credibility. To achieve these goals, the latter monetary policy regime seemed to be the most suitable. First, since monetary emission is possible only through purchasing base foreign currency (the US dollar in the Lithuanian case), the way would be blocked for political and other interest groups to influence the

Bank of Lithuania concerning the issue of money, including depriving the bank of the possibility of financing the budgetary deficit. Second, under the automatic monetary emission regime, potential losses would be avoided in the event that inappropriate policy was pursued as a result of the inexperience of employees or their lack of skills. These, psychological rather than economical, motives were presented as the most decisive arguments on the eve of introducing the CBA. Third, it was expected that a fixed exchange rate regime and the complete backing of the national currency by gold and convertible foreign currency reserves, which guarantees the exchange of any amount of litas to the base currency and vice versa, would result in greater confidence in the national currency, which had only recently been introduced.

In effect, the introduction and maintenance of the CBA since April 1994, alongside other programmes of economic reform, has led to improvements for Lithuanian macroeconomic stabilization – a fall in the inflation rate, economic recovery, the growth of domestic investment, a reduction in interest rates, and a moderate official unemployment rate (Table 7.1).

The restrictive nature and transparency of monetary operations were positive factors in the process of inflation decrease. Inflation dropped from 72.2 per cent in 1994 to 8.9 per cent in 1997, and even to 5.1 per cent in 1998. Real GDP growth began in 1995 and in 1997 it reached 7.3 per cent, but the Russian crisis influenced the slight decrease in GDP growth rate to 5.1 per cent in 1998. Foreign exchange reserves are also growing, mostly due to increased

Table 7.1   Main macroeconomic indicators of Lithuania

Indicators	1993	1994	1995	1996	1997	1998
Real GDP (growth in %)	−16.2	−9.8	3.3	4.7	7.3	5.1
GDP per person, current prices (USD)	797	1136	1622	2128	2587	2887
Average annual CPI (%)	410.2	72.2	39.6	24.6	8.9	5.1
Foreign exchange reserves (excluding gold) (USD mill.)	341.7	525.5	757.1	772.3	1010	1409
Foreign exchange reserves as months of imports	1.6	2.4	2.3	1.9	1.9	2.7
Gross fixed capital formation (% in GDP)	23.1	23.1	23.0	23.0	24.4	25.8
Current account balance (% in GDP)	−3.1	−2.1	−10.2	−9.2	−10.2	−12.1
Unemployment rate (average annual), %	4.4	3.8	6.1	7.1	5.9	6.4

Sources: Bank of Lithuania, *Balance of Payments of the Republic of Lithuania*, no. 4, 1997; Bank of Lithuania. *Balance of Payments of the Republic of Lithuania*, no. 4, 1998.

borrowing from abroad as well as to privatization of big Lithuanian enterprises for foreign investors.

On the other hand, the CBA in Lithuania revealed several disadvantages related to liquidity problems in the banking sector and, to some extent, to the sphere of monetary base regulation. In the case of serious external shocks (for example, large capital outflows or inflows) which influence sharp fluctuations in exchange reserves and, consequently, the monetary base and money supply, an active monetary policy could be helpful. Thus, restrictions on conducting monetary policy operations were the main cause of these shortcomings.

1. *The restrictive nature of the CBA with regard to avoiding the banking crisis*   Under the CBA, the central bank has virtually no means of performing the lender-of-last-resort function, and this restricts the central bank from ensuring the stability of the financial system. When indicators of a crisis situation appear in the financial market, insolvency of one or several banks may cause a liquidity crisis in other banks, and limitations of the CBA prevent the central bank from taking discrete monetary policy measures to sustain the liquidity of solvent banks. Such a situation existed in Lithuania at the end of 1995 and the beginning of 1996, when the cessation of activities of two banks threatened to result in a detrimental decrease in the liquidity of other Lithuanian banks. In an attempt to avoid the further spread of the crisis, the Bank of Lithuania had to perform a lender-of-last-resort function, that is, certain banks were granted liquidity loans, government securities were purchased from banks and the rate of the required reserves was reduced. The first two operations were carried out incompletely, as only foreign exchange in excess of the full cover of the monetary base may be used for lender-of-last-resort operations.

2. *The restrictive nature of the CBA in the sphere of the regulation of money supply*   The currency board regime predetermines the fact that changes in the monetary base are directly related to foreign currency flows. This means that the CBA protects the economy from inflation, that is, the central bank is not able to finance the state budgetary deficit or otherwise execute an expansive monetary policy. But the CBA is an unsuitable measure of inflation control after the start of mass foreign currency inflow to the country. Capital inflows precondition a corresponding increase in money amount that threatens a growth in inflation. Limited by the CBA, the central bank has almost no monetary policy measures to regulate the after-effects of capital inflows. The central bank would be in the same desperate situation in the event of a sudden capital outflow which may cause a monetary deficit, diminished liquidity of the banking system and so on.

Table 7.2   Foreign investment, loans and increase in reserve assets (USD m)

Year	Direct investment	Portfolio investment	Loans	Increase in international reserve assets
1993	30.2	0.6	255.8	284.2
1994	31.3	4.5	237.5	183.8
1995	72.5	86.6	435.2	231.8
1996	152.4	214.6	571.8	15.3
1997	354.5	180.5	848.9	237.8
1998	925.5	−42.7	1144.7	399.0

Source: Bank of Lithuana, *Balance of payments of the Republic of Lithuania*, no. 4, 1997.

Although before 1997 speculative capital inflows were rather small (Table 7.2), the central bank could not avoid mostly short-term fluctuations in reserve money, caused by fluctuations in foreign currency inflows. For example, during the first two months of 1996, reserve money decreased by 23 per cent; after the introduction of the CBA in April 1994, during the first three months of its functioning, reserve money had increased by 23 per cent.[3]

In the meantime, increasing fluctuations in capital inflow (Table 7.2) and a rapidly increasing current account deficit (Table 7.3) were important reasons for the central bank to return to regulating measures of money supply. Portfolio investments increased by 2.5 times in 1996, compared with those in 1995, decreased by 50 per cent in 1997, compared with those in 1996, and resulted in portfolio capital outflow in 1998. Despite this fact, there is a possibility that

Table 7.3   Current account deficit (USDm)

Year	Trade balance	Balance of services	Income balance	Balance of current transfers	Balance of current account	Current account/ GDP (%)
1993	−154.6	−55.1	8.3	115.9	−85.7	−3.1
1994	−204.8	−54.5	8.6	156.8	−94.0	−2.1
1995	−698.0	−12.9	−12.9	109.3	−614.4	−10.2
1996	−896.2	120.8	−91.0	143.8	−722.6	−9.2
1997	−1147.5	134.5	−198.4	230.0	−981.4	−10.2
1998	−1518.4	240.7	−255.5	235.0	−1298.1	−12.1

Sources: Bank of Lithuania, *Quarterly Bulletin*, no. 4, 1997. Bank of Lithuania, *Balance of Payments of the Republic of Lithuania*, no. 4, 1998.

speculative capital inflow will increase in the future because the gap between interest rates in Lithuania and most other foreign countries still remains, while the number of financial instruments would have to increase with the development of money and capital markets. Significant short-term capital inflows and outflows cause fluctuations in the money supply, so to neutralize these external shocks the central bank should be given the right to use monetary policy instruments to change the monetary base.

Great anxiety is also caused by the growth in the current account deficit: in 1996 it amounted to 9.2 per cent of GDP; in 1997, 10.3 per cent; and in 1998, 12.1 per cent. Economic theory maintains that the main measures for decreasing the current account deficit are devaluation of currency and fiscal limitations. The central bank cannot make use of the currency devaluation measure under the CBA conditions since this right is retained by parliament. However, currency devaluation is not an acceptable measure at present because of other reasons. First of all, when calculating the exchange rate according to the purchasing power parity factor, the litas still remains unvalued against other convertible currencies, in spite of the difference between inflation in Lithuania and that in the base currency country, the USA, which has existed for several years. This happened because when the litas was pegged to the US dollar, according to the purchasing power parity, 1 litas equalled about 1 US dollar (Nauseda 1997), while the official exchange rate was fixed at as much as 4 litas to 1 US dollar. Second, devaluation of currency is always followed by such evils as rapid growth in inflation and a decrease in real income. Also, bearing in mind the inflexibility of prices of raw materials and products imported into Lithuania, one may forecast that imports can increase at a greater rate than exports, and this may worsen the current account balance even more. In this case, fiscal rather than monetary measures might be preferable, with a complete decline in the budget deficit. In this respect Lithuania has extra reserves, since although it had a budget deficit, in fact, the deficit was not large and amounted to only 1.2 per cent of GDP in 1997 and 1.3 per cent in 1998.

Taking into consideration the negative experience of South-East Asian and certain CEE countries concerning an increasing internal consumption of foreign loans manifested by a huge current account deficit and 'overheating' of the economy, the Bank of Lithuania has started to apply the required reserve requirements for domestic bank liabilities to foreign credit institutions. This helps to make foreign currency loans more expensive and thus slows down their growth.

Finally, two factors can be discerned on the basis of which we can conclude that a CBA is not of vital importance to the Lithuanian economy, and could be replaced by some other framework.

The first factor is that the expected level of confidence in the litas in the domestic market was not achieved. The lack of confidence in the litas could be illustrated by the time deposit ratio (which reveals which currency is preferred as the savings function within the country) in foreign and national currencies before the introduction of the CBA (April 1994) and during the period of its functioning. On the eve of its introduction, resident time deposits in litas accounted for 55 per cent, and foreign currencies for 45 per cent; after a year (March 1995), time deposits in litas decreased to 33 per cent of total time deposits, while foreign currencies increased to 67 per cent. By the end of 1996, confidence in the litas increased: time deposits in litas amounted to 43 per cent.[4] But in 1997 and 1998, foreign currencies were again preferred by residents as a means of saving: time deposits in foreign currencies accordingly amounted to 64 per cent and 68 per cent, while time deposits in litas amount to only 36 per cent in 1997 and 32 per cent in 1998. This happened despite the fact that the interest rate on time deposits in litas was higher than that in foreign currencies: for example, in June 1997, the interest rate on time deposits in litas was 8.78 per cent, and in foreign currencies, 5.54 per cent; at the end of 1998, the amounts were, respectively, 6.06 and 4.53 per cent.[5] Thus, the increase in confidence in the national currency in 1996 was replaced by a decrease in 1997 and 1998, after criticism of the CBA was voiced again among economists.

It should be noted first of all that the CBA, contrary to that in Estonia, was introduced in spite of objections made by most economists. Therefore, during the entire period of its operation, despite possible negative consequences for the Lithuanian economy, criticism of the regime never ceased, and it gave rise to a certain lack of confidence from both the domestic community and foreign investors in the national currency, the monetary authorities and the whole Lithuanian financial system. Thus, the public were psychologically prejudiced against the pursued monetary policy regime, reasoning that the CBA was not appropriate for Lithuania and was forced on Lithuania by international organizations.

The second factor is related to the insufficient confidence in the economic reforms attained among foreign investors. When the CBA was introduced, it was expected that such a monetary policy regime would become one of the most important factors promoting foreign investor confidence and thus increasing the inflow of foreign direct investment (FDI). However, the flow of foreign investments into the country was rather small before 1997 (by 1 January 1997, the cumulative FDI equalled USD 700 million). According to the FDI per capita, Lithuania lagged behind most transition countries and its rate was the lowest when compared with other Baltic states – Latvia and Estonia (Table 7.4). Only since 1997, has the increase in FDI become more significant, and the cumulative FDI to Lithuania amounted to USD 1041 million at the beginning of 1998 and reached USD 1625 million by the beginning of 1999.[6]

Table 7.4   Cumulative FDI inflows per capita (USD)

	Lithuania	Latvia	Estonia	Poland	Czech R.	Hungary	Romania
1 October 1997	263	340	735	535	796	1655	106*

Note: *1 July 1997.

Source: Republic of Lithuania, *Programme of Stimulation of Foreign Direct Investment*, January 1998.

The plans of the Bank of Lithuania to phase out the CBA, publicized in 1997, had no negative influence on the increasing activity of foreign investors. In January 1999, cumulative direct investment in Lithuania increased to USD 440 per capita. This confirms the opinion that the flows of FDI are conditioned first of all by entirely different factors (overall image of the country, political conditions, stability of the legislation, criminal situation, strength of the financial system, removal of bureaucratic obstacles and so on) and not by the functioning of the CBA. Therefore, the replacement of this monetary policy regime by another one, taking into consideration that a fixed exchange rate will be retained, should not influence foreign investors' decisions negatively.

The CBA in Lithuania was introduced as a transitional arrangement to support economic reforms. Due to considerable success in recent years in macroeconomic stabilization and the development of financial markets, the time has come to relax the currency board rules and so gradually abandon this monetary policy regime. Integration into the EU and internal pressures in Lithuania demonstrate the significance of restoring to the Bank of Lithuania the instruments for pursuing a discrete policy. The question is how to implement the abandonment of the CBA without losing the achieved macroeconomic and financial stability and at the same time for the monetary authorities and policymakers to retain some credibility.

CHANGE OF MONETARY POLICY GOALS AND INSTRUMENTS

The Bank of Lithuania has chosen to make a gradual exit from the CBA,[7] taking into account all the complexity and importance of this process. During the transformation of the monetary policy regime to that of a standard central bank, the credibility achieved under the CBA must be retained. On the one hand, it is necessary to convince the public as well as foreign investors that the monetary authorities have the strategy and experience to change the monetary policy regime and to operate effectively under new monetary conditions. On the other hand, the monetary authorities themselves have to participate in the learning process to be able to act in a suitable manner under different shocks. In addition, eventual abandonment of the CBA enables a choice to be made of the most appropriate time to introduce discrete monetary policy instruments with respect to macroeconomic changes and financial sector development within the country, as well as to external factors, for example, progress achieved in negotiations concerning EU membership and changes in the financial markets in the world. This applies especially to the macroeconomic and financial situation in Russia, since trade relations with this large neighbour country remain intensive and influence Lithuania's macroeconomic indicators.

The decision to change the existing monetary policy framework requires an assessment and any necessary adjustments in setting up monetary policy goals and targets, as well as appropriate instruments for achieving set goals, taking into account the experience of EU countries and the likely strategy and instruments that will be used by the European Central Bank.

Currently the ultimate (final) goal of monetary policy in Lithuania is preconditioned by the monetary policy regime based on a fixed exchange rate and the CBA. Therefore, the stability of the national currency with emphasis on its external stability is the ultimate goal of the bank's monetary policy. Such a final goal is logical because Lithuania is a small, very open economy country seeking to integrate into the EU markets as soon as possible. The extent of openness of the Lithuanian economy is indicated by the ratio of the foreign trade turnover to GDP, which fluctuated around 120 per cent in 1994–96. Therefore, the maintenance of a stable litas rate with respect to foreign currencies conforms with Lithuania's political and economic goals.

The central bank cannot establish independently other monetary policy goals and targets that would realize the final goal, and it has a very limited number of central banking instruments at its disposal that do not contradict the CBA. Both intermediate goal and operational target merge into one goal – that of the currency exchange rate. The instruments employed by the central bank include a requirement for commercial banks to keep the required reserves in the central bank as well as fixing the rate of such reserves. In special cases, the central bank could extend liquidity loans for commercial banks that have encountered serious problems of liquidity. In addition, the fact that the central bank has performed these operations means that a modified and flexible CBA exist in Lithuania.

Meanwhile, the final goal of the monetary policy in EU countries is maintenance of price stability. The goal of price stability is also stated in the Maastricht Treaty, with the provision that this will be the main goal of the European central banking system. Thus, it differs from the final monetary policy goal in Lithuania, since external and internal currency stability cannot always be coordinated.

EU member states employ a variety of ways and instruments to realize their final goal, and they have each selected one of the following as an intermediate goal: money amount, exchange rate or inflation (Ketter 1998).

The money supply goal is employed in the central bank strategy of such countries as Germany, France, Italy and Greece. Indicators of money supply and the definition of indicators are set, taking into account the way that specific conditions of each country would best reflect the liquidity situation. The essence of the money supply goal may be defined as a monetary emission whose purpose is to provide money stock for the normative (not the current) increase in prices, which is based on the probability of a price increase over the medium term. In some countries, M3 indicators are employed; in others, M2. In addition, the definition of these indicators may differ slightly from one country to another. Some central banks declare their goal publicly (for example, the Bundesbank declares M3 to be its annual goal); others only publicize tendencies of money supply growth (for example, the central bank of France).

Smaller countries, whose economic development has a greater dependence on foreign trade, apply the exchange rate goal to their monetary policy. This monetary policy objective is used in the Benelux countries, Denmark and Austria. Some countries have pegged their currency to the Deutschmark, while others have established the limits of fluctuation of their currencies by pegging against the currencies of their main trade partners.

In countries where money supply or exchange rate goals were not suitable (because of speculative attacks on the currency or other disturbances in the foreign currency market) the inflation goal is chosen. These countries are the United Kingdom, Sweden, Finland and Spain. In order that the final goal of price stability will be achieved, they employ certain indicators that determine inflation – consumer or retail price indices as well as additional intermediate targets – money supply M0 and M4 (the United Kingdom) or exchange rate (Spain, Finland) (Ketter 1998).

When pursuing these set goals, central banks of EU countries can utilize a number of instruments of monetary policy – they can perform open market operations, apply requirements of required reserves for banks and also have permanent lending and borrowing facilities.

This short survey on monetary policy goals aspired to in EU countries and the instruments of their implementation show that monetary policy in Lithuania, characterized by its declared monetary policy goals and the instruments being employed, differs greatly from that of EU countries. The intermediary goal – exchange rate stability – may correspond to the goal declared in certain European countries, but operational targets and the reserve of instruments used for the implementation of the declared goal are completely different. Meanwhile, the ability to join EMU and to execute the corresponding and reliable monetary policy is an important precondition for accession to the EU.

Therefore, the Bank of Lithuania, when formulating its monetary policy programme, on the one hand has provided for a gradual expansion of monetary policy instruments, and on the other hand has reduced the currency board requirements, which will bring its monetary policy model more in line with EU standards.

First, the bank has undertaken to expand monetary policy instruments which still survive under the CBA. The first step was to apply repo agreements for securities between the Bank of Lithuania and commercial banks. By this means it was attempting to fulfil the following tasks: (i) to start applying reversible open market operations that are broadly used in the EU; (ii) to regulate the liquidity of the banking system more effectively, both when seeking to ensure normal settlements of the banks with customers and when attracting free bank funds in the event of a surplus; (iii) to induce the development of a national money market, since repo agreements should provisionally restrain free bank funds from flowing to Western money markets; and (iv) to increase the attractiveness of government securities, since if no other instruments appear in the money market, then they will remain the only one (Shiaudinis 1997).

The second step was the modification of lender-of-last-resort loans in the system of short-term loans for commercial banks collateralized by securities, that is, Lombard loans were introduced. At the beginning of 1998, rules were prepared that regulated one of the most important types of Lombard loans – the extension of overnight lending. That is, settlement of accounts provided to a certain bank and made by the Bank of Lithuania during the last clearing of the day in the event that the bank falls short of funds in its correspondent account. The bank must back this payment with a pledge of government securities. Currently, some European central banks extend such loans. In the European Monetary Institute's *The Single Monetary Policy in Stage Three*, it is foreseen that such loans will be also extended by the ECB. In addition, the ECB plans to extend intra-day lending when loans are issued and repaid during the same working day. In Lithuania, intra-day lending will be introduced only after the general volume of clearing has increased.

After the CBA was introduced, the Bank of Lithuania had at its disposal such instruments of monetary policy as required bank reserves, kept in the central bank. Thus at least partial liquidity of the banking system was assured, and with the help of the require reserve rate it was possible to regulate bank borrowing in the domestic market. The system of required reserves will be applied by the ECB to all European credit institutions. This is why the Bank of Lithuania has recently improved the required reserve rules in an attempt to provide equal conditions to both domestic and foreign banks in Lithuania. Also, the Bank of Lithuania, when seeking to promote long-term saving and to increase the interest rates of long-term deposits whose term is longer than one year, declined the requirement of required reserves for deposits in any currency.

After certain experience has been accumulated in the application of monetary policy instruments, it is planned to reduce the main standards of the CBA. First of all, an attempt will be made to change the rule that money issued by the Bank of Lithuania must be backed only by gold reserves and convertible foreign currency. A provision has been made that reserve money may be backed by other assets, such as rediscounted bills or other liabilities, government securities, loans guaranteed by the government or credit institutions and so on. However, the issued litas will have to be backed by gold and convertible currency reserves of the bank in such quantities that will ensure the continuous settlements with foreign countries. Usually, for the transition countries it is recommended that foreign exchange reserves should back the import volume for three months. However, the bank's foreign exchange reserves (excluding gold) at the end of 1997 satisfied import demand for only 1.9 months, although central bank reserve money was backed by exchange reserves of 128 per cent (in October 1996). There is insufficient backing of reserve money by foreign exchange reserves, when calculated in import months, because in Lithuania, a very open economy country, the imports are very high (in 1996, imports as a share of GDP quite often reached 60 per cent). In spite of this, the accumulation of foreign exchange reserves, which would back the volume for 3–4 import months, still remains an important task for the bank.

Another important feature of the abandonment of the CBA is to grant the bank the legal right to determine the base currency or currency basket as well as to establish the official litas exchange rate in respect of the chosen base currency. Currently, it is foreseen that the Bank of Lithuania, after talks with the government, may change the base currency and official exchange rate of the litas only when there are extraordinary circumstances threatening the stability of the Lithuanian economy; in other cases this can be done only by parliament.

Thus the CBA rules would be abrogated and the bank could legitimately execute the functions of a traditional central bank when regulating the supply of money and ensuring the liquidity of the banking sector.

With the increase in the Bank of Lithuania's powers to execute a discrete monetary policy, the bank's goals and monetary policy strategy will have to be adjusted.

The final goal, after the CBA is abandoned, remains the same – external currency stability. The most important intermediate goal also remains the same – exchange rate stability. However, the operational goal within the period of the functioning of the CBA remains the limit of net foreign reserves of the bank (up to October 1997 it was established by the IMF). Meanwhile after the

CBA has been abandoned, net domestic assets will become the operational goal of monetary policy, since in the presence of a fixed currency exchange rate the central bank may control only internal credit. Such a hierarchy of monetary policy goals currently exists in Latvia (Krzak 1997).

If later the Bank of Lithuania has to choose a policy of litas rate fluctuation when seeking to suspend the speculative pressure of foreign capital flows on the exchange rate, it is planned that the reserve money indicator should become the monetary policy guide. The choice of this indicator is justified because its control is much easier than that of indicators M1 and M2. However, as the experience of central banks of developed countries shows, an attempt is usually made to orientate towards the money supply indicators on a wider scale (M2 and M3) since they characterize the liquidity situation in the money market more fully and allow the final goals of monetary policy to be reached more effectively.

RESTRAINTS OF MEETING THE MAASTRICHT CRITERIA

The prospects of applicant countries for participation in EMU will be evaluated using the same convergence criteria as for the present EU members. Indeed, convergence criteria are not base requirements for admission to the EU, a 'benchmark' for accession to the EU, and we can analyse their satisfaction only within the framework of EMU participation (Daviddi and Ilzkovitz 1997). First, in order that candidate countries can become EU members, they must meet a set of political and economic market economy conditions that were established by the European Council in Copenhagen in July 1993 (Backe and Lindner 1996). Formally, Maastricht criteria should not be applied to candidate countries as long as these countries do not comply with the conditions for accession to the EU.

However, it is useful to establish to what extent the Lithuanian economy already meets Maastricht requirements in order to assess which direction economic development should take when seeking to fully implement these criteria later.

Strict Price Stability

Lithuania must achieve long-term price stability – annual inflation (growth of consumer prices) must not exceed more than 1.5 per cent point of the inflation average of the three most stable EU countries.

Taking into consideration the rapid annual inflation decrease in 1997 and 1998 (see Table 7.1), it seems that Lithuania should overcome this convergence criterion within a few years. In the Lithuanian government's programme for 1997–2000, it is anticipated that annual inflation will be reduced by up to 7 per cent, but this target has already been exceeded and in 1998 the average annual inflation was only 5.1 per cent.

However, achieving a low inflation target is considered by experts to be a complex and long-term task. This is because of an inertia resulting from inflation expectations and a wide range of labour contracts and financial assets (Krzak 1996). It is difficult to evaluate how long Lithuania will be able to maintain a low inflation level, because it could be influenced by several factors:

- In future, increasing energy prices, abrogation of tax incentives and reduction of subsidies should increase the pressure on inflation.
- More rapid economic growth should be accompanied by a certain average inflation. Since Lithuania's GDP per capita lags considerably behind the EU countries (in 1996, GDP per capita amounted to only USD 4245[8], according to purchasing power parity; while in EU countries in 1994, GDP per capita had been USD 19 740[9]), more rapid economic growth is necessary if it is to approach the level of EU countries. In 1996, GDP growth was 4.7 per cent; in 1997, 7.3 per cent; and in 1998, 5.1 per cent. The government of Lithuania foresees that GDP growth in the next few years should reach the same or even higher rates. High rates of economic growth may influence the slight increase in inflation.
- In contrast to other transitional countries, Lithuania cannot make use of such additional inflation reduction factors as the reduction or prohibition of state budget crediting, since the state budget deficit has been backed by the issue of government securities.
- Because the Bank of Lithuania has a paucity of monetary policy instruments, its influence in reducing inflation is not strong. Abandonment of the CBA would enable the central bank to regulate inflation by means of newly introduced monetary policy instruments.
- The increasing current account deficit can have an indirect influence on inflation growth if the litas is devalued in the desire to promote exports.

In the case of devaluation, the inflation rate will depend directly on the monetary policy that is followed. According to estimations made by the central bank's experts, if the currency is devalued by 50 per cent, the level of inflation would increase from 17 (without indexation of earnings) to 24 per cent (with total indexation of earnings).[10] It is evident that in the case of currency devaluation, it will be very difficult to maintain a low inflation level.

Currency Exchange Rate Stability

Fluctuations in the country's currency exchange rate, when compared with currencies of other EU countries, cannot exceed normal fluctuation margins for at least two years; nor can the currency be devalued when compared with other EU currencies.

Execution of the criterion of currency exchange rate stability in Lithuania is influenced by the fixed exchange rate regime when the litas is pegged against the US dollar. Lithuania has chosen the US dollar as the anchor currency which makes most international settlements in convertible currency. This generates problems in the sense that when the US dollar's rate fluctuates in relation to European national currencies and the ecu (euro), the exchange rate of the Lithuanian national currency (the litas) also fluctuates, and frequently exceeds the limits of currency exchange rate floatation permissible within the terms of the Maastricht Treaty (see Fig. 7.1). For example, in August 1997, compared with the beginning of 1996, the litas fluctuation rate in respect of the Deutschmark was 21 per cent and of the ecu, 15.8 per cent. The new monetary policy strategy will make a significant impact on the realization of this criterion, which is why it is important to change the anchor currency and to peg the litas against the EU currency (currency basket or euro) in order to ensure a litas fluctuation rate within the required limits.

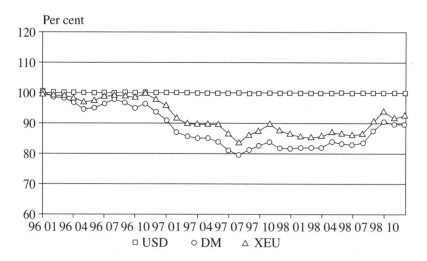

Sources: Bank of Lithuania, Quarterly Bulletin no. 4, 1997; Bank of Lithuania, Monthly Bulletin, no. 12, 1998.

Figure 7.1   Development of official foreign exchange rates

Table 7.5   Ratio of national budget balance to GDP (%)

Year	1993	1994	1995	1996	1997	1998
Ratio	0.3	–2.0	–2.1	–2.2	–1.2	–1.3

Sources: Bank of Lithuania, *Balance of Payments of the Republic of Lithuania*, no. 4, 1997;
Bank of Lithuania, *Balance of Payments of the Republic of Lithuania*, no. 4, 1998.

State Budget Discipline

The first indicator reflecting this criterion is the ratio of the planned or actual annual state budget, which should not exceed 3 per cent of GDP in market prices; exceeding the ratio is permissible only in exceptional circumstances or as a temporary phenomenon, or it must be clearly shown that the 3 per cent ratio will be reached as soon as possible. The second indicator – the state debt ratio – cannot exceed 60 per cent of GDP in market prices or at least it should be reduced and approaching the reference value.

It is very difficult to analyse how this convergence criterion can be met as the methodology for setting the Lithuanian state budget differs fundamentally from those in the EU countries.

If we analyse the Lithuanian national budget in terms of the current system, we can see that the indicators are quite good, complying fully with Maastricht requirements. At the beginning of the reform in 1993, there was a surplus; in 1997 there was a small deficit which did not exceed 3 per cent of the GDP limit (Table 7.5).

However, the official national budget does not include all the financial means used by the state, since they are disseminated among many state funds. Only state and municipality budgets are included in the national budget, while a state social insurance fund and about 20 (their number changes constantly) extrabudgetary funds exist separately. In 1997, state expenditures exceeded revenues by approximately 1.2 billion litas – 3.5 per cent of GDP.[11] Thus, the consolidated state deficit has already overstepped the limit permitted under the Maastricht criterion. But in 1999, the situation should change positively. The government has planned to refuse most extra-budgetary funds in the near future.

There is a similar situation with respect to state debt. Calculation of international debt is clear and transparent. But the rules of assessment for internal debts which would allow a precise definition of what state liabilities must be included in the composition of internal debt have still not been adopted. Referring to ministry of finance data, at the end of 1997, state debt amounted to almost USD 2030 million (22 per cent of GDP). During 1997, state debt increased by 10 per cent. This increase was conditioned by the growth in foreign debt (11.5 per cent), which is 70 per cent of the total state debt.[12]

However, the internal debt does not include state commitments to compensate the depreciated savings of residents, and that will amount to about USD 875 million. In addition, debts of the social insurance fund and of municipalities to banks, other economic entities and the budget are not included (Starkevichiute 1998). After an accounting of internal debt in compliance with international standards has been made, the internal debt will also increase considerably. Thus, the state debt is higher than has been declared officially. However, this indicator is considerably smaller than the reference one.

Capital Market Stability

Nominal interest rate of the country's long-term government securities or other commensurate securities should not exceed the interest rates of long-term securities of the three most stable EU countries by more than two percentage points.

An analysis of the criteria of capital market stability is virtually impossible, since there is no market for long-term loans in Lithuania. To cover the 1998 budget deficit, the government issued only short-term (up to one year) securities. The government has already issued long-term bonds for the restructuring of state banks, but they are not traded in the secondary market, so they cannot be used for capital market stability criterion assessment.

Therefore, realization of this criterion depends on whether reforms in financial and capital markets will be carried out sufficiently rapidly. Plans to introduce long-term securities to the market are already in the preparation state. The introduction of legal registration of mortgages and deeds will provide an opportunity to develop a mortgage system by establishing mortgage banks and issuing mortgage bonds. But the CBA was an obstacle to the issuance of mortgage bonds. Market research into Lithuanian commercial banks, insurance companies and investment funds show that institutional investors are not yet ready to invest in long-term securities. The main reasons given are: plans of the Bank of Lithuania to exit from the currency board regime and to change their anchor currency, as well as high expectations of an inflation increase due to a possible devaluation of the national currency. These factors increase the exchange rate risk of investment in long-term securities. Therefore, the existing monetary policy regime – the CBA – should be changed as soon as possible to provide a more open and stable environment for the development of a long-term securities market.

SUMMARY

The European Council has set a considerable number of economic requirements and conditions for countries in transition that are striving for EU membership. One of them is the capability of a candidate country to assume all membership commitments, including participation in EMU. Lithuania, one of the few transition countries basing its monetary policy on a CBA, faces the task of evaluating the current monetary policy regime and making decisions concerning its further strategy.

The CBA has played a significant positive role in Lithuania's economy. The CBA was one of the most important factors in financial stabalization, and as a result the following reforms have been: (i) independence of the central bank from political and other interest groups was ensured, since money could be issued only by purchasing the base currency, the US dollar; (ii) pursuit of an inappropriate monetary policy and mistakes due to the inexperience of the central bank's employees and their lack in skills were avoided; (iii) the business and domestic confidence in a fixed currency rate was partially achieved, because all issued money was backed by gold and reserves of convertible currency.

However, there are now external and internal reasons and conditions which make the further functioning of the CBA inappropriate:

- the CBA is incompatible with the standards of EU central banking, which is why it is necessary to approximate the model of Lithuanian monetary policy to that of EU countries gradually;
- the inadequacy of the CBA is revealed during banking crises when the central bank cannot perform the lender-of-last-resort function properly;
- the CBA hampers the regulation of money supply; this function is important when capital flows become more intensive;
- the introduction of the CBA has not fully justified expectations of increased confidence in the litas;
- the CBA is not an indispensable instrument for attracting foreign capital.

On the basis of these reasons it is anticipated that the CBA will gradually be abandoned, and central banking instruments will be developed.

After the CBA has been abandoned, the final monetary policy goal of the Bank of Lithuania will be the stability of the national currency when orientating to the external stability of the litas. The choice of such a final goal is conditioned by the fact that Lithuania is a small country with a very open economy. This is why the intermediate objective – the currency exchange rate – should not change either. However, the limit of net foreign reserves, which is the operational goal within the period of the CBA, should be replaced by a limit to net domestic assets. In order that these goals are attained, the central bank should gradually increase the number of monetary policy instruments when taking into consideration what instruments are available to the ECB. The Bank of Lithuania already applies repo agreements for securities between the bank and commercial banks, and one of the most important types of Lombard loans (overnight loans) is being implemented; it has also improved the rules of required reserves when seeking to provide both domestic and foreign banks in Lithuania with equal conditions. In the near future, after the main regulations of the CBA have been changed, that is, when issued money can be backed not only by gold and convertible foreign currency but also by other assets of the Bank Lithuania and when the bank has been given the right to determine base currency and bring the litas rate in line with this currency, then other instruments of discrete monetary policy can be introduced.

The possibilities of Lithuania complying with the Maastricht criteria in the future have been analysed in the last section. Compliance with the price and currency exchange rate stability criteria will depend partly upon the future monetary policy strategy, particularly the possibility of a litas devaluation and the choice of the new base currency (currency basket). The best option may be to follow the criterion of state budget discipline, but the exact estimation has so far been hindered by the means of setting the state budget and the calculation of internal debts, which are so different from the one used in EU countries. The criterion of capital market stability cannot be evaluated properly, because of an undeveloped financial sector and particularly because of the lack of institutions and instruments of a capital market.

NOTES

1. Eesti Pank, 'The 1997–1998 programme for the economic policy of the government of Estonia and Eesti Pank', Press release, 11 November 1997, http:/www.ee/epbe.
2. Bank of Lithuania (1997).
3. Bank of Lithuania, *Monthly Bulletin*, no. 12, 1996; Bank of Lithuania, *Quarterly Bulletin*, no. 4, 1997.
4. Bank of Lithuania, *Monthly Bulletin*, no. 12, 1996.
5. Bank of Lithuania, *Monthly Bulletin*, no. 12, 1998.
6. Bank of Lithuania, *Balance of Payments of the Republic of Lithuania*, no. 4, 1998.
7. 'Monetary policy programme for 1997–1999 of the Bank of Lithuania' (1997).
8. Statistical Department, Government of the Republic of Lithuania, *Survey of the Lithuanian Economy*, November 1997.
9. See Krzesniak (1997).
10. The forecasts were made by the Bank of Lithuania and the Academy of Sciences in 1998.
11. Starkevichiute (1998).
12. Bank of Lithuania, *Quarterly Bulletin*, no. 4, 1997.

BIBLIOGRAPHY

Backe, P. and I. Lindner (1996), 'European Monetary Union: prospects for EU member states and selected candidate countries from Central and Eastern Europe', *Focus on Transition*, no. 2, Oesterreiche Nationalbank.

Bank of Lithuania (1997), 'Monetary policy programme for 1997–1999 of the Bank of Lithuania', *State News*, no. 10, Vilnius.

Daviddi, R. and F. Ilzkovitz (1997), 'The Eastern enlargement of the European Union: major challenges for macro-economic policies and institutions of Central and East European Countries', in Salvatore Baldone and Fabio Sdogati (eds), *EU–CEECs Integration: Policies and Markets at Work*, Milan: FancoAngeli, pp. 15–40.

Ketter, G. (1998), 'Monetary policy: strategy and instruments for the future European Central Bank', *Monetary Studies*, no. 1, Bank of Lithuania.

Krzak, M. (1996), 'Persistent moderate inflation in Poland and Hungary', *Focus on Transition*, no. 2, Oesterreiche Nationalbank.

Krzak, M. (1997), 'Estonia, Latvia and Lithuania: from plan to market – selected issues', *Focus on Transition*, no. 2, Oesterreiche Nationalbank.

Krzesniak, A. and W. Maciejewski (1997), 'Implications of trade policy liberalisation for Poland's trade with the European Union', in Salvatore Baldone and Fabio Sdogati (eds), *EU–CEECs Integration: Policies and Markets at Work*, Milan: FrancoAngeli, pp. 99–142.

Nauseda, G. (1997), 'The issue of the litas stability in the law on the credibility of the litas and monetary policy programme for 1997–1999', *Monetary Studies*, no. 1, Bank of Lithuania.

Shiaudinis, S. (1997), 'Repurchase agreement', *Monetary Studies*, no. 1, Bank of Lithuania.

Starkevichiute, M. (1998), 'Government has concealed the real economic situation in Lithuania', *Respublika*, 1 May.

8. The currency board regime in Bulgaria and its sustainability

Tatiana Houbenova

INTRODUCTION

The failure of discretionary monetary policy to prevent accelerating inflation during 1995–97 forced the adoption of a currency board arrangement (CBA). At the beginning of the banking crisis, the monetary authorities were faced with a dilemma: weakening confidence in the national currency could not be countered with an interest rate increase which would further harm an already weak banking system and put additional pressure on the budget. At the same time, liquidity had to be provided to banks (both solvent and ailing) facing withdrawals in an attempt to prevent the crisis from becoming systematic. Even with this constraint, monetary policy was inconsistent and ultimately provoked the inflationary consequences of the banking crisis. The attempts to use the exchange rate as a nominal anchor while providing uncollateralized refinancing to insolvent banks caused an irreversible depletion of foreign reserves. Once the official reserves fell below a certain threshold, the banking crisis turned into a general confidence crisis. The belated attempts to use the interest rate to stabilize money demand failed in spite of its drastic jump to more than 800 per cent on an annual basis.

During the autumn of 1996, it had become clear that in order to restore confidence in domestic currency, a dramatic shift in policy was needed. A complete regime change centred on a CBA was deemed necessary to restore confidence in public institutions and give credibility to monetary and fiscal policies. The CBA was put in place as a key element of a macroeconomic stabilization programme, characterized by a move to a transparent, *rule-based* approach to policy making. The CBA and all its relevant parameters were determined in the new law on the Bulgarian National Bank (BNB). The law determined the exchange rate and the restrictions on the financial relations between the BNB and the state, and the BNB and the banking system.

DESIGN OF THE CBA

The key features of a CBA include the peg currency, the level of exchange rate, the currency board's structure and the exact operating principles and instruments. Bulgaria's CBA is a narrow one that ensures full cover of the monetary base. This effectively prevents the monetary authorities from extending credit, except on the basis of any excess of international foreign reserves over the amount required to cover the monetary liabilities. However, even this opportunity is tightly regulated by law, which explicitly states that the BNB shall not extend credit to banks, except in a narrowly defined role as lender of last resort, or to the state or to any state agency, except against special drawing right (SDR) purchases from the International Monetary Fund (IMF). Consistent with this setup, the BNB ceased open market operations and eliminated the repurchase facility prior to the adoption of the CBA. Since one of the key objectives of the CBA was to contribute to the transparency of the policy regime, it was decided to create two principal financial departments within the BNB, following the Bank of England model.[1] (See Table 8.1.)

The *Issue Department* holds all the BNB's monetary liabilities which must be covered at all times by foreign exchange assets and gold and redeemed for

Table 8.1   Structure of BNB accounts under the CBA

Assets	Liabilities
Issue Department	
Foreign reserves	Monetary liabilities
Foreign currency assets	Notes and coins issued
Domestic monetary gold	Commercial bank settlement
	account
Accrued interest receivable	Government deposits
	Banking Department deposit
	Accrued interest payable
Banking Department	
Deposit at Issue Department	Credit from the IMF
Claims on government	Other long-term liabilities
Claims on commercial banks	Accrued interest payable
(net of provisions)	Capital and reserves
Other assets (non-monetary gold,	
participation in international	
financial institutions, fixed assets)	
Accrued interest receivable	

the peg currency at the official exchange rate[2] on demand and without limit. The monetary liabilities are themselves interchangeable. The *Banking Department* has at its disposal a deposit with the Issue Department, for the purpose of collateralized lending to commercial banks in circumstances where the banking system as a whole is at systemic risk. These loans are to be limited to the amounts deemed necessary, and are deployed only in exceptional circumstances.[3] The Banking Department is also responsible for enforcing reserve requirements, monitoring financial markets and the payment system, with a view to minimizing the risk of liquidity problems.

The BNB continues to act as fiscal agent for the Ministry of Finance (MoF) through a specially created Fiscal Services Department. The MoF maintains almost all of its reserves in an account at the BNB where they are a liability of the Issue Department and must be fully covered by foreign assets. As a result of this setup, government use of deposits at the BNB will appear as an increase in net claims on the government, while the government is in fact using its own foreign assets.

DEVELOPMENTS SINCE ADOPTION OF THE CBA

By introducing the currency board regime in Bulgaria, an explicit legislative and executive policy commitment has been made in favour of regulating the money supply by backing the monetary base with a 100 per cent coverage of foreign assets and by fixing the exchange rate of the Bulgarian lev to the Deutschmark. For the attainment of stability and credibility of the CBA, the functioning of the monetary system is expected to be carried out consistently under the accepted rules within the medium-term period under consideration.

The monetary stabilization of the Bulgarian economy was based on the discontinuance of the discretionary monetary policy, which has contributed to a considerable extent to the inertia of high inflation with all its unfavourable consequences for economic trends and the business environment. The adoption of the new monetary rules and the suspension of the autonomous role of the BNB as a central bank led to profound changes concerning the discretionary issuance of money and the BNB's former instruments of refinancing the government and the commercial banks. The aim is to guarantee monetary and financial stabilization by resorting to a fixed exchange rate regime, disinflation and progressive realignment of the relative prices to the price level of the country whose currency has been chosen as a 'nominal anchor'.

Together with the transition of the monetary and credit system to a clear and transparent structure, an additional feature of the CBA is the elimination of the instruments of the central bank policy which regulated the liquidity of the economy. The suspension of any form of politicized money supply through direct or indirect financing of the state budget and the refinancing of the commercial banks may be expected to contribute to the improvement in financial discipline at all levels of economic activities in the foreseeable future. In particular, the maintenance of exchange rate parity will imply restriction of the monetary financing of fiscal deficits. In addition, the currency board regime is expected to derive its credibility from the provision of a better potential for servicing the state debt.

The transition to a CBA has been provided for by adequate legislative and institutional arrangements since mid-1997, encompassing the existing central bank and the commercial banks. Thus, after a prolonged and deep banking and financial crisis, the restoration of the credibility of the banking system has begun. In order to guarantee the credibility of the CBA, the BNB has been restructured and deprived of its former policy instruments with the exception of the minimum reserve requirements of the commercial banks. The lender-of-last-resort facilities allowed to the BNB (especially to its Banking Department) are restricted to systemic and emergency situations and are limited to the amount of forex reserves in excess of the backing requirement (the reserves) of the Banking Department.

In its integrity, the modifications of the 'pure' orthodox type of CBA as approved by Bulgarian legislation may allow for a higher degree of adaptability of the monetary sector because the BNB may:

1. act as the regulative centre of the settlements' system of the commercial banks;
2. govern the currency reserves of the Department of Issue of money under the currency board rule;
3. regulate the commercial banks' activities in compliance with the prudential banking rules through its Department of Banking and act as a lender of last resort in systemic risk cases; and
4. supervise banking and non-banking financial intermediation and provide for the stability of the CBA.

In order to evaluate the results and prospects for the monetary sphere after the introduction of the CBA in July 1997, three main aspects of the new monetary regime are of interest:

- evaluation of the trends of the money-supply changes as being crucial for the revival of the economy;
- possibilities and prospects for the development of the money demand with regard to expectations of the progress of the structural reforms and the dynamization of economic growth; and
- analysis of the factors and prerequisites expected to contribute to monetary stabilization.

The Bulgarian economy is still undergoing profound structural adjustment through privatization, and the strengths of the currency board regime and its contribution to monetary stabilization are not to be derived solely from interaction between the fixed exchange rate commitment and the fiscal stance. The sequencing of the structural policies under the CBA will be of great importance for achieving lower inflation rates, diminishing the state budget deficit and credible policies in favour of setting the ground for enhancing economic growth.

The currency board regime may be expected to be dependent to a great extent on the further progress of the transformation of the Bulgarian economy towards market-orientated development. Thus monetary stabilization through the currency board regime has to meet the challenges as well as be supported by the accelerated structural adjustment of the Bulgarian economy up to the year 2000.

Dynamics and Main Characteristics of the Money Supply

The money supply mechanism has changed considerably under the currency board regime. The main factor of its dependence is the dynamics of the capital flows and the forex reserves of the country. The major positive result of the introduction of the CBA is the increased amount of forex reserves and the guaranteed backing of the monetary base. This has occurred as a result of the external financing support provided by the international organizations on the basis of the fifth standby agreement with the IMF. The recovery of the BNB's credibility has been made possible on the basis of the support for the servicing of the foreign debt and the domestic debt under the CBA rules.

The fiscal flexibility achieved under the CBA has become the most significant contribution to monetary stabilization. But similar to the experience of other countries, this fiscal flexibility is the result of increasing the foreign debt by means of newly borrowed official credit. Thus management of foreign debt has become extremely important for the sustainability of the CBA.

The problem in the medium term will be how to combine the servicing of the foreign debt with the maintenance of a volume of forex reserves of the BNB, allowing for the full backing of the domestic money liabilities and thus guaranteeing the sustainable functioning of the CBA.

The increased dynamics of reserve money is another important feature of the CBA. The trends of nominal and real changes of this money aggregate by the beginning of 1998 are indicative of the improved liquidity of the economy after the introduction of the CBA. Some excess reserves of the banking system have been accumulated. (See Figure 8.1.) The challenge for the monetary sphere will be to undergo the proper restructuring of the money demand, which is yet to be balanced more adequately with the money supply.

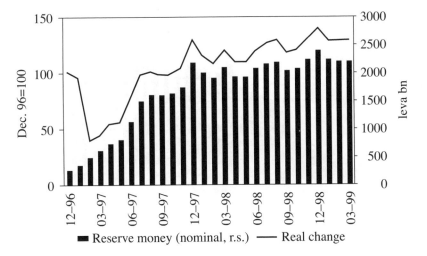

Figure 8.1   Reserve money

Typical characteristics of the money supply since the introduction of the CBA are the rising volume of monetary assets and the ongoing remonetization of the Bulgarian economy. A substantial rate of growth in M1 has been observed. In real terms this most liquid monetary aggregate increased considerably by the end of 1998. Nevertheless, the overall reduction in the inflation rate since the introduction of the CBA has made possible a countervailing process of the real remonetization of the economy. (See Figure 8.2.)

In the medium term, the *forex reserves* of the BNB will be maintained at a relatively higher level than the one achieved in 1997. A higher volume of forex reserves than five months of the imports would guarantee the sustainable functioning of the CBA but this could be made possible only by increasing the export revenues or borrowing new loans from the international capital markets.

Due to the strict dependence of the liabilities of the BNB on the forex assets available, the role of the velocity of money circulation will increase. (See Figure 8.3.) The 'GDP broad money' ratio, as an indicator of the money velocity, is a second main prerequisite for the sustainability of the CBA especially with the prospect of the decelerated dynamics of growth of the forex reserves. After reaching values of 1.5 to 2 in 1992–96, the indicator of the velocity of money increased to four by the end of 1997 and is gradually decreasing, reflecting the stabilization of the demand for money.

The changes in the monetary aggregate M2 in 1997 and 1998 are favourable, but still higher growth of less-liquid money (quasi-money) as an

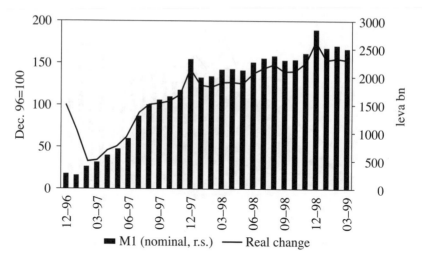

Figure 8.2   Monetary aggregate M1

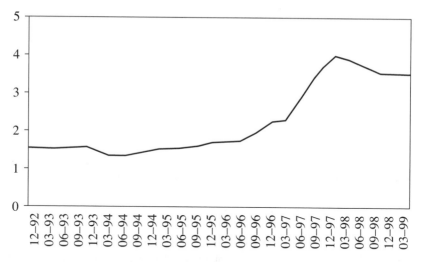

Figure 8.3   Broad money velocity (GDP/M3)

indicator of improving financial intermediation has to be achieved. The expectations of more active foreign banks' supply of services in the domestic market make it possible to forecast a trend of rising competition and improved financial services.

Since the introduction of the CBA, a positive trend of the remonetization is the growth of the monetary aggregate 'broad money'. The real growth indices

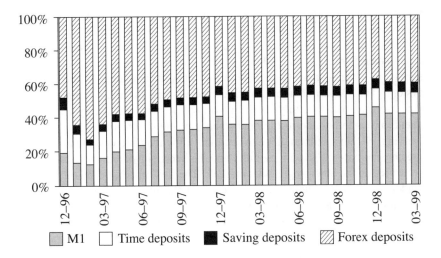

Figure 8.4   Structure of M2

(1995 = 100) of broad money have increased from 28.6 in June 1997, up to 37 in December 1997 and 40.2 at the end of 1998 (see Figure 8.4). The future growth of broad money will be more moderate due to the disinflation process and improved money transmission.

The currency substitution has undergone some reduction since the CBA implementation. The 'deposits in foreign currency/broad money' ratio may be expected to continue to decrease under a sustainable development of the CBA.

A specific feature of the CBA in Bulgaria is the interrelation of the net domestic assets and the dynamics of the reserve money. The net domestic assets of the BNB as assets of its Banking Department represent loans to the commercial banks and liabilities of the government. Any direct loans of the BNB to the government have already been suspended and the reduction in the former liabilities will follow a stable trend of fiscal consolidation. In the case of insufficient state budget revenues, the government may resort to its fiscal reserve which has reached a relatively high level of nearly 45 per cent of the liabilities of the Issue Department. The need to manage the fiscal reserve properly will be of crucial importance for the stabilization of the money supply. The specific feature of the Bulgarian CBA is the possibility of keeping the fiscal reserves of the government as deposits with the BNB Department of Issue. Nevertheless, the maintenance and management of the fiscal reserves has been transferred completely to the competencies of the government. The BNB has been deprived of any usage of open market operations or purchases of government securities. Thus an imperative for the medium-term stability of the money supply is to limit the endogenous factors of its growth. The maintenance of the stability of the fiscal reserves within the due limits as well as their proper operational management contribute to the sustainability of the currency board regime.

The potential resort of the BNB to its 'lender-of-last-resort' facility under circumstances of systemic risk may allow for some flexibility of the money supply in order to help to overcome the liquidity problems of the banking system. The Department of Banking reserves are the main source of the lender-of-last-resort facility. Their growth will remain satisfactory but special attention has to be paid to the maintenance of the reserves in the future. The banking system's vulnerability to incipient runs may increase as a result of greater international capital mobility and the banks' involvement in trade with securities on the emerging capital markets. The flexibility attained through the lender-of-last-resort facility may ensure that the monetary system develops utilizing a combination of the automatic currency board monetary rule and some application of monetary measures of a discretionary nature. This unorthodox type of CBA in Bulgaria should allow for more adequate management of banking crisis risks. Some degree of duality of the monetary regime makes the adequate application of any instruments of intervention necessary in the case of a systemic risk.

Under the CBA, the BNB has retained the minimum reserve requirements as the only instrument of direct control of the monetary base and the liquidity of the banking system. The changes expected in the approaches to the evaluation and monitoring of the reserve requirements will make possible a more differentiated and efficient management of the money supply through the banking system.

It is difficult to predict the total demand for reserves because of the ongoing process of restoration of the banks' credibility and the delay in the revival of the banks' credit activities. The introduction of a better reserve-operating mechanism is to be undertaken in order to influence appropriately the money supply and money growth through the reserve requirement ratio. For the banking system the problem will be to what extent the changes expected to be introduced in the mechanism of required reserves may have a regulative, but not restrictive, effect on the banks' credit activities.

A more important aspect of the required reserves is their usage as the only instrument of the BNB for influencing the money multiplier. The reserve money multiplier model of money control will remain a better indicator of the economic activity than the banks' credits or interest rates in the medium term. Under the CBA an important function of the required reserves will be to provide liquidity of the banking system to act as a buffer to liquidity shocks. In principle, any changes in the ratios of required reserves cause restructuring of the banks' portfolios. The sustainability of the CBA will be supported by the stable maintenance of the required reserve ratio and by relinquishing its usage as a monetary instrument of fine-tuning.

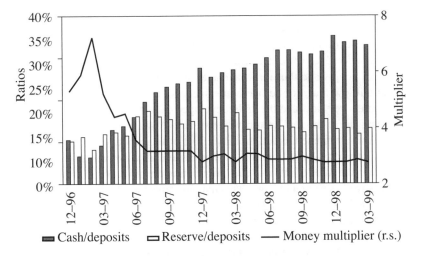

Figure 8.5   The money multiplier and its components

The money multiplier is a complex indicator of the money supply and the money transmission process (see Figure 8.5). The general trend is the reduction of the broad money multiplier: from 5.3 at the end 1996 it has decreased to 3.6 in June 1997, then respectively to 2.77 and 2.76 in December 1997 and December 1998.

Substantial changes can be observed in the two main components of the money multiplier. Liquidity preferences dominate, as a result of a fixed exchange rate and low interest rate levels, while the reserves to deposits ratio seems to be declining, reflecting an improvement in bank management.

In the medium term, the dynamics of the money multiplier will be influenced by some reduction in the bank reserves to deposits ratio. Any further growth in the money multiplier may not be expected, because of the following factors:

- the banks will refrain from higher credit exposure;
- the changes due to be introduced in the deposit insurance schemes will require the maintenance of greater amounts of bank reserves; and
- the low interest rates will cause higher values of the bank reserves to deposits ratio.

Of great importance for the money supply is the dynamics of the net foreign assets of the BNB and the commercial banks. The growth of the BNB's foreign assets is substantial. Some further increase in the net foreign assets may be expected as a result of capital inflow and official balance-of-payments support financing. The privatization revenues could also contribute.

The net foreign assets of the commercial banks have also increased substantially since the introduction of the CBA. The excess reserves of the commercial banks will continue to reflect the trend of growth of the net foreign assets, although at a reduced rate. This trend allows for some contraction in the domestic money supply and thus may have a deflationary effect on the economy. The capital outflow may not be overcome successfully as long as the real interest rates remain very low and the underdeveloped capital markets continue to serve the financing of the real sector only partially. Any further delay in economic growth may combine the deflationary effect of the capital outflow with higher rates of inflation. On the contrary, economic revival will eventually cause some increase in the rates of interest, thus stimulating the reduction in the net foreign assets as well as capital inflows. This may improve the supply of bank credit as well. Thus it is to be expected that the CBA will influence the money supply indirectly in order to restore the stability of monetary relations.

Problems of Money Demand under the CBA

In spite of the relatively short period of functioning of the currency board regime, some trends of the money demand raise the problem of the speed of achieving some positive effects of the CBA's adjustment mechanism. On one hand, the money demand is positively influenced by the suspension of direct credits to the government and the state budget. The demand for money may not correspond fully to that associated with market equilibrium, at least in the short run.

The adjustment of the money demand has been slower than that of the money supply due to factors such as:

- inadequate money transmission mechanism;
- underdeveloped financial markets; and
- the isolation of Bulgaria from international capital mobility.

With regard to money demand, the adjustment process is more difficult as capital control and underdeveloped financial intermediation limit capital mobility. It may be expected that the adjustment of the money demand will occur more gradually through further changes in the rate of absorption and the eventual worsening of the trade balance.

With the introduction of the CBA, the sharp drop in interest rates has decreased the burden of the interest-related expenditures of economic agents. Nevertheless, the reduced interest rates are not stimulating enough for the growth in money demand. The economy has not yet emerged from the deep crisis and the money demand will need some time to recover under the conditions of strict observance of the prudential banking criteria.

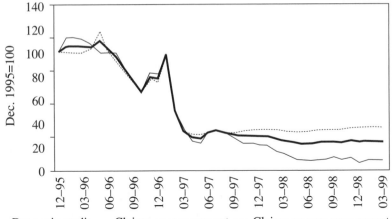

Figure 8.6   Domestic credit dynamics in real terms

Domestic credit has remained depressed (see Figure 8.6). This is due to the overall economic destabilizationn at the beginning of 1997 and the difficulties of economic recovery. The suspension of government borrowing from the BNB has limited the crowding-out effect of government credit.

It is to be expected that the share of government credit will continue to decrease, while the non-governmental sector will increase (see Figure 8.7). It

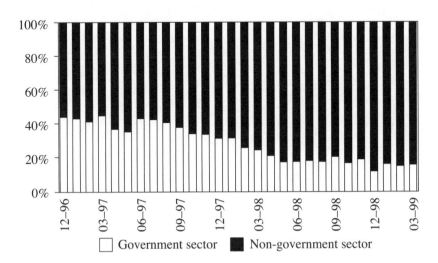

Figure 8.7   Structure of domestic credit

is much more likely that the demand for credit will grow more gradually because of the peculiarities of the ongoing privatization and the high degree of segmentation of the real economy.

An important advantage of the CBA in the future will be the interest rate policy, which is based on the convergence of the interest rate level with the 'nominal anchor' level. The interest rate level reduced as a result of a shock after the introduction of the CBA. The fall in the nominal and real interest rates is a trend that has already contributed substantially to monetary stabilization. The main problem in the future will be whether the application of the yield of the three-month government securities as the basic interest rate can continue to serve any market-orientated monetary development.

The preservation of a higher interest rate differential between the credit and the deposit rates is typical of the difficulties faced by financial intermediation in successfully achieving the transformation of savings into investments (see Figure 8.8). The interest rate differential is expected to be decreased further.

In real terms, the interest rates (both on credits and on deposits) remain unstable though slightly positive. The methodical approach to estimation of the basic interest rate must be considered a crucial issue of the choice of monetary growth path in the future. There might be a risk that higher growth in demand for money may cause greater fluctuations in the interest rates. The development of the financial market would also be dependent on the market formation of the rates of interest. The basic interest rate policy of the present type will become even more vulnerable with increased capital mobility and the growing needs of economic agents for increased liquidity.

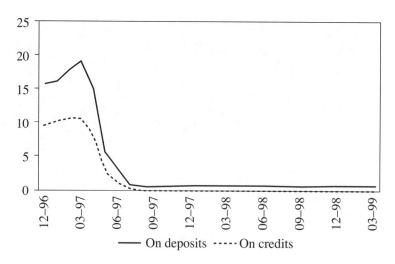

Figure 8.8   Nominal monthly interest rates

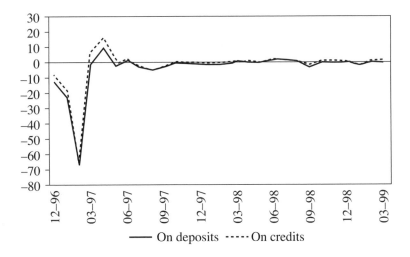

Figure 8.9   Real monthly interest rates

The prospects for any change in the approach towards the estimation and announcement of the basic interest rate remain uncertain. The undeveloped money and capital market and the problems of the money transmission mechanism will delay the transition to market-orientated determination of the basic interest rate. It is expected that the basic interest rate will be preserved at the annual level of 5 to 7 per cent (see Figure 8.9). This may be possible because of the availability of excess reserves, the fiscal consolidation and the maintenance of the fiscal reserves at a stable level due to foreign financing.

PREREQUISITES AND CONDITIONS FOR THE ACHIEVEMENT OF MONETARY STABILIZATION

Achievement of the Stability of the Monetary Sector

In the medium term, the difference between monetary stabilization as a policy outcome of proper measures taken by the currency board and the consolidation and stability of the monetary sphere and its interrelations with the real sector may be of crucial importance for the better management and performance of the currency board.

The still-existing uncertainty about the process of economic transformation through the privatization of the main state-owned banks as well as the delayed inflow of fresh foreign investments into the Bulgarian economy may cause a wider amplitude of fluctuations in the process of monetary stabilization.

In addition to the inflation restriction, monetary stabilization will depend on the adequate management of other sources of monetary disequilibria. Under the CBA, the limited availability of foreign capital inflows so far may raise the importance of the following factors of monetary stabilization:

1. Making sustainable the reduction in the interest rate expenditures of the economy by providing for adequate servicing of the public debt on a long-term basis.
2. Improving the market access of the economic agents and the competition rules and increasing the export revenues.
3. Overcoming the burden of bad credit and improving banking liabilities and asset management in order to improve the liquidity of the economy.
4. Consolidation and recapitalization of the banking system through privatization, with foreign participation as well.
5. Better management of the credit and market risks at all levels of the economy.

The stability of the monetary system will still remain dependent on overcoming the debt crisis, the avoidance of any bank's insolvency and the delay in the revival of economic growth. Summarizing the analysis of the factors for achieving the consolidation of the monetary sector, it is important to underline that while at the start of the CBA the reduction in the interest rates and the fixed exchange rate to the German mark have contributed to the stabilization, in the medium term it will be the interdependence with the real sector that will play the decisive role for the outcome of sustainable monetary adjustment.

Money Transmission and the Prospects for its Normalization

The main reasons for the still inadequate money transmission in the Bulgarian economy are the delay in the market-orientated transformation, inconsistent financial reform and lack of proper functional and institutional development of the money, credit and capital markets. Because of this, the behaviour of the main price variables in the economy (the rate of interest and the exchange rate) have become inadequate to reflect the dynamics of the adjustment process and have acted in a pro-inflationary manner, thus leading to the necessity for the CBA. The most difficult problem yet to be solved will be the choice of an appropriate financial mix as regards money transmission. Although since mid-1997 the focus may seem to have been on financial market development, the banking institutions have to play a key role in the medium term. Banks remain crucial for channelling resources and for the restructuring of the non-financial sector. Financial sector reform has entered the stage of restructuring and together with sound, transparent solutions in corporate governance is yet to contribute to the generation of higher levels of domestic savings.

Under the currency board rules, the regulative mechanisms of interest rate determination at the government securities market and the fixed exchange rate of the Bulgarian lev will set the conditions for balancing money supply and demand while the financial markets are still in the process of being organized. The return to a market determination of the main price variables in the Bulgarian economy will occur under the CBA by passing eventually through two phases:

1. The improvement in money transmission by raising the credibility of the financial intermediaries (both banking and non-banking).
2. The development of functioning money and capital markets that may make possible the abandonment of the fixed exchange rate regime in the long term.

The improvement in the money transmission mechanism may be enhanced by:

- the expected acceleration of the privatization process through new approaches and mechanisms;
- the further restructuring of the real sector and the growing share of the private sector's contribution to GDP;
- the consolidation of the commercial banks and the recapitalization of the banking sector; and
- increasing the role of the organized capital market in the privatization process and as a source of external financing of the enterprises and other economic entities.

In the medium term, the factors contributing to the improvement in money transmission under the CBA will involve:

- the consolidation of the banks' portfolios in order to provide for the acceptance of prudential banking rules compatible with international standards and the official creditors' requirements;
- the availability of an information base within banks, relating to real economic agents and the potential of commercial banks' debt restructuring; and
- the privatization of banking institutions, with foreign capital involvement.

The financial sector reform is proceeding more slowly than expected at the start of the CBA but a rational process of readjustment may be the better result of such a delay. Banking sector supervision and the management of systemic risks will be crucial for the avoidance of a banking crisis, which in general is detrimental to the credibility of the currency board. Two possible alternatives for normalizing money transmission in the Bulgarian economy may be considered in the medium term.

Under the first alternative the banking system would meet the challenges of its recapitalization and consolidation at a moderate speed of privatization, with foreign participation and by adhering to the stringent conditions while maintaining strict control over lending to the real sector. Money transmission would depend mainly on the Bulgarian banking system's potential to restructure itself to market-orientated conditions and its relations with the real sector.

Under the second alternative there would be a more radical involvement of foreign banks and intermediaries in the improvement of the money transmission mechanism through development of the monetary sector. Thus a greater degree of fluctuation in financial market trends in the medium term may occur. So far this alternative seems to reveal more clearly the segmented corporate interests in the banking and economic systems and the effect on the money transmission process. The lack of a national strategy for the development of the banking system until now may create risks of opportunistic behaviour by foreign investors in the banking section in the foreseeable future. Nevertheless, the process of improving money transmission will be actively supported by the entry of foreign financial intermediaries into the banking and non-banking services in Bulgaria.

INDICATORS OF CURRENCY BOARD STABILITY

The currency board limits the possibilities of fast response to a systemic crisis in the financial system. This entails the construction of a system of indicators to assess currency board stability and developments in monetary indicators. An analysis of the financial system should be based on the fundamental assumption that major problems stem from volatility and dramatic changes in variables and indicators rather than from their levels. The analysis of their absolute levels gives a limited meaning to economic processes. Balance-sheet indicators are based on selected coverage coefficients for individual items within the Issue and Banking Departments and on indicators from BNB monetary statistics. Some of these have been used by countries operating under currency board arrangements or fixed exchange rates. A careful analysis of these indicators reveals some adverse trends. (See Table 8.2.)

First, we look at the ratio of quasi money to reserves of the central bank (issue department). This indicator must be close to unity. When it is far above unity, there is greater risk associated with conversion service; when it is below

Table 8.2 Volatility of balance-sheet indicators and major monetary variables since adoption of the CBA

	07–97	12–97	03–98	06–98	09–98	12–98	03–99
Quasi-money to assets of Issue Dept (MQ/R)	0.93	0.78	0.77	0.66	0.73	0.69	0.71
M2 to assets of Issue Dept (M2/R)	1.30	1.30	1.23	1.09	1.20	1.24	1.21
M1 to assets of Issue Dept (M1/R)	0.37	0.52	0.46	0.43	0.48	0.55	0.50
M2 to deposit of Banking Dept (M2/BD)	5.75	11.36	9.61	6.19	7.52	8.34	7.53
M1 to deposit of Banking Dept (M1/BD)	1.64	4.53	3.60	2.43	2.97	3.73	3.09
Quasi-money to deposit of Banking Dept (MQ/BD)	4.11	6.84	6.01	3.76	4.55	4.62	4.44

	MQ/R	M3/R	M1/R	M2/R	BD/R	BD/MQ	BD/M3	M0/(R-Au)	M3lev/R
Mean square deviation	10.05	5.29	8.48	5.50	27.47	23.52	26.2	9.03	5.23
in % from period's	M0	M3	MQ	Rate spread	mm	BD	DG	R	BD/M3lev
average	11.87	9.04	17.06	15.53	4.36	23.34	48.64	11.53	29.97

Indicators
M0   Reserve money;
M1   Narrow monetary aggregate;
M2   M1 plus MQ;
M3   Broad money;
MQ   quasi-money lev component;
M3 lev Broad money lev component;
mm   monetary multiplier.

unity, this is a signal of low confidence in the banking system and the national currency. The substantial fall in this indicator since early 1998 is indicative of demonetization of the economy due in part to low confidence in the banking system and low income on deposits. M3/R and M2/R display similar dynamics. The fact the M2 and even broad money could be backed by the reserves of the Issue Department is indicative of demonetization and setbacks in the banking system rather than stability. The possibilities for refinancing are reduced to the amount of the Banking Department deposit BD with the Issue Department. Even though all indicators that can be used for manipulation, that is, BD/M0, BD/M1, BD/MQ, BD/M3, BD/R, and especially BD/MQ lev and BD/M3 lev, decrease, their volatility is more disturbing rather than their levels. As the table shows, these indicators too often move within the range between 24 per cent and 30 per cent which is assumed to be dangerous. Even though the Banking Department deposits pulse in line with the dynamics of the tranches disbursed by the IMF, this is of no importance – the problem lies with the volatility of these indicators.

The government deposit with the Issue Department is extremely volatile (48.64 per cent). Although such a dynamic is understandable, it causes concern. The classical CBA involves abandonment of monetary policy and discretion. This is a specific form of monetary constitution whereby money supply is determined by the automatic mechanism of the balance-of-payments dynamics. In the case of the Bulgarian currency board model this is only partly true. It may be argued that there exists a specific type of transmission mechanism in the context of the Bulgarian CBA. Monetary policy is taken over by fiscal policy and the government can manipulate money supply through its deposit at the Issue Department. The dynamics of this deposit may be interpreted as an indicator (measure) of the government's monetary policy and acts as a buffer between changes in the monetary base and foreign exchange reserve dynamics. A growth in this deposit constrains reserve money and its dramatic fluctuations cause sharp changes in reserve money dynamics. Essentially it performs a sterilizing function and injects or withdraws liquidity in and out of the economy.

The existence of this deposit gives the public sector an advantage over the private sector, because only the former is backed by the reserves of the Issue Department, which constitute public wealth. The government's deposit at the Issue Department reflects budgetary dynamics and receipts from the IMF. Also it is the result of governmental policy in the government securities market (the volume of issues). The deposit affects money supply in two ways: through volumes by reducing reserve money, and through prices by the impact of the nominal base interest rate. This reflects directly on real interest rates and, in turn, on motives for saving and investment, on the quantity and quality of investment, and hence on economic growth. In this mechanism we may discover the two classical transmission channels of monetary policy under a central bank: directly through the monetary base and through the interest rate.

IMPLICATIONS OF A CBA FOR THE BANKING SYSTEM

A key feature of bank activity after the CBA implementation was the pursuit of financial stability and improved capital adequacy. Development in general economic conditions caused significant changes in the structure and composition of reported incomes. Before the adoption of the CBA their magnitude was strongly affected by unpredictable events and extremely volatile financial conditions, but afterwards the fixed exchange rate of the lev to the Deutschmark precluded formation of large accounting gains resulting from valuation adjustments.

The stable interest rate level ensured a relatively constant margin on commercial loans, but resulted in a lower yield on government securities, the most commonly used investment instrument over the last two years. Except for the short period from August to October 1998, developments in the international markets did not affect the price of Bulgarian debt dramatically, which in turn precluded sizeable income formation from revaluations. Consequently net income from interest, fees and commissions and income from securities trading proved to be the major sources of self-financing and capital formation.

Higher income from financial operations reflects a wider range of bank services offered and improved efficiency in operating bank activities. At the same time, financial institutions faced a number of difficulties. The deteriorating position of a number of enterprises, mainly in the public sector, combined with tentative development of some of the newly privatized companies, limited the range of creditworthy customers. An additional problem arose for a part of the banking system from acquisitions of tangible assets and securities serving as collateral on non-performing credits. Domestic market conditions do not provide for the sale of chattels and real estate at acceptable prices in the short term, while the faltering and rather symbolic development of stock trading forced banks to hold large volumes of low liquid corporate securities in their portfolios for long periods.

Recently the banking system has faced two major challenges: the introduction of international accounting standards, and more rigorous supervision and capital requirements. In these conditions banks had to operate under new rules of transparency and publicity and had little room for manipulating their financial position parameters. These changes, underpinned by decisive banking supervision actions, reduced violations to a minimum and created improved conditions for controlling risks in the system.

By operating in a new financial, accounting and supervisory environment and following a pattern of conservative behaviour, banks were ready to face the crisis in the international financial markets: they had a healthy share of high-liquid assets, a good capital position and a flow of customers.

At the end of 1998 the Bulgarian banking sector comprised 34 banks classified into three groups according to system significance, asset size and the type of shareholder capital. Based on these criteria, banks are divided into the following three major groups. *Group I* includes banks of systemic significance, with the largest balance-sheet asset size. It includes seven banks making up 70.4 per cent of total banking system assets. *Group II* includes 17 small banks with majority private shareholder capital controlling 19 per cent of banking system assets. *Group III* includes ten subsidiaries and branches of foreign banks, comprising 10.6 per cent of banking system assets.

By establishing a CBA, the authorities subordinate other policy objectives to defending the exchange rate parity and allow interest rates to play a major role in the CBA adjustment mechanism. Because the backing rule limits the monetary authorities from sterilizing capital flows, a balance-of-payments deficit or rapid capital outflows will automatically be translated into domestic liquidity tightening and higher interest rates, which will, in turn, contribute to a reversal of the deficit or outflow.

Although a CBA does help to stabilize inflation and interest rates over the medium to long terms, banks operating under a CBA are likely to face relatively high day-to-day interest rate volatility. In other words, banks have to accept the burden of adjustments. Moreover, interest rates may increase sharply to defend the fixed exchange rate if the country experiences systemic capital outflows. In that case, if the interest rates remain high for a long period, small and undercapitalized banks may find it difficult to stay liquid and become insolvent.

Apart from limiting the scope for sterilization operations and smoothing monetary operations, the CBA backing rule also restricts the monetary authorities from providing lender-of-last-resort (LOLR) support to banks. Since this support is often required to mitigate the effects of a liquidity crisis and containing spreading risks, its absence may allow problems of an individual bank to spread system-wide more easily.

Since the CBA was established to achieve stabilization objectives, the fixed exchange rate must be credible to serve as a meaningful nominal anchor that can influence inflation expectations among the public. Weak banking conditions could be detrimental to the CBA. Thus, for example, unsound banks are generally willing to take higher risks and, hence, do not usually respond to monetary signals (especially interest rates) in a predictable manner. In other words, the existence of unsound banks may imply a larger magnitude of interest rate adjustments in response to shocks than would occur otherwise.

High and volatile interest rates are detrimental to banks' liquidity positions,

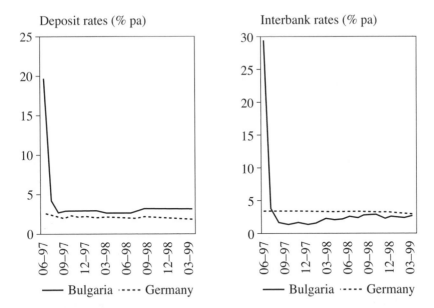

Figure 8.10   Deposit and interbank interest rates

especially for small and undercapitalized banks, and may exacerbate problems in the banking system. In this context, the market may believe that the authorities will for go the CBA's fixed exchange rate and backing rule to protect the weak banking system. Such a belief could easily lower the credibility of the CBA and the stabilization programme as a whole, and further increase liquidity pressure among banks. Weak and unsound banks could also slow down the processes of interest rate convergence and financial intermediation since the commercial banks facilitate interest rate arbitrage. Although the deposit rate almost converged to the German level, the interbank rate fell even lower, reflecting increased liquidity in the banking sector. (See Figure 8.10.)

The slow pace of interest rate convergence and financial intermediation could undermine the credibility of the entire stabilization programme and, in particular, the nominal exchange rate anchor. Because of the slow interest rate convergence, interest costs remain high and the public may not be willing to incorporate a lower inflation path into their inflation expectations, thereby slowing down the stabilization process.

Despite the successful stabalization after the CBA was introduced, the currency to broad money and deposit ratios increased sharply and financial intermediation was delayed (see Figure 8.11). The slow process of financial intermediation could prevent the authorities from achieving their targeted levels of credit to the non-government sector and, hence, economic growth.

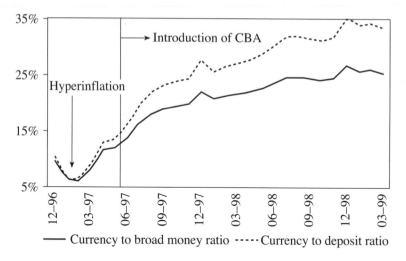

Figure 8.11   Currency to broad money and deposit ratios

This lower than projected performance may pressure the authorities to resort to other measures, including abandoning the CBA or devaluing the currency. In order to prevent such fears and to minimize the trade-offs between maintaining bank soundness and CBA credibility, some additional elements should be considered.[4]

- *Limiting the effects of inflation volatility*   Because inflation influences the values of collateral and bank assets and liabilities directly and, thus, complicates the assessment of credit risk, large inflation volatility makes bank portfolio management difficult. Moreover, a country that uses a CBA as a stabilization anchor needs to take into account the potential effects of disinflation and/or deflation on the value of a banking system's assets.
- *Lender-of-last-resort support*   Following the practice of traditional central banks, a CBA needs to provide limited LOLR support and, hence, to establish explicit facilities. The BNB may provide Lombard credit at a penalty rate against collateral of securities to sound banks suffering temporary liquidity. However, if these facilities are not sufficient (especially during systemic crisis) a contingency credit line with international banks may need to be established (as in Argentina) to avoid further widening of liquidity shortage.
- *Buffer liquidity by required reserves*   Experience during the banking crises in Argentina and Lithuania proved the benefit of imposing high reserve requirements that could be relaxed to provide liquidity during

times of pressure. However, that could be costly to banks and detrimental to bank soundness unless the required reserves are remunerated at market interest rates, which is not the case for Bulgaria.

- *Stricter prudential regulations* Because the monetary authorities subject to a CBA regime are limited in their ability to provide LOLR support and banks tend to face higher liquidity and interest rate volatility due to the limited scope for monetary operations, it is essential for banks to be able to withstand shocks better than in the case of other monetary arrangements. That is why the capital adequacy and liquidity ratio requirements are higher than recommended by the Basle Committee's Accord for internationally active banks. All the CBA countries have imposed stricter prudential regulations and supervision than the ordinary standards.

- *Deposit insurance* Losses of an individual bank could easily trigger a deposit run against which LOLR facilities are limited. As from 1 January 1999, a new deposit insurance law was put in place with the intention of reducing the potential fiscal cost of bank failure and limiting the moral hazard associated with all insurance schemes. Funding will come from initiation fees and annual premia, calculated on the total deposit base, investment income, and the fund's share of closed bank's assets in case of subrogation.

FINANCIAL SECTOR DEVELOPMENTS

Bulgaria's financial system, dominated by the banking sector throughout the transition period, was at the heart of the severe economic crisis in 1996 and early 1997. Years of lack of appropriate supervision, and delay in structural reform culminated in the banking crisis when runs on banks exposed the general insolvency of the banking system. Using a combination of closures, recapitalization, privatization, strengthened supervision and the adoption of sound macroeconomic policy, confidence in the banking system was gradually restored. These reforms had a significant impact on the sector: the banking system became solvent and compliance with supervisory regulation has improved; further privatization and consolidation are under way; and a limited self-financing deposit insurance system was recently established.

Structure of the Financial Sector

The banking system in Bulgaria consists of a relatively large number of banks (34) but a handful of state-owned banks (six) still dominate, even though recent progress in bank privatization is increasing the role of private banks. As in other transition economies, Bulgaria's monobanking system was split into a two-tiered system at the beginning of the economic reform. The banking system is highly concentrated and relatively specialized. Seven big banks held 71 per cent of banking system assets and 76 per cent of deposits at the end of 1998. In this group the biggest bank is nearly three times as large as the second-largest bank and accounts for about one-third of banking assets. Domestic private banks (17) serve narrow interests and account for 19 and 16 per cent of assets and deposits, respectively. Foreign banks and branches (ten) hold 10 and 8 per cent of each, and deal mainly with foreign direct and portfolio investors.

The development of the non-bank financial sector was hampered by inconsistent and insufficient progress in structural reform prior to CBA introduction. Recently the foundation has been put in place for the sustainable and sound development of this sector. Following the liberalization of the foreign exchange market in 1991, foreign exchange bureau were the most important non-bank financial institution, but after the adoption of the CBA both their numbers and activity declined substantially. The privatization funds, which emerged in the context of the first wave of mass privatization, were converted into investment funds and are in the process of being listed on the stock exchange. Voluntary pension funds have been in existence for a while but have been acting mainly as mutual funds and are of insignificant size. The recently adopted new pension law clarifies their role and supervisory regime. Financial brokerage houses flourished in the early 1990s, but the economic crisis shifted their role towards the marketing of domestic government securities to portfolio investors and issues targeted to the public.

Domestic Financial Markets

The development of domestic financial markets since the beginning of transition was strongly affected by repeated periods of macroeconomic instability and associated foreign exchange crises, the deficit financing needs of the budget and the hesitant approach to structural reforms.

The economic significance of the financial markets was severely diminished during and after the 1996/97 crisis, although there were no operational breakdowns. The crisis and the growing budget deficit caused a dramatic reduction in newly issued government securities, and a substantial drop in the volumes in the interbank money market (see Figure 8.12).

The successful macroeconomic stabilization programme launched in April 1997 initiated the recovery of both these markets. However, secondary market transactions are still insignificant while delay of progress in structural reform marginalized the role of the stock exchange, kept institutional and foreign investors away, and prevented the development of a market for corporate debt.

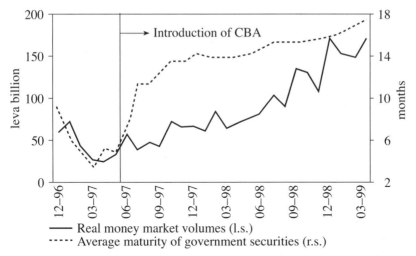

Figure 8.12   Real money market volumes and average maturity of government securities

Government Securities Market

Institutional arrangements for the operation of primary and secondary markets for government securities were put in place in the early 1990s. Auctions are conducted by the BNB on behalf of the MoF. Starting from April 1996, a system of primary dealers was introduced to encourage further development of the primary and secondary markets in terms of volume, depth, transparency and liquidity.

The primary securities market has grown since the CBA was introduced. After the adoption of the CBA, confidence in the government was restored – by March 1999 the average maturity of outstanding deficit-financing issues reached 18 months.

Secondary market transactions in government securities have been relatively unimportant, but domestic securities have been used actively as collateral for interbank transactions.

Interbank Money Market

Developments in the interbank money market were closely linked to those in the market of government securities and were strongly affected by the banking crisis. The very active interbank market during 1991–95 was almost destroyed with the emergence of bank insolvencies. In early 1996, deteriorating bank liquidity and the low confidence among banks triggered a downward trend in money market volumes. Financial stabilization following the introduction of the CBA encouraged the re-emergence of the interbank money market and the peg to the Deutschmark initiated a trend towards integration of Bulgaria's interbank market with the European financial market. Initially, increased bank liquidity and uncertainties as to the implications of the new monetary regime for bank operations kept volumes relatively low. Banks held large amounts of unremunerated excess reserves on settlement accounts with the BNB and interbank interest rates fell to historically low levels. As liquidity management improved, banks began placing resources abroad which led to interest rate convergence. This trend was reinforced when Deutschmark positions were excluded from open foreign exchange position limitations, and further, when conditions for access to minimum required reserves were eased. Consequently, money market interest rates moved closer to rates prevailing in the international Deutschmark money market.

As for the foreign exchange market, given the relatively open character of the Bulgarian economy, and the large share of deposits denominated in foreign currency (54 per cent of total deposits as of March 1999), it plays an important role in the economy. In addition to the interbank market, foreign exchange bureau dominated the cash transactions, and it is very difficult for the BNB to establish proper control over them. Activity in the interbank foreign exchange market suffered a dramatic drop at the onset of the crisis: the total volume fell by more than one-third. Following the implementation of a stabilization programme, activity returned to pre-crisis levels while the BNB assumed a passive role.

Stock Market

The Bulgarian stock exchange – Sofia (BSES) is still developing but expected to gain in importance. Following the consolidation of several small stock exchanges, BSES was established in 1997. It is segmented into official and free markets, with strict listing requirements for the official market. While only a few companies are listed and market capitalization is small, it has facilitated the consolidation of ownership process which followed privatization.

Prospects for its development are favourable. The market capitalization is likely to increase with the second wave of mass privatization, as the number of listed companies rises.

CONCLUSIONS

1. The achievement of *financial stabilization* is an immense success, although it has failed to produce the desired effect on the real sector so far.

As practice shows, if not underpinned by serious structural reforms, financial stabilization is only temporary.

2. The *real sector* has not yet adapted to the new environment. The principle of hard budget constraints is not observed everywhere. The practice of covering losses with state funds has not yet been eradicated. The heavy tax burden forces small and medium-sized private companies to conceal their income. Access to credit is still limited, reflecting both poor quality of investment projects and extremely prudent lending policies of banks. Under conditions of reduced credit supply, companies (predominantly state owned) seek alternative sources for financing, even through higher intercorporate indebtedness, particularly strong in the energy sector.

3. The *fixed exchange rate* gives no reason for concern so far; moreover, it ensures stability. The foreign exchange market is functioning smoothly without exerting pressure on the national currency. Calls for devaluation are unsustainable. Given a highly import-intensive export output and relatively low labour costs, overvaluation of the real effective exchange rate (within certain limits) is unlikely to impair the trade balance severely. Problems rather lie with low competitiveness of export output consistent with poor quality and lack of marketing strategies.

4. The process of *remonetization* is slow. Monetary and credit aggregates have stagnated. The share of domestic assets in broad money is declining continuously, already accounting for less than 20 per cent. Under the CBA, money supply depends mostly on real money demand which reflects the state of the financial sector. In the context of Bulgaria's currency board, the fiscal sector exerts a strong influence on the monetary sector. Government deposit with the Issue Department has been increasingly volatile. The existence of this deposit puts the public sector in a better position than the private sector because it is backed by foreign exchange reserves, which are national wealth. Movements in this deposit can be interpreted as *quasi-monetary policy* pursued by the government, while it provides a buffer between stagnating reserve money and growing foreign exchange reserves. Growth in government deposit constrains reserve money growth while dramatic fluctuations in the deposit cause even more dramatic changes in reserve money. Excessive growth of government deposits has negative implications triggered by liquidity withdrawals. The decision on how to use accumulated budget resources is imperative.

5. *Confidence in the banking system* is still low. Interest rates do not encourage saving and deposits increase rather slowly. The percentage share in GDP fell dramatically: from 72 per cent in 1994 to 50 per cent in June 1997 and currently to about 22 per cent. This severely limits the possibilities for domestic investment growth. At least USD 700–800 million

(drawn during the crisis) still remain outside the banking system. It is crucial to incorporate these funds into the legal economic turnover.

6. The *state of the banking system* has improved, but there are other problems that need to be addressed. The percentage share of credit portfolio in bank assets has shrunk and its quality is improving slowly. The reason behind this is the still low capital base of most banks and their reluctance to take risks associated with investment lending. Banking staff is insufficient to ensure efficient asset management. Foreign banks have intensified their activity over recent months, buying cheap lev funds in the interbank market, converting them into foreign exchange and investing abroad, generating profits from the interest differential.

NOTES

1. 'The role of the CBA in Bulgaria's stabilization', IMF, PDP/99/3.
2. Initially: 1000 leva = 1 Deutschmark. As from 1 January 1999: 1955.83 leva = 1 euro. From 5 July 1999: 1.95583 leva = 1 euro.
3. Should such a loan be extended, the effect would be a reduction in the Banking Department's deposit at the Issue Department, a corresponding credit to the account of the relevant commercial bank at the Issue Department, and an equivalent claim on the commercial Bank recorded in the assets of the Banking Department.
4. International Monetary Fund, *Bank Soundness and CBA: Issues and Experience*, IMF, PPAA/97/11, Washington, DC: IMF.

9. EMU convergence criteria and international flows of capital: the dilemmas for Polish macroeconomic policy

Boguslaw Grabowski and Jerzy Pruski

INTRODUCTION

From the very beginning, Poland has sought to join the European Union (EU) at the earliest possible date. The same priority was given to joining the North Atlantic Treaty Organization (NATO). The first goal was broadly recognized and immediately accepted by all political parties while the second received strong nationwide support after a short period of discussion by the left-wing party. As a result of such priorities in Polish foreign policy as well as an open attitude from the EU, the Polish Association Agreement with the EU was signed in 1991. Three years later Poland submitted a formal application for full EU membership. In 1996, Poland finalized negotiations and became a member of the Organization for Economic Cooperation and Development (OECD). Poland was invited to join NATO in 1997 and became a full member on 12 March 1999. Finally, in 1998 Poland was invited to join full accession talks with the EU, which have been continuing since then.

On 1 January 1999, 'euroland' was established. The group of founder members of the European Monetary Union (EMU) consisted of 11 countries. After fulfilling the Maastricht criteria, Denmark, Sweden and the UK postponed their decision about participation in EMU. Greece is expected to join EMU after meeting macroeconomic criteria. This group of four countries constitutes the expected second wave of EMU membership. The Czech Republic, Cyprus, Estonia, Hungary, Poland and Slovenia may create the third wave of EMU enlargement.

The latest group of countries, with Greece, will be eligible to join EMU only after meeting the convergence criteria specified in the Maastricht Treaty. These conditions impose a serious challenge for countries such as Poland, and for their economies. In order to meet the criteria, Poland like other countries, will have to improve the performance of its economy significantly in terms of disinflation, fiscal consolidation and competitiveness. Substantial progress in these fields will pave the way for sustainable growth without inflation. It will also allow macroeconomic policies among membership countries to be coordinated to a large extent.

On the other hand, however, the improved performance of the applicant economies makes them more attractive, since their credibility is increasing, for inflows of foreign capital including short-term portfolio capital. All applicant states belong to the group of emerging market economies which, as evidence from different regions shows, are extremely vulnerable to financial crises caused by international flows of capital. In fact, Hungary and the Czech Republic have already experienced this problem. As a result, they have faced higher inflation and a lower rate of economic growth. Thus the huge inflows of capital with their potential danger of financial crises constitutes one of the most important obstacles for applicant economies to overcome in order that the Maastricht convergence criteria are fulfilled in a prompt and efficient way.

Therefore, in the event of globalization of financial markets, macroeconomic policy, whose ultimate aim is to fulfil the convergence criteria, faces several dilemmas. First, the applicant states have to consider the framework for monetary policy and the exchange rate regime.[1] Second, the need for structural reforms calls for a more expansionary fiscal policy, while the current account deficit indicates a more restrictive fiscal policy. Third, assuming given restrictiveness of fiscal policy, the pace of disinflation depends upon the restrictiveness of monetary policy, but a higher real interest rate disparity stimulates additional inflows of capital. Fourth, all applicant states eventually have to decide their preferred time framework for joining EMU.

PERFORMANCE OF THE POLISH ECONOMY, 1992–1997

For the last few years Poland has been able to combine strong economic growth with a substantial decline in inflation. From 1992 to 1997, the real GDP rate of growth increased from 2.6 to 6.9 per cent while the inflation rate (consumer price index, CPI, at end of year) decreased from 44.3 to 13.2 per cent. Developing real activity led to a decline in the unemployment rate from 16.4 per cent in 1993 to 10.5 per cent in December 1997. (See Table 9.1, and Figures 9.1–3.)

During the 1992–97 period internal demand and exports were the main driving force of the sharp increase in industrial production. Private consumption was growing due to the real wage increase and to improved credit availability. Investment was rising rapidly, driven by strong demand, firms' strong desire to update equipment and expand capacity, and more recently by foreign

Table 9.1   Growth rate, inflation and unemployment in Poland, 1992–1997

	1992	1993	1994	1995	1996	1997
Real GDP (% change)	2.6	3.8	5.2	7.0	6.1	6.9
Consumer prices (% change):						
end period	44.3	37.7	29.5	21.6	18.7	13.2
average period	43.0	35.3	32.2	27.8	19.9	14.9
Unemployment ratio (%)	14.3	16.4	16.0	14.9	13.2	10.5

Sources: National Bank of Poland; Central Statistic Office.

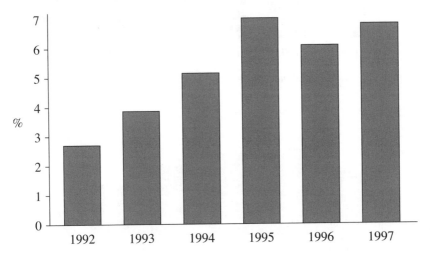

Figure 9.1   GDP growth rate in Poland, 1992–1997

direct investment (FDI). Moderate fiscal expansion added to these factors in boosting economic growth. (See Tables 9.2–5.)

However, the strong internal demand, growing faster than internal supply (GDP), has had a negative effect on the current account. Despite a significant increase in exports and cross-border trade, rapidly growing imports reduced the current account from a surplus of 3 percent of GDP in 1995 to a deficit of 3.2 per cent of GDP in 1997. So far, this deficit has been covered mostly by FDI. Despite the growing importance of portfolio investments, they have still financed only a relatively small share of the current account deficit.

Since the beginning of 1997, macroeconomic policy responded to the growing current account deficit mostly by tightening the monetary policy whereas the restrictiveness of the fiscal policy increased only slightly. During

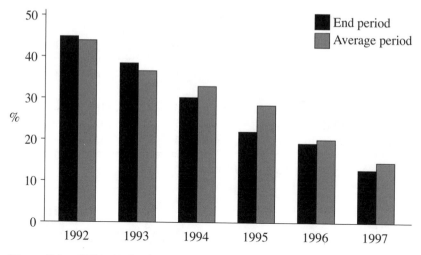

Figure 9.2   CPI in Poland, 1992–1997

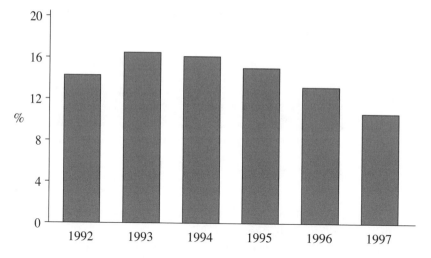

Figure 9.3   Unemployment rate in Poland, 1992–1997

this period the National Bank of Poland (NBP) increased its open market interest rate and its basic interest rate several times. As a result the real interest rate increased to 10–12 per cent by the end of 1997 (Table 9.6).

In addition, the monetary policy was tightened by the increase of the obligatory reserves from 17 to 20 per cent for demand deposits and from 9 to 11 per cent for term deposits. At the same time the obligatory reserves for foreign

Table 9.2   Domestic economy: demand and supply in Poland, 1992–1997

	1992	1993	1994	1995	1996	1997
GDP Growth rate (%)	2.6	3.8	5.2	7.0	6.1	6.9
Industrial production (% change)	2.8	6.4	12.1	9.7	8.3	13.3
Domestic demand (% change)	–0.1	6.9	4.6	7.1	12.8	9.8
Goods export volume (% change)	3.7	5.9	20.0	20.1	13.2	17.9

Sources: National Bank of Poland; Central Statistic Office.

Table 9.3   Domestic demand in Poland, 1992–1997

	1992	1993	1994	1995	1996	1997
Domestic demand (% change)	–0.1	6.9	4.6	7.1	12.8	9.8
Private consumption (% change)	2.3	5.2	4.3	3.6	8.6	8.5
Investment spending(% change)	2.3	2.9	9.2	16.9	22.7	18.5
Public consumption (% change)	6.4	3.4	2.8	2.9	3.3	3.0

Sources: National Bank of Poland; Central Statistic Office.

Table 9.4   Private consumption and its sources in Poland, 1992–1997

	1992	1993	1994	1995	1996	1997
Private consumption (% change)	2.3	5.2	4.3	3.6	8.6	8.5
Real wages (% change)	na	–1.8	5.6	4.5	7.1	4.8
Credit outstanding to individuals:						
nominal (% change)	67.1	88.0	48.0	68.1	107.8	56.1
real (% change)	24.1	52.7	15.8	40.3	87.9	41.2

Sources: National Bank of Poland; Central Statistic Office.

Table 9.5   Investments and corporate credit in Poland, 1992–1997

	1992	1993	1994	1995	1996	1997
Gross fixed investment (% change)	2.3	2.9	9.2	16.9	22.7	18.5
Corporate credit outstanding:						
nominal (% change)	27.0	30.6	23.5	32.4	35.2	29.4
real (% change)	–16.0	–4.7	–8.7	4.6	15.3	14.5

Sources: National Bank of Poland; Central Statistic Office.

Table 9.6   Nominal and real NBP interest rates, 1989–1997 (%)

	1989	1990	1991	1992	1993	1994	1995	1996	1997
Nominal rate	61.3	103.8	53.9	39.0	35.4	33.7	31.5	22.0	24.5
real rate:									
CPI deflator[1]	−78.2	−41.6	−4.0	−3.7	−1.6	3.2	8.1	2.9	10.0
PPI deflator[2]	−78.6	−34.4	13.4	5.7	−1.2	4.5	10.6	9.7	12.2
GDP deflator	−58.7	−64.7	−0.9	0.4	3.8	4.1	2.6	2.9	10.8

Note: For 1989–95 the basic NBP interest rate refers to average annual interest rate of refinancing credit and for 1996–97 it refers to interest rate of rediscount credit for the end of the year.
1.   Consumer price indices for the 12-month period ending December.
2.   Producer price indices for the 12-month period ending December.

Source: Z. Polanski, *Polish Monetary Policy in the Second Half of 1990: Current Problems and Strategic Challenges*, Warsaw: NBP, 1998.

deposits increased from 2 to 5 per cent. As a result of these measures the rate of growth of credit for the non-financial sector decreased from 42.4 per cent in 1996 to 33.2 per cent in 1997 (from 107.8 to 56.1 per cent for households and from 35.2 to 29.4 per cent for corporate clients).

However, the effectiveness of the monetary policy in curbing internal demand has been limited because of the small impact of the central bank interest rates on the interest rates in commercial banks as well as the low credit demand elasticity with respect to interest rates. The limited response of the banks' interest rates has been caused by the existing overliquidity in the banking sector and its specific structure inherited from the central planning economy (that is, the important role played by two large banks with underdeveloped credit activity compared to the amount of deposits).

On the other hand the low demand for credit elasticity on interest rates relates to both households and corporate clients. With respect to households, the low credit elasticity results from a rapid expansion of real wages and the large potential of postponed consumption from the first period of transition. In addition, it is caused by the lack of institutional factors which would strengthen the propensity to save (such as a capital pillar in the pension system, a system of voluntary health insurance, the development of a building society sector or a private education system). The weak response of corporate clients to changes in interest rates is explained by the small role played by external financing in the firms' activity (low leverage ratio) and also by the large share of state ownership in the economy. (See Table 9.7).

In 1997, the maintenance of the increasingly restrictive monetary policy was relatively easy due to the developments on the world financial market and the floods in Poland. At first, the Czech crises undermined confidence in the

Table 9.7   Sources of investment financing in Poland, 1992–1997 (structure in %)

	1992	1993	1994	1995	1996	1997
Fixed capital investment in corporate sector	100	100	100	100	100	100
Own funds	58.1	63.2	62.4	66.3	64.5	63.4
Government budget financing	5.6	4.7	4.2	2.4	2.9	2.9
Bank loans	10.8	8.7	10.3	12.9	15.2	16.3
Others:	25.5	23.3	23.1	18.4	17.4	17.4
including foreign funds and FDI	na	9.8	9.0	5.9	5.5	na

Source: K. Moscibrodzka, 'Dangerous interest rates', *Nowe Zycie Gospodarcze*, No. 25, 1998.

East European markets, among others in the Polish zloty. The uncertainty related to the Polish financial market was further enforced by the floods in south-western Poland in July, and more strongly by financial crises in Asia and the parliamentary election in Poland towards the end of the year. Therefore the basically healthy economy, with its high real interest rates, did not experience significant inflows of foreign capital and an appreciation of the currency. Consequently the monetary authority, while maintaining a crawling band exchange rate regime, faced a unique opportunity to conduct an independent monetary policy.

The restrictive monetary policy was assisted by the increasingly restrictive fiscal policy in terms of tightening the central government deficit. This deficit decreased from 3.8–4.6 per cent of GDP in 1995–96 to 3.3 per cent in 1997. However, the general government deficit decreased only slightly, mostly as a result of the increased deficit of the local governments and other government funds financing flood damage. (See Table 9.8.)

The policy mix described above reduced the growth of domestic demand from 12.8 per cent in 1996 to 9.8 per cent in 1997 which was still above the GDP growth rate (6.9 per cent). However, the current deficit increased from 1.3 per cent of GDP in 1996 to 3.2 per cent in 1997, which was below the forecast level of 5 per cent. (See Tables 9.9 and 9.10.)

LATEST DEVELOPMENTS AND POLICY RESPONSE

For 1998 the government[2] decided to tighten fiscal policy with an overall budgetary sector deficit of 3.5 per cent (with a central government deficit of 2.8 per cent). However, the planned budget and even its early, monthly results

Table 9.8   Structure of general government deficit in Poland, 1992–1997 (% of GDP)

	1992	1993	1994	1995	1996	1997
General government:	−7.1	−4.5	−3.7	−3.0	−4.4	−4.2
central government*	−8.1	−5.0	−4.2	−3.8	−4.6	−3.3
including cash deficit	−6.0	−2.8	−2.7	−2.6	−2.5	−1.3
local governments	0.0	0.0	0.0	0.1	−0.1	−0.4
government funds	0.8	0.3	0.4	0.5	0.3	−0.5
others	0.3	0.2	0.1	0.2	0.1	0.0

Note: *Cash deficit plus change in liabilities of government entities, issue of restructuring bonds, accrued interest, exchange rate differentials and capital transaction balance.

Sources: Ministry of Finance and Central Statistic Office.

Table 9.9   GDP, domestic demand, current account, exports and imports in Poland, 1992–1997 (USDm)

	1993	1994	1995	1996	1997
GDP growth rate (%)	3.8	5.2	7.0	6.1	6.9
Domestic demand (% change)	6.9	4.6	7.1	12.8	9.8
Current account (% of GDP)	−0.1	2.3	3.3	−1.0	−3.2
Merchandise exports	13 585	16 950	22 878	24 420	27 233
Merchandise imports	15 878	17 786	24 705	32 574	38 522
Unclassified transactions on	na	na	7 754	7 153	6 061

Sources: National Bank of Poland; Central Statistic Office.

Table 9.10   Investment and savings in Poland, 1992–1997 (% of GDP)

	1992	1993	1994	1995	1996	1997
Gross domestic investment	15.9	16.2	16.3	18.3	20.6	23.1
Gross national savings	12.9	13.8	15.9	18.7	17.7	18.0
Net foreign balance	−3.1	−2.5	−0.4	0.4	−2.9	−5.1

Sources: National Bank of Poland; Central Statistic Office.

were not sufficient conditions for an immediate easing of monetary policy which would lower the uncovered interest rate disparity against the foreign financial markets. Simultaneously the strength of the external and internal risk factors weakened significantly, allowing a huge inflow of foreign capital from February 1998. As a result the central bank foreign reserves increased in 1998

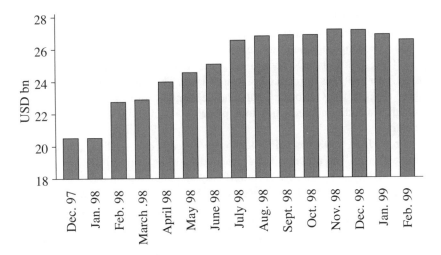

Source: National Bank of Poland

Figure 9.4   Gross official reserves (USD bn)

by about USD 6 billion (2 billion in February) to the level of USD 27.4 billion. (See Figure 9.4.)

In order to prevent huge inflows of capital as well as reach the inflation target for 1998 at the level of 9.5 per cent, the newly elected Monetary Policy Council (MPC), at its initial meeting in late February 1998, made some very important decisions concerning the direction of monetary policy, including:

- widening the exchange rate band of the zloty and allowing the rate to be determined by the market within the band; this step eliminated much of the exchange rate rigidity and created conditions for a more effective monetary policy;
- reducing the 'crawling devaluation' of the zloty, thus setting conditions for a continuous disinflation;
- shifting the emphasis from the monetary base to interest rates in the process of controlling the money supply; and
- changing the rules of conducting open market operations by adopting the rate on 28-day open market operations as the reference rate, thus shortening the maximum maturity period of NBP money bills from 270 to 28 days.

In October 1998 the MPC announced its Medium-Term Monetary Policy Strategy (1999–2003). Under the new strategy, the monetary authority adopted direct inflation targeting as the underlying precept of monetary policy and decided to increase further the exchange rate flexibility.

The exchange rate band was extended twice in 1998: in February from ±7 to ±10 per cent and in October to ±12.5 per cent. Further widening of the band to ±15 per cent was introduced in March 1999. The rate of crawl was lowered three times in 1998 (February, July and September), from 1 to 0.5 per cent per month. An additional reduction took place on March 1999, to 0.3 per cent per month.

From June 1998 the MPC began the process of a gradual reduction in interest rates. The process was correlated with the falling inflation rate and better budgetary results. Most importantly, the intervention interest rate, was reduced from 24 per cent in February to 15.5 per cent in December 1998 and to 13 per cent in January 1999. Changes in the term structure of open market operations and interest rate levels allowed for a significant adjustment of the long-term interest rates in response to an inflow of foreign capital, with a much smaller decrease in the short-term interbank interest rates. The interest rates on five-, two- and one-year treasury bonds decreased from 22–24 per cent in February to 9.5–11 per cent at the end of 1998, while the one-month interbank market rate decreased from about 24 per cent to about 16 per cent.

Therefore the expansion of credit in the commercial banking sector, which is mostly correlated with the one-month interbank interest rate, still remained under control. The twelve-month rate of credit growth decreased from 33.2 per cent in December 1997 to 27.5 per cent in December 1998.

Nevertheless, the increased exchange rate risk with a different structure of interest rates may appear insufficient to offset the interest rate disparity and to prevent the further inflows of portfolio capital in the medium term. As a result, the zloty appreciated significantly in the first half of 1998. However, in the second half of the year (due to the Russian crisis) and in the first months of 1999 (because of the Brazilian turmoil and the worsening macroeconomic situation in Poland) foreign investors faced a substantially increased risk which effectively prevented the inflow of foreign portfolio capital. On the other hand, increased flexibility of the zloty exchange rate and the extensive scope of the longer-term interest rate arbitrage helped the Polish economy to pass smoothly through the turmoil on the world financial markets caused by the Russian crisis. (See Figure 9.5.)

Increased flexibility of the exchange rate (and its real appreciation) with more exogenous money supply and its better control allowed for deeper disinflation. The inflation rate measured by the CPI decreased to 8.6 per cent in December 1998 (4.9 per cent in PPI) and 5.6 per cent in February 1999. The execution of tighter central government budget (eventually 2.5 per cent of GDP) along with falling oil and raw material prices on the world market as

Source: National Bank of Poland.

Figure 9.5 PLN/USD exchange rate deviations from central parity (%)

well as substantial decrease in foreign demand on Polish export helped in this achievement.

The real sector of the economy performed much worse in 1998. The GDP rate of growth decreased from 6.5 per cent in the first quarter to 5.2, 5.0 and 2.9 per cent in the next three quarters to reach 4.8 per cent in the whole of 1998. this was caused mostly by the external demand decrease and partially by the policy of cooling down the internal demand.

Due to the successful cooling of internal demand, the current account deficit had fallen below 3 per cent of GDP by August 1998, then skyrocketed from September to reach about 4.6 per cent of GDP for the whole year. The abrupt fall in external demand caused by the Russian crisis as well as the slow-down in the EU economies reflected this phenomenon.

EMU CONVERGENCE CRITERIA

The EMU convergence criteria create a convenient framework for analysing the distance of the Polish economy from the member state economies. They also provide indications about necessary developments in Polish macroeconomic policy.

Table 9.11   Inflation in EU countries and Poland, 1996–1997 (%)

	EU[1]	EMU[2]	Lowest inflation countries[3]	Reference value	Poland
1996	2.4	2.1	1.0	2.5	18.7
1997	1.8	1.5	1.2	2.7	13.2

Notes:
1. Average inflation in 15 countries.
2. Average inflation in 11 countries.
3. Average inflation in the three countries with the lowest inflation rate.

Sources: European Monetary Institute, *Convergence Report*, March 1998; Central Statistic Office.

Inflation convergence Criterion

With the exception of Greece, with inflation running at 4.2 per cent, all member state economies reached the reference value of inflation. The reference value increased slightly from 2.5 per cent in 1996 to 2.7 per cent in 1997 due to the different composition of countries with the lowest inflation and a moderate increase in their inflation rate. (See Table 9.11.)

Notwithstanding the satisfactory overall performance of the Polish economy, there still exists a huge distance in terms of a necessary reduction in the inflation rate. Compared with the EMU average inflation, the difference amounted to 16.6 and 11.7 percentage points in 1996 and 1997, respectively. With the inflation rate for EMU at 0.8 per cent[3] and for Poland 8.6 per cent, the difference dropped to 7.8 percentage points by the end of 1998. In order to reach the criterion the rate of inflation in Poland has to be reduced to below 3 per cent within 5–7 years. The National Bank of Poland announced recently that its inflation target for 2003 was below 4 per cent.

Disinflation has to be consistent with a relatively high rate of economic growth. To reach the goals the structure of the fiscal–monetary policy mix has to change considerably and some kind of income policy has to be implemented to curb the expansion of wages drastically. The continuous process of disinflation without affecting the real sector of the economy constitutes a tremendous challenge for applicant economies. In addition, experience from emerging markets shows that capital inflows might slow down the pace of disinflation.

The logic for the inflation criterion was that this would enable the euroland countries to live with the common monetary policy resulting from EMU. But the criterion neglects the fact of huge price-level differentials between the 'core' and aspiring countries mostly arising from a difference in price level in the non-tradables sector. With a similar level of inflation the process of price-level convergence will last for about 20 years in the case of Poland. The 'dual inflation' model of Balassa[4] and Samuelson[5] shows that relatively higher inflation in a country with a lower price level need not necessarily undermine its competitiveness. Also, the relatively higher inflation is a natural counter-part of the real economic convergence.

The problem can be resolved through EMU countries' tolerance of some-what wider inflation differentials or aspiring countries' acceptance of sub-par growth required to meet the inflation standard. The third possibility is that the dual inflation process is somehow short-circuited, such that the rapid produc-tivity growth in the tradables sector is not allowed to feed through fully into wages, or higher wage growth in the tradables sector is not passed through to the non-tradables sector.

In all cases it is clear that inflation convergence will pose a major challenge for aspiring countries and the international capital inflow will intensify this challenge.

The General Government Deficit Criterion

With regard to the government fiscal position, Denmark, Ireland and Luxembourg recorded a budgetary surplus while 11 countries achieved deficits below the 3 per cent reference value specified in the Maastricht Treaty. Only Greece exceeded the reference value, with a deficit level of 4 per cent. (See Figure 9.6.)

Poland, with a general government deficit of 4.4 and 4.2 per cent in 1996 and 1997, respectively, was close to the reference value. In 1998 the central government deficit was reduced to 2.5 per cent of GDP while the estimated overall budget deficit slightly exceeded 3 per cent. In a budget planned for 1999 the central government deficit is expected to be about 2.15 per cent of GDP.

However, from the beginning of 1999 the government initiated some important institutional reforms. These include a three pillars pension system reform (with introduction of the obligatory and voluntary capital pillars), health-care system reform (with the introduction of a health-care insurance system) and administration reform (with the decentralization of public finance). In addition, the government is running coal and steel industry restructuring projects. Although all of these reforms are necessary for the long-term stability of the public finance sector, they create additional expenditures for the government budget in the short run. According to the estimates, the total cost of institutional reforms incurred by the budget accounts for 1 per cent of GDP.

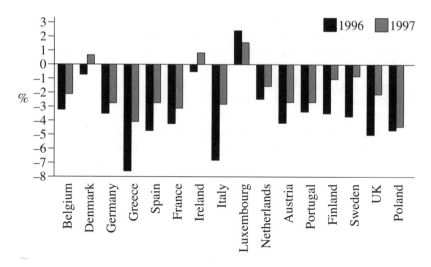

Source: European Monetary Institute, Convergence Report, March 1998 Central Statistic Office.

Figure 9.6   General government surplus/deficit in EU countries and Poland, 1996–1997

Therefore, despite the government's determination to consolidate fiscal policy, the costs of institutional and structural reforms might result in lower than required restrictiveness of fiscal policy. Consequently Poland would deviate not only from the Maastricht criterion, but from the desired fiscal–monetary policy mix as well. In such a scenario the excessive burden of disinflation in 1999–2000 would be carried by monetary policy. This in turn might create an instrument instability problem (excessive appreciation of the zloty and too high interest rates), a further surge of foreign capital and a deterioration of the current account. Consequently the sustainability of economic growth and disinflation might be undermined, which would have implications for the fulfilment of the Maastricht convergence criteria.

The Public Debt Criterion

Only France, Luxembourg, Finland and the United Kingdom recorded gross debt ratios below the reference value of 60 per cent in 1997. With respect to Belgium, Greece and Italy, the debt-to-GDP ratios were above 100 per cent. Almost all member countries experienced accelerated progress in reducing debt ratios. However, in a number of countries the reduction was related to one-off measures. (See Table 9.12.)

Table 9.12   General government gross debt in EU countries and Poland, 1996–1997 (% of GDP)

	EU debt[1]	EMU debt[2]	Reference value	Poland
1996	73.3	71.4	60.0	51.1
1997	71.0	69.2	60.0	48.1

Notes:
1. Average debt in 15 countries.
2. Average debt in 11 countries.

Sources: European Monetary Institute, *Convergence Report*, March 1998; Central Statistic Office.

Poland, with a debt-to-GDP ratio of 51.1, 48.1 and 46.3 per cent, respectively, in 1996, 1997 and 1998 is well below the reference figure. However, the methodology for calculating general government debt in Poland is not fully compatible with that applied to the EU. Recalculation of Poland's public debt according to EU standards would give necessarily higher results. As an example, general government debt should have been increased by the indebtedness of the health-care sector in the range of 7–8 billion zlotys and compensation payments of 10 billion zlotys to pensioners and budgetary employees. Assuming the need for both a relatively high rate of economic growth and more restrictive fiscal policy, maintaining the appropriate gross debt ratio should not, however, be a serious problem for the economy in future.

The Exchange Rate Criterion

Ten member countries have experienced a two-year reference period of participation in the Exchange Rate Mechanism (ERM). The periods of membership for the Finnish markka and the Italian lira were shorter, as these currencies joined and rejoined the exchange rate mechanism in October 1996 and November 1996, respectively. The Greek drachma, the Swedish krona and the pound sterling remained outside the ERM. Each of the 12 ERM currencies, with the exception of the Irish punt, was normally traded close to its unchanged central rates against other ERM currencies. The three currencies remaining outside ERM experienced higher fluctuations against other EU currencies.

The Polish zloty follows a crawling peg exchange rate regime against a basket of two currencies: the US dollar with a weight of 45 per cent and the euro with a weight of 55 per cent. Currently the central rate devalues by 0.3 per cent per month and the zloty may fluctuate within the bank ±15 per cent bank from the central rate.

After Poland has joined the EU, the Polish zloty is expected to follow ERM2 for the two-year reference period, with an expected band of fluctuations of ±15 per cent from the central rate against the euro. The MPC decided in its Medium-Term Monetary Policy Strategy that this should be preceded by a period of freely floating exchange rate. This arrangement will help to bring the market rate closer to the equilibrium rate, prior to its renewed fixing within ERM2. The floating exchange rate will be introduced following a period of gradual expansion of the bank of permitted exchange rate fluctuations and the gradual reduction of the crawling devaluation within the framework of the presently existing exchange rate system.

The increased flexibility of the zloty will guarantee increased control over the money supply despite foreign capital inflow, and enable monetary policy to be conducted according to the direct inflation targeting rule. The flexible exchange rate system is also the precondition for coping with the problem of the considerable excess liquidity of the banking sector, spurred by the rapid increment in official foreign exchange reserves in the last four years.

On the other hand, even in the flexible exchange rate system, exchange rate misalignment may occur because of the differing speeds of adjustment of the exchange rate and goods prices. Additionally, while switching to a flexible exchange rate one should remember that the exchange rate is perhaps the most efficient transmission mechanism from monetary policy to inflation, at least in emerging economies. Thus the central bank will be left with an interest rate as the only monetary policy instrument, for which the transmission mechanism is not yet fully effective.

The Long-term Interest Rate Criterion

The reference value of the long-term interest rate, calculated as the arithmetic average of the long-term interest rates in the three countries with the lowest inflation plus 2 percentage points, changed significantly from 9.1 per cent in 1996 to 7.8 per cent in 1997. Similarly the average long-term interest rates decreased for the EU countries to 6.3 per cent and for the EMU countries to 5.9 per cent in 1997. This was due to a further reduction in inflation, further stabilization of exchange rates and a significant consolidation of fiscal position in the respective countries. Only Greece, with an interest rate of 9.8 per cent, has not fulfilled the long-term interest rate criterion. (See Table 9.13.)

This criterion is far from being fulfilled for the Polish economy. However, in 1998 much progress was made in this respect. With the long-term interest rate at the end of 1998 at about 10 per cent, the difference dropped to about 6 percentage points with respect to EMU ten-year government bonds. The potential success in the process of interest rate convergence will depend on the results in disinflation and fiscal consolidation.

Table 9.13   Long-term interest rates in EU countries and Poland, 1996–1997 (%)

	EU[1]	EMU[2]	Lowest inflation countries[3]	Reference value	Poland
1996	7.8	7.2	7.1	9.1	18.3
1997	6.3	5.9	5.8	7.8	19.5

Notes:
1. Average inflation in 15 countries.
2. Average inflation in 11 countries.
3. Average inflation in the three countries with the lowest inflation rates.

Sources: European Monetary Institute, *Convergence Report*, March 1998; Central Statistic Office.

However, in transition economies a higher dynamic of internal demand and a higher inflation rate create pressure for maintaining higher real and nominal interest rates. As a result, the uncovered interest rate disparity with a dominant tendency of local currencies to appreciate might cause an excessive inflow of portfolio capital (unless there is increased risk) that would reduce domestic interest rates and increase appreciation pressure. This may create a situation whereby there is no interest rate level that would guarantee internal and external equilibria at the same time. The only solution to this dilemma is to achieve a structural government budget surplus and to earmark it for an earlier foreign debt repayment. In order to make the earlier debt repayment efficient in terms of lower pressure for the zloty exchange rate, the budgetary surplus has to be sufficiently large. Regardless of government intentions, the possibility of achieving a significant budgetary surplus may be questioned on the grounds of the need for additional budgetary expenditures in the field of the initiated institutional reforms as well as the required restructuring in the coal and steel industries and agriculture.

Other Factors

According to Article 109j(1) of the Maastricht Treaty, the other factors of convergence include the development of the ecu, the result of the integration of markets, the situation in current accounts, the examination of unit labour costs and other price indices. However, for applicant economies the development of the balance of payments on current account is of special importance because of its influence on the sustainability of economic growth and disinflation.

In spite of the fact that at the beginning of the 1990s the majority of EMU countries experienced a current account deficit only four countries, (Greece, Germany, Austria and Portugal) showed a deficit at the end of 1997. All remaining countries experienced a current account surplus. With respect to the Polish economy, the current account surplus of 3.3 per cent of GDP in 1995 turned into a deficit of 1.0 per cent in 1996 and further deteriorated to 3.2 per cent in 1997 and to 4.6 per cent in 1998. An even further worsening of the current account position is expected in 1999, mostly due to external demand shock.

Despite a restrictive macroeconomic policy mix as well as a flexible exchange rate system, we shall observe a tendency towards a high and persistent current account deficit in Poland (as in other aspiring countries) in the years before accession. This will be caused by the persistent and growing capital account surplus due to the inflow of foreign capital (FDI with connected credits and portfolio investments) which may even reach 8–10 per cent of GDP. The macroeconomic and structural policies should, however, guarantee the best possible structure of this surplus with most FDI and long-term portfolio investments. So far 80–100 per cent of the current account deficit in Poland has been covered by FDIs.

CONCLUSIONS

The comparison presented above describes the current distance of the Polish economy from the EMU convergence criteria. Within the feasible period of approximately 5 to 7 years, the actual reference values have to be achieved. The targets related to the government budgetary position seem to be much more easily attainable compared with inflation, long-term interest rates and the current account position. However, quite apart from current distance, the fulfilment of the convergence criteria in the future requires a well-formulated long-term macroeconomic policy. As a result, the economy should follow a sustainable path of high growth rate, accompanied by permanent disinflation and external equilibrium. However, the huge inflow of foreign capital constitutes the most serious potential obstacle for a smooth and balanced convergence process.

NOTES

1. H. Wagner, 'Central banking in transition countries', IMF Working Paper, WP/98/26.
2. According to the new Polish constitution, effective from 17 October 1997, the planned budget deficit is decided by the government and cannot be changed by parliament or financed by the central bank. Accumulated public debt cannot exceed 60 per cent of GDP.

3. European Central Bank, *Monthly Bulletin*, February 1999.
4. B. Balassa, 'The purchasing power parity doctrine: a reappraisal', *Journal of Political Economy*, **72**, 1964, pp. 548–96.
5. P. Samuelson, 'Theoretical notes on trade problems', *Review of Economics and Statistics*, **23**, 1964, pp. 1–60.

10. The Asian financial crisis and lessons for CEE economies

David G. Dickinson and Andrew W. Mullineux

INTRODUCTION

The Asian financial crisis can be traced, in chronological terms, to the collapse of the pegged exchange rate regime in Thailand in mid-1997. Whether this was the catalyst for a contagious bout of 'Asian financial flu' where the symptoms were more important than the causes, in itself indicating the speculative nature of much international capital movement, or whether the result of the Thai crisis was to highlight the domestic economic inadequacies of several of the economies of the region is a matter of intensive debate. However, what is clear is that the financial crisis had sustained real effects with large falls in output (in the Association of South-East Asian Nations (ASEAN) region as a whole the International Monetary Fund (IMF) has reported a 9.4 per cent drop in 1998), although the performance for 1999 and the outlook for the year 2000 is more optimistic. Financial crises elsewhere (in Russia and Brazil) have created additional clouds on the horizon and the global financial system seems currently to be in a state of shock. As a result, finding the reasons for the crisis, and the appropriate policy response, is a matter of concern to the international policy community and as we shall discuss here, an issue of great interest to the economies of Central and Eastern Europe.

This chapter takes the view that the inadequacies of the economic, legal and regulatory structure (particularly in the financial system) lie at the heart of the problems which have been observed in Asia. However, we also accept that financial markets can exacerbate a crisis both in terms of their reaction to shocks and to the policy measures that are taken in response to problems in currency markets. Thus, in terms of the conventional literature on currency crises we argue that the reasons for the problems in East Asia are related to domestic fundamentals (where we interpret this to include institutional and policy-making structures) as in the first-generation-type models, but that these problems can generate multiple equilibria as modelled in the more recent second-generation frameworks where sudden shifts in expectations can push the financial markets from a stable position into a crisis (see Flood and Marion (1998) for a recent survey of the literature). Hence expectational forces caused the crisis but these expectations were driven by fundamentals reflecting the deficiencies in the underlying domestic economic environment. What is more, recognizing the importance of expectations also has implications for the speed at which the economy can recover from the initial shock.

The chapter is divided into four further sections. In the next section we review the alternative explanations which have been offered for the financial crisis in the region. In the third section we look at the short-run effects of the crisis while in the fourth section we consider how the relative underdevelopment of the financial system and a lack of proper regulation could have created the conditions for a crisis to start and offer policy conclusions which relate to longer-term restructuring of the financial sector to improve its efficiency and to prevent similar crises occurring in the future. There is a concluding section which contains a summary of the chapter and draws together the lessons for the Central and Eastern European (CEE) economies.

EXPLANATIONS FOR THE CRISIS

Much of the early economic analysis of financial crises focused on problems in a country's banking/financial system, ignoring international linkages. This is probably because in the immediate post-war (post-1945) era, such linkages were not particularly strong. Exchange controls were, for example, widespread. The linkages have however, become progressively stronger since the late 1960s, and the terms 'globalization' and 'global capital markets' are now widely used. The current period is often compared with the pre-1930 period of the twentieth century. Kindleberger (1996) is replete with examples demonstrating the importance of these international linkages in the early part of this century. Thus the process of globalization can be seen as a move back to an international economic system which had been displaced after the Great Depression.

The Asian financial crisis has created a debate as to whether this return to an older style of international economic relations is a good thing or not. The increasing international nature of financial markets can be a positive influence on the development of domestic economies, providing finance for capital investment and improving the efficiency of the domestic financial system and resource allocation. However, such a development carries with it risks associated with the potential instability created by unfettered capital flows. That some of the apparently most successful economies of the 1990s should suffer from these risks appears to be a serious indictment of the role of international financial markets. Even if international capital markets are found not guilty of the charge that they destabilized otherwise healthy economies, there will be many lessons from the problems which a number of Asian economies experienced. It is these lessons which we shall wish to draw out for CEE economies.

The analysis of the reasons for the Asian financial crisis has followed two broad themes. One has argued that the crisis indicated major domestic failings with regard to the way in which these economies operated (many authors have followed this line of reasoning, for example, Corsetti et al. 1998; Mishkin 2000; Burnside et al. 1998) while the other highlights the speculative nature of international financial markets and the inadequacy of the policy response by the IMF (Radelet and Sachs 1998). We shall consider each of these.

For many of the South-East Asian countries, it has been argued that there had been considerable 'overinvestment' and consequently, given the 'underdeveloped' ('emerging') equity capital markets in the region, 'overborrowing', largely from banks, but also from 'near' or 'secondary' banks, such as the finance companies in Thailand. Beyond this, the finance for investment came mainly from outside the economy, the domestic banking system therefore engaging in potentially risky foreign currency borrowing and domestic currency lending (Kaminsky and Reinhart (1999) have documented that currency and banking crises are usually closely connected). Large domestic firms were also able to tap the international capital markets directly. However, there are two forces which will work against these flows continuing. The first is that eventually the international banking community will become wary of overextending their credit lines to particular economies. The second is that, as the foreign currency exposure of the domestic banks and corporations grows there will be the possibility of speculative attack on the pegged currency (against the US dollar) which these economies adopted (and which, of course, encouraged the international borrowing in the first place). However, it has been suggested that neither of these countervailing forces operated for the Asian economies because private sector exposure to foreign currency risks was associated with government guarantees.

Thus Burnside et al. (1998) have argued that the currency crisis was the result of expected large prospective deficits associated with implicit bail-outs of the bankrupt domestic banking system which would be required if the currency peg collapsed. To support this view they argue that the fragility of domestic banking systems was well known prior to the crisis which eventually brought them down. This argument is also complementary to the Krugman (1997) explanation for the excessive international capital inflows into the affected countries prior to the crisis. His argument is based upon the implicit government guarantees underpinning the lending which took place, introducing a moral hazard problem such that international banks were less concerned with the risks that their lending entailed.

Other fundamentals may also have been working to encourage excessive capital inflows. Inappropriately low (often negative) real interest rates ('cheap money') will generally encourage overinvestment and overlending (Fry 1997). In this respect, the low nominal rates prevailing in Japan in the mid-1990s, and the capital outflows from Japan to the Pacific and South-East Asian region throughout the 1990s, seems likely to have exerted a downward pressure on interest rates in the affected economies. Alternatively, lack of regulation of the banking sector created a lax environment in which speculative investors could operate (Mishkin (2000) highlights the poor regulatory framework in these economies). Furthermore the close business relationships between the political, financial and corporate establishments created conditions where excessive investment was likely to take place (Dickinson (2000), discusses this in some detail; see also Rajan and Zingales (2000)).

Allied to the fundamentals are expectations. Recent analysis of currency crises (see Obstfeld 1996) has highlighted how the potential for multiple equilibria has created the potential for self-fulfilling crises. This work is in contrast to the Krugman (1979) explanation of the inconsistency between a country's fiscal deficit and its pegged exchange rate. Hence, although the root cause of the currency collapse is the fundamentals in the domestic economies, the actual collapse of the currency is triggered by self-fulfilling expectations which force the issue. The basic idea here is that the attack on the currency creates costs for the policy makers which eventually lead them to abandon the peg, even though it would be sustainable in the short term without the currency attack. Note, however, that the expectational mechanism operates to determine the timing of the currency collapse but is not the underlying reason for it.

The alternative model to explain the currency crisis argues that international capital markets were excessively optimistic about the Asian economic miracle and tended to act as a herd in 'getting into the markets'. Then when expectations about the health of these economies changed, the markets again acted in a herd-like manner but in the reverse direction. The resulting currency collapse and associated banking and corporate sector problems were brought about by the irrationality of financial market participants. One of the most comprehensive analyses of the Asian crisis which favours this argument has been by Radelet and Sachs (1998). They present a wealth of evidence to show that the crisis can be attributed to financial panic where a run on a currency occurs because that is what economic agents expect. This was further exacerbated by a disorganized approach to dealing with the resulting financial/macroeconomic problems (essentially by the IMF). In this regard they are critical of the overtight monetary and fiscal conditions which were imposed on the crisis economies. They argue that this made matters worse by increasing the severity of the resulting bank credit contraction. In support of their analysis, Radelet and Sachs offer the view that much of the investment which was financed by international banks (and which went to the private sector) was profitable and hence it would have been sensible to continue financing projects rather than to starve them of funds. In other words, the policy response forced the crisis-hit economies into a worse equilibrium than they need have experienced.

One of the main observations in support of this second argument is that the crisis displayed contagion effects. Other countries in the region with sound fundamentals (for example, Hong Kong and Singapore) were subject to speculative pressure while some which had no connection with the Asian crisis (for example, in Latin America) were also subject to attack. Masson (1998) has introduced a useful taxonomy for distinguishing the form of currency instability that can (appear to be) be contagious. First, there are the 'monsoonal' effects, by which is meant common external effects such as interest changes in developed economies. Second, there are 'spillover' effects which are represented by contagion of macro fundamentals across countries (brought about, for example, by trade relations). Finally there are (pure) contagion effects representing the transmission of bubbles or noise (which distorts asset prices away from fundamental value) across economies. Interpreting this in the context of the Asian crisis, one can argue that spillover (regional) effects were the reason for speculative attacks on the Hong Kong and Singapore dollars, while the contagion to other, more distant economies can be explained by reassessment of the fragility of financial systems in the emerging market economies.

However, the existence of bubbles in the domestic stock and real estate markets in the East Asian economies is also suggestive of the volatile nature of financial markets, driven not by fundamentals but by market psychology (see Shleifer (2000) for a nice review of the importance of these ideas in stock markets). The existence of bubbles as a source of the Asian financial crisis is a controversial issue. That (asset-price) bubbles did exist in a number of Asian economies prior to the crisis is well documented (see Corsetti et al. 1998) This certainly seems to have been the case in Japan in the early 1990s and subsequently in Thailand prior to the onset of the June 1997 crisis. There is, however, some disagreement about the extent to which Malaysia, Indonesia and South Korea were also suffering from 'bubbles' prior to contagion from the Thailand crisis in the summer of 1997. Recent work has looked at this issue (see, for example, Baig and Goldfajn 1998; Jeanne and Masson 1998) and found evidence for the existence of pure contagion effects of bubbles in Asia during the financial crisis.

A key issue is the extent to which such bubbles were the result of excessive exuberance or whether it was a product of poor regulation of financial markets and the failure of monetary policy to take the impact of such bubbles into account. We would argue that these latter effects are as much to blame for the asset price inflation as any market behaviour. Given wealth effects, asset-price inflation can quickly impact on the real economy, generating excessive demand and general price inflation. The policy of pegging the exchange rate does restrict policy makers in their monetary policy stance and, with the benefit of hindsight, it certainly seems that action should have been taken to calm the financial markets prior to the onset of the currency crisis. The IMF is known to have urged the Thai government to take action to deal with an increasing trade deficit in 1996 brought about by domestic demand growth and an appreciating real exchange rate.

To summarize, our view of the Asian crisis is that it was driven by fundamentals, relating to underdeveloped financial markets, poor regulation and inappropriate relationships between business, finance and political groups. That speculative pressure generated the crisis is without question but this was driven by the underlying fundamentals of the domestic economy and not by herd behaviour of the financial markets. However, we would argue that such behaviour can have important short-run effects and the next section analyses these and their policy implications.

THE SHORT-RUN EFFECTS OF THE CRISIS AND THE POLICY IMPLICATIONS

The prelude to the Asian financial crisis was one which saw asset-price inflation in a number of countries and overheating of the economies. We have already argued that such conditions required a policy response some time in advance of the onset of the crisis but that the exchange rate policy adopted prevented appropriate action from being taken. In this section we consider both the effects of the crisis and the policy implications.

The immediate aftermath of the collapse of the currency is panic in the financial markets. Those who cash their chips in first get the most for them, while those that wait in an orderly queue risk losing substantial amounts of money as asset prices fall. Once asset-price deflation takes hold, the banks find that they have overlent since the market value of the collateral underwriting the loans no longer covers the loans extended. Property developers begin to go bust, and banks' bad and doubtful debts begin to accumulate. It becomes clear that the government does not have the resources to guarantee the scale of expected losses in the banking sector. At this stage it is clear that banks' provisioning policy is important. We shall return to this point in the section on prevention of crises.

Unfortunately, the problems do not stop here, for there will be an impact on the real economy through (negative) 'wealth effects' on consumption and investment. There will also be an impact through the 'credit channel' in the sense that banks will become less willing to lend due to the need to divert capital to address the emerging bad-debt problem. A 'credit crunch' ensues, which leads to an increase in bankruptcy rates and a worsening bad-debt problem. Attempts to improve bank balance sheets by liquidating assets used as collateral exacerbate the situation by putting further downward pressure on asset prices and making it difficult for firms to protect their financial integrity as well as making a banking crisis more likely. This type of transmission mechanism is emphasized by Edison et al. (1998).

It is also the case that 'directed' lending and traditional associations (for example, between the largest banks and the chaebol in South Korea or lending to 'key' industries encouraged by governments) are important in this deflationary process. If the banks tend, for whatever reason, to support the larger enterprises, then small and medium-sized enterprises (SMEs) will suffer from tighter credit rationing. Given their dependence on banks for external finance, widespread SME failures can be expected. The 'credit crunch' is often exacerbated by increases in nominal interest rates. A brief review of literature on past crises (including the 1930s) would indicate that domestic interest rates should be reduced in financial crises. An increase is thus likely to be imposed from outside due to international linkages, for example, the need to stabilize a falling exchange rate. Under a variable rate loan system, rising nominal interest rates make loans more difficult to service and increase banks' exposure to credit risks (making them yet more cautious about lending). This further increases the incidence of bad debts as more and more households and firms become unable to service their loans. There will also be a similar effect on fiscal deficits as the cost of servicing government debt increases.

So far we have ignored depositor and shareholder responses to the increasingly evident deterioration in the banks' asset quality. In the absence of adequate deposit insurance, it is rational for depositors to panic and so, eventually, panic they will. In the Pacific and South-East Asia there have, so far, only been isolated incidences of 'bank runs' despite the obvious insolvency of many of the institutions. However, as shareholders begin to sell shares, banks find it costly to raise the capital necessary to cover the accumulating bad debts. Further, if, as in Japan, it is common for banks to be involved in cross-shareholding networks, declining bank share prices will undermine the assets of firms holding bank shares and, if the stock market itself begins to slide (possibly as a result of international linkages), then the assets of the banks holding large equity portfolios will be further impaired. To the extent that banks hold stocks and shares as collateral, their asset-price risk exposure is further increased. If, in addition, as in Japan, banks rely on unrealised capital gains to meet the Basle capital adequacy ratios, then declining share prices will eventually threaten their solvency.

In addition to the domestic reaction we must also take account of the significant impact of the withdrawal of international capital as a result of the bubble bursting. The bubble has attracted borrowing from abroad, which seemed fairly risk free because of the pegged exchange rate regime. However, these loans become impossible to service, let alone repay, given the collapse of the currency. There is no possibility that the investments made (outside the real estate sector) will be profitable enough at the new exchange rate. Thus the flow of international capital dries up as soon as the crisis hits. This also creates a problem for rescue of the bankrupt domestic banking sector which might be achieved through foreign purchase of existing commercial banks. As Thailand has found, there is substantial reluctance from international banks to buy into the domestic system unless the terms are very favourable. This reflects the perceived riskiness of such an inward investment strategy in the face of a highly uncertain economic and political environment.

Political instability seems to be an extremely important influence on capital flows. In work on the transition economies of Central and Eastern Europe, Dickinson and Mullineux (1996) found that capital inflows increased following the establishment of stable political regimes. This was particularly evident in Poland. Certainly outflows from Thailand and South Korea in response to the crisis seem to have been exacerbated by the uncertainty surrounding the stability of the government (note these reflect not only withdrawal of international capital but also capital flight). The key concern seems to have been over the incumbent governments' abilities to manage the economy effectively. Once political uncertainty enters the equation, the restoration of political stability appears to be a prerequisite for re-establishing macroeconomic stability and pushing forward the banking sector reform programme. Such stability will not only encourage less capital flight but create the incentive to make further investment in the domestic economy.

Exchange rate depreciation and loss of foreign exchange (through capital flight) exacerbates the domestic banking and wider financial crises. The domestic crisis is thus worsened by international financial linkages. Just as a panic involving an individual bank can lead, through panic and contagion via interbank exposures, to a domestic systemic banking crisis, a domestic financial crisis, through panic and contagion via international interbank linkages, can lead to a regional crisis (as in the Pacific and South-East Asia). In this respect the policy of Malaysia should be commented upon. She adopted a method of dealing with the issue by effectively cutting herself off from the global financial economy. While this might buy her time to sort out the domestic financial sector problems and hence avoid the additional problems of international financial contagion and overshooting the exchange rate, the decision seems to be motivated as much by political as economic calculation. Such a policy can only be a short-term stabilization measure and attempts to use it to shore up political positions are not likely to encourage a restoration of capital inflows when the current restrictions are eased.

The picture painted above is a dramatic collapse from one equilibrium to another. The first is characterized by high investment, a rapidly growing economy and asset-price inflation (a bubble) which is sustained for as long as the economy grows, the bubble is expected to continue and the exchange rate peg is maintained. The other is low investment equilibrium, where a banking crisis creates a credit crunch, bankruptcies generate a further collapse of investment, asset-price deflation exacerbates the credit crunch, and the international financial markets add to the domestic economic woes by withdrawing financial support. However, the latter equilibrium is itself a temporary one since the effect of panic in financial markets and banking sector response to the onset of the crisis is to make things much worse. Over time as the banking sector problems subside and confidence is restored in the economy, there will be a revival. This will also be fuelled by the increasingly competitive position of domestic industry as a result of the exchange rate depreciation and by the return of international capital. This is exactly the profile we have observed in some of the Asian economies most affected by the crisis. But what are the policy implications of this story of the short-run response to the onset of the crisis?

Clearly the main responsibility of policy makers in the short run is to re-establish confidence in the economy and to mitigate the impacts of asset-price deflation. The first actions should therefore be to restore stability. This, however, is not straightforward. The initial response (promoted by the IMF) was to increase interest rates. With the benefit of hindsight it can be argued that this was overdone. The problem is that an increase in interest rates will make matters worse rather than better as has been explained. Once the bubble collapses it is not just a matter of raising interest rates a small amount to stabilize financial markets. The herd instinct will take over and, irrespective of the underlying fundamentals, there will be a collapse in capital inflows into domestic financial institutions. The initial response should be to stabilize the financial markets by replacing the loss of private sector funding with international agency funding. The IMF clearly has a role to play here as lender of last resort. Of course, there are well-known moral hazard problems with such a role but Calomiris (1999) has presented some interesting ideas on how to overcome these problems.

The above analysis of the short-run effects of the crisis and the appropriate policy response is a second-best solution, since there are always going to be deadweight losses resulting from a crisis. Better to prevent the crisis in the first place. This requires policy to be flexible. Stockman (1999) suggests that flexible exchange rates are the appropriate exchange rate regime for a globalized financial system. However, for many emerging market economies there is value to be had from imposing a pegged exchange rate in order to achieve a credible stabilization policy. The real problem becomes one of exiting from the pegged exchange rate regime. Eichengreen (1998) has pointed out the difficulties associated with this strategy. Given the analysis of the lead into the crisis which we have given, we would suggest that it is important for policy makers to be transparent in their decision making. Thus we would argue that a number of indicators should be monitored (Kaminsky et al. (1998), have presented a detailed analysis of leading indicators of currency crises) and that once thresholds have been reached the policy is changed. This may allow for some speculation close to a threshold but the impact is limited by the policy response which will be triggered once the threshold is reached. Such a policy may appear to be rather mechanistic. We would suggest that it be operated flexibly; that is to say, policy may or may not be changed according to judgement at the time the threshold is reached.

To summarize, our analysis of the short-run effects of the crisis has highlighted the potential for over-reaction both in the banking sector (brought about by the need to build reserves against loan losses) and, more generally, the financial markets and as a result of herd behaviour. This implies that attempts to stabilize the financial markets through interest rate increases may do more harm than good. Far better, in our view, is a policy which is flexible and can respond to events prior to the crisis with a view to preventing it from happening.

FINANCIAL SECTOR DEVELOPMENT, GOVERNANCE AND REAL INVESTMENT

In this section we outline our analysis of what went wrong in the Asian economies prior to the crisis. In other words, what were the fundamental factors which drove some of the economies into a currency and banking crisis? We shall focus here on why there was such overinvestment by considering how financial structure has an impact upon corporate governance and hence why firms' objectives were severely distorted. In so doing we are able to draw policy lessons for the longer term.

In making investment decisions, firms should increase capital stock until the value of the firm is maximized. However, there may be other reasons why firms invest which have more to do with increasing the size of the firm than its profits. This will be the case particularly when corporate governance mechanisms are not operating effectively. The choice of firms' financial structure can be an important determinant of this.

In a world without distortions (such as differential taxation, market imperfections or bankruptcy costs) the way in which that investment is financed is immaterial to the optimum level of capital. This was the argument put forward by Modigliani and Miller (1958) (MM) in seminal work. However, this result is not likely to hold for a number of reasons. In particular, the problem of asymmetric information and the resulting agency problems (whereby managers may have different objectives from the owners), imperfections in the capital markets (such as a limited access to different types of finance) and positive bankruptcy costs (which cannot be diversified away) all cause the breakdown of the MM result. Although most attention has been paid to the financial structure of firms, at a macroeconomic level, these arguments suggest that the development of the overall financial system can be important to the way in which firms behave and are governed. For example, a bank-dominated financial system may be associated with ownership arrangements and management relationships which can encourage cronyism and corruption. Such arrangements will not be conducive to well-judged decisions about future investment strategy. Alternatively a market-based system may focus on short-term profits at the expense of longer-term projects.

Beyond the overall financial system structure there are other ways in which the external environment can affect the firms' decision making. First, we consider the overall health of an economy. At a time when the economy is growing strongly then bankruptcy costs are reduced. To justify this, note that bankruptcy costs relate to the additional costs imposed by having to liquidate the assets of the firm. But the ability to sell assets is a function of the state of the economy and we would expect the discount necessary to find a buyer would fall as the economy grows strongly, for two reasons: (i) the risk premium will reduce since the probability of market expansion exceeds that of contraction; and (ii) the market for capital goods will be relatively liquid, reducing the liquidity premium. In addition, as the general well-being of the economy increases, the probability of bankruptcy reduces (although note that this does not necessarily imply that bankruptcies themselves decline since this depends on the number of new projects (enterprises) created). Hence there may be lower costs involved in making poor investment decisions; this could encourage excessive investment being undertaken.

Furthermore, monitoring of the actions of managers (by banks or share-holders) can reduce the agency problems which motivate some of the reasons for the importance of financial structure. But part of the cost of monitoring is information gathering. In a strongly growing economy, then, there are incentives to reduce these costs since the benefits of acquiring information are reduced. Low interest rates may have a similar effect since monitoring costs are not likely to be related to interest rates.

If there is also the possibility for monitor capture then we can move from lack of corporate governance to bad governance. This can become apparent when there is cross-ownership of shareholdings between banks and enterprises. The problems will be further exacerbated when regulatory and supervisory agencies develop too slowly and hence are unable to provide an appropriate level of monitoring of the banking system. However, the external environment is a major determinant of whether and how these problems become serious. Thus in a rapidly growing economy (or where interest rates are low) the existence of high returns to most investment masks the inefficiency resulting from the lack of governance mechanisms. It is only when the economy starts to run into difficulties that the negative impact of inappropriate business relationships starts to surface. These conditions then feed on each other as banks and other financial institutions attempt to save themselves from the consequences of their past decisions. In other words, it is vital to have properly functioning corporate control mechanisms during the good times even if they do not seem to have major effects, since the misallocation of finance and the lack of corporate governance will cause later problems.

A further issue which appears as a result of underdeveloped financial markets is the increasing short-term nature of financial commitments, largely through debt, which firms take on. This reflects that the limited supply of long-term debt finance (corporate bonds markets are not well developed) and the consequent need for firms to resort to the short-term end of the market. Quite clearly this increases the risks which firms face since they are exposed to the possibility that debt will not be renewed at maturity. In addition there is less incentive for debt holders to monitor the actions of the firm properly, since the planning horizon is shortened as debt maturity declines and much lending has real estate as collateral; this seems to provide adequate insurance in rising asset markets. The lack of variety in domestic financial assets also creates an incentive for firms to look to foreign markets for investment finance. This can create problems since foreign debt holders are unlikely to monitor, either as effectively, or at as low a cost, as domestic lenders. Hence there will be more emphasis placed on short-term maturities. Thus, firms are more likely to make high-risk investments, which are not in debt-holders' interest, as a consequence of a lack of corporate control.

A third area of concern relates to the role of the government sector. It is well recognized that it is important for markets to be given as much freedom as possible to promote economic efficiency. Hence when governments interfere in promoting finance for industrial investment they interfere with market mechanisms in two ways. Initially such directed investment may result in funds being transferred into less-productive sectors than would be found in a free market. In addition, the government may increase total investment beyond its optimum level, thus generating intertemporal inefficiencies. Beyond this, however, we can argue that such direct intervention creates distortions in the control mechanisms. First, managers may find that they can ignore the constraints which debt might impose upon them. Second, the very act of government intervention will reduce the monitoring capacity of financial structure. Holders of debt may well expect the government to underwrite the debt. In order to correct this distortion it is important for government to play a limited role in directing investment, concentrating on (infrastructure) projects where an element of public good appears.

A further issue of great significance is the overall legal framework within which financial markets (or more generally the private sector) operates. Recent work by La Porta et al. (1998) and Demirguc-Kunt and Maksimovic (1998) highlight this issue. La Porta et al. provide an analysis of the legal rules governing the relationship between corporations and their shareholders and creditors in 49 countries and Demirguc-Kunt and Maksimovic how differences between financial and legal systems generate different growth performance. Of particular interest to our work are the structures operating in the Asian countries which have experienced the effects of the financial crisis. Thus (English) Common Law, which has the greatest legal protection for shareholders and creditors, is used as the basis of the legal system in Malaysia, Singapore and Thailand. Meanwhile Indonesia and the Philippines use French Civil Law which has the weakest protection. Japan, South Korea and Taiwan have a system which is similar to the German Civil Law and which provides an intermediate position between the other two. On this basis there appears to be significant diversity across the region and hence the legal system does not seem to have been a major factor. However, as pointed out by Demirguc-Kunt and Maksimovic, it is not the legal system itself, but how well it is enforced that is important. On this basis we observe that those countries which are less effective in enforcing laws are the ones most exposed to the financial crisis. Note that a number of countries (Thailand is an early example) have revised (or are considering revision of) bankruptcy laws to provide greater protection to creditors and to speed up the restructuring of banks and industrial firms.

Of particular interest is that generally the ownership concentration (based on the percentage of shares owned by the largest three shareholders for the ten biggest firms in each country) is rather high for several countries in the region (Malaysia, Thailand, Indonesia and the Philippines). The figures for Japan and South Korea are very low but reflect the nature of the cross-shareholding which make both countries unique. Taiwan has very dispersed share ownership and is also the country which has been least affected by the problems afflicting the region. A possible rationale for this relates to the interaction between the business community and the political process. When ownership is concentrated there is opportunity for inappropriate relationships to arise. Government policy may be tailored to fit the particular objectives of big business. Hence we could have a situation arise where the government preserved a pegged exchange rate system in order to protect a business community which was heavily exposed to foreign currency borrowing.

We can use the above analysis to explain contagion effects which, as pointed out earlier, have apparently occurred during the Asian financial crisis.

We would argue that since we can characterize the fundamentals of each economy as being similar, then it is this similarity that is driving the apparent bubble contagion. Although Thailand was the first economy to suffer effectively this was the trigger which forced international investors to revise their view of a number of similar economies with similar structure. Hence the problems in South Korea, Indonesia and Malaysia reflect the underlying problems of lack of financial development, poor regulation and the potential for crony capitalism, resulting in the consequent corporate governance issues which we have discussed in this section.

To conclude this part of the section, it may appear that part of our argument implies that the problems were inevitable, since we have argued that strongly growing economies are likely to experience, to a greater extent, the sort of problems we have identified. We would not wish for this to be our central message. Essentially we are arguing that, since the problems are likely to be greater for strongly growing economies there is even more reason for policy makers to take appropriate action to prevent their worst consequences. Note that this conclusion holds whether the economy is open to international capital markets or not, although the consequences of the problems are far greater when a country has abandoned any controls over capital movements.

We now turn to consider the implications of our analysis for policy response to the crisis. We focus, particularly, on the structural issues since we have argued that this has been a root cause of the problems. We start with banking sector problems and an overhaul of the regulatory system.

Beyond the need to achieve immediate financial stability, which as we have argued will need international assistance, it is necessary to tackle the domestic bank bad-debt problem. This has been the most difficult part of the process. Thailand, which has struggled with this still unresolved issue, closed 57 finance companies once the crisis hit but has delayed far longer dealing with the large commercial banks. They have tried to encourage foreign investment into the banking sector but, so far, with little success, probably because the risks are still perceived to be too great and hence foreign interests require too large a (risk) discount on the underlying value of the bank. Indonesia has had to face up to the need to close banks and take others into state ownership but its piecemeal approach sparked a run on deposits. Japan is famous for its dithering, brought about by political inertia. The need for state involvement is fairly clear and hence there is a cost to the taxpayer. But vested business interests are probably the most likely cause of the delays, at least outside of Japan, where taxpayer opposition was evident. There has to be an element of punishment for shareholders and one method is for the state to buy the bank for a nominal sum and then clear it of bad debts to sell on later. This has been used successfully in the past, for example, in Sweden. The cost of this strategy can be quite low since the government can wait until market conditions improve before turning the bank back into private hands and hence selling assets into a rising market.

It has been argued that a proper deposit insurance system should be in place for the future. However, it is important to recognize that such a scheme can create problems itself. In particular, there is a moral hazard problem that a bank with deposit insurance will engage in excessively risky loans in order to maximize shareholder return. A risk-related premium schedule and a guarantee for only smaller deposits would assist in avoiding the moral hazard issue, but it will never be fully resolved. Hence reducing the coverage of the scheme over time is desirable as a disciplining device (but difficult to operate in practice). What should not be allowed is an implicit lender-of-last-resort function to be taken on by the central bank so that any failing bank feels it has a safeguard. Of course there is always the 'too big to fail' argument and this may require special regulatory response, perhaps through extra disclosure requirements and higher premiums, and by penalizing shareholders through nationalization prior to restructuring.

In order to prevent a recurrence of the crisis, banks should be required to hold sufficient capital to cover non-diversifiable (credit and market) 'risks', acknowledging that we live in a world of uncertainty (and hence should err on the side of caution and 'worst-case' scenarios in setting minimum risk-related capital adequacy ratios). The amount of capital banks need to cover their risk exposures varies over the business cycle. In periods of rapid growth (as experienced by the Asian 'Tiger economies' in the couple of decades before the crisis) banks can be tempted to run down capital and tend to fail to build up general loan loss provisions against future bad loans. During drawn-out, and seemingly continuous, expansions (the business cycle persists, but people live in perpetual hope that the last recession was indeed the last ever), a sort of Ponzi finance starts to develop, under which banks lend to borrowers who can only possibly pay if growth continues at currently prevailing rates. Even a slowdown can make it difficult for borrowers to service loans (as in Thailand). Such developments are clearly magnified if the rapid growth period culminates in an asset-price 'bubble', which bursts; again as in Thailand. Bad financial habits can thus become endemic, and when the slowdown ('growth recession') occurs and the incidence of bad and doubtful debts increases, banks are revealed to be underprovisioned. Banks should be forced to build up loan loss reserves in good times (a buffer stock) so that they can be nourished by them in the winter of the recession; this has the added benefit of reducing the ability of the banking system to fuel the bubble economy. The bad and doubtful debt provisions should, therefore, display an anti-cyclical pattern. More commonly, banks find themselves being forced to make provisions when they can least afford to and, as a result, the credit crunch is exacerbated. However, like other (over)optimists, banks also tend to believe in the 'premature death' of the business cycle. Supervisors should adopt a pessimistic stance.

Banks should abide by overexposure and overconcentration rules, particularly important when the business community is dominated by a relatively small number of individual families. They should not lend too much to individual borrowers or sectors of the economy, otherwise the borrowers can hold the bank (indirectly the government) to ransom, because the bank cannot afford to let them fail. Mismatching by maturity and currency are major sources of risk and should be monitored carefully by supervisors. Generally, the trend is towards letting banks engage in whatever financial activities they wish, provided they have enough capital to cover non-diversifiable risks. Prohibitive and prescriptive rules are being swept away. With good cause, however, supervisors encourage diversification of lending (and increasingly diversification into wider financial services, that is, 'universal banking' and 'bancassurance') to reduce average risk. Increasingly they also keep close watch on exposure to property, stock and futures markets, since these have been sources of numerous recent bank losses (with property market exposure causing the most frequent and biggest problems of the last couple of decades).

Increasingly, supervisors worldwide are adopting variations on the US CAMEL (capital adequacy, asset quality, management quality, expected earnings and liquidity) system for judging the quality of banks. Asset quality is particularly important since there is a danger that inexperienced domestic banks operating in emerging markets might effectively develop into 'pyramid schemes', attracting deposits by posting competitive interest rates and yet doing very little lending and thus not developing an asset portfolio to support their commitments to depositors. Such banks can often make a profit if they can take advantage of slow payment systems to benefit from inflation, but they face severe difficulties if inflation falls dramatically as a result of successful macroeconomic stabilization programmes (for example, Brazil and Russia in the early 1990s).

Another trend is to require greater disclosure of information (increased 'transparency') in the hope that this will create greater market discipline, perhaps by creating the opportunity for credit-rating agencies to develop and for institutional investors and other shareholders to become more active. However, enhanced reporting requirements are not enough, since it is not just the quantity of data that matters. Quality assurance is also required. This is where the auditing process comes into play. The UK relies heavily on the auditing of company (including bank) accounts. The USA puts greater emphasis on on-site expectations of banks than the UK, and is probably right to do so given the potential conflicts of interest faced by auditors, whose employing accounting firms are also trying to sell consultancy services. On-site inspections by supervisors are, however, expensive. Some countries have lists of recognized bank auditors who are required to revolve periodically so that they do not become too close to bank management. The appropriate frequency of on-site inspections is difficult to gauge. Particular attention needs to be paid to disclosure rules relating to bad and doubtful debts, which the banks must be prevented from hiding. The US system requires disclosure of loans on which interest and principal has not been paid for so many days. The longer the period since the last payment, the greater the provisioning required. The system is scaled with various thresholds and seems eminently transferable to other countries.

With an adequate flow of rigorously audited information, a comprehensive funded deposit insurance scheme with risk-related premia, and sufficient capital to cover non-diversifiable and non-insured (through derivatives) risks, there should be few surprises emanating from the banking sector. Exceptions might arise due to undetected internal fraud. Hence supervisors should also ensure that 'internal controls' are adequate and that managers and traders have 'incentive-compatible contracts'. Some academics and regulators are also considering forcing the senior management of banks to enter into contracts with the regulators, with dire financial consequences for the managers if they break those contracts (see, for example, Kupiec and O'Brien 1995). Again the idea is to achieve an incentive-compatible solution; building on the concept underlying the risk-related capital adequacy ratios recommended by the Basle Committee (which effectively 'tax' risk taking by requiring banks with more risks in their asset portfolios to hold more capital to cover those risks), which are being adopted increasingly widely in domestic banking sectors around the world. It is probable, however, that banks in developing, transition and emerging market economies should hold more capital to cover the risks they are exposed to than the *minimum* levels recommended by the Basle Committee.

Finally, the appropriate institutional structure for financial supervision is currently unclear. Many countries have dedicated banking commissions, which propose revisions to bank regulation and undertake supervision. In other countries these tasks are undertaken by the central bank or the finance ministry. As banks diversify, the question arises as to whether a single financial service regulator is preferable to having a number of sectorally orientated (for example, banking, insurance, securities and so on) regulators. In the UK in 1998, responsibility for banking supervision was removed from the Bank of England (though it remains responsible for assuring systemic financial stability) and vested in a new Financial Services Authority, which is to be made responsible for supervising (most of) the wider financial system. In 1998 Japan made a similar move, transferring responsibility for supervising banks and securities firms from the finance ministry to a new financial supervisory agency. In both countries newly independent central banks were left to concentrate on setting monetary policy.

Apart from bank regulation we have also argued that the limited nature of the financial sector in terms of the type of institutions, has been a contributory factor to the crisis. In other words, development of the financial sector has not kept pace with the real sector. Thus a further policy issue concerns promoting the creation of non-bank financial institutions and markets. The development of financial markets is not something which is evidently under the control of policy but there are various measures which can assist in widening the scope of the financial markets. First, tax systems often imply favourable treatment of bank lending relative to other forms of finance. Hence any distortion should be corrected. As an intermediate stage it may also be desirable to use the tax system to favour other non-bank sources of finance such as corporate bonds. The development of stock markets should also be given priority, itself not necessarily easy given that many firms are in a fairly parlous financial state.

Transparency of financial accounting is an obvious requirement of a properly functioning stock market. In addition, companies should be required to provide basic information about the way that they are run. For example, it is now standard practice to provide information on the size of the board, the age of directors and compensation packages (at least in the aggregate). But information about the individual pay of directors, their equity holdings (particularly in related enterprises or in the financial sector) and the role and identity of non-executive directors (if they exist) and whether they are members of other boards of directors, would also assist in making corporate decision making clearer. The role of cross-shareholdings is a particularly important issue when this involves potential conflicts of interest (for example, when banks and firms hold each other's equity). So is the link between the corporate sector and political parties. Information on donations above a certain level should be routinely included in company statements.

It is interesting to speculate what would have happened in these economies if there had been a much more diversified ownership and financial structure of enterprises. Clearly there is no guarantee that this would have prevented the excesses that led to the bubble economy, but it could be argued that the relationship between financial, business and political communities would have been at least more transparent. A thorough review of the legal framework with a view to promoting (small) investor protection should be undertaken. Some of the measures outlined above, designed to make corporate decision making more transparent, will assist in this regard. However, it is very important to ensure that the rule of law is upheld. One way of doing this would be to set up an independent watchdog which has the sole aim of monitoring the legal framework governing investment in financial assets, with a view to highlighting any anomalies and irregular behaviour. Such agencies appear regularly in developed financial markets. A further mechanism for promoting a more open system of corporate governance would be to establish a set of rules which firms would be expected to follow in reporting to and taking account of the interests of their shareholders. The issue of corporate governance is one which is being examined increasingly in developed economies with a view to ensuring that powerful interests do not ride roughshod over minority groupings. Recently in the UK we have had the Cadbury Committee report on corporate governance (for an excellent review of its conclusions, see Dimsdale and Prevezer 1994) as well as further reviews by the Greenbury and Hempel committees. One suggestion has been to give more powers to non-executive directors as monitors of the company performance. It has also been suggested that executive pay should be related to profitability and not to volume of sales or company size. The role of stakeholders has also been highlighted (these can include a company's workforce, its customers and the general public). While each of these recommendations has been devised in the context of developed stock market systems they reflect a general concern that the creation of financial institutions and markets is not a sufficient condition for efficient allocation of capital. It has been argued that lack of financial development has been one of the causes of the problems seen in South-East Asia. But a general recommendation to promote financial development will not solve the problem. These markets must work properly and using the experience of the UK (for example) can help to make this happen.

CONCLUSIONS AND IMPLICATION FOR CEE ECONOMIES

In this chapter we have reviewed the causes of the Asian financial crisis of 1997–98. We have considered the extent to which explanations have relied upon fundamentals compared to pure expectational forces. In the case of the former, little blame for the crisis can be attributed to the speculative nature of financial markets while in the latter case the countries affected can feel rightly aggrieved that their economies have been so damaged.

We take a middle approach which identifies the core reasons for the financial crisis as being due to domestic economic fundamentals but that expectational forces did matter as a propagation mechanism. Thus there were multiple equilibria and the crises can be attributed to a switch from one equilibrium to another. Furthermore we do not attribute much of the resulting regional problems to pure contagion effects. In particular, the identification of institutional problems in one country caused a crisis of confidence in neighbouring countries which had similar institutional structures (we can class these as spillover effects). Thus while the bubble bursting was the initial cause of the crisis, there was no direct contagion of this bubble from one country to another.

The major lessons which can be drawn from the Asian crisis are that institutional features are a very important determinant of economic performance and that failure to impose proper regulatory and legal control over the operation of the financial sector will have real consequences. What then are the observations we can make about lessons for the CEE economies? There are a number which we would wish to flag up.

1. *There are very significant dangers in pegging the exchange rate while liberalizing the financial sector* The credibility of the pegged exchange rate created the perception of riskless currency transformation. As a consequence, large-scale capital inflows were encouraged, intermediated through the banking system. A more developed financial system would have been able to diversify the risks involved by promoting equity investment as well as through debt. Once the currency peg was broken, the domestic financial (banking) system was under enormous stress.

2. *If it is desirable to have a currency peg there must be mechanisms through which exit from the system is both orderly and transparent* When there is a need to use a pegged exchange rate for stabilization purposes there should also be a clear mechanism for moving to a more flexible system. One indicator which could be used is the level of capital inflows, or the foreign currency exposure of the domestic banking system (which could, potentially, reduce the incentive for the domestic banks to acquire foreign currency debt). Widening of target bands is one way of transitioning from a pegged to a flexible exchange rate system in a relatively smooth way.

3. *There must be proper regulation of the banking system with appropriate measurement of, and provisioning against, the risks faced* It has been argued that banks may well understate the risks of lending in fast-growing economies, possibly because they are inexperienced, but also because the costs of mismeasurement are relatively low. The regulatory authorities must ensure that regulations are made tough enough that the incentives are in place to prevent banks understating the risks they face.

4. *Development of non-bank financial institutions is to be encouraged* The over-reliance on the banking system, the potential for regulators to be captured by the banks, and the close relationship between finance, banks and politicians, can all create the potential for failure of corporate governance mechanisms. Encouraging a liquid and encompassing stock market, where foreign equity holders can exert proper control, with small shareholders' rights protected, will encourage a much more efficient role for financial markets.

5. *Liberalization brings risks as well as rewards* Although capital inflows offer large benefits for economies which are starved of funds for capital investment these can bring risks (volatile financial markets, potential reversal and currency crises) which need to be properly managed. As we have argued, it is important for regulation to be strict enough, and for

monetary policy to be flexible enough, to deal with these risks. If the risks are recognized then decisions can be made in an appropriate way.

6. *State involvement invariably leads to distortions in financial markets* One response to the Asian crisis has been to argue that exposure to the whims of international capital is not to be encouraged. Malaysia appears to have been relatively successful in its navigation through troubled waters by imposing and then slowly relaxing capital controls. Now there is a recovery in Asia there seems to be less enthusiasm for structural reforms and discussion is focusing on how to develop a sustainable pegged exchange rate regime. However, this is not a lesson for CEE economies. There is still much to be done to protect the financial systems of the crisis-hit Asian economies against the consequences of another crisis. The state should rapidly withdraw from any direct involvement in the running of the financial system and should ensure that there are no perceptions of future government guarantees which will distort resource allocation. Its role should be to ensure that the legal system protects all investors while making them aware of the risks involved in their decisions.

The challenges facing the CEE economies are great as they integrate more fully into the European Union. They will need to adapt to specific problems which have not been discussed in this chapter. However, if they can learn the lessons from the Asian economies they will, at least, be in a better position to deal with the impact of greater exposure to the international capital markets, and as a consequence avoid some of the dangers which these markets bring.

REFERENCES

Baig, T. and I. Goldfajn (1998), 'Financial market contagion in the Asian crisis', IMF Research Department, Working Paper, WP/98/155.
Burnside, C., M. Eichenbaum and S. Rebelo (1998), 'Prospective deficits and the Asian currency crises', Centre for Economic Policy Research Discussion Paper Series, no. 2015.
Calomiris C. (1999), 'Building an incentive-compatible safety net' *Journal of Banking and Finance*, **23**, 1499–519.
Corsetti, G., P. Pensenti and N. Roubini (1998), 'What caused the Asian currency and financial crisis? Part 1: A macroeconomic overview', National Bureau of Economic Reseach Working Papers Series, no. 6833, Cambridge, MA, NBER.
Demirguc-Kunt, A. and V. Maksimovic (1998), 'Law, finance and firm growth', *Journal of Finance*, **53**, 2107–37.
Dickinson, D.G. (2000), 'Investment, finance and firms' objectives: implications for the recent experience of South East Asian economies', in D.G. Dickinson, J.L. Ford, M.J. Fry, A.W. Mullineux and S. Sens (eds), *Finance, Governance and Economic Performance in Pacific and South East Asia*, Cheltenham: Edward Elgar.

Dickinson, David G. and Andy W. Mullineux (1996), 'Currency convertibility, policy credibility and capital flight in Poland and the CSFR', Chapter 5 in Thomas D. Willet, Richard Sweeney and Clas Wihlborg (eds), *Capital Account Issues in Liberalising Economics*, Boulder, CO: Westview Press.

Dimsdale, N. and M. Prevezer (1994), *Capital Markets and Corporate Governance*, Oxford: Clarendon Press.

Edison, H.J., P. Luangaram and M. Miller (1998), 'Asset bubbles, domino effects and "lifeboats": elements of the East Asian crisis', International Finance Discussion paper Series, Federal Reserve Board, no. 606.

Eichengreen, B. (1998), 'Kicking the habit: moving from pegged rates to greater exchange rate flexibility', *Economic Journal*, **109**, C1–C14.

Flood, R. and N. Marion (1998), 'Perspectives on the recent currency crisis literature', National Bureau of Economic Research Working Paper Series, no. 6380.

Fry, Maxwell J. (1997), *Money, Interest and Banking in Economic Development*, 2nd edn, Baltimore, MD: Johns Hopkins University Press.

Jeanne, O. and P. Masson (1998), 'Currency crises, sunspots and Markov-switching regimes', Centre for Economic Policy Research Discussion Paper Series, International Macroeconomics, no. 1990.

Kaminsky, G., S. Lizondo and C. Reinhart (1998), 'Leading indicators of currency crises', *IMF Staff Papers*, **45**, 1–48.

Kaminsky, G.L. and C.M. Reinhart (1999), 'The twin-crises: the causes of banking and balance-of-payments problems', *American Economic Review*, **89**(3), June, 473–500.

Kindleberger, Charles, P. (1996), *Manics, Panics and Crashes: A History of Financial Crises*, New York: John Wiley & Sons, Inc.

Krugman, P. (1997), 'What happened to Asia?', mimeo, Cambridge, MA: MIT.

Kupiec, Paul H. and James M. O'Brien (1995), 'Recent developments in bank capital regulation of market risks', Finance and Economic Discussion Series, 95–51, December, Washington, DC: Federal Reserve Board.

La Porta, R., F. Lopez-de-Silanes, A. Shleifer and R.W. Vishny (1998), 'Law and finance', *Journal of Political Economy*, **106**, 1113–55.

Masson, P. (1998), 'Contagion: monsoonal effects, spillovers, and jumps between multiple equilibria', IMF Research Department, Working Paper, WP/98/142.

Mishkin, F. (2000), 'Financial policies and the prevention of financial crises in emerging market countries', paper prepared for National Bureau of Economic Reseach conference 'Economic and Financial Crises in Emerging Market Countries', Cambridge, MA: NBER.

Modigliani, F. and M. Miller (1958), 'The cost of capital, corporation finance and the theory of investment', *American Economic Review*, **48**, 261–97.

Obstfeld, M. (1996), 'Models of currency crises with self-fulfilling features', *European Economic Review*, **40**, April, 1037–47.

Radelet, S. and J. Sachs (1998), 'The onset of the East Asian financial crisis', National Bureau of Economic Research Working Paper Series, no. 6680.

Rajan, R.G. and L. Zingales (2000), 'Which capitalism? Lessons from the East Asian crisis', Working Paper, Chicago: University of Chicago (forthcoming in *Journal of Applied Corporate Finance*).

Shleifer, A. (2000), *Inefficient Markets: An Introduction to Behavioural Finance*, Oxford: Oxford University Press.

Stockman, A. (1999), 'Choosing an exchange rate system', *Journal of Banking and Finance*, **23**, 1483–98.

11. Joining EMU as an irreversible investment

David G. Dickinson and Jean-Baptiste Desquilbet

INTRODUCTION

The Central and Eastern European (CEE) and the European Union (EU) countries are conducting their negotiations for the former to join the latter. A key issue is the assessment of the benefits of accession for both sides. Certainly from a political perspective there is considerable enthusiasm for the project. From an economic point of view there is also substantial evidence that membership of the EU will significantly benefit the CEE economies. One influential study which considers this is Baldwin et al. (1997).[1] They argue that the trade aspects of enlargement are important and positive but, much more significant is a reduction in the risk premium and hence real interest rates in CEE countries. As they point out, accumulation effects (from increases in the capital stock) are much larger, in the long run, than allocation effects (from more efficient use of current resources).

Beyond reductions in real interest rates, we have much evidence to suggest that improved trade opportunities can have a major beneficial impact on growth (for example, see Baldwin and Seghezza 1996; Cameron et al. 1998; Coe et al. 1997). Another potentially important channel is through foreign direct investment (FDI) and the resulting productivity improvements. Membership of the EU is seen as one way of making the CEE countries more attractive as production bases for multinational enterprises. Certainly later entrants to the EU such as Spain, Portugal and Ireland seem to have benefited from this effect. Hence FDI may be particularly important for the CEE transition economies although the current evidence on the effects of FDI has been mixed (see Djankov and Hoekman 1998). Thus in assessing the benefits of EU membership we should consider the pattern of trade and capital flows and how these may change in response to membership of the EU.

However, many of the benefits of EU membership will only be fully realized once the CEE countries have adopted the single European currency. In particular, convergence of real interest rates between CEE economies and the

EU is, at least partly, related to the decision to participate in European Monetary Union (EMU). This is not something which Baldwin et al. consider although, as mentioned, they place great emphasis on the likely fall in real interest rates which will accompany membership of the EU. While it is true that membership of the EU is likely to bring down real interest rates from their current levels (for example, by giving increased future economic stability and hence a reduction in any risk premium required by investors) we may note that adoption of the single European currency has been the main impetus to convergence of interest rates among the current member countries. Furthermore, the trade and foreign direct investment benefits of membership will only be fully realized once CEE countries are using the single European currency.

The approach we shall use to analyse this decision, concerning membership of the single currency, is adapted from the recent literature on irreversible investment. We argue that this is a useful way to proceed since it allows us to highlight that uncertainty about, rather than the size of, the future costs and benefits of joining the eurozone are important in determining the timing of the decision to join EMU (note that Baldwin et al. also emphasize the importance of timing of the EU membership decision). Of course the size of benefits and costs are important but if we assume that, in the long run, the net benefits of membership are positive, it is the stochastic pattern of these net benefits which will be crucial to the timing of the membership decision. Thus it is the future stochastic behaviour of the economy which will determine the option value of the policy decision to join the single currency. Hence we introduce a further perspective on the issue of EMU membership, by highlighting the factors which are important in influencing the uncertainty about costs and benefits of that membership.

The chapter is divided into three further sections. In the next section we consider the basis for modelling the decision to join the eurozone as an irreversible investment and relate the optimum decision to current domestic economic volatility. In the third section we discuss measurement of this uncertainty and hence consider what is the optimum policy option for CEE countries which join the EU. The fourth section draws together the main conclusions and looks at extensions to the analysis.

CHOICE OF CURRENCY REGIME AS AN IRREVERSIBLE INVESTMENT

As the CEE countries approach accession to the EU they face a variety of choices with regard to the currency regime. They can choose a flexible exchange rate, peg against one currency or a basket of several, or choose to follow a path which will result in replacement of their domestic currency with the single European currency. Of course, how quickly the last option can be implemented is not just a decision of the CEE countries but a function of the speed at which they are able to meet the various convergence criteria attached to membership of the single currency. In this respect, the choice that they make on exchange rate policy will have to be made in advance of their accession, since the process of convergence needs to be started well in advance.[2]

The early literature on optimum currency areas (Mundell 1961; McKinnon 1963) emphasized the trade benefits but also highlighted the need for business cycles to be consistent across countries. These ideas have been used extensively in discussing the decision of existing EU members to join EMU. They are also relevant in discussing the stochastic nature of the net benefits of membership of the single European currency. We can identify a number of factors which are important.

1. *Patterns of trade* Maintaining the stability of exchange rates with major trading partners should enhance trade (although the evidence on this is mixed see, for example, Kenan and Rodrick 1986; Chowdhury 1993). Thus trade relations with existing EMU members (relative to those who are outside) is important in determining the benefits of pegging to, or eventually adopting, the euro. However, as Frankel and Rose (1996) point out, trade patterns may not be exogenous to the choice of currency regime so that maintaining stability with another currency may increase trade between those countries. In addition, trade will depend upon the macroeconomic health of the trading partners. For example, a Europe which is growing will enhance trading relations with potential new members. Alternatively, a world recession will have a negative affect.

    Hence the actual response of trade to the exchange rate regime which CEE countries adopt, is a source of uncertainty. We can make some estimate of this by considering the existing pattern of trade. Increasing exchange rate uncertainty with a major trading partner would be expected to have a negative impact while the reverse should also hold true. So we can use these existing patterns of trade as a benchmark for assessing the impact of CEE economies joining EMU.

2. *The performance of the euro* The choice of pegging to the euro (and eventually adopting the currency) means that the domestic economy's relationship to other trading partner currencies is also determined. For example, the Czech Republic can peg its currency to the euro but its relationship to the US dollar will then depend upon the relative economic performance of Europe and the United States and also the policy taken by the respective central banks towards managing the euro/dollar exchange rate. Also the possibility of the euro becoming an international reserve

currency will have important repercussions on countries which are pegging to it.[3] We can view these issues as influencing the uncertainty about the benefits of membership of the single currency.

3. *The relative flexibility of the domestic economy* As has been widely discussed in the context of EMU, a single currency requires other nominal values to be flexible. Thus pegging a currency against economies which are less flexible will imply that the burden of adjustment to asymmetric shocks will fall upon the more flexible economy. This may not be costly if flexibility is maintained. But the decision to join the EU may affect the relative flexibility of the CEE economies. For example, the performance of EU labour markets has been a cause for concern and how membership of the EU will adversely affect CEE labour markets is consequently important.[4] If CEE economies become less flexible as a result of EU membership then they will be subject to greater real volatility as nominal (exchange rate) flexibility falls. Hence any (asymmetric) shock will be the source of greater uncertainty. Note that the probability of an asymmetric shock is greater the less integrated the economy is with the EU (trade and business-cycle patterns are not closely related). So this implies that the early stages of EU membership are likely to exhibit a greater chance of asymmetric shocks and hence greater volatility surrounding the benefits of euro membership.

4. *The development of the financial sector* As has been observed with the recent financial crisis in South-East Asia, problems arise when the financial sectors fails to develop at a speed consistent with the real sector. Increasing reliance on foreign borrowing, encouraged by a pegged exchange rate, can create an unsustainable situation. The importance of FDI in providing a source of investment finance is also relevant here. The greater this flow, and indeed it is seen as one of the potential benefits of EU membership, the faster the economy can grow. Although portfolio investment can be a mechanism for improving access to finance and hence promoting investment, it also creates additional volatility in that such flows are (probably) easier to reverse. Note also that financial sectors at different stages of development create a greater possibility of asymmetric (monetary) shocks. A financial sector which is relatively underdeveloped is one which is likely to be the cause of greater concern than one which is well developed and which has well-managed banks and strong regulatory agencies.[5]

This is certainly not a comprehensive list but will serve for the particular focus we wish to take here. We assume that membership of a single currency is economically desirable, and concentrate instead on how current economic volatility affects when that decision should be made. The logic, which is taken from the irreversible investment literature (see Dixit and Pindyck 1993), is as follows. A country has a policy choice about the exchange rate regime. It can choose to keep the regime as it currently is or to give up its own independent currency in favour of a single European currency. But the decision to join a single currency is irreversible. This does not mean that a country could not withdraw from such an arrangement (although this could be very difficult and itself incur costs) but that it will not recover the costs of joining in the first place. We can think of these costs as being those incurred in order to meet the convergence criteria which are imposed on potential members of the common currency area. They can involve, for example, the need to cut government deficits and the impact of adopting an exchange rate pegged to the euro in preparation for monetary union. These will have adverse consequences for the economies involved since the real sector does not adjust instantaneously. Thus we shall observe increased unemployment, lower growth rates and social costs from reduced government expenditure. We would expect the current level of economic instability to be a determining factor of these costs since a higher level will make the achievement of the necessary conditions more difficult.

The other side of the modelling process is to consider the (net) benefits of joining the single currency. These will depend upon the impact of the single currency on trade and on financial market performance. But the key aspect which we wish to emphasize is that the stochastic flow of these benefits will be related to the level of economic volatility which the countries are currently facing. Thus we can argue that the benefits to trade will depend upon how much trade is currently disrupted by domestic economic volatility. Similarly the reduction in real interest rates will be related to the current level of the risk premium which is, itself, a function of current domestic economic instability. Third, the actual process of joining EMU will immediately impart a significant amount of economic stability into the new member. Domestic resource allocation should be more efficient and growth will be enhanced as a result. Hence we have a situation where both the costs and benefits of membership of the single European currency are a function of the current level of domestic economic stability. We have also noted that these benefits are dependent upon the evolution of the EU and, more generally, the global economy. Hence sudden changes in economic fortunes of EU countries will have important effects on the decision to pursue EMU among the CEE economies as they approach accession to the EU. This is not something we shall consider directly in this chapter although these effects could be important. We now formalize these ideas.

We start with how the benefits of enhanced trade relate to the decision to join EMU. We suggest that there is a positive relationship between the impact on trade and adopting the euro as current economic volatility increases. This is based upon the idea that uncertainty inhibits trade and that adoption of the euro will reduce volatility of the domestic economy. Furthermore, since there will be a significant increase in trade into the EU we would expect that membership of the eurozone will enhance this trade. But the benefits will be related to the current level of economic instability since the greater this is, the larger is the gain to be had. Hence:

$$B^T = T_0 + T(V) \qquad T'(V) > 0, \, T''(V) < 0, \, T(V) \to T^* \text{ as } V \to \infty$$

where B^T is the benefits from increased trading opportunities from membership of EMU and V is the current volatility of the domestic economy. The constant term T_0 will vary in size according to the existing trade patterns of the economy. If there is significant trade with EU countries then T_0 will be relatively large and $T'(.)$ will be relatively small. A similar observation will hold if we assume that the economies' main CEE trading partners also join the eurozone. Note that we build into the functional specification that there is an upper bound on these trade-enhancing effects as would generally be assumed.

With regard to the impact on the real interest rate then we argue that these effects can be represented in the following way:

$$B^R = R_0 + R(V) \qquad R'(V) > 0; \, R''(V) > 0, \text{ for } R(V) < V_R^*$$
$$\text{and } R''(V) < 0, \text{ for } V > V_R^*.$$

So B^R is related to the current level of economic volatility, where B^R are the benefits of reducing real interest rates. Here we suppose that the marginal net benefits of real interest rate reductions are increasing in volatility at relatively low levels of V but eventually this effect will disappear. Hence we are arguing that small increases in volatility can increase real interest rates quickly at low levels of volatility but that there is likely to be an upper bound on the real interest rate even in highly volatile economies. Furthermore we would expect that the growth effects of real interest rate reductions will have an upper bound. Given both these assumptions, the above representation of the relationship between domestic volatility and the benefits of real interest rate reductions seems reasonable.

A third effect of EMU membership will come from the resource allocation effects of the additional stability which the CEE economies achieve as a result of joining the eurozone. We can assume that the eurozone will be, on average, more stable than the economy of any single CEE economy. One of the reasons for this is that there is much less possibility of problems brought about by the movement of international capital (the CEE economies will be protected once they adopt the euro). Although some CEE countries have relatively stable economies we would still expect that they will benefit from more stability. For other more volatile economies the gains will be significant. The impact of stability on growth will be positive and we expect that the greater the domestic economic volatility the greater the benefit of EMU membership from more efficient use of resources. Hence we can write the benefits from membership in the following way:

$$B^S = S(V) \qquad S' > 0, S''(V) < 0; B^S \to S^* \text{ as } V \to \infty.$$

Note that we assume that the benefits are related positively to the level of domestic volatility and that this effect is diminishing as V increases. The reasoning here is that volatility has a smaller marginal effect on the actual way in which the economy operates as it increases.

We now turn to the costs of membership. As we have pointed out above, one of the key factors which determines the cost of joining EMU is the relative flexibility of the domestic economy, particularly its labour markets. As markets become more flexible we would expect the impact of meeting convergence criteria to be smaller. However, as an economy is more volatile then it will clearly be more difficult to achieve convergence with other EU economies and hence the cost of meeting the necessary criteria will increase. We represent this reasoning with the following specification:

$$C^M = C_0(\Phi) + C(V) \qquad C'(V) > 0, C_0' > 0, C''(V) < 0, C_0'' < 0,$$
$$C_0(\Phi) \to C_0^* \text{ as } \Phi \to \infty, C(V) \to C^* \text{ as } V \to \infty$$

where C^M is the cost of membership of the eurozone and $C_0(\Phi)$ is the fixed cost of membership which will depend upon the degree of flexibility in the economy Φ, and $C(V)$ is the cost of membership related directly to the level of domestic volatility. Note that both relationships are assumed to be bounded as Φ and V go towards ∞.

The final cost which we need to introduce, and which emanates from our view of the decision to join EMU as an irreversible investment, is that joining at some stage will remove the value of the option to join at a later date. The analysis of irreversible investment decisions demonstrates that the option value is higher the greater the degree of uncertainty about the future benefits of joining. We argue that this uncertainty is directly related to the current level of domestic volatility. Hence we can write the cost of exercising the option to join EMU as the following:

$$C^{opt} = C_{opt}(V) \qquad C_{opt}'(V) > 0, C_{opt}''(V) \geq 0.$$

We now can write down the condition for a country to join the single currency in terms of the specification above. Essentially a country should adopt the euro if the benefits from joining are greater than the costs of doing so. This requires:

Net benefits $= B^T + B^R + B^S - C^M - C_{opt}$
$= T_0 + T(V) + R_0 + R(V) + S(V) - C_0(\Phi) - C(V) - C_{opt}(V) \geq 0.$

If we ignore the impact of volatility then we have the requirement that $T_0 + R_0 - C_0(\Phi) \geq 0$, and we would argue that this condition is met for all the CEE economies, mainly due to the large value associated with R_0. However when we have the terms relating to V the issue is less clear-cut. Essentially we require the impact of volatility on the benefits to exceed the costs associated with that volatility. Note that $C_{opt}(V)$ can go to zero as V goes to zero. But costs (including the option value) may exceed benefits in the short run.

Figures 11.1 (a), (b) and (c) show the relationship between volatility and net benefits from trade growth, the reduction in the risk premium and the impact of increased economic stability, respectively. We can add the three net benefits together to obtain a total net benefits schedule. The precise form of this schedule will depend upon the relative speeds at which the various effects approach their upper bounds.

The minimum level of net benefits for a currently very stable economy is given by $TB_0 = (T_0 + R_0 + S_0)$; maximum net benefits obtainable, for an economy which is currently very unstable, are given by $TB^* = (T^* + R^* + S^*)$. At any level of V the slope of the total net benefit function is $T'(V) + R'(V) + S'(V)$ which is always positive for $0 < V < \infty$. But the rate at which the slope is changing depends upon $T''(V) + R''(V) + S''(V)$. If the stabilization component of net benefits is relatively dominant then this expression will be positive at values less than but close to V^*. If, however, the trade and risk premium components are more important then positive values of the combined second derivative will be at significantly smaller values than V. In Figure 11.2 we show a situation somewhat closer to the second than the first case where the switch to decreasing marginal benefits is given at a level of volatility V_B^*.

We now consider the total costs which are $TC = [C(\Phi) + C(V) + C_{opt}(V)]$. Given our assumptions about these functions then we know that the total costs will have an initial level of $TC_0 = C_0(\Phi)$, and will then increase with volatility, but the rate at which they increase depends upon the relative impact of meeting the convergence criteria (the cost of the investment) and the cost of losing the policy option in the future. Our assumptions about the behaviour of the option price mean that $C''(V) + C_{opt}''(V)$ may be positive or negative at low values of volatility. We shall assume that it is negative but that the option value effect will take over and hence the costs will increase at an increasing rate with volatility. The form of the total cost function is shown in Figure 11.3. We show a case where the level of volatility at which the costs start to increase at an increasing rate as V_c^*. Beyond this level of volatility the costs increase without bound because the option value also increases without bound.

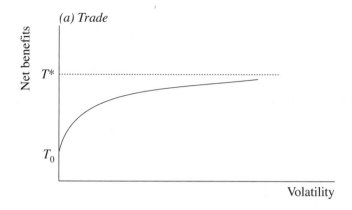

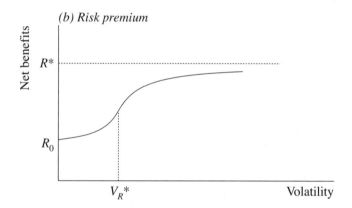

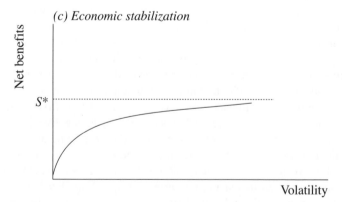

Figure 11.1　Relationship between volatility and net benefits

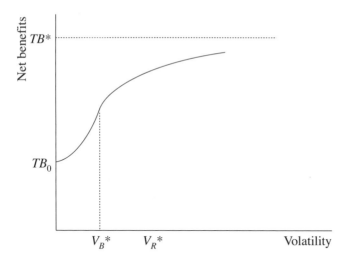

Figure 11.2   Total net benefits of joining the single European currency

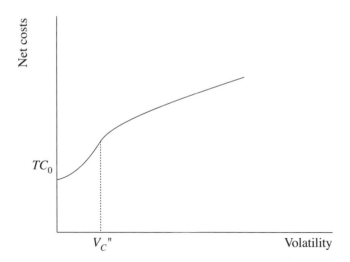

Figure 11.3   Total net costs of joining the single European currency

We now turn to a consideration of the comparison of net benefits and costs in order to identify the interaction between domestic economic volatility and the decision to join EMU. Consider first the situation shown in Figure 11.4(a). The initial level of total benefits exceeds that of costs. Also benefits grow at a rate with volatility such that only when the option value becomes dominant do we find it not in the interests of the country to join EMU but to stabilize the

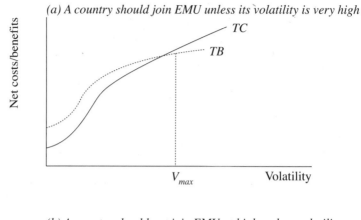

(a) A country should join EMU unless its volatility is very high

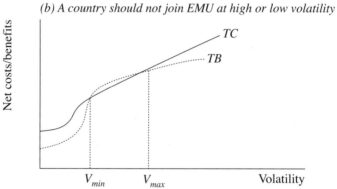

(b) A country should not join EMU at high or low volatility

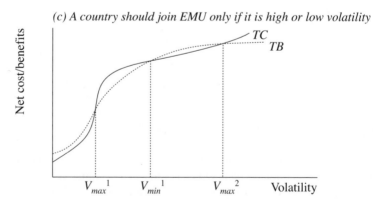

(c) A country should join EMU only if it is high or low volatility

Figure 11.4   Interaction between domestic economic volatility and decision to join EMU

economy first. This can be viewed as the pure irreversible investment case where, once volatility reaches V_{max} the option value is so large that it is optimal to delay the investment decision.

In the case shown in Figure 11.4(b) we have total costs exceeding total benefits when volatility is zero (perhaps because of an inflexible domestic economy or due to the option value of the decision being positive). Now we have two values of volatility, one at V_{min} which marks the minimum level of volatility which is necessary for the economy to find it worthwhile to join while at V_{max} then this marks the maximum level of volatility which it is optimal for the country to join. The rationale for this result is that when TC_0 is greater than TB_0 then a country should not join until it is achieving significant benefits from the stabilizing aspects of EMU membership. Once again, though, at very high levels of volatility the option value of waiting becomes dominant.

In Figure 11.4(c) we show the case where there are a number of possibilities. At low levels of volatility the country should join the eurozone. Essentially the benefits of trade growth and risk premium reduction are such as to make it worthwhile. However, once $V > V^1_{max}$ the costs of volatility (convergence criteria particularly) are too high. At still higher levels of volatility the increase in these costs falls (they are quite insensitive to volatility after a certain level) and the benefits of achieving the stabilization associated with EMU start to take over. Hence countries should join again. However, at levels of volatility above V^2_{max} the option value of waiting for greater stability has the dominant influence.

Although we do not consider this explicitly, it is, of course, feasible for the EU to make the costs of membership so high that it is, effectively, never economically sensible for the CEE countries to join. In this case the net costs schedule would shift upwards (parallel to the existing line) such that it always lies above the net benefits schedule. In a similar vein, the EU could reduce the incentive for high volatility countries to join by increasing the net costs per unit of volatility, causing the net costs line to pivot upwards. This would be achieved by making the convergence criteria very tough. Although we do not model this, there may be a rationale for such behaviour if the EU believes that allowing unstable countries to join would increase the instability of the whole single currency area. However, as we can see from our previous analysis, this action may very well be counterproductive in that it means the exclusion of some high-stability countries. To see this, imagine the *TC* schedule pivoting upwards in Figure 11.4(c). Then the volatility V^1_{max} would fall while V^1_{min} and V^2_{max} would get closer together and may disappear altogether. Thus only very high-stability countries will find it in their interest to join. The impact of tougher convergence conditions which increase the fixed costs of membership are even more of a problem. If we look at Figure 11.4(b) we see that making these costs too high will exclude the high-stability countries completely. Of course, the argument for setting these high hurdles is that the eurozone stability is maintained. This is undoubtedly true but the analysis above shows the dangers of being too restrictive in terms of the membership conditions. In any event our analysis shows that the convergence criteria should increase the cost of volatility, not impose an equal lump-sum cost on all economies.

There are many other cases we could consider but the above analysis shows that the timing of the decision to join EMU is not a simple one, at least in terms of the economics. However, in order to obtain a better understanding of the implications of this analysis we now turn to an evaluation of the actual performance of a number of the CEE economies which are looking towards EU accession in the near future, so as to offer suggestions as to which seem to fall into each of the categories identified above.

ASSESSING THE DECISION OF CEE COUNTRIES TO JOIN EMU

In this section we consider the performance of selected CEE economies and use this to evaluate what the optimal timing for them joining EMU might be. Recall that we do not investigate whether these countries should join EMU; we assume that the benefits in terms of increased trade and, more importantly, reduced real interest rates, as well as enhanced political stability and social cohesion brought about by having the EU provide a solid foundation for economic development and well-functioning welfare programmes, ensure that membership of EMU is economically desirable.

As is clear from the previous discussion, the issue of optimal timing involves assessing the level of uncertainty about the benefits which will accrue as a result of joining EMU and to compare these with the (uncertain) costs including the option value of the EMU decision. There are a number of factors which we have identified as being important determinants of the behaviour of the benefits of euro membership and which will have a key role in determining the stochastic dynamics of benefits. These are trade patterns, particularly relative to EMU members, the flexibility of the domestic economy, once again relative to those which are members of the eurozone, and the development of the financial sector. We have argued that the current level of economic volatility can be used in conjunction with these key structural conditions to evaluate the stochastic flow of net benefits and hence the optimal timing decision.

Flexibility of the Domestic Economy

We consider first the growth and inflation performance of each of the CEE economies to assess their overall level of economic stability. First we examine the overall performance of the economy using GDP (constant prices).[6]

Table 11.1 *GDP annual growth for seven CEE economies, 1990–2000*
(forecast)

	BL	CZ	EO	HN	LN	LV	PL
Mean	−3.147	−1.478	−1.115	0.426	−2.807	−4.038	2.788
Median	−1.500	0.320	2.250	1.540	1.895	2.055	4.800
Maximum	4.00	6.43	10.60	5.10	7.30	6.500	6.96
Minimum	−11.70	−15.90	−21.64	−11.89	−21.30	−35.20	−7.17
Std dev.	6.1027	6.8434	9.2917	5.0518	9.9657	13.1284	5.0569

Note: BL = Bulgaria; CZ = Czechoslovakia; EO = Estonia; HN = Hungary; LN = Lithuania; LV = Latvia; PL = Poland.

The pattern observed is similar across the CEE economies with an initial fall in output followed by a recovery. The summary statistics, along with the graphs, suggest that Poland has been the most successful of the transition economies for the period of the data, followed by Hungary, although the recent strong performance of the Estonian economy (signalled here by the median) should not be disregarded. The other Baltic states are lagging somewhat behind, while the Czech Republic has lost its position as the most successful of the CEE transition economies due to the recession in 1996–97. Note that we do not have figures for the last two years but the Czech economy has now shown signs of recovery. (See Table 11.1 and Figure 11.5.)

We now turn to consider the inflation performance, Table 11.2 indicates that all economies have experienced significant levels of inflation during the 1990s, although the Czech Republic has been by far the best performer overall and Bulgaria, by some distance, the worse (for which we do not have continuous data). However as shown in Figure 11.6, below all economies have experienced much greater price stability in the latter part of the decade.

It has been suggested that a key aspect of membership of the EU and also EMU is the fall in real interest rates. We now consider the path of real interest rates for the selected CEE economies. The real interest rate is calculated using the bank lending rate and the quarterly rate of consumer price inflation (both quoted on an annual basis). From Figure 11.7 we may observe significant variability which reflects the wide variation in inflation rate across quarters. This variability creates uncertainty which surely will reduce both savings and investment and hence economic growth. In order to get a better perspective on the level of real interest rates we report, in Table 11.3, the descriptive statistics for the whole period. We may note that real interest rates have not been excessively high during the period. However, as economies have stabilized there is a marked trend towards higher and more stable real interest rates. The major exceptions to this are Hungary and Bulgaria, both of which have struggled to

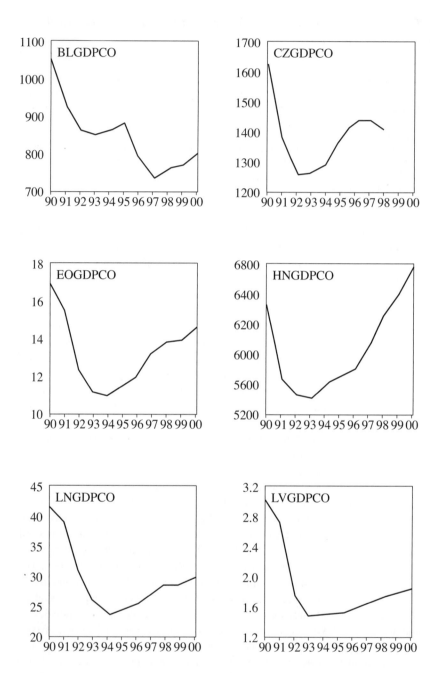

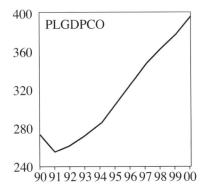

Note: See Table 11.1 for abbreviations.

Figure 11.5 GDP at constant prices, 1990–2000 (annual)

Table 11.2 Consumer price inflation 1992–2000 (quarterly on an annual basis)

	BL	CZ	EO	HN	LN	LV	PL
Mean	52.975	7.536	28.781	19.628	47.028	29.329	25.272
Median	42.468	7.403	18.717	15.760	16.373	10.328	20.990
Maximum	236.9	19.37	198.3	93.9	302.7	191.2	96.6
Minimum	–24.5	–2.42	0.002	–14.92	–3.07	–4.76	–0.74
Std dev.	58.74	4.898	40.22	25.02	79.74	49.16	18.64

Note: See Table 11.1 for abbreviations.

get inflation under control. Hence it seems that low real interest rates require macroeconomic stability. This confirms the idea that uncertainty is not good for savings and investment and hence EU and EMU membership should reduce real interest rates by reducing uncertainty.

Overall we may observe that the CEE economies still exhibit a greater degree of volatility than is associated with membership of the EU. Hence we would expect to see EU membership generate reductions in real interest rates as predicted by Baldwin et al. (1997). Furthermore, joining the eurozone should bring significant benefits in terms of increase in macroeconomic stability. But in order to fully assess the costs and benefits of EMU for these economies we need to consider the trade benefits. We now turn to a consideration of the trade patterns and hence the likely trade benefits of eurozone membership.

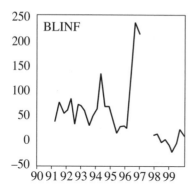

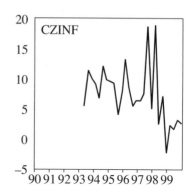

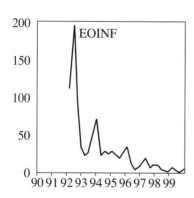

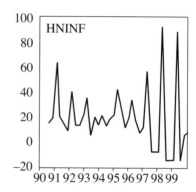

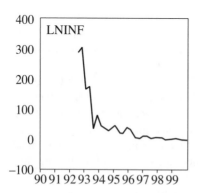

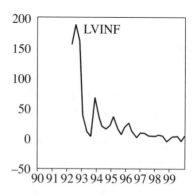

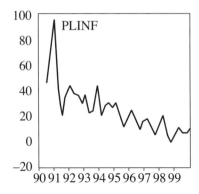

Note: See Table 11.1 for abbreviations.

Figure 11.6 *Consumer price inflation, 1990–2000 (quarterly on an annual basis)*

Table 11.3 *Real interest rates for seven CEE economies, 1992–2000 (quarterly)*

	BL	CZ	EO	HN	LN	LV	PL
Mean	1.93	4.87	−1.21	6.30	5.26	16.62	7.08
Median	6.24	5.33	3.09	11.93	9.57	12.04	7.79
Maximum	53.24	13.73	15.13	28.80	52.94	71.30	29.18
Minimum	−111.13	−5.80	−54.34	−73.65	−73.53	−1.24	−30.54
Std dev.	31.16	4.29	15.97	21.32	26.31	15.54	12.17

Note: See Table 11.1 for abbreviations.

Trade Patterns

We consider in Table 11.4, the trade patterns of the six CEE economies (Czech Republic, Estonia, Hungary, Poland, Lithuania and Latvia). The table shows the pattern of imports and exports for the economies for 1993 and 1996, with trade with industrial countries as a proportion of total trade identified and also the most important trade partners shown.

The first point to note is the significant increases in trade for all economies during the period. For Poland, which is by far the largest economy of the six studied here we can see imports more than doubling and exports up by 75 per cent (in US dollar terms). For Estonia and Lithuania, growth is in the region

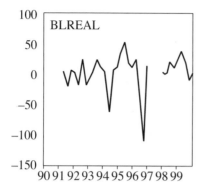

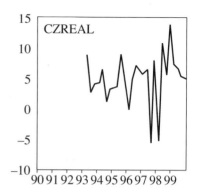

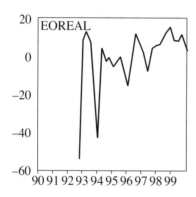

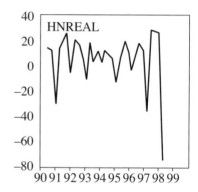

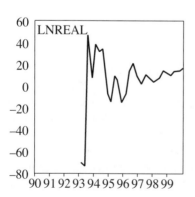

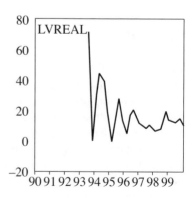

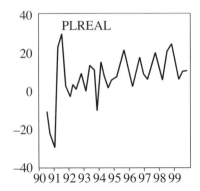

Note: See Table 11.1 for abbreviations.

Figure 11.7   Real interest rate, 1990–2000 (quarterly)

of a factor of three or four. Thus trade has been closely related to growth in the economy.

The pattern of trade shows how important are the markets of industrialized countries, particularly those in the EU. Note that by 1996 industrial countries accounted for 60–75 per cent of imports and exports to the CEE economies studied. Germany is the most important trade partner for all the economies. Other EU countries also figure as important trade partners. Hence we can conclude that these economies are well integrated with the EU and hence, on trade grounds, joining EMU does not imply a period of instability.

However, certain features indicate risks. The increasing reliance on Germany, particularly, and other EU countries generally means that the economic fortunes of some CEE countries are closely linked to the EU. A more diversified set of trading relationships would reduce the risks of continuing low growth in the EU region. In addition, for the Baltic states, particularly Latvia and Lithuania, Russia still features as an important trade partner (although this is declining and certainly may be affected by the continuing problems for the Russian economy). However, in order to assess the way in which trade patterns present risks we need to consider the exchange rate regime which CEE countries have operated during the period. We consider this by analysing the behaviour of the value of the domestic currencies relative to the Deutschmark (DM).

Figure 11.8 shows the behaviour of the exchange rate. Note that this will have been influenced significantly by the exchange rate regime which we now review. Lithuania has been using a currency board with a peg to the US dollar

Table 11.4   Trade Patterns for six CEE economies, 1993 and 1996

	Total (US$m)		Industrial countries (%)		Most important trade partners % of total (imports, exports)
	Imports	Exports	Imports	Exports	
1993					
Czech Republic	12 550	11 448	59.5	60.2	Germany (25.3, 30); Slovakia (17.8, 20.2); also Austria, France, Italy, UK and Poland
Estonia	896	805	76.2	80.4	Finland (27.9, 20.7); Russia (17.2, 22.6); also Germany, Sweden, Latvia
Hungary	12 387	8 598	64.8	66.0	Germany (21.5, 25.3); Italy (11.9, 8.6); Russia (10.3, 7.5); also Austria, France, Czech R.
Latvia	960	1 040	29.5	34.1	Germany (9.8, 6.4); Lithuania (9.7, 4.1); also Lithuania, Finland
Lithuania	1 375	1 154	57.3	72.4	Germany (24.2, 15.3); Russia (25.4, 4.3); also Holland, UK, Poland
Poland	18 834	14 143	75.9	74.6	Germany (28.1, 36.4); Italy (7.8, 5.2); Russia (6.8, 4.6); also US, France, UK, Holland, Czech R.
1996					
Czech Republic	27 824	21 916	67.7	62.8	Germany (29.8, 35.9); Slovakia (9.6, 14.3)
Estonia	3 209	2 077	71.8	56.9	Finland (29.1, 18.3); Russia (13.4, 16.4)
Hungary	16 209	13 145	68.2	69.0	Germany (23.6, 29.0); Italy (8.1, 7.9); Austria (9.1, 10.6)
Latvia	2 101	1 424	54.6	46.4	Germany (13.9, 14.0); Lithuania (6.3, 7.5); Russia (20.3, 23.2)
Lithuania	4 404	3 281	52.0	36.4	Germany (15.7, 13.1); Russia (26.0, 23.8)
Poland	37 137	24 440	73.2	71.6	Germany (24.7, 34.3); Italy (9.9, 5.6); Russia (6.8, 6.8)

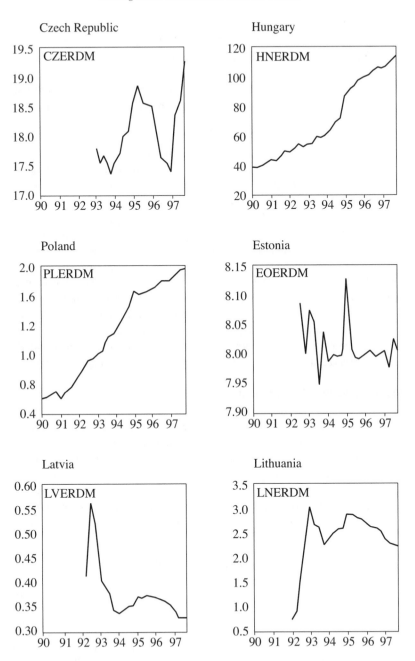

Figure 11.8   Exchange rate behaviour, 1989:Q1 to 1998:Q1 (domestic currency price of DM)

since 1994. Poland has used a crawling peg against a basket of currencies (mainly DM and USD) since 1992, as has Hungary since 1995 while the Czech Republic pegged its exchange rate to a basket (mainly composed of DM) but abandoned this during the currency crisis of 1996. Estonia has used a currency board with a peg to a basket (mainly DM and USD) while Latvia has pegged to a basket with a greater weight given to the US dollar than Estonia.

We may observe from Figure 11.8 the effects of the currency crisis in the Czech Republic. Significant appreciation of the currency preceded the collapse of the peg. However, since the float of the Czech koruna the currency has performed in a reasonably stable manner. For Hungary we can observe a continued depreciation of the currency managed through the crawling peg policy, a policy and outcome which is similar to the experience of Poland. For the Baltic states we may observe the stability imparted by the currency board in Estonia and Lithuania (where the latter country pegs to the US dollar) while Latvia has experienced a significant appreciation followed by relative stability. Overall we can observe that foreign exchange markets have been relatively stable, where we interpret this as either a stable value or trend to the currency. Such stability may very well have created conditions conducive to the trends in trade patterns which have been previously observed. We may conclude that the performance of the CEE economies is consistent with the Frankel and Rose (1996) observation that trade patterns respond to the exchange rate regime.

Financial Sector Development

A third area which we have identified as being important in assessing the degree of uncertainty which transition economies face in moving towards EMU is the degree of financial sector development. The ability of transition economies to attract international capital is an important component of the benefits of EMU. However, in the presence of a poorly functioning and under-developed domestic financial system there is the prospect that such capital will be used inefficiently. One way of evaluating this possibility is to consider the

Table 11.5   Net foreign investment (gross for Poland), 1993:Q1 to 1998:Q1

	Czech R.	Estonia	Hungary	Latvia	Lithuania	Poland
Mean	361.5556	57.25789	633.7222	53.57895	32.04500	145.8000
Median	309.0000	48.70000	354.5000	65.00000	16.50000	144.0000
Maximum	1590.000	122.1000	3701.000	178.0000	151.6000	252.0000
Minimum	125.000	25.80000	213.0000	–49.00000	1.200000	27.00000
Std dev.	337.4997	27.25449	826.7819	58.37552	36.53911	72.07681

Table 11.6   Equity inward investment, 1993:Q1 to 1998:Q1

	Czech R.	Estonia	Hungary	Lithuania
Mean	237.7222	14.05333	4.800000	3.405882
Median	182.5000	4.500000	20.50000	1.800000
Maximum	1154.000	96.90000	82.00000	20.70000
Minimum	−145.0000	−18.00000	−201.0000	−0.200000
Std dev.	283.6856	26.97792	78.26564	5.114742

Table 11.7   Private inward debt flows, 1993:Q1 to 1998:Q1

	Czech R.	Estonia	Hungary	Latvia	Lithuania
Mean	92.40000	16.57500	379.8333	−1.714286	20.35000
Median	126.0000	6.850000	369.0000	4.000000	19.15000
Maximum	412.0000	108.5000	1359.000	14.00000	87.80000
Minimum	−375.0000	−40.00000	−516.0000	−27.00000	−47.00000
Std dev.	214.9916	36.67095	596.1392	14.09154	38.34645

recent history of capital inflows and outflows. The rationale for this is that smaller inflows of capital, being driven by direct investment intentions, are likely to have fewer problems than inflows based on debt or equity finance. Note that all the economies we consider have completely or almost completely liberalized the capital account as well as adopted current account convertibility, generally at the outset of their transitions.

The general message of the statistics presented in Tables 11.5–7 is that capital flows have been positive but quite volatile. Indeed, for those economies which have experienced relatively more inflows (Hungary and the Czech Republic) they have also experienced more volatility. If financial systems are underdeveloped then they are less able to withstand the effects of such volatility. One point to which we alluded to above is that foreign ownership of the domestic banking system is one way of bringing proper management practices into place quickly. Initially this trend was resisted by the CEE countries (they are not alone in this) but we now find significant foreign ownership in several of the banking systems in CEE economies (for example, Poland and the Czech Republic). Given the concerns that the EU may import instability as the CEE economies join, it is certainly sensible for the EU to include some measures for the domestic banking systems within the general convergence criteria for the CEE economies to meet prior to EMU membership.

We have already pointed out that a move towards EMU by CEE countries could create problems if capital outflows impose burdens upon the financial

Table 11.8   Trade balance, 1993:Q1 to 1998:Q1

	Czech R.	Estonia	Hungary	Latvia	Lithuania	Poland
Mean	−784.1579	−159.0000	−765.2222	−130.6000	−155.0600	−387.4000
Median	−760.0000	−141.4000	−732.0000	−130.0000	−166.1500	−373.5000
Maximum	367.0000	−15.00000	−377.0000	39.00000	122.0000	−53.00000
Minimum	−1845.000	−332.8000	−1700.000	−333.0000	−396.6000	−829.0000
Std dev.	592.5812	99.25222	318.4670	95.94099	127.0727	264.7272

sector and the potential for a currency crisis. A key issue in this respect is balance of payments and the recent experience of the CEE economies is shown in Table 11.8, once again reported as descriptive statistics.

We may observe that these economies have experienced mainly current account deficits. As we have seen, exchange rates have increasingly come under pressure with significant depreciation, partly as a result of these balance-of-payments problems. But such deficits are likely to appear in the presence of substantial capital inflows. Hence membership of EMU is likely to create a situation of persistent capital inflows with resulting current account deficits. For such an environment to be sustainable it is necessary for the capital to be invested productively. The South-East Asian crisis has emphasized the importance of proper regulation of financial markets and the problems of investment in real estate and stock markets creating speculative bubbles (see Chapter 10 in this volume by Dickinson and Mullineux). Hence the volatility of the economy will increase as financial markets remain underdeveloped and consequently so does the uncertainty about the benefits of joining EMU.

To conclude, we observe from this brief analysis of the data that all the countries we have considered have been very successful in achieving economic stability. The most successful in this respect, the Czech Republic, did suffer from a currency/financial crisis but has since recovered. Trade seems to moving closer towards the EU, although the Baltic states are lagging somewhat in this respect. However, the general performance of these economies with respect to attracting private capital inflows has not been outstanding and there is clearly the potential for major increases. We may expect such inflows to have positive benefits for the economies concerned but also to increase the volatility of their economic development.

In terms of our previous analysis we could tentatively classify Poland as a relatively stable economy, the Czech Republic, Hungary and Estonia as more unstable while Latvia and Lithuania are the most unstable.[7] The rationale for this is that overall, Poland has been the best-performing economy in the recent past (although it has taken time to achieve stability) while the Czech Republic is going the other way. Hungary has had a mixed performance but on the whole seems to be improving. Of the three Baltic states, Estonia has been the most successful in repositioning its economy towards the EU and in control-ling inflation, while, despite the currency board system there has not been great evidence of a very dynamic economy in either Latvia or Lithuania. Hence we may find that, depending on the actual convergence criteria which are set, along the lines of our analysis in the second section (Figure 11.4(c)) the first three economies may not find it in their interests to pursue member-ship of the eurozone at an early stage while the last two could find it a more attractive proposition to move quickly to adopting the euro. This is a situation which may require the EU to think carefully about the criteria it sets for membership of the eurozone.

CONCLUSIONS

This chapter has argued that, while the benefits of joining a single currency may certainly be greater than any costs which will be incurred, this ignores the issue of timing of membership. By analysing the decision as an irreversible investment we have argued that uncertainty about the net costs and benefits of membership (which are closely related to the stochastic behaviour of the domestic economy) are crucial determinants of the optimal timing of the membership decision. Beyond linking the stochastic flows of net benefits to the current level of domestic economic volatility, the chapter identifies exist-ing trade patterns, exchange rate performance and financial sector develop-ment as important factors in assessing the optimal decision to make.

First we have argued that the decision to join the euro may be related to current economic conditions in a non-linear way. Thus we could have a situa-tion where countries with relatively low and high volatility may find it worth-while to participate in EMU while those in the middle region do not. Alternatively we can find conditions under which the reverse holds and only countries in the middle range of volatility should join. We find that trade patterns are broadly consistent with euro membership and that, where they are not, there is evidence to support that they will respond in an appropriate way. Thus trade relations with EU countries (particularly Germany) are strong and those with other EU economies are growing. Since membership of the EU is likely to increase these relationships, then trade flows are likely to support early membership of the single currency. However, there are further sources of uncertainty which need to be taken into account. Exchange rate policy has generally been in favour of close links to the DM and hence the euro. However where emphasis has also been placed upon the US dollar in determining exchange rate targets, this policy is likely to result in instability relative to the euro in the first stages of membership of the EU. In addition, the development of the financial sector is also unpredictable although there does appear to be increasing convergence with international standards of efficiency and regulation (see other chapters in this volume). Figures on foreign direct investment indicate that some countries (Poland, Hungary, Czech Republic) have been much more successful in attracting inflows. Portfolio investment has been much less and this may explain the relative stability in the foreign exchange markets. The future is likely to see the balance switch towards portfolio investment and thus instability will inevitably increase. Hence development of the financial sector allied to appropriate regulatory mechanisms is crucial to ensure that increasing capital inflows are used efficiently.

Hence the main sources of uncertainty facing the CEE economies as they decide upon the timing of membership of the single currency will come from the underdeveloped nature of the financial system. Consequently strict convergence conditions for this sector of the economy should be set. We would suggest that such convergence conditions are at least as important as the standard Maastricht criteria and that CEE economies which do not satisfy them may very well join EMU before it is optimal for them to do so. What then would such convergence conditions entail? We have highlighted that the sustainability of capital inflows is the key factor. Recent experience in Asia illustrates that international capital inflows into domestic debt instruments may be a major source of instability and increase the probability of a currency crisis. Furthermore, such a currency crisis will often be associated with a banking crisis when the banking sector is the key agent of financial intermediation. Thus an important indicator of financial sector development would be the composition of capital inflows. We would suggest that significant emphasis be placed on development of debt and equity markets and that achieving an EU-wide average in terms of the composition of finance for industry in terms of equity, corporate and bank debt be set as a convergence condition.

NOTES

1. See also, for example, Keuschnigg and Kohler (1998) for a methodologically similar study of the effects on Austria of EU enlargement which also concludes that the economic benefits are large and positive.
2. This issue has been a focus of attention for countries which are joining the eurozone. For example, De Grauwe (1996) considers whether inflation targeting is superior to a pegged exchange rate as a way of achieving inflation convergence. Canzoneri et al. (1996) consider a similar issue.
3. This issue is discussed in, for example, Alogoskoufis et al. (1997).
4. This is considered by Burda (1998) who highlights the dangers of importing EU labour market rigidity into the still fragile market stuctures of the CEE transition economies.
5. We might view foreign ownership as being a good signal that the commercial banking sector is well managed, although this is by no means always the case since, typically, foreign banks regard direct investment in emerging market economies as very speculative.

6. The data here is taken from the IMF *World Economic Outlook* while IMF *International Financial Statistics* provides the remainder of the data used in this section. Note that we do not have complete data for all countries considered.
7. Bulgaria is an outlier in this regard and we do not consider it in any detail since it seems that the option value of joining EMU is dominant at the moment.

BIBLIOGRAPHY

Alogoskoufis, G.G., R. Portes and H. Rey (1997), 'The emergence of the euro as an international currency', Centre for Economic Policy Research Discussion Paper (International Macroeconomics), no. 1741, October, London: CEPR.

Baldwin, R.E., J.F. Francois and R. Portes (1997), 'The costs and benefits of eastern enlargement: the impact on the EU and Central Europe', *Economic Policy*, April, 127–76.

Baldwin, R.E. and E. Seghezza (1996), 'Growth and European integration: towards an empirical assessment', Centre for Economic Policy Research Discussion Paper (International Trade), no. 1393, May, London: CEPR.

Burda, M. (1998), 'The consequences of EU enlargement for Central and Eastern European labour markets', *European Investment Bank Papers*, **3**(1), 65–82.

Cameron, G., J. Proudman and S. Redding (1998), 'Productivity convergence and international openness', Bank of England Working Paper, no. 77, March, London: Bank of England.

Canzoneri, M.B., C. Nolan and A. Yates (1996), 'Feasible mechanisms for achieving monetary stability: a comparison of inflation targeting and the ERM', Bank of England Working Paper, no. 52, July, London: Bank of England.

Chowdhury, A. (1993), 'Does exchange rate volatility depress trade flows? Evidence from error-correction models', *Review of Economics and Statistics*, **75**, 700–706.

Coe, D., A. Hoffmaister and E. Helpman (1997), 'North–South R&D spillovers', *Economic Journal*, **107**, 134–49.

Commission of the European Communities (1990), 'One market, one money', *European Economy*, October, no. 44.

De Grauwe, P. (1996), 'Inflation targeting to achieve inflation convergence in the transition towards EMU', Centre for Economic Policy Research Discussion Paper (International Macroeconomics), no. 1457, September, London: CEPR.

Dixit, A. and R. Pindyck (1993), *Investment under Uncertainty*, Princeton, NJ: Princeton Univeristy Press.

Djankov, S. and B. Hoekman (1998), 'Avenues of technology transfer: foreign direct investment and productivity change in the Czech Republic', Centre for Economic Policy Research Discussion Paper (Transition Economies), no. 1883, London: CEPR.

Frankel, J. and A.K. Rose (1996), 'The endogeneity of the optimum currency area criteria', National Bureau of Economic Research Working Paper Series, no. 5700, August, Cambridge, MA: NBER.

Giavazzi, F. and F. Torres (eds), *The Transition to Economic and Monetary Union in Europe*, Cambridge: Cambridge University Press.

Grafe, C and C. Wyplosz (1997), 'The real exchange rate in transition economies', Centre for Economic Policy Research Discussion Paper (Transition Economies), no. 1773, December, London: CEPR.

Halpern, L and C. Wyplosz (1992), 'Equilibrium exchange rates in transition economies', Working Paper WP/92/125, Washington, DC: International Monetary Fund.

Karatzas, G. and S. Shreve (1988), *Brownian Motion and Stochastic Calculus*, Berlin: Springer-Verlag.

Kenen, P. and D. Rodrick (1986), 'Measuring and analysing the effects of short-term volatility in real exchange rates', *Review of Economics and Statistics*, **68**, 311–19.

Keuschnigg, C. and W. Kohler (1998), 'Eastern enlargement of the EU – how much is it worth for Austria', Centre for Economic Policy Research Discussion Paper (International Trade), no. 1786, January, London: CEPR.

McDonald, I. and D. Siegel (1986), 'The value of waiting to invest', *Quarterly Journal of Economics*, **101**, 709–27.

McKinnon, R. (1963), 'Optimum currency areas', *American Economic Review*, **53**, 717–24.

Mundell, R. (1961), 'A theory of optimum currency areas', *American Economic Review*, **51**, 509–17.

PART II

Financial Sector Development

12. Financial stability and economic development in transitional economies

Maxwell J. Fry

INTRODUCTION

In most countries, central banks are responsible for financial stability as well as monetary policy and the national or wholesale payment systems. For example, the Bank of England's mission statement specifically recognizes the promotion of financial stability as one of the Bank's core purposes. Gerry Corrigan, former President of the Federal Reserve Bank of New York, also recognized this important role when referring to the 'trilogy' of central banking functions and responsibilities: monetary policy, banking supervision and payment systems.

In the transitional economies, expertise formed one serious constraint to ensuring financial stability in the early years (Knight et al. 1997). Not only was expertise scarce in the central bank but also within the financial sector as a whole. Unsurprisingly, therefore, the rapid transformation from a mono-banking system into a two-tier banking system produced casualties, instability and fragility. Many gaps existed in the financial landscape in terms of institutions and markets that typically constitute financial sectors in the industrial countries. Central bankers also faced uncompetitive and uncooperative commercial banking systems.

Much has changed over the past decade in the transitional economies. But some transitional economies have adapted to their new environments more quickly and successfully than others. So there is perhaps more diversity now than there was at the outset. Nevertheless, there are several common features of the process of financial liberalization and financial development in the transitional economies. For example, the prevalence of insolvent commercial banks poses serious threats of systemic instability. Here I examine some aspects of financial instability and fragility that still exist in many transitional economies.

Increased vigilance is imperative in the transitional economies because of the potential for increased financial system fragility that accompanies the global trend towards market-based financial structures. The convergence hypothesis argues that state-based and bank-based financial systems are becoming increasingly uncompetitive in the global environment (Peréz 1997; Vitols 1997, pp. 221–55). The modern financial institution is a lightly regulated financial supermarket offering a range of financial products to a mobile pool of consumers seeking short-term relationships on the basis of price competition. The development of direct financial markets, particularly secondary markets for government securities and corporate paper, is increasingly important for the competitive survival of financial systems in this age of globalization.

While the market-based financial structure may dominate international finance at the end of the twentieth century, it tends to substitute efficiency for stability and short-term profit for long-term relationships aimed at sustained productivity gains. Globalization introduces new problems for national financial regulators in terms of surges in international capital flows that can be, and have been in several countries, highly destabilizing. In the belief that financial structures may well be converging on the market-based model, I focus on aspects of the liberalization and globalization process that may confront transitional economies over the next decade as their central banks undertake further financial liberalization.

MARKET DEVELOPMENT

This section concentrates on the dangers created by gaps that exist in financial structures of most transitional economies. Evidence suggests that financial stability is enhanced by the existence of a broad variety of financial markets and financial institutions. As Malcolm Knight (1997, p. 10) points out:

> Each financial market – as well as the legal and regulatory framework that supports markets – performs a different role that can contribute toward achieving a robust financial system. If a key market, law, or regulatory practice is missing or does not operate efficiently, financial soundness and the robustness of the system will be adversely affected. . . . most emerging market economies have significant 'gaps' in the structure of their financial systems. However, the presence or absence of a given financial intermediary or market, the extent to which it offers close substitutes for bank liabilities and assets, and the degree to which it functions efficiently can affect the soundness of the banking sector. In this sense, gaps in the market can have a large impact on the robustness of a country's financial system – that is, on the financial system's ability to return to a stable equilibrium following a major shock.

Vested interests created under controlled market conditions are bound to oppose reform. Financial restriction involves protecting the commercial banks, from which government can expropriate significant seigniorage, and discouraging direct markets. Not too surprisingly, when the government develops direct markets not only for its own debt but for private debt as well, commercial banks face a competitive threat. Non-bank investors can be intimidated to some extent from participating in direct markets by fear of reprisals in some form or another from their banks.

This suggests that financial liberalization could advantageously be accompanied by some explicit efforts to develop financial markets. In many developing and transitional countries, establishing voluntary domestic markets for government debt may be particularly efficacious. Markets for government debt provide the central bank with the opportunity to adopt indirect market-based techniques for implementing monetary policy. Abandoning direct controls in favour of indirect market-based techniques can be expected to improve efficiency if, as a result, all agents face the same market constraint in the form of the market interest rate in their lending and borrowing decisions. A unified market system improves the efficiency with which investible funds are allocated. Formerly, this allocation took place under fragmented market conditions in which agents faced different price signals.

Although government deficits are generally not conducive to economic growth, voluntary private sector purchase of government debt appears to be the least damaging method of financing any given deficit (Fry 1997a). Both economic and social efficiencies are improved not only through the use of the market-pricing mechanism but also through the transparent presentation of the costs of government expenditures. When the costs of borrowing are borne openly by the public and not hidden through the use of captive buyers, the true resource costs of government spending can be incorporated into both economic and social choices. Even politicians' choices can change when they are properly informed.

A move towards developing voluntary domestic markets for government debt offers benefits in terms of lower inflation and higher saving and growth. High growth, in turn, alleviates the deficit. There is, therefore, some hint of a virtuous circle in which greater use of voluntary domestic markets lowers inflation and raises growth, both of which reduce the government's deficit. In general, developing and transitional country governments make too little use of voluntary private sector lenders. While the typical Organization for Economic Cooperation and Development (OECD) country finances about 50 per cent of its deficit from voluntary domestic non-bank lenders, the typical developing country finances only about 8 per cent of its deficit from this source.

Establishing a voluntary market for government debt involves a fundamental change in the approach to financing the government deficit. Typically, the change occurs from a system in which most institutional interest rates are fixed and the government is financed at favourable fixed rates by unwilling captive buyers of its debt. In such a system, bank rates and all other institutional interest rates, including the treasury bill yield, are simply announced by the minister of finance. Captive buyers hold treasury bills and other government securities to fulfil their ratio requirements, and the central bank takes up any shortfall.

In the process of developing a voluntary market, privileged access and captive buyers are eschewed in favour of a level playing-field philosophy. Government now competes on the same terms and conditions as private agents for available saving and so faces the economy's opportunity cost of borrowing. It has to accept the interest cost consequences of its borrowing and this should exert fiscal discipline that may have been absent when borrowing was kept artificially cheap. The economic principle behind the change is that a level playing field maximizes the efficiency with which scarce resources are allocated throughout the economy. This change in approach necessarily involves many practical changes in the way government debt is sold.

A 'clean' auction in which all bills are sold at whatever price the market dictates yields four advantages:

1. It informs the government of the true opportunity cost of its borrowing.
2. It avoids recourse to the central bank and so avoids the road back to inflationary finance.
3. It provides important feedbank signals from the market for monetary policy purposes.
4. The treasury bill yield can and soon will be used as a crucial reference rate for the pricing of other financial claims in new markets.

Central banks may well become involved in the debate, since they stand to benefit on at least three counts:

1. Cutting the government off from central bank financing clearly reduces the inflationary threat of deficits.
2. Developing voluntary domestic markets for government debt enables the central bank to use indirect market-based instruments of monetary policy.
3. By divorcing fiscal and monetary policy in this way, the central bank is bound to attain more independence regardless of any legal provisions.

It is not enough to persuade the main political actors that inflationary finance and financial repression are growth-reducing ways of financing deficits. It is also essential to persuade the main political actors that debts and deficits must be kept within sustainable bounds after inflationary finance and financial repression are abandoned. Hence, the primary macroeconomic prerequisite for developing voluntary domestic markets for government debt is a sustainable government deficit.

The development of markets for government debt has never occurred overnight. The important first step for any country is to gain investor confidence in government debt and to build and maintain a good reputation for issuing and honouring debt. The process is necessarily one of learning-by-doing as much on the part of the authorities as on the part of the private sector. It is usually also a process of learning from one's mistakes.

Cole et al. (1995, p. 19) identify four stages in the typical development process:

1. The controlled system.
2. Initial liberalization.
3. Retrenchment after crisis.
4. More aggressive development.

The first step invariably takes the form of some interest rate liberalization. The crisis can take various forms: exchange rate of balance-of-payments problems, recession, excessive liquidity or fraud. The reaction is to 'shoot the messenger' and reimpose controls. After the crisis abates, a second attempt is launched in the light of the previous experience.

A typical element of sequencing has been the reduction in excessive reserve and liquid asset ratio requirements, although abolition has often been resisted on the grounds that such ratios still serve prudential purposes.[1] To the extent that they remain binding, liquid asset ratio requirements maintain captive buyers and so distort price signals emanating from treasury bill auctions and impede the market development process.

Inevitably, it takes time for any government to establish a new track record of sound finance. At the start of any initiative to develop voluntary domestic markets for government debt, the authorities are bound to face a suspicious and unwilling private sector. Their record is one of confiscation; the promise of attractive market yields is unlikely to be believed before some credibility has been earned. This implies that market yields on government debt will embody a significant risk premium, mainly taking the specific form of an inflation-risk premium. Once the debt has been sold, the private sector may reason, the government will have an incentive to inflate its way out of its obligations returning to the old confiscatory pattern.

Initially, therefore, voluntary lenders demand a risk premium from government. From the government's perspective, it is paying too high an interest rate immediately after the switch to voluntary domestic market financing. From the private sector's perspective, caution dictates the extraction of a risk premium before it can be enticed to lend. One solution that can help reconcile the government's commitment to turn over a new leaf with the private sector's doubts that this has really happened is for the government to issue debt that is automatically adjusted for changes in the price level, that is, index-linked debt, at the outset of its reform.[2]

Aggressive competition among banks should prevent them from intimidating or deterring non-banks from using direct markets, so measures to ensure vigorous competition may be needed at the start of the market development programme. At the same time, prudential supervision and regulation can play a vital role in maintaining stable rather than unstable competitive conditions.

To enhance competition, measures to broaden the investor base are crucial. They may include advertising as well as improving access for non-bank participants at treasury bill auctions. Indeed, if the major investors remain commercial banks, portfolio adjustments by the banking system as a whole in response to changing business conditions may be constrained or disruptive. If there are no other holders of treasury bills, the banking system will perforce have to hold the same volume even though it would now prefer to reduce such holdings in favour of loans to the private sector. In such a case, treasury bill yields must adjust by possibly large amounts. With a broad and deep market for treasury bills, however, banks can use these assets as shock absorbers against fluctuations in both deposits and loan demand. Under such conditions, it is typical to find that banks decrease their holdings of government securities and increase their loans during economic upswings (Fry and Williams 1984, pp. 92–3).

If the banking system holds the lion's share of government securities, secondary market development is inevitably retarded if not stifled completely because of the lack of diversity among the holders of government debt. The homogeneity of banks implies that they will frequently all be on the same side of the market. Hence, trading remains thin, yields fluctuate excessively and spreads stay high. For example, bid–ask spreads are far lower in highly liquid markets, such as Australia (0.03 per cent) and Japan (0.02 per cent), than they are in illiquid markets, such as India (1 per cent), Indonesia (1.5 per cent), Malaysia (0.25 per cent) and Thailand (0.75 per cent) (Lynch 1995, p. 330).

Foreign participation enhances competition and efficiency in several respects. However, before domestic debt markets can be opened to foreign investors with any realistic expectation of foreign participation, they must meet international standards with respect to the market microstructure, for example, trading practices, registry, transfer and settlements systems and so on, and have established a track record.

While no foreign demand exists for some government bonds because of their low yields and high risk, some governments (for example, Korea) have restricted foreign acquisition of bonds that yield rates above the world level. Whether due to lack of demand for unattractive fixed-income securities offering yields below the world level or government restrictions on supply, the general pattern of capital account liberalization over the past two decades exhibits a preference for opening the equities market to foreign investors before the debt market. This preference may reflect, in part, a belief that foreign equity participation does not involve payment of a country-risk premium to foreigners and, in part, a belief that capital flows into and out of equity markets are less speculative or destabilizing than capital flows into and out of debt markets. In fact, destabilizing capital flows tend to use bank deposits denominated in both local and foreign currencies and may be generated just as much if not more by residents than by non-residents.

One source of reluctance to permit foreign investors to participate in domestic fixed-income securities markets emanates from a concern that the country will pay an unnecessary and expensive currency-risk premium. To the extent that foreign investors are already permitted to participate in equity markets as well as to undertake foreign direct investment (FDI), the relevant comparison is between returns that foreign investors are obtaining in these two markets relative to returns in the bond market. Given the typical incentive package encouraging FDI, the cost to the host country of this form of capital flow may well exceed the cost of funding through domestic bond markets by a considerable margin.

Given the relatively small size of fixed-income markets in most developing and transitional countries, foreign inflows would in any case be limited by their negative impact on yields.[3] While bubbles and herd instincts can produce large stock price rallies under illusions that future dividends will rise too, higher bond prices are necessarily *always* accompanied by the sobering reality of lower yields because coupon payments remain constant.

Foreign participation in domestic bond markets broadens the investor base, permits foreign investors greater diversification than is possible through international bonds, stabilizes aggregate capital flows since more portfolio reallocation can occur among financial assets of the same country, supports bond issuers that are too small for the international market, improves depth and liquidity, improves risk management for investors which simultaneously benefits issuers, increases market sophistication through the transfer of technology, and imposes additional fiscal discipline on the government through the threat of capital withdrawal. In many developing and transitional countries, the main problem is not a potential oversupply of foreign investment into domestic bond markets but rather the lack of a well-functioning bond market into which foreign investment can flow.

PERVERSE BORROWERS, WILDEBEEST BANKERS AND PRUDENTIAL SUPERVISION

My second point focuses on the additional burden that financial liberalization places on prudential regulation and supervision. Several interest rate liberalization experiments have failed to produce the desired results. The basic problem lies in the perverse reaction to higher interest rates by insolvent (or non-profit-motivated) economic agents – governments, firms or individuals. By definition, an insolvent agent (one whose liabilities exceed its assets) or 'distress borrower' is unable to repay its loans. Hence, it is not deterred from borrowing by a higher cost. It simply continues, if it can, to borrow whatever it needs to finance its losses. These inevitably increase with an increase in the interest rate which drives up the agent's cost of servicing its loans. Therefore, such agents exhibit loan demand functions that respond positively to the interest rate.

Perverse upward-sloping demand functions may be responsible, in part, for the observation that real deposit rates in 85 developing countries for which any data exist ranged from –458 to +234 per cent over the 1971–95 period.[4] The standard deviation of these 1329 annual observations is 32 per cent.

José De Gregorio and Pablo Guidotti (1995, pp. 436–7) claim that real interest rates are not a good indicator of financial repression or distortion. They suggest that the relationship between real interest rates and economic growth might resemble an inverted U curve:

> Very low (and negative) real interest rates tend to cause financial disintermediation and hence tend to reduce growth, as implied by the McKinnon–Shaw hypothesis. . . . On the other hand, very high real interest rates that do not reflect improved efficiency of investment, but rather a lack of credibility of economic policy or various forms of country risk, are likely to result in a lower level of credibility of economic policy or various forms of country risk, are likely to result in a lower level of investment as well as a concentration in excessively risky projects. (De Gregorio and Guidotti 1995, p. 437)

In fact, the point made by De Gregorio and Guidotti holds up well with the data from my sample of 85 developing countries. First I estimated the relationship between the annual rate of economic growth YG and the real rate interest RR in equations of the basic form $YG = \beta_0 + \beta_1(RR + \beta_2) \cdot (RR + \beta_2)$. Since the parameter β_2 was not significantly different from zero, although its negative value implies that growth is maximized at some positive real interest rate, I drop it from the estimate reported here. A pooled time-series fixed-effect estimate including both the squared real interest rate and the absolute value of the cubed real interest rate gives the following result (t-statistics in parentheses):[5]

$$YG = -0.033\ RR^2 + 0.008\ |\ RR\ |^3.$$
$$(-3.949) \qquad (3.598)$$
$$\bar{R}^2 = 0.163$$

No intercept is reported because the fixed-effect model estimates separate constants for each country; this equation estimates 85 intercepts. The effect of a rising real interest rate on growth produced by equation 12.1 is illustrated in Fig. 12.1. Evidently, growth is maximized when the real interest rate lies within the normal or non-pathological range of, say, −5 to +15 per cent.

Pathologically high positive real interest rates, possibly triggered by fiscal instability, indicate a poorly functioning financial system. Distress borrowing crowds out borrowing for investment purposes by solvent firms, so producing an epidemic effect (Fry 1995, pp. 305–6; McKinnon 1993, pp. 38–41; Rojas-Suárez and Weisbrod 1995; Stiglitz and Weiss 1981). Funds continue to be supplied because of explicit or implicit deposit insurance. The end result is financial and economic paralysis.

There has been increasing recognition that prudential regulation and supervision is a key prerequisite for financial stability. In their absence, financial systems are prone to financial crises, as witnessed by Chile, which experienced high real interest rates in the 1980s:

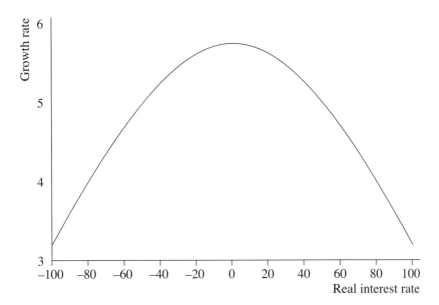

Figure 12.1   Real interest rates and economic growth rates in 85 developing countries, 1971–1995

'These incredibly high interest rates on peso loans represented, in large part, the breakdown of proper financial supervision over the Chilean banking system. Neither officials in the commercial banks themselves nor government regulatory authorities adequately monitored the creditworthiness of a broad spectrum of industrial borrowers' (McKinnon 1991, p. 383).

Before interest rate liberalization can produce the beneficial allocative and inflation-reducing effects, pathological borrows with perverse credit demands must be removed from the pool of potential borrowers and banks put on a sound footing. These are tasks for improving the prudential supervision and regulation of banks. Essentially, those firms whose liabilities exceed their assets and whose management is not affected positively in some form by better economic performance of their firms should be excluded from the process of credit allocation through the market mechanism. Their behaviour in a market environment is inappropriate.

The same criteria – solvency and profit motivation of management – also applies to the banks themselves. Rapid growth in banking creates yet another potential problem in the form of a knowledge bottleneck. For example, even a short visit makes one immediately aware of the considerable investment in human capital now being undertaken to achieve the objective of establishing Bangkok as a regional financial centre for Indochina. Obviously, financial expertise and experience cannot be acquired overnight. This suggests that prudential regulation and supervision is all the more important in rapidly growing financial sectors than in those growing less dramatically.

One solution to the knowledge bottleneck lies in foreign banks.[6] If prudential supervision and regulation is weak or stretched, however, wisdom might counsel granting licences only to large, reputable foreign banks that would be least likely to risk adverse publicity from sharp, if not illegal, practices (Fry 1997b). As recognized by Mauritius and the Seychelles, there can also be some advantages in inviting foreign banks from several different economies to establish offices. This strategy may not only introduce a wider range of banking innovations but also deter the formation of a foreign bank cartel.

In several countries, rapid expansion of lending by newly liberalized banks has resulted in just as high levels of non-performing assets as did directed credit policies under financial repression. Most banking systems simply lack the expertise needed to make good commercial judgements. In any case, they cannot acquire more of such expertise at the moment financial liberalization occurs. Hence, prudential regulation and supervision are double imperative at the outset of financial liberalization to curtail the worst excesses of inexperienced and untrained bankers (Villanueva and Mirakhor 1990; Vittas 1992).

Experience indicates that interest rate liberalization typically raises at least two major questions. The first is how to curb or counter an explosion in consumer lending after financial liberalization, particularly when it takes the form of the abolition of credit ceilings. The second is how to confront the herd instinct possessed by bankers throughout the world.

International evidence suggests that easier access to consumer credit lowers private saving ratios in the medium term (Jappelli and Pagano 1994; Liu and Woo 1994; Patrick 1994). A burst of consumer lending following financial liberalization may also jeopardize monetary control or squeeze out investment lending. Perhaps the pragmatic answer lies in imposing high downpayment requirements for mortgages and loans for durable consumer goods at the outset of the liberalization programme. Subsequently such requirements can be gradually reduced, particularly when the economy is in no danger of overheating.

Many newly liberalized banking systems have become overly enthusiastic about property development, credit card lending and housing only to find that expected returns failed to materialize. Loan officers exhibiting such fads and fancies can be compared to a herd of wildebeest moving from one watering hole to another. As one hole runs dry and the surrounding grass is overgrazed, the herd moves on to a new source of water and pastures. The first to arrive at the new watering hole do well, the laggards struggle to survive.[7] This herd instinct among bankers takes the form of bank lending surging into particular sectors or activities only to withdraw again after delinquency and default rates rise. Loan officers have an incentive to follow the herd when it comes to sectoral lending decisions. To be wrong in the company of most other loan officers is excusable. To be wrong in isolation may not be forgiven so readily.

Occasionally this herd instinct degenerates into lemming-like behaviour when bankers all rush into a new activity with virtually no consideration of the risks involved. The macroeconomic problem is that such credit surges produce bubbles in which prices are increased solely as a result of the credit injections. When the bubbles burst, banks are left with collateral worth considerably less than the loans that are now non-performing. The end result is financial crisis.

Application of risk-weighted capital adequacy requirements provides one specific way of containing systemic risk inherent in overexuberant financial sector growth, the herd instinct, and herd- or lemming-like lending behaviour. The aim is to deter excessive lending concentration to (a) a single sector of the economy, such as construction or real estate, (b) a single region of the country, or (c) a single borrower. These capital requirements would gradually raise the marginal cost of excessive growth in loans of all particular types. Thus, a bank that increased risk through rapid expansion of any loan category by either changing the composition of its portfolio or increasing its total portfolio size would incur increased risk weighting on all loans in its high-growth categories.

Such a system could start with an increased risk weighting on all loans in any category whose growth exceeded, say, 15 per cent in real terms by, for example, 2 percentage points by which the actual percentage growth of this loan category exceeded the benchmark. For example, a 20 per cent growth of loans in any specific category would involve an increase in risk weighting of 10 percentage points on each additional loan of this type. In this way the price mechanism can be used, for example, to increase the financial institutions' marginal cost of property lending, so raising interest rates on such loans and deterring speculative real estate booms. A more sophisticated version of this proposal is to assess a bank's portfolio in terms of the covariance of individual loan default probabilities. The score in this exercise would then produce an adjusted capital adequacy requirement.

While capital-adequacy ratios are designed to counteract credit risk, market or interest rate risk can be equally if not more important in market-based financial systems. Recently, therefore, the Basle Committee for Banking Supervision accepted the use of in-house value-at-risk (VaR) models for determining minimum regulatory capital requirements against market risk and the incorporation of covariances between basic market-risk categories (Goodhart et al. 1998, ch. 5).

Market VaR models estimate future potential losses on given portfolios caused by fluctuations in interest rates, exchange rates, equity and commodity prices. The output is an expected maximum loss over a given time period for a given confidence interval. The Basle Committee adopted a two-week holding period, a 99 per cent confidence interval and a one-year data window. Over a one-year period (250 trading days), this implies that expected losses (violations) would exceed the VaR estimate on 2.5 occasions ($250 \cdot 0.01$). The Basle Committee defines a green zone for 0–4 violations, a yellow zone for 5–9 violations and a red zone for 10 or more violations. Regulators impose penalties when the number of violations over the past year fall outside the green zone.

While results differ, sometimes considerably, depending on the choices of confidence interval, holding period and length of data window, they also depend on the model used to predict the frequency distributions of portfolio returns. The three main techniques are the historical simulation based on past outcomes, the variance–covariance approach that assumes a given (usually the normal) distribution, and Monte Carlo simulations that use random-generated risk factor returns based on either historical data or an adopted parametric distributions (again, usually the normal distribution). In assessing the alternative techniques, Goodhard et al. (1998, ch. 5) conclude that historical simulation addresses the facts that financial market returns are not normally distributed and that non-linear relationships exist between portfolio returns and risk factor returns. The main disadvantage of historical simulation lies in its sensitivity to the data window. This simply illustrates the point that the past is rarely a good indicator of the future.

Because assessing a bank's in-house VaR model is far from easy, the US

Federal Reserve System has suggested an approach that would shift this responsibility on to the banks themselves. Under such a system, the bank commits itself not to exceed a given portfolio loss over some future time period; this pre-committed amount then constitutes the bank's regulatory market-risk minimum capital requirement. Violation invokes monetary or non-monetary penalties based on such predetermined graduated ladder of responses. Under this system regulators do not evaluate the model, as they do under the Basle approach, because they focus on the outcomes rather than on the way these outcomes are achieved. Such a scheme can be seen as an incentive contract between regulators and the regulated.

In examining trends in financial regulation, Goodhart et al (1998) argue that regulations themselves are becoming more market based. Specifically, increasing complexity now forces the regulators to adopt systems that attempt to reinforce financial institutions' own internal regulatory structures rather than to superimpose external constraints. For example, the shift from balance-sheet ratio constraints towards capital adequacy provisions recognizes that financial institutions were able with increasing ease to remove activities from their balance sheets. Similarly, the acceptance of institutions' own value-at-risk models for capital adequacy recognizes that well-run financial institutions can be steered towards public welfare objectives, such as systemic stability of the financial system, more effectively by regulations based on best-practice internal control mechanisms than on any externally imposed restrictions. Of particular relevance in the present context is the authors' conclusion that the institutional arrangements of national regulatory systems are of second-order importance compared with the substantive issues of how to regulate effectively in a global market environment to protect consumers from poor business practice, fraud and systemic financial instability.

THE CASE OF CHINA

The end of China's Cultural Revolution in December 1978 heralded a gradual process of economic liberalization and reform. In the financial sector, the monobank system was abandoned in favour of a two-tier banking system in which the People's Bank of China (PBC) became the central bank and its commercial lending activities were transferred to four specialized banks. While China's financial sector has changed since 1978, the credit plan remains the key instrument of monetary policy. Credit ceilings are set for each specialized bank and subceilings are also imposed for specific types of loans, such as working capital and fixed investment loans. Although banks have some discretion in varying interest rates, China's interest rates are basically determined by administrative fiat (Tseng et al. 1994, pp. 13–18). In large part, reluctance to liberalize interest rates springs from the desire to contain losses in China's state-owned enterprises, the main borrowers from China's state-owned financial institutions.

Inconsistencies between the development of a market-based economy and the use of credit ceilings as the main instrument of monetary policy have become increasingly apparent. Since 1993, therefore, the Chinese authorities have accelerated the pace of financial sector reforms. Part of these reforms include greater flexibility in, and are scheduled to lead eventually to market determination of, interest rates (Tseng et al. 1995, pp. 18–19).

The main problem lies in the fact that the PBC and China's state-owned banks have undertaken and continue to undertake large quasi-fiscal activities. When these costs are consolidated with the central government deficit, the consolidated government deficit rises from a reported level of just over 2 per cent of GDP to an average of 6–7 per cent of GDP since 1989, rising to 7–9 per cent in 1993 (World Bank 1995b, pp. xi–xiii). Were the inflation tax and financial repression as sources of government revenue abandoned without concomitant increases in conventional tax revenue or reductions in government expenditure, the government's fiscal position might become unsustainable and unstable. Furthermore, state-owned enterprises might well react in a perverse fashion by increasing their demands for credit in step with increases in the interest rate.

Past quasi-fiscal activities of the PBC and the state-owned banks, hereafter referred to as China's banking system, taking the form of extending policy loans to state-owned enterprises have produced a legacy of bad debts. In the form of interest rate controls that have squeezed spreads between time deposit and loan rates to zero or even inverted them, these quasi-fiscal activities have reduced the banking system's reported capital/asset ratio. Not only has the banking system's balance sheet been impaired as a result of past quasi-fiscal activities, the government expects its banking system to continue providing policy loans, either directly or indirectly, in the future. Hence, the banking system faces both stock and flow problems. This section questions the sustainability of such quasi-fiscal activities in the light of proposed interest rate liberalization.

China's financial system is dominated by its central bank, the PBC, and its four state-owned specialized banks, the Industrial and Commercial Bank of China, the Agricultural Bank of China, the Bank of China, and the People's Construction Bank of China. While they coexist with three policy banks (the State Development Bank of China, the Agricultural Development Bank of China, and the Export–Import Bank of China), four nationwide commercial banks, six regional banks and numerous deposit-taking non-bank financial institutions (urban credit cooperatives, rural credit cooperatives, financial trust and investment corporations, finance companies and finance leasing companies), these four state-owned specialized banks distributed 78 per cent of all loans and collected 72 per cent of all deposits in 1995 (People's Bank of China 1996, p. 88, and Table 6, pp. 93–4).

Despite China's move towards a market economy in several respects, the credit plan still directs financial resources through the state-owned banks to state-owned enterprises to a large extent under a non-market allocative mechanism. Mehran et al. (1996, p. 69) report that the state-owned enterprises absorb over 80 per cent of total bank credit to the economy. These enterprises also post losses of about 6 per cent of GDP (p. 68).

To contain these state-enterprise losses, the state-owned banks have been used to conduct quasi-fiscal activities in the form of extending loans at subsidized interest rates and to loss-making, insolvent state-owned enterprises. Some loan rates of interest have been held below deposit rates of comparable maturity within the state-owned banking system (Mehran et al. 1996, p. 47). Between April 1990 and January 1995, for example, the margin between deposit and loan rates of maturities exceeding 10 years ranged from –0.36 to –4.32 percentage points.

One effect of the wafer-thin spreads between average deposit and loan rates of interest has been a declining profit rate. Eric Girardin (1997, Table 6, p. 32) reports a decline in state-bank profits from 1.2 per cent of assets in 1987 to 0.3 per cent of assets by 1993. A consequence of declining bank profitability has been the decapitalization of the state-owned banks from a capital/asset ratio of 6.5 to 3.3 per cent for the Industrial and Commercial Bank of China and from 7.3 to 2.8 per cent for the People's Construction Bank of China between 1989 and 1994 (Girardin 1997, p. 32). Given an estimate suggesting that at least 20 per cent of state-owned banks' loan portfolios are non-performing, the situation raises issues of sustainability and stability.

In effect, the losses of state-owned enterprises have now produced insolvency in all the state-owned specialized banks. While this is not catastrophic because seigniorage revenue and financial repression can still keep the financial sector afloat, continued balance-sheet impairment implies that an increasing proportion of this seigniorage and financial repression revenue must be allocated to bank losses, thus leaving a dwindling proportion available to boost government revenues. As Tamar Atinc and Bert Hofman (1996, Figure 1, p. 3) demonstrate, government revenue has declined continuously from almost 35 per cent of GDP in 1978 to 12.1 per cent in 1995 (see also International Monetary Fund 1996, Table 38, p. 73). Hence, the fiscal situation is far from buoyant and can ill afford revenue loss from seigniorage or financial repression.

In practice, China has found it impossible to satisfy its intertemporal budget constraint with conventional tax revenue. Indeed, this has been possible only by relying on revenue from the inflation tax and reducing interest costs through financial repression, as do many other developing and transitional countries. In a sample of 43 developing countries, the inflation tax yielded 2 per cent of GDP and financial repression decreased government interest costs by an additional 2 per cent of GDP over the 1979–93 period (Fry et al. 1996, p. 36). In China's case, the inflation tax yielded about 8 per cent of GDP with 25 per cent inflation in 1994; financial repression reduced interest costs by approximately the same magnitude.

In the Chinese context, it is useful to consolidate central and commercial banks and to treat them for analytical purposes like the monobank they replaced. Hence, the level of and remuneration on required reserves is irrelevant. This will no longer be the case, however, once interest rates are liberalized and private sector competition introduced into China's commercial banking system. The consolidated balance sheet of China's banking system shows negative values under 'other items, (net)' since the first quarter of 1995 (*International Financial Statistics*, September 1996 CD-ROM). At the end of March 1996, this negative figure had reached –159 billion yuan.

In present value terms, the negative net worth of China's banking system produced from the monetary survey can be reduced by the amount of currency in circulation which has a far smaller present value than its face value, since it pays no interest. The present value of this liability item is the present value of maintaining the currency and preventing forgery and so on. Here I subtract the entire value of currency in circulation from the monetary survey liabilities making the assumption that currency maintenance costs are zero.

On the other hand, in present value terms, the negative net worth of China's banking system must be enlarged by the amount of non-performing or bad loans on the bank's books. Taking an estimate of 20 per cent of non-government loans as effectively uncollectable reduces assets and hence reduces net worth (Girardin 1997, p. 30). Here I reduce domestic credit by 20 per cent of its non-government component. I also add the value of bonds issued by banks to quasi-money to obtain an estimate of total interest-paying liabilities. These modifications indicate that the banking system had interest-paying liabilities that exceeded interest-earning assets by 457 billion yuan, equivalent to about 8 per cent of GDP at the end of March 1996.

In one way or another, the cost of servicing the excess interest-paying liabilities must be met through seigniorage revenue or financial repression. In China, seigniorage is currently raised only through currency in circulation because interest comparable to interest paid on deposits and charged on loans is paid on bank reserves. In July 1993, for example, the interest rate on both required and excess reserves was set at 9.18 per cent compared with commercial bank rates of 9 per cent on 6-month working capital loans and 10.98 per cent on both 12-month working capital loans and 12-month deposits (People's Bank of China 1996, Tables 9–10, pp. 96–7).

The government expects the banking system to provide policy loans to loss-making enterprises at subsidized interest rates as well as to service its negative net worth. A considerable proportion of these policy loans are never repaid. Hofman (1995, Table 3, p. 12) estimates that transfers from the Chinese banking system in the form of interest subsidies and loan default averaged over 5 per cent of GDP over the 1992–94 period. If these transfers continue and, at the same time, depositors were not taxed implicitly through financial repression, the entire cost would have to be met from seigniorage revenue.

That inflation has not risen to over 40 per cent, as predicted by the financing model presented in Fry (1998), is due to the fact that the Chinese authorities have extracted revenue from sight deposits. This has been achieved using the basic instrument of financial repression – setting the sight deposit interest rate by administrative fiat. Since July 1993, for example, the sight deposit rate has been 3.15 per cent compared with the 12-month time deposit rate of 10.98 per cent and the 3-year time deposit partially indexed yield of about 16 per cent (People's Bank of China 1996, Table 10, p. 97). These sight and 3-year time deposit rates produce almost exactly the 12 percentage point cost-minimizing gap between sight and time deposit rates of interest estimated in Fry (1998). Hence, China's banking system has extracted the inflation tax from depositors as well as from currency holders.

Proposed interest rate liberalization in China (People's Bank of China 1996, p. 82) would undermine the existing method of extracting seigniorage. Seigniorage revenue from deposits would be competed away as sight deposit rates were raised. In the absence of fiscal reform designed to reduce the government's consolidated deficit, financing the policy loan programme and debt default equal to about 5 per cent of GDP through seigniorage would necessitate an inflation rate in excess of 40 per cent. 'Good-bye financial repression, hello financial crash' is the verdict of Carlos Diaz-Alejandro (1985) on the Latin American experiments with interest rate liberalization since the mid-1970s. Were no accompanying measures taken, the same verdict would be applicable to interest rate liberalization in China.

One solution is to combine interest rate liberalization with the imposition of a non-interest-earning reserve requirement solely against sight deposits. This reserve requirement retains sight deposits as a source of seigniorage revenue and ensures that, even after interest rate liberalization, the competitively determined sight deposit interest rates would remain well below time deposit rates. The model presented in Fry (1998) indicates that such an *intramarginal* tax on currency and sight deposits will not affect the *aggregate* demand for M2 and therefore will not affect the ability of the banking system as a whole to extend the same real volume of loans as it does under present arrangements. What the non-interest-earning required reserve does is to influence the desired composition of money holding between currency, sight and time deposits.

CONCLUSION

One common prerequisite for financial stability is a level playing field. Specifically, a level playing field necessitates the exclusion of uneven, that is, insolvent, players. This is the key role of prudential supervision and regulation in the development process. The case study of China indicates that at least this transitional economy still exhibits a Himalayan topology.

NOTES

1. In practice, resistance often springs from reluctance to lose seigniorage revenue.
2. Much of the literature on indexation (for example, Dornbusch and Simonsen 1983; Gleizer 1995; McNeils 1988) concentrates on its role in a stabilization programme rather than as a specific instrument for use in the process of developing voluntary domestic markets for government debt. For articles focusing more on the market development and fiscal aspects of price-indexed debt in such countries as Australia, Canada and the United Kingdom, the interested reader may consult the Bank of England (1996).
3. The World Bank (1995a, p. iii) notes that total market capitalization of Pacific Asian bond markets equalled USD 338 billion, that is, 22 per cent of GDP or one-third of the size of equity markets, at the end of 1994.
4. Not all countries report data for the entire period. Here I use the geometric average of commercial bank deposit and loan rates, since these are the most prevalent interest rate data reported in the March 1996 *International Financial Statistics* CD–ROM. For symmetry, I use continuously compounded rates throughout this chapter. The real interest rate is defined as the continuously compounded nominal interest rate minus the continuously compounded inflation rate.
5. The estimation procedure, which is asymptotically full-information maximum likelihood, automatically corrects for heteroscedasticity across equations and therefore, in this case, across countries (Johnston 1984, pp. 486–90).
6. Herbert Grubel (1977) provides one of the most comprehensive frameworks with which to assess the costs and benefits of permitting foreign banks to establish branches.
7. I am grateful to Andrew Mullineux for providing this analogy.

REFERENCES

Atinc, Tamar Manuelyan and Bert Hofman (1996), 'China's fiscal deficits, 1986–1995', Toronto: University of Toronto, AERIL Tax Program, August.
Bank of England (1996), *The UK Index-linked Gilt-edged Market: Future Development*, London: Bank of England, Papers from the Conference on Indexed Bonds.
Cole, David C., Hal S. Scott and Philip A. Wellons (1995), 'The Asian money markets: an overview', in David C. Cole, Hal S. Scott and Philip A. Wellons (eds), *Asian Money Markets*, New York: Oxford University Press, pp. 3–38.
De Gregorio, José and Pablo E. Guidotti (1995), 'Financial development and economic growth', *World Development*, **23** (3), March, 433–48.
Diaz-Alejandro, Carlos (1985), 'Good-bye financial repression, hello financial crash', *Journal of Development Economics*, **19** (1–2), September–October, 1–24.

Dornbusch, Rudiger and Mario Henrique Simonsen (1983), *Inflation, Debt, and Indexation*, Cambridge, MA: MIT Press.

Fry, Maxwell J. (1995), *Money, Interest, and Banking in Economic Development*, 2nd edn, Baltimore, MD: Johns Hopkins University Press.

Fry, Maxwell J. (1997a), *Emancipating the Banking System and Developing Markets for Government Debt*, London: Routledge.

Fry, Maxwell J. (1997b) 'Financial sector development in small economies', Alison Harwood and Bruce L.R. Smith (eds), in *Sequencing? Financial Strategies for Developing Countries*, Washington, DC: Brookings Institution, pp. 167–87.

Fry, Maxwell J. (1998), 'Can seigniorage revenue keep China's financial system afloat?', in Donald J.S. Brean (ed.), in *Taxation in Modern China*, New York: Routledge.

Fry, Maxwell J., Charles A.E. Goodhart and Alvaro Almeida (1996), *Central Banking in Developing Countries: Objectives, Activities and Independence*, London: Routledge.

Fry, Maxwell J. and Raburn M. Williams (1984), *American Money and Banking*, New York: John Wiley.

Girardin, Eric (1997), *The Dilemmas of Banking Sector Reform and Credit Control in China*, Paris: OECD Development Centre.

Gleizer, Daniel L. (1995), 'Brazil', in Stephan Haggard and Chung H. Lee (eds), *Financial Systems and Economic Policy in Developing Countries*, Ithaca, NY: Cornell University Press, pp. 212–56.

Goodhart, Charles A.E., Philipp Hartmann, David Llewellyn, Liliana Rojas-Suárez and Steven Weisbrod (1998), *Financial Regulation: Why, How and Where Now?*, London: Routledge.

Grubel, Herbert G. (1977), 'A theory of multinational banking', *Banca Nazionale del Lavoro Quarterly Review*, (123), December, 349–63.

Hofman, Bert (1995), 'Fiscal decline and quasi-fiscal response: China's fiscal policy and fiscal system, 1978–1994', Washington, DC: World Bank, Paper prepared for the CEPR/CEOII/OECD Conference on Different Approaches to Market Reforms, Budapest, 6–7 October.

International Monetary Fund (1996), 'People's Republic of China – recent economic developments', Washington, DC: International Monetary Fund, IMF Staff Country Report No. 96/40, May.

Jappelli, Tullio and Marco Pagano (1994), 'Saving, growth, and liquidity constraints', *Quarterly Journal of Economics*, **109** (1), February, 83–109.

Johnston, Jack (1984), *Econometric Methods*, 3rd edn, New York: McGraw-Hill.

Knight, Malcolm (1997), 'Developing countries and the globalization of financial markets', Washington, DC: International Monetary Fund, Monetary and Exchange Affairs Department, August.

Knight, Malcolm et al. (1997), 'Central bank reforms in the Baltics, Russia, and the other countries of the former Soviet Union', Washington, DC: International Monetary Fund, Occasional Paper 157, December.

Liu, Liang-Yn and Wing Thye Woo (1994), 'Saving behaviour under imperfect financial markets and the current account consequences', *Economic Journal*, **104** (424), May, 512–27.

Lynch, David (1995), 'Links between Asia-Pacific financial sector development and economic performance', Sydney: Macquarie University, PhD thesis, October.

McKinnon, Ronald I. (1991), 'Monetary stabilization in LDCs', Lawrence B. Krause and Kim Kihwan (eds), in *Liberalization in the Process of Economic Development*, Berkeley and Los Angeles: University of California Press, pp. 366–400.

McKinnon, Ronald I. (1993), *The Order of Economic Liberalization: Financial Control in the Transition to a Market Economy*, 2nd edn, Baltimore, MD: Johns Hopkins University Press.

McNelis, Paul D. (1988), 'Indexation and stabilization: theory and experience', *World Bank Research Observer*, **3** (2), July, 157–69.

Mehran, Hassanali, Marc Quintyn, Tom Nordman and Bernard Laurens (1996), 'Monetary and exchange system reforms in China: an experiment in gradualism', Washington, DC: International Monetary Fund, Occasional Paper 141, September.

Patrick, Hugh T. (1994), 'Comparisons, contrasts and implications', in Hugh T. Patrick and Yung Chul Park (eds), *Financial Development of Japan, Korea, and Taiwan: Growth, Repression, and Liberalization*, New York: Oxford University Press, pp. 325–71.

People's Bank of China (1996), *China Financial Outlook '96*, Beijing: China Financial Publishing House.

Peréz, Sofía A. (1997), '"Strong" states and "cheap" credit: economic policy strategy and financial regulation in France and Spain', in Douglas J. Forsyth and Ton Notermans (eds), *Regimes Changes: Macroeconomic Policy and Financial Regulation in Europe from the 1930s to the 1990s*, Providence, RI: Berghahn Books, pp. 169–220.

Rojas-Suárez, Liliana and Steven R. Weisbrod (1995), 'Financial fragilities in Latin America: the 1980s and 1990s', Washington, DC: International Monetary Fund, Occasional Paper 132, October.

Stiglitz, Joseph E. and Andrew Weiss (1981), 'Credit rationing in markets with imperfect information', *American Economic Review*, **71** (3), June, 393–410.

Tseng, Wanda, Hoe Ee Khor, Kalpana Kochhar, Dubravako Mihaljek and David Burton (1994), 'Economic reform in China: a new phase', Washington, DC: International Monetary Fund, Occasional Paper 114, November.

Villanueva, Delano P. and Abbas Mirakhor (1990), 'Strategies for financial reforms: interest rate policies, stabilization, and bank supervision in developing countries', *International Monetary Fund Staff Papers*, **37** (3), September, 509–36.

Vitols, Sigurt (1997), 'Financial systems and industrial policy in Germany and Great Britain: the limits of convergence', in Douglas J. Forsyth and Ton Notermans (eds), *Regimes Changes: Macroeconomic Policy and Financial Regulation in Europe from the 1930s to the 1990s*, Providence, RI: Berghahn Books, pp. 221–55.

Vittas, Dimitri (ed.) (1992), *Financial Regulation: Changing the Rules of the Game*, Washington, DC: World Bank, EDI Development Studies.

World Bank (1995a), *The Emerging Asian Bond Market*, Washington, DC: World Bank, June.

World Bank (1995b), *China: Macroeconomic Stability in a Decentralized Economy*, Washington, DC: World Bank, August.

13. Payment systems and economic development in transitional economies

Maxwell J. Fry

INTRODUCTION

It was noted that in most countries, central banks are responsible for national payments systems, as well as monetary policy and financial stability. For example, the Bank of England's mission statement specifically recognizes the promotion of sound and efficient payment and settlement arrangements as an important element of the Bank's core purposes. Gerry Corrigan, former President of the Federal Reserve Bank of New York, also recognized this important role when referring to the 'trilogy' of central banking functions and responsibilities: monetary policy, banking supervision and payment systems.

In the transitional economies, central bankers have faced uncompetitive and uncooperative commercial banking systems. Despite or because of this, central banks in the transitional economies are more heavily involved in their countries' payment systems than are central banks in the industrial countries.

There is now a general appreciation among both central and commercial bankers that the operation of payment and settlement arrangements is not something that can simply be left for the 'back office' to sort out. Because of their role as the 'plumbing' of the financial and banking system, how efficiently and safely these arrangements operate has become an issue with wider strategic and policy implications for central banks. This Chapter has two basic objectives. The first is to examine the reasons why central banks are interested in payment systems. The second is to provide an overview of the role of central banks in the payment system reforms in transitional economies; Poland is used as the main example.

CENTRAL BANK OWNERSHIP AND OVERSIGHT OF PAYMENT SYSTEMS

Table 13.1 records ownership of the major payment systems across a sample of 70 countries that responded to a recent questionnaire (Fry et al. 1999).

Table 13.1   Central bank ownership of payment systems (percent of countries in each group)

Type	Industrial	Transitional	Developing
RTGS			
Sole	56	86	100
Joint	6	14	0
None	38	0	0
DNS			
Sole	6	44	47
Joint	44	44	37
None	50	12	16

Ownership is particularly important to the extent that payment systems pool or absorb participants' payment risks. Unsurprisingly, there is considerably less central bank ownership of payment systems in the industrial countries. While 62 per cent of central banks in industrial countries own or part own their country's real-time gross settlement (RTGS) systems, central banks in transitional and developing countries own or part own all the existing RTGS systems. While 50 per cent of deferred net settlement (DNS) systems in industrial countries are entirely privately owned, a large majority of DNS systems in transitional and developing countries are owned or part owned by their central banks.

The questionnaire collected information on the role of the central bank in the country's payment arrangements. Table 13.2 provides an overview of the nature of central bank involvement in the payment systems in the sample. Evidently, the majority of central banks possess formal powers of oversight over their country's payment systems, a minority use informal arrangements, while some exert both formal and informal powers.

Table 13.3 shows the questionnaire answers on pricing of central bank payment services. Evidently central banks in the industrial countries tend to

Table 13.2   Central bank oversight of payment systems (percent of countries in each group)

Type	Industrial	Transitional	Developing
Formal	50	77	70
Informal	25	23	21
Both	25	0	9

Table 13.3   *Pricing of central bank payment services (percent of countries in each group)*

Type	Industrial	Transitional	Developing
Free	5	8	61
Subsidized	0	25	3
Full-cost recovery	90	42	27
Target rate of return	0	17	0
Other	5	8	9

price their services on the basis of full-cost recovery, whereas central banks in developing countries typically provide their services free of charge. The distortions so created may appear small at present. Experience from the industrial countries suggests, however, that the sooner such distortions are removed, the less likely are a country's inhabitants to fall into expensive habits, such as writing cheques for sums smaller than the costs of the cheque processing.

INCREASING CENTRAL BANK INVOLVEMENT IN PAYMENT SYSTEMS

Over the last two decades, central banks have tended to play a more important role in payment systems. There are several reasons for this change. The most important are rapid technological changes, growth of financial activity and consequent growth in volumes and values of payment transactions, and the integration (globalization) of financial markets. As a result, liquidity and credit risks for central banks, commercial banks and other participants involved in payment systems increased dramatically; payment systems became an important potential source of domestic and cross-border financial crises. In this new situation, promoting stability and efficiency of payment systems, developing measures to reduce risk and ensuring that payment system arrangements and changes in such arrangements do not jeopardize monetary management have become important central bank objectives.

An efficient payment system is essential in any economy and determines, to some extent, its growth. In this context, the speed and certainty of fund transfers from the payer's account to the payee's account are the key elements. Central banks try to achieve these objectives in two ways: by operational involvement or through a regulatory role. The degree to which central banks are involved in operational activities differs across countries. Undoubtedly, the payment system, as an important part of the financial system, should be overseen. The role of central banks in this area usually consists of developing rules of operation for the system to eliminate or reduce systemic risk.

In general, central bank interest in the stability of payment systems is manifested in attempts to reduce the probability of a situation in which a large participant in the payment system cannot meet its obligations. Such a situation can cause serious difficulties for the safe functioning of the system and for other participants. Eliminating this kind of risk, known as systemic risk, is the primary central bank objective in the field of payment systems.

In implementing monetary policy, central banks pursue intermediate targets such as growth rates of monetary aggregates or, in many cases, short-term interest rates. On the one hand, the efficiency of indirect instruments depends on the stage of development and functioning of financial markets used to transmit monetary policy signals. On the other hand, the payment instruments used in payment systems, the facilities available for market participants, as well as the rules and procedures for payments influence the speed, risks and cost of transactions in financial markets. For example, open market operations require well-developed markets but also payment systems that ensure the transfer of securities through book entries and the rapid settlement of funds through accounts at the central bank.

The various central bank interests in payment system operations produce conflict. For example, one way of eliminating systemic risk is to adopt an RTGS system, but there are some consequences of such an approach for monetary policy. One important issue involves the cost of liquidity. There are also issues relating to granting intraday overdrafts for RTGS payments, pricing and guaranteeing payment finality. These problems are important in the context of the trade-off between risk reduction and the effectiveness of monetary policy. An additional link between the payment system and monetary policy consists of required reserves maintained by commercial banks for monetary policy purposes. Since such reserves can usually be used for settlements during the day, they contribute to the smooth functioning of the payment systems. Moreover, changes in payment systems can contribute to changes in the velocity of money and banks' demand for reserves. Central banks must take such changes into account when implementing monetary policy.

Another important issue relating to the efficiency of payment systems is payment float, which arises largely because of delays in the execution of payment transactions. To some extent the availability of funds depends on the instrument used by the participants involved in the transaction. For cash this availability is immediate, for large-value electronic transfers it is usually less than one day, for other instruments from two or more days.

We can distinguish between credit float and debit float. Credit float arises when a bank debits a client's account before transferring the funds to the beneficiary's bank or when the receiving bank delays crediting the beneficiary's account. Such float represents an interest-free loan from bank customers to their banks, so banks have an incentive to delay the processing and crediting of payments to customer accounts (Veale and Price 1994, p. 147). Debit float arises from processing cheques or other debit instruments when a bank credits the payee before receiving money from the payer's bank or when the payer's account is debited with delay after funds are paid to the payee's bank. In such a case, bank customers receive the benefit of float at the expense of banks.

Both kinds of float can also exist in the central bank/commercial bank account relationship. Inefficient processing of transfers by the central bank could cause the delay, for example, when instructions have to be transmitted from one central bank branch to another. Hence, commercial banks may provide interest-free loans to the central bank if the central bank debits the account of a bank instructing it to transfer funds before crediting the payee bank's account. Conversely, the central bank provides an interest-free loan to the banking system when it credits a bank's account for funds owed before it debits the payer bank's account. In any event, one of the parties to a payment transaction is either granting or receiving interest-free credit. John Veale and Robert Price (1994, p. 149) provide the matrix showing distinguishing credit/debit and central bank–bank/bank–customer float reproduced in Table 13.4.

The volume of float can be important for several reasons. For example,

Table 13.4   Credit and debit float

Relationship	Credit float	Debit float
Commercial banks and their customers	Generated by credit payments such as giro or payment orders. The commercial bank benefits at the expense of the the customer	Generated by debit payments such as cheques. Customers benefit at the expense of commercial banks
Central bank and commercial banks	Generated by credit payments when the account of the payer bank at the central bank is debited before the account of payee bank is credited. The central bank benefits at the expense of the commercial banks because commercial bank reserves are decreased	Generated by debit payments when the account of the payer bank at the central bank is debited after the account of the payee bank is credited. The commercial banks benefit at the expense of the central bank because commercial bank reserves are increased

Source: Veale and Price (1994, Table 1, p. 151).

lenders may not be able to charge borrowers for the credit they have extended, borrowers can decide when and how much they borrow and banks may take advantage of float to cover some of their costs. From the central bank's viewpoint, float can affect the level and volatility of banks' reserves and complicate the operation of monetary policy. Central banks have a strong incentive to minimize payment float, especially in industrial countries where the principle that money has a time value is well developed. Typically, central banks attempt to reduce float by speeding up paper-processing procedures and introducing funds availability schedules.

The effectiveness of a payment system is also very important for financial stability. Disruption in the payment system can decrease public confidence in the financial sector. Hence, to maintain confidence in the financial sector, the central bank must promote a sound and efficient payment system. The payment system constitutes one source of risk to commercial banks. Liquidity problems of one of the participants may cause problems for other participants and for the entire system. On the one hand, timely information from the payment system may provide warning signals. On the other hand, some information about an individual bank may cause problems if published by the supervisory authorities. Hence, cooperation between payment system and bank supervisors is essential. Such cooperation can help central banks to distinguish between serious problems, which may cause insolvency, and temporary liquidity problems. For example, central banks usually have information about whether a commercial bank is experiencing difficulty in maintaining reserve balances at the required level or about its reliance on intraday credit to fund payments.

Although eliminating systemic risk has been an important objective for some years, central banks have also been concerned about the relationship between payment systems and monetary policy. This springs from the fact that monetary policy interventions are routed through the payment systems, so the efficiency of payment systems is essential for monetary policy implementation and for its effective transmission through the economy. The main goal of central banks' monetary policy, usually authorized by law, is price stability and soundness of the financial system. To achieve its goals, central banks use different instruments. In some countries, direct instruments such as credit controls and credit ceilings are used, but recently there has been a general shift towards indirect, market-orientated instruments such as open market operations, Lombard facilities, and rediscount window and reserve requirements.

The discussion so far stresses the importance of payment systems and explains why central banks' interest in payment systems has increased considerably in recent years. But is this true for all countries? Maybe central banks focus on payment systems only in some industrial countries with decades or even centuries of experience with developed financial sectors and strong economies that are integrated into the global economy. To what extent are central banks in transitional and developing countries involved in their payment systems? What is the effect of little or big central bank involvement in payment systems? What are the common approaches of central banks to their payment systems?

The views on the role of central banks should play in payment systems are very diverse. This is quite understandable when one recognizes that the different conditions in each country – differences in payment instruments, the domestic financial sector, legal systems, technical infrastructure, stage of institutional development, country size and so on – make each payment system unique. So in some countries central banks are active providers of payment services, competing with commercial banks, while in other countries central banks do not play such a role, as in Slovenia and the United Kingdom. The US Federal Reserve Banks provide a wide variety of payment services that include collection of cheque payments, electronic fund transfers, securities transfer and custodial services for US government securities. The Deutsche Bundesbank makes its payment systems available to all credit institutions, many of which operate their own giro systems. The Bundesbank operates an RTGS System (ELS) as well as a liquidity saving system (EAF), which combines gross and net features, for large-value payments. The Bundesbank's payment systems are important transfer points for inter-network payments. At the other end of the spectrum are a number of countries in which the initiative is left primarily to the private sector. In the United Kingdom, for example, the Bank of England's role consists in making accounts available under certain conditions for settlement purposes, while payment processing is carried out mainly by the private sector. In Slovenia the central bank does not provide interbank clearing facilities. As the central bank does not operate a special clearing house for interbank payments, these facilities are provided by commercial banks.

ROLES OF THE CENTRAL BANK IN TRANSITIONAL ECONOMIES

Changes in payment systems during the last two decades, global integration, growth of value and the volume of transactions have not been identical in all countries. Typically, analyses of these issues are made from the viewpoint of the industrial countries. But countries that have just started to introduce economic reforms and to rebuild their payment systems are usually interested in basic payment system issues.

The aim of this section is to analyse the role central banks can play in payment systems in some transitional countries. Poland is chosen as an example, but the situation in most other transitional countries is similar. While not all the experiences of these countries will be relevant for other countries that are currently developing their payment systems, many of the more important problems appear to be.

The political, economic and financial changes in the 1990s in countries such as China, Poland, Russia and Tanzania have put significant strains on their payment systems. The structure of the banking systems in these countries was similar: at the outset of the payment system reforms, all these countries possessed a government-owned monobanking system. Initially, there was only one bank (the state or national bank) in China and Russia. In addition to the national bank, some government-owned and controlled banks focusing on providing agriculture credits, on raising domestic saving or on import and export transactions existed in Poland and Tanzania. However, there was deliberately no competition between these banks.

The role of the national banks in these countries at this stage of development was very different from the role of central banks in market-orientated economies. National banks were responsible for issuing money, for filfilling the state budget, for maintaining accounts of enterprises and households, and for providing settlement services and credits to enterprises. In Russia, the national bank was also involved in collecting taxes. Another major purpose of the national bank was to monitor the state plan. This plan determined all production and distribution decisions that are made separately by individual firms and households in a market economy. Usually, public saving was channelled to enterprises requiring credit under the state plan. Credit was automatic and payments were assured through the monobanking system.

Until the beginning of the reforms in China, Poland and Russia, payment systems were characterized by a clear separation of cash and non-cash circuits. The cash circuit was for households and the non-cash circuit for enterprises – usually state owned and obliged to use a bank account. The main non-cash payment instruments consisted of the credit transfer (credit instrument initiated by the payer) and the payment demand order (a debit instrument initiated by the payee following shipment of goods). The national bank debited the payer's bank immediately after receiving a credit transfer order but credited the payee's bank with a lag. In the case of a debit instrument, the payee's bank was credited before the payer's bank was debited.

In both cases this resulted in payment system float that either decreased commercial bank reserves at the national bank (credit float) or increased commercial bank reserves (debit float). Erratic procedures and delays in processing payments produced large and variable float. In China, Poland and Russia, payment clearing relied on the physical transport (by postal services) of detailed paper documentation for each transaction. Because of the size of the countries, transport between the initial debt or credit entry and the registration in the books of the other bank involved in the transaction often took several weeks, so creating enormous float in China and Russia.

Another common feature of payment systems in these countries was the decentralization of commercial banks' current accounts. This meant that every branch of a commercial bank (where commercial banks existed) kept a clearing account with the local branch of the central bank. Moreover, each branch had to maintain its individual reserve requirements. Reserves were maintained in separate accounts that could not be used for payment purposes. Banks often had large surpluses of funds in some branches and at the same time were paying a penalty for reserve shortfalls in other branches.

The reform of the banking sectors in these countries has required large changes in the arrangements discussed above. This has involved redefining the operational and regulatory roles of the national bank, introducing appropriate accounting procedures and creating new arrangements for the payment system. Although the starting points in such countries as China, Poland and Russia were similar, the next section examines the Polish reforms in more detail.

THE CASE OF POLAND

In 1990, Poland launched an adjustment programme known as the Balcerowicz Plan to reduce inflation and liberalize the economy. To support the economic reform, both the National Bank of Poland (NBP) and the financial sector required reform. Under the new Banking Law of 1989 that ended the monobank system, the NBP became the central bank and its commercial banking functions were spun off into nine state-owned commercial banks. There followed very rapid development of the banking sector and by 1992 some 100 private banks had been established.

One aspect of the reform of this young banking system was the creation of a new payment system. The objectives were to accelerate settlement, to reduce risk and to increase the efficiency of monetary policy. Although these aims were expressed at the start of the economic reform process, serious discussions about payment system risk and inefficiencies of the existing payment system, for example, large and volatile float, unreliable timing of execution of payment orders, inefficiencies caused by decentralization of banks funds, problems with operating monetary policy and so on, started in 1991 after two large payment frauds.

At that time there was a distinction between the socialized and private sectors. State-owned enterprises were obliged to use bank accounts and to make non-cash payments. Households were served by the banking sector mainly as a savings depository. Banks did not provide them with any payment services. As a result, there was a non-cash circuit for payments in the social-ized sector and a cash circuit for payments of the private sector and house-holds. Because of high inflation and demands for cash, the President of the NBP prohibited the use of cash between economic units for payments exceed-ing a certain amount. The currency/GDP ratio declined considerably from 1989 to 1994.

At the beginning of the banking reform, most non-cash payments were executed within the NBP. The NBP operated through independent branches serving their customers and keeping their own books. Each NBP branch main-tained accounts for all other branches. Book entries on these accounts were controlled by a centralized computer system working with data delivered by branches. Payment documents were sent directly from branch to branch by standard postal services, sometimes taking several days.

Until 1992, bank branches maintained their current accounts at 49 regional branches of the NBP. Banks had to transfer funds between their branches and had to maintain reserve balance accounts. For credit transfers, the originating bank debited the customers' accounts and then sent a list of credit transfers to the regional NBP branch, which debited the originating bank and credited an interbank clearing account with the NBP. After some days the branches of other banks received the credit transfers and sent a list to their regional NBP branch. This NBP branch credited the receiving banks' current accounts and debited the interbank clearing account. Credit transfers were the most popular payment instruments, so the NBP usually had a credit float on its books. Commercial banks had no incentive to speed up the process because they benefited from delaying transmission of the payment document lists. So the banks were able to debit customers' accounts before they were debited by the NBP.

The transition to a two-tier system transformed what had been an internal float between branches of the central bank into a float involving different insti-tutions. Technical difficulties and the lack of profit orientation on the part of newly created state-owned commercial banks produced long delays in execut-ing transactions. Furthermore, the volume of transactions increased dramati-cally because of the creation of many new private enterprises. Payment system regulations failed to penalize such delays in processing.

Positive float, that is, an excess of gross debit transfers over gross credit transfers, was less frequent than negative float.[1] This float was large – reach-ing 10 per cent of reserve money in early 1990 – and variable.[2] Difficulties in predicting movements in the float complicated monetary management in Poland. It was almost impossible to set the size or even the direction of appro-priate monetary operations because it was impossible to forecast demand for bank reserves, money and credit aggregates.

Although net float was negative, that is, credit float exceeded debt float, both the commercial banks and the NBP assumed significant credit risk, especially when banks granted immediate credit to the payee from debit transfers; the payer was debited only after its bank received the cheque. In 1991 a large-scale cheque-kiting scam was uncovered. A private holding company, ART-B, used guaranteed cheques to finance its activity. They increased the value of the debit float to such an extent that net float in the banking system became positive. When the NBP introduced new rules on cheques, which forced banks to receive telecommunication confirmations of balances on payers' accounts before crediting payees, banks realized that there was no money in ART-B's account. The company failed, as did one of the commercial banks that had guaranteed the cheques.

After the ART-B case, implementation of new arrangements became a matter of urgency. In these circumstances the role of the central bank was crucial and the NBP implemented the following measures:

- Consolidated banks' clearing accounts into a single account per bank (April 1991 to September 1992). The consolidation of clearing accounts has reduced banks' need for excess reserves, has facilitated banks' liquidity management, and has fostered the development of the money market.
- Implemented a communication infrastructure providing a network between banks.
- Introduced the 'no overdrafts' rule. This means that banks' payment orders are executed only if there are sufficient funds in the payer's current account. Some rules concerning cheques (notification by telex) were also introduced which decreased debit float from almost 11 per cent of reserve money in June 1991 to about 2.6 per cent in October 1991. However, these new rules did not change the clearing and settlement mechanism (through branches of NBP) that deterred, almost completely, cheque use in Poland. The float continued but became negative (banks credited the central bank).
- Prepared the rules for the National Clearing House. The NCH started its activity in April 1993. The NCH operates two clearing systems: paper based and electronic. At the same time, current accounts of the NCH members were moved to the NBP head office.
- Established a new department (Interbank Settlements Department) responsible for managing the new settlement system and overseeing the interbank payment system.
- Implemented the SORBNET (RTGS) system operated by the Interbank Settlement Department.
- Implemented an automated book-entry securities system for dematerialized treasury bills issued by the Ministry of Finance. Transactions in the treasury bill market are conducted on a DVP basis.

From a theoretical viewpoint, the introduction of the new payment system in April 1993 should have speeded up the processing of payment instructions and decreased the float in the banking system. There was indeed a significant decrease in the positive float on the central bank's books. However, this was matched by a large increase in the commercial banks' positive float against their customers. This implies that the implementation of the new, much more effective, system shifted the float from the central bank to the commercial banks. It also shows that commercial banks did not use the new possibilities to speed up the transfer of funds between their clients. One of the reasons for such behaviour was the lack of competition in the banking sector. Nevertheless, these funds did enable banks to create an interbank money market that became the main source of liquidity. Naturally, this had some consequences for the policy of the central bank concerning liquidity in the RTGS system. The introduction of an RTGS system increases the demand for reserves that central banks may wish to satisfy by creating additional liquidity, for example, through intraday credit facilities.

In Poland the policy of the central bank is to decrease the liquidity of the banking sector because banks are able to use required reserves, which are high in Poland compared with other European countries. for settlement purposes. Hence, reserves and the interbank money market are the main sources of liquidity. However, Polish banks hold considerable levels of excess reserves, which may constitute expensive liquidity for payment purposes.

The implementation of these measures took some years. When the NBP started to design a new payment system, there were not enough internal resources and experience to develop a modern payment system quickly. Development of the Polish payment system has been accomplished step by step. The first step was to dismantle the old system and to establish a paper-based clearing-house and gross settlement systems. The second step was to introduce electronic systems both through the Clearing House and the NBP (RTGS SORBNET system).

In some countries, the central bank oversees payment systems in a regulatory role. In others, the central bank takes a much more active part in developing and running payment systems, particularly large-value transfer systems (LVTS). Where commercial banks have existed for centuries, central banks tend to play a more passive role than they do in countries that until recently possessed a monobanking system.

IMPLICATIONS FOR TRANSITIONAL ECONOMIES

For transitional economies one might draw the following conclusions from the material presented above:

1. Initial conditions and changes introduced on a step-by-step basis to date suggest that central banks in transitional economies probably assume, and need to assume, more responsibilities than central banks in market economies in leading and coordinating payment system reforms. The commercial banks were not strong enough to develop new payment systems on their own. Resources and skilled personnel were lacking, as was experience in the young private sector. The costs of the reform were too high for new small banks. Furthermore, the central bank was able to receive and coordinate financial help and technical assistance from other central banks and international institutions. Perhaps as a consequence, the similarities in the sequencing of banking system reforms in transitional economies have been quite striking.

2. Because of the lack of resources, the shortages of skilled personnel and the lack of experience in the private sector, the central bank must play important roles in all aspects of payment system design and development. Consequently, the central banks in transitional economies typically assume prominent operational roles.

3. Emerging economies can adopt successful systems and practices from the industrial countries to suit their own needs. These countries can learn from the experiences of, as well as the mistakes made in, industrial countries and they can choose different design options for modernizing their payment systems that were not available to industrial countries.

4. There are some similarities in transitional economies' starting points:
   - monobank or state-owned banking system;
   - cash-based economies;
   - underdeveloped, in technological and institutional terms, payment systems;
   - insufficient recognition of the important of the time value of money and of opportunity costs in general;
   - absence of competition;
   - insensitivity to customer needs.

5. There are some similarities in sequencing of payment system development, for example, accounts in branches of the central bank, consolidation of these accounts, paper-based systems and RTGS adoption. Many countries chose an evolutionary approach and did not leap-frog to the latest technology. Users and suppliers in industrial countries have experience with non-cash payment systems and infrastructures that support non-cash payments. These conditions do not exist in many transitional and developing countries. Rapid change in payment systems may not be practical from financial, institutional or human resource standpoints. Initial efforts should be implementable and practical. The critical payment design issue is to identify the most important payment applications and

develop a system that can easily be installed and used in commercial and central banks.

6.   Many transitional countries suffer legal problems, for example, physical authentication by means of signature is or was the only legally acceptable method of authentication of a payment.

7.   In market economies, banks have profit incentives to develop payment services that meet the needs of their customers. So market forces influence the development of payment services. In transitional economies, the situation is different because the profit incentive is still in its infancy. One consequence is that there is little customer pressure for improved payment services.

8.   The central and commercial banks provide and promote different types of payment services in transitional economies because individuals still rely heavily on cash. This implies that considerable potential exists for commercial banks to expand their markets by developing the banking habit.

9.   China and Russia still face major control problems within their central banks that necessitates strong centralized control. In the absence of such severe internal control problems, the central banks of Poland and Tanzania have been able to focus on cooperating with the commercial banks to promote reforms in their payment systems.

10. Changes in the timing of debits and credits influencing the size and variability of float have caused serious problems for monetary control in the transitional economies.

11. Unfortunately data for transitional countries are still inadequate. Particularly because of insufficient data concerning the share of cash payments, velocity and float, there is no doubt that large one-time changes in payment systems arrangements in transitional and developing countries necessitate the close attention of central banks to the linkages between payment systems and monetary policy.

For the industrial countries, one general conclusion is that the key lies in regular contact and information-sharing among those responsible for payment systems, monetary policy and supervision and surveillance of banks and financial markets. This is particularly important when major operational changes are contemplated and when markets and systems are under strain. With close cooperation and communication, there should at least be opportunities to prevent problems developing into crises and to reduce the incidence of 'nasty surprises'.

CONCLUSION

As noted in the conclusion to Chapter 12, a prerequisite for financial stability is a level playing-field. First, in my opinion, central banks in the transitional economies could usefully promote the development of a secondary market for government debt; the government should certainly compete with other borrowers on a level playing field. This enables monetary policy to be separated from fiscal policy and promotes financial stability. Second, a level playing field necessitates the exclusion of uneven, that is, insolvent, players. This is the key role of prudential supervision and regulation in the development process. While an efficient payment system fosters economic development in its own right, it also promotes it indirectly by facilitating monetary policy. An efficient payments system also contributes to overall financial stability and so, in this way too, promotes economic development.

NOTES

1. Negative float means that credit float exceeds debit float, the situation one would anticipate in a system where credit transfers predominate over debit transfers.
2. Balino et al. (1994, Figure 6, p. 403) compare float as a percentage of reserve money in Poland and the United States, 1990–92. Float in Poland ranges from 2 to 10 per cent of reserve money while float in the United States ranges from 0.05 to 0.5 per cent of reserve money.

REFERENCES

Balino, T., J. Dhawan and V. Sundararajan (1994), 'Payment system reform and monetary policy in emerging market economies in Central and Eastern Europe', *IMF Staff Papers*, **41** (3), September, 383–95.
Fry, M.J., I. Kilato, S. Roger, D. Shepherd, F. Solis and J. Trundle (1999), *Payment Systems in Global Perspective*, London: Routledge.
Veale, John M. and Robert W. Price (1994), 'Payment system float and float management', in B.J. Summers (ed.), *The Payment System: Design, Management and Supervision*, Washington, DC: International Monetary Fund.

14. Mobilization of savings in transition countries: the case of Lithuania

Dalia Vidickienė, Salomėja Jasinskaitė and Rasa Melnikienė

INTRODUCTION

Notwithstanding the huge importance of saving for the economy, savings regularities in transition countries still remain one of the least investigated subjects. The scanty literature that does analyse specific features of saving in transition countries restricts itself to a mere mention of such abstract factors making an impact on the savings behaviour as 'choice of reform sequencing' and reform strategy, that is, 'big bang or gradualism' (De Melo et al. 1995; Schmidt-Hebbel and Serven 1997). However, these factors relate only to what has already occurred and are suitable only for a comparative analysis of countries.

Such an analysis is of little practical use when searching for ways to increase the scale and rate of saving. Therefore, it is not surprising that the process of saving in transition countries has so far been ignored, while depreciation and compensation of savings are being addressed for political reasons, since the theory of economics cannot provide an answer concerning the basis for optimal decisions.

This chapter analyses changes to the savings rate in transition countries and the need for these countries to mobilize domestic savings. The chapter has four further sections. The next section includes a survey of the main modern theories of saving and evaluates whether they can predict savings behaviour in transition countries. After analysing the actual situation during the first years of reform, we shall investigate the main reasons for the decrease in the savings rate. The third section analyses the characteristic features of savings behaviour in Lithuania, and considers the main factors that predetermine a change in the savings rate. The fourth section presents an analysis of the degree of Lithuania's financial integration, and analyses the preferred foreign to domestic savings ratio for economic growth and financial stability in Lithuania. The final section offers a summary and conclusions.

Table 14.1   Gross domestic savings in CEE transition countries (% of GDP)

	1989	1990	1991	1992	1993	1994
Lithuania	25.8	25.5	31.5	17.8*	16.0*	16.3*
Latvia	37.9	38.8	27.0	24.0	24.4	25.0
Estonia	25.9	22.3	30.1	17.1	25.0	25.0
Bulgaria	31.4	22.0	35.8	22.9	16.7	20.0
Czech Republic	30.6	29.9	36.7	25.3	20.1	22.0
Hungary	29.9	28.0	19.4	15.7	10.7	12.0
Poland	42.7	36.0	21.9	16.5	15.9	17.0
Romania	29.5	20.8	24.1	23.4	21.7	21.0
Slovakia	28.5	24.2	28.2	19.8	22.4	23.0
Slovenia	33.0	32.6	27.4	26.2	25.0	25.0
Belarus	37.4	30.2	32.9	32.7	33.2	29.0
Russia	34.7	29.5	40.2	35.8	32.7	25.0
Ukraine	27.3	25.5	16.9	11.8	7.9	10.0

Note: According to World Bank data, the savings rate in Lithuania was 20.4 per cent in 1992, 10.6 per cent in 1993, and 12 per cent in 1994.

Sources: World Bank data. * Department of Statistics, Government of the Republic of Lithuania, Lithuanian National Accounts in 1990–1996, Vilnius, 1998.

DETERMINANTS OF SAVING: THEORETICAL PERSPECTIVE

The characteristic feature of the transition process in Central and Eastern European (CEE) countries is a decrease in the savings rate in transition economies. While during the pre-reform period the savings rate in these countries accounted for 33 per cent on average, during the transition period it gradually started to decrease, in some countries by as much as two- or threefold during the early reform years. (See Table 14.1).

Results from the first years of the transition period should be regarded with caution because it is unclear whether this accurately portrays the evolution of savings or includes for the most part a statistical artefact. On the one hand, a relatively large and dynamic informal economy (whose size is estimated to be about 20–40 per cent of the formal economy) as well as methods of national accounting that are not adapted to the market economy, could lead to a serious underestimation of GDP and of household and corporate savings.

On the other hand, there are reasons why private savings can fall in response to transition. So, the tendency of a decrease in the savings rate in the early phase of transition could be explained as follows:

- the savings rate in the socialist economy was too high;
- uncertainty during the transition period was too high to induce precautionary saving; and
- the lack of incentives for saving in the early period of transition.

The first reason is related to the fact that in the socialist economy the amount of savings was determined not by market equilibrium but whether a desired commodity or service could be acquired under conditions of universal deficit. Scientists who analysed the economies of socialist countries in this respect emphasized repeatedly that under central planning, saving was residually determined given the investment demands implied by the plan's growth targets and assumed incremental capital–output ratios. There is some evidence that the implied savings rates amply exceeded desired saving, until the onset of liberalization loosened the rigidity of the binding consumption constraints (Kornai 1959, 1980, 1992; Welfe 1989; Quandt 1989). To the degree that consumption was indeed below its desired level, the transition caused a welfare-increasing decline in saving from disequilibrium to equilibrium levels.

The second reason – a huge uncertainty about the future – has created preconditions for the radical change to guides that adjust the savings behaviour of the population in transition countries. In the transition period, not only did the sources of savings and the spheres of their employment become unpredictable, but also the value of savings itself. As a consequence of hyperinflation, which is characteristic of all transition countries at the beginning of reforms, household savings accumulated during the socialist period depreciated significantly. The psychological shock that resulted, followed by tremendous economic losses, have not only reduced the propensity to save, but have also taught people to save under completely different criteria.

The traditional view is that saving depends mainly on income and wealth, while investment depends on profitability and risk. However, a huge uncertainty in the transition period created a situation whereby saving was determined by the same factors that were determinants for investment. Saving in the form of money and, later, in the form of real assets, became highly risky. Money savings depreciated due to inflation even if deposited in banks, because the real interest rate was negative. In addition, a large number of banks and financial companies that accepted deposits went bankrupt. Therefore, savings were usually irrevocably lost, since there was no system of deposit insurance.

Since at the beginning of the reform period it became clear that the only winners were those people who had transformed their savings from a monetary form to one of real assets, other people and even companies soon followed suit. As a result, in most transition countries the property form of saving started to predominate over that of money. All commodities became more expensive and, in fact, any purchase became a good means of protecting savings against inflation. Since the market was understocked, at first it was not difficult to sell unnecessary commodities. However, the empty market inherited from socialism was soon filled to overflowing, with the result that such accumulated property became non-liquid or less valuable. When the price structure started to change and inflation had decreased markedly, it became as complicated to save in kind as through starting business. Thus, saving in the transition period became complicated, demanding an evaluation of savings risks and profitability.

Because of the fear of depreciation of savings, or even their absolute loss, most households reduced their savings to a minimum, leaving themselves only a very small amount as an emergency fund for use in the case of sudden disaster (illness, funerals, unemployment and so on). Inevitably, this factor reduced the savings rate.

The third reason – the lack of incentives for saving – is closely related to the socioeconomic policy of the state, especially in the early phase of transition. First of all, such an important savings stimulus as private savings for pensions (accumulated in large amounts in industrial countries), which can later be used to increase investment, has not been presented in transition countries. Some authors (for example, Baross 1979) have noted that pension schemes, by increasing the possibility of financial independence in old age, may motivate the public to save more in other forms. Hubbard (1986), using microdata for the United States, found that 'an increase in private pension wealth of one dollar reduces nonpension net worth by sixteen cents'. This estimate was consistent with the range of 10 to 19 cents found by Gultekin and Logue (1979). Ando and Kennickell (1987) found that

> [T]hose families participating in private pension programmes do not seem to change their behaviour towards assets and liabilities other than the value of pension fund reserves, so that contributions to pension funds, by both employers and employees, and interest earnings on pension reserves appear to constitute additional savings for those families. (p. 208)

Another important motive for personal saving, is that people aspire to own their own homes. However, in the majority of transition countries this dream, especially for urban residents, remains unrealized for two reasons: (i) in most transition countries, particularly in those which were incorporated into the former Soviet Union, there is a housing shortage; and (ii) at the beginning of the reform, residual flats and houses were one of the most important commodities in which savings were invested, and such premises command very high prices. In most transition countries the preferential (subsidized) mortgage loan scheme is either not yet functioning or is still only in the early stages. This is why saving for even a very modest house or flat independently seems an impossible dream for most households. As a consequence, some of the income, which could be directed towards the accumulation of a downpayment for a house or a flat, is instead used for improving current consumption.

Thus, these three reasons (too high savings rates under the socialist economy, uncertainty about the future and lack of incentives in the early transition period) all explain the reduction in aggregate saving. In addition, it is important to indicate that each of these reasons operates in a different time dimension. The first is related to the past, the second to the present and the third to the future. When functioning at the same time they create a three-dimensional time continuity, which is why their impact becomes stronger.

The reasons confirm the presumption that a sudden decrease in the propensity to save is an undoubted fact of transition economies rather than a statistical artefact. Under certain macroeconomic theories, any large change in the amount of savings in an economy may cause macroeconomic imbalances. Economic theory also stresses the important role of savings in capital accumulation and economic growth in the long term. But despite these theoretical propositions, domestic savings mobilization in transition countries still remains a macroeconomic question of minor importance in practice.

Ignorance about matters related to domestic savings mobilization could be influenced by various factors.

The first factor includes difficulties of finding theoretical models that are suitable to analyse and forecast the rate of saving in transition countries. First of all, because of the peculiarities of transition countries, it is difficult to apply the two paradigms of saving/consumption that are most frequently used in modern economic literature – the life-cycle hypothesis and the permanent-income hypothesis.

The life-cycle hypothesis, fathered by Modigliani and Brumberg (1954, 1979), introduces age-related consumer (or household) heterogeneity. In this hypothesis, individuals are assumed to maximize the present value of their lifetime utility, subject to a budget constraint that is equal to their current net worth plus the present value of the labour income that they expect to earn over their remaining working life. Within this framework, variations in aggregate saving could result from changes in demographics, income growth, interest rates and inflation, and changes in budget deficits that shift tax burdens to future generations. There could also be an impact on the availability of foreign saving on domestic saving.

The permanent-income hypothesis (PIH) abstracts from consumer heterogeneity by focusing on the consumption of an infinitely-lived consumer or, equivalently, an infinite sequence of finitely-lived generations linked through intergenerational transfers (including bequests). Conception is equal to permanent income – the annuity value of the sum of non-human assets and human capital (the discounted value of labour income), net of the discounted value of taxes (see Friedman 1957, Hall 1978, and Flavin 1981 for the most popular formulations of PIH). As a variant of PIH, the Ricardian-equivalence hypothesis, by making use of both the consumer's and the government's budget constraint, derives permanent income as net of the discounted value of government spending (Barro 1974).

Empirical investigations carried out in a number of countries demonstrate that mathematical models constructed according to these hypotheses often served to explain and predict the savings behaviour of the people of developed countries. However, when applying these models to the analysis of saving in developing countries, it emerged that in this case, dependency upon the age of the population as well as constant income is expressed much more weakly. Among the main reasons causing difficulties in applying life-cycle models in developing countries, macroeconomic instability is mentioned as well as the fact that household income in developing countries may be more uncertain than in industrial countries because a relatively large portion of households in developing countries derive their income from agriculture and other primary commodities where incomes are subject to larger fluctuations.

Application of both theories in transition countries becomes even more complicated. The fundamental starting-point of these two theories is people's ability to evaluate their likely income and to plan in detail their future income for the rest of their life (life-cycle hypothesis) or at least for some longer period. But the predominant characteristic feature of transition countries is uncertainty, and this has already been the case for more than ten years. People find it difficult to predict their future income since it is largely subject to the general economic situation and schemes introduced during social security and health-care reforms; these schemes are still rather vague in most transition countries.

Future uncertainty also manifests strongly when forecasting individual and family income. New phenomena for transition countries – unemployment, bankruptcy – make a very strong impact on a psychological level. In addition, differentiation of earnings correlating to the education and skill levels of an employee still remains unsettled.

Second, numerous theories have been developed that analyse the propensity to save when facing possible changes that affect income rate, taxation, interest rate and other factors that influence the consumption rate (Skinner 1988; Zeldes 1989; Epstein and Zin 1989; Weil 1989, 1990; Kimball 1990). However, nowadays it is already apparent that the application of such theories in the analysis of saving processes in transition countries is complicated. All these theories are based on the hypothesis that greater uncertainty about the future reduces current consumption and hence increases saving, whereas empirical studies (Table 14.1) demonstrate that notwithstanding high uncertainty about the future, the savings rate decreases markedly in transition countries.

It is clear that the tendency for a change in savings rates in transition countries is determined by other factors than the ones in these models, so it is difficult to predict savers' behaviour change in response to planned measures.

The second factor explaining why such limited attention is paid to the domestic savings mobilization process is the steady increase in the openness of transition economies. Once transition countries have completed the transformation from a closed- to an open-type economy, they should theoretically become a constituent part of the global capital market and thereby be able to increase their investments by drawing on the global pool of savings. Thus, domestic savings mobilization is less important. Nevertheless, to implement these expectations in reality is not so simple.

First of all, this is related to the fact that savings investment is one of the most inert phenomena when analysing it with respect to space mobility. According to empirical investigations, until now capital markets have been the markets that are least integrated on a world scale.

Feldstein and Horioka (1980) argued in a seminal contribution that, in a world of high capital mobility, an increase in saving in any one economy could lead to an increase in investment in all countries depending on each country's initial capital stock and the marginal product of capital. This would suggest a low coefficient on saving in the following cross-section regression of domestic investment on domestic saving:

$$(I/Y)_i = a + b(S/Y)_i \qquad (14.1)$$

A high coefficient on domestic saving would imply that most of the incremental saving in an economy is invested in the same economy. The Feldstein–Horioka results for the Organization for Economic Cooperation and Development (OECD) countries for the 1960–74 period showed that the coefficient on saving was large and significantly different from zero, although not from unity. Numerous subsequent studies have shown the existence of a high correlation between saving and investment across industrial countries. (See Bayoumi (1996) for a comprehensive review of these studies and various extensions.)

During the last few years, the degree of integration of capital markets has increased. Later studies (for example, Frankel 1989 and Feldstein and Bacchetta 1989) showed that the correlation between domestic saving and domestic investment became much weaker from the early 1980s onwards, particularly within the European Community. The main reason for this change is that by the mid-1980s, a large number of countries had removed most of their capital controls and liberalization of financial markets was becoming more general, enabling capital to flow more freely across national borders.

Another reason for the breakdown in the correlation was that large public sector budget deficits (especially in the United States) created current account deficits, with high interest rates necessary to attract the inward flows of capital needed to finance the deficit.

However, rapid transition to open economies could produce negative macroeconomic consequences. In particular this concerns the growth of current account deficits in transition countries. According to the national accounting identity, a current account deficit is the result of investment over domestic saving. Taking into consideration the increased investment demand needed for modernizing and restructuring most branches of the economy in transition economies, a significant decrease in the propensity to save (Table 14.1) and, consequently, a decrease in domestic saving, lead to a rapid growth in the current account deficit. This problem is especially urgent for those countries where, compared with other transition countries, investment risk is lower and financial instruments are more developed and integrated into the global capital market, as well as for very small economies (for example, the Baltic countries) (Table 14.2).

Countries running a large current account deficit should use different policies to fight this macroeconomic imbalance. Alongside the widening of the export base, replacing imports with domestic goods, strengthening barriers on capital inflows (especially short term) and so on, an increase in domestic savings is one of the most important instruments to decrease the current account deficit. In the light of current account deficit sustainability, this instrument is particularly essential for countries where an increase in the current account deficit has been conditioned by saving decline rather than investment demand. Therefore, domestic savings mobilization should be regarded as an important economic policy task.

Table 14.2   Current account deficit in selected transition countries (% of GDP)

	1994	1995	1996	1997
Czech Republic	−2.2	−2.9	−8.3	−6.1
Estonia	−7.0	−4.6	−10.1	−13.0
Hungary	−9.8	−5.7	−3.8	−2.2
Latvia	5.5	−0.4	−8.8	−8.0
Lithuania	−2.1	−10.2	−9.2	−10.3**
Poland	2.5	−2.0*	−6.0*	−8.0*
Slovakia	5.2	2.2	−11.0	−6.7

Sources: Focus on Transition, Oesterreische Nationalbank, 1/1998. *Bank for International Settlements; **Bank of Lithuania.

When evaluating whether the government can influence the savings rate growth, it is evident that greater opportunities lie in the elimination of the third reason, given above, for the tendency of the savings rate to decrease, that is, with the help of institutional innovations to create saving incentives.

In the next section, the evolution of savings trends, their macroeconomic consequences and instruments to mobilize domestic savings under transition are analysed more thoroughly for the case of Lithuania.

RECENT SAVINGS TRENDS IN LITHUANIA

After the start of economic reforms, a tendency to a decrease in the savings rate, characteristic of all CEE countries, was apparent in Lithuania. An especially severe and sudden drop was witnessed in the first years of the reform – 1992 (and in 1993, with reference to World Bank data, see note in Table 14.1) when the savings rate almost halved (Table 14.3).

The main reasons for the sudden decrease in the savings rate in the first years of the reform were the economic decline as well as the consumption boom. Significant economic decline (real GDP in 1993 decreased by 16.2 per cent) influenced the savings rate decrease both in private and government sectors. Economic decline has had a particular impact on the decrease in real income, which resulted in a fall in the standard of living and, subsequently, in a decrease in private sector saving. The government savings rate fell in relation to the consolidated fiscal deficit in Lithuania (nearly 4 per cent in 1989, 5.5 per cent in 1990 and more than 3 per cent in 1993[1]).

Liberalization of foreign trade as well as complete convertibility of the local national currency created perfect conditions for offering consumers import commodities not previously available. After legalizing private ownership of capital goods, the availability of a variety of local production goods and services also increased rapidly. When the long-lasting period of universal deficit ended, consumers were keen to satisfy their needs. The subsequent consumption boom overwhelmed not only households but also companies. With the opportunity to acquire capital goods and raw materials at the market

Table 14.3   Gross domestic saving in Lithuania (% of GDP)

1989	1990	1991	1992	1993	1994	1995	1996	1997	1998
25.8*	25.5*	31.5*	17.8	16.0	16.3	14.5	15.3	16.3	16.1

Sources: Department of Statistics, Government of the Republic of Lithuania, *Lithuanian National Accounts, 1990–1996, 1997*, Vilnius, 1998; *World Bank data.

rather than through the centralized supply system, most companies sought to invest all available financial means by purchasing relatively cheap capital goods and raw materials in Russia and other republics of the former Soviet Union.

Also we should note that national accounts indices in the transition period do not completely reflect the process of saving that has taken place in Lithuania. First of all, national accounts do not reflect saving in kind, the scale of which was very large at the start of the reform, according to expert opinion. Transition from saving in the form of money to saving in kind was a natural defensive reaction of households and companies after the onset of hyperinflation. At the start of the reform many households saved by purchasing durable consumer goods that could be put aside for future consumption. Such a form of saving was not reflected in macroeconomic indices. Funds spent on acquiring commodities for future consumption were attributed to the consumption and not the saving category. This reduced the savings rate as reflected in the statistics, although in reality it was larger. It is difficult to assess by exactly how much the savings rate was higher than those official statistics show, since special investigations were not carried out at the time.

After inflation had been severely curbed (in 1994 and later), saving in kind also fell. Nevertheless, a certain difficulty remains in measuring the amount of savings. This is related to the fact that, according to the System of National Accounts (designed through the joint efforts of Eurostat, the United Nations, the OECD, the International Monetary Fund and the World Bank, and introduced into Lithuania in 1992), if a firm purchases a consumer durable, this is classified in the national accounts as an investment, since the 'services' from the investment can be sold in the future to provide an income (the owner and the customer of the services generally being one and the same firm). If the private consumer purchases a consumer durable, this would be treated as consumption. Bearing in mind that measuring the amount of household savings is based on expenses required to purchase consumer durables not only for everyday consumption but also for the activities of unincorporated companies, the amount of savings recorded in the statistics is diminished. As the number of small-scale enterprises is increasing rapidly, the main investments of which are made through purchasing consumer durables, (for example, hotels, cafes and restaurants buy furniture, refrigerators, video and audio equipment and so on), the real savings rate tends to be distorted when the current national accounting methods are employed.

Statistical data show that the main source of savings during the transition period in Lithuania was the corporate sector. The general government sector experienced a steady decline in the savings rate. Meanwhile, the problem of the high negative household savings rate is being constantly addressed (see Table 14.4).

Table 14.4   Gross domestic saving in Lithuania by institutional sectors (% of GDP)

	Non-financial corporations	Financial corporations	General government	Households
1993	31.6	43.2	81.3	–47.8
1994	29.3	58.6	28.7	–26.2
1995	29.3	41.8	27.6	–22.2
1996	35.0	58.5	15.2	–24.4
1997	34.7	48.2	14.5	–23.3

Sources: Department of Statistics, Government of the Republic of Lithuania, *Lithuanian National Accounts, 1990–96, 1997*, Vilnius, 1998; *Lithuanian National Accounts, 1991–92 at Current Prices*, Vilnius, 1994.

When we try to analyse in greater depth the amount of savings and factors determining it in other sections, we face accounting problems. As a consequence of the restoration of independence and Lithuania's orientation towards a free market economy, traditions of overall accounting or exhaustive enumeration have collapsed. The setting up of small businesses and privatization are phenomena that have caused many problems relating to accounting and statistics. The number of economic units coming into the area of statistical observation, as well as the share of activities not covered by statistical surveys, have expanded greatly. A large proportion of the private sector units belong to the informal ('hidden') economy. According to the survey data, organized by the Methodical Publishing Centre of the Department of Statistics of Lithuania, in 1992–96, this unaccounted share made up 23.4 per cent of GDP.

Indeed, in 1997 the Department of Statistics declared the adjusted GDP estimations, calculated according to the requirements of the 1995 European Account System; more detailed price indices were applied, and the evaluation methods of commercial activity production were also changed after other corrections were made. Having conducted a special survey to estimate the scope of the hidden economy, the results obtained were used for assessing its GDP share for ten activities. However, in this case, as in other countries, illegal activities were not estimated.

It is likely that this reason – the artificial reduction of GDP due to a large informal sector – is the main one when explaining the high negative savings rate in the household sector. Savings estimates, especially in the household sector, tend to be calculated as residuals in Lithuania, therefore saving rates may be poor approximations of their true value.

Also, one must bear in mind that the main source of household income is still salaries and wages. Because, when seeking to modernize their production processes, many enterprises do not pay dividends to their shareholders but rather invest as much profit as they can, the income of households is lower and that is why they are forced to reduce the amount that they can save.

There are also problems related not to the methods but to the collection of preliminary data. Unincorporated household enterprises do not report to the statistical office, and data is based on income tax files; consequently there is a problem of understatement of income/expenditures, which is to be expected. Furthermore, the classification of economic activity is made at aggregate levels and has not been currently updated.

There are many methodical problems relating to the estimates of savings in the governmental sector, since state revenue and expenditures have not been included in one consolidated budget until now. In addition to the budget that reflects the main revenue and expenditures of the state and municipalities, there is a separate social insurance fund budget as well as some 20 other budgets (their number changes constantly) of different target funds. The method for consolidating all these budgets has not yet been decided and is subject to frequent adjustments in cooperation with the Department of Statistics and the ministry of finance. According to data provided by international organizations, the consolidated fiscal balance in Lithuania was negative throughout the 1993–97 period (it fluctuated around 3–4 per cent[2]) as well as in 1998. This had an impact on the savings rate decline in the general government sector.

To identify the basic factors that influence savings and evaluate their impact, a regressive analysis of the dependence of the domestic savings rate was performed on the factors that are most usually referred to in theoretical works as the 'basic saving determinants'. However, this did not reveal any regular pattern. The analysis demonstrated that the 1993–96 savings rate, which was calculated as the gross saving as a percentage of GDP, was independent of the following eight indices: (i) GDP growth; (ii) inflation; (iii) real interest rate paid on short-term deposits in banking institutions in local and in (iv) foreign currencies; (v) fiscal balance as a percentage of GDP; (vi) current account balance as a percentage of GDP; (vii) foreign direct investment as a percentage of GDP; and (viii) broad money as a percentage of GDP.

Such results were conditioned by several factors. First, the data base was not very reliable and the time series were very short. As the Lithuanian national accounts have been kept using a new methodology since 1993, the data of the previous years (calculated according to the former methodology) were not comparable. A short period characterized by national accounts indices calculated according to the uniform methodology, and inexact accounting, make the employment of mathematical methods very difficult.

An absence of distinct tendencies in savings behaviour could also be influenced by the fact that the economic and social reforms that were undertaken increased the saving risk markedly, and changed saving motives and incentives, as we emphasized above.

Because of high and unpredictable inflation, saving in the form of money resembled a lottery. Fluctuations in the interest rates paid on deposits by banks differed greatly from changes in inflation. Therefore, even after 1993, when the national currency was introduced, it was very difficult to predict what the real interest rate would be in the near future.

During the first years of reform, saving was highly unprofitable, especially savings in a foreign currency. The interest rate of time deposits in litas became positive (2 per cent) only at the beginning of 1997, but in the second half of the same year the interest rate became negative again (between −3 and −4 per cent.)[3] The real interest rate of time deposits in foreign currency was always negative, but in spite of that these deposits continued to account for the larger part of total resident time deposits (the portion of time deposits in foreign currencies increased to 68 per cent in 1998) (Table 14.5).

In analysing the composition of total deposits, it is apparent that the comparative weight of deposits in foreign currency in 1994–95 decreased because of the reduction in deposits in foreign currency held by corporations. The latter fact was largely conditioned by the ban on making payments in foreign currency within the territory of Lithuania, imposed in 1994. Meanwhile, foreign currency deposits held by households increased, notwithstanding the negative interest rate, and in 1998, they accounted for 47.9 per cent of all household deposits (see Table 14.5).

These depositing trends demonstrate that in order to protect those savings held in an emergency fund from the huge uncertainty that predominates in the economic reality of Lithuania, deposits are made in hard foreign currency (usually in US dollars). This testifies to the fact that, in spite of the CBA introduced in April 1994, confidence in the local currency and the state economic

Table 14.5   Deposits in foreign currencies in commercial banks (%)

End of period	1993	1994	1995	1996	1997	1998
Resident deposits (compared with total resident deposits)	69.7	40.0	36.7	35.8	33.4	36.8
Resident time deposits (compared with total resident time deposits)	39.8	66.0	59.9	56.5	64.0	68.0
Household deposits (compared with total household deposits)	34.5	41.9	38.8	44.1	45.3	47.9

Source: Bank of Lithunia, *Quarterly Bulletin*, 1993–98

Table 14.6 Savings as a percentage of disposable income

	1992	1993	1994	1995	1996	1997	1998
Gross domestic saving as a percentage of disposable income	20.1	15.3	15.7	14.3	15.2	16.3	16.2
Net saving as percentage of net national disposable income	–	7.4	7.8	6.2	6.2	7.2	–

Sources: Department of Statistics, Government of the Republic of Lithuania, *Lithuanian National Accounts, 1990–96, 1997*, Vilnius, 1998; *Lithuanian National Accounts, 1991–92 at Current Prices*, Vilnius, 1994; Bank of Lithuania, *Balance of Payments of the Republic of Lithuania*, no. 4, 1998.

policy in general is low. Even a high premium for depositing in local currency is not a sufficient incentive to deposit savings in litas. For example, the interest rate on time deposits fixed for 3-6 months in December 1994 was 20.9 per cent for litas and 16.03 per cent for foreign currencies; in December 1996 it was 11.2 per cent for litas and 8.8 per cent for foreign currencies; and in December 1998 it was 7.4 per cent in litas and 4.7 per cent in foreign currencies.

Notwithstanding a significantly reduced inflation, rapid growth of GDP and other favourable changes in the economy, economic agents consider the savings risk to be very high. Attempts made by most of them to use savings as a source of income were defeated. A negative real interest rate of savings deposited in banks, bankruptcies of banks and financial institutions, and the loss of a huge portion of savings because the deposit insurance system did not exist, have all had an adverse effect on the propensity to save. Since 1994, the situation has stabilized and savings equals about 15–16 per cent of disposable income (Table 14.6).

THE ROLE OF DOMESTIC SAVINGS MOBILIZATION

During the first years of reform, a decrease in saving in the form of money did not cause great macroeconomic problems since part of capital formation was from 'natural' savings. The stock of raw materials, accumulated as a protection against inflation, was exhausted only in 1995. Thus, until then the negative value of changes in inventories reduced the statistical domestic investment rate and helped to avoid large domestic saving and domestic investment imbalances (Table 14.7).

However, since 1995 the gap between domestic saving and investment has

Table 14.7   Domestic investment in Lithuania (% of GDP)

	1992	1993	1994	1995	1996	1997	1998
Domestic investment	8.8	19.2	18.4	24.7	24.5	26.5	28.3
Changes in inventories	−20.3	−3.9	−4.7	+1.7	+1.5	+2.2	+2.5

Sources: Department of Statistics, Government of the Republic of Lithuania, *Lithuanian National Accounts, 1990–96, 1997*, Vilnius, 1998; *Lithuanian National Accounts, 1991–1992 at Current Prices*. Vilnius, 1994.

widened considerably. Domestic involvement has reached nearly 25 per cent of GDP, while the savings rate even decreased in 1995, to 14.5 per cent. In the 1996–98 period, saving increased by only 1 percentage point. Taking into consideration Lithuania's need to achieve rapid growth, it is first necessary to stimulate domestic investment growth. Since the domestic savings rate has not yet shown any sign of rapid increase, the only way to satisfy investment demand may be to attract foreign savings.

The possibility of attracting foreign savings generally depends on the financial openness of the country. One way of assessing the country's degree of financial integration in the world economy is to measure the extent to which domestic savings and investment rates are correlated. For that purpose, we could use the savings–investment regression proposed by Feldstein and Horioka (1980) (see equation (14.1)). The authors argue that under the null hypothesis of perfect financial interaction, b should be zero for small countries. The savings–investment regression for Lithuania was calculated using the quarterly data of the 1993–97 period. According to these calculations, the b value for Lithuania is rather small, equal to 0.309, which shows a fairly strong financial integration in the world economy.

On the other hand, bearing in mind that the Lithuanian capital market is still weak in comparison with developed countries (a lack of different types of securities, weak performance of investment funds, non-existence of private pension funds and so on), this conclusion is questionable. Therefore, there is a conceptual problem when using the Feldstein–Horioka regression to test transition countries' financial openness. According to Montiel (1994), although zero capital mobility implies that I/Y and S/Y would be highly correlated, the converse is not true. In other words, if investment and savings rate correlations are low, this does not imply perfect integration.

To be more sure about the true financial openness, Montiel suggested using other ways to assess capital mobility, for example, by measuring gross capital flows. He argues that 'a country enjoying a high degree of financial

Table 14.8   Gross capital flows to GDP in Lithuania (annual average %)

	1993	1994	1995	1996	1997	1998
Capital flow ratio	5.5	4.3	5.7	6.8	7.8	7.0
Capital flow ratio (excluding loans on behalf of the state)	–	2.5	4.2	5.9	7.5	6.5

Sources: Calculations based on the data from Bank of Lithuania, *Balance of Payments of the Republic Lithuania*, 1997, 1998.

integration with the rest of the world should, on average, experience large gross capital flows' (1994, p. 314). Therefore, one could expect that small gross capital flows imply a low degree of financial openness in a country.

An assessment of Lithuania's financial integration, using the gross capital flows approach, was performed by calculating the capital flow ratio (Table 14.8). Two different capital flow ratios were calculated. In the first case, the capital flow ratio was the capital flow value (the sum of inflows and outflows) divided by two and then divided by GDP. In the second case, the capital flow value was changed with respect to non-market flows – the loans received on behalf of the state as well as the amounts repaid were eliminated from the capital inflows. Thus, the second capital ratio reflects the degree of financial openness more accurately.

To evaluate the data it is necessary to compare them with the capital flow ratios in other countries, for example, with those in developing countries. According to Montiel's calculations (1994), gross capital flows to GDP in 88 developing countries in the 1980–89 period fluctuate from 1.5 per cent in India to 140.16 per cent in Panama. The capital flow ratio of 33 developing countries is less than the capital ratio in Lithuania in 1997. If the modal range of 5–10 per cent were used as a benchmark for an intermediate degree of capital mobility, then Lithuania could be placed among the low–intermediate countries, although (with the exception of the 1998 results), the level of financial integration is increasing. But even the highest calculated ratio – 7.8 per cent is still below the average gross capital ratio of 11.9 per cent for 88 developing countries.

Given this result, it is unlikely that the needed investment growth will be financed only by foreign savings in the near future. Moreover, the increase in Lithuania's current account deficit is very undesirable. Indeed, the current account deficit in 1995 grew rapidly (Table 14.2) and reached 12.1 per cent in 1998. A further increase in the current account deficit could produce very serious consequences, resulting in currency and financial crises.

If savings and investment evolutionary trends are compared, it could be concluded that the most important reason for the savings–investment gap is the decrease in savings, which lasted from the beginning of reforms up to 1995. The slight increase in domestic savings in 1996-98 could not satisfy the growing investment demand. With increased financial liberalization in the country, the current account deficit is likely to increase further. In order to change this tendency, it would be necessary to apply instruments regulating investment from abroad. The Lithuanian authorities have suggested measures that will result in restricting capital flows. For example, a tax on loans received by Lithuanian economic entities from abroad could be imposed. Another proposal is that the interest rate on short-term loans received from non-residents should not be included in tax calculations. But such restrictions on capital inflows reduce the possibilities of receiving finance from foreign sources and can influence private sector development negatively, since domestic financial institutions will not be able to satisfy the financial needs of the real sector.

So, taking into consideration the situation related to the current account deficit in Lithuania, domestic savings mobilization becomes an important instrument for regulating external balances. A greater dependence on domestic savings should help to reduce the gap between savings supply and investment demand. Consequently, one of the major tasks for policy makers is to encourage higher rates of saving.

In the current economic and social climate in Lithuania, compulsory means of saving by increasing taxes – which would not only increase public savings but also reduce household and firm consumption – would be unpopular. It is more appropriate to achieve a higher public savings rate by consolidated fiscal budget restraints. The first step has already been taken by the Lithuanian government when it planned a balanced state budget in 1999.

Government savings constitute only a small part of domestic savings (11 per cent of all gross savings in 1997), so it is more urgent to stimulate households' propensity to save and to achieve a positive change in the savings rate. For this purpose, the best way is to apply instruments of government regulation, which will create new savings incentives and suggest new forms of saving.

The creation of the following savings incentives is urgent:

- the introduction of a preferential housing credit system using contractual saving schemes and increased accessibility of this system to a wider community;
- the introduction of a private pension savings scheme and its promotion with tax incentives; and
- an increase in the role of private investment funds as well as other institutional savers in the economy.

The introduction of long-term credit schemes for the construction and purchase of flats and houses would probably mobilize saving in Lithuania and at the same time would contribute to the development of the construction industry. Only recently have commercial banks started to offer loans for housing for longer periods – up to 10 years. However, experience shows that this type of loan provided by commercial banks is not popular, since household income is insufficient for them to be able to repay the loan plus 10–15 per cent annual interest during the 10 years. A significant increase in saving could be expected only when the loan can be repaid over a longer period (15–30 years) together with the requirement that the borrower should accumulate a down-payment (20–30 per cent of the value of the house) on a contractual saving scheme basis.

Another important institutional innovation that would mobilize saving is the introduction of private pension schemes. The main problem for such schemes is that there is insufficient confidence in them. People are afraid that private funds will go bankrupt and all savings lost, as happened with banks and other financial institutions at the beginning of the reform. Indeed, pension funds will face problems of safe investment – because of an insuffiently developed financial sector, investment choice barely exists. In practice, the only safe investment currently is government bonds, issued for a short period (up to one year). Such a situation impedes the establishment of private pension funds, although the draft law on private pension funds has already been prepared. This difficult situation could be resolved only by a more rapid development of capital market institutions and instruments.

SUMMARY AND CONCLUSIONS

CEE countries in transition carrying out essential restructuring of their economies encounter an increased investment demand. But during the transition period they experienced a considerable fall in domestic savings. In order to attain long-term growth aspirations, they will either have to confront the gap between domestic savings supply and investment demand or rely mostly upon foreign savings. Both measures could be employed, but the latter is restrained by the country's current account sustainability.

The savings behaviour characteristic of transition countries was also apparent in Lithuania. In the transition period, Lithuania experienced a sharp decline in its saving rate. This was related to a decrease in the savings rate in both the private and public sectors. The regressive analysis of dependence of the domestic savings rate on the factors that are usually referred to as the basic saving determinants did not reveal any regularities. The absence of distinct tendencies of savings behaviour could be explained by the unreliability of the data base and a short time series, as well as by increased uncertainty that changed usual saving habits. Savings began to be determined by the same factors as investment – by profitability and risk – rather than by income and wealth.

As the domestic savings rate does not show a tendency to increase rapidly, investment demand could be satisfied only by the employment of foreign savings. The possibility of attracting foreign savings generally depends on the financial openness of the country. Although an assessment of Lithuania's financial integration into the world economy using a savings-investment regression (Feldstein and Horioka 1980) has shown rather strong financial integration, this conclusion is subject to doubt if we recall the weak level of development in the Lithuanian capital market. Montiel (1994) has stated that because of conceptual problems when using the Feldstein–Horioka regression, it is useful to use other approaches to assess the degree of financial integration. According to the capital flows approach, Lithuania in the 1995–98 period could be considered as a country of low-intermediate, but increasing, level of financial integration with the outside world.

Thus it is unlikely that in the near future essential investment growth will be financed by foreign savings at a desirable level. Moreover, it could have a negative result on external balances because of a huge increase in the current account deficit. Therefore, domestic savings mobilization becomes an important factor for macroeconomic balances.

The most important domestic savings mobilization measures in Lithuania should be related to the introduction of institutional innovations into the housing crediting schemes, as well as increasing the role of institutional savers – private investment funds, private pension funds and others – in the economy.

NOTES

1. IMF, *World Economic Outlook*, 1996.
2. IMF, *World Economic Outlook*, 1996, 1997.
3. Bank of Lithuania, *Lithuania under Conditions of Unstable International Financial Markets*, Vilnius, 1998.

REFERENCES

Aghevli, Bijan B., J.M. Boughton, P.J. Montiel, D. Villanueva and G. Woglam (1990), 'The role of national saving in the world economy', International Monetary Fund Occasional Paper 67, Washington, DC: IMF.

Ando, A. and A.B. Kennickell (1987), 'How much (or little) life cycle is there in micro data? The cases of the United States and Japan', in R. Dornbusch, S. Fischer and J. Bossons (eds), *Macroeconomics and Finance: Essays in Honor of Franco Modigliani*, Cambridge, MA: MIT Press.

Bank of Lithuania (1998), *Lithuania under the Conditions of Unstable International Financial Markets*, Vilnius (in Lithuanian).

Baross, D. (1979), 'Private saving and provision of social security in Britain, 1946–75', in G.M. von Furstenberg (ed.), *Social Security versus Private Saving*, Cambridge, MA: Ballinger.

Barro, R. (1974), 'Are government bonds net wealth?', *Journal of Political Economy*, **82**, 1095–117.

Bayoumi, T. (1996), *Financial Integration and Real Activity*, Manchester: Manchester University Press.

De Melo, M., C. Denizer and A. Gelb (1995), 'From plan to market: patterns of transition', manuscript.

Department of Statistics, Government of the Republic of Lithuania (1997), *Uncalculated Economy: Attitudes, Investigations Problems*, Vilnius. (in Lithuanian).

Epstein, L. and S. Zin (1989), 'Substitution, risk aversion and the temporal behaviour of consumption and assets returns: a theoretical framework', *Economica*, **57**, 937–69.

Feldstein, M.S. and P. Bacchetta (1989), 'National saving and international investment', National Bureau of Economic Research, Working Paper no. 3164, Cambridge, MA: NBER.

Feldstein, M. and C. Horioka (1980), 'National saving and international capital flows', *Economic Journal*, **90**, 314–29.

Flavin, M. (1981), 'The adjustment of consumption to changing expectations about future income', *Journal of Political Economy*, **89**, 974–1009.

Frankel, J.A. (1989), 'Quantifying international capital mobility in the 1980s', National Bureau of Economic Research Working Paper no. 2856, Cambridge, MA: NBER.

Friedman, M. (1957), *A Theory of the Consumption Function*, Princeton, NJ: Princeton University Press.

Gultekin, N.B. and D.E. Logue (1979), 'Social security and personal saving: survey and new evidence', in G.M. von Furstenberg (ed.), *Social Security versus Private Saving*, Cambridge, MA: Ballinger.

Hall, R.E. (1978), 'Stochastic implications of the life-cycle hypothesis', *Journal of Political Economy*, **96**, 971–87.

Hubbard, R.G. (1986), 'Pension wealth and individual saving: some new evidence', *Journal of Money, Credit and Banking*, **18**.

Kimball, M.S. (1990), 'Precautionary saving in the small and the large', *Econometrica*, **58**, 53–73.

Kornai, J. (1959), *Overcentralization in Economic Administration*, Oxford: Oxford University Press.

Kornai, J. (1980), *Economics of Shortage*, Amsterdam: North-Holland.

Kornai, J. (1992), *The Socialist System*, Princeton, NJ: Princeton University Press.

Modigliani, F. and R. Brumberg (1954), 'Utility analysis and the consumption function: an interpretation of cross-section data', in K.K. Kurihara (ed.), *Post-Keynesian Economics*, New Brunswick, NJ: Rutgers University Press.

Modigliani, F. and R. Brumberg (1979), 'Utility analysis and the consumption function: an attempt at integration', in A. Abel (ed.), *The Collected Papers of Franco Modigliani*, Vol. 2, Cambridge, MA: MIT Press.

Montiel, P.J. (1994), 'Capital mobility in developing countries: some measurement issues and empirical estimates', *World Bank Economic Review*, **8** (3), September, 311–50.

Quandt, R.E. (1989), 'Disequilibrium econometrics for centrally planned economies', in C. Davis and W. Charemza (eds), *Models of Disequilibrium and Shortage in Centrally Planned Economies*, London and New York: Chapman & Hall.

Schmidt-Hebbel, K. and L. Serven (1997), 'Saving across the world: puzzles and policies', World Bank Discussion Paper no. 354, Washington, DC.

Skinner, J. (1988), 'Risky income, life-cycle consumption, and precautionary saving', *Journal of Monetary Economics*, **22**, 237–55.

Weil, P. (1989), 'Equity premium and risk free rate puzzles', *Journal of Monetary Economics*, **24**, 401–21.

Weil, P. (1990), 'Nonexpected utility in macroeconomics', *Quarterly Journal of Economics*, **105**, 29–42.

Welfe, A. (1989), 'Saving and consumption in the centrally planned economy', in C. Davis and W. Charemza (eds), *Models of Disequilibrium and Shortage in Centrally Planned Economies*, London and New York: Chapman & Hall.

Zeldes, S. (1989), 'Consumption and liquidity constraints: an empirical investigation', *Journal of Political Economy*, **98**, 305–46.

15. The Polish banking sector and EU regulations

Andrzej Raczko

INTRODUCTION

The process of the integration of the Polish banking sector with that of the European Union (EU) can be evaluated from the point of view of the aims towards which both sides are orientated. The strategic goal of the Union countries consists in the creation of a uniform market, that is, the establishment of a legal and organizational environment in Poland, which would ensure that the functioning of companies is subject to standards analogous to those prevailing in the EU. The uniform conditions are supposed to apply both to banks and to companies who are their clients. From this point of view, the Polish banking sector should conform to EU safety standards and should also deliver at least the basic basket of products and services. This represents an area where the Polish objectives are convergent with those of EU countries. We must not, however, forget about another aspect – the unrestrained operation of foreign banks in Poland will constitute competition for the Polish banking sector. We are thus faced with the problem of how we should prepare the already functioning banks for the new conditions. In addition, the adaptation of the existing banks to the requirements of market competition raises the question of the pace at which the changes should be introduced.

The purpose of this chapter is to evaluate the speed and the sequence of the adaptation endeavours with regard to the Polish banking sector with a view to establishing not only a stable and safe system but also creating an environment which would allow the existing Polish banks to cope successfully with the competition from foreign banks.

We shall start with the provisions of the European Accord, which took effect as of 1 February 1994. In keeping with the Accord, which has divided the unification process of Polish banking into two stages (Daniluk 1996), the chapter is composed of two parts, each devoted to one stage of the adjustment of the banking sector towards meeting EU standards. The first and essential part relates largely to the changes already introduced in the Polish banking sector. Apart from the assessment of the fulfilment by Poland of the obligations imposed by the treaty, this historically orientated analysis will also contain a commentary on the extent to which the introduction of European standards facilitated the solution of specific problems faced by the Polish banking sector in the years from 1994 to 1998.

The second part represents a short commentary, including a projection of the consequences of the complete adaptation of the Polishing banking sector to EU standards. The point of departure in this discussion is the White Paper, which sets out the expectations of the EU countries in relation to the countries of Central Europe.

THE FIRST STAGE OF THE IMPLEMENTATION OF THE KEY SETTLEMENTS OF EUROPEAN ACCORD

The analysis of the processes of adaptation to EU standards should commence with the presentation of the developmental stage of the banking sector as 1994 approached. The reforms, started in 1989, had created the possibility, over the five years, for the crystallization of fundamental institutions and the creation of a legal framework facilitating the functioning of banks. They constituted the backbone of the banking system, which was subsequently adjusted to EU standards. This course of events was extremely significant and it brought specific consequences both in terms of the absorption of EU standards and in terms of the unique qualities of the Polish banking sector.

We must bear in mind that although the European Accord became effective in Poland in February 1994, its provisions had already been known and agreed upon in December 1991. Thus, the changes which had been effected in the banking sector since the beginning of 1990 had to some extent anticipated the provisions of the European Accord, formally introduced in 1994.

When analysing the provisions of the European Accord relating to the first stage of implementation, we should mention five major objectives which should have been achieved:

- Ensuring the functioning of foreign banks under principles that were not less favourable than the principles applicable to Polish banks and permitting foreign banks to introduce innovative products in compliance with the Polish regulations prevailing at that time (arts 44, 45, 47).
- Introduction of an efficient banking supervision and appropriate prudential regulations (arts 83, 85).
- Gradual introduction of institutions, norms and customs corresponding to EU standards (arts 68, 69).
- Gradual liberalization of flows of current foreign currency payments and capital payments (arts 59, 60, 61, 62).

- Ensuring stability of the financial system by means of proper institutional solutions (art. 84).

Development of the Foreign Bank Sector in Poland

The EU's postulate regarding the creation of an environment facilitating the undertaking of business activities by foreign banks (not less favourable than for Polish banks) was given full effect. Foreign banks enjoyed a variety of privileges, not only tax related but also with regard to the range of operations (all of them obtained a full foreign exchange licence), with, additionally, foreign banks being permitted to index their equity. Share capital contributed in foreign currencies was converted in the consecutive balance-sheet years according to the then-current exchange rate. It was only in 1996 and 1997 that the final conversion of capital into zlotys was made. The National Bank of Poland (NPB) permitted two legal forms in which foreign banks could function: the status of a branch of a foreign bank in Poland (for example, ING, Société Générale), or the status of a joint-stock company established according to Polish law, owned by a foreign bank. The latter possibility was preferred by the NBP.

The opening of banks as branches of a foreign bank required additional agreements between the NBP and the foreign bank. The agreements concerned two issues: the amount of credit line granted to the Polish branch by the foreign-based head office (playing the role of own funds) and the obligation of the Polish branch to provide access to data relating to its operations, pursuant to the NBP reporting requirements. Of particular significance here was the amount of credit line, since it was on the basis of this amount that prudential norms were defined for the branch, especially loan concentration ratios.

The fulfilment of the EU's postulate regarding the creation of an environment facilitating the undertaking of business activities by foreign banks resulted in a rapid increase in branch numbers as well as in employment (see Tables 15.1 and 15.2). Such banks also made a significant contribution to the training of Polish bank personnel as well as pioneering the introduction of new

Table 15.1   Number of branches in the commercial bank sector

	1993	1994	1995	1996	1997	1998*
Polish commercial banks	1426	1441	1472	1437	1460	1529
Foreign banks	10	13	29	143	169	280

Note: *September 1998.

Source: General Inspectorate of Bank Supervision.

Table 15.2   Employment in the commercial bank sector

	1993	1994	1995	1996	1997	1998*
Polish commercial banks	119 045	127 708	134 048	129 102	130 823	130 595
Foreign banks	688	997	2000	15 099	16 272	17 535

Note: *September 1998.

Source: General Inspectorate of Bank Supervision.

banking products on the Polish market (mainly in the area of investment banking). On the other hand, foreign banks became serious competitors against Polish banks, especially in the area of foreign operations, and the provision of services to foreign firms in Poland as well as to the best Polish clients (Kosinski 1998). The expansion of foreign banks was accelerated in late 1996 and 1997. The large number of such banks and the exhaustion of the formula of a specialist bank having a small number of branches servicing only corporate clients led to losses incurred by the foreign banks which had started operating in 1995 and the following years (see Table 15.3). The comments concerning the changes in the strategy of foreign banks will be addressed later in the chapter.

New possibilities for foreign banks were created by the privatization of big banks owned by the state treasury. The results of this process have had a great influence on the development of the banking sector in Poland. As they are interconnected with the process of adaption to EU standards, we shall discuss this problem later.

The operational activities of foreign banks in Poland as well as the introduction of innovative products did not meet any substantial barrier in the form of Polish provisions and regulations. This was the result of a very prudent operational approach by foreign banks. The internal prudential norms of foreign banks in Poland were more restrictive than the norms imposed by the

Table 15.3   Net Profitability in the commercial bank sector (%)

	1993	1994	1995	1996	1997
Polish commercial banks	−2.00	0.90	12.20	16.80	12.46
Foreign banks	39.50	24.70	15.00	15.30	9.70

Source: General Inspectorate of Bank Supervision.

NBP and the procedures applied in Polish banks. Indeed, elements of discrimination against Polish banks and their customers (for example, the obtaining of a limit by a Polish bank required the fulfilment of additional conditions) could be detected.

Considerable prudence was also exercised by foreign banks in introducing new products. This can be very well exemplified by the innovations introduced by foreign banks with regard to investment banking (commercial papers (CPs) adapted to the Polish environment, known as KWITs). At the onset, CPs were offered only to reputable foreign companies in Poland.[1] It was only after the establishment of efficient secondary trading that the instrument was offered to leading Polish companies. Later on, it was adopted by Polish banks and became part of a standard basket of services.

Banking Supervision and Prudential Norms

It seems obvious that the construction of an efficient system of banking supervision and a rapid harmonization of prudential norms are in the joint interest of the EU and Poland. The reality, however, was more complicated in this respect. The possibility of introducing prudential norms was largely limited by the level of development of the Polish banking sector at the beginning of the 1990s (Hewelt 1995). The adaptation processes were especially important in relation to four areas (Sleszynska and Lewandowski 1996):

- determining the rules for obtaining bank licences;
- introduction of prudential forms;
- establishment of banking supervision as an efficiently functioning institution capable of monitoring the prudential norms;
- monitoring the introduced prudential norms.

Rules for obtaining banking licences

At the start of the 1990s, the Polish banking sector authorities, when determining the licensing policy, had to reconcile, on the one hand, the necessity of ensuring a high level of competition and on the other the appropriate prudential standards for banking operations.

The Banking Act, introduced in 1989, provided for very liberal rules governing the establishment of banks. The model of a joint-stock company was adopted as the basic legal form (exclusive of state and cooperative banks). The licences for banking operations were granted by the president of the NBP, subject to the fulfilment of relevant technical requirements (appropriate premises, qualified personnel), legal requirements (bank statutes), a business plan and, first and foremost, a sufficient founding capital. The Banking Act did not specify the minimum level of equity, the specification of which rested with the president of the NBP and the minister of finance. The act did provide, however, that the founding capital may not be derived from a credit and may not be in anyway encumbered (the licensing procedure was compatible with the First Banking Directive 77/780/EEC).

The Banking Act did not prohibit the possibility of capital being contributed in kind, and did not impose any additional conditions on contributions in kind, other than those set out in the Commercial Code. The underdeveloped real estate market and the substantial variation in the valuation of contributions in kind gave rise, in a number of cases, to the necessity of significantly revaluating the relevant contributions in kind and subsequently the equity of the given banks.

What had a decisive significance for the development of the banking sector was the adoption of the strategy of a gradual attainment by Polish banks of the minimum equity threshold (ecu 5 million) required by the Second Banking Directive 89/646/EEC. In 1989, PLN 600 thousand was sufficient to establish a bank, in 1992 the limit for newly launched banks was raised to PLN 7 million and in 1994 to PLN 13 million (see Table 15.4).

The NBP's strategy of low equity thresholds resulted in a rapid increase in the number of new banks. In total, during the first three years, 72 licences were issued to Polish banks and nine licences to foreign banks (see Table 15.5). The subsequent rises in the minimum equity thresholds decelerated the further growth in the number of banks, however it contributed only insignificantly to bank merges. In the begining the consolidation processes had a forced character and in the majority of cases consisted in state banks taking over banks which were going bankrupt.

The liberal licence-granting policy, and above all the low equity requirements, substantially departing from EU standards (they became a norm in Polish law only after the latest update of the Banking Act in 1997), led to the creation of a very diversified banking sector (see Table 15.6). On the one hand, the banking sector was characterized by a very large number of banks, while

Table 15.4   Structure of core capital in the Polish banking sector: commercial banks* (no. of banks)

Core capital (million)	1993	1994	1995
Below 2.5	25	12	5
2.5–5.0	16	16	19
5.0 and over	42	50	57

Note: *Not including banks in the process of liquidation.

Source: General Inspectorate of Bank Supervision.

Table 15.5   Structure of the Polish banking sector (no. of banks)

	1993	1994	1995	1996	1997	1998*
Commercial banks	87	82	81	81	81	83
Direct state-owned banks	18	18	16	11	7	7
Indirect state-owned banks	11	11	11	13	7	7
Private Polish banks	48	42	36	32	39	38
Foreign banks	10	11	18	25	28	31
Cooperative banks	1653	1612	1510	1394	1295	1208

Note: *September 1998.

Source: General Inspectorate of Bank Supervision.

Table 15.6   Structure of core capital in the Polish banking sector (%)

	1993	1994	1995	1996	1997
Commercial banks	91.8	94.2	94.9	95.2	95.0
Direct state-owned banks	60.9	60.5	56.3	43.2	24.1
Indirect state-owned banks	4.5	6.0	6.4	12.6	7.9
Private Polish banks	24.1	24.2	24.4	19.3	39.1
Foreign banks	2.3	3.5	7.8	20.1	23.9
Cooperative banks	8.2	5.8	5.1	4.8	5.0

Source: General Inspectorate of Bank Supervision.

on the other, the majority of assets, loans and deposits in the banking sector belonged to big state banks (see Tables 15.7–9). A high level of competition could be observed on the corporating banking market, with a concurrent slow pace of development in retail banking.

As a result, the second half of the 1990s saw the creation of a banking sector with a relatively large number of small banks characterized by a low operational efficiency (measured in terms of assets per employee), and a small network of branches, with limited financial resources necessary for the development of new banking products (especially in the case of retail banking). Additionally, the problem of cooperative banks, a leftover from the command economy period, was still unsolved (and also the problem of the large BGŻ bank central to this issue). These banks (numbering about 1600 at the start of the 1990s) were used to provide financing for individual farmers. The capital of each such bank did not exceed a few thousand dollars. Some

Table 15.7   Structure of assets in the Polish banking sector (%)

	1993	1994	1995	1996	1997	1998*
Commercial banks	93.4	94.7	95.2	95.4	95.5	95.8
Direct state-owned banks	76.1	70.8	63.0	51.1	39.1	37.6
Indirect state-owned banks	4.3	5.3	5.8	15.4	10.9	10.5
Private Polish banks	10.4	15.4	22.7	15.1	30.5	31.5
Foreign banks	2.6	3.2	4.2	13.7	15.0	16.2
Cooperative banks	6.6	5.3	4.8	4.6	4.5	4.2

Note: *September 1998.

Source: General Inspectorate of Bank Supervision.

Table 15.8   Structure of net loans in the Polish banking sector (%)

	1993	1994	1995	1996	1997	1998*
Commercial banks	92.9	93.9	94.5	93.9	94.5	94.8
Direct state-owned banks	76.6	69.1	58.5	42.0	27.9	26.2
Indirect state-owned banks	2.7	3.9	5.2	19.3	15.3	13.7
Private Polish banks	10.9	15.9	25.0	16.6	33.1	33.5
Foreign banks	2.7	4.4	5.8	16.0	18.2	21.4
Cooperative banks	6.6	5.3	4.8	4.6	4.5	4.2

Note: *September 1998.

Source: General Inspectorate of Bank Supervision.

Table 15.9   Structure of deposits in the Polish banking sector (%)

	1993	1994	1995	1996	1997	1998*
Commercial banks	92.4	94.1	94.5	94.5	94.8	95.0
Direct state-owned banks	75.6	71.6	65.6	57.2	49.5	44.1
Indirect state-owned banks	5.5	5.7	5.7	12.9	8.5	12.2
Private Polish banks	9.2	14.1	20.2	12.2	24.1	25.7
Foreign banks	2.1	2.7	3.0	12.2	12.7	13.0
Cooperative banks	7.6	5.9	5.5	5.5	5.2	5.0

Note: *September 1998.

Source: General Inspectorate of Bank Supervision.

of them qualified for bankruptcy. Attempts to create a new structure of cooperative banks, based on the German model (the Raiffeisen bank), were not completed.

Prudential norms

The introduction of prudential norms is a good example of the depth of changes which have to be effected in various areas connected with the principles of banking operations. The adaptation measures were applied in relation to the principles of bank accounting, the reporting system for bank supervision and bank auditing.

The primary EU prudential norm adopted by the Polish banking sector was the solvency ratio (Directive 87/647/EEC). The introduction of this ratio was desired for two reasons:

- to determine the extent of solvency of Polish banks, and
- to encourage bank management boards to undertake measures aimed at structuring assets (in terms of risk) and own capital (proper accumulation of profit) in a manner that would bring them in line with the EU norm (8 per cent pursuant to art. 10 of Directive 89/299/EEC).

An immediate introduction of the ratio formula in the form prescribed by Directive 87/647/EEC was both impossible and impractical. It was impossible for technical reasons, for example, because of the respective definition of banks' own funds comparable to the definition included in the directive. It was impractical because of the rather obvious result of calculating the ratio. The small own capital of state-owned banks represented a decisive factor in the occurrence of a very low ratio for such banks. In its policy assumptions, the NBP expected that banks would attain 3 per cent ratio in 1991, 6 per cent in 1992 and 8 per cent in 1993. The logic of introducing a solvency ratio was supported by three underlying factors:

- It was possible to introduce this ratio as a strict norm to be adhered to by banks starting their operations.
- In the case of state-owned banks, the supervision institution was able to analyse and react to not only the level of the ratio itself but also the changes in the ratio occurring in the course of time.
- The supervision institution gained an instrument with which to impose a proper structure on a bank's asset portfolio.

The last factor was especially important. In an economy which was going through a period of systemic transformation, it was necessary to introduce instruments which would force banks to limit their exposure to assets carrying a high level of risk. What counted most was the loan policy. The transformation of the system led to the collapse of a number of large state-owned companies operating in unprofitable sectors. The safety of the banking sector necessitated the discontinuation of the provision of loans to such companies. The solvency ratio (introduced under NBP regulations in 1990) was clearly different from the EEC formula in terms of the risk weights. The Polish solvency ratio assigned risk weights of 140 per cent for watch loans and 300 per cent for doubtful loans. This was a clear manifestation of the central bank's preferences in relation to its loan policy.[2]

A proper calculation of the solvency ratio necessitated a proper assessment of the asset value. This was especially important in the case of loan-related debt. The necessity of accounting for loan-related debt in terms of its net value led to the necessity of specifying the principles of establishment of provisions for bad loans. The general banking risk fund, envisaged by the financial system, did not provide sufficient protection against potential losses incurred in connection with bad loans, therefore the NBP decided to introduce obligatory principles of setting up specific provisions for bad loans (Regulation 19/92 of the president of the NBP). The scale on which provisions were set up was so extensive that in many cases it led to the threat of banks having to report losses. For this reason, a decision was made to introduce a period of a few months in which banks were allowed to attain full compliance with the required number of provisions. The introduction of this adaptation period for banks required a change in the formula for calculating the solvency ratio. In May 1993, a regulation by the president of the NBP (7/93) brought into effect new principles for calculating the ratio. High-risk weights (140 per cent and 300 per cent) were given up. Simultaneously, new norms for the solvency ratio of new banks were adopted at the respective levels of 15 per cent and 12 per cent in the first two years. The solvency ratio calculated according to the new principles was still low for some state-owned banks. This was the combined result of two factors – low own funds and bad loans. Further development in the banking sector and adaptation to EU standards was conditional on a quick solution to both these problems.

In 1993 a package of solutions was adopted which opened the way for an injection of additional capital to state banks and at the same time laid the groundwork for solving the problem of bad loans (see Table 15.10). A key element of the package was the act on financial restructuring of enterprises and banks (dated 3 February 1993). The act created the possibility of a definitive solution to the problem of bad loans by way of bank conciliatory proceedings, a public sale of loan-relate debt and a conversion of the debt into shares of the indebted companies. On the other hand, the act also made it possible to inject additional capital into banks by means of special restructuring bonds (see Table 15.11). From the financial point of view, there was a rise in own

Table 15.10   Share of bad loans in total loans (%)

	1993	1994	1995
Commercial banks formed on NBP basis (9)	32.7	27.2	16.1
State-owned banks (6)	32.0	33.9	27.2
Other Polish banks	26.4	22.5	14.9
Foreign banks	2.5	1.3	19.7
Cooperative banks	22.7	21.3	11.7

Source: General Inspectorate of Bank Supervision.

Table 15.11   Restructuring bonds programme (PLNm)

Bank	
Bank Depozytowo-Kredytowy SA	179.0
Bank Gdanski SA	160.9
Bank Przemyslowo-Handlowy SA	159.8
Bank Zachodni SA	144.5
Pomorski Bank Kredytowy SA	136.4
Powszechny BankGospodarczy SA	125.6
Powszechn Bank Kredytowy SA	193.7
Powszechna Kasa Oszczednosci BP	573.4
Bank Gospodarki Zywnosciowej	1956.5
Bank Polska Kasa Opieki SA	370.0
Total	3999.8

Source: Ordinance of Ministry of Finance, 27 July 1993.

capital of state-owned banks, financed with 15-year state treasury bonds. The issuance of these bonds was based on the transformation of part of the Polish Stabilization Fund (about USD 1 billion), granted to Poland and unutilized, into the Polish Banks' Privatization Fund (about USD 400 million). The resources from the latter fund were available for funding the issuance of the restructuring bonds.

The injection of additional capital into banks and the restructuring of the loan portfolio allowed most state-owned banks to attain a solvency ratio of more than 8 per cent. The expected ratio was not attained by Bank Gospodarki Zywnosciowej or by several cooperative banks (see Tables 15.12 and 15.13).

Table 15.12   Solvency ratio: commercial banks (no. of banks)

Solvency ratio	1992	1993	1994	1995	1996	1997	1998*
8% and over	85	69	64	68	73	73	75
0%–8%	11	5	3	2	1	2	4
Below 0%	8	13	15	11	7	6	4

Note: *September 1998.

Source: General Inspectorate of Bank Supervision.

Table 15.13   Solvency ratio: cooperative banks (no. of banks)

Solvency ratio	1993	1994	1995	1996	1997	1998*
8% and over	1300	1188	1144	1074	1119	1115
0%–8%	133	115	151	195	137	76
Below 0%	220	309	215	125	39	17

Note: *September 1998.

Source: General Inspectorate of Bank Supervision.

The subsequent adjustments of the method of calculating the solvency ratio were of a technical nature. The new banking law (1997) introduced a uniform method of calculating banks' own funds, modelled on the division into core capital and soft capital, and the principles of classifying subordinated liabilities. What remained, however, was an elaborate table of risk weights (under the Polish method of calculating the ratio there are six risk weights), as well as the principle of classifying own liabilities as part of own funds on the basis of an individual NBP permit. In 1999, plans were made for expanding the principles of calculating the solvency ratio in relation to specific off-balance-sheet items (interest rate forward contracts and foreign currency forward contracts). The essence of the difference between the method of calculating the solvency ratio according to Polish regulations and according to the EEC directive still consists in the principles of determining provisions for bad loans. The Polish system is based on centralized NBP regulations which, although liberalized (Regulation No. 13/93), make individual determination of the provision fairly unlikely. In addition, such provisions are set up for a specific purpose and are thus subject to taxation. As a result, the method of calculating the solvency ratio is more restrictive than under the EU standard. Under Polish law, the solvency ratio must be calculated every month (not twice a year), thus making it possible to carry out an ongoing monitoring of banks' solvency. Such a solution appears to be justifiable as long as loan operations continue to be more risky than in EU countries.

The problem of specific provisions was similar to the problem of adaptation of credit exposure. It was possible to reach the target standard stage by stage. Initially, the limits were more rigorous than those applicable under the EU norm. The total exposure (loans and other claims, including off-balance-sheet items) arising from a single agreement was set at no more than 10 per cent of the bank's own funds; the total exposure in relation to a single customer was, however, set at no more than 15 per cent of own funds. Such restrictive norms, especially given the banks' low own funds, effectively limited the banks' loan operations (for example, in the first half of the 1990s none of the banks was able to finance the construction of a ship). This limit could be increased to 50 per cent of own funds if an individual permit was obtained from the president of the NBP. This system led to a significant development of syndicate loans. It had a positive effect because creditworthiness was assessed not only by one but by a number of banks. On the other hand, however, syndicate loans were granted for a relatively short period (from one to three years). Thus, the financing of long-term investment projects was made difficult. Such a system also led to an expansion in the function of the NBP, which acted as a 'Superloan' committee giving permission to grant big loans (the 50 per cent limit). In addition, the system played a crucial role in the gradual departure from the so-called central loans relating to large investment projects guaranteed by the government. The most significant element in the system was the lack of a global limit for big loans. This encouraged the development of banks specializing in financing a specific sector of the economy, whose loan operations were concentrated on providing service to large corporate customers. The consolidation processes in the sector, combined with the privatization of banks, made it possible to introduce concentration limits complying with EEC Directive 92/121/EEC. The new limits ceased to restrict the operations of big banks significantly and instead became a crucial stimulant for consolidation processes in the case of specialized banks. The norms were incorporated into the new banking law (1997).[3]

When adapting the limits for capital operations as specified in the Second Banking Directive 89/646/EEC to Polish banks, it was necessary to take into account the extent of the development of the capital market. Public trading in securities and the institutions connected with it, were set up in 1991. The visible weakness of the capital market in terms of, above all, the liquidity of trading as well as the significant fluctuations of rates, forced banks to proceed very cautiously with their capital market investments. The main threat, however, in the opinion of bank supervision bodies, was the banks' inclination to capital-expose themselves to manufacturing and retail companies whose shares were not admitted to public trading. The danger of banks' tying up their financial resources in this type of investment was the reason why very strict limits were introduced. Banks' exposure on the capital market (both in shares and bonds) was not permitted to be larger than 25 per cent of a banks' own funds. With the permission of the NBP president, this limit could be increased to 50 per cent of own funds.

The limit very soon became an impediment to the development of investment banking. Polish banking law did not envisage any separate regulations for investment banks. Banks invested the permissible limit in ways connected with the strategic expansion of the given bank (capital investments leading to a controlling state in leasing companies, brokerage offices and investment funds).[4] Of necessity, banks did not become long-term strategic investors. Banks' operations on the capital market were confined mainly to playing the role of a passive agent for issuance of securities or bonds, distributing these financial instruments among customers. Banks also became involved in underwriting, but as a rule, this did not apply to the whole issue but only to the part necessary to close the issue successfully. Sometimes the issue agent also acted as an arranger of secondary trading. In the case of stock exchange-listed companies a crucial role was also played by the so-called commercial bills, that is, short-term debt securities issued by listed companies. These bills, because of the ease of assessment of the standing of the company (information about listed companies was in the public domain) readily found purchasers in the financial sector. Also, secondary trading in such securities functioned very well. The bank that deserves special praise for its contribution in the promotion of commercial bills was Polski Bank Rozwoju.[5]

The functioning of strict limits in relation to banks' capital operations led to the occurrence of substitute investment banks in the form of large listed companies (for example, Elektrim, Universal). They began to function as financial holdings. To some extent, this process was engendered by the authorities dealing with privatization, which championed the concept of transforming large companies that were involved in foreign trading into financial holdings maintaining control over firms dealing in the manufacturing of export products. A similar principle was used in the construction of the privatization programmed based on National Investment Funds (NIFs), where the investment funds acted as holdings for subsidiary manufacturing companies.[6]

Apart from the restrictive limits imposed on capital market operations, another impediment of banks' operations on the capital markets was constituted by the late introduction of acts regulating bond trading (the bonds act was passed in June 1995) and investment funds (dated August 1997). As a result, banks, instead of developing their own operations on the capital market, began to set up sister companies actively operating on this particular market. Similarly, the Polish banking sector was not conducive to the creation of a *sensu stricto* investment bank which would deal with financing the capital investment projects of large corporations by means of long-term debt instruments. Nor was this trend reversed at the moment of liberalization of limits and approach to EU standards. The new banking law (1997) introduced a 15 per cent limit calculated in relation to the bank's own funds with regard to a stake of shares held in non-bank companies. The global limit for this type of investment was raised to 60 per cent of own funds. An exemption from this limit was offered to pension funds and to companies that provided services to the banking sector (for example, banking telecommunications firms, and clearing). The NBP and the Securities Commission retained the power (Bank Supervision Commission) to limit exposure to debt instruments. The biggest difference between the limits prescribed by the Second Banking Directive and the limits introduced in Poland consists in the fact that the Polish solution disregarded the definition of a significant state of shares, thus relating the limits exclusively to the entities in which the given bank has a significant shareholding. The lack of such a provision prevents the banks from conducting operations typical of an investment bank. Accordingly, the adopted solution will promote a development of the continental model rather than the Anglo-Saxon model. To some degree, this caution on the part of the Polish authorities was reflected in the financial problems of a well-known stock exchange-listed company, Universal, whose financial standing did not allow for a timely redemption of short-term bonds and led to banks filing a petition announcing the company's bankruptcy (the most active part in this procedure was played by the Austrian bank in Poland – Raiffeisen Centro Bank).

Organization of bank supervision

An effective enforcement of prudential regulations depended on the proper organization of bank supervision and on proper empowerment of the supervision bodies. The formal basis for the operation of bank supervision was laid down in the banking law (1989). Very quickly, a system of reporting was prepared which made possible the calculation of prudential norms for every bank as at the end of month. In order to facilitate the calculation of suitable formulas, a uniform accounting chart of accounts was introduced. This far-reaching interference with the accounting system also had its negative aspects. It hampered the introduction of new banking products which had not been envisaged by the standard chart of accounts (such problems required a bank to obtain a decision from the bank supervision body). Apart from the system of reporting, a system of direct control was introduced. Bank supervision could also include viewing reports prepared by auditors. Under the new banking law (1997), a new banking supervisory body was established in the form of the Bank Supervisory Commission (its executive body is the General Inspectorate of Bank Supervision, which had already existed in the earlier structures of the

NBP). The Commission is a body furnished with a very wide range of powers: it has the right to carry out an analysis of the current liquidity of a bank, examine banks' financial statements, and determine the norms of banking risk pursuant to the banking law. The Commission has the right to make recommendations to banks. If a bank does not follow these recommendations and if, in the opinion of the Commission this may pose a threat to depositors' interests, the Commission is empowered to motion for the dismissal of the bank's management board, suspend the management board in its duties, limit the scope of operations of the bank and even annul the permit under which the bank operates.

The scope of empowerment of the Bank Supervisory Commission goes beyond the customary standards. It makes possible a very thorough interference in the manner in which a bank fu tions. Under extreme circumstances, the Commission has the right to limit t... entitlements of even the owners of a bank by, for example, withholding payment of dividends or by prohibiting the establishment of new organizational units. This solution should be treated as a temporary one. The appearance of a large number of small banks with limited prospects of development and limited accumulation of capital gives rise to the necessity for restrictive forms of banking control. The acceleration of consolidation processes and the concomitant restructuring of the Polish banking sector should lead to the liberalization of bank supervision.

Introduction of Institutions, Norms and Customs Corresponding to the Functioning of EU Banks

Apart from an efficiently operating bank supervision body, another key factor was the transparency of the information regarding the functioning of banks. From this point of view, what was important was the adaptation of the Polish regulations governing account, audits and chartered auditors. The Polish Act on accounting, which took effect from September 1994, harmonized the Polish regulations towards compliance with the Fourth and Eighth Council Directives (78/660/EEC, 84/253/EEC). Bank accounting, however, required adaptation to specific directives, Directive 86/635/EEC about reports of a credit institution and directives connected with consolidated reports and supervision (86/635/EEC and 83/350/EEC). The compliance of the Polish regulations was ensured by resolutions adopted by the Bank Supervisory Commission (Resolutions 1/98 and 2/98). Of no less importance than the adaptation of Polish accounting regulations was the launching of the operations of prestigious international auditing firms (see Table 15.14). The audits of financial statements, made by these firms, paved the way for Polish banks to start a wider cooperation with foreign banks (interbank limits, issuance bonds, listings on foreign stock exchanges).

Table 15.14   Leading auditors of commercial banks

Auditor	No. of banks
KPMG	15
Deloitte & Touche	5
Price Waterhouse	3
Coopers & Lybrand	12
Arthur Andersen	10

Source: Gazeta Bankowa, June 1997.

The standards of European banking necessitated the creation of a banking guarantee fund (94/19/EEC). In the Polish sector, it was launched as early as 1995 (Act on the Banking Guarantee Fund dated 14 December 1994). The principal difference between the Polish guarantee fund and the EU prescription consisted in the amount of deposits embraced by the guarantee. In Poland, the 100 per cent guarantee covered deposits of up to ecu 1000 and 90 per cent related to deposits of up to ecu 5000. These amounts departed significantly from the recommended amount (ecu 20 000). The reason for this was the actual financial resources of banks. The annual contribution amounted to 0.4 per cent of total assets weighted against risk ratios. Additionally, banks were obliged to set up a guarantee fund amounting to 0.4 per cent of the value of the accepted term and demand deposits. Under the terms of the guarantee fund, banks are obliged to offer the money from these funds towards payment of guaranteed deposits. The annual contribution, apart from being a guarantee for deposits, can also be used for supporting rehabilitation programmes for the benefit of banks which run into financial difficulties.

The approximation to the prescribed amount of guarantee at the level recommended by EU standards will have to proceed gradually (Smykala 1996). It will not be possible to sustain a high contribution concurrently with a drop in banking margin. Some state-owned banks would not have been able to pay such a high contribution and a special lower contribution was applied in their case (0.2 per cent of the value of weighted assets). The limited financial resources of banks caused a situation whereby the NBP will have to contribute some funds to the guarantee fund. Any progress in the area of increasing the guaranteed amount will be conditional on the reduction in the number of banks going bankrupt. The problems of small commercial banks which found themselves in a very difficult financial situation were solved by means of such banks being taken over by big commercial banks (the NBP guaranteed financial support for such operations). The main reason why payments were made from the guarantee fund was the bankruptcy of small cooperative banks. In such cases, the cost of rehabilitation was greater than the payments from the fund. The large number of cooperative banks and their financial standing do not give grounds for projecting a decreasing stream of payments from the guarantee fund.

Another standard, apart from the guarantee fund, which the EU countries would especially like to see implemented quickly, was the procedure aimed at counteracting money laundering (Directive 91/308/EEC). The amendment of the banking law in 1992 made it possible to introduce a proper procedure, Regulation 16/92 issued by the president of the NBP, which sets out the principles which should be applied by banks in this respect. The main difference in the Polish procedure is the amount of the transaction which is subject to registration: PLN 20 000 in Poland rather than the equivalent of ecu 15 000.

Apart from the implementation of specific EU directives relating to the functioning of the banking sector, there are also a number of measures which were not directly defined in EU directives but which are indispensable for an efficient functioning of the banking sector: for example, the organization of an interbank clearing system and a system which enables banks to monitor and adjust their financial liquidity.

The clearing system inherited from the command economy, apart from being characterized by low efficiency (money transfer took a few days) was also a favourable ground for financial abuse (the notorious ART. B scandal in Poland). The clearing system was reformed in two stages. In the first stage in 1993, KIR (the national clearing house) was set up. The organizational structure of KIR made it possible to receive payment orders from banks, and carry out their sorting and delivery to the beneficiary bank's branch within 24 hours. KIR's task also involved the preparation of banks' settlement specifications, which were later delivered to the NBP Interbank Settlements Department. In practice, the bank-clearing process was completed within a day. The clearing process was possible if the bank held sufficient funds on its account with the NBP.

Such a system of clearing required a proper planning of liquidity by banks and a well-developed interbank market. Interbank operations were one of the most quickly developed banking operations whose technological standard was equal to foreign banks. The flexibility of the system of regulation of interbank liquidity was broadened by means of a few innovations:

- a simple system of provision of a line of Lombard credit offered by the NBP;
- dematerialization of the trading in treasury bills via a system of accounts operated by the NBP;
- organization of open market contingent operations; and
- banks could make settlements using funds accumulated on obligatory service accounts and account for the reserve on a monthly basis.

In the second stage of reforming the clearing system a decision was made to abandon the paper-based system in favour of an electronic system. The new system, known as Eliksir, made it possible to increase the number of clearing sessions in any one day. Thus a customer's transfer could be completed in one day. The principles of regulating liquidity remained the same. However, the innovative technical facilities allowed the bank to obtain current information regarding the amount of transfers incoming from other banks. This contributed to a more effective regulation of liquidity and to a greater intensity of dealers' activities on the interbank market during the whole day.

Liberalization of Flows with regard to Current Foreign Currency and Capital Payments

The changes in the extent of the convertibility of money were closely correlated with the situation of the balance of payments and the amount of foreign exchange reserves in Poland (Pietrzak 1995). The stabilization programme, whose objective was to bring under control the hyperinflation which had set in at the end of the 1980s, introduced a fixed exchange rate which acted as an anti-inflation anchor. The restrictive stabilization programme was reflected in the foreign exchange law (1989), which introduced a strict administrative control over current and capital turnovers. The objective of this measure was to guarantee a central control over foreign currency reserves. Apart from a small number of exceptions, without a special foreign exchange permit, neither corporate nor non-corporate non-residents were permitted to hold foreign exchange on foreign bank accounts. It was also impossible either to take out or to grant a loan abroad, or to make capital investments. The current foreign exchange turnover was subject to the control of Polish foreign exchange banks which held the exclusive right to mediate in foreign exchange operations between domestic and foreign entities. Every foreign exchange contract had to be expressed in a currency which was recognized by the NBP as convertible. Companies were obliged to collect all foreign exchange receivables from abroad within three months. Companies were not permitted to hold convertible currencies, that is, there was an obligation of immediate sale of foreign currencies to foreign exchange banks. In the case of a payment for an import, companies bought foreign currencies in a foreign exchange bank, which was then able to make a transfer exclusively on the basis of a document proving the existence of an obligation of the domestic company towards a foreign entity. The foreign currency buy and sell rates offered by foreign exchange banks could not deviate by more than 2 per cent from the exchange rate set by the central bank.[7] Foreign exchange banks could buy foreign exchange at the central bank but only for the purpose of covering the foreign payments of their customers. This rigid system permitted internal exchange

(Pytkowska 1996) only in the case of individual persons, who were allowed to purchase and sell foreign currency at licensed banks or exchange offices and to deposit the currency in accounts in Polish banks.

The liberalization of the exchange of foreign currency went in two directions – enabling domestic companies to manage their foreign exchange rationally, and creating favourable conditions for foreign exchange trading for the benefit of foreign investors (Krakowiak 1995). The amendment of the foreign exchange law in 1995 put an end to the obligation for companies to sell their foreign exchange. Companies were permitted to deposit their foreign currency in foreign exchange banks. Concurrently, a mechanism was introduced whereby foreign exchange banks were able to purchase foreign exchange from the central bank at a special foreign exchange session called 'fixing'. This session allowed Polish banks to close their foreign exchange positions and at the same time it led to the fixing of the official exchange rate of the zloty. The system of crawling devaluation (crawling peg mechanism) remained in operation. However, there was a significant broadening of the permissible band of deviation of the fixing rate from the central rate (7 per cent). A floating exchange rate created the possibility of stiffer competition among foreign exchange banks and led to an increase in the turnover of Polish forex trading. In practice, foreign exchange turnover was shaped by the NBP and the offers placed at the fixing session. Thus, the foreign currency exchange rate was determined by the scale of inflow of foreign capital and by the intervention exchange rate policy of the NBP.

Domestic companies were permitted to purchase the shares and the CPs of companies whose business was registered in Organization for Economic Cooperation and Development (OECD) countries, in amounts not exceeding ecu 1 million. They were also allowed to incur long-term loans abroad. A unique approach was adopted in the liberalization of foreign exchange trading in relation to non-residents, whereby a special type of bank account was introduced – the so called 'free-transfer' foreign exchange account (Ofiarski 1995). Non-residents were permitted to deposit into these accounts Polish zlotys derived from profits generated in direct and portfolio capital investments. It was possible to convert such deposits into foreign currencies and to transfer them abroad.

The further liberalization of foreign exchange turnover required a decisive step in the form of departure from the internal convertibility of the zloty and recognition of the Polish currency as one which can be used to enter into export and import contracts.[8] This step should lead to a situation where the territory of Poland will cease to be the only area of convertibility of the zloty (Durjasz 1995). The adoption of this measure can already be seen in the newest foreign exchange law, which took effect on 1 January 1999. The foreign exchange law brought a further liberalization of foreign exchange trading with OECD countries. In the case of these countries, the new rules abandon the limits for portfolio and direct investments made by domestic companies. The legislators did, however, leave some limits aimed at counteracting speculative operations based on the Polish currency. A limit of ecu 50 000 was introduced for short-term loans (up to three months) granted in Polish zlotys to non-residents. A limit of PLN 0.5 million was also imposed on the amount of three-month Polish zloty term deposits held by non-residents. Non-residents were also prohibited from selling these deposits with maturities longer than three months and amounts exceeding PLN 0.5 million and then converting the money into foreign currencies and transferring it abroad.

The legislators retained certain essential elements which had been part of the previous prevailing foreign exchange law. First and foremost, what remained in force was the prohibition on holding money in zlotys and in foreign currencies abroad. Foreign exchange banks and brokerage offices retained their mediation role in foreign trading. Foreign exchange banks were still furnished with the power to exercise control, especially in respect of transfers abroad related to the balance of payments.

Independence of the Central Bank

Although the unification of the Polish banking sector towards compliance with EU standards does not determine the structure of the institutions which conduct economic policy, it does, however, require a proper efficiency of operation of institutions guaranteeing the control over the stability of the financial system. The beginnings of the process of system transformation, in particular the implementation of the stabilization package, required that the central bank should be provided with a significant amount of independence. The law on the NBP from 1989 ensured the autonomy of the central bank. The president of the NBP was nominated by the country's president and appointed by parliament. The term of office was six years, with little possibility of dismissal. The vice-presidents of the NBP management board, designated by the NBP president, were then approved by the country's president. The management board managed the current operations of the NBP. All essential decisions regarding the monetary policy were left in the hands of the NBP president (interest rates of the central bank, amount of obligatory reserves). The scope of the bank's activities was defined in the monetary policy plan which was subject to review by the government and to acceptance by parliament. By statute, a limit was imposed on the extent to which the NBP could finance the budget deficit (limits on the amount of treasury securities purchased by the NBP). Bank supervision also became part of the NBP structure. The extent of NBP independence was substantial. By applying the Cukierman method, the level of independence in the years from 1950 to 1989 was assessed at 0.10 points, whereas in the period from 1990 to 1993 the indicator was 0.83 (Cukierman et al. 1992; Strzelec 1994).

The independence of the central bank was a contributory factor in suppressing inflation and the bank did not impede the government as long as the fight against inflation was on the government's priority list. The inflow of foreign capital in the second half of the 1990s caused a significant deceleration in the pace of devaluation in relation to the rate of inflation, which led to a deterioration in the balance of payments. It was at that time that differences in the conceptual approaches to the economic policy could be observed: the NBP wanted to restore the equilibrium in the balance of payments by suppressing internal demand (a policy of high interest rates); the ministry of finance sought to solve the problem by accelerating the pace of devaluation of the zloty. As a result, the situation gave rise to a competence dispute between the central bank and the ministry of finance as to which of these institutions is responsible for the rate policy and to what extent. This was the first test of the extent to which an independent bank is capable of reaching agreement with the government on its policy (Wojtyna 1996).

The potential conflict between the president of the central bank and the minister of finance, especially if it is fuelled by personal ambitions, could have been detrimental to a coordinated economic policy. In the amendments to the law on the NBP (1998), an essential change was made in that the Monetary Policy Council was set up (Kowalski 1997). The Council replaced the NBP president as the body responsible for monetary policy, and it also became a controlling body for the NBP. In addition to the president of the NBP (who presides over the Council sessions), the Council comprises nine members, of whom six are nominated by parliament and the three remaining by the country's president. The term of office of the members is the same as in the case of the NBP president. Like the president, they cannot be recalled before the end of tenure. The new solution was more flexible. The composition of the Council reflects the existing political structure and thus, the decisions of the Council to some extent take account of various opinions in respect of monetary policy. The meetings of the Council with the media, as well as the views presented by particular members of the Council, contribute to the transparency of the decisions made by this body. It must be stressed that the Council, apart from key decisions related to interest rates and the rate of obligatory reserve, also takes other decisions of no lesser importance, connected with the mechanisms of the central bank's influence on the financial system. For instance, the Council changed the principles of foreign exchange fixing, the method of calculating the obligatory reserve and the principles affecting the banking sector by means of open market operations. The first year of the Council's activities was characterized on the one hand by the consistency of certain actions, for example, the gradual reduction in interest rates (as a result, the interest rates were lowered by as much as 10 per cent over the year); on the other hand the Council was faced with external shocks such as the financial crisis in Russia and the rapid drop in exports in the fourth quarter of 1998. However, the consistently pursued policy allowed the Council to maintain control over the exchange rate. As a result, there was no rapid drop in the exchange rate, but rather a gradual decline in the currency exchange rate at a pace faster than inflation.

THE SECOND STAGE OF THE ADAPTATION OF THE POLISH BANKING SECTOR

The second stage of the adaptation of the Polish banking sector was formally started in February 1999 and is scheduled to end in 2006. Although the postulates contained in the White Book and directed to potential EU members do not guarantee an automatic acceptance into the community, their message is unambiguous: the countries that are applying for membership should have a sufficiently mature economic system that they can function properly within the structure of the uniform internal market (Kantecki 1998). In relation to the Polish banking sector, the following conditions must be fulfilled:

- complete unification in respect of prudential norms, the adoption of principles of bank accounting such that supervision over bank branches is exercised by the supervision body of the bank head office's mother country, irrespective of their location;
- unrestricted opening of branches of foreign banks and introduction of a full range of their products;
- introduction of cross-border services; and
- full liberalization of foreign currency and capital turnover coupled with full convertibility of the currency.

The fulfilment of these conditions is tantamount to a simultaneous lifting of the 'protective umbrella' over banks operating in Poland. The principle of supervision exercised by institutions of the mother country causes a situation whereby all limits, including the limits on loan concentration, will be calculated in relation to the capital of the whole bank, thus increasing significantly the possibility that branches of foreign banks will be able to grant large loans. The substantial difference between the amount of own funds possessed by foreign banks and the funds held by banks operating in Poland will also act in favour of the former with regard to capital market operations. The insubstantial own funds and the limitations imposed on exposure on the capital market excludes the possibility that domestic banks can operate effectively as investment banks.

This barrier will not, however, occur in the case of foreign banks. In addition, foreign banks will be able to use their potential to make placements of debt securities issued by Polish companies, among others also abroad.

The subordination of branches of foreign banks to supervision by the mother country will ensure that deposits will also be guaranteed in that country. Thus, the branches of foreign banks will reduce their operational costs because of a lower contribution to the guarantee fund.

An unrestricted flow of capital and the convertibility of the zloty will deprive domestic banks of the privilege of mediation in foreign exchange turnover. This means that domestic companies will be able to deposit their foreign exchange funds and to make settlements via the mediation of a foreign bank.

Strategy of Foreign Banks

The exposure of domestic banks to competition from foreign banks could have a varying intensity depending on the strategy adopted by foreign banks. If we assume that it will be a continuation of the strategy applied so far, we can envisage the following scenario. Foreign banks will concentrate their expansion on such areas of banking operations where they will be able to take advantage of their technological superiority, which is determined by:

- modern information systems (transaction settlement in real time);
- modern techniques of communication with customers (home banking);
- a network of foreign branches (quick realization of foreign exchange transactions);
- marketing techniques in attracting customers;
- support for the analytical division of the head office;
- experience in introducing new products; and
- image and reputation of the company.

The main objective will be to achieve dominance in corporate banking. So far, the success of foreign banks in this area has consisted in taking over a part of foreign exchange transactions and the servicing of the leading Polish companies. The scale of taking over Polish corporate clients will be constrained by the level of risk that foreign banks will be willing to accept. In other words, we should expect that loan exposure will be limited to companies which have high creditworthiness.

Another direction of development in foreign bank operation will be connected with investment banking. In such areas, foreign banks will discount their competitive advantage arising from access to world capital markets. The possibilities for raising funds via the Polish stock exchange are limited.

Therefore, not only big companies but also medium-sized domestic companies are striving to list their shares and bonds on world capital markets.

The third direction of development will be connected with the comprehensiveness of the range of products and services offered by foreign banks. Even now, we can see steps taken by foreign banks which are aimed at creating interconnected financial institutions (insurance companies, investment funds, brokerage offices). The customization of the bank offer will also consist in an attempt to meet those needs of the customer that domestic banks will be able to satisfy only to a small extent. For instance, many Polish exporters require their foreign partners to make instant payment for the sold products. Foreign banks can offer credit to Polish exporters' trading partners, which in turn will allow Polish companies to generate higher returns.

The fourth direction of development of foreign banks concerns the expansion of banking services. At present only a small part of Polish bank income derives from banking services, and this source of income is not sufficiently appreciated. The pricing policy of foreign banks is different – they offer attractive interest rates and at the same time they introduce comprehensive systems of fees for banking services.

We should expect a special strategy in the case of retail banking. Foreign banks will focus on taking over the servicing of only the higher-income-bracket individuals. This strategy follows, on the one hand, from the willingness to reduce the costs of customer service, and on the other hand, in the case of such customers, foreign banks are able to take advantage of their superiority on account of the wide range of services they can offer. A good example of this is City Bank SA, which launched its credit card on the market, addressing the product exclusively to wealthy customers. The product, despite offering much worse financial terms than Polish banks (for example, interest rate on the credit), met with significant interest because of the package of associated banking services.

The change in the circumstances under which foreign banks operate in Poland (see Table 15.15) and the possibility of executing cross-border services, raises the question of the method used by foreign banks in their expansion in Poland. The full adaptation of Polish regulations to EU standards facilitates the expansion of branches of foreign banks in Poland, which leads to two crucial questions:

- whether foreign banks will depart from the strategy employed so far, that is, opening small (in term of capital) banks in the form of joint-stock companies operating under Polish law, which involves issuing a banking licence granted by the Polish central bank and banking supervision exercised by the NBP; and
- whether foreign banks will be interested in the process of privatization and then in taking over Polish state-owned banks.

Table 15.15   Performance indices of commercial banks (%)

	Cost/income		Net interest income/assets		Return on assets		Return on equity	
	1995	1996	1995	1996	1995	1996	1995	1996
Banks with Polish shareholder majority	86.5	81.1	3.65	4.87	1.48	2.29	21.74	27.14
Banks with foreign shareholder majority	76.6	83.9	12.98	5.51	5.72	2.21	42.79	15.79
Banks with 100% foreign shareholders	77.9	90.6	10.08	3.77	2.75	1.22	17.69	8.17

Source: Bank i Kredyt, 5, 1998 (Table 6, p. 8).

The saturation of the Polish market with one-branch banks with a limited profile of operations means that this strategy of entering the Polish market will not be employed. A limited expansion, whose main aim will be to ensure banking services for foreign customers in Poland, will be realized by means of rendering cross-border services. The take-over of small banks will be of interest to foreign banks only to a limited extent. Such banks generally provide services to local customers, who are not within the circle of interest of foreign banks. There may be some exceptions to this rule in cases where banks which support themselves with an existing network of a medium-sized bank have the intention of developing a specific type of retail operation (this can be exemplified by Ford Bank SA, which intends to offer credit for car purchases). The existing foreign banks in Poland will, however, be interested in participating in the privatization of the banking sector, in order, among other reasons, to

Table 15.16   Structure of share capital of commercial banks (%)

	1996	1997	1998*
Direct State Treasury	30.59	21.99	19.29
NBP	7.87	2.94	2.59
State-owned firms	10.94	5.59	4.91
Private firms	8.79	9.94	7.23
Foreign investors	29.79	41.52	48.07
Individual investors	12.02	18.02	17.91

Note: *September 1998.

Source: General Inspectorate of Bank Supervision.

Table 15.17   Structure of foreign share capital, September 1998 (%)

| Country | Share in | |
	Foreign capital	Total capital
USA	29.50	14.18
Germany	29.36	14.12
Holland	15.20	7.30
France	7.82	3.76
Austria	7.62	3.66
Others	10.50	5.04

Source: General Inspectorate of Bank Supervision.

broaden their customer base (see Tables 15.16 and 15.17). It is also quite likely that the ING scenario will be emulated, where the bank took over Bank Slaski – a state-owned bank with a well-developed network of branches. A merger of both banks did not occur; instead there was a division of functions. The provision of services to big corporate clients was taken over by the ING branch in Poland, whereas Bank Slaski has mainly taken upon itself a specialization in retail services.

Weaknesses of Polish Banks

Taking into account the probable scenario of the expansion of foreign banks, we must turn our attention to a number of factors connected with the structure of the Polish banking sector, which significantly hamper the domestic banks' efforts to meet the challenges of foreign competition. The development of the banking sector to date has led, on the one hand, to the formation of a group of big state-owned banks, subjected to gradual privatization and managing a substantial part of the total assets of the whole sector, and on the other hand to a group of small private banks founded by Polish state-owned companies or by private companies.

The group of domestic private banks manages a small part of the assets of the whole sector, and to a large extent, such banks provide services to specialized sectors of economic activity or to small business. Because of this, these banks are especially sensitive to fluctuations in the economic climate. The small accumulation of profit in these banks does not facilitate a quick expansion of operations and technological development. In the case of stiffer competition and a drop in interest rates and banking margins, such banks may run into financial problems.

When analysing the structure of the banking sector, we must remember that the group of banks which are in the worst financial position are cooperative banks and Bank Gospodarki Zywnosciowej SA (BGZ), which is interrelated with them. As mentioned above, the majority of cooperative banks are in a position qualifying them for liquidation and BGZ has also been reporting an accumulated loss. Because of the size of this bank, it is difficult to envisage its bankruptcy, so it will be necessary to implement a restructuring programme with financial support from the government (Kulawik 1996).

A large number of small banks does not pose a threat to the banking sector, if we take into account the capital weakness of big state-owned banks. Their capital resources are relatively small, if we consider the necessity of incurring significant investment outlays connected with the upgrading of banking technology. In other words, the available capital resources will be insufficient for big banks to take over small private banks (Solarz 1998).

The technological weakness of domestic banks is, to a certain extent, the consequence of domestic banks' adaptation to the requirements of Polish customers at the beginning of the 1990s. A large cash turnover necessitated the setting up of expensive branches which had to meet specified safety norms. Additionally, a lack of upgraded information systems fulfilling the requirements set by the NBP caused a situation whereby information systems with a dispersed data base were installed. Such a solution forced banks to set up a back office in each branch, with employees involved in the clearing and processing of particular operations. As a result, domestic banks are characterized by high operational costs and an excessively large workforce plus a number of large branches, instead of a network of many small branches. Foreign banks were not burdened with such defects. Above all, foreign banks focused on corporate customers and limited their cash operations to a minimum. Foreign banks started their operations as one-branch units, therefore their information systems were based on a concentrated data base. The expansion of foreign banks into multibranch structures occurred only when it was possible to create a fixed real-time telecommunication link among all units.

CONDITIONS FOR A SUCCESSFUL ADAPTATION OF POLISH BANKS TO EU STANDARDS

The remarks presented below concern the conditions which must be met in order to prevent the 'black scenario' of adaptation of the Polish banking sector, under which privatization will result in the take-over of the best Polish banks by foreign banks. In turn, the competition from foreign banks will drive small banks to the brink of bankruptcy (Jaromin 1998). The prevention of a financial collapse of the small banks must eventually lead to the involvement of Polish taxpayers' money and to significant problems in Polish banking supervision.

The prevention of such a scenario requires first of all the consolidation and appropriate privatization of the banking sector. In 1996, a consolidation act was brought into effect, which opened the way to bank mergers. In the majority of cases, consolidation processes concerned big state-owned banks (Konopielko 1997), whereas they should embrace, above all, small banks. Attempts at starting such a process can be traced to the creation of the G11 group of small banks intending to enter into closer cooperation with one another. The effort aimed at injecting banks with additional capital should be concentrated on providing small banks with a strategic investor. The privatization of state-owned banks should proceed by stages, and not only should emphasis be placed on the amount of the price generated on the sale of the sold shares but also attention should be paid to the business plan specifying the future development path of the bank which is being privatized. The privatization process also requires a specification as to whether any banks, and if so which ones, should remain in the hands of the state.

It is also essential to complete the process of unification of prudential norms. Past practice shows that banking supervision bodies were very cautious about new banking products and foreign exchange operations. This approach was reflected in the risk-limiting norms introduced in relation to some types of banking activities, for example, the limiting of foreign exchange positions. The unification of prudential norms should enable domestic banks to introduce the same products as will be offered by foreign banks. Because of this, it is necessary to implement the directive regarding capital adequacy (93/6/EEC). This directive assesses various types of banking risk and based on this, it designates the minimum amount of capital that a bank should have for the given type of banking activity (Zielinski 1996). The introduction of this norm will allow Poland to abandon the strict limiting of particular types of banking risk.

Also the system of provisions for bad loans should undergo a change. The system that is in place now does not make it possible to set up adequate provisions proportional to the scale of loan operations (also known as hidden reserves) and additional provisions connected with a rapid deterioration in the quality of assets (open provisions). Such a division of provisions allows banks to exclude hidden provisions from taxation. The introduction of this division would enable Polish banks to compensate for the drop in their profit connected with a drop in banking margin.

The factors discussed above determine the circumstances under which the

Polish bank sector can adapt its products and technology to the standards of foreign banks over the next six years.

NOTES

1. The introduction of this product represented a good example of an innovation customized to the specific circumstances of the transition economy. The demand for this product came from foreign companies operating in Poland, which, because of the threat of rapid devaluation were not willing to tie up their own foreign exchange resources. At the same time, the restrictive credit policy applied to Polish companies (recession) by Polish banks led to excess liquidity in the domestic banks, which they willingly invested in CPs, provided that the CPs offered a higher yield than treasury bills.
2. With the permission of the NBP, own capital also included deposits with maturities longer than one year. This made it possible to increase the value of the ratio for large state-owned banks.
3. A big loan means a value in excess of 10 per cent of the bank's own funds. The maximum total exposure is 25 per cent of own funds per customer. The global value of big loans 800 per cent of own funds.
4. The low limit also partially explained why banks preferred offices in the form of internal organizational units rather than separate joint-stock companies.
5. This bank was absorbed by Bank Rozwoju Eksportu.
6. The NIFs acted as para-banking institutions, taking loans from banks and granting them to particular subsidiary-level companies.
7. Initially, a fixed exchange rate of the zloty against the dollar was maintained, adjusted by means of one-off one-shot devaluations. In 1991 the exchange rate of the zloty was linked to the basket of five currencies with a concurrent introduction of the crawling peg mechanism for devaluation at the rate of 1.8 per cent per month.
8. This step was required not only from the point of view of EU standards but also in connection with Poland's inclusion in the OECD.

REFERENCES

Cukierman, Alex, Steven B. Webb and Bilin Neyapit (1992), 'Measuring the independence of central banks and its effects on policy outcomes', *World Bank Economic Review*, **3**, 353–98.

Daniluk, Dariusz (1996), 'The Polish banking system and EU regulations – framework, scope and rate of modification in the light of the European Accord', *Bank i Kredyt*, **6**, 17–28.

Durjasz, Pawel (1995), 'The move to full convertibility: risks and opportunities', *Bank i Kredyt*, **6**, 4–15.

Hewelt, Przemyslaw (1995), 'Selected issues on the strategy of banking supervision in Poland against the experience of developed countries', *Bank i Kredyt*, **1–2**, 38–43.

Jaromin, Józef (1998), 'Polish banks – survival conditions', *Bank i Kredyt*, **5**, 11–12.

Kantecki, Antoni (1998), 'Commercial banks on the horizon of economic development perspectives and EU integration', *Bank i Kredty*, **5**, 81–3.

Konopielko, Lukasz (1997), 'Empirical analysis of the consolidation in the banking sector', *Bank i Kredyt*, **12**, 35–8.

Kosinski, Bogdan (1998), 'Foreign banks in the Polish banking sector', *Bank i Kredyt*,, **5**, 20–23.

Kowalski, Tadeusz (1997), 'Selected economic and institutional aspects of the act on the National Bank of Poland and the banking act of 29 August', *Bank i Kredyt*, **12**, 4–20.

Krakowiak, Michal (1995), 'The deregulation of international foreign exchange operations', *Bank i Kredyt*, **6**, 27–31.

Kulawik, Jacek (1996), 'Restructuring conditions of cooperative banks', *Bank i Kredyt*, **4**, 12–17.

Ofiarski, Zbigniew (1995), 'Escrow accounts and free foreign accounts', *Bank i Kredyt*, **7–8**, 51–7.

Pietrzak, Edmund (1995), 'The convertibility of the zloty: what and when?', *Bank i Kredyt*, **6**, 60–74.

Pytkowska, Beata (1996), 'Zloty convertibility vs IMF standards', *Bank i Kredyt*, **7–8**, 36–43.

Sleszynska-Charewicz, Ewa and Dariusz Lewandowski (1996), 'The banking prudential regulations', *Bank i Kredyt*, **6**, 67–80.

Smykala, Bernard (1996), 'Deposit insurance in Polish law. From state guarantee to Deposit Insurance Fund', *Bank i Kredyt*, **1–2**, 43–57.

Solarz, Jan K. (1998), 'Scenarios of domestic banks' capital increase', *Bank i Kredyt*, **5**, 24–7.

Strzelec, Agnieszka (1994), 'Independence of the National Bank of Poland, 1989–1993', *Bank i Kredyt*, **7**, 4–15.

Wojtyna, Andrzej (1996), 'Central bank independence and theoretical and practical aspects of monetary and fiscal policy coordination', *Bank i Kredyt*, **6**, 87–101.

Zielinski, Tomasz (1996), 'Solvency ratio and capital adequacy', *Bank i Kredyt*, **11**, 63–9.

16. Banking sector restructuring and debt consolidation in the Czech Republic

Roman Matoušek

INTRODUCTION

A decade has passed since the Central and Eastern European (CEE) countries began the transition to establishing market-based economies integrated with the rest of the world. The development of a broad-based financial sector has been seen as an integral component of the transition. The approach and progress towards development of a viable financial sector vary among the countries and are dependent on a number of factors:

- the country's starting point (particularly its historical experience with market-based economic systems and the degree to which its economy had been centrally planned and controlled);
- the macroeconomic setting;
- the pace of other reforms – institutional and legal environment (commercial and civil law, bankruptcy law, accounting standards and so on); and
- political consensus in support of market-based institutions.

Banking reforms took place in the Czech Republic at the beginning of 1990, when the so-called 'two-tier' banking system was established. The banking sector has undergone a rapid process of liberalization. Interest rate ceilings on credit were removed, barriers to entry on private domestic banks and later also on foreign banks were abolished, allocation of credit was no longer made on the basis of government decisions, and regulation and supervision were strengthened. Nevertheless, even though all essential liberalization steps that are considered essential for improving functional efficiency and competitiveness within the banking sector have been taken, the outcomes are still modest. Past experience in Visegrad countries has shown that the common feature for developing a sound and efficient banking system requires a balance of the two central aspects of the financial sector: internal efficiency (profit maximization, the quality and cost of the services provided) and efficient resource allocation.

Taking the transition countries as a whole, there have been several distinct stages leading to a gradual improvement in internal efficiency and optimal resource allocation within the banking sectors, or in other words, to the promotion of a viable banking sector.

The first stage was characterized by the establishment of a two-tier banking system based on market principles. In this period, a completely new legal and institutional framework had to be established (commercial law, bankruptcy law, accounting standards). Changing the macroeconomic environment – price liberalization, devaluation of the currencies, the privatization process – also had a substantial effect on the financial market.

The second stage emerged as the period in which a number of mutually interrelated steps, influencing the present and future development of the banking sector, had to be taken – opening banking sectors to domestic and foreign banks in order to enhance competitiveness and a dramatic liberalization of the banking sector. CEE countries have been undergoing a complex process of liberalization similar to that in European Union (EU) countries in the 1970s and 1980s. Setting the basic regulatory and supervisory framework, new operational guidelines and principles for banks' prudential behaviour, and the consolidation and recapitalization of state-owned banks burdened by inherited non-performing loans from centrally planned economies was on the agenda.

The third stage was characterized by sorting out the problems that had accumulated from the previous two stages. Policy makers have been faced with basic dilemmas in the process of ensuring a viable banking sector. Applied methods of consolidation, recapitalization and privatization, ways of recaptilizing or whether to recapitalize at all before privatization, whom to privatize, and the sequencing and speed of these steps within the banking sector were some of the crucial points for discussion.

The final stage will be when banking sectors operate on market principles (that is, when protective umbrellas are removed) and regulatory and supervisory standards are fully compatible with those in standard market economies. the Czech banking sector has already undergone two stages of its development and is coping with the third. However, there is still a long way to go before the accomplishment of the final stage, that is, the EU standard.

THE DEVELOPMENT OF THE CZECH BANKING SYSTEM – PROS AND CONS

The growth of banking institutions and employment in the financial sector accelerated in the period from 1990 to 1993. The development reflected the dramatic liberalization of the banking sector including the removal of interest rate ceilings, the opening to newcomers, the improvement of regulatory frameworks, and the creation of new operational guidelines and principles for banks' prudential behaviour. This rapid growth was also accelerated by demand factors because of a gap between the supply and the demand of banking products. However, from 1995 up to now – the third stage – the banking sector has found itself as a whole in difficulties.

Expansion of the Banking Sector

As of 1 January 1990 the monobanking system was replaced by the two-tier banking system. Two commercial banks were carved out from the former Czechoslovak State Bank – Komerční Banka in the Czech Republic and Všeobecná Úverová Banka in the Slovak Republic. In addition, the following banks were already operational: Česká Spořitelna (Savings Bank), Zivnostenská Banka, Československá Obchodní Banka (Czechoslovak Trade Bank) and Investiční a Poštovní Banka (formerly Investiĉní Banka). Afterwards it was widely accepted that the more banks operating within the financial market, the better, since this would result in the system as a whole being more competitive and efficient.[1]

The rapid growth of new commercial banks in the 1991–92 period brought a certain degree of competition into the financial market but later the financial position of these banks was considerably impaired. The growth of commercial banks in the 1990–94 period and their gradual decline since then can be seen in Table 16.1.

The Czech Republic (among other countries) had a unique opportunity to start building a banking system almost from scratch. Nevertheless, there are

Table 16.1 Number of banks in the Czech Republic (as of the end of year)

	1990	1991	1992	1993	1994	1995	1996	1997	1998	1999
Total banks	9	24	37	52	55	55	53	50	45	42
State financial institutions	4	4	1	1	1	1	1	1	1	1
State-owned banks	1	1	4	4	4	6	6	6	5	4
Czech-controlled banks	4	15	21	28	28	25	18	15	14	10
Foreign-controlled banks and branches	0	4	11	18	21	23	23	24	25	27
Banks under conservatorship	0	0	0	1	1	0	5	4	0	0
Unlicensed banks	0	0	0	0	2	5	7	11	18	21

Source: Czech National Bank.

several questions regarding the expansion and openness of the banking system. First, commercial banks were carved out of the former Czechoslovak State Bank (central bank). This step was identical for most of the former communist countries undergoing a transformation of domestic banking sectors. But if we look at the current situation within the segment of the biggest commercial banks we can see different shortcomings in the applied measures.[2] In Poland, nine state-owned regional banks were established rather than one or two large banks. The advantage of such a policy is, at least for the first stage of development, to avoid creating 'capture banks'. Decentralization led to the coverage of major regions in the country and the allocation of credit was monitored more effectively. This might be explained by better knowledge of debtors and regional conditions. On the other hand, experience shows that a regional break-up limits the competitiveness within a given market since banks play a dominant role. The European Bank for Reconstruction and Development (EBRD), for example, suggests that the break-up of state banks should be organized on a sectoral rather than geographical basis. However, such an organization reduces the advantages of portfolio diversification and increases the probability of a default risk.

Second, this almost 'free entry' of the small and medium-sized commercial banks into the banking sector, which was adopted mainly because of the perceived benefits of competition, has in fact been detrimental. Partly unrestrained access has induced a situation in which too many banks serve a limited market. In addition, these newly operating banks were mostly poorly capitalized and managed. At present the growth of operating banks is almost zero – the banking supervision body stopped issuing new banking licences in September 1993 in order to create a breathing space for established banks to consolidate their position.[3]

Third, as for foreign entry, the situation is quite different. There is a general consensus that the activities of foreign banks are in the first stage of transition, and have little impact on the banking sector in question. This might be explained by their specific role, whereby these banks provide services primarily to their home-country clients who are getting established within the unfolding market economy. Later these banks expand and provide services not only for their home-country clients but also for domestic firms and individual clients. For banks from EU countries applying for a banking licence to operate within the Czech system, the Czech National Bank (CNB) should apply slightly different rules. It is necessary to adopt a strictly selective policy in order to avoid a negative impact on the banking sector from newcomers, but, as noted, the entry of foreign banks has generally had a positive effect on the domestic banking system. Hence, if there are some highly regarded foreign banks wishing to operate in the Czech Republic, no obstacles should be imposed by the CNB. Furthermore, if the CNB continues to apply a restrictive

Financial sector development

Table 16.2   Share of banks in total assets (%)

	1993	1994	1995	1996	1997	1998	1999
Large banks	82.30	77.18	71.72	68.87	66.97	64.47	62.06
Small banks	8.90	4.44	4.92	5.20	2.61	2.70	1.85
Medium-sized and banks	7.20	11.67	16.46	18.84	24.20	25.71	29.37
Specialized banks	na	1.47	2.11	3.09	3.32	4.10	4.65
Banks under conservatorship	na	5.24	4.79	4.00	2.90	3.02	2.07
Total	100.00	100.00	100.00	100.00	100.00	100.00	100.00

Source: Czech National Bank.

policy on foreign banks, this undoubtedly sends a negative signal to the European Commission, when those wishing to obtain licences do not know what criteria to meet. In other words, this situation can cast doubts on whether the Czech Republic will be able to meet one of the essential criteria involved in the 'Second Directive', that is, to enable a non-domestic credit institution to operate in any member country.

A significant feature of the Czech banking system is a relatively high degree of concentration. This characteristic is similar to developed countries, but the major Czech banks perform well below the standard of these countries. The explanation for the high concentration is also determined, as has already been mentioned, by the adopted policy at the outset of banking reforms. Turning to the data analysis, we can see that these big banks have decisive market shares in assets, deposits and credit (Table 16.2). The balance sheets of the biggest commercial banks show that Česká Spořitelna has the most personal deposits but like financing corporations its activities are limited. Its lending activities are mainly within the interbank bank market. Komerční Banka (KB), Investiční and Poštovní Banka (IPB), and Československá Obchodní Banka (CSOB) have a different structure. These banks are involved primarily in corporate lending. The KB and the IPB are also gradually increasing their share in the collection of deposits from households.

As for the small banks, they differed from the major banks in two basic ways: they lacked a more substantial base of primary deposits of their own and were engaged disproportionately in highly risky trades. Small banks had to build up a branch network from scratch and deal with the traditional inclination of depositors who preferred established major banks. Small banks first became dependent on central bank refinancing and later on the interbank deposit market. As interest rates on this market were high at the start, these banks concentrated on having a high proportion of credit and other claims with a presupposed above-average return which were, however, burdened by a substantial degree of risk.

The first failure within the group of small banks led to a reduction in the growth of liabilities, deposits in particular, and later even their decline. From the end of 1995, many small banks were unable to support the drop in deposits. The composition of bank resources and the poor quality of credit portfolios put heavy pressure on their liquidity, which the banks were unable to overcome with their own liquid assets. Despite the fact that the banking supervision body applied remedial measures and implemented revitalizing programmes for the banks, its efforts to stop this unfavourable development were, in most cases, not successful. The CNB banking supervision body sometimes even encountered unwillingness on the part of bank owners to try radical solutions to problems, or found that the problems originating in the initial period of a bank's activity exceeded its capability to remedy them.

Bad Loans as the Main Flaw in the Czech Banking System

The transition towards the standard market economy disclosed a number of problems which the Czech banking sector had to cope with. One of these was portfolio restructuring, stimulated by the dominance of inherited bad loans on state bank balance sheets which would worsen bank liquidity and solvency once hard-budget constraints were imposed. A poor portfolio adversely affects the soundness of the banking system.

Despite efforts to cope with the bad loans that had been made in the previous years and despite the recent recovery and growth which contributed to the improved financial position of the firms in the real sector of the Czech economy, the credit portfolio of commercial banks has continued to be unfavourably affected by a high proportion of such loans. Although some of them as a heritage of the past, an increasing number are 'new' bad loans, especially, but not exclusively, from the initial stage of transition.

The increasing number of non-performing loans has two basic aspects. Either the bad loans can result from adverse local and industrial conditions, or they are a result of the greater propensity of banks to take risks. Factors leading to bad loans' can be categorized as either controllable or uncontrollable.

If the major factors are controllable then banks can avoid losses. First of all, they must improve their credit policy, that is, credit analyses, loan structuring and so on, and further, they must have better management. On the other hand, it is very difficult to influence uncontrollable factors since the losses are less predictable. They are conditional on a number of external factors, which are apparent, for example, in the agricultural sector.

Indentification by the banking supervision body of credit quality was

Table 16.3   Classified loans (% of total credit)

	1994	1995	1996	1997	1998	1999
Total classified loans	36.53	33.04	29.33	26.98	26.67	32.15
Weighted Classification	21.52	20.26	18.82	17.42	16.37	16.88
Classified credits adjusted for collateral	na	17.01	14.72	14.43	14.89	18.80
Reserve and provisions surplus or shortage	na	−0.28	0.10	1.12	1.99	0.55

Note: Excluding *Konsolidační Banka* and banks under conservatorship.

Source: Czech National Bank.

significantly complicated by the absence of a unified system for the classifi-cation of credit portfolios. In 1993, the CNB issued recommendations for this area, but banks respected them only to a certain extent. It was not until 1994, when the CNB issued a crucial provision on the principles of classification of credit claims and on the creation of reserves and provisions for such credit, that it was possible to identify poor-quality credit in bank portfolios. This led to substantial growth in recorded classified credit in all problem banks by the end of 1994, when their share in total credit roughly tripled, representing about one-third of credit in bank portfolios.

The data in Table 16.3 provide the identification of trends in the classified client credit of commercial banks in the Czech Republic in the period from 1994 to 1998. These banks also have corresponding trends in reserves and loan loss provisions. One might observe a gradual decline in total classified loans to total credit. However, this decline should be explained by the fact that the CNB did not include banks under conservatorship.

Parallel to the volume of classified credit, there was also a corresponding decrease in the amount of risk-weighted classified credit, that is, in the amount of reserve requirements. The data indicate that despite the growing volume of reserves and loan-loss provisions, the ratio of actual to required reserves continued to diminish in the covered period.

The trends in both of these ratios suggest that bad loans and the resulting vulnerability of commercial banks are a huge burden for banks. This conclu-sion must, however, be qualified by at least three arguments:

- As discussed above, the interpretation of data in time series must allow for the institutional changes which have materialized over time.
- According to the legal regulations in force up to mid-1995, the possibil-ities of writing off non-performing loans were severely restricted. As a

result, commercial banks stockpiled classified credit on the one hand and unused reserves and loan-loss provisions on the other.

* The ratios of classified credit and of accumulated reserves and loan-loss provisions varied widely across groups of banks.

In considering the Czech banking system, it is quite obvious that a relatively high level of non-performing loans and especially loss loans can be expected. This is caused by several factors. The roots of classified loans lie above all in recent inadequate management, although a large number of non-performing loans are a legacy of the previous economic period (1970–89). With respect to a given situation, commercial banks should be forced to create adequate provisions for loans and high loss reserves. However, commercial banks are sharply limited as regards the creation of reserves for loss loans by exploiting a tax deduction. In accordance with Act 593/1992 Sb, a bank could create the reserves, which allowed a tax deduction of up to 10 per cent of such loans that are not repaid to the lender according to the terms of the initial agreement; only 2 per cent of such loans are due for repayment over more than one year. This was modified (Act 132/1995 Sb) in July 1995, allowing for a substantial increase in the number of ways that reserves and loan-loss provisions can be created.

A further issue is the question of how to apply the write-off method and tax treatment of loan losses. The Czech banking accounting system did not allow loan losses to be written off before a borrower announced his or her bankruptcy. This had a direct impact on the financial position of a bank. For example, a bank could report a profit even if de facto due to the repayment failure of borrowers its gross profit is negative.

Financial Distress – the Group of Small and Medium-sized Commercial Banks

A rapid credit expansion at the start of their activities was one cause of the problems of some small banks. All banks with solvency problems created most of their credit portfolios before the end of 1993. This is particularly evident for banks that become operational before 1992, where the credit share recorded in 1993 made up more than 80 per cent of all credit as of the first half of 1996; the highest credit risk exposures also originated in the initial period of their activity. The riskiness of such credit was quite apparent when it came due and debtors were unable to meet their obligations.

An earlier disclosure of the extent of the problem did not emerge even after auditors' reports on problem banks, an important factor in verifying the quality of assets and amount of bank losses. With only some exceptions, these reports did not signal any major problems until the end of 1994.

The development of a market mechanism accompanied by vast shifts of property, the development of financial and capital markets, the opening up of borders facilitating substantial migration and other factors associated with the overall economic transformation following 1989, created a hotbed of crime in general, including in the banking area. Along with new banking instruments, funding and guarantee schemes, new technologies for data transfer and its processing and new business partners, various frauds were perpetuated in banks.

An increase in banking criminal activity was facilitated by the fact that from the beginning, insufficient control mechanisms were implemented in banks, bank employees lacked experience in new banking transactions and the types of fraud with which they might be confronted and which had already been detected in advanced countries. Also, the general weakening of morals as a heritage of the past regime contributed to the increased criminality.

Legislation stipulating the rights, obligations and scrutiny of participants in the banking market and other financial markets, has been undergoing significant changes, as have the criminal and legal spheres. Gradually, as know-how is acquired, legal means are being established for a more effective fight against financial criminal activity, including organized crime, concurrent with the restructuring of the police and court systems. The professional level and capacities of the police and courts are not sufficient to investigate and try the larger, more complicated cases.

It can be said that one of the causes of the small bank failures is banking criminality. Many fraudulent financial schemes have been introduced into the Czech Republic and successfully implemented in banks. Apart from 'intermediary' frauds, 'transfer' fraud, fraud involving letters of credit, cheques, credit cards and computer fraud, a new type of fraud, the 'primary bank guarantee' as appeared in the Czech Republic, and proved fatal for Banka Bohemia. This type of fraud has many forms and is based on the use of banker inexperience in effecting secured transactions. The CNB has also encountered a similar type of fraudulent operation.

In the Czech Republic there have been a large number of false bills of exchange in high denominations, and considerable efforts have been made by various persons to sell them to domestic banks (usually underpriced and for an intermediary commission for the discounting bank). If these involve well-known foreign firms and the counterfeit looks plausible, including signatures and a well-established foreign bank, then the possibility of 'success' with inexperienced banks is quite high.

The so-called 'capital deposit confirmation' method is another type of new financial fraud being plied at a large number of Czech banks. An embezzler extracts from a bank confirmation that he or she has deposited capital with it, which is acceptable since this does not originate from criminal activity and will not be used for some time, and then tries, with this confirmation, to obtain credit from another bank, or effect another operation which would bring profit. However, the 'deposited capital' is usually nothing more than, for example, the uncovered bill of exchange itself, or forfeited deposit certificates, which the embezzler places into the care of the respective banks. This kind of fraud is again associated with a 'commission' for a willing banker, while the bank as such is harmed by the damage to its good name and by possible legal disputes with the victims of the fraud.

Apart from these specific kinds of banking fraud, which have placed some banks in difficulty to a greater or lesser extent, there is danger for the banking sector because there are non-transparent groups of persons and firms acting together to withdraw money from banks and shift it to the priority areas of their entrepreneurial interest (to industry in particular). These groups are deliberately created as a non-transparent, mutually connected network of persons and firms, frequently changing firm names, their headquarters, persons in management and authority, and so on. In banks they exist in various roles: as direct or indirect owners, members of statutory authorities or business partners, and often all the roles are played together.

Some of the methods used are as follows: the sale to banks of illiquid securities (mostly shares of satellite firms existing only on paper) with a future buyback agreement that is not met, leaving the bank with an illiquid asset or unpaid debt; the purchase of a security from a bank with a commitment to buy back, and a bank obligation to sell this security back at a much higher price than the purchasing one; funding of a group by a bank in the form of 'hidden long-term interest-free crediting', presented as an advance for the purchase of securities for a bank. These and similar transactions account for hundreds of millions to billions of crowns, meaning, for a bank, a considerable real or potential loss, which may lead to the loss of bank liquidity and its failure. This kind of financial criminal activity is extremely difficult to detect through the usual methods, since it can be concealed for a long time, for example, by entering assets as other categories, or not entering some assets and liabilities at all, so that the financial loss is not evident from the financial statements.

The CNB has filed complaints in cases where it has detected unusual operations[4] being repeatedly executed in banks, which as a result have impaired the bank's financial position and its creditor interests. Other complaints are being prepared.

It is necessary to amend criminal and legal regulations in order to punish the offenders effectively. In this respect, during the procedure dealing with the amendment to the penal law, the CNB suggested changing or adjusting the definition of acts constituting an offence and the levels of punishment.

As regards banking legislation, an amendment under preparation to the act on banks specifies the issue of possible deliberate misuse of a bank by its own shareholders, in its provision authorizing the CNB to carry out a detailed scrutiny of new shareholders, including members of the group to which they belong, in terms of their creditworthiness, transparency and financial stability. An amendment to the act in this area also enables the CNB to take effective action against a shareholder or group of shareholders, should they have a detrimental influence on a bank's performance (the right to deprive a shareholder of his or her voting rights, to order a sale of shares to a person meeting CNB criteria and so on). The CNB expects this strict procedure against undesirable shareholders, common in advanced countries, to be supported by legislators.

METHODS OF BANKING CONSOLIDATION AND RESTRUCTURING

The assumption of bad claims from the portfolio of state-owned commercial banks has been the main feature of bank rehabilitation. The great volume of non-performing loans in the portfolio of the state-owned commercial banks is due to the legacy of the past. In addition, these banks signalled problems of undercapitalization. Cleaning up the bank portfolio from the non-performing credit inherited from the past, solving new problems arising in the banking sector during the transformation process, and a further restructuring of banks in conjunction with their preparation for privatization are essential steps in this stage. The restructuring, consolidation and stabilization programmes in the banking sector were implemented outside the state budget through the creation of some non-standard, so-called 'transformation' institutions, which were given a direct state guarantee of financial resources provision and loss and operating costs coverage. As a result, the indirect potential liabilities of the state in the banking sector emerged.

The bank recapitalization, consolidation and stabilization programmes were implemented over time in three steps.

Consolidation Programme I

If the government along with the central bank wanted to set up a competitive, efficient and credible environment in the banking sector, then it was more than desirable to 'clean up' the portfolio of those banks. The government and the central bank (formerly the Czechoslovak State Bank) had to decide which strategy should be adopted for recapitalization of the banks listed above and their consequent privatization. Generally speaking, two basic approaches – centralized and decentralized – could be taken into account.

The essence of the first consists in the concentration of all the bad debts into one institution established for this special purpose. The second method relies on banks to manage their bad portfolios themselves. A further possibility is a hybrid of these two approaches.

The government and the central bank decided to adopt the centralized approach and, consequently, a bank was established to collect and manage these non-performing loans. The Consolidation Bank (Konsolidační Banka – KOB) was founded in February 1991 by the federal ministry of finance as a bank with 100 per cent state participation.[5] In the early stage of its activity, the KOB was supported financially by the former Czechoslovak State Bank, the Czech Savings Bank and the Czech Insurance Company.

The original reason for establishing the KOB, as we have already mentioned, was to manage poor-quality loans. Its first important activity consisted in handling the so-called 'perpetual inventory loans' (TOZ) especially from Komerční Banka Praha, Československá Obchodni Banka (Czechoslovak Trade Bank), Investiční Banka and Všeobecná Úverová Banka Bratislava. The write-off of TOZ had been desirable because of the unavoidable recapitilization of these banks to enable their activities to be expanded. TOZ were issued at the beginning of the 1970s. The purpose of this 'credit' was to extend the financial means of state-owned companies. TOZ were unsecured loans with a very low interest rate of 3 per cent (which jumped to 6 per cent in 1986) on the loans and were also without a given maturity. In 1990 these loans were commercialized. The interest rate increased by almost four times up to 23 per cent. The volume of this credit transferred to the KOB was CZK 110 billion, which represented 80 per cent of total TOZ. The new interest rate of this transferred credit has been kept at 1–5 per cent above the discount rate and its repayment term is 8 years.

The key event that extend the activities of the KOB occurred at the beginning of 1992. The National Property Fund (Fond Národního Majetku – FNM) released a total amount of CZK 50 billion. Of this amount, CZK 22.8 billion was transferred for loan write-offs and CZK 7.8 billion in bonds for bank recapitalization to the Czech banks already mentioned. This allowed these banks to write off large amounts of non-performing loans.At the end of 1992, the KOB then took over the risk credit for CZK 15 billion. These loans were largely from Komerční Banka Praha, Investiční Banka and Všeobecná Úverová Banka Bratislava. The KOB paid 80 per cent of their nominal value for this credit. We can see from Table 16.4 that after these activities the number of clients jumped sharply.

In February 1993, with the split of the Czechoslovak Federation, the Consolidation Bank, State Monetary Institution in Prague was created, which would follow the activities of the Czechoslovak Consolidation Bank in the Czech Republic.

The new strategy of the KOB meant that it was transformed as an instrument for implementing government investment programmes in the economy.

Table 16.4   *Konsolidační Banka: net public expenditure, 1993–1998*
               (CZK bn)

	1993	1994	1995	1996	1997	1998*
New programme outlay	7.2	14.7	10.0	8.1	29.2	37.0
Received from	0	−7.8	−6.2	−4.8	−5.3	−8.3
programmes (−)						
Interest expense	0.7	1.6	2.0	2.2	4.4	7.0
Interest income (−)	−0.2	−1.2	−1.3	−1.4	−1.8	−5.6
Net public	7.7	7.3	4.5	4.1	26.5	30.1
expenditure						

Note: *Estimation.

Source: *Konsolidační Banka.*

Accordingly, KOB activities were extended to include banking activities. From the end of 1994, in connection with the decision on the reorientation of the bank, the new strategy was adopted, assuming a considerable extension of activities and transactions. The CNB extended the range of KOB authorization activities and by the end of 1995 the bank was licensed to perform a full range of banking activities. Under the new strategy, the KOB was characterized by its supervisory board as a bank with certain development features. The main features of the new strategy and reorientation of the bank were:

* Transformation of the bank into a joint-stock company, fully state owned, with liabilities guaranteed by the state.
* Active management of the so-called 'block of old loans' taken from commercial banks. Prudent restructuring of these loans to selected large clients with good potential. An instrument for supporting the process of reviving the Czech economy through the implementation of important projects and transactions.
* Implementation of large-scale development and public service projects, in particular in the fields of infrastructure and the environment.

The loans count for a large portion of the asset portfolio of the KOB. The loan portfolio is divided into two categories of loans. The block of old loans consists of TOZ loans taken over by the bank in 1991, debts purchased before December 1992 from commercial banks and restructured loans, most of them being long-term loans. The new loans consist of loans bought in 1993 from commercial banks and loans granted by the KOB. Over the years the bank has extended its activities and transactions. The KOB granted 'new loans' in 1993 and 1994 mainly in two areas: Financing the development of production and technology of companies with a large volume of exports and bridging the time gap between production and financial sources of bank clients (especially agriculture) – see next subsection.

The recapitalization of banks has been done through the bond issue of the National Property Fund (NPF). The cost of Consolidation Programme I was covered from the privatization proceeds of the NPF. At the end of 1992, the former Czechoslovak government took over from the Investiční Banka the loans that were allocated to the Council for Mutual Economic Assistance (CMEA) countries. Moreover, in order to clean the portfolio of Československá Obchodní Banka (CSOB), from the claims and afterwards the guarantees issued in the past in the high-risk territories, Česká Inkasní (Czech Encashment Corporation Ltd) was set up at the end of 1993. Česká Inkasní has started its operations as a subsidiary of the ministry of finance.

The NPF has covered most of the financial costs of banks' rehabilitation programmes carried out by the government in the past years. It was established in 1991 as one of the temporary institutions organizing the large privatization programme of state property. The NPF does not have the right to decide how to conduct state property privatization, it only conducts the privatization based on government decisions. The fund is not a government institution and is controlled directly by Parliament. The gains from privatization are the property of the NPF and can be used only for such purposes as are specified by the law. The law presumes that they shall be used mostly for the elimination or reduction of 'debts' inherited from the past, such as the bad debts of privatized companies, or for the solution of environmental problems. However, the privatization gains are used largely for the replenishment of sources of the state budget and for the implementation of government investment policies in the economy. A substantial part of NPF expenditures was used for the refinancing of bank restructuring and reorganization.

The third institution having an impact on the consolidation process has already been mentioned – Česká Inkasní, Czech Encashment Corporation Ltd (CE), owned by the ministry of finance. The CE was set up on 23 December 1993 with the objective of repurchasing and administering claims of the Czech Trade Bank (CSOB) against entities in countries presenting high political risk. In return, the CSOB provides funds of equal amount as the claims transferred (bought). The CE differs from other companies in the following:

- it owns neither tangible nor non-tangible assets;
- all operational expenses including salaries are paid by the CSOB;
- a substantial proportion of its assets include long-term outstanding claims

Table 16.5   Česká Inkasní: net public expenditure, 1993–1998 (CZK bn)

	1993	1994	1995	1996	1997	1998*
Claims taken	26.7	3.8	0.0	1.3	0.0	0.00
Total claims (cumulative)	26.7	30.5	30.5	31.8	31.8	31.80
Interest expenses	–	–	3.5	3.2	2.8	1.40
Interest income (–)	–	–	–0.4	–0.1	–0.1	–0.02
Net public expenditure	26.7	3.8	3.1	4.4	2.7	1.40

Note: *Estimation.

Source: *Česká Inkasní.*

which by the end of 1993 were in the credit and guarantee portfolio of the CSOB (the CE bought these claims from the CSOB as part of the transformation programme approved by the government); and

- CE activities are backed by the NPF, which is obliged to subsidize the difference between the value of the claim including interest and the amount collected, until the year 2003. However, related to an expectation of deficiency of privatization incomes, the NBP compensation to the CE may be shifted to the state.

According to the government agreements, from its beginnings until the end of 1997, the CE received CZK 19.037 billion from the NPF, of which CZK 9.341 billion represented principal payments, and CZK 9.696 billion was paid in interest. The amount of CZK 1.066 billion paid as interest was generated from CE bank activity. During the 1994–97 period, CE income from bank activity was CZK 2.912 billion, of which only CZK 1.819 billion was repayment of principal and interest from clients and CZK 407 million was from the shares sale. Total expenses for the period were CZK 2.460 billion. Nevertheless, in 1997 the CE disclosed a total loss of CZK 7.49 billion. the main cause of this loss was the creation of loan loss provisions, which amounted to CZK 7.636 billion.

The losses and debt of the CE should be analysed in connection with the NPF's refinancing obligation. Therefore, the whole load is shifted directly to the NPF. In Table 16.5 we present the debt and loss evaluation of the CE for the period from 1993 to June 1998.

Consolidation Programme II

The main reason for adopting the measures within Consolidation Programme II was to prevent these problems from weakening the confidence in banking institutions. Although the share of all small banks in the bank market was only 9 per cent in 1993, the continuing bankruptcies of small banks have gradually undermined public confidence in the banking sector.

Another stimulus for the effort aimed at small bank consolidation is their contribution in the area of client services. In some respects, these banks substantially improve the level of banking services in the Czech Republic. They often offer an individual approach to clients, new products such as home banking, a high-quality and manageable payment system, and short-term investment programmes or current accounts with advantageous interest. They introduce such services either exclusively of much earlier than major banks. A banking sector composed only of major banks, where the introduction of each new product involves high costs and complex management and banks with exclusive orientation towards large corporate clients would develop slowly and have a lower level of client services. Moreover, not all small banks have problems and client distrust could also threaten those banks which are, in principle, 'sound'.

Of crucial importance for the implementation of Consolidation Programme II, were the audits of annual accounts representing the basic legislative support for banking supervision interventions in compliance with the act on banks. Based only on the 1995 bank audit results, when, in compliance with the CNB provision on bank performance reports, auditors were obliged to conduct a general examination of bank portfolios with respect to their quality and determine the necessary volume of provisions and reserves, conditions were created for more radical action by the banking supervision body, directed at solving the problem of banks that recorded insufficient reserves and whose capital was insufficient to cover the losses.

Since 1994 we have witnessed the failure of several small and medium-sized commercial banks. These banks had obtained their financial resources largely via the interbank market, and the biggest banks in the Czech Republic are (were) the main creditors of these small and medium-sized banks. It is not surprising that the big banks were involved in rescue activities when these events occurred. A particularly prominent role was played by Česká Spořitelna (Savings Bank) and Československá Obchodní Banka (Czechoslovak Trade Bank). Although Česká Spořitelna allegedly lost a huge amount of credit, especially to AB Banka and Bohemia Banka, we cannot find any sign of systemic risk or rather systemic crises in the banking sector as a whole.[6] (See Table 16.6.)

The small and medium-sized commercial banks have no direct impact on the Czech banking system since the total assets of these banks amount to only 5 per cent of total assets within the banking sector. Nevertheless, the decline of small banks cannot be ignored, since it could cause not only systemic risk (crisis) in this segment of the banking sector, but also a decline in confidence in the banking sector.

Table 16.6 Small banks under liquidation, conservatorship and prepared for merger (October 1998)

Name of bank	Start of operation	CNB administration	Liquidation	Method
Agrobanka	01–07–90	17–09–96	08–10–98	Takeover by GE
AB Banka	01–04–91	–	05–03–96	Licence revocation (15–12–96)
Banka Bohemia	29–01–91	31–03–94	18–07–94	Licence revocation (18–07–94)
Bankovní dům Skala	13–12–90	–	10–12–97 to 30–04–98	Takeover by Union Banka, licence revocation (31–03–97)
Coop Banka	24–2–92	23–04–96	–	Takeover by Foresbanka; licence revocation
Česka Banka	15–01–92	–	19–03–96 to 27–06–96	Licence revocation (15–12–95); bankruptcy (28–06–1996)
Ekoagrobanka	01–11–90	16–01–96	01–01–98	Takeover by Union Banka, licence revocation (31–05–97)
Evrobanka	01–10–91	–	–	Takeover by Union Banka, licence revocation (30–06–97)
Krediní a průmyslová banka	01–10–91	30–09–93 to 31–08–95	–	Licence revocation (02–10–95); bankruptcy (02–10–95)
Kreditní Banka Plzeň	01–01–90	–	01–10–96	Licence revocation (08–08–96)
Podnikatelská Banka	18–12–92	06–06–96	–	na
První Slezká Banka	12–01–93	–	24–07–96	Licence revocation (13–05–96); bankruptcy (20–11–97)
Realitbanka	01–11–91	10–07–96	–	Licence revocation (17–4–97); bankruptcy (24–03–97)
Velkomoravská	03–11–92	10–07–96	–	Licence revocation (24–10–98); bankruptcy (02–07–96)
Pragobanka	01–10–90	–	–	Licence revocation (24–10–98); bankruptcy (19–11–98)
Universal Bank	12–02–93	–	–	Licence revocation (10–02–1999); bankruptcy (12–02–99)

Source: Czech National Bank.

Even if the failure of some commercial banks in the Czech Republic is still a possibility, we do not envisage that the decline in small banks could lead to an epidemic in the banking system as a whole. This is, of course, a matter of *ad hoc* judgement; the reason for this assumption lies in the 'too big to fail', or rather, 'too important to fail', doctrine. These 'big' banks are too important to the Czech banking system; we presume they have such a strong foothold that they are able to deal with whatever disturbances there maybe within the banking system. In fact, the state is a shareholder in these banks and thus the government will support these big banks if a solvency problem arises, for example, Česká Spořitelna.

The main weaknesses of the small and medium-sized banks can be identified as follows, excluding those where financial crime is present:

- insufficient capital;
- lack of primary deposits;
- inappropriate assets–liabilities mismatch;
- no transparency of shareholders;
- a problem of adverse selection due to relatively high interest rates; and
- inadequate management in many cases.

In the light of these problems, one of the possible ways of resolving them would be a merger of these small banks with bigger, healthier banks. However, we argue that this solution has not been widely adopted in the Czech banking sector. Reasons for being sceptical can also be found in the experience in other countries. First of all, it is desirable to analyse the benefits of mergers. Banks aspire to membership of a core bank group for the following reasons:

- to secure unrealized economies of scale;
- to carry out the rationalization of branch networks;
- to enable the demands of large customers to be met;
- to match the size of other banks in international banking; and
- to meet foreign bank competition in their home country.

Applying these factors to the Czech banking sector, there is minimal incentive for mergers or take-overs by domestic banks. The same situation can be seen in mergers of foreign commercial banks. We observe that there is absolutely no incentive to be active in these operations. One possible explanation is that the advantages are not significant, at most marginal. The small banks mentioned have a few or no branches and their clients are mainly small private companies, which are not good performers. The process of mergers and acquisition in the Czech Republic can be seen in Table 16.6.

Nevertheless, one way to proceed might be to eliminate undesirable banks by increasing the minimum capital requirement for banks – a measure that would have a relatively quick and positive impact on the banking structure. Above all, it is desirable to emphasize the measure prior to taking this step; there is a need to clarify which size banks, in terms of capital levels, should be 'eliminated'. Unfortunately, the secondary consequence of this step is that a few of the small banks which do not have any difficulties at present would also have to either increase their capital or merge with a larger bank.

An indirect way of increasing capital was applied in the Czech banking system. Since a number of small banks have a great volume of bad loans, the CNB decided, in the framework of a consolidation programme, to oblige these banks to increase their capital in order to cover their bad loans. If they are not able to do so, the CNB will put these banks under forced (special) administration and look for a strategic partner. If no other investor can be found relatively quickly, Konsolidacni Banka will take over the bank temporarily. It is worth noting that the above-mentioned method, that is, forced administration, is an operation often used as a temporary solution for failed banks. During this period the authority seeks bridge banks, new banks or other institutions which will ensure the stability of the bank in question. These operations have a positive effect, in the sense of avoiding a further deterioration in the financial position of the bank in question. For example, such a method was applied when Barings failed in 1995. The bank was under the administration of the Bank of England and then sold to ING, the Dutch banking and insurance group (see Lastra 1996).

The last, but not necessarily least, way of dealing with failed institutions is to revoke the banking licence of the particular bank. Such a step avoids a further deterioration in this situation. On the other hand, it could have negative consequences as far as the credibility of the banking sector is concerned. In addition, this solution can be costly. Therefore, any hasty decision on the part of the banking supervisory body or other authorities could be very harmful. But when a bank has failed as a result of fraud, liquidation is the appropriate response.

Stabilization Programme

Undoubtedly, all these ways of sorting out the troubled institutions involve the cost of solving such problems. The CNB decided to run the so-called Consolidation Programme II and later the government announced a further programme helping small and medium-sized commercial banks – the Stabilization Programme.

Consolidation Programme II was implemented by the CNB at the end of 1995 and the beginning of 1996, and was focused on small and medium-sized banks. The objective of the Stabilization Programme was to solve the remaining problems in the banks by an injection of additional private capital and recapitalization through profit generation.

Česká Finanční (Czech Financial Corporation, Ltd – CF), was created as a CNB subsidiary in February 1997. The corporation was created for the purpose of implementing the consolidation and stabilization programmes and to administer the CNB non-performing credit and property participation taken from small banks. The Stabilization Programme was initiated in 1996 and it is to be terminated in the year 2003, when all the loss and asset write-offs will be made good by the NPF to the Consolidation Bank. Since the privatization is almost complete and its income is expected to be low, it is doubtful whether the NPF will be able to compensate the Stabilization Programme at its termination. Therefore, there is some probability that the costs will have to be covered by the government. Moreover, the Consolidation Bank has issued its own bonds to finance the Stabilization Programme for small and medium-sized banks, and consequently there may be additional costs transferred to the state. The consolidation programme administered by the CF is financed from the CNB compensation.

Within the framework of the bank Stabilization Programme, in which six banks participated, the CF bought CZK 10.633 billion assets in nominal value of which CZK 7.536 were loans and CZK 3.097 were shares. In addition, in 1997, the CF bought assets within the framework of the Consolidation Programme for small and medium-sized banks amounting to CZK 11.466 billion, of which CZK 8.3609 billion was credit, and the remaining CZK 3.097 billion were shares. Moreover, the CF acted as a bank, with the power to revoke licences. The CF is financed by the CNB and the Consolidation Bank. In 1997, the CNB provided CZK 9.638 billion at 17.5 per cent interest and the KOB provided CZK 12.3 billion at a lower interest rate related to the PRIBOR rate.

In February 1998, the government decided to increase the CF financing by CZK 5 billion. In April 1998, the CF transferred CZK 9 billion as a capital injection to Agrobanka (AGB). The total amount of cash transfer from the CNB to the CF to buy the AGB assets during 1998 was CZK 22 billion. By the end of 1997, CAK 17.499 billion (71 per cent) of the total CF assets (CZK 24.6 billion) were overdue by periods of from 30 days to one year (35 per cent of total assets were more than a year overdue). Only CZK 0.23 billion, about 1 per cent of the total assets were (realized) paid during the year, of which 0.9 per cent were from the Consolidation Programme assets.

Through the CF, a special institution set up for this purpose as a subsidiary of the CNB, the government temporarily purchased the bad assets at face value, up to 110 per cent of respective bank capital. These had to be bought back within a period of 5–7 years, and the banks did not have to pay interest. The programme was initially financed through the extension of short-term credit

Table 16.7   Debt and profit/loss evaluation of CF, 1997–1998 (CZK bn)

	AGB	SP		CP		Total	Net interest income	Profit/loss
		Credits	Shares	Credits	Shares			
1997	0	8.678	2.140	8.820	2.590	22.191	0.113	−2.374
1998	22.3	10.420	2.140	12.840	3.097	50.840		

Source: CF, Annual Report.

from the CNB to the CF. Further, the CF was refinanced at market cost through the Consolidation Bank, which issued bonds for this purpose. The CNB also extended credit to the CF, together with the transfer of bad assets bought by the central bank during the second stage of the Consolidation Programme.

Accordingly, following the restructuring, consolidation and stabilization of the banking sector, as analysed above, the Czech government had a high implicit fiscal exposure in the banking sector.

The bank also began to participate in the consortium loans in cooperation with large financial institutions. The loans granted by the KOB were based on bank policy and the government's decision for restructuring and revitalization programmes of some enterprises, such as Aero, the aviation holding company, and the revitalization of Ekoagrabanka. Following the government decision, the KOB has been associated with a programme for consolidating the stability of the banking sector adopted at the end of 1996. Using sources provided by the NPF, the KOB granted a loan of CZK 12.3 billion to the CF to refinance the risky assets purchased from banks.

Only the net interest expenses shown in the Table 16.7 should be included in expenses in the 'true' budge deficit, since the costs of stabilization programme financing are already accounted for in the KOB calculations. In a broader picture of fiscal operations analysis, which includes the CNB quasi-fiscal operations, the cost of the Consolidation Programme borne by the CNB should be included as expenses.

THE COST AND EFFECTS OF THE CONSOLIDATION AND STABILIZATION PROGRAMMES

Effects of the Programmes

The most important contribution of Consolidation Programme I was the effect on the national economy. Due to the recapitalization and partial consolidation of major banks during the first phase of economic transformation, they could more easily fulfil their intermediating function between depositors and credit recipients, and service financial transactions during the critical period of privatization and the entry of new firms into the market. Despite some problems, this suppressed the risk of a system crisis in the banking sector and the destabilizing effects of such a crisis on a sector of the real economy undergoing exacting structural and institutional changes.

Other effects of consolidation and recapitalization were important to the banks themselves and their development. Due to partial 'clearing' of bank portfolios, bank balances were not hampered so much by the creation of provisions and reserves. The speedy transfer and concentration of bad debts in one institution reduced the costs which would have been covered by banks if they had been forced to 'handle' both revolving credit on inventories and classified credit individually. The consolidation and recapitalization of the banking sector would not have been possible without the help of the government or the NPF. During the subsequent development of the transformation, it was broadly accepted that the costs of bank consolidation and recapitalization would become returnable to the NPF as the banks, when their portfolios had been cleared, would be able to contribute more widely and rapidly via their credit operations to at least a partial restructuring of credited enterprises. Following their privatization, the NPF should have collected higher prices than would otherwise have been the case. But we shall see that this did not occur (see below).

Moreover, the government is exposed in the banking sector through the retained shares of ownership. In the Czech Republic, the government retains a large share of ownership in the three big commercial banks – 45 per cent in the Czech Savings Bank (CS), 65.7 per cent in the Czech Trade Bank (CSOB) and 48.74 per cent in Komerční Banka (KB). The balance sheets of these banks show a substantial percentage of classified loans, of which the government has its share. Within the framework of the preparation of banks for privatization, the government may be obliged to assume, at least, its share of non-performing loans carried by these institutions. Already in December 1998, in preparing the CS for privatization, the government decided to help the bank with its bad loans problem and capital adequacy requirements. Therefore, it was decided that the KOB would have to issue CZK 5.5 billion of subordinated loans, money that the KOB has to borrow. The KOB loss will be covered by the state. Further, the KOB will buy CZK 10.5 billion of bad debt from the CS for CZK 4 billion. CZK 2.5 billion of these loans are secured loans which are already provided for. Moreover, in 1999 the KOB is taking over CZK 15 billion of the CS's 'social loans'.

The privatization of the other two banks, the CSOB and the KB should be completed by the year 2000 (end 1999). With the government's planned intervention for helping the CS, it is expected that it will do the same for the other

Table 16.8 Government exposure in loss and classified loans in three big banks (% of total assets)

	1997		November 1998	
	Loss loans	Classified loans	Loss loans	Classified loans
KB	13.50	18.52	15.10	33.2
CSOB	15.05	23.06	10.69	24.4
CS*	7.79	9.23	7.85	18.8
Total	36.33	50.81	33.64	74.4
As percentage of GDP	2.80	4.00	2.60	5.80

Note:　*At the end of 1998 the government had to pay CZK 4 billion of CS losses guaranteed by state, and CZK 10.5 billion of CS bad assets were transferred to the KOB.

Source:　Banks' Annual Reports.

two banks. Therefore, the amount of government loss loans in the two banks, at least, should be included in the government's accounts.

According to the annual reports of the above-mentioned banks and the government share of ownership in each of them we can calculate government exposure to non-performing loans in the three big banks (see Table 16.8). As shown in the previous section, the government measures for bank consolidation and stabilization took the form of bank asset transfers, bond transfers, placement of deposits, enterprise debt assumption or loss and debt compensation, and were implemented through the special government guaranteed institutions, such as the KOB, the CE, the CF and the NPF. Therefore, the costs of the bank rehabilitation were not properly registered and accounted for in the government budget.

During the Stabilization Programme of small and medium-sized banks, the CNB also took over claims and participation shares of the problem banks included in the programme. Through the NPF, the government issued a guarantee to the CNB that covers the losses occurred for the Stabilization Programme. If the state were to take over the claims and losses of the CNB it would have to increase the government debt and budget deficit by a significant amount.

The method used to rescue Ekoagrobanka was employed as a model. This approach, quite common in standard economies, was an illustration of rapid intervention. Its use was only made possible by an amendment to the act on the CNB allowing a capital decrease in a problem bank. Thereby, scope was created for the bank's take-over by another investor without having to negotiate the purchase of actually worthless shares from former shareholders. In future possible rescues of problem banks, it will be necessary to prevent shareholders, if a bank has financial problems, from calculating on a capital decrease as an acceptable recourse, which will not present any great danger to the main shareholders. For this reason, this approach has to be applied relatively early.

A specific problem is the absence of any institution which would – with state support, common in similar situations abroad – participate in the rescue of threatened banks. If no private sector entity is interested, such an institution would go into banks, salvage and sell them. This method is not only more orderly from the system point of view, but usually also cheaper. To date, negotiations with 'state institutions' (for example, KOB, Česká Inkasní) regarding such activity have been unsuccessful.

Another, similar problem is the non-existence of a mechanism for purchasing less sound assets prior to the commencement of potential problems. The CNB has already prepared a model for a centralized solution of bad debt problems with possible state support. This model presupposes the establishment of a unit for the purchase and management of non-performing bank assets, whose founders might be the CNB and the MF, with perhaps the participation of the International Financial Corporation (IFC).

This unit would, based on bank requirements, purchase their bad debts, or possibly other assets, for which it would pay in cash an estimated sum. The remaining value (possibly decreased by 10–20 per cent) would be transferred to a subordinated debt of the unit towards a bank. This method would also enable a certain degree of state support of such operations to a precisely determined volume (strengthening the credit of a subordinated debt, the purchase of a certain part of non-performing assets for higher than the market price and so on).

Cost of the Programmes

The banking sector development described above is also associated with the fact that in recent years the state has incurred substantial expense connected to banking sector stabilization. These included operations directed at the banks' clearing of assets linked with the pre-transformation economy and those connected to the transformation.

In the first case, these were costs of Consolidation Programme I, generated by the transfer of revolving credits on inventories into the KOB, recapitalization of banks from NPF funds and the rescue of the CSOB's balance through the CE. The total cost of these operations will be known after all credit cases have been concluded, that is, after the repayment or writing off of credit granted. At present, the preliminary CNB estimate of these costs is about CZK 60 billion. (See Table 16.9).

With regard to banking sector problems originating in the transformation stage, the first expense arose in connection with Kreditní a průmyslová Banka, AB Banka and Bank Bohemia. In 1996, the consolidation process continued via steps described above. Other potential costs arose, generally divided as follows.

First, costs for deposit compensation above the DIF limit in První Slezská Banka, Podnikatelská Banka, Velkomoravská Banka and Realitbanka. These are not cases of net losses, as the expense will have to be decreased by the share from sales of assets. In some cases, the CNB opted for support of a take-over of a problem bank by a sound bank. In addition to reducing banking sector destabilization in the public mind, this solution also required comparatively lower costs. Support was procured for take-overs of the following banks: COOP Banka, Bankovní Dům Skala, Ekoagrobanka and Evrobanka.

Table 16.9 Assessment of costs for banks' consolidation and stabilization (CZK bn)

Type of programme	Type of expense	Costs
Consolidation Programme I	Establishing KOB	6
	Reserves for KOB	31
	Transfering debts from state-owned banks	22
	Loss of KOB	14–15
	Compensation of the losses in 1996	5.1
	Transfer of assets from CSOB to CF	20
	Estimation of losses from Slovak encashment	10
Consolidation Programme II	Financial support of the small and medium-sized banks	40.3
	Loss of AGB	12–20
Stabilization Programme	Interest compensation*	2.5
Total		160.9–171.9

Note: *Costs for the first two years of programme. In seven years, costs are estimated to be CZK 16 million.

Source: Hospodářské noviny.

*Table 16.10   Net public costs of consolidation and stabilization
programmes, 1993–1998 (CZK bn)*

	1993	1994	1995	1996	1997	1998*
Konsolidacni Banka (KOB) net public expenditure	7.7	7.3	4.5	4.1	26.5	30.1
Česká Inkasní (CI) net public expenditure	26.7	3.8	3.1	4.4	2.7	1.4
Česká Financni (CF) net public expenditure					0.6	1.8
National Property Fund (NPF) net public expenditure (excl. KOB CI)	4.2	8.2	4.3	1.9	2.0	2.9
State guarantees net hidden subsidy (risk adjusted)	0.1	–0.4	1.3	14.9	51.5	26.7

Notes: *Estimated.

Source: Ministry of Finance.

Second, reduction of economic effects on the banking sector resulting from some bank bankruptcies. In this case, support was provided to those banks who were unable to meet their commitments. These operations, carried out from 1994, have involved about CZK 30 billion, but it is difficult to determine the precise amount. The costs will depend on the efficiency of the administration of both acquired and residual assets. With regard to assets administered by the CNB, a specialized team was created to achieve maximum revenues. (See Table 16.10.)

In addition, some bad debts were used to finance unsuccessful privatization projects and subsequently appeared on NPF accounts (for this reason, this is not a net loss). Although the reporting discipline of banks is not good in this area, the volume of such credits exceeds CZK 10 billion. Some of this credit was granted by banks that no longer exist.

CONCLUSION

The rapid transfer and concentration of bad loans into one institution – the KOB – during Consolidation Programme I undoubtedly reduced costs that accompanied non-performing loans. That cost reduction must be seen in terms of the higher efficiency of restructured banks as well as from the point of view of the process of privatization. The situation in Hungary showed unambiguously that a 'wait and see' approach is not feasible. Poland's approach has been based on the decentralized method, that is, each state-owned bank set up a special division that has managed non-performing loans. There, this approach has slowed down the privatization process of state-owned banks.

Nevertheless, a key question, which runs as a theme to the whole analysis, is a moral hazard problem. Broadly speaking, a phenomenon of the moral hazard in the banking environment arises when managers have an incentive to increase risk, that is, in our case, to increase the likelihood of creating bad loans. This incentive is above all caused by the fact that a government sets up a central institution, which gives certain guarantees to take over bad loans. Thus a question is whether or not the presence of the KOB, the CE, or the CF that is, a central institution, which at least at the beginning of its activity, guaranteed to take over bad loans from state-owned banks, creates this potential jeopardy of moral hazard. Undoubtedly, the first period of the KOB's business activities seems to have been a classical example of a moral hazard problem. As indicated earlier, the KOB was established to take over the bad loans of commercial banks. However, there was no transparent environment regarding the rules as to how the KOB would proceed in its activities in the near future. Furthermore, core commercial banks, in which the Czech government has had a substantial share, might have depended on some rescue plan from the government in case of a deterioration in their portfolio. In other words, although there could have been a moral hazard problem, we cannot find any indication of it in the commercial banks in Consolidation Programme I. Due to the above measures, the Czech Republic banking sector has generally been cleaned up and has made a good recovery.

However, foreign experience shows that no banking sector is secure beforehand against the possibility of problems emerging in individual banks or their groups, or even against bank crises on a small or large scale. Bank crises are frequent even in advanced market economies. It is thought that the main reason lies with the discrepancy between the rapidity and extent of financial operations on one hand and the degree of flexibility and adaptability of the real economy on the other. Moreover, a new dimension is emerging, the ongoing globalization in the conditions of an information society. This is why the main target in this area is the prevention of system crisis at both national and international levels. This orientation should also include the creation of cushion 'bumpers', special funds, whose use would stop an emerging crisis or at least moderate its extent.

Thus, the risk to the development of the Czech banking sector involves this generally valid component, multiplied, moreover, by the specific domestic position. This position originates not only in the character of the economic transformation, but also in the still inadequate regulation of the environment in which banks operate. We have in mind both the earlier mentioned legislative problems, but also, primarily, the character and composition of the domestic financial market, where banks are undoubtedly the most strictly regulated entities. However, they are affected by the consequences of the inefficient regulation of other parts of the financial market (capital, in particular). For example, the present 'struggle for majorities' can potentially weaken the financial strength of banks and decrease their credibility.

Obviously, the development of Czech banks is proceeding very quickly and their financial force and know-how are currently at an incomparably higher level than several years ago. Nevertheless, it is necessary to take into account that in the Czech banking sector, even the strongest and soundest banks are in international terms only banks which 'are not too unsound'. Domestic banks still have a long way to go to approach the level of banks in most advanced countries.

The elimination of obviously insolvent banks does not guarantee the survival of other banks. If people are uncertain, as in the case now, even comparatively good banks are exposed to the risk of liquidity crises, which can easily be generated even by completely unjustified information. In the next stage also, bank activities will be exposed to the above-average risky environment of the Czech economy, and to increasing competition on the bank market, which is suppressing interest margins. They will also be affected by the ongoing regulation of other parts of the financial system and by the not quite adequate legal infrastructure.

An analysis of the banking sector, its development, present position and the measures directed at its consolidation, makes it possible to identify the causes of its problems. The analysis shows that, in addition to limitations in the banking sector itself and its relationship to subjects in the real economy sector, there are causes of a more general nature related to the overall financial sector and its institutions: banks, investment funds and companies in particular, as well as capital market institutions insurance companies and pension funds, and the legislative and institutional framework within which both financial and non-financial sectors operate.

It follows that recommendations and measures proposed to consolidate banking sector development further should have a wider orientation, that is, focus on more general problems of the functioning of financial institutions and their environment.

The main limitation of the current position consists in the fact that the processes of changing the legislative and system frameworks, of forming financial market institutions and enforcing consistent observance of contracts and 'rules of the game' of a market economy have lagged far behind the growth of the financial sector, increased by the weight and branches of its subjects as well as by the diversification and sophistication of its products. The liberalization of the financial markets, and also their increasing technological level, call for a correlative adjustment of legislation and of controlling and regulatory institutions.

NOTES

1. The argument, widely used by the private sector, was based on the false idea that foreign banks could strengthen competitive pressures within the banking sector. There has been no evidence in EU countries that foreign banks have influenced competitive pressures on domestic banks substantially.
2. We shall not discuss other important issues such as the privatization process.
3. Only three foreign banks obtained licences from the CNB – Midland Bank, Westdeutsche Landesbank and GE Capital Bank (West Deutsche Landesbank's licence was revoked because the bank did not start operations).
4. The CNB has already filed complaints in the cases of Kreditní a Prùmyslová Banka and Banka Bohemia, and more recently in the cases of První slezská Banka and Ekoagrobanka.
5. Unfortunately, in the first phase of its establishment, the KOB obtained a banking licence for only six months. This undoubtedly caused the problem of finding adequate management for this short period, since there was no guarantee that the licence would be renewed. The reasons for this uncertainty was the scale of all the unresolved problems connected with the technical aspects of managing this bank. A further alternative, which was also taken into account, was to transfer only these non-performing loans to a special kind of account.
6. In the interbank market, the largest lender is Česká Spořitelna.

BIBLIOGRAPHY

Begg, D. and R. Portes (1992), 'Enterprise debt and economic transformation in Central and Eastern Europe', Centre for Economic Policy Research Discussion Paper no. 695.

Benston, G.J. (1985), 'An analysis of the causes of savings and loans association failures', Monograph Series in Finance and Economics, New York University.

Caprio, G. and D.Klingebiel (1996), 'Bank insolvency: bad luck, bad policy, or bad banking?', Paper prepared for the World Bank Annual Bank Conference on Development Economics,Washington, DC, 25-26 April.

Chew, D. (ed.) (1991), *New Developments in Commercial Banking*, Oxford: Basil Blackwell.

Dewatripont, M. and J. Tirole (1993), *The Prudential Regulation of Banks*, Cambridge, MA: MIT Press.

Foster, G. (1986), *Financial Statement Analysis*, 2nd edn, Englewood Cliffs, NJ: Prentice-Hall.

Freixas, X. and J.C. Rochet (1997), *Microeconomics of Banking*, Cambridge, MA: MIT Press.

Fry, M. (1988), *Money, Interest and Banking in Economic Development*, Baltimore, MD: Johns Hopkins University Press.

Frydman, H., E.I. Altman and D. L. Kao (1985), 'Introducing recursive partitioning for financial classification: the case of financial distress', *Journal of Finance*, March.

Hrnčíř, M. (1992), 'Money and credit in the transition of the Czechoslovak economy', in H. Siebert (ed.), *The Transformation of Socialist Economies,* Kiel: Kiel Symposium.

Lastra, R.M. (1996), 'Central Banking and Regulation', Financial Market Group, London: London School of Economics.

Mullineux, A.W. (1993), 'Privatization and banking sector reform: lessons from Poland', Department of Economics, Discussion Paper, University of Birmingham.

17. Market efficiency in transition economies: equity markets and EU accession

Nicholas Horsewood and Douglas Sutherland*

It is largely an issue of financial contagion. The real economic links between east Europe and Russia are much less than before, but investor sentiment generally has been hit. ... We have seen stock markets falling across the region, bond yields edging up and currencies weakening. (Philip Poole, Chief Economist for European Emerging Markets at ING Barings, *Financial Times*, 29 May 1998)

INTRODUCTION

Over the last decade a considerable amount of research has focused on the efficiency of financial markets, with the majority of studies concerning bilateral exchange rate data from advanced countries.[1] Given the recent behaviour of the Russian stock market, which has declined more than 70 per cent during the last half year and underlies the sentiment expressed in the above quotation, it is of interest to examine the time-series patterns of equity indices from the main Central and Eastern European (CEE) economies to ascertain how much information can be gleaned from them. Despite the growth of analysis into the efficiency of financial markets, there has been relatively little research into the behaviour of the newly created stock markets in CEE economies. This chapter provides an investigation into the long-run relationships between four stock market indices from CEE economies and between the FT 100 index, taken to be the leading European market index and a key measure of investors' sentiment in advanced countries. Comparisons can be made between their long-term trends which, under certain assumptions, have important implications for the efficiency of these markets.

In a world of integrated equity markets, it has been argued that individual stock prices may possess common long-run relationships.[2] There are several

* We wish to thank the Know How Fund of the British Foreign Office for initiating the research and Jose Palacin for providing the data. We are grateful to Karen Croxson for constructive comments.

reasons why different countries' stock prices may have significant co-movements. The presence of strong economic ties and policy coordination between the relevant countries can indirectly link their stock prices over time. As the CEE economies are to some extent experiencing similar problems regarding their transition to market economies with common policy prescriptions being proposed, the possibility that long-run relationships exist between their stock markets is a real one and is the main focus of attention of this study.[3] Furthermore, certain CEE countries have embarked on the process of accession to the European Union (EU). In attempting to meet the EU membership conditions one would expect implicit policy coordination to have been adopted, suggesting a further possible source for the presence of long-run relationships among the stock market indices. This raises the issue as to the means by which long-run relationships are brought about. If the transition experience is similar one would expect policy coordination for all CEE economies and a co-movement among their indices. Alternatively, if EU accession is the main factor influencing policy linkage then cointegration should be present only among those CEE economies attempting to satisfy entry criteria, with or without the FT100. Finally, if country experiences are dissimilar enough to break these potential long-term relationships then no cointegration should be found.

Stock market indices from Russia, the Czech Republic, Poland and Hungary are used in the following empirical analysis. A widely held perception about CEE equity markets is that price indices or returns are frequently subject to extended deviation from fundamental values with subsequent revisions. Support for such a view is based upon the high transactions costs, including those associated with the accrual of information, in emerging markets. Consequently, the existence of prolonged periods of disequilibrium in the thin trading environment associated with CEE equities, superficially suggesting inefficiencies and the possibilities of profit-making opportunities, may in fact be due to high transaction costs prohibiting arbitrage behaviour rather than inefficiencies.

Descriptions of the stock exchanges of the selected CEE economies and their related indices are provided in the next section. Time-series analysis is employed to examine the efficiency of the CEE equity markets. The basic statistical techniques are presented in the third section. The empirical investigation, contained in the fourth section, begins by testing each stock market index for the presence of unit roots, employing augmented Dickey–Fuller tests and variance ratio tests. Relationships between the various stock markets are estimated and the possibility of cointegration among the different stock indices investigated. Further tests of the relationships between the stock market indices are presented in the fifth section. The final section concludes the analysis.

DATA

The European Commission has recently entered into negotiations with five Central and Eastern European countries on the possibility of accession to the European Union; the Czech Republic, Hungary, Poland, Estonia and Slovenia have participated in the discussions along with Cyprus. The cost of entry for each country is currently being calculated, where one major element of the adjustment process is capital mobility and associated stock market efficiency. Four CEE economies have been selected – Russia, Poland, Hungary and the Czech Republic – and the interrelationship between the equity indices in the countries examined.[4] Daily data were employed in the testing procedures as the frequency of the data allowed for the possibility of inefficiency in the markets. One problem with high frequency data in emerging markets relates to the possibility of the non-trading of equities. The sample period, from 1 September 1995 to 2 April 1998, was chosen to minimize this problem. To ensure valid cross-country comparability of results, the test are conducted using returns measured in US dollars. Consequently the time-series behaviour of the stock market index includes the effect of both the movement in the equity market and the exchange rate behaviour.[5] As equity prices tend to be more volatile than the exchange rate, it is likely that the results reflect stock market movements. As background to understanding the performance of the various markets, Table 17.1 provides information on the capitalization and turnover for the CEE countries.

Russia

In terms of market capitalization, the Moscow stock exchange is the largest of the CEE economies. The first exchanges started to operate in Russia during 1991, though it was only in the period from 1994 to 1996 that the legislative base was created. The Russian Trading System (RTS) was created by the

Table 17.1   Capitalization and turnover, end 1994

Market	Capitalization (US$m)	Turnover ratio	Repatriation of income	Repatriation of capital
Russia	30 000	n/a	n/a	n/a
Czech Republic	12 589	12.1	Free	Free
Hungary	1 604	21.6	Free	Free
Poland	3,057	176.7	Free	Free

Source: IFC (1995).

National Association of Stock Market Participants in 1995 as an electronic off-exchange trading system, linking more than 400 companies and banks. Assistance was given by NASDAQ, who also supplied the trading software for the RTS. Daily trading volume grew steadily from USD 2 million at the inception of the trading system to close to USD 100 million at the beginning of 1998. Against the backdrop of complete collapse in Russian financial markets, during the second half of 1998 daily trading volumes have concurrently fallen to the levels seen in 1995.

The RTS index is the main index of the Moscow stock exchange and it is displayed in Figure 17.1(a). Investors in Russian equities experienced the first sharp increase in 1995 when the index tripled in value. The driving force behind the first boom, which is mostly outside our sample period, was domestic capital. In early 1996 the index increased gently with foreign investors entering the Moscow stock exchange for the first time. During 1997 the RTS index fluctuated around an upward trend until November when the market was hit by the Asian crisis. Foreign investors began reassessing the risk associated with emerging markets and the demand for Russian equities declined considerably.

The booms and slumps of the Moscow stock market can be observed in Figure 17.2(a) which presents the first difference of the RTS index, equivalent to daily returns. To enable further comparisons, four-week differences have been calculated and are given in Figure 17.3(a). Statistics corresponding to the RTS index are presented in Table 17.2 and the Jarque-Bera test for normality indicates that the series appears non-normal, where the row labelled 'probability' presents the probability of the null hypothesis of normality being true. Such a finding is consistent with the booms and slumps witnessed in financial time series as is evident from the summary statistics relating to the FT index. The high volatility of the Moscow stock market is captured by the RTS having the largest standard deviations out of all the stock market indices.

Poland

The Warsaw Stock Exchange joint-stock company, established in 1991, is a self-regulated organization based upon the French model. As the privatization process has progressed the composition of the Warsaw Stock Exchange has changed, with 96 listed companies in 1997 compared to just nine in 1991. As the Polish privatization programme occurred through financial intermediaries, in terms of capitalization its stock market is the second smallest of the major CEE economies, with the market values of the largest companies lagging behind those listed on the Moscow, Budapest and Prague exchanges. The existence of the National Investment Funds, holding more than 500 companies, has restricted the development of the Warsaw stock exchange.

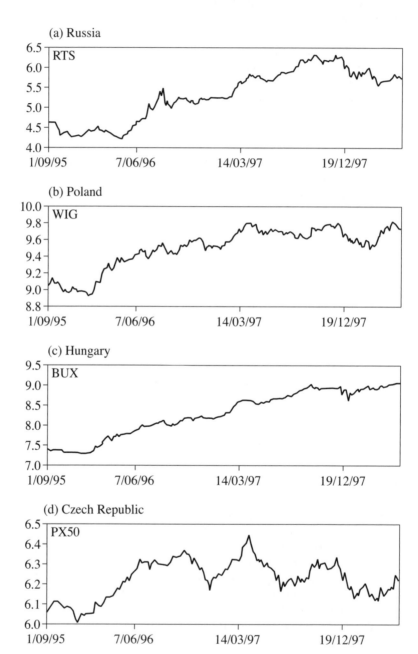

(a) Russia

(b) Poland

(c) Hungary

(d) Czech Republic

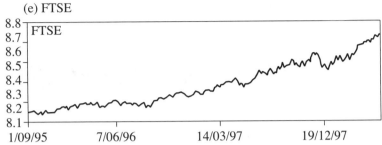

Figure 17.1 Stock market indices

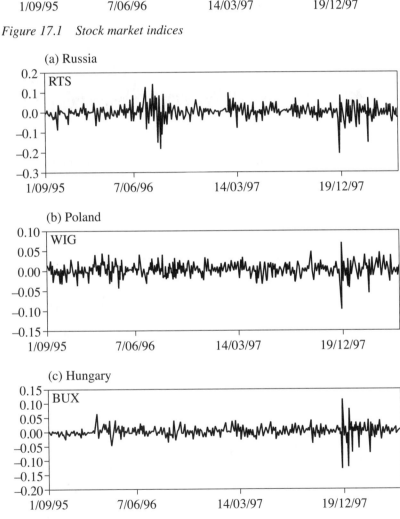

Figure 17.2 Daily returns

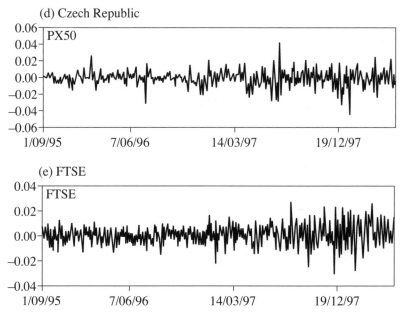

Figure 17.2   continued

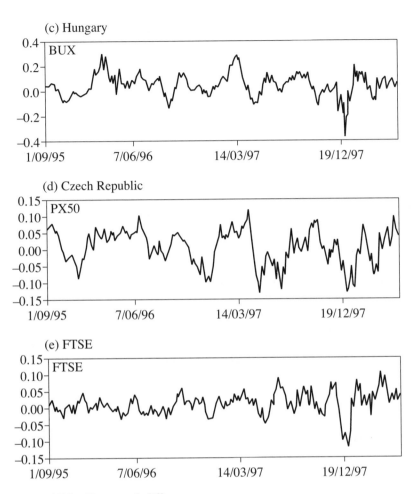

Figure 17.3   Four-week differences

The WIG is the main index of the Polish stock market and it is presented in Figure 17.1(b). As can be gleaned, in common with the RTS the WIG rose sharply in early 1996 and then also fluctuated around a steady upward trend. The effects of the Asian collapse can be identified in late 1997. Unlike the RTS, the WIG recovered from the problems of the stock market falls in South-East Asia and by the end of the sample period had reached the levels previously witnessed in 1997. Foreign investors returned to the Warsaw stock market as it was more secure than the majority of other emerging markets due to its highly regulated nature, which led to further funds flowing into Poland as a result of the flight to relative security.

Table 17.2   Summary statistics

	RTS	WIG	BUX	PX50	FTSE
Mean	5.314	9.502	8.302	6.229	8.357
Median	5.266	9.559	8.264	6.234	8.308
Maximum	6.349	9.830	9.092	6.444	8.710
Minimum	4.200	8.917	7.280	6.005	8.149
std dev.	0.661	0.247	0.573	0.094	0.148
Skewness	−0.253	−0.940	−0.353	−0.328	0.556
Kurtosis	1.729	2.827	1.822	2.297	2.117
Jarque–Bera	52.744	100.420	53.124	26.024	56.855
Probability	0.000	0.000	0.000	0.000	0.000
Observations	676	676	676	676	676

The first difference and the four-week difference of the WIG are given in Figures 17.2(b) and 17.3(b), respectively. Increased variability of daily and four-week returns can be observed at the beginning and at the end of the sample period. Table 17.2 contains the basic statistics for the WIG index and, as expected, there is evidence of non-normality in the series. Although the Warsaw stock market was behind Moscow and Prague in terms of capitalization, it was the leader in terms of absolute trading value until mid-1997 which explains the relatively low standard deviation of the index.

Hungary

The Budapest stock exchange opened in 1990[6] and the number and the variety of registered firms have increased over time. In 1997, 49 companies were listed, two of which were foreign firms. The stock market index (BUX) comprises 22 firms, with the main companies having declared continually increasing profits.[7]

The Budapest stock market has experienced a strong upward trend from the beginning of 1996, attracting cash from foreign investors. The BUX index is graphed in Figure 17.1(c) Although a relatively small market, the influx of foreign funds was influenced by the high level of profits declared by Hungarian companies and the weakness of the forint, making firms appear relatively cheap. Since the beginning of 1996 the Hungarian stock market has been viewed as the leader of the CEE economies with average trading per session exceeding USD 20 million in the first half of 1997. Capitalization of the stock market tripled over the twelve months to the end of 1997, representing 35 per cent of GDP. The effects of the Asian stock market collapse can be discerned directly from Figures 17.2(c) and 17.3(c), which plot daily returns and four-week returns, respectively. Although the variability of the returns increased, by early 1998 the BUX index appeared to have overcome the influence of the Asian crisis and reverted to its previous upward trend. Summary statistics for the Hungarian stock market are presented in Table 17.2 with the second highest standard deviation indicating its volatility.

Czech Republic

The Prague stock exchange was established in 1992 and the first trading session was held in April 1993. Its development has differed from that of the Budapest and Warsaw markets as the majority of private companies transformed via the privatization programme were directly listed on the stock market. Of the CEE equity markets, the Prague stock exchange boasts the greatest number of companies with more than 1750 issues registered on the three markets.[8]

The index of the Prague stock exchange (PX 50) has displayed a pattern independent from the trends of the other CEE countries. The PX 50 index rose sharply in late 1995 and early 1996 as a result of Western investors moving into the Czech market. Since June 1996 the index has tended to fluctuate around a slight downward trend. The booms and slumps in the index reflect an unstable political system and uncertainty surrounding domestic economic reform. Scandals connected with the collapse of a number of banks, including Agrobank the biggest totally private bank, adversely affected the Czech PX 50. The economic performance of the flagship companies has been varied with lower profits declared in 1997. The fall of the Czech government in November 1997 and the associated uncertainty of the further privatization programme can be clearly identified. The recent revival of the index reflects the improved perception of the Czech stock market as a result of the establishment of the Securities Commission. Although the standard deviation of PX50 is lower than that of other CEE market indices, the Jarque–Bera statistic still provides evidence of non-normality in the series, as can be seen in Table 17.2. The low standard deviation in the Prague Stock Exchange is attributed to several factors: first, the fact that the sheer scale of issues has left the market indifferent to many; second, lax disclosure rules and oversights; and third, concentration of ownership in investment funds combined with unreported off-bourse trades between them. These factors have resulted in very low turnover on the stock exchange, with up to 90 per cent of trades taking place off-market.

The time-series pattern of the equity indices can be seen in Table 17.3, which presents the partial autocorrelation of the index from each stock market. A number of studies have taken the existence of more than first-order autocorrelation as a prima facie evidence of inefficiency in asset markets (see Poterba and Summers (1988) for a discussion of these types of results). Under

Financial sector development

Table 17.3   Partial autocorrelations

	ρ_1	ρ_2	ρ_3	ρ_4	ρ_5	ρ_{10}	ρ_{15}	ρ_{20}	ρ_{25}
RTS	*0.998*	*−0.066*	0.007	−0.030	0.047	−0.042	−0.032	−0.001	0.032
WIG	*0.995*	*−0.072*	−0.004	−0.011	−0.023	0.010	−0.024	−0.002	−0.013
BUX	*0.996*	*−0.010*	−0.004	0.012	0.000	0.001	0.003	−0.012	−0.008
PX50	*0.994*	*−0.181*	0.000	−0.017	0.015	−0.031	−0.004	0.037	0.012
FTSE	*0.993*	*−0.021*	0.012	0.027	0.009	−0.015	0.010	−0.003	−0.011

rational expectations and no transaction cost, information concerning the value of an asset should be incorporated immediately into its price, implying that only the first partial autocorrelation should be significant. The existence of a long autoregressive lag structure for a stock market index indicates a slow accrual of information and, under certain assumptions, is inconsistent with efficiency. As previously discussed, transaction costs of equities are high, the presence of more than first-order autocorrelation may not indicate inefficiency but rather that the gains from trade are less than the costs associated with rebalancing a portfolio. This view is consistent with the stock markets of CEE economies where markets are thin and information costs are large, especially for daily data. Even though these are real concerns in CEE economies, the partial autocorrelations are consistent with an AR(1) process for the Hungarian BUX, while the size of ρ_2 for the remaining CEE markets is weak and implies that the information content of the second lag is not particularly high. No other partial autocorrelation coefficients are significant for the stock market indices.

The autocorrelations of the first difference of the logarithm of each series are presented in Table 17.4. As the stock market indices are compounded, the transformation is equivalent to the daily return of each series. The autoregressive pattern of the five stock market indices indicate some evidence of permanence for all series. The first-order autocorrelation is also the slope coefficient of a regression of returns on a constant and its first lag. This therefore means, as the coefficient of determination is the square of the slope coefficient, that the predictability of the daily return varies from 0.3 per cent in Hungary to almost 9 per cent in the Czech Republic. Both the Czech Republic and Polish markets display a common time-series behaviour with similar patterns of autocorrelation and a highly significant Q-statistic. Such a pattern can be consistent with either predictability in relative returns or irrationality of investors (Richards 1996). This finding is slightly surprising as the above discussion suggests that the institutional features of the Warsaw and Budapest stock exchanges are similar, with both markets recovering from the Asian financial collapse in the period covered in the analysis. Changes in the

Table 17.4 Autocorrelations of second moments

	ρ_1	ρ_2	ρ_3	ρ_4	ρ_5	Q_5	Q_{10}	Q_{15}	Q_{20}
RTS	*0.104*	–0.002	0.038	*–0.085*	–0.012	13.42	20.34	31.45	41.61
WIG	*0.222*	0.046	0.040	–0.039	–0.046	38.45	41.96	46.31	51.94
BUX	0.058	0.007	*–0.058*	–0.056	–0.045	8.11	19.05	41.18	42.96
PX50	*0.298*	0.048	0.042	–0.020	–0.033	64.10	77.19	88.07	90.34
FTSE	*0.115*	–0.024	–0.006	*–0.064*	*–0.109*	20.29	35.80	50.54	51.79

Ljung–Box Q-statistic as lag length is increased expose significant autocorrelation at long lag lengths for both the BUX and RTS indices, at 12 and 22 lags, respectively.

ESTIMATION PROCEDURES

The non-stationarity of time-series data has led to the development of a number of statistical tests to identify the existence of unit roots within a series. Although a large number of tests exist in the literature, the majority of the test statistics are based on the work of Dickey and Fuller (1979, 1981).[9]

Dickey–Fuller Tests

Dickey and Fuller present a class of statistics for testing whether a pure AR(1) process (with or without drift) has a unit root. Let the time-series variable, y_t, satisfy the following data-generating process:

$$y_t = \beta_0 + \beta_1 t + \rho y_{t-1} + \varepsilon_t \tag{17.1}$$

where $\varepsilon_t \sim \text{IID}(0, \sigma_\varepsilon^2)$, t is a trend and the initial condition, y_0, is assumed to be a known constant (zero, without loss of generality). A unit root describes the situation where $\rho = 1$ and results in conventional statistical distributions being inappropriate. To test the null hypothesis of non-stationary versus the alternative hypothesis of stationarity requires ordinary least squares (OLS) estimation of the reparameterized version (17.1):

$$\Delta y_t = \beta_0 + \beta_1 + \gamma y_{t-1} + \varepsilon_t \tag{17.2}$$

where H_0: $\rho = 1$ is equivalent to H_0: $\gamma = 0$. The test for non-stationarity is implemented through the usual t-statistic of γ but using the asymptotic distributions tabulated in Fuller (1976) and Dickey and Fuller (1981).

In cases of a higher-order AR process the augmented Dickey–Fuller (ADF) test is carried out on the reparameterized model:

$$\Delta y_t = \alpha + \beta_t + \gamma y_{t=1} + \sum_{i=1}^{p} \beta_i \Delta y_{t-i} + \varepsilon_t$$

where the lag length p is determined to remove autocorrelation. According to DeJong et al. (1992) and Banerjee et al. (1993), the ADF test provides more robust results than any other unit root test in the presence of serially correlated errors, which are modelled by the autoregressive terms. The order of integration of a series defines the number of times it has to be differenced to achieve stationarity.

Variance Ratio Test

An alternative way of evaluating the presence of a stochastic trend in a time series is by measuring its degree of persistence. Assuming that the expected return is constant, under rational expectations the random walk model can be expressed as:

$$y_{t+1} = \mu + y_t + \varepsilon_{t+1}.$$

The average return over q periods, R_{t+1}^q, is approximately:

$$R_{t+1}^q = (y_{t+q} - y_{t+1}) = q\mu + (\varepsilon_{t+1} + \varepsilon_{t+2} + \ldots + \varepsilon_{t+q}).$$

The assumption of rational expectations implies that the forecast errors, ε_t, are independent and have zero mean. Hence the expectation of the future return over the q periods based on time period t is given by:

$$E_t(R_{t+1}^q) = q\mu.$$

Assuming a constant variant of ε_t, σ^2, then:

$$\text{var}(R_{t+1}^q) = q\sigma^2.$$

The variance ratio test compares returns at different time horizons and is defined as:

$$VR(q) = \frac{\text{var}(R_t^q)/_q}{\text{var}(R_t^a)/_a}$$

where a denotes the base data frequency. From the above information, if the stock prices indices are trend stationary, VR approaches zero as q goes to infinity. Alternatively, if the series is a random walk, the value of the VR should be equal to one.

A number of modifications have been made to the variance ratio test to take account of autocorrelation and heteroscedasticity, both of which are prevalent in financial time series.[10] The advantage with the modified statistic is that it follows a standard normal distribution, even though adjustments have been made for autocorrelation and heteroscedasticity.

Cointegration

A system of non-stationary individual stock prices in levels may possess common stochastic trends. Two or more non-stationary time series, being of the same order of integration, are described as cointegrated if a linear combination of these variables produces a stationary series. The existence of cointegration between non-stationary stock market indices would imply that the indices have a tendency to move together in the long run. Standard asset-pricing models preclude cointegration between national indices in integrated markets, as asset prices or price indices should respond differently over time to shocks. Rejection of the null hypothesis of no cointegration would therefore imply that markets are inefficient, segmented or both. Granger (1986) demonstrated that market efficiency, in which the price of an asset incorporates all available information, has the important implication that the prices from two efficient markets cannot be cointegrated.

Consider the dynamic model:

$$\Delta y_t = \alpha_0 + \alpha_t \Delta y_{t-1} + \beta_0 \Delta x_t + \beta_1 \Delta x_{t-1} - \gamma(y_{t-1} - a - bx_{t-1}) + \varepsilon_t.$$

Let Y_t be the index of the Russian stock market and X_t represent the index of the Polish stock market with lower cases denoting logarithms. If the equity market indices are cointegrated then, according to the Granger Representation Theorem, they can be expressed in the form of the above dynamic model. Cointegration implies that part of the daily return in the Russian stock market is predictable, that is, $\gamma(y_{t-1} - a - bx_{t-1})$, even if the lagged Russian returns and the growth of the Polish stock market are excluded. However, if an asset incorporates all available information, its price change cannot be predictable. For the Russian and Polish equity markets to be efficient, the two stock markets cannot be cointegrated.

The above argument assumes that the Russian and Polish equity market indices are different assets. If countries explicitly fix their exchange rates or implicitly link their economic policies, while possessing similar economic structures, then it may not be sensible to view the stock market indices as different assets. Consequently, the equity indices could be cointegrated even though they were determined in efficient markets.

There are a number of ways to investigate the possibility of cointegration between two economic time series with the simplest being the first part of the Engle–Granger two-step modelling procedure. Assuming all variables are of the same order of integration, the technique of OLS is employed to estimate a static relationship between the variables believed to be cointegrated. The residuals from the static regression equation are then tested for their order of integration using an ADF test, with stationarity indicating cointegration.

Problems exist with the Engle–Granger technique as more than one cointegrating vector may exist. To allow for this possibility, a multivariate approach was developed by Johansen (1988) where the non-stationary time-series variables are estimated in a vector autoregressive model:

$$\Delta X_t = D + \sum_{i=1}^{p} \Gamma_i \Delta X_{t-i} + \Pi X_{t-1} + \varepsilon_t \qquad \varepsilon_t \sim \text{NIID}(0, \sigma^2)$$

where X_t denotes the vector of non-stationary variables and D represents the deterministic factors. The information on the coefficient matrix between the levels of the series Π is decomposed as $\Pi = \alpha\beta'$ where the relevant elements of the α matrix are the adjustment coefficients and β matrix contains the cointegrating vectors. Two test statistics exist to determine the cointegrating rank, that is the number of cointegrating vectors, of Π: the trace statistic and the maximum eigenvalue. Adjustments can be made to both statistics for degrees of freedom.

UNIT ROOT AND COINTEGRATION TEST RESULTS

Given the various tests discussed above, the stock market indices will be examined in a univariate setting to establish the order of integration of each series. Further analysis will be undertaken in a bivariate and in a multivariate system to investigate co-movements between the series.

Individual Stochastic Trends

The augmented Dickey–Fuller test statistics are presented in Table 17.5, with the numbers in parentheses indicating the minimum number of lags required to remove autocorrelation. As discussed earlier, the tests are applied to all series in logarithmic form. For all five stock market indices the null hypothesis of non-stationarity cannot be rejected in levels but it can be rejected once the data has been first differenced, implying that all indices appear to be integrated of

Table 17.5   Augmented Dickey-Fuller tests

Stock indices	Null: single unit root		Null: two unit roots	
RTS	−1.304	(23)	−4.684	(22)
WIG	−1.874	(1)	−20.721	(0)
BUX	−2.128	(12)	−4.684	(0)
PX50	−1.846	(1)	−19.080	(0)
FTSE	−2.279	(1)	−23.190	(0)

order one. Based on the Aikaike information criteria and the diagnostic test statistics from preliminary regressions, a maximum of 25 lags was used with ADF tests. Certain problems arose with the dependent variable lag length required to remove the autocorrelation present in the Russian stock market index, which is not surprising given the higher degree of autocorrelation displayed by the RTS series (see Table 17.4).

Results from the variance ratio (VR) tests provide contrasting information on the time-series properties of the equity indices and are presented in Table 17.6. For all the series the maximum length of the interval is 25, covering the possibility of a monthly difference in the data. For all intervals the VR test indicates that the Hungarian BUX index and the Russian RTS index are insignificantly different from unity, implying a random walk at all lag lengths. The VR test for the FT index follows a similar pattern with the exception of the first two lags, which display persistence and may be a consequence of high frequency data. For Poland and the Czech Republic, the VR tests of their respective stock market indices find both series to have more persistence than a random walk at all intervals.

Given the autocorrelations presented in Table 17.4, the finding of persistence in the Polish index and the Czech index is not surprising. In summary, the four indices from CEE countries and from the UK are either a random walk or have more persistence than a random walk, results consistent with each series being non-stationary in levels.

Common Stochastic Trend

Given the existence of a unit root in the five stock market indices, the issue is whether long-term relationships exist among the CEE stock markets, providing evidence of inefficiencies. Table 17.7 displays bilateral cointegration tests for combinations of the four CEE indices and the FT100, with the number of lags of the ADF test shown in parentheses. The ADF test statistics cannot reject the null hypothesis of non-stationarity in the residuals for all combinations which provides preliminary support for the efficiency of the CEE stock

Table 17.6   Variance ratio tests

Lag	RTS		WIG		BUX		PX50		FTSE-100	
	VR	Z	VR	Z	VR	Z	VR	Z	VR	Z
2	1.11	1.50	1.22	3.43	1.06	0.49	1.30	6.19	1.12	2.68
3	1.14	1.36	1.33	3.54	1.08	0.50	1.43	5.97	1.14	2.11
4	1.18	1.41	1.40	3.61	1.07	0.34	1.52	5.77	1.15	1.73
5	1.17	1.16	1.46	3.69	1.04	0.17	1.56	5.38	1.12	1.25
6	1.15	0.98	1.48	3.55	1.00	0.01	1.58	4.92	1.07	0.66
7	1.15	0.91	1.48	3.30	0.96	−0.16	1.59	4.53	1.02	0.12
8	1.16	0.89	1.47	3.04	0.95	−0.19	1.59	4.17	0.96	−0.32
9	1.17	0.88	1.47	2.88	0.94	−0.21	1.59	3.92	0.91	−0.59
10	1.19	0.95	1.46	2.73	0.94	−0.22	1.60	3.80	0.90	−0.65
11	1.22	1.04	1.46	2.60	0.95	−0.18	1.64	3.82	0.90	−0.64
12	1.26	1.17	1.46	2.52	0.96	−0.13	1.68	3.92	0.91	−0.55
13	1.29	1.27	1.46	2.44	0.99	−0.02	1.72	3.98	0.91	−0.49
14	1.32	1.36	1.47	2.40	1.02	0.07	1.76	4.03	0.92	−0.44
15	1.35	1.43	1.48	2.39	1.04	0.13	1.79	4.07	0.92	−0.42
16	1.37	1.46	1.48	2.34	1.06	0.19	1.82	4.11	0.92	−0.41
17	1.38	1.47	1.49	2.33	1.08	0.22	1.85	4.13	0.91	−0.42
18	1.38	1.44	1.50	2.31	1.08	0.23	1.88	4.15	0.90	−0.46
19	1.38	1.40	1.51	2.30	1.08	0.22	1.91	4.15	0.89	−0.52
20	1.38	1.37	1.52	2.29	1.08	0.23	1.92	4.12	0.87	−0.57
21	1.38	1.34	1.53	2.29	1.09	0.24	1.93	4.08	0.86	−0.59
22	1.38	1.33	1.55	2.31	1.10	0.26	1.95	4.04	0.86	−0.61
23	1.40	1.34	1.57	2.34	1.11	0.28	1.96	4.02	0.85	−0.62
24	1.41	1.35	1.58	2.36	1.12	0.30	1.98	4.01	0.85	−0.62
25	1.42	1.36	1.60	2.39	1.13	0.32	1.99	4.00	0.84	−0.62

markets, even though high frequency data are employed from markets with considerably lower trading volumes than in advanced countries.

Johansen Technique

The finding of no cointegration within a bilateral relationship does not rule out the possibility of cointegration within a multilateral system. The results from the Johansen technique of cointegration are presented in Table 17.8 and there is rejection of cointegration according to the trace and the maximum eigenvalue statistics.

Cointegration analysis using the Johansen technique for developed and over emerging markets (see, among others, Kasa 1992, and Choudhry 1997, respectively) has suggested that long-run relationships are present in the high-dimensional systems that have been tested. One of the implications of their

Table 17.7   Bilateral cointegration test results

	BUX	PX50	RTS	WIG
BUX				
PX50	−0.842 (7)			
RTS	−1.860 (2)	−1.690 (1)		
WIG	−0.745 (4)	−1.209 (3)	−2.423 (17)	
FTSE	−1.663 (7)	−1.715 (0)	−0.209 (4)	−1.015 (7)

Table 17.8   Multilateral cointegration test results

H_0: rank = p	−Tlog(1−μ)	using T−nm	95%	Tsum log(.)	using T−nm	95%
$p = 0$	21.19	20.4	33.5	49.88	48.02	68.5
$p \le 1$	14.55	14.01	27.1	28.69	27.62	47.2
$p \le 2$	9.79	9.425	21.0	14.14	13.61	29.7
$p \le 3$	4.329	4.167	14.1	4.346	4.184	15.4
$p \le 4$	0.01776	0.0171	3.8	0.01776	0.0171	3.8

respective findings is that with the presence of a single common stochastic trend the expected gains from international diversification are reduced, even if the speed of adjustment is slow. On a simplistic level, the evidence presented here indicates that potential gains from portfolio diversification across CEE countries are present. On a second level, these results beg an additional question. Are the CEE economies not subject to the single, common world-growth factor or policy coordination that have been proposed as the reasons why different countries' stock prices have long-run relationships? One answer to this may be that the sample period was insufficient to capture these effects. Another potential explanation is that there are sufficient differences between the economic policies employed in the four CEE economies during the sample period that there is no possibility of implicit coordination.[11]

An alternative interpretation for the failure to identify any co-movement that seems to be present in other groups of markets is that these markets are in fact efficient. This is not as surprising a claim as first appears. The Johansen–Juselius maximum-likelihood critical values in high-dimensional systems with finite samples can be subject to size distortion (Godbout and Norden, 1997[12]). Reducing the frequency of the data results in evidence of cointegration in the Johansen and Juselius test statistics (the maximum eigenvalue and in particular the trace test), but the Reinsel and Ahn statistics, which correct for size distortion in finite samples, will continue to indicate no sign of cointegration.

Although there is no co-movement among all the indices, a subset of them

Table 17.9a   Multilateral cointegration test results: EU accession countries and FTSE

H_0: rank = p	$-T\log(1-\mu)$	using T–nm	95%	Tsum log(.)	using T–nm	95%
$p = 0$	17.03	16.93	27.1	32.98	32.79	47.2
$p \le 1$	11.90	11.98	21.0	15.96	15.86	29.7
$p \le 2$	4.049	4.025	14.1	4.062	4.038	15.4
$p \le 3$	0.01237	0.0123	3.8	0.01237	0.0123	3.8

Table 17.9b   Multilateral cointegration test results: EU accession countries

H_0: rank = p	$-T\log(1-\mu)$	using T–nm	95%	Tsum log(.)	using T–nm	95%
$p = 0$	14.2	14.14	21.0	18.30	18.22	29.7
$p \le 1$	3.971	3.9542	14.1	4.102	4.084	15.4
$p \le 2$	0.1311	0.1306	3.8	0.1311	0.1306	3.8

may cointegrate. If the CEE countries requesting EU membership have pursued similar economic policies to meet conditions for EU accession then there would be another route for implicit policy linkage. Hence one would expect to find a long-run relationship between the stock market indices of the three CEE economies. Table 17.9 provides multivariate cointegration tests for the Hungarian BUX, the Polish WIG and the Czech PX 50 indices, with and without the FT index. There is no evidence of cointegration with either subset of indices. One interpretation of this finding is that the CEE economies are adopting a number of different approaches to achieve the economic conditions for EU membership and so there is no common factor to coordinate policies. Alternatively, the CEE countries may not be placing great emphasis on the EU requirements, which explains the lack of a long-run relationship.[13]

CAUSALITY TESTS

Although the results presented in the previous section indicated that there was not a long-run relationship among CEE equity markets or subsets of them, the hypothesis of contagion, as mentioned in the initial quotation, and so popular a term among economic journalists, needs to be investigated. It can best be examined by considering the short-run dynamics between the indices. As no definitive test exists to examine the dynamic relations between variables, Granger causality tests are carried out to investigate the

Table 17.10   Granger causality test results

	BUX	PX50	RTS	WIG	FTSE
BUX	–	7.72 (0.00)	1.77 (0.12)	1.73 (0.13)	1.46 (0.20)
PX50	0.69 (0.63)	–	2.07 (0.07)	1.21 (0.30)	2.12 (0.06)
RTS	2.95 (0.01)	1.44 (0.21)	–	1.58 (0.16)	1.03 (0.40)
WIG	1.19 (0.31)	3.17 (0.00)	1.58 (0.16)	–	0.48 (0.79)
FTSE	3.71 (0.003)	6.50 (0.00)	3.19 (0.008)	7.71 (0.00)	–

nature of predictability of daily returns within CEE stock market indices and will be interpreted as measuring some form of contagion. The added advantage of undertaking the analysis on first differences of the indices is that all variables are stationary and conventional critical values can be adopted for hypotheses tests. Granger causality focuses on the following equation:

$$\Delta y_t = \alpha + \sum_{i=1}^{p} \alpha_i \Delta y_{t-i} + \sum_{i=1}^{p} \beta_i \Delta x_{t-i} + \varepsilon_t$$

and tests the hypothesis that all the coefficients on lagged Δx are jointly zero. As has been recognized for some time, the term causality in the title of the test is misleading. The test investigates whether the returns of one asset, Δy, can be predicted by the lagged returns of another series, Δx, and no direct linkage is claimed, which is similar to the view expressed by certain economic journalists.

Table 17.10 presents the Granger causality tests for all bilateral combinations of the series, with the figures in parentheses denoting the probability of the null hypothesis of the coefficients on lagged Δx jointly zero being true. Daily returns on the London stock market Granger, cause the returns of each of the four CEE equity indices but no evidence of reverse causality exists, illustrating that events on the European and world stock markets influence, rather than are caused by, the first difference of the indices in Hungary, Russia, Poland and the Czech Republic. Further evidence of contagion is found with the daily returns of the Czech PX 50 index being forecast by both the Polish WIG and the Hungarian BUX indices. As economic reform in the Czech Republic appears relatively unstable, it is likely that events in certain CEE markets are going to have major effects on the PX50 index. Over the sample period for the econometric analysis, contagion from the Russian stock market appears not to be statistically significant and does not influence the returns of the other CEE equity indices.

CONCLUSION

The selected indices from CEE stock markets all appear to be integrated of order one, but evidence from the variance ratio tests indicate that not all the series follow a simple random walk. Given the previous work on stock market indices, both advanced and emerging, this finding is not particularly surprising. The stochastic properties of the various series reveal a division in the CEE economies, which is also present in the subsequent reaction of these equity markets to the 'contagion' from South-East Asia. Small corrections were seen in Poland and the Czech Republic (10 and 15 per cent, respectively) and much larger falls in Hungary and Russia, of 40 and 90 per cent, respectively, where higher-order autocorrelation was present.

Linear combinations of the indices were analysed in bivariate and multivariate settings and no long-run relationships could be found, which initially appeared to conflict with studies on other emerging markets. One interpretation of this finding is that the CEE stock markets are efficient. Alternatively, the transition approaches adopted in each CEE country are so diverse that there is no common policy to bring about a common evolution and produce a long-run relationship.

When the subset of indices from economies applying for EU membership were analysed, no cointegrating vector could be found. Again the diversity of approaches may explain the results. Equally the market participants may not be convinced either by the overriding commitment of each country to EU membership or even the actual possibility of accession taking place.

The daily returns in CEE markets were predicted by returns from the London stock exchange, capturing events in the advanced markets. Although this relationship is expected, the failure to find contagion from emerging markets on the London stock market is surprising and superficially goes against the recent events experienced by world bourses and the economic collapse in Russia. Recalling that Granger causality is the measure of contagion employed, if advanced markets are efficient only current information will be important in determining the stock indices. As contemporaneous first differences of the Russian RTS index are excluded from the hypothesis test, the failure to find no contagion from the Russian fallout can be explained as the other markets have between one and three hours to react after the close of the RTS.

NOTES

1. See among others, Hakkio and Rush (1989), Baillie and Bollerslev (1989) and Dwyer and Wallace (1992).
2. Choudhry (1997) provides an account of the main economic means by which long-run relationships can be established between stock market indices.
3. Carlin and Landesmann (1997) use variations in the extent of policy changes to explain cross-country differences in restructuring behaviour.
4. Due to the very limited number and type of companies represented on TALSE, the Tallin stock market, and the very underdeveloped nature of the Ljubljana stock exchange these markets were excluded from the analysis.

5. The Czech Republic, Poland and Hungary all had fixed exchange rate regimes (pegged) in place prior to the period of analysis, although the Czech National Bank was forced to float the koruna during 1997. Russia converted from a floating exchange rate regime to an exchange rate corridor in July 1995.
6. On the eve of the First World War the Budapest stock exchange was the largest in Europe.
7. The flagship companies were from the pharmaceutical industry (Gedeon Richter, Egis), the chemical industry (TVK, Borsodchem), the MOL fuel distributor and the OTP bank.
8. The three markets being primary, parallel and free markets.
9. See among others, Phillips and Peron (1988), and Elliot et al. (1996).
10. See among others, Campbell et al. (1997) for an excellent exposition of variance ratio tests, especially the refinements undertaken to correct autocorrelation and heteroscedasticity.
11. See, for example, Zecchini (1997), who addresses many differences in transition progress.
12. Godbout and Norden re-examined the results in Kasa (1992) and found no evidence of cointegration among international stock markets.
13. Bernard and Durlauf (1996) caution that cointegration techniques to measure convergence may not be appropriate for time series in transition.

REFERENCES

Baillie, R., and T. Bollerslev (1989), 'Common stochastic trends in a system of exchange rates', *Journal of Finance*, **44**, 167–81.
Banerjee, A., J. Dolado, J.W. Galbraith and D.F. Hendry (1993), *Co-integration, Error-correction, and the Econometric Analysis of Non-stationary Data*, Oxford: Oxford University Press.
Bernard, A.B. and S.N. Durlauf (1996), 'Interpreting tests of the convergence hypothesis', *Journal of Econometrics*, **71**, 161–73.
Campbell, J.Y., A.W. Lo and A.C. MacKinley (1997), *The Econometrics of Financial Markets*, Princeton, NJ: Princeton University Press.
Carlin, W. and M. Landesmann (1997), 'From theory into practice? Restructuring and dynamism in transition economies', *Oxford Review of Economic Policy*, **13** (2), 77–105.
Choudhry, T. (1997), 'Stochastic trends in stock prices: evidence from Latin American markets', *Journal of Macroeconomics*, **19** (2), 285–304.
DeJong, D., J. Nakervis, N. Savin and C. Whiteman (1992), 'The power problems of unit root tests in time series with autoregressive errors', *Journal of Econometrics*, **53**, 323–44.
Dickey, D. and W.A. Fuller (1979), 'Distribution of the estimates for autoregressive time series with a unit root', *Journal of the American Statistical Association*, **74**, 427–31.
Dickey, D.A. and W.A. Fuller (1981), 'Likelihood ratio statistics for autoregressive time series with a unit root', *Econometrica*, **49** (4), pp. 1057–72.
Dwyer, G. and M. Wallace (1992), 'Co-integration and market efficiency', *Journal of International Money and Finance*, **11**, 318–27.
Elliot, G., T.J. Rothenberg and J. Stock (1996), 'Efficient tests for an autoregressive unit root', *Econometrica*, **64** (4), 813–36.
Frydman, R., K. Murphy and A. Rapaczynski (1998), *Capitalism with a Comrade's Face: Studies in Postcommunist Transition*, Budapest: Central European University Press.
Fuller, W.A. (1976), *Introduction to Statistical Times Series*, New York: John Wiley.
Godbout, M.-J. and S. Norden (1997), 'Reconsidering co-integration in international

finance: three case studies of size distortion in finite samples', Bank of Canada Working Paper no. 97–1.

Granger, C.W.J. (1986), 'Developments in the study of co-integrated economic variables', *Oxford Bulletin of Economics and Statistics*, **48**, 213–28.

Hakkio, C.S. and M. Rush (1989), 'Market efficiency and cointegration – an application to the sterling and Deutschmark exchange markets', *Journal of International Money and Finance*, **8** (1), 75–88.

International Finance Corporation (IFC) (1995), *Emerging Stock Markets Factbook 1995*, Washington, DC: International Finance Corporation.

Johansen, S. (1988), 'Statistical analysis of cointegration vectors', *Journal of Economic Dynamics and Control*, **12**, 231–54.

Kasa, K. (1992), 'Common stochastic trends in international stock markets', *Journal of Monetary Economics*, **29**, 95–124.

Phillips, P.C.B. and P. Perron (1988), 'Testing for a unit root in time series regressions', *Biometrika*, **75**, 335–46.

Poterba, J.M. and L.H. Summers (1988), 'Mean reversions in stock prices: evidence and implications', *Journal of Financial Economics*, **22**, 27–59.

Richards, A.J. (1996), 'Volatility and predictability in national stock markets: how do emerging and mature markets differ?', *IMF Staff Papers*, **43** (3), 461–501.

Zecchini, S. (ed.) (1997), *Lessons from the Transition: Central and Eastern Europe in the 1990s*, London: Kluwer Academic Publishers.

18. Risk and optimal interest margins: the case of commercial banks in Central Europe

Daniel Goyeau, Alain Sauviat and Amine Tarazi

INTRODUCTION

The banking systems in Central and Eastern Europe have experienced dramatic changes in recent years with the transition process towards a market economy. Reforms aimed at building an institutional environment in which banks could efficiently but also soundly perform their activities. With higher financial fragility in most market economies and the implementation of more stringent prudential rules, the steps towards a decentralized resource allocation system in the banking industry had to fit in with the new international standards for solvency regulation.

Bank intermediation nevertheless appears as a major challenge for the economic development of these countries. Because of their narrowness due to the persistence of severe asymmetric information problems among borrowers and lenders, financial markets are still unable to perform their funding function satisfactorily. In this context, at least in the short run, banks have the heavy task of channelling savings and meet the private sector demand for funds.

One can then question the ability of the banking system itself to fulfil its functions efficiently in an environment with strong moral hazard incentives and information problems. Also a connected issue that arises, in the light of integration with the European Union is whether European and international standards for prudential regulation should actually be implemented in transition economies if fair competition with Western banks is to be reached. If prudential rules and safety nets in general are prerequisites to prevent systemic risk they can also induce counterproductive effects resulting in credit contraction spreading to the real economy (credit crunch). In addition, the trade-off between the efficiency and the stability of the banking system may have to be assessed differently in the case of transition economies where banking systems have to play a major role in funding the investments required to boost the economy.

The aim of this chapter is to analyse bank behaviour in Central and Eastern Europe in a framework where decisions are taken in a risky environment. More precisely we study both theoretically and empirically their reaction in terms of margin setting with respect to the risks they are exposed to and the prudential constraints they have to cope with.

The stress is mainly put on standard intermediation activity that consists in directly funding and generating real investment projects. Other banking activities such as services and market trading which are less developed in transition economies and which require the existence of efficient and broad capital markets are neglected.

In the next section we consider the case of a bank operating under imperfect competition and uncertainty. In the model the bank is exposed to both credit risk and interest rate risk. Because of the often reported cases of moral hazard behaviour related to asymmetric information in these economies, these two categories of risk at least needed to be taken into account. Our aim, however, is only to assess the implications of risk in terms of price setting in the sense that the strategic responses of banks to deal with asymmetric information problems are not derived.

In the third section, we use individual bank data for a large number of countries to analyse the empirical determinants of interest margins. Proxies of the theoretical variables from the model in the second section are introduced in the various regressions (level of interest rates, loan defaults, maturity risk, capital constraints and operating costs). Particularly, econometric tests are run to assess the effect of more stringent capital regulation on the banks' decisions to invest in loans.

The final section provides a brief summary of the main results and raises some implications for the future of banking systems in Central and Eastern Europe.

DETERMINANTS OF INTEREST MARGINS: THEORETICAL APPROACH

The Model

Consider a bank which maximizes its end-of-period wealth utility W in a single-period horizon. At the beginning of the period the liability side of its balance sheet shows a given amount of equity capital K and a given amount of deposits D and the asset side consists in risky non-tradable loans C and risk-free traded assets T (government bonds):

$$T + C = D + K. \tag{18.1}$$

On the deposit market, supply is assumed to be perfectly elastic. The bank can determine the optimal amount of deposits it issues but not the level of their interest rate i_d: the bank is a quantity setter on the deposit market. On the loan market, however, the bank determines the interest rate on the loans it grants i_c. A monopolistic structure is assumed for the loan market where the bank is therefore price setter. Thus, we simply consider a bank facing a downward-sloping loan demand function $C(i_c)$ ($C' < 0$, $C'' \leq 0$) and serving a fixed interest rate as a monopoly.[1] Moreover, the decision to grant loans depends on the the alternative allocation of funds the bank can consider by holding safe assets T which provide a riskless interest rate i.

Thus, the bank has two control variables to maximize its end-of-period income (and therefore wealth): D, the amount of deposits and i_c, the interest rate loans. The bank, however, faces uncertainty (on the actual costs of deposits and the actual rate on loans) and it also has to satisfy a capital adequacy requirement.

If we assume that deposits have a shorter maturity than the reference period (one period), the interest rate at which deposits have to be rolled over within this period is unknown to the bank. This means that the bank is exposed to interest rate risk since it funds loans with a maturity longer (at a fixed-rate basis) than the maturity of deposits it issues (at a variable-rate basis). Thus, within the structure of this model the sources of interest rate risk are located solely on the liability side of the balance sheet. On the asset side the maturity and the rate on loans are determined at the beginning of the period once and for all. Therefore the actual *ex post* return on loans depends on the actual end-of-period customer repayments of interest and principal to the bank. We assume here that the bank is exposed to credit risk measured by the amount of non-performing loans in its balance sheet.

More precisely, credit risk is modelled with γ, which is the proportion of non-performing loans in the loan portfolio at the end of the period. γ is a random variable with support $[0, 1]$ with a probability distribution function known by the bank. We shall consider in what follows, without loss of generality, that non-performing loans pay nothing to the bank (neither interest nor principal).

Interest rate risk is taken into account considering random changes in the rate paid on deposits i_d and furthermore with the assumption of a positive relationship between the rate on deposits and credit risk.[2] We therefore have:

$$i_d = i_d(\gamma) + \varepsilon \tag{18.2}$$

where $i'_d(\gamma) > 0$ and ε is a white noise independent of γ, defined over $[\underline{\varepsilon}, \overline{\varepsilon}]$ and with a probability distribution $h(\varepsilon)$ known by the bank.

Eventually, the bank has to satisfy a capital constraint that is $K \geq kC$ where k^{-1} is the maximum leverage which the bank is allowed to achieve (capital/loans ratio). This minimum capital-to-loans ratio is similar to a Cooke-type ratio (risk based) assuming that there are two categories of weights in this simple model, a maximum 100 per cent weight on all loans and a minimum 0 per cent weight on risk-free assets.

The bank's end-of-period profit π is given by:

$$\pi = iT + (1 - \gamma)i_c C - \gamma C - i_d D - G_c(C) - G_d(D) \qquad (18.3)$$

where $G_c(C)$ and $G_d(D)$ stand for (respectively) the administrative cost of loans and the administrative cost of deposits which are assumed to be separable such that $G'_j > 0$ and $G''_j > 0$, $j = c, d$. The level of profit increases or decreases the amount of the initial equity capital and determines the bank's end-of-period level of wealth. If the bank is allowed to fail (limited liability) its end-of-period wealth can be written as:[3]

$$W = \text{Max } (0, K + \pi). \qquad (18.4)$$

Since the bank can fail, depositors are protected by a deposit insurance system. Because they are insured, depositors do not require a risk premium on the rate paid on their deposits. The insurance system can either be explicit (flat rate paid by the bank to the insurer on the amount of issued deposits) or implicit (*ex post* public intervention). In any case we assume here a 0 per cent fixed rate insurance premium which fits both types of systems.[4]

Now consider $U(W)$ the von Neumann–Morgenstern utility function of the bank defined over its wealth. The bank is assumed to be risk averse ($U' > 0$, $U'' < 0$) and its aim is to maximize its end-of-period expected utility of wealth:

$$E[U(W)] = \int_0^1 \int_{\underline{\varepsilon}}^{\bar{\varepsilon}} U[W(\gamma, \varepsilon)] f(\gamma) h(\varepsilon) d\gamma d\varepsilon. \qquad (18.5)$$

When the bank fails, because of limited liability, its utility level is $U(0)$. This occurs for all combinations of γ and ε such that:

$$\pi < -K \Leftrightarrow i(K + D - C) + (1 - \gamma)i_c C - \gamma C$$

$$- \left[i_c(\gamma) + \varepsilon \right] D - G_c(C) - G_d(D) < -K$$

$$\Leftrightarrow \varepsilon > \hat{\varepsilon}(\gamma) = \left\{ \begin{array}{l} (1 + i)K - (1 + i)C + (1 - \gamma)(1 + i_c)C \\ + \left[i - i_d(\gamma) \right] D - G_c(C) - G_d(D) \end{array} \right\} \Big/ D \qquad (18.6)$$

where $\hat{\varepsilon}$ stands for the critical value of ε for which, given a certain value of the default rate γ, the rate on deposits is affected by a sufficiently high ε shock to bring the bank to fail, $\hat{\varepsilon}'(\gamma) < 0$. In other words, we consider that the interest rate risk occurring on the liability side of the balance sheet can bring the bank to fail on its own, that is when $\hat{\varepsilon}(\gamma) < \bar{\varepsilon}$ for all values of γ. Equation (18.5) can thus be rewritten as:

$$
\begin{aligned}
E[U(W)] &= \int_0^1 \int_{\underline{\varepsilon}}^{\hat{\varepsilon}} U[W(\gamma,\varepsilon)] f(\gamma) h(\varepsilon) d\gamma d\varepsilon \\
&+ \int_0^1 \int_{\hat{\varepsilon}}^{\bar{\varepsilon}} U[W(0)] f(\gamma) h(\varepsilon) d\gamma d\varepsilon \\
&= \int_0^1 \int_{\underline{\varepsilon}}^{\hat{\varepsilon}(\gamma)} U[W(\gamma,\varepsilon)] dF(\gamma) dH(\varepsilon) \\
&+ U[W(0)] \int_0^1 \left\{ 1 - H[\hat{\varepsilon}(\gamma)] \right\} dF(\gamma)
\end{aligned}
$$

(18.7)

where $F(\gamma)$ and $H(\varepsilon)$ are, respectively, the cumulative distribution functions of $f(\gamma)$ and $h(\varepsilon)$. The first term of the right-hand side of equation (18.7) is the bank's expected utility when there is no failure and the second term is the implicit subsidy the bank obtains from the insurer when the latter has to repay depositors in case of failure.[5]

The Optimal Bank Behaviour

The bank maximizes its expected utility equation (18.7) by fixing the interest rate on loans i_c and the amount of issued deposits D satisfying the capital adequacy requirement limiting its leverage C/K. As a first step we shall consider that the capital constraint is not binding in the sense that the bank's optimal choice lies on the loan demand curve at a point which is below the maximum amount of loans it could grant from a regulatory point of view. The first-order conditions, in this case, are:

$$
\frac{dE[U(W)]}{di_c} = \int_0^1 W'_{i_c} \int_{\underline{\varepsilon}}^{\hat{\varepsilon}} U'(W) dF(\gamma) dH(\varepsilon) = 0
$$

(18.8a)

$$
\frac{dE[U(W)]}{dD} = \int_0^1 \int_{\underline{\varepsilon}}^{\hat{\varepsilon}} W'_D U'(W) dF(\gamma) dH(\varepsilon) = 0
$$

(18.8b)

where $W'_{i_c} = [(1 - \gamma)(1 - \eta^{-1})(1 + i_c) - (1 + i) - G'_c] C'(i_c)$, η is the elasticity of loan demand with respect to i_c[6] and $W'_D = i - i_d(\gamma) - \varepsilon - G'_D$.[7] The optimal values i_c^* and D^* are the solutions of the implicit equations (18.8a) and (18.8b) (η and G'_c are evaluated at i_c^* and G'_D is evaluated at D^*). The bank will grant an amount of credit $C^* = C(i_c^*) \leq K/k$ and invest an amount $T^* = K + D^* - C^*$ in risk-free assets.

The solutions are studied in three cases where we consider simplifying assumptions to facilitate the interpretation of the obtained results.

- The bank is *risk neutral* (U' = constant)
  (a) *Without limited liability*:

$$(1 - \overline{\gamma})(1 - \eta^{-1})(1 + i_c) = (1 + i) + G'_c \qquad (18.9a)$$

$$i = i_d(\overline{\gamma}) + G'_D \qquad (18.9b)$$

where $\overline{\gamma} = E(\gamma)$, η and G'_c are evaluated at i_c^* and G'_D is evaluated at D^*. Condition (18.9a) implies that the expected marginal return on loans (net of default risk) is equal to its marginal cost (opportunity cost of not investing in safe assets plus administrative costs).[8] Condition (18.9b) shows that the expected marginal return on deposit issued funds (invested in the risk-free asset) equals the expected marginal cost of deposits (interest payments plus administrative costs).[9] The bank sets a higher rate on loans (and grants a lower amount of loans) when the risk-free rate and/or the average default rate and/or administrative costs of loans increase. It issues more deposits in the first case and fewer deposits in the two other cases. These conditions, here derived with the average probability of loan defaults, are similar to those obtained in the original model developed by Klein (1971) and Monti (1972). Optimal asset and liability management are separated in the sense here that loan rate setting is independent of deposit quantity setting.[10]

  (b) *With limited liability*, we obtain:

$$(1 - \overline{\gamma}^r)(1 - \eta^{-1})(1 + i_c) = (1 + i) + G'_c \qquad (18.10a)$$

$$i = i_d(\overline{\gamma}^r) + \overline{\varepsilon}^r + G'_D \qquad (18.10b)$$

where $\overline{\gamma}^r = E[\gamma | \varepsilon \leq \hat{\varepsilon}(\gamma)] < \overline{\gamma}$ and $\overline{\varepsilon}^r = E(\varepsilon | \varepsilon \leq \hat{\varepsilon}(\gamma)] < 0$.[11] Interest rate risk is now determinant in setting D^*. Moreover, since $\overline{\gamma}^r$ and $\overline{\varepsilon}^r$ depend on the values taken by i_c^* and D^*, decisions taken for assets are no longer separated from those taken for liabilities. With limited liability the bank can now underestimate the negative outcomes of its profit which leads to an increase in the amount of loans granted (at a lower interest rate) and to an increase in the quantity of issued deposits. We here obtain results which are similar to those of Dermine (1986), who introduced limited liability in the Klein–Monti model.[12]

• The bank is *risk adverse* ($U'' < 0$), without limited liability:

$$\int_0^1 W'_{i_c} \int_{\underline{\varepsilon}}^{\overline{\varepsilon}} U'(W) dF(\gamma) dH(\varepsilon) = 0 \qquad (18.11a)$$

$$\int_0^1 \int_{\underline{\varepsilon}}^{\overline{\varepsilon}} W'_D U'(W) dF(\gamma) dH(\varepsilon) = 0. \qquad (18.11b)$$

Risk aversion also implies a breakdown in the separateness between asset and liability optimal decisions. The slope of the wealth utility function W depends on the values taken by i_c^* and D^* and jointly determines optimality conditions. Risk aversion implies a safer bank behaviour with a lower amount of granted loans (at a higher rate) and a lower quantity of issued deposits (downsizing). This framework is very close to that of Wong (1997) and we can usefully refer to his comparative statics results to consider the impact of changes in the determinants i_c^*.[13] When a concave utility function is considered, direct effects related to changes in parameter values (substitution effect) can be distinguished from indirect effects incurred by subsequent marginal utility changes (income effect). Thus, the loan rate is positively related to market power (measured by the inverse of loan demand elasticity η), as well as to credit risk and interest rate risk (both captured by a Rothschild–Stiglitz mean preserving spread on the distributions of γ and of ε.[14] If constant absolute risk aversion is imposed (sufficient condition) the loan rate is also positively linked to the risk-free rate and to administrative costs.

In our model the bank is risk averse and it can benefit from limited liability. Conditions (18.8a) and (18.9a) express the opposite impacts of these two assumptions on the behaviour of the bank, and the optimal rate i_c^* as well as the optimal deposit quantity D^* depend on all the exogenous parameters. *Ceteris paribus*, risk aversion causes the bank to decrease the size of its balance sheet whereas limited liability has the opposite effect. If risk aversion is sufficiently high, limited liability will probably modify the extent but not the sign of the changes induced by parameter movements. In other words, the underestimation of positive outcomes because of risk aversion will outweigh the underestimation of negative outcomes due to limited liability.

Until now we have assumed that the model parameters were such that the capital adequacy constraint was not binding. If this is not the case the bank can only grant an amount of loans limited to $C^k = K/k$ at the rate equal to $i_c^k = C^{-1}(K/k)$. Then, the bank determines the size of its balance sheet by issuing the optimal level of deposits which in turn determines the quantity of safe assets held. The first-order condition is then:

$$\frac{dE[U(W)]}{dD} = \int_0^1 \int_{\underline{\varepsilon}}^{\varepsilon^k} W_D' U'(W) dF(\gamma) dH(\varepsilon) = 0 \qquad (18.12)$$

where

$$\hat{\varepsilon}^k = \left\{ \begin{matrix} \left[(1+i)(1-k^{-1}) + (1-\gamma)(1+i_c^k)k^{-1}\right]K \\ -G_c(K/k) + [i - i_d(\gamma)]D - G_d(D) \end{matrix} \right\} \Big/ D.^{15}$$

If we assume risk neutrality ($U'(W) = $ constant) and unlimited liability (substituting $\hat{\varepsilon}$ for $\hat{\varepsilon}^k$) then equation (18.12) is equivalent to equation (18.9b) and prudential regulation does not effect the optimal quantity of deposits D^{*k} (and therefore the optimal quantity of safe assets T^{*k}). In all other cases the capital constraint is determinant in the setting of D^{*k}, because with risk aversion and/or limited liability the parameters of (18.12) are connected to the regulatory fixed quantity of loans. When only limited liability is taken into account the equivalent of equation (18.10b) can be obtained by substituting $\overline{\gamma}^{rk} = E[\gamma|\varepsilon \leq \hat{\varepsilon}^k(\gamma)]$ and $\overline{\varepsilon}^r$ by $\overline{\varepsilon}^{rk} = E[\varepsilon|\varepsilon \leq \hat{\varepsilon}^k(\gamma)]$ for $\overline{\gamma}^r$. It can be shown that $d\overline{\gamma}^{rk}/dk > 0$ and $d\overline{\varepsilon}^{rk}/dk > 0$. The quantity of issued deposits is positively linked to the degree of leverage authorized by regulation and a more stringent capital adequacy ratio causes the bank to decrease D^{*k}. Similarly, when risk aversion is introduced we can see that the capital constraint operates in equation (18.11b) through the bank's marginal utility $U'(W)$ which depends on the amount of loans granted and therefore on the authorized degree of leverage. However, the effect of capital regulation on the optimal quantity of issued deposits cannot be estimated without further assumptions on the utility function (higher substitution effect involving a switch from loans to deposit-funded riskless assets versus higher-income effect due to a decrease in the level of utility implying an increase in $U'(W)$).

Margin on Loans and Global Interest Margin

Optimal bank behaviour can be captured through two types of margins which can be estimated with the implicit solutions obtained for the loan rate and for the quantity of issued deposits: margin on loans (*mic*) which is the spread between the interest rate on loans and the interest rate on deposits and a global interest margin (*mig*) computed as the difference between the implicit rate on assets i_a and the implicit rate on liabilities i_p. For simplicity, margins are defined *ex post* in the sense that they incorporate the actual realizations of γ

and of ε (*ex post* margins are equal in expectation to *ex ante* margins – expected or constrained by regulation):

$$mic = i_c - i_d = i_c - i_d(\gamma) - \varepsilon \qquad (18.13)$$

where $i_c = i_c^*$ or $i_c = i_c^k$ if the capital constraint is binding

$$mig = i_a - i_p = \left\{[iT + i_c(1 - \gamma)C]/(T + C)\right\} - i_d D/(K + D)$$
$$= \left\{iK + [i - i_d(\gamma) - \varepsilon]D + [(1 - \gamma)i_c - i]C\right\}/(K + D) \qquad (18.14)$$

where $i_c = i_c^*$, $C = C^*$, $D = D^*$ or $i_c = i^k$, $C = C^k$, $D = D^{*k}$ if the capital constraint is binding. The global interest margin can be rewritten as a function of the margin on loans and the margin on safe assets ($mit = i - i_d$):

$$mig = (1 - \gamma)c \, mic + t \, mit + k'i_d \qquad (18.15)$$

where c, t and k' are, respectively, the relative shares of loans, safe assets and capital (net of loan losses) in the bank's balance sheet.[16]

Since in our model the rate on deposits i_d is given, the comparative statics conclusions determined for the loan rate i_c also hold for the margin on loans (*mic*).[17] However, the impact of parameter changes on the global interest margin (*mig*) is not clear since both price effects (the bank sets the rate on loans) and quantity effects (the bank sets the quantity of deposits) have to be taken into account. Thus in our model global margin behaviour cannot be determined straightforwardly since it depends on price effects, quantity effects and eventually on balance-sheet structure (c, t and k') effects (asset and liability reshuffling).

EMPIRICAL ANALYSIS

The Sample and the Data

The empirical analysis of the link between bank interest margins and the independent variables identified in the theoretical model is carried out for nine Central and Eastern European countries (Croatia, Estonia, Hungary, Latvia, Lithuania, Poland, Slovenia, Slovakia and the Czech Republic). The banking data come from Bankscope Fetch-IBCA which provides series from individual bank balance sheets and income statements. Interest rate series are those published by the EBRD (1997).

Table 18.1   Concentration ratios for the banking systems in the sample

	Number of commercial banks	$CONC_A$ (1995)	$CONC_D$ (1995)
Poland	37	44.80	44.74
Czech Republic	25	59.66	64.29
Slovenia	16	64.36	62.83
Hungary	29	52.91	54.95
Slovakia	13	79.84	80.59
Croatia	29	68.20	73.42
Lithuania	13	76.54	76.53
Latvia	20	44.05	41.96
Estonia	11	70.76	71.25

Notes
$CONC_A$ = Market share of the three largest commercial banks in terms of total assets.
$CONC_D$ = Market share of the three largest commercial banks in terms of customer deposits.

More precisely, the samples include commercial banks only, that is, institutions relying more heavily on loan and deposit activities in order to focus on intermediation banking generating interest margins. Annual data for the 1992–96 period were gathered for a sufficiently significant number of banks operating in the considered countries. The information contained in balance sheets and income statements for the smaller banks was insufficient to run our regressions. Nevertheless, it is interesting to note that accounting standards in most of the countries under study allowed the computation of the necessary variables (particularly the ones capturing credit risk) sometimes with more accuracy than for banks established in Western Europe.

Compared to Western countries the considered banking systems include a relatively low number of commercial banks and are highly concentrated in terms of both total assets and total deposits (see Table 18.1). The three-largest commercial banks weighted, in 1995, from 44 to 80 per cent in aggregate assets or deposits.

Apart from being highly concentrated, banking markets are still strongly segmented in these countries (see OECD reports 1996a, b and 1997a, b). This is particularly the case in the Czech Republic, mainly because of historical and institutional matters. For instance, the Ceska Sporitela can still rely on a particularly wide network (branching) inherited from the past. The Komercni banka still benefits from having taken over the commercial activities of the previously established state-owned bank. On the whole, it seems that non-competitive behaviour in the banking sector can be witnessed either because of large market shares of state-owned banks or because of concentrated shareholdings in recently privatized banks. Therefore, the monopolistic structure retained in our theoretical framework seems to fit banking markets in transition economies conveniently.

The Empirical Specification of the Model

The empirical tests which were run to study the determinants of bank interest margins involve two groups of variables. The first group contains the variables which explain the desired spread, under uncertainty, between the rate on loans and the cost of liabilities. In other words, this set of variables reflects the mark-up required by banks to compensate their exposure to interest rate risk and credit risk. The second group of variables is assumed to capture the effects of active portfolio reshuffling (marketable asset/loan substitution) as well as the effects of operating costs and prudential regulation.

In the theoretical model developed in the previous section, the two control variables were the rate required on loans and the amount of deposits (liabilities). Thus, both the size and the structure of assets (risky loans/risk-free assets) can be determined. The rate on risk-free assets being defined exogeneously, the model enables to define not only the margin required solely on loans but also the margin required on the entire balance sheet (total assets). The empirical analysis therefore consists in estimating both a loan margin equation and a global interest margin equation using the same independent variables. Note that previous empirical studies on Western banking systems (see, for instance, Angbazo 1997 for a recent study in the case of the USA) consider the estimation of a global margin only. The data available for transition countries in Bankscope allow a direct estimation of margins required on loans.

Empirical Variables

The interest rate required on loans is defined as the ratio of interest received on customer loans to the amount of customer loans net of loan loss reserves. This implicit measure of the rate on loans is estimated for all the banks in the sample except for those established in Hungary and Slovakia due to a lack of the required data. Therefore, only a global margin equation can be estimated for these two countries.

The interest rate on liabilities is measured as the implicit cost of liabilities estimated as the ratio of interest paid to customers to total assets. An alternative variable, apparently more consistent with our theoretical model, is the cost of deposits only (interest paid on customer (non-marketable) deposits/total customer deposits). But because banks can actually collect funds under various forms, the cost of total liabilities can better capture bank liability structure heterogeneity, enabling cross-market estimations.[18] For instance, some banks (money-centre banks relying on heavy branching) will exhibit high deposit-to-total-assets ratios. Others, benefiting from higher ratings and therefore able to borrow funds on international capital markets will have different liability structures. Also, for banks with lower ratings, relying mainly on domestic money markets, the cost of funds will be higher.

The interest margin on loans is defined as the difference between the implicit rate on loans and the implicit rate on liabilities and the global interest margin (net interest income) is measured by the ratio of net interest revenues to total assets.

The ratio of loan loss reserves to gross loans is used as a proxy of credit risk. Estimations were also carried out using the ratio of loan loss provisions to gross loans. Using either balance-sheet (loan loss reserves) or income statement (loan loss provisions) information led to approximately the same results.

Transformation activity implies that banks are exposed to both interest rate risk and liquidity risk. Interest rate risk arises because, given their maturity and their rate definition (fixed rate, floating rate), assets and liabilities will be affected differently by market interest rate movements. A measure of interest rate risk should therefore capture the existing maturity or duration gap between assets and liabilities sensitive to market rate changes. A standard measure used in empirical studies to proxy interest rate risk is the net position in short-term assets deflated by the value of equity capital (see, for instance, Flannery and James 1984; Yourougou 1990; Angbazo 1997). Liquidity risk is the risk for the bank of not having sufficient cash to meet customer deposit withdrawals. This dimension of risk can be captured through the ratio of liquid assets to liabilities or the ratio of net liquid assets to total assets (Angbazo 1997).

Unfortunately, such interest rate risk and liquidity risk measures cannot be computed from the data available for our set of countries and for the banks included in our country samples. In fact the variables that can be computed can only implicitly capture effects related to bank balance-sheet structures and thus to transformation risk without explicitly distinguishing interest rate risk from liquidity risk. Also, introducing two variables in the estimations to evaluate both type of effects separately (interest rate risk and liquidity risk) raises collinearity problems. Therefore only one indicator was taken into account to measure both types of risks jointly and which we call maturity (or transformation) risk.[19]

The bank's measured exposure to transformation risk is thus simply the ratio of loans to the bank's customer and short-term funding. This variable stands more for liquidity risk than for interest rate risk since it divides the amount of non-tradable assets by short-term liabilities. Moreover, loans are considered as a whole with no distinction on the basis of their maturity or rate definition (fixed or floating). Nevertheless, maturity transformation in transition economies (ratio of long-term loans to short-term deposits) is on average relatively low compared to Western economies and has recently experienced a sharp decline.[20] Under these conditions the exposure to interest rate risk should be quite low.

The variable which is supposed to capture substitution effects (marketable assets substituted for loans) induced by changes in market interest rates is the interest rate on three-month treasury bills. For the Czech Republic, Estonia and Slovakia (that is, countries for which series were not available), the inflation rate was considered instead as a proxy (consumer price index).

The capital ratio is measured by the ratio of equity capital to total loans. This variable is a convenient proxy of the Cooke ratio if loans are considered as risky assets with a weight equal to 100 per cent and if all the other assets held by banks are assumed to be risk free (weight equal to 0 per cent).

The variable reflecting changes in administrative costs is defined as the sum of personnel expenses[21] and non-interest expenses deflated by total assets (the size of the bank). An alternative measure would have been to deflate costs by the amount of loans only. Over the recent period most of the banks in the countries under study have experienced a significant increase in the ratio of administrative costs to loans. Therefore such a variable would have better taken this effect into account. We preferred, however, to divide overall costs by total assets in order to consider deposit costs as well and to allow the inclusion of different patterns in bank balance-sheet structures.

The Results

The results of the two bank interest margins equations can be found in Table 18.2. The determinants of margins should be considered carefully for Slovenia, Slovakia, Lithuania and Estonia since the number of observations is relatively weak for these countries.

On the whole the model fits the data with a satisfying explanatory power for the determination of the margin on loans (the goodness of fit coefficients (R^2) are higher than 60 per cent except for Estonia (47 per cent) and for Slovenia (34 per cent)). Most of the time the coefficients are lower for the second equation (global interest margin) but remain sufficiently high compared to previous studies.

In most countries banks react by increasing their interest margin when facing a higher rate on the government bond market (opportunity cost variable). Thus an increase in the return on risk-free assets induces banks to charge a higher rate on their risky assets that is on their loans. Since in our model banks are loan-rate setters and assuming that the demand of loans remains unchanged, this effect should imply a decrease in the investment in loans and

Table 18.2 Determination of margins on loans (1) and global interest margins (2)

	Poland (1)	Poland (2)	Czech Republic (1)	Czech Republic (2)	Slovenia (1)	Slovenia (2)	Hungary (2)	Slovakia (2)
Intercept	-16.75**	-1.32	14.67**	2.31**	115.32	3.20**	0.29	-1.40
	(-3.83)	(-0.88)	(8.09)	(4.08)	(1.19)	(3.35)	(0.24)	(-0.86)
Opportunity cost	0.62**	0.07*	0.38**	0.07*	4.60	0.03	0.04	0.42**
	(5.31)	(1.73)	(3.35)	(1.98)	(1.23)	(0.80)	(0.96)	(3.26)
Credit risk	0.35**	0.06*	0.44**	-0.01	-8.75*	0.01	0.03*	0.07**
	(3.62)	(1.92)	(6.96)	(-0.01)	(-1.71)	(0.01)	(1.85)	(2.17)
Maturity risk	-0.01	0.05**	-0.18**	-0.01	-2.61**	0.02*	0.04**	0.02*
	(-0.08)	(3.93)	(-13.10)	(-0.11)	(-2.39)	(1.64)	(5.64)	(1.99)
Capitalization (leverage)	0.08**	0.02*	0.20**	0.01	2.95	-0.05*	0.01**	0.01
	(2.30)	(1.96)	(8.20)	(0.78)	(1.02)	(-1.90)	(2.16)	(0.80)
Administrative costs	1.72**	0.46**	-0.52**	-0.09*	14.49	-0.12	0.03	-0.53*
	(4.17)	(3.20)	(-3.28)	(-1.73)	(1.23)	(-1.21)	(0.41)	(-1.86)
R^2	0.64	0.39	0.77	0.16	0.34	0.24	0.33	0.47
Observations	54	54	70	70	20	20	72	30

	Croatia (1)	Croatia (2)	Lithuania (1)	Lithuania (2)	Latvia (1)	Latvia (2)	Estonia (1)	Estonia (2)
Intercept	-3.98	0.76	18.86**	3.65	-1.73	2.47	-4.54	-1.98
	(-0.31)	(0.34)	(2.23)	(0.84)	(-0.13)	(1.06)	(-0.50)	(-0.83)
Opportunity cost	1.46**	0.23**	0.26**	0.08**	0.83	0.04	0.18	-0.01
	(8.52)	(7.40)	(5.48)	(3.14)	(1.46)	(0.54)	(1.64)	(-0.18)
Credit risk	-0.23	-0.10*	-0.18	-0.15	0.71**	0.01	0.93	0.18
	(-0.72)	(-1.86)	(-0.94)	(-1.51)	(2.32)	(0.29)	(1.61)	(1.24)
Maturity risk	-0.01	0.02	-0.01	-0.07*	-0.49*	0.15**	-0.02	0.06**
	(-0.01)	(1.54)	(-0.12)	(1.84)	(-1.90)	(3.40)	(-0.23)	(2.07)
Capitalization (leverage)	-0.07	-0.01	-0.06	-0.03	-0.01	-0.00	0.23**	0.08**
	(-1.10)	(-1.28)	(-0.72)	(-0.62)	(-1.11)	(-0.11)	(2.69)	(3.46)
Administrative costs	-1.35	-0.01	-0.29	0.06	2.22**	-0.13	0.80	0.24
	(-1.54)	(-0.02)	(-0.31)	(0.12)	(3.24)	(-1.08)	(1.20)	(1.39)
R^2	0.70	0.68	0.70	0.63	0.62	0.28	0.55	0.59
Observations	35	35	24	24	44	44	19	19

Notes: (): t-statistics; coefficients with ** or * are significantly different from 0 at 5 and 10 per cent, respectively. Equations estimated using SURE (dependent variable: margin on loans in (1) and global interest margin in (2)).

an increase in the purchase of more attractive risk-free assets (substitution effect).

The credit risk proxy is both significant and positive for Poland, the Czech Republic, Hungary, Slovakia and Latvia. This variable is therefore determinant for bank margin setting. When they face a higher probability of loan default banks require a higher premium paid by potential borrowers. The estimated regression coefficients are more significant in equation 1 than in equation 2, which is consistent with our theoretical model. Banks react instantaneously by charging a higher rate on loans but the implication on their global net interest revenue will depend on their asset structure. However, it can be noted that the coefficients are significant at the 5 per cent level only in the case of four estimations out of eight. Thus, whether bank managers take credit risk into account or not in their pricing strategies is an issue for which no clear and straightforward answer can be provided for the considered countries as a whole.

Maturity or transformation risk does not play a significant role in bank loan margin determination. In the first equation estimated for the different countries, maturity risk is either not significant or when it is the obtained sign is opposite to the predicted one. However, except for the Czech Republic and Croatia the coefficients in equation 2 (global margin determine) are all significant with the predicted positive sign. Thus, banks with a more developed intermediation and transformation activity benefit from higher average interest on their assets. But on the whole, maturity risk is not directly taken into account in the risk premium charged on loans and the results obtained in equation 2 cannot be interpreted on behavioural grounds. These surprising results obviously come from the difficulties in defining and measuring a relevant indicator of this risk.

Administrative costs are not linked to margins in the case of Slovenia, Hungary, Croatia, Lithuania and Estonia. For the other countries the signs of the significant coefficients are sometimes positive (Poland and Latvia), sometimes negative (the Czech Republic and Slovakia), and a negative effect of operating costs on desired or required margins is inconsistent with our theoretical model as it is built. A possible explanation relates to moral hazard effects which cannot explicitly be taken into account here. If a higher operating cost implies a higher level of *ex post* monitoring of borrowers, for instance (lower probability of non-performing loans), then the default risk premium charged on loans can be lower. On the whole, the fact that the sign of the coefficient is not clearly identified is not surprising since the process of structural reorganization is not yet achieved in these countries. The majority of banks have recently experienced an increase in their administrative costs relative to the quantity of loans because of the decrease in loan investment and to a lesser extent because of an increase in the proportion of highly qualified staff.

The variable which is a proxy for the Cooke ratio (capitalization) has a significant effect with the expected positive sign only for Poland, the Czech Republic, Hungary and Estonia. Thus, a higher capital ratio is compensated for these countries by a higher mark-up on the rate required on loans. Two types of lesson can be drawn from our results. If during the period covered by our estimations more stringent capital ratios were imposed on banks to catch up with international standards, their behaviour might have been to offset lower leverage by setting higher margins on their loans. In this case a possible effect is a credit crunch for the economy as a whole and a lower proportion of loans in bank balance sheets. If, on the other hand, lower leverage is related to strategic choices made by unconstrained banks willing to improve their own solvency and their rating, then the increase in margins can come from a lower cost of borrowed funds.[22]

With the estimation of the equation determining the margin on loans we were able to identify a certain number of price effects. In the case of a monopolistic structure on the loan market, price effects imply opposite quantity effects with magnitudes depending on the value of the interest rate elasticity of loan demand. Therefore, a change in the rate on loans should induce quantity effects due exclusively to changes in demand behaviour (the bank faces a loan demand curve with the reciprocal of the interest rate elasticity).

To assess the magnitude of quantity effects we regress the amount of loans deflated by the value of total assets on the set of independent variables used to estimate margin equations.[23] The results of these estimations are reported in Table 18.3.Since the expected signs in the margin equation (Table 18.2) were all positive those in Table 18.3 should all be negative. However, if in the line of the theoretical model only demand effects operate, a variable with no significant price effect (in Table 18.2) should not exert significant quantity effects (in Table 18.3). The presence of significant positive price effects which are not coupled with significant negative quantity effects can be interpreted in terms of credit rationing.

The risky loans/risk-free assets arbitrage behaviour of banks clearly illustrates this case. For a first group of countries (Hungary, Latvia and Estonia) we have no price effects and no quantity effects. For a second group (Poland, the Czech Republic, Croatia, Lithuania) only price effects coefficient are significantly different from 0. Thus, banks react to changes in the market risk-free rate by modifying rates on loans without, however, an increase or a decrease in the quantity of granted loans. Eventually, for a third group (Slovenia) we get only quantity effects.

Thus, the different banking systems do not react similarly in terms of loan quantity setting and/or price setting and thus in terms of credit rationing to changes in market risk-free interest rates.

The same interpretation holds for credit risk. An increase in credit risk

Table 18.3 Quantity of granted loans

	Poland	Czech Republic	Slovenia	Hungary	Slovakia
Intercept	57.88**	59.47**	51.09**	43.34**	64.10**
	(5.76)	(7.34)	(3.63)	(3.73)	(2.13)
Opportunity cost	-0.12	0.31	-1.45**	0.37	1.48
	(-0.49)	(0.52)	(-2.90)	(0.91)	(0.61)
Credit risk	-0.62**	-0.02	-2.01**	-0.42**	-0.85
	(-2.99)	(-0.07)	(-3.84)	(-2.66)	(-1.55)
Capitalization (leverage)	-0.45**	-0.38**	0.78**	-0.17**	-0.19**
	(-3.60)	(-2.31)	(2.74)	(-2.13)	(-4.50)
Administrative costs	1.11	0.18	4.09**	-0.83*	-5.69
	(1.09)	(0.27)	(3.22)	(-1.74)	(-1.02)
R^2	0.42	0.16	0.63	0.29	0.32
Observations	54	70	21	73	30

	Croatia	Lithuania	Latvia	Estonia
Intercept	60.80**	70.52**	24.59**	48.79**
	(18.80)	(4.83)	(4.40)	(5.41)
Opportunity cost	0.01	-0.07	0.02	-0.18
	(0.09)	(-0.70)	(0.12)	(-0.97)
Credit risk	-0.86**	-0.43	-0.44**	-0.52
	(-10.07)	(-1.21)	(-3.93)	(0.59)
Capitalization (leverage)	-0.18**	-0.16	0.01	-0.34**
	(-7.20)	(-0.98)	(1.09)	(-3.44)
Administrative costs	-0.12	-1.08	0.59**	0.87
	(-0.40)	(-0.76)	(2.04)	(1.26)
R^2	0.64	0.13	0.27	0.32
Observations	35	24	44	19

Notes: (): t-statistics; White heteroscedasticity-consistent standard errors and covariance; coefficients with ** or * are significantly different from 0 at 5 and 10 per cent, respectively. Dependent variable: customer loans/total assets.

involves a contraction in the quantity of loans in balance sheets in the case of Poland, Slovenia, Hungary, Croatia and Latvia. Significant positive price effects were obtained in Table 18.2 for only three of these countries (Poland, Hungary and Latvia). The fact that only quantity effects could be obtained for Slovenia and Croatia suggests that beyond demand effects there may be a case for credit-rationing effects.

The leverage variable (loans/equity) is significant for all the countries under study except for Lithuania and Latvia. A decrease in leverage is linked to a fall in the ratio of loans to total assets except in the case of Slovenia, where the opposite sign is obtained in the regressions. For these three countries (Lithuania, Latvia and Slovenia) no price effects could be identified in Table 18.2. On the whole, the obtained positive links for all the other banking systems cast doubts on their ability to perform their intermediation activity efficiently, whether or not banks were actually constrained in their leverage choices (prudential regulation or strategic unconstrained decisions).

Administrative costs do not affect the investment in loans in most cases. For the few countries where they do, the signs of the estimated coefficients are opposite to the expected ones. The same ambiguous results were obtained in the estimation of price equations (Table 18.2).

CONCLUSION

The aim of this chapter was to analyse the behaviour of banks in Central and Eastern Europe in terms of their interest margins. Within an imperfect competition setting under uncertainty we first derived the effects of changes in the conditions of interest rate risk, credit risk, capital constraints, risky assets/risk-free assets arbitrage opportunities, and administrative costs.

The theoretical determinants of interest margins derived from our model were then empirically analysed using a sample of commercial banks for nine countries in Central Europe. Except for Lithuania and Estonia, for which no reliable estimations could be run, the results show that three determinants significantly affect bank margins (arbitrage opportunities related to changes in risk-free market interest rates, credit risk and the level of equity capital (leverage)).

An increase in market (risk-free) interest rates is an incentive for banks either to increase the required rate on their risky loans or to lower the quantity of loans in their balance sheets. Therefore the funding of public deficits may well reduce that of private investment projects by banks. Similarly, higher loan defaults imply higher risk premia charged on loans and/or narrower access to credit. Eventually, higher capital ratios either constrained by regulation or freely set by bank managers in order to improve solvency and reputation, also negatively affect credit conditions for borrowers.

On the other hand, maturity risk and operating costs (administrative costs) seem less clearly taken into account by banks in their margin behaviour. Obviously, a possible explanation is that maturity transformation activity is in general relatively weak in these countries and that the process of restructuring of the banking system is far from being achieved. However, weak transformation is a threat to the development of long-term private investment projects. But then to develop their investments in long-term loans, banks will need first, a less unstable macroeconomic environment and second, to charge further higher rates.

On the whole it appears that only a certain number of factors affect current conditions on the credit market and that others are still not explicitly integrated in supply decisions (maturity transformation and operating costs).

A limit of our study is related to the simple framework used in this chapter. The empirical analysis showed that quantity effects and price effects were not always connected consistently. Such results may highlight credit rationing behaviour and suggest that our model could be improved by explicitly considering incentive problems (adverse selection or moral hazard.[24] Also, during the period covered by our sample the analysed banking systems experienced severe difficulties mostly involving public intervention (bank recapitalization, transfer of bad loans, and so on). Consequently, the incentives for banks to price correctly the risks they were taking and to manage and integrate costs thoroughly in their pricing policies in general may have been altered.

NOTES

1. There is no loss of generality in considering the bank as a monopoly for the purpose of our model (see note 6).
2. This is a usual assumption often considered in the literature (from Sealey 1980 to Wong 1997). From a macroeconomic point of view we can assume that an overall increase in interest rates (which affects i_d) leads to a decrease in business and therefore to higher loan defaults. Sealey argues that the business cycle implies similar positively related movements in loan defaults and the supply in deposits. This assumption is made by Wong, who introduces a negative link between i_d and γ, which we consider less relevant, however, in a model where deposit supply is perfectly elastic.
3. When profit is negative, the capital constraint is not necessarily satisfied any more since the value of equity capital diminishes. We assume here that the bank is declared bankrupt when its capital is completely absorbed by incurred losses and not as soon as it drops below the level required by regulation.
4. Assuming a fixed rate insurance system implies that the bank benefits from an implicit subsidy because the insurer does not take the bank's actual level of default risk into account. Specifying a zero-rate premium makes this subsidy effective in all cases without altering the results that would be obtained with a positive fixed rate.
5. The probability of bank failure can be written $p = \text{prob}(W < 0) = \text{prob}(\varepsilon > \hat{\varepsilon}) = 1 - H(\hat{\varepsilon})$. If there is no limited liability $\bar{\varepsilon}$ substitutes for $\hat{\varepsilon}$ in equation (18.7) where the last term (which is positive) disappears (since $H(\bar{\varepsilon}) = 1$.
6. If our framework was one of oligopolistic competition, the optimality condition of a Cournot symmetric equilibrium would have required multiplying the elasticity η by n the number of banks on the loan market (see, for instance, Freixas and Rochet 1996).

7. Differentiating $E[U(\pi)]$ with respect to the two choice variables shows that the sum of the first derivative of the first term of the right-hand side of equation (18.7) with respect to $\hat{\varepsilon}$ (the failure limit is modified with a change in i_d or in D) and the derivative of the second term (the expected utility of the insurance subsidy in case of failure is also a function of i_d and D) equals 0.

8. A solution such that $i_d^* > 0$ requires $\eta > 1$.

9. Assuming that $i > i_d(\bar{\gamma})$, condition $G_D'' > 0$ is sufficient to guarantee a result with a finite level of issued deposits.

10. This condition would of course not hold if the assumption of separateness of administrative costs of loans and administrative cost of deposits is relaxed.

11. $\bar{\gamma}^r = \int_0^1 \int_{\underline{\varepsilon}}^{\hat{\varepsilon}'} \gamma dF(\gamma) dH(\varepsilon) < \bar{\gamma}, \quad \bar{\varepsilon}^r = \int_0^1 \int_{\underline{\varepsilon}}^{\hat{\varepsilon}'} \varepsilon dF(\gamma) dH(\varepsilon) < \bar{\varepsilon} = 0.$

12. In Dermine (1986) several cases are studied with different deposit insurance schemes (risk-based/flat-rate deposit insurance). In our model the value of the insurance premium is underestimated and therefore limited liability implies an underestimation by the bank of negative profit outcomes (an overestimated premium would imply an overestimation of negative outcomes and a correctly estimated premium would fully neutralize the implications of limited liability).

13. Wong (1997) considers a regulatory constraint defined as $K > kD$ which is slightly different from ours. In his model this constraint is always binding and therefore his solution is not equivalent to (18.11b).

14. Substituting $s\gamma + (1 - s)\bar{\gamma}$ for γ and $v\varepsilon$ for ε the impact of credit risk and that of interest rate risk on i_c^* are obtained by implicitly differentiating (18.11a) with respect to the parameters of s and v and evaluating the derivatives at, respectively, $s= 1$ and $v = 1$.

15. $\hat{\varepsilon}^k = \hat{\varepsilon}(C^k, i_c^k)$.

16. Since a portion of safe assets is financed with equity capital (which is free) *mit* underestimates the actual margin on safe assets which explains whey we have $k'i_d$ in (18.12).

17. Which is relevant only when the bank does not fail.

18. Our variable definition implies that the cost of liabilities can differ across banks. This assumption is not contradictory with our theoretical model where banks are assumed to be price takers on the deposit market. It simply implies that they are price takers on their own market.

19. Another solution would have been to define country-specific and/or bank-specific interest rate risk and liquidity risk measures depending on the available information in the data set. To preserve homogeneity in the estimations a common simple definition was retained for all the banks in our samples.

20. In Hungary in 1995 short-term loans accounted for more than 75 per cent of total business loans. In the Czech Republic, short-medium-term loans accounted for 47 per cent (28 per cent) of total business loans in 1995 (see Borish et al. 1996, p. 47 for more details). However, by the end of 1995, 80 per cent of the granted loans were for short periods against 70 per cent in 1993–94, implying a fall of the transformation ratio from 50 to 30 per cent. In Hungary the same ratio was equal to 47 per cent in 1993, falling to 40 per cent in 1996 (OECD 1996a and 1997a).

21. The theoretical model suggested that the administrative cost of loans should be separated from the administrative cost of issuing deposits. Unfortunately the data set does not provide information allowing for such a distinction.

22. With this second interpretation we no longer refer to our theoretical model in which the risk of insolvency is not linked to the cost of liabilities. This second interpretation is, however, retained in many empirical studies (see, for instance, Angbazo 1997).

23. Except maturity risk. The regression coefficients obtained when this variable (loans/customer and short-term funding) is included in the estimations are very highly significant. This can obviously be explained by the fact that, because changes in total assets and in short-term funding were relatively small and correlated over the period, the independent variable (loans/total assets) did not differ much from this variable. We therefore preferred to omit this variable which only contributed to boosting the value of R^2.

24. Such an extension is suggested in Wong (1997). In his model the proportion of non-performing loans is related to the rate charged on loans by the bank. However, incentive problems are not taken into account explicitly in his model.

REFERENCES

Allen, L. (1988), 'The derminants of bank interest margins: a note', *Journal of Financial and Quantitative Analysis*, **23**, June.

Angbazo, L. (1997), 'Commercial bank net interest margins, default risk, interest-rate risk, and off-balance sheet banking', *Journal of Banking and Finance*, **21**.

Borish, M.S., W. Ding and M. Noël (1996), 'On the road to EU accession: financial sector development in Central Europe', World Bank Discussion Paper no. 345.

CEPII (1996), 'Credit crises and the role of banks during transition: a five-country comparison', Working Paper no. 96-108.

Claessens, S. (1996), *Banking reform in Transition-Countries*, World Development Report, Washington, DC: World Bank.

Dermine, J. (1986), 'Deposit rates, credit rates and bank capital: the Klein–Monti model revisited', *Journal of Banking and Finance*, **10**.

European Bank for Reconstruction and Development (EBRD) (1997), *Transition Report*, London: EBRD.

Flannery, M.C. and C.M. James (1984), 'The effects of interest rate changes on the common stock returns of financial institutions', *Journal of Finance*, **39**, 1141–53.

Freixas, X. and J.C. Rochet (1996), *Microeconomics of Banking*, Cambridge, MA: MIT Press.

Klein, M.A. (1971), 'A theory of the banking firm', *Journal of Money Credit Banking*, **3**, May.

Monti, M. (1972), 'Deposit, credit and interest rate determination under alternative bank objective functions' in Shell and Szego (eds), *Mathematical Methods in Investment and Finance*, Amsterdam: North-Holland.

Organization for Economic and Cooperative Development (OECD) (1996a), 'La république tchèque', (The Czech Republic), *Etudes Economiques de l'OCDE*, Paris: OECD.

Organization for Economic and Cooperative Development (OECD) (1996b), 'La république slovaque' (The Slovak Republic), *Etudes Economiques de l'OCDE*, Paris: OECD.

Organization for Economic and Cooperative Development (OECD) (1997a), 'La Hongrie' (Hungary), *Etudes Economiques de l'OCDE*, Paris: OECD.

Organization for Economic and Cooperative Development (OECD) (1997b), 'La Slovénie' (Slovenia), *Etudes Economiques de l'OCDE*, Paris: OECD.

Sealey, C.W. (1980), 'Deposit rate-setting, risk aversion, and the theory of depositary financial intermediaries', *Journal of Finance*, **35**.

Wong, K.P. (1997), 'On the determinants of bank interest margins under credit and interest rate risks', *Journal of Banking and Finance*, **21**.

Yourougou, P. (1990), 'Interest rate risk and the pricing of depositary financial intermediary common stock: empirical evidence', *Journal of Banking and Finance*, **13**, 797–810.

19. The impact of market structure and efficiency on bank profitability: an empirical analysis of banking industries in Central and Eastern Europe

Céline Gondat-Larralde and Laetitia Lepetit*

INTRODUCTION

On 1 January 1998, the European Union (EU) enlargement process was reactivated, as five Central and Eastern European (CEE) countries[1] – Hungary, Poland, the Czech Republic, Slovenia and Estonia – were invited by the EU to enter into negotiations leading to their membership. Even if some regional integration has been achieved as trade and investment flows progressively and significantly increased, the CEE countries still retain some of the characteristics of transition economies, making their near-term entry problematic. However, such a scheme would constitute the ultimate phase of a decade-long economic transition process.

Current and past changes in the competitive process have considerably reshaped the world banking industry. Nowadays, competition is considered by banking authorities more as an efficiency-enhancing factor than as a potentially destabilizing element. Within such a remodelled financial environment, CEE economies have initiated a profound metamorphosis of their banking industry. They have done so by creating a new economic agent, the banking firm, after abandoning the socialist financial system based on centralized payments and on soft budget constraints. First, authorities implemented a rapid deregulation and liberalization phase, giving priority to the competitive aspect of banking restructuring. Subsequently, CEE economies have been (and some of them still are) confronted with a consolidation trend. Even though the vulnerability of banking systems remains an Achilles' heel of transition

* We would like to thank Professors D. Lacoue-Labarthe, A.W. Mullineux, A. Sauviat and A. Tarazi, and Dr F. Strobel for their valuable comments and support.

economies, we should highlight the significant progress that the CEE banking systems have achieved in the recent past.

The objective of this chapter is to provide a synoptic view of the development of banking sectors in the CEE countries, focusing particularly on the evolution of their market structure and their competitive environment since the beginning of the transition process. As in Western Europe, but in a more distinct way, most banking industries in Central and Eastern Europe are dominated by groups of core banks – most often descendants of the old 'monobanking' system, still (or until recently) state owned, though progress is being made with privatization. Emphasizing the existence of anti-competitive behaviour in CEE markets, our empirical results for the 1992–96 period show that the market concentration index is a significant determinant of bank profitability. Governments should thus closely monitor future mergers. But our results also show that each bank's efficiency has a strong influence on its performance, and that state-owned banks are the less profitable institutions, while banks whose capital is predominantly foreign owned earn the highest return on equity. This in turn suggests that authorities should accelerate the privatization process while encouraging foreign banks' presence.

After examining the evolution of the structure of banking industries in CEE countries in the next section, we try to assess to what extent individual performance can be explained by banking market structure. In the third, we focus on the relationship between market structure, efficiency and performance, and its analysis in banking. In the fourth section, we estimate this link in the case of CEE banking industries and check whether the classical results obtained in the US case or, more recently, in Western Europe are confirmed. The final section concludes.

THE REORGANIZATION OF BANKING STRUCTURE AND BEHAVIOUR IN CENTRAL AND EASTERN EUROPE

Banking efficiency and stability are key, though antithetical, features of the successful transition of a centrally planned economy towards a market economy. In the absence of a significant development of financial markets, the financing of economic activity and efficient resource allocation are closely dependent on banking systems. In the late 1980s, regulators in CEE countries undertook reforms aimed at authorizing banks to set up a financial intermediation activity. However, banks' inexperience in risk management led the authorities to react and to implement new regulations in the early 1990s.

Radical Structural Reforms at the Start of the Transition Process

Before the beginning of the transition process, the structure of all CEE banking systems was similar: each monobanking system comprised a state bank combining commercial and central banking functions, and several specialized financial institutions including trade, investment and savings banks. The latter, although formally autonomous, were in fact tightly controlled by the ministry of finance. In such a context, the state monopolized banking activities; thus, banks mainly fulfilled a function of accountants of financial transactions dictated by the planning authorities.[2] Competition between banks hardly existed.

Between 1987 and 1992, two-tiered banking systems were gradually implemented in the CEE countries (see Table 19A1.1 in Appendix 19A1), using two different channels simultaneously. First, regulators allowed the 'rehabilitation'[3] of state banks by transferring some parts of their asset portfolios to newly created banks whose capital was, directly or indirectly, predominantly owned by the CEE states. Those banks then moved in the same environment as the specialized financial institutions already existing before transition, which were granted the right to undertake commercial banking activity as well. On the other hand, regulators implemented a rather liberal policy concerning bank chartering – at least in the early years of the transition process – in order to enhance the set-up of privately owned commercial banks (the 'new entry' approach).

Countries from Central Europe have generally given priority to the first approach – the rehabilitation of structure inherited from the previous system. Table 19A1.1 displays significant differences across countries. In contrast to Hungary and (to a lesser extent) Poland where economic reforms preceded political changes, Czechoslovakia until the Velvet Revolution in 1989, conformed to the Soviet economic model, relying on an extremely centralized management of its economy. In Poland, the break-up of the previous financial system resulted in the emerging of a significantly larger number of banks throughout the country, which could assess regional economic needs more efficiently. On the other hand, Baltic countries, like Estonia or Latvia, counted much more on new entry by privately owned commercial banks, even before their declaration of independence. In 1992, when the Estonian Central Bank officially relinquished its commercial banking activity, 42 commercial banks were sharing a particularly narrow market.

The set-up of two-tier banking systems has almost immediately resulted in a significant increase in the number of commercial banks (see Table 19.1). However, new entries by banking firms did not establish a truly competitive environment. Newly created banks remain, at least at the beginning of the transition process, of rather modest size, as their branching network and customer panel remain limited. CEE banking systems are in fact dominated by the large banks directly inherited from the previous system. Those banks, directly or indirectly owned by the states, had market shares representing 78.9 per cent of total deposits in 1993 in the Czech Republic and 87.2 per cent in Poland, while privately owned banks shared only 19.9 per cent and 12.8 per cent in those

Table 19.1   *Number of chartered commercial banks (excluding foreign banks' representative branch offices) in Central and Eastern Europe, 1990–96*

	1990	1991	1992	1993	1994	1995	1996
Croatia[a]	na	na	na	43	50	53	57
Estonia	na	na	42	21	na	16	na
Hungary[b]	23	32	30	37	37	35	na
Latvia	na	14	50	62	56	42	35
Lithuania	na	na	na	na	na	12	12
Poland	68	85	88	86	81	81	81
Slovak Rep.	na	na	15	18	19	24	24
Czech Rep.	21	33	41	47	48	45	na
Slovenia	na	26	30	32	33	31	29

Notes: na   data not available.
[a]   excluding savings and loan associations.
[b] *Source:*   Anderson and Kegels C. 1998.

Source: National Central Banks unless specified.

markets respectively (Buch 1996). Foreign banks' penetration in CEE markets remained limited in the early years of the transition process as Western firms hesitated for some time before investing significantly in those new markets.[4] Moreover, some governments, such as the Polish one, quickly restricted the entry of foreign banks, for fear of cut-throat competition for their domestic financial institutions. In 1993, there were only eight banks with foreign participation in the Czech Republic, 20 in Hungary and seven in Poland (Buch 1996).

As a result, CEE banking systems remain highly concentrated (see Table 19.2). The average value of the Herfindahl–Hirschmann index for the 1993–96 period is above 0.10 in all CEE countries, which indicates that these markets can be considered as relatively concentrated.[5] Polish, Hungarian and Latvian banking systems are the least concentrated markets in Central and Eastern Europe, and this situation might be partly explained by the way two-tiered banking systems were implemented (see Table 19A1.1); for instance, in Poland, the monobank system has been split up into nine regional banks, whereas in the Czech Republic only two banks were thus created.

A New Role for the Banking Firm

The bulk of structural reforms implemented to liberalize CEE banking systems did not result in a genuinely competitive environment, in the sense that those

Table 19.2   Concentration levels of CEE banking systems, 1993–1996

| | HERF index* | | | | | CR3** |
	1993	1994	1995	1996	Average	Average
Hungary	0.1291	0.1581	0.1505	0.1569	0.1491	54.63
Latvia	0.2126	0.1168	0.0996	0.1025	0.1206	46.82
Poland	0.1308	0.1203	0.0994	0.1425	0.1222	48.17
Croatia	0.2209	0.2082	0.1947	0.1937	0.2032	67.88
Estonia	0.5650	0.2417	0.2051	0.2601	0.2813	75.33
Lithuania	0.2900	0.2191	0.2112	0.1584	0.2139	64.02
Slovak Rep.	0.3417	0.2696	0.2619	0.2238	0.2704	81.96
Czech Rep.	0.2423	0.1854	0.1526	0.1548	0.1956	64.88
Slovenia	0.1611	0.2061	0.1885	0.1757	0.1845	63.29

Notes:
*   HERF index = Herfindahl–Hirschmann index = the sum of squared market shares of assets of each bank, calculated for each country.
**   average value of the CR3 index, calculated for the 1993–96 period with CR3 = (total assets of the three largest banks/total assets of all banks in the country) × 100.

Source: Calculations carried out by the authors with data extracted from the database Bankscope, Fitch-IBCA.

markets remained highly concentrated; however, it triggered some slow but profound changes in bank behaviour.

The expansion of financial intermediation in CEE banking systems can be partially assessed by studying deposit raising by banks. It implies some changes in agents' habits in CEE countries, where payments were mainly made by paper money and where bank cheques were not very widespread. In 1993 and in 1996, there are some relevant differences in the ratio of bank deposits of non-financial agents to GDP (see Figure 19.1). In 1996, the Slovak and the Czech Republics are similar to some Western European economies such as Greece, as bank deposits are worth 61 per cent and 64 per cent of their GDP, respectively. On the other hand, banks in Croatia, Hungary, Slovenia and Poland raise deposits which represent only one-third of GDP. Baltic banks seem to fall behind the rest of Central and Eastern Europe, as bank deposits represent less than a quarter of each country's GDP in 1996. One of the reasons for such heterogeneity in terms of deposit raising by banks may lie in the differences in the size of CEE banking networks; the Czech Republic, with 2900 inhabitants per bank branch office in 1995 (Buch 1996) has a banking network equivalent to the French one (2767 inhabitants per bank branch network), while Poland and Hungary, with 32 120 and 10 700 inhabitants per

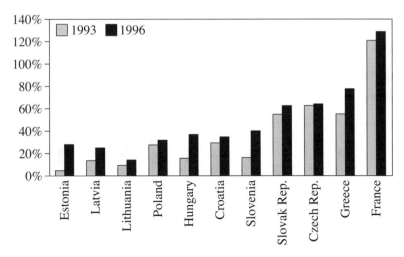

Source: Calculation carried out by the authors with data extracted from Bankscope, Fitch-IBCS and the *International Financial Statistics* of the IMF (1998). Non-financial agents are defined as non-financial firms and households.

Figure 19.1   Ratio of bank deposits of non-financial agents to GDP, 1993 and 1996 (%)

bank branch office, respectively, have significantly less dense networks; this undoubtedly slows the pace of bank development.

The development of financial intermediation can also be partially assessed by the amount of credit allocated by the banks to the whole economy. The CEE banking systems that display the larger ratios of bank deposits to GDP are logically those which allocate the most loans. Slovak and Czech banks allocate loans to non-financial agents worth 46 per cent and 56 per cent of their respective GDP in 1996 (see Figure 19.2). On the other hand, in Poland, Hungary, Croatia and Slovenia, those loans amount from 19 to 28 per cent of their respective GDP. However, credit allocated to the government has not been recorded in these figures; and credit allocated to the government represents 56 and 43 per cent of total loans allocated by banks in Hungary and Poland, respectively, but only 3 and 23 per cent in the Czech and the Slovak Republics, respectively. The extent of loans allocated to the government in Hungary and Poland significantly explain the relatively low amount of credit allocated to the private sector. Table 19.3 shows that loans allocated to households by banks still remain low, while state-owned firms receive between 15 and 22 per cent of total bank loans.

The two indicators used below, although incomplete, show that banks in the CEE countries perform their financial intermediation function unequally.

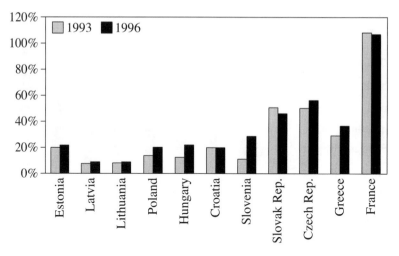

Source: See Figure 19.1.

Figure 19.2   Ratio of bank loans of non-financial agents to GDP, 1993 and 1996 (%)

Table 19.3   Distribution of domestic credit by category of agents, 1995 (%)

	Government	Firms		Households	Others	Total loans
		Private	State owned			
Czech Rep.	3	54	15	11	17	100
Slovak Rep.	22	39	22	7	10	100
Hungary	56	32.5[a]		11	0.5	100
Poland	43	31	21	5	0	100
Slovenia	21	57[a]		21	1	100

Note: Domestic credits consist of credits granted to the government and to the private sector.
[a]   Data only available for all firms, without distinguishing between private and state-owned firms.

Source: Borish et al. (1996).

However, all CEE countries had to cope with a massive 'bad loans' accumulation in bank balance sheets. In 1994, non-performing loans represented 39, 30 and 29 per cent of total bank loans in the Czech Republic, in Hungary and in Poland, respectively (Anderson and Kegels 1998). First, there has been no general forgiveness plan concerning the debt accumulated during the socialist period so the core banks have inherited bad-quality loans from the collapse of the socialist financial system and might be 'captured' by some of their borrowers. Second, some 'pocket banks' have entered banking markets although this phenomenon varies significantly across countries. But overall, banks lacked experience, especially in terms of risk management (for example, screening, and monitoring activities) and in terms of enforcing loan contracts, whereas the restructuring of firms – newly privatized or about to be so – was far from being completed. In late 1992, as the overall banking situation was giving cause for concern, CEE governments promptly intervened by implementing some write-offs and recapitalization programmes.

Write-offs and Recapitalization as a Prerequisite

Cleaning up bank balance sheets rapidly proved to be indispensable. A complete collapse of CEE banking systems, with potentially disastrous consequences on the whole economy, was then feared. Moreover, the integration of CEE economies within the EU implies a smooth, sound but competitive functioning of banking systems. Given the amount of bad loans and the low level of capital of CEE banking institutions, cleaning up their balance sheets could not be considered without massive government intervention. With the notable exception of Estonia, it has mostly consisted of writing off irretrievable loans and recapitalizing the main troubled banks as well as restricting entry into banking markets and strengthening prudential regulation and supervision. During this phase, significant differences appeared in the methods chosen by CEE governments (and the impact on the behaviour of banking firms).

The problem of bad loans inherited from the previous socialist system mainly affected state-owned banks, which developed as a result of the breaking-up of the monobanking system. The Czech, Slovak and Slovenian governments all opted for a centralized management of cleaning-up and recapitalization programmes. Non-performing loans have been transferred to an agency specially created by the authorities (see Table 19A1.1), for example, the Bank of Consolidation (KOB) in the Czech Republic and the Banking Agency for Rehabilitation (BRA) in Slovenia. On the other hand, in 1993–94, Poland and Hungary opted for a more decentralized version of such schemes; after several ineffective bail-outs in the early 1990s, the Hungarian government forced banks to confront their bad loans. In return for recapitalizing them (with long-term treasury bonds), the Polish government required banks to set up special departments charged with recovering what they could from irretrievable loans. Polish banks helped troubled borrowers to restructure themselves, but were not forced to take equity stakes in them.

The recapitalisation process of large banks was generally followed by privatization programmes,[6] which appear to be the cornerstone of the current phase of the transition process. As authorities have rapidly opted for limited new entry conditions for foreigners, foreign penetration is currently closely linked to the privatization process.

Simultaneously, the cleaning-up of CEE banking sectors has required a reduction in banking overcapacity which appeared in the first phase of the transition process. Authorities then let some banks fail. In Central Europe, liquidations generally affected small or medium-sized institutions, whereas in Estonia in 1992–93, or in Latvia in 1995, banking crises ended with the disappearance of a substantial number of important actors.[7] Regulatory entry conditions have been strengthened since then.

Between 1992 and 1995 the number of commercial banks in most CEE countries declined (see Table 19.1). Thus, the concentration levels in CEE banking markets, which were already high according to international standards, have increased while a consolidation process (initiated by banking firms themselves, as in the Baltic states at the present moment, or by governments in order to create 'domestic champions' to be able to compete with Western banks) is in progress. For instance in 1996, in Poland, a bank holding was created, on the government's initiative, by merging the group Pekao SA and three regional banks.

So CEE banking systems are still highly concentrated. Not so long ago, the privatization process did not result in the weakening of the role of the state and its influence in the banking sector. The massive flow of foreign investments since 1995–96 has allowed foreign banks to appear, no longer as institutions looking for specific niches, but as direct competitors of domestic institutions.[8] Foreign shareholding in banking sector capital is larger than 20 per cent in Poland and in the Czech Republic (Bednarova and Szymkiewicz 1998). One could easily conclude that because those markets are highly concentrated,[9] they are not efficient. However, after the banking crises all CEE countries have gone through, banking authorities have given first priority to the implementation of a stable banking system.

In such a context, it seems relevant to study the relationship between market structure, efficiency and performance in CEE banking markets. Empirical analyses carried out for the United States and Western European banking markets will serve us as prime references.

ANALYSING AND INVESTIGATING THE RELATIONSHIP BETWEEN MARKET STRUCTURE AND PERFORMANCE IN BANKING

By trying to isolate the determinants of firms' profitability, some US inter-industry empirical analyses in the 1940s and 1950s[10] highlighted a positive relationship between the level of concentration of an industry and the performance of incumbent firms; this link is particularly significant in sectors with high entry barriers. Economists then tried to interpret this result and to analyse its potential normative consequences, in particular in terms of competition policy.

The Structuralist Approach: the Structure–Conduct–Performance (SCP) Hypothesis

This model[11] developed by industrial organization theory, tries to explain the impact of the structure of a market on incumbent firms' strategies and its final impact on their performance, while borrowing some of the results of oligopoly theory. Differences between firms' performance are only transitory and it is the market, through its entry conditions and its degree of concentration, which is the main focus of this approach. The SCP paradigm indeed stipulates that, other things (for example, management) being equal, firms in two different sectors that share a similar market structure should have a similar performance.

High concentration in a market allows incumbent firms to adopt non-competitive behaviour. Firms in the same market may collude and may set prices less favourable to consumers (thus earning monopoly rents)than prices set when there is perfect competition; while in a market characterized by no or small entry barriers[12] (and exit barriers), the mere threat of entry restrains the ability of incumbent firms to maintain oligopolistic behaviour. For instance, the theory of contestable markets developed in the 1980s[13] denies, under very restrictive conditions, that there is any link between concentration and market power: when there are no barriers to entry and exit in a market, firms in an olipolistic position – and in an extreme case, one monopoly firm – cannot develop any market power and their performance should be similar to the performance obtained in a perfectly competitive market.

The Causal Link between Market Structure and Performance is Challenged

For the advocates of the efficient structure (ES) hypothesis, such as Demsetz (1973),[14] the SCP model is fundamentally incorrect because the essential variable determining a firm's profitability is its efficiency. This argument reverses the explanatory pattern of the traditional model and endogenizes the market structure of an industry. As some differences in firms' efficiency persist, the most efficient firms (and only those firms, because they have lower costs) can expand at the expense of other firms. In the end, the market in which they operate should be more concentrated. So it is between a firm's profitability and its market share, and not between a firm's profitability and the level of concentration of the market in which it operates, where there is a positive correlation. Consequently, the concentration phenomenon emerges not from collusive behaviour, but from the mere competitive process between firms. As Berger et al. (1999, p. 157) noted, 'efficiency gains are made by changing input or output quantities in ways to reduce costs, increase revenues, and/or reduce risks to increase value for a given set of prices. This is in contrast to market power gains ... in which value is created by institutions changing prices to their advantage'.[15]

What Is the Relationship between Market Structure and Performance in Banking?

In the early 1960s, after the US regulators decided that antitrust laws should be applied to the banking industry, economists started to emphasize the importance of a positive link between the level of concentration of a (local) market and bank performance in terms of profits or prices. The US banking industry then perfectly lent itself to such analyses: although it consisted of more than 12 thousand banking entities, it was, however, highly concentrated on a local basis. The various surveys recounting most SCP studies on banking do not find a relationship as significant as in inter-industrial studies. For Rhoades (1982), as for Gilbert (1984) (even if the latter raises some important objections[16]), there is a positive relationship between concentration and performance, while Osborne and Wendell (1983), emphasizing methodological discrepancies, refuse to accept that such a link exists in the US banking industry.

Discriminating Between the Two Potential Explanations of a Positive Link Between Concentration and Performance

In the early 1980s, new stakes in terms of regulation appeared: was concentration in banking markets to be promoted? This kind of analysis, which tried to discriminate between both explanations (SCP hypothesis versus ES hypothesis) of a positive link between market structure and performance in banking, enjoyed a renewal of interest, as their competitive policy implications are opposite. The first studies trying to discriminate between both explanations included a new explanatory variable in the tested regressions: the market share of each banking firm.[17] In most cases (for instance, See Smirlock 1985 or Evanoff and Fortier 1988), the introduction of such a new variable significantly diminishes the impact of concentration on bank profitability. But one should emphasize a potential misinterpretation: this result supports the ES hypothesis if one assumes – and this is questionable – that a large firm's market share reflects only its relative efficiency (the more efficient a bank gets, the higher its market share is), and not its relative market power.[18]

One possible solution to this dilemma consists in directly testing the relationship between performance and efficiency, as the most recent studies do. For instance, Berger (1995) introduces two efficiency measures (accounting for X-efficiency[19] and scale efficiency of each banking firm) in the estimated equation. Moreover, some of those recent studies test the basic premise of the ES hypothesis: does the efficiency of a bank have an impact on the structure of the market in which this institution operates? Actually, if one wants to validate the ES hypothesis, firm efficiency should have a positive influence on market concentration and/or on its market share. The previous empirical results are not modified fundamentally once direct measures of firm efficiency are introduced in the tested equations. However, those results suggest that the market share of a firm is not an adequate proxy for its efficiency (as in Smirlock 1985), but rather a proxy for its relative market power. Above all, it seems that neither the SCP hypothesis, nor the ES hypothesis, could significantly explain bank profitability in the USA.

Other studies have recently attempted to transpose this kind of analysis to European banking (see, for instance, Molyneux and Thornton 1992; Molyneux and Forbes 1995; Goldberg and Rai 1996), each national banking market becoming the reference level. Even if there are only a few of them, and they use different countries' samples, it seems that their results validate the anticompetitive behaviour hypothesis.[20]

From the prospect of a potential integration of some CEE countries into the European Union, trying to assess to what extent the performance of CEE banks is explained by their market structure and/or their efficiency seems to be a relevant task. So far, we believe that no empirical study of this kind has been performed for CEE banking markets; we shall address this issue in the next section, first relying on the methodology developed by Weiss (1974, see note 17), and then applying the methodology used by Berger (1995).

EMPIRICAL ANALYSIS OF THE RELATIONSHIP BETWEEN MARKET STRUCTURE, EFFICIENCY AND PERFORMANCE IN CEE BANKING INDUSTRIES

Data Description and Methodology

We carried out an empirical analysis for eight CEE countries[21] (Croatia, Estonia, Latvia, Lithuania, Poland, the Czech and the Slovak Republics and Slovenia) using pooling data for the 1992–96 period. As in Molyneux and Forbes (1995), we consider each country as one banking market. Our sample contains 146 commercial banks in 1996, 154 in 1995, 134 in 1994, 96 in 1993 and 56 in 1992 (for a detailed review of the number of banks for each country,

Table 19.4   Average return on assets (ROA), 1992–1996 (%)

	All banks	State-owned banks	Foreign banks	Private domestic banks
Croatia	–0.12	–1.61	na	–0.13
Estonia	0.08	–2.26	na	4.40
Latvia	1.77	–3.33	6.93	1.35
Lithuania	–1.26	–1.58	na	0.67
Poland	1.30	2.52	3.66	2.80
Czech Rep.	0.34	0.99	1.18	–1.54
Slovakia	1.44	0.61	2.20	0.64
Slovenia	2.77	1.12	1.22	1.75

Source: Bankscope Fitch–IBCA.

see Table 19A1.2 in Appendix 19A1). Even if there are institutional differences in the definition of a commercial bank between countries, we consider that this category is sufficiently homogeneous. We use BankScope, the database produced by the rating agency International Bank Credit Analysis Ltd (Fitch–IBCA), which contains yearly data extracted from bank balance sheets and income revenue statements.

The performance of banks in this study is measured by their return on assets (ROA). In Table 19.4, significant differences in ROA can be observed on a national average basis, as well as in terms of different bank categories (private-owned, state-owned and foreign banks). On average, for the 1992–96 period, banks in Slovenia, in Latvia and in Poland outperform other banks in our sample. In all CEE countries, foreign banks are the most profitable while banks whose capital is predominantly owned by the state are the least profitable. Consequently, we introduce dummy variables in our tests to account for these characteristics.

First, in order to assess the relationship between banking market structure and performance, we estimate the following equation:

$$\Pi_{ijt} = a_0 + a_1(HERF_{jt}) + a_2(MS_{ijt}) + a_3(BQETAT_{ijt}) \\ + a_4(BQETRG_{ijt}) + a_5(FPTA_{ijt}) + a_6(\text{Log}(TA)_{ijt}) \quad (19.1)$$

where the dependent variable is:

Π_{ijt} = net income divided by total assets of bank i (ROA) operating in market j during the year t,

and the explanatory variables are:

$HERF_{jt}$ = concentration of market j measured by the Herfindhal–Hirschmann index (on assets).

$BQETAT_{ijt}$ = dummy variable which equals 1 when banks are predominantly state owned, otherwise 0 (see Table 19A1.2).

$BQETRG_{ijt}$ = dummy variable which equals 1 when banks' capital is predominantly foreign, otherwise 0 (see Table 19A1.2).

MS_{ijt} = market share in terms of assets (%) of bank i operating in market j.

$FPTA_{ijt}$ = capital ratio (%) of bank i operating in market j (capital divided by total assets).

$Log(TA)_{ijt}$ = logarithm of total of assets of bank i in market j.

The independent variables included in equation 19.1 are similar to those used by Smirlock (1985), Molyneux and Thornton (1992) and Molyneux and Forbes (1995) in their studies of the link between structure and performance in banking. As a measurement of the concentration of each banking market, we use the Herfindahl–Hirschmann[22] index (*HERF*) on assets, and we first consider that the market share of each bank (*MS*) in terms of assets is a proxy for each bank's efficiency: according to Smirlock (1985), the more efficient a firm gets, the larger is its market share. The traditional SCP hypothesis is validated if $a_1 > 0$ and $a_2 = 0$, while the ES hypothesis is validated when $a_2 > 0$ and $a_1 = 0$. The variables *BQETAT* and *BQETRG* allow us to check whether state-owned banks are less profitable ($a_3 < 0$) and foreign banks more profitable ($a_4 > 0$), as suggested by the results in Table 19.4. The control variables, the capital ratio and the logarithm of total assets, are included to account for the fact that risk strategy and size differ from bank to bank. The sign of the coefficient of Log(*TA*) should be positive if banks enjoy a size and a diversification effect. Generally, there is a negative relationship between banks' profitability and capital ratio (*FPTA*).

This methodology, which includes the market share in the tests in order to account for each bank's relative efficiency, has been criticized. As Shepherd (1982) emphasized, a bank's market share may reflect its relative market power, especially if it offers well-differentiated products and can use its influence to set its prices. For instance, Berger (1995) and Goldberg and Rai (1996), by directly including efficiency measures as well as market structure measures (concentration of each market *and* market share of each bank in each market), have attempted to assess more precisely the relationship between market power, efficiency and profitability in banking. Using the methodology developed by Berger (1995), we have completed our empirical study by estimating another equation which includes direct measures of efficiency.

In order to test the competing SCP and ES hypotheses, Berger (1995) develops a series of tests to incorporate efficiency directly into the model. Four hypotheses are actually tested:

- Two so-called 'market-power' (MP) hypotheses:
  1. the traditional SCP hypothesis; and
  2. the relative-market-power (RMP) hypothesis which stipulates that only firms with large market shares and selling well-differentiated products and services may be able to exercise market power while pricing these products and services and thus, earn supernormal profits.

  The difference between SCP and RMP is that the latter need not occur in concentrated markets.

- Two explanations in terms of efficiency (ES):
  1. the X-efficiency version of the efficient-structure hypothesis (ESX), according to which banks which enjoy superior management or production technologies incur lower costs and, as a result, earn higher profits. Those firms should thus obtain large market shares that may result in high concentration levels; and
  2. the scale-efficiency version of the ES hypothesis (ESS), which states that banks have similar production and management technology but operate at different levels of economies of scale. Those which operate at optimal scale will have the lowest unit costs and the highest unit profits. Those firms are also assumed to have a large market share, a situation that may lead to high levels of market concentration.

According to the two ES hypotheses, the positive relationship between market structure and performance is not of direct origin but rather 'spurious' (according to Demsetz 1973, see note 14), as firm efficiency simultaneously determines profits and market structure.

The equation tested by Berger (1995) to determine which one of the four hypotheses is valid is:

$$\Pi_{ijt} = a_0 + a_1(HERF_{jt}) + a_2(MS_{ijt}) + a_3(XEFF_{ijt}) \\ + a_4(Log(TA)_{ijt}) + a_7(FPTA_{ijt}) \tag{19.2}$$

where:

$XEFF_{ijt}$ = a measure of X-efficiency, reflecting the ability of bank i (located in market j) to produce a given bundle of output at minimum cost through superior management or technology.

$Log(TA)_{ijt}$ = a measure of scale efficiency, reflecting the ability of banks to produce at optimal scale, given similar management and production technology.

If either of the MP hypotheses holds true (SCP or RMP), then the expected signs of the coefficient are $HERF > 0$ if the SCP holds, or $MS > 0$ if the RMP holds. On the other hand, if the efficient-structure hypothesis is verified, the expected signs of the coefficients are as follows: $XEFF > 0$, $\text{Log}(TA) > 0$, $HERF = 0$ and $MS = 0$. Moreover, a necessary condition for the efficient-structure hypothesis to hold is that efficiency affects market structure. The following two equations are also tested:

$$HERF_{jt} = b_0 + b_1(XEFF_{ijt}) + b_2(\text{Log}(TA)_{ijt}) + b_5(FPTA_{ijt}) \quad (19.3)$$

$$MS_{ijt} = c_0 + c_1(XEFF_{ijt}) + c_2(\text{Log}(TA)_{ijt}) + c_5(FPTA_{ijt}) \quad (19.4)$$

The efficient-structure hypothesis is strictly valid if it can be established that more efficient banks are more profitable and have larger market shares. Thus, the coefficients of $XEFF$ and $\text{Log}(TA)$ should be positive in equations (19.3) and (19.4).

The data are pooled for the years 1992 to 1996 and equations (19.1)–(19.4) are estimated for the whole sample.

Empirical Results

Tables 19.5 and 19.6 outline the empirical results for equations (19.1) and (19.2), using the technique of ordinary least squares and White's methodology to correct t-statistics for heteroscedasticity.

The empirical results given by the estimate of equation (19.1) support the validity of the traditional SCP hypothesis: the coefficient of the *HERF* variable is significantly positive while the coefficient of the *ms* variable is not significantly different from zero. These results are consistent with those in the study carried out by Molyneux and Forbes (1995) on 18 European countries for the 1986–89 period. It is worth noticing that the coefficient of the variable measuring the market concentration has a relative high value (0.1925), if it is compared with the values of coefficients in Molyneux and Forbes (on average, it equals 0.0004). It seems that concentration of banking markets in CEE countries is a relevant determinant of bank profitability.

Table 19.5   Estimate of equation (19.1) for all banks in the sample,
*   1992–1996*

Equation (observ.)	Constant	HERF	MS	FPTA	LOG(TA)	BQETAT	BQETRG	R^2
(19.1)	−24.5601**	0.1925**	−0.0453	0.1680**	1.6120**	−2.7947**	0.5752**	0.106
(577)	(−7.040)	(3.811)	(−0.966)	(5.803)	(6.165)	(−2.135)	(1.986)	

Note: (.) t-statistic in brackets, corrected for heteroscedasticity by White's methodology.
** coefficients are significant at 5% level.

Table 19.6   Estimate of equation (19.2) for all banks in the sample,
1992–1996

Equation (observ.)	Constant	HERF	MS	XEFF	LOG(TA)	FPTA	R^2
(19.2)	−12.0382**	0.1421*	−0.0405	5.1918**	0.5042**	0.1324**	0.103
(446)	(−2.6966)	(1.9007)	(−1.1287)	(2.1886)	(2.0178)	(2.7315)	

Note: (.) t-statistic in brackets, corrected for heteroscedasticity by White's methodology; ** coefficients are significant at 5% level; * coefficients are significant at 10%.

In equation (19.2), we have included a direct measure of X-efficiency,[23] and keep the control variable Log(*TA*) to account for size effect. This methodology allows us to consider the market share variable *MS* as a measure of individual market power and not as a measure of each bank's efficiency.

The estimate of equation (19.2) confirms the validation of the SCP hypothesis as in equation (19.1), though in a weaker manner – as the *HERF* coefficient is significant and positive only at the 10 per cent level. Bank mergers and acquisitions in CEE countries should thus be closely monitored by banking regulators and allowed only if they can be shown to be in the public interest (as mergers among smaller banks can actually enhance competition). But equation (19.2) more strongly emphasizes the influence of each bank's efficiency on its profitability. This result is rather different from those of similar studies implemented for Western European banking markets, but is consistent with some results in the study by Goldberg and Rai (1996) (using a sample of large banks across 11 European countries over the 1988–91 period) which validates the X-efficiency hypothesis in some markets. Although some collusive behaviour may exist in CEE banking markets, it seems that each bank's profitability is more likely to be driven by its efficiency. However, the estimates of equations (19.3) and (19.4) (not included in this chapter) highlight that the second condition necessary to fully validate the efficient-structure hypothesis does not hold here: market structure variables ($HERF_j$ and MS_{ij}) are not positively influenced by efficiency measures.

Another important result highlighted by the estimate of equation (19.1) – but not validated by equation (19.2) – is the significantly negative coefficient of the *BQETAT* variable, which reflects the fact that banks with predominantly state-owned capital are less profitable than the other banks in the sample. This result is not consistent with those found by Molyneux and Thornton (1992) and Molyneux and Forbes (1995) in which state-owned Western European banks are, on the contrary, more profitable than the others. This finding may be explained by the fact that since state-owned banks in CEE countries have inherited the doubtful and bad loans left by the socialist system, they may be partly captured by some of their main customers – they may be locked into relationships with (previously or still) state-owned enterprises; in addition, their main shareholder has been much slower in implementing corporate governance principles. In the context of a forthcoming integration of CEE countries within the EU, it is in CEE governments' interest to accelerate the path of the privatization process. This study also emphasizes the fact that banks whose capital is predominantly held by foreigners are more profitable than other banks. Policy aiming at limiting foreign stakeholding in domestic banks, as implemented after the beginning of the transition process, is not desirable in CEE countries, from a stability as well as a competition point of view.

With regard to the *FPTA* explanatory variable, an increase in a bank's capital ratio has a positive impact on its profitability in regressions (19.1) and (19.2). This result is not consistent with Molyneux and Forbe's (1995) study in which there is a negative relationship between these two variables in Western European banking. Bail-out and write-off programmes implemented by CEE governments as early as 1992 may partly explain the positive link between capital ratio and return on assets.

The significantly positive coefficient of the Log(*TA*) variable in equations (19.1) and (19.2) highlights that CEE banks enjoy size effects.

To sum up our findings,[24] first we would like to emphasize that the SCP hypothesis is validated in CEE banking markets. This result does not conflict with the observation that individual efficiency plays a significant role in determining profitability levels. But our results do not allow us to completely validate the ES hypothesis, as we do not find that market structure variables ($HERF_j$ and MS_{ij}) are positively influenced by our efficiency measure.[25] Finally, we find that state-owned banks and foreign-owned banks are at the two extreme ends of the profitability spectrum.

As several studies[26] have emphasized, the relationship between market concentration and performance in banking might be non-linear. So we decided to split our sample into two subgroups: less concentrated (Latvia and Poland) and more concentrated (Croatia, Estonia, Lithuania, Slovakia, Slovenia and the Czech Republic) banking markets.[27] Our results are displayed in Tables 19.7 and 19.8.

The results emphasized in equation (19.2) are still valid, but only in CEE countries' most concentrated banking markets, as the coefficients of both variables *HERF* and *XEFF* are positive and significant. An additional increase in the level of concentration of those markets would increase monopoly rents. Potential mergers in already highly concentrated banking markets should be carefully regulated, as we have emphasized.

Table 19.7   Analysis of the impact of concentration levels on bank performance, 1992–1996 (equation (19.1), differentiating between concentration levels)

Equation (observ.)	Constant	*HERF*	*MS*	*FPTA*	LOG(*TA*)	*BQETAT*	*BQETRG*	R^2
(19.1) LC	–38.7978**	0.3495	–0.0033	0.1782**	2.7019**	–4.3315	1.4078	0.146
(202)	(–5.104)	(1.247)	(–0.021)	(2.674)	(5.177)	(–1.457)	(0.733)	
(19.1) HC	–17.440**	0.2728**	–0.0612	0.1484**	0.8746**	–1.6404	0.8400**	0.151
(375)	(–2.739)	(3.153)	(–1.232)	(3.214)	(2.216)	(–1.568)	(9.690)	

Notes
(.)   t-statistic in brackets, corrected for heteroscedasticity by White's methodology
**   coefficients are significant at 5% level.
LC   least concentrated banking markets (Latvia and Poland).
HC   highly concentrated banking makets (Croatia, Estonia, Lithuania, Slovakia, Slovenia and the Czech Republic).

Table 19.8   Analysis of the impact of concentration levels on bank performance, 1992–1996 (equation (19.2), differentiating between concentration levels)

Equation (observ.)	Constant	*HERF*	*MS*	*XEFF*	LOG(*TA*)	*FPTA*	R^2
(19.2) LC	–5.6143*	0.0316	–0.0046	–0.9776	0.5474**	0.0629**	0.103
(160)	(–1.7091)	(0.4384)	(–0.1377)	(0.5984)	(2.8394)	(2.8128)	
(19.2) HC	–21.7034**	0.3358**	–0.0537	10.3284**	0.6239**	0.1562**	0.18
(286)	(–2.8228)	(3.1066)	(–1.0981)	(2.5801)	(1.5422)	(2.6398)	

Notes
(.)   t-statistic in brackets, corrected for heteroscedasticity by White's methodology.
**   coefficients are significant at 5% level.
*   coefficients are significant at 10% level.
LC   least concentrated banking markets (Latvia and Poland).
HC   highly concentrated banking makets (Croatia, Estonia, Lithuania, Slovakia, Slovenia and the Czech Republic).

CONCLUSION

Implementing simultaneously efficient and stable banking systems is a prerequisite for transition economies to switch successfully to market economies and for them to join the European Union. CEE countries have evolved from a monobanking system towards a system in which the banking firm is considered to be making a genuine contribution to the financial intermediation process. However, banking systems are still dominated by the (previously or still state-owned) banks that emerged from the monobanking system. Since they remain highly concentrated, some further measures of competitive patterns, such as measures of contestability of banking markets, are thus necessary to comprehend the true nature of banking competition in CEE countries.

Our empirical work on eight transition economies between 1992 and 1996 shows that there is a positive relationship between the market power of banks and their performance (SCP hypothesis with or without direct measures of X-efficiency). It also highlights, in contrast to most other studies carried out on Western European banking markets, that efficiency is a prominent determinant of CEE banks' profitability and that state-owned banks are the least profitable institutions while foreign banks, on the contrary, earn the highest return on equity. The privatization process in Central and Eastern Europe should be reinforced in order to overcome the domination of state-owned banks and it would not be desirable to set up regulatory policies aimed at limiting the presence of foreign banks there. Besides, it would be rather difficult to implement the various privatization programmes without foreign capital. Finally, bank mergers should be closely monitored, particularly those encouraged by authorities in order to build institutions sufficiently large to compete with Western European banks. The admission of CEE economies into the European Union, planned not before 2002 for some of them, could trigger the completion of a genuinely competitive banking system.

NOTES

1. In this chapter, Central and Eastern European (CEE) countries refers to the Visegrad countries (Hungary, Poland, the Czech and Slovak Republics), Slovenia, Croatia and the three Baltic states (Estonia, Latvia and Lithuania) but does not include Romania and Bulgaria, or the other countries from the former USSR.
2. The funds allocated to state-owned firms were distributed with little regard to the value of the return on investment projects or the creditworthiness of borrowers: those credits, thus, were deemed equivalent to indirect subsidies. See, for instance, J. Kornai (1990), *The Road to a Free Economy. Shifting from a Socialist Economy: The Example of Hungary*, New York: W.W. Norton & Company.
3. According to the terminology developed by Claessens (1996).
4. The strong recession that ensued from the transition in all CEE countries, but also specific problems such as those linked to the Polish debt problem for instance, first encouraged Western banks to adopt cautious behaviour, even if some limited technical assistance and training agreements were signed between Western and CEE firms. The twinning agreements signed by some Western banks and the Polish regional banks, under the aegis of the Polish government, were exceptional at the beginning of the transition process.
5. The US Department of Justice, in charge of antitrust matters, considers a market with a Herfindahl–Hirschmann index (HHI) smaller than 0.10 as not concentrated, a market with an HHI between 0.10 and 0.18 as moderately concentrated, and a market with an HHI bigger than 0.18 as highly concentrated.

6. The differences in privatization methods chosen by governments seem to have had a significant impact on the incentive schemes of firms. For instance, the large – but partial-scope privatization (with vouchers) of main Czech firms from 1993 onwards did not necessarily result in genuine structural reforms. One wonders if, apart from truly strategic investors, it has not delayed the implementation of an efficient microeconomic governance.

7. For example, the liquidation of the Estonian Tartu Commercial Bank (1993) and of the larger Latvian bank, Baltija Banka (1995).

8. See the strategy of the retail bank Citibank in Hungary, for instance.

9. In order to complete the analysis of the competitive pattern in CEE banking markets, contestability measures are needed here.

10. For instance, see J. Bain (1951), 'Relation of profit rate to industry concentration: American manufacturing 1936–40', *Quarterly Journal of Economics*, **65**, August, 293–324.

11. See F.M. Scherer and D. Ross (1990), *Industrial Market Structure and Economic Performance*, Boston, MA: Houghton Mifflin.

12. There is no consensus on how to define and measure the entry barriers in a market. Several definitions exist, depending on whether one adopts a normative point of view, like Bain (1956), or a comparative approach like Stigler (1968) and in the theory of contestable markets.

13. See W.J. Baumol, J. Panzar and R. Willig (1988), *Contestable Markets and the Theory of Industry Structure*, revised edn, New York: Harcourt Brace Jovanovich.

14. H. Demsetz (1973), 'Industry structure, market rivalry and public policy', *Journal of Law and Economics*, **16**, April, 1–9.

15. A. Berger, R. Demsetz and P. Strahan (1999), 'The consolidation of the financial services industry: causes, consequences and implications for the future', *Journal of Banking and Finance*, **23**, 135–94.

16. Gilbert (1984) bases his analysis on the most rigorous studies, in particular those carried out on surveys detailing the prices of products set by each bank (even if this approach neglects the fact that the banking firm is a multiproduct firm in which cross-subsidies cannot always be neglected).

17. In accordance with the methodology developed by I.W. Weiss (1974), 'The concentration–profits relationship and antitrust' in W. Goldschmid, M. Mann and J. Weston (eds), *Industrial Concentration: The New Learning*, Boston, MA: Little Brown & Co., pp. 184–233.

18. Some firms, because they benefit from reputation rents, or from a particularly dense network, for example, may develop higher-quality products, so they can set up higher prices and then, finally, earn higher profits. See D. Ravenscraft (1983), 'Structure–profit relationship at the line of business and industry level', *Review of Economics and Statistics*, **55**, February, 22–32, or W.G. Shepherd (1986), 'Tobin's q and the structure–performance relationship: comment', *American Economic Review*, **76**, December, 1205–10, or more recently, Berger (1995) for the product differentiation hypothesis or relative market power (RMP) hypothesis.

19. See the next section for a definition of X-efficiency and scale efficiency.

20. The result is valid even if the market share of each bank is introduced in the tested equation in Molyneux and Forbes (1995). This result is invalidated in the study by Goldberg and Rai (1996).

21. Hungary has been excluded from the analysis because some data were not available.

22. The Herfindhal–Hirschmann index (*HERF*) on assets, calculated for each country, is defined as the sum of squared market shares of assets of each bank.

23. The methodology used to calculate the values of *XEFF* is outlined in Appendix 19A2.

24. Similar results have been found using Herfindahl–Hirschmann indices and market shares calculated on a deposits basis. The explanatory power of our regressions is rather weak (R^2 equalling 0.106 and 0.082, respectively) but is similar to the studies we refer to (on average, R^2 is about 10 per cent, as in Smirlock (1985), Molyneux and Forbes (1995), and Berger (1995).

25. Results are not shown here.

26. See Heggestad (1977), Jackson (1992), Berger and Hannan (1989), Goldberg and Rai (1996), for instance.
27. The banking markets considered as highly concentrated (HC) are those with a Herfindahl–Hirschmann index bigger than 0.18. See the second section, above, for more details.

BIBLIOGRAPHY

Anderson, R. and C. Kegels (1998), *Transition Banking*, Oxford: Clarendon Press.
Bain J. (1956), *Barriers to New Competition*, Cambridge: Cambridge University Press.
Bednarova E. and K. Szymkiewicz (1998), 'L'évolution des systèmes bancaires polonais et tchèque: une approche comparative' (The evolution of the Polish and Czech banking systems: a comparative approach), Working Paper, 15th International Conference of Banking and Monetary Economics, Université de Toulouse I, June.
Berger, A. (1995), 'The profit–structure relationship in banking – tests of market power and efficient-structure hypotheses', *Journal of Money, Credit and Banking*, **27**(2), May, 404–31.
Berger, A. and T. Hannan (1989), 'The price–concentration relationship in banking', *Review of Economics and Statistics*, **71**, May, 291–9.
Bonin, J., M. Kalmal, S. Istvan and P. Wachtel (1998), *Banking in Transition Economies*, Cheltenham, UK and Northampton, MA, USA: Edward Elgar.
Borish, M.S., W. Ding and M. Noël (1996), 'On the road to EU accession: financial sector development in Central Europe', Discussion Paper no. 345, Washington DC: World Bank.
Buch, C. (1996), Creating efficient banking systems, Tübingen: JCB Mohr.
Claessens, S. (1996), 'Banking reform in transition-countries', World Development Report, Washington DC.
Dietsch, Michel (1992), 'Coûts et concurrence dans l'industrie bancaire' (Cost and competition in the banking system), Report for the Conseil National du Crédit et l'Association Française des Banques, March.
Evanoff, D. and D. Fortier (1988), 'Reevaluation of the structure–conduct–performance paradigm in banking', *Journal of Financial Services*, **1**(3), June, 277–94.
Gilbert, R.A. (1984), 'Bank market structure and competition', *Journal of Money, Credit and Banking*, **16**(4), November, 617–45.
Goldberg, L. and A. Rai (1996), 'The structure–performance relationship for European banking', *Journal of Banking and Finance*, **20**, 745–71.
Gondat-Larralde, C. and A. Tarazi (1998), 'Entry conditions, structure and performance in banking, lessons from Western experience and an empirical analysis of Central and Eastern Europe', in A. Mullineux and C. Green (eds), *Economic Performance and Financial Sector Reform in Central and Eastern Europe*, Cheltenham, UK and Northampton, MA, USA: Edward Elgar, pp. 136–61.
Heggestad, A. (1977), 'Market structure, risk and profitability in commercial banking', *Journal of Banking and Finance*, **32**(4), 1207–16.
Jackson, W.E. (1992), 'The price–concentration relationship in banking: a comment', *Review of Economics and Statistics*, **2**, May, 373–9.
Molyneux, P., Y. Altunbas and E. Gardener (1996), *Efficiency in European Banking*, New York: John Wiley & Sons.
Molyneux, P. and W. Forbes (1995), 'Market structure and performance in European banking', *Applied Economics*, **27**, 155–9.

Molyneux, P. and J. Thornton (1992), 'Determinants of European bank profitability', *Journal of Banking and Finance*, **16**, 1173–8.

Osborne, D. and J. Wendell (1983), 'Research in structure, conduct and performance in banking 1964–79', Research Paper 83–003, College of Business Administration, Oklahoma State University, July.

Rhoades, S. (1982), 'Structure–performance studies in banking: an updated summary and evaluation', Staff Study no. 119, Board of Governors, Federal Reserve System, Washington, DC.

Sgard, J. (1996), 'Credit analysis and the role of banks during transition: a five-country comparison', CEPII Working Paper no. 96–08, Paris: CEPII.

Shepherd, W.G. (1982), 'Economies of scale and monopoly profits', in J. Craven (ed.), *Industrial Organization, Antitrust and Public Policy*, Dordrecht: Kluwer Nijhoff, pp. 79–95.

Smirlock, M. (1985), 'Evidence on the (non) relationship between concentration and profitability in banking', *Journal of Money, Credit and Banking*, **17**(1), February, 69–83.

Stigler, G.J. (1968), *The Organization of Industry*, Homewood, IL: Richard Irwin.

Tirole, J. (1988), *The Theory of Industrial Organization*, Cambridge, MA: MIT.

APPENDIX 19A1

Table 19A1.1   The set-up of two-tiered banking systems in CEE countries

Set up of a two-tiered banking system (year)	Banking system created directly from the previous monobanking system	Period of enhanced liberalization of entry conditions	Recapitalization programmes
Hungary (1987)	3 banks created from the previous state bank + 2 specialized banks already in business + several joint ventures initiated between the Hungarian National Bank and foreign banks	1989–92	Decentralized implementation in 1993–94
Poland (1989)	9 regional banks created from the previous state bank + 6 specialized banks	1989–91 (1992–94: restrictions concerning foreign banks)	Decentralized implementation in 1993
Czechoslovakia, then Czech Rep. since 1993 (1990)	3 banks (including one in Slovakia) created from the previous state bank + 3 specialized banks already in business	1990–93 (temporary moratorium in 1994)	Centralized implementation by the KOB* in several failures in 1995–96
Estonia (1992)	Branch offices of the 4 Soviet specialized banks + Bank of Estonia created as early as 1990	1988–92 (temporary moratorium in 1993)	Banking crises in 1992 and in 1994

Note: *KOB: Konsolidacni Banka, the Consolidation Bank of the banking sector.

Financial sector development

Table 19A1.2   Number of commercial, state-owned and foreign banks in the sample, by country

	1992	1993	1994	1995	1996	State-owned banks in 1996*	Foreign banks in 1996**
Poland	16	24	30	35	32	4	12
Latvia	4	9	16	20	19	2	3
Croatia	13	20	28	29	26	2	0
Estonia	0	4	7	9	8	1	0
Lithuania	1	7	8	7	10	3	0
Slovak Rep.	5	6	10	13	13	2	2
Slovenia	6	9	13	16	15	2	4
Czech Rep.	11	17	22	25	23	6	9
Total	56	96	134	154	146	22	30

Note
*   State-owned banks are banks whose capital is predominantly held by the State.
**   Foreign banks are banks whose capital is predominantly held by foreigners.

Source: Bankscope Fitch–BCA.

APPENDIX 19A2.   X-EFFICIENCY MEASURES

In this study we use a version of the 'distribution-free' method (DFA) (see Berger 1995) to estimate individual X-efficiency. The DFA specifies a functional form for the frontier and separates the specific distributions for the inefficiencies and random errors. This method assumes that X-efficiency differences across banks should persist over time, while random errors should be ephemeral and average out over time.

The cost equations for each of five periods of a panel data set are specified as:

$$\ln TC = \alpha_0 + \sum_{i=1}^{3} \alpha_i \ln(y_i) + \sum_{j=1}^{3} \beta_j \ln(p_j) + \frac{1}{2} \sum_{i=1}^{3} \sum_{k=1}^{3} \alpha_{ik} \ln(y_i)\ln(y_k)$$

$$+ \frac{1}{2} \sum_{j=1}^{3} \sum_{h=1}^{3} \beta_{jh} \ln(p_j)\ln(p_h) + \sum_{i=1}^{3} \sum_{j=1}^{3} {}_{ij}\ln(y_i)\ln(p_j) + \ln(x) + \ln(\varpi)$$

$$\tag{19A2.1}$$

where *TC* represents the total operating and interest costs of each bank n, y_1 total loans, y_2 deposits, y_3 securities and equity investment, p_1 is the price of labour defined as staff expenses divided by total assets, p_2 is the price of physical capital defined as other non-interest expenses divided by total assets and p_3 is the price of financial capital defined as interest paid divided by resources. The term $\ln(x)$ is the systematic error component which appears as X-inefficiency factor, and $\ln(\varpi)$ is a random error term. (For specific restrictions imposed on the parameters of the equation, see Molyneux et al. 1996 or Dietsch 1992.)

For each bank and time period, an average of the residual from (19A2.1) for that bank for the four other periods is formed. This average residual, $\ln(\bar{x}_n)$, is an estimate of $\ln(x_n)$ for the bank n, given that the random error $\ln(\varpi)$ will tend to cancel each other out in the averaging. This average residual of each bank is used in the computation of X-efficiency. The efficiency score is given by the following equation:

$$XEFF = \exp[\ln(\bar{x})_{min} - \ln(\bar{x}_n)] \tag{19A2.2}$$

where $\ln(\bar{x})_{min}$ is the minimum $\ln(\bar{x}_n)$, that is, the average residual for the bank with the lowest average cost residual, which is assumed to be the most efficient bank. Therefore, *XEFF* is an estimate of the ratio of predicted costs for the most efficient bank to predicted costs for any bank. Nevertheless, this measure of efficiency is not completely correct if the random error terms $\ln(\varpi)$ do not cancel each other out fully during the period, especially for banks at the

Table 19A2.1   Estimates of XEFF, *1992–1996 (truncated at 5%)*

	Average	Median	Maximum	Minimum	Standard error
Poland	0.607	0.540	1	0.370	0.370
Latvia	0.476	0.473	0.671	0.290	0.134
Croatia	0.548	0.542	0.733	0.290	0.102
Estonia	0.529	0.517	0.635	0.386	0.075
Lithuania	0.528	0.550	0.702	0.384	0.102
Slovakia	0.502	0.514	0.640	0.350	0.085
Slovenia	0.634	0.570	1	0.448	0.203
Czech Rep.	0.487	0.461	1	0.290	0.154

Source: Calculations carried out by the authors with data extracted from the database Bankscope, Fitch–IBCA.

extreme values of $\ln(\bar{x}_n)$, which may have had persistently 'lucky' or 'unlucky' errors that did not fully average out. To alleviate this problem, we have computed truncated measures of X-efficiency, where the value of the average residual of the qth $((1 - q)$th) quantile was given to each observation for which the value of the average residual is below (above) the qth $((1 - q)$th) quantile value. We have used one value of q: 5 per cent.

The values of *XEFF* are displayed in Table (19A2.1).

20. Convergence between the financial systems of EU member states and applicant transition economies

Victor Murinde, Juda Agung and Andrew W. Mullineux*

INTRODUCTION

Most policy makers and academics agree that the restructuring of the financial system is an integral element of the ongoing economic transformation in Eastern and Central Europe (Mullineux 1998; Walter 1998). This is particularly important because, as Doukas et al. (1998) have observed, one distinct feature which all transition economies had in common during the central planning era was that a market-orientated financial system was almost completely absent. Apart from some informal financing activities, the financial sector comprised a 'monobank system' (state bank, savings banks, specialized banks and so on) which played a limited role compared to a traditional banking system (Buch 1996). Although the savings banks accepted deposits from households and the state banks had accounting and credit disbursement roles, the final decisions on the distribution of credit rested with the central planning agencies, which allocated credit to selected enterprises in order to attain output targets. Bank managers had no incentive to undertake credit risk analysis because the credit lines were underwritten by the state; moreover, the managers were not constrained by capital budgeting criteria (for example, using financial ratios to analyse the efficiency of investment).

At the genesis of the transition period, there was no blueprint for developing a banking sector (Bahra et al. 1997). However, most transition economies started by creating a two-tier banking system, comprising on the one hand a central bank to oversee monetary policy and bank supervision, and on the

* The research for the chapter was undertaken with support from the European Commission's PHARE (ACE) Programme 1997–99 under Contract Numbers 96-6152-R and 96-6159-R. However, the interpretations and conclusions expressed in this chapter are entirely those of the authors and should not be attributed in any manner to the European Commission.

other hand some commercial banks to perform some form of financial inter-mediation. Thereafter, the process of privatization of all or some of the exist-ing banks and new entry was used to encourage further the development of the commercial banking system.

However, as private banks started to operate on the basis of market criteria and as privatization of firms increased, there was a marked increase in the amount of credit default. Clearly, the inherited bad loans problem affected almost every transition economy, but in some cases the accumulation of bad loans by the banking sector became an epidemic (Buch 1996). It is useful to note, therefore, that although the banking systems of these transition economies shared a broadly common central planning heritage, they have had different experiences of bank development during the transition process, and also inherited different levels of bad loans from the previous period of directed lending (Buch 1996). The procedures for dealing with the inherited bad loans also varied considerably across the transition economies (Buch 1996; Mullineux 1998). Consequently, the banks have grown at very different rates throughout the 1980s such that by 1993 (as we explain in the next section) there were marked differences in the level of bank development in each of the transition economies. Since January 1993, when the European Union (EU) launched the European single market, the transition economies have more purposely redefined their reforms, especially with the banking sector, in order to prepare for subsequent entry into the EU as members.

This chapter investigates whether there has been some convergence in the banking systems of transition economies in terms of a systematic shift in the output of banking operations in these economies, taking January 1993 as the initial conditions period. In addition to shedding light on the growth behaviour of the banking sectors in these economies, the chapter is motivated by the fact that one of the main expectations of transition economies was that the launch-ing of a single market in Europe in January 1993 would impact positively on their budding financial systems by facilitating their future membership. In contrast to the literature on economic growth models (for example, Sala-i-Martin 1996) where convergence is tested with respect to the growth rate of national output, the chapter reinterprets the convergence tests for banking systems with respect to the growth rates of bank output. It thus follows the literature on the cost and output behaviour of banks, relating to economies of scale and scope.

In the chapter, econometric tests for convergence are conducted in two steps. In the first step, the idea of absolute convergence used in the literature on economic growth (for example, Barro and Xala-i-Martin 1995) is adopted in order to consider a group of transition economies which are assumed to have structurally similar banking systems: the only difference among the banking systems is the initial quantity of bank output as at 1993. In other words, a relatively homogeneous group of transition economies is used to test for convergence of the banking systems across these economies. The econometric test for convergence used here underpins the concept of convergence that banking systems with lower bank output (that is, loans), expressed relative to their steady-state levels at 1993, tend to grow faster: over time, 1993 to 1997, the bank output growth rates across all the transition economies tend to converge, suggesting that the banking systems are converging.[1] In the second step, the idea of absolute convergence is maintained but two groups of economies are distinguished, namely the transition economies on the one hand and the EU countries on the other. The banking systems in these two groups of economies have different starting values at the initial period 1993; the transition economies have low initial values of bank output, while the EU countries have high initial values of bank output. Since each of the banking systems have some similar underlying features, the growth rate of bank output in the transition economies is larger, given the lower initial value (at 1993). This implies that convergence takes place in the sense that transition economies have lower starting values of bank output and higher bank output growth rates, and these tend to catch up with or converge to those of the EU.

In both the first and second steps, the loan activities of banks, which tie down the product (output) of banking operations, are disaggregated into three tiers: loans to the private sector, loans to public enterprises and loans to the government sector. The analysis also draws from the literature which addresses the main controversy of defining output in a banking firm (Murinde 1992). This literature argues that deposits may be regard as bank output. In this case, the convergence test is applied to determine whether there has been a shift towards a sustained increase in bank output (this time defined by deposits), given an initial level, in a manner that suggests that the banking systems are converging. Hence the convergence tests will also shed light on whether the banking systems are converging on the supply side (loans) or on the demand side (deposits), or both.

The chapter makes at least three major contributions. First, it proposes and implements a novel application of convergence tests with respect to the banking systems of transition economies, among themselves and on the EU. Second, it covers the period (1993–97) in which there has been substantial financial innovation, liberalization and regulatory reform in the transition economies as well as the EU member countries which the transition countries aspire to join in due course. Third, the chapter yields evidence which complements the experience of the genesis and later developments in the banking systems of the transition economies detailed below. Two main conclusions emerge. First, it is shown that in the transition economies, and for most of the 1993–97 period, the banking systems of Central and Eastern Europe exhibited convergence in terms of their loan portfolio to the private sector and the government sector, but not the public enterprises. Second, it is found that these banking systems also exhibit convergence in terms of their liabilities with respect to demand deposits as well as foreign liabilities, but not time and saving deposits. Taking the results on both the demand and supply sides of banking operations, the findings emphasize some reasonable degree of convergence among the banking systems of the transition economies in Central and Eastern Europe.

The remainder of the chapter is structured into five sections. The next section briefly reviews the experience with banking sector restructuring in the transition economies, with the question: what have they achieved? The approach taken to model convergence in this chapter is discussed in the third section. The fourth section reports the estimation and testing results with respect to the transition economies as a group, while the fifth section reports the evidence with respect to the transition economies and the EU. The final section concludes.

THE EXPERIENCE WITH BANKING SECTOR RESTRUCTURING IN TRANSITION ECONOMIES

As noted in Mullineux (1998), it has become increasingly evident that the restructuring of the banking sector should be given a very high priority in the stabilization and restructuring of formerly centrally planned economies. The increasing amount of funding allocated by development banks, such as the World Bank (International Bank for Reconstruction and Development: IBRD) and the European Bank for Reconstruction and Development (EBRD), for the purpose of recapitalizing and privatizing banks, resolving bank debt problems and sponsoring the transfer of banking 'know-how', bears witness to this, as does the prominence given to banking sector reform in more recent International Monetary Fund (IMF) programmes.

At the outset of the transition, the centrally planned economies had extremely rudimentary financial systems which had only recently been transformed, from the Soviet 'mono-banking' model, to a 'two-tier' banking system. They had only just begun to develop a third tier of cooperative and private sector banks, which were often joint ventures with 'Western' banks. Apart from such banks the financial sector was extremely underdeveloped. There were no capital markets or wholesale money and interbank markets of any significance and few non-bank financial intermediaries, such as insurance companies and pension funds, managing portfolios of shares in private companies and holding government debt (bonds). This was because, at the beginning of the transition and before the launch of privatization programmes, the industrial and retailing sectors were state owned, the service and welfare sector was underdeveloped, and tax revenue was derived largely from enterprises.

In the second half of the 1980s, first Hungary, then Bulgaria and then other transition economies took on board the 'two-tier' model and they tried to find a 'third way' by introducing market forces into a central planning framework. Hungary went further by granting licences to joint ventures between the newly created commercial banks and foreign banks. This move was followed in some other transition economies, including the then Soviet Union, which also began to allow the establishment of numerous cooperative banks, and a third tier of banks was created. The development of this third tier accelerated with the establishment of numerous domestically owned private sector commercial banks following the collapse of communism in Central and Eastern Europe in 1989. The state-owned commercial banks, however, continued to dominate the banking systems in the transition economies, and privatization of the state-owned commercial banks only gathered pace in the mid-1990s. Poland has now privatized a number of major banks with the financial support of the EBRD and Hungary has also made significant progress in this area, also with the EBRD's financial assistance. But privatization also recently gathered pace in the Czech Republic.

It should be noted that the 'mono bank' system was always a misnomer since most of these economies had a number of specialized (for example, investment, agricultural and trade finance) banks, as well as a national bank and also a savings bank, whose degree of independence from the national bank varied. When two-tier banking was introduced, not only were new commercial banks created, but the specialized and savings banks were usually also permitted to undertake commercial banking business. The new commercial banks were often regionally based (as in Poland) or allocated state-owned enterprises (SOEs) on an industrial sectoral basis (as in Bulgaria), which led to a degree of de facto regional concentration. In Poland, for example, nine regional state-owned banks (SOBs) were established alongside a number of formerly specialized banks.

At the time of their creation, the commercial banks clearly lacked experienced staff with well-developing lending (risk-appraisal) skills, as well as the facilities to collect deposits from the public and to provide modern money transmission services. The general public was used to receiving rudimentary services from the state savings banks, whose key function was to collect savings and channel them, via the national banks, to help fund planned expenditure. Under monobanking, the national banks' roles included the disbursement of planned budgetary allocations, the collection of taxes, and monitoring the use of the allocated credits (that is, a governance role). It was thus an arm of the planning agency, the finance ministry and a central bank rolled into one.

The abandonment of central planning in favour of 'capitalism' requires the introduction of an alternative means of allocating 'credits', or 'capital'. In capitalist countries the banks are by far the most important allocators of capital through the advancement of loans (debt contracts) to enterprises and households. In some capitalist economies 'capital markets' (stock exchanges) also play an important, but normally subservient, role in the allocation of capital (see Doukas et al. 1998). These markets allocate debt and equity capital directly to enterprises, who issue securities such as bonds and 'shares', without the use of an intermediary such as a bank. The proportion of capital allocated in this way has grown significantly over the last two decades as a result of 'securitization' involving 'disintermediation'. We need not enter here into the reasons for this development, but can note that it is only in the USA that the future role of banks has, prematurely and due to special factors prevailing in the late 1980s and early 1990s (in our view), been seriously called into question by some commentators.

It seems likely that, due to information asymmetry, banks will remain the main source of finance for small and medium-sized enterprises (SMEs) for the foreseeable future (even in the USA). It is only in countries at an advanced stage of financial development that capital markets, rather than banks, play a significant role in allocating capital and it should be noted that these markets satisfy the debt and equity needs of only the larger enterprises.

The focus of financial sector reform in transforming economies should therefore be first, to establish a well-functioning banking sector and then, subsequently, to develop capital markets. The latter will anyway begin to develop as a result of the execution of privatization programmes and the issuance of government securities (treasury bills and bonds). The restructuring of the banking sector does, however, require the development of wholesale money markets, including an interbank market. These markets facilitate increased efficiency in the allocation of capital by banks, which is the prime goal of the reform process. This is because banks with insufficient profitable lending opportunities and a surplus of (retail) deposits should be able to lend to banks in the opposite position. It is also evident that a rapid transfer of know-how (to practitioners and supervisors) concerning lending techniques and risk control, via asset and liability management, in commercial banking is required if a more efficient allocation of capital is to be achieved.

In capitalist economies, the financial sector not only allocates capital but also monitors is use and imposes sanctions on its misuse. This latter 'corporate governance' function is crucial since if capital, once allocated, is not efficiently used, then it should be withdrawn and reallocated. It is through this process that continuous restructuring and development occurs under capitalism. For the process to work effectively, a legal system has to be developed covering property rights, privatization and restitution, debt and equity contracts, and bankruptcy *inter alia*.

The transforming economies had to construct such a legal system from scratch and this ensured that the transition progressed at a tortuous pace in the early stages. If the banks are to play a key role in corporate governance, the question of who should monitor the activities of the monitors arises. The need for bank regulation and supervision is widely accepted (although not undisputed) and rests on the existence of a market failure. As the SME finance, this is usually attributed to information asymmetry and the resulting moral hazard, adverse selection and public choice problems. We lack the space to explore these issues here and merely note that international 'best practice' and a desire to join the European Union, made it necessary for the transition economies considered in this study to develop a bank regulatory and supervisory system conformable with that of the EU, whose members have themselves been harmonizing their strategies (Mullineux 1992, ch. 1). Again this had to be done virtually from scratch, although in this case there were internationally agreed (Basle Committee) standards on which to model the legalization, rather than the bewildering array of legal models available covering the aforementioned spheres.

Given their key importance in the early stages of transition, the corporate governance responsibility will fall primarily on banks. As the capital markets develop, as a result of privatization, other institutions, such as the investment funds created in connection with voucher-based mass privatization programmes in Poland and the Czech Republic, will begin to share this role. As major shareholders, the investment funds will have the potential to influence management behaviour and should be given the incentive to do so. In the 'West', and especially in countries where the capital markets are most developed, particularly the UK and the USA, institutional shareholders, such as insurance companies and pensions funds, are playing an increasingly important role in corporate governance. In more bank-orientated countries, such as Germany and Japan, the banks are major shareholders and wield influence as both debt and equity holders, though in recent years banks in these countries have begun to reduce their equity stakeholding in corporates.

It has been noted that the need to establish a legal, regulatory and supervisory infrastruture, and the lack of known-how, made instant banking sector restructuring impossible, but another important factor hindered the process. This was the SOBs inheritance, from the previous (central planning) regime, of debt contracts with SOEs.

In the early stages of the transition it soon became apparent that many of the SOEs were uncompetitive and inefficient and that a large proportion of the loans to them were bad, or at best doubtful. The loans had been made under a directed credit regime, rather than in pursuit of profit, but the banks could not simply cut off supplies of finance in the new regime because they would have revealed themselves to be insolvent. Further, bankruptcy laws were not in place and the banks had no legal claims on the property of the borrowers since the practice of taking collateral against loans, and the law on property rights in general, had not been developed.

In an ideal world the new, democratically elected, governments would have acknowledged the state's responsibility for the debts inherited from the previous regime, taken on the debt (as national debt by swapping it for government bonds) and then recapitalized the banks. The SOBs would then have started with a 'clean slate' and been able to develop genuinely commercial relationships with SOEs and private sector borrowers. Already severe budgetary problems would, however, have been aggravated. These problems were becoming worse as demands for state expenditure (to put in place a social safety-net for example) were increasing and state revenues (from the 'profits' of struggling SOEs) were falling. Belatedly, the case for external assistance in the funding of the recapitalization of banks was recognized, and in most cases considered inadequate anyway.

The cost of postponing comprehensive bank restructuring was an accumulation of bad debts in banks. More and more doubtful debts went bad as the 'transition recessions' worsened. It should be noted, however, that there was a severe transition (Phillips curve) trade-off between inflation and unemployment. If the banks had been freed of their debt burden and bankruptcy law had been introduced rapidly, then many more SOEs would have been closed (rather than commercialized and restructured) and unemployment would have risen even more rapidly, possibly engendering political instability. By postponing the resolution of the bank bad-debt problem, however, capital was misallocated because it continued to be lent to inefficient firms and was not released for lending to new, and potentially more efficient, enterprises. The restructuring of the economy was therefore slowed down and mass privatization of SOEs (as well as the privatization of SOBs) was also hindered because the SOEs had inherited debts to banks from the previous regime and they also needed financial restructuring prior to privatization. The resolution of the bank bad-debt problem and the possibility of launching an early and successful mass privatization programme were therefore interrelated.

It should be noted that in the countries which experienced hyperinflation (for example, Poland and Russia) the bad-debt problem was initially resolved by the wiping out of the real value of old loans. This had temporary benefits in the early phase of the banking sector reform. However, the aforementioned inexperience in lending, and the fact that, without substantial restructuring, the SOBs remain tied to SOEs, soon led to a re-emergence of bank bad-debt problems.

MODELLING CONVERGENCE OF BANKING SYSTEMS

Convergence has mainly been modelled using time-series, cross-section and panel data techniques with respect to economic growth models. Strictly, there is no universally agreed definition of the term convergence, although what is generally meant by it is easily understood. Baumol et al. (1994) identify seven concepts of convergence; these use Barro-type tests, as in Barro and Sala-i-Martin (1995), or cointegration analysis to test whether convergence has occurred or not. However, there are two predominant concepts of convergence in the growth literature (Quah 1993). One concept, referred to as beta convergence, implies regression to the mean and applies if a poor country tends to grow faster than a rich one, such that the poor country tends to catch up with the rich one in terms of the level of per capita income (Barro and Sala-i-Martin 1992). The other concept, known as rho convergence, concerns cross-sectional dispersion and applies if the dispersion, measured as a change in the standard deviation of a given variable (for example, ln Y for GDP), declines over time. The relationship between beta convergence and rho convergence is that the former tends to generate convergence of the type implied by the latter, that is, if poor countries grow faster than rich ones, there is reduced dispersion of incomes overall (see Bernard and Durlauf 1996). The regression tests take the following form:

$$x_{i,t+1} = a + b_y(y_{i,t} - y_i^*) + e_{i,t+1} \qquad b_y < 0, \qquad (20.1)$$

where $x_{i,t+1} = y_{i,t+1} - y_{i,t}$, and $y_{i,t}$ is the logarithm of per capita GDP of country i at time t; y_i^* is the steady-sate level of country i, and by construction $e_{i,t+1}$, is the error term that is uncorrelated across i and with regressors. The parameter restriction, $b_y < 0$, is the main implication tested in the convergence literature; it suggests that a country positioned further below the steady-state level tends to grow faster.

Inspired by the above literature, this chapter applies the procedure for modelling convergence in the context of the banking systems in the transition economies of Central and Eastern Europe first, as well as on the EU. The literature on the microeconomics of the banking firm has focused on the existence of economies of scale and economies of scope in the banking industry. In contrast to the neoclassical growth model and endogenous growth models used in the growth literature, the early studies on the banking firm started with a standard log linear Cobb–Douglas production function of the following form:

$$q = y_0 + \alpha k + \eta m \qquad (20.2)$$

where q is an output measure (for example, loans), and k and m are factor inputs into the bank production process. However, this entailed a strong assumption regarding the shape of the cost function, that is, returns to scale area assumed to be increasing everywhere ($\eta < 1$), constant everywhere ($\eta = 1$) or decreasing everywhere ($\eta > 1$), thus a u-shaped curve is not possible. Recent studies are therefore based on a multiproduct translog production function:

$$q = y_0 + \sum_i \alpha_i k_i + 0.5 \sum_i \sum_j \eta_{ij} m_j k_i \qquad (20.3)$$

where $\eta_{ij} = \eta_{ji}$ for all i, j. The key output of the banking firm comprises loans to the business sector, loans to public enterprises and loans to government sectors. It is also plausible to consider the obverse argument in the literature and redefine bank output in terms of demand deposits, time and saving deposits and foreign liabilities.

The modelling procedure used for testing for convergence, based on equation (20.3), was initially based on cross-section tests of unconditional and conditional convergence. The cross-section unconditional convergence tests were constructed as follows:

$$g_{i,T} = \alpha + \beta q_{i,0} + \varepsilon_{C,T} \qquad (20.4)$$

where $g = q_t - q_{t-1}$, and T is a fixed horizon. Conditional convergence tests are constructed by modifying equation (20.4) to include control variables:

$$g_{i,T} = \alpha + \beta q_{i,0} + \pi w_{i,T} + \varepsilon_{i,T} \qquad (20.5)$$

where $w_{i,T}$ denotes a vector of control variables.

However, one main limitation of our database is that it consists of unbalanced short-panel data; to resolve this problem we use the dynamic panel data programme by Arellano and Bond (1988). Thus, we introduce dynamic behaviour and incorporate both time-series and cross-section variation. In addition, recent studies indicate that the standard procedure for the estimation of the dynamic panel data regression model involves casting the equation in first differences and then using instrumental variables (see Arellano and Bond 1991; Arellano and Bover 1995). However, Ahn and Schmidt (1997), among others, have shown that instrumental variable estimators may not be able to exploit some additional moment conditions. Hence, rather than using cross-section estimation, we used the dynamic fixed-effects panel data specifications using the generalized method of moments (GMM) estimator (Arrelano and Bond 1991),[2] to estimate the following equation with respect to the growth of output of the banking sector, based on equation (20.4):

$$g_{i,t} = \alpha + \beta_1 g_{i,t-1} + \beta_2 g_{i,t-1} + \beta_3 q_{i,0} + \varepsilon_{i,t} \qquad (20.6)$$

where $g_{i,t} = \ln q_{i,t} - \ln q_{i,t-1}$, the growth rate of bank output measures, that is, loans to government sectors, loans to public enterprises, or bank loans to the private sector, and $q_{i,0}$ is the initial level of bank output measures (at 1993).

As earlier noted, the literature on the cost and output behaviour (the micro-economics) of the banking firm stresses the controversy regarding the definition of bank output, and points out the possibility of redefining bank output in terms of deposits. In this context, we extend the above convergence tests for the banking systems in transition economies, as well as transition and EU banking systems, and redefine bank output in terms of three types of deposits: demand deposits, time and savings deposits and foreign liabilities. To test for convergence of the banking systems, we apply the GMM estimator of the dynamic fixed effects model with panel data to estimate the equation (20.6) with respect to the growth of output of the banking sector, in terms of demand deposits, time and savings deposits and foreign liabilities.

The econometric results for equation (20.6) for various bank output measures are reported in the next two sections.

ESTIMATION AND TESTING RESULTS FOR TRANSITION ECONOMIES ONLY

For the first stage of the empirical exercise, the data are taken from the International Financial Statistics Database (IFS) published monthly by the International Monetary Fund and cover the 1993–97 period for ten transition economies in Central and Eastern Europe: Azerbaijan, Croatia, the Czech Republic, Estonia, Latvia, Lithuania, Poland, Russia, the Slovak Republic and Ukraine.[3] Bank output is defined in terms of loans, classified into three types: bank loans to government sector, observed in terms of claims on general government by domestic money banks (line 12a of IFS); bank loans to public enterprises, observed in terms of claims on non-financial public enterprises by domestic money banks (line 12c of IFS); and bank loans to the private sector (households and firms), observed in terms of claims on the private sector by domestic money banks (line 12d of IFS). As an alternative, based on the previous discussion, output is defined in terms of deposits of domestic money banks, classified into three types: demand deposits of domestic money banks (line 24 of IFS); time, savings and foreign currency deposits of domestic money banks (line 25 of IFS); and foreign liabilities of domestic money banks (line 26c of IFS).

The estimation and testing results for the convergence hypothesis with respect to bank loans to the government sector, bank loans to public enterprises, and bank loans to the private sector are reported in Table 20.1.

The results reported in the table suggest that there has been a tendency towards convergence among the banking systems of the transition economies in terms of loans to the government sectors. It would appear that over time (during 1993–97) and across the ten countries the banking systems have

Table 20.1 *GMM estimation results for convergence of bank loans:*
CEE countries (dependent variable: growth rate of loans
proportion (g))

	Loans to government sectors	Loans to public enterprises	Loans to private sector
constant	−0.340**	−0.030	−0.393
	(−3.857)	(−0.327)	(−0.973)
$g(-1)$	0.301**	−0.419	12.502**
	(9.020)	(−0.441)	(2.157)
$g(-2)$	0.039**	0.200	(1.953)*
	(2.388)	(0.674)	(1.660)
q_0	−0.098**	0.126	−0.929**
	(−3.158)	(1.159)	(−2.950)
Wald test	51.01	2.922	10.407
df	3	3	3
Sargan test	0.767	0.345	0.006
df	1	1	1

Number of countries   10
Number of observations   48
Sample   1993–97

Notes:
*Significant at 10%; ** Significant at 5%.
Values in parentheses are *t*-statistics.
q_0 is the initial level of share of the components.

shifted towards convergence, if bank output is defined in terms of their own activities to government. The results for the 'loans to government equation' shows the expected negative sign on the initial level of bank loans to government (at 1993), tied down by variable q_0, with statistically significant estimates. The dynamics in the specification are validated by statistically significant estimates for both the first and the second periods. Overall, therefore, the results are consistent with our definition of convergence bank output across the homogeneous group of transition economies, in terms of the growth rate of bank loans to government sectors versus the initial level at 1993.

It is found, however, that in terms of loans to public enterprises, the results reported in Table 20.1 do not suggest that there has been a tendency towards convergence among the banking systems of the transition economies. The expected negative sign on the initial level of bank loans to public enterprises (at 1993), tied down by variable q_0, is not validated; rather, the results show a positive sign with statistically insignificant estimates. The dynamics in the specification also bear statistically insignificant estimates for both the first and the second periods. Overall, therefore, the results are not consistent with our definition of convergence of bank output across the homogeneous group of transition economies, in terms of the growth rate of bank loans to public enterprises versus the initial level at 1993. This finding is likely to be a result of attempts to resolve the inherited bad-debt problem affecting the relationship between the larger (still state owned or now privatized) state-owned banks and state-owned enterprises, whose number has shrunk as privatization has progressed.

In terms of bank loans to the private sector, the results reported in Table 20.1 suggest that there has been a tendency towards convergence among the banking systems of the homogeneous group of transition economies. It would appear that over time (during 1993–97) and across the ten countries the banking systems have shifted towards convergence, if bank output is defined in terms of their loan activities to the private sector: the results bear the expected negative sign on the initial level of bank loans to the private sector (at 1993), tied down by variable q_0, with statistically significant estimates. In addition, we find that the dynamics in the specification are validated by statistically significant estimates for both the first and the second periods. Thus, the results are consistent with our definition of convergence of bank output across the homogeneous group of transition economies, in terms of the growth rate of bank loans to the private sector versus the initial level at 1993. It should be noted, however, that the evidence of convergence based on lending to the private sector will also have been biased by the growth in the private sector as a result of ongoing privatization. Hence, the need to confirm the finding by looking at deposits as an alternative measure of bank output.

For the alternative definition of bank output, the estimation and testing results for the convergence hypothesis with respect to demand deposits, time and savings deposits, and foreign liabilities are reported in Table 20.2. The evidence in the table suggests that there has been a tendency towards convergence among the banking systems of the transition economies in terms of demand deposits. It would appear that over time (during 1993–97) and across the ten countries the banking systems have shifted towards convergence, if bank output is defined in terms of their mobilization of demand deposits. The results for the 'demand deposits equation' show the expected negative sign on the initial level of demand deposits (at 1993), tied down by variable q_0, with statistically significant estimates. The dynamics in the specification are validated by statistically significant estimates for only the second period, suggesting that the first period is merely transitory. Overall, therefore, the results are consistent with our definition of convergence of bank output

Table 20.2   *GMM estimation results for convergence of bank deposits: CEE countries (dependent variable: growth rate of deposits proportion (g))*

	Demand deposits	Time and saving deposits	Foreign liabilities
Constant	−0.092*	−0.065*	−1.266
	(−1.914)	(−1.817)	(−1.450)
$g(-1)$	0.091	0.193	−3.746
	(0.799)	(0.595)	(−1.294)
$g(-2)$	0.184*	−0.124	−0.689
	(2.265)	(−0.774)	(−1.307)
q_0	−0.052*	−0.045	−0.935*
	(−1.654)	(−0.922)	(−1.656)
Wald test	22.041	6.951	3.191
df	3	3	3
Sargan test	0.000	0.164	0.018
df	1	1	1

Number of countries   10
Number of observations   48
Sample   1993–97

Notes:
*Significant at 10%.
Values in parentheses are *t*-statistics.
q_0 is the initial level of share of the components.

across the homogeneous group of transition economies, in terms of the growth rate of demand deposits versus the initial level at 1993.

However, it is found that in terms of time and savings deposits, the results reported in Table 20.2 do not suggest that there has been a tendency towards convergence among the banking systems of the transition economies. The GMM estimate suggests that although the coefficient on the initial level of time and savings deposits (at 1993) is convergence, as expected, the *t*-statistic does not show significant estimates. In addition, the dynamics in the specification do not bear statistically significant estimates for both the first and the second periods. This finding may reflect the emergence of alternative (to bank) savings instruments (for example, investment funds following voucher-based privatizations).

Finally, in terms of foreign liabilities, the results reported in Table 20.2

suggest that there has been a tendency towards convergence among the banking systems of the homogeneous group of transition economies. It would appear that over time (during 1993–97) and across the ten countries the banking systems have shifted towards convergence, if bank output is defined in terms of their foreign liabilities: the results bear the expected negative sign on the initial level of foreign liabilities (at 1993), tied down by variable q_0, with statistically significant estimates. However, the dynamics do not seem to play a role; they bear statistically insignificant estimates for both the first and second periods. Overall, the results are consistent with our definition of convergence of bank output across the homogeneous group of transition economies, in terms of the growth rate of foreign liabilities versus the initial level at 1993.

EVIDENCE FOR TRANSITION ECONOMIES AND THE EU

The data for the second stage of the empirical exercise are also taken from the International Financial Statistics Database (IFS) published monthly by the International Monetary Fund and cover the 1993–97 period for seven transition economies in Eastern Europe, namely Croatia, the Czech Republic, Estonia, Latvia, Lithuania, Poland and the Slovak Republic,[4] as well as 11 EU member countries, namely Belgium, Denmark, Finland, France, Germany, Italy, the Netherlands, Norway, Spain, Portugal and the United Kingdom. Bank output is defined in terms of loans, classified into two (rather than three) types: bank loans to government sector, observed in terms of claims on general government by domestic money banks (line 12a of IFS); and bank loans to the private sector (household and firms), observed in terms of claims on the private sector by domestic money banks (line 12d of IFS). As an alternative, based on the previous discussion, output is defined in terms of deposits of domestic money banks, classified into three types: demand deposits of domestic money banks (line 24 of IFS); time, savings and foreign currency deposits of domestic money banks (line 25 of IFS); and foreign liabilities of domestic money banks (line 26c of IFS).

A panel for the above transition and EU countries is estimated using ordinary least squares (OLS) as well as GMM procedure, allowing dynamics and a dummy for Eastern Europe as regressor. The estimation and testing results for the convergence hypothesis with respect to bank loans to the government sector and bank loans to the private sector are reported in Table 20.3.

It is found that in terms of loans to government sectors, the results reported in Table 20.3 do not suggest that there has been a tendency towards convergence among the banking systems of the transition economies and the EU. The expected negative sign on the initial level of bank loans to government sectors

Financial sector development

Table 20.3   OLS and GMM estimation results for convergence of bank loans: CEE and EU countries (dependent variable: growth rate of loans proportion (g))

	Loans to government sector		Loans to private sector	
	OLS	GMM	OLS	GMM
Constant	−0.179**	−0.047	−0.018	−0.013
	(−2.860)	(−0.525)	(−1.709)	(−1.530)
$g(-1)$	0.185	0.406	0.470**	0.497**
	(0.980)	(1.570)	(2.890)	(4.260)
q_0	−0.032	0.026	−0.150**	−0.121**
	(−1.390)	(0.530)	(−6.019)	(−3.260)
dum	0.018	−0.116	0.002	0.005
(Eastern Europe)	(0.261)	(−1.420)	(0.12)	(0.215)
Wald test	5.346	2.499	40.00	18.28
df	2	2	2	2
Sargan test	−	2.753	−	2.276
df	−	2	−	2

Number of countries   18
Number of observations   87
Sample   1993–97

Notes:
**Significant at 1%.
Values in parentheses are t-statistics.
q_0 is the initial level of share of the components.

(at 1993), tied down by variable q_0, is not validated; rather, the GMM results show a positive sign with statistically insignificant estimates. The dynamics in the specification also bear statistically insignificant estimates. Overall, therefore, the results are not consistent with our definition of convergence of bank output across the group of transition and EU economies, in terms of the growth rate of bank loans to government sectors versus the initial level at 1993. The transition economies have hardly converged on the EU model. This implies that the transition economies still have a lot to do in the field of achieving reduced fiscal deficits and establishing means of financing them through bond markets.

In terms of bank loans to the private sector, the results reported in Table 20.4 suggest that there has been a tendency towards convergence among the

Table 20.4   OLS and GMM estimation results for convergence of bank
deposits: CEE and EU countries (dependent variable: growth
rate of deposits proportion (g))

	Demand deposits		Time and savings deposits		Foreign liabilities	
	OLS	GMM	OLS	GMM	OLS	GMM
Constant	−0.061	−0.058	−0.104**	−0.105**	−0.171**	−0.305**
	(−0.902)	(−0.630)	(−2.600)	(−3.210)	(−3.480)	(−3.640)
$g(-1)$	−0.048	−0.991*	0.576**	0.602**	−0.123	−0.861*
	(−0.160)	(−2.240)	(4.460)	(2.610)	(−0.720)	(−2.420)
q_0	−0.019	−0.058	−0.055	−0.055	−0.230**	−0.368**
	(−0.480)	(−1.110)	(−1.400)	(−1.330)	(−5.840)	(−5.460)
dum	−0.019	−0.086	0.043	0.053**	−0.200**	−0.255*
(Eastern Europe)	(−0.340)	(−1.170)	(1.720)	(2.910)	(−3.620)	(−2.230)
Wald test	0.238	6.572	28.08	9.643	61.375	29.849
df	2	2	2	2	2	2
Sargan test	–	3.305	–	−0.770	–	0.199
df	–	2	–	2	–	2

Number of countries   18
Number of observations   87
Sample   1993–97

Notes:
*Significant at 5%; **Significant at 1%.
Values in parentheses are *t*-statistics.
q_0 is the initial level of share of the components.

banking systems of the transition and EU economies. It would appear that over time (during 1993–97) and across the sample of transition and EU countries (18 in all) the banking systems have shifted towards convergence, if bank output is defined in terms of their loan activities to the private sector. Both the GMM and OLS results show the expected negative sign on the initial level of bank loans to the private sector (at 1993), tied down by variable q_0, with statistically significant estimates. The dynamics in the specification are validated by statistically significant estimates. Overall, therefore, the results are consistent with our definition of convergence of bank output across the group of transition and EU economies, in terms of the growth rate of bank loans to the private sector versus the initial level at 1993.

For the alternative definition of bank output, the estimation and testing results for the convergence hypothesis with respect to demand deposits, time and savings deposits, and foreign liabilities are reported in Table 20.4. The evidence in the table rejects convergence among the banking systems of transition economies and the EU in terms of demand deposits. It would appear that over time (during 1993–97) and across the 18 countries the banking systems have not shifted towards convergence, if bank output is defined in terms of their mobilization of demand deposits. Although the results for the 'demand deposits equation' show the expected negative sign on the initial level of demand deposits (at 1993), tied down by variable q_0, the estimates are not statistically significant. However, the dynamics in the specification are validated by statistically significant estimates. Overall, therefore, the results are not consistent with our definition of convergence of bank output across the homogeneous group of transition economies, in terms of the growth rate of demand deposits versus the initial level at 1993.

It is also found that in terms of time and savings deposits, the results reported in Table 20.4 do not suggest that there has been a tendency towards convergence among the banking systems of the transition economies and the EU. The expected negative sign on the initial level of bank time and savings deposits (at 1993), tied down by variable q_0, is not validated, although the expected negative sign is obtained (with statistically insignificant estimates, though). The dynamics in the specification do bear statistically significant estimates. The dummy for Eastern Europe is statistically significant, suggesting that their classification as a distinct group is justified. Overall, therefore, the results are not consistent with our definition of convergence of bank output across the group of transition economies and the EU, in terms of the growth rate of time and savings deposits versus the initial level at 1993. Taken together, the results suggest that the financial sector is still heavily bank dominated in the transition and some EU economies, and that convergence can be expected to accelerate as non-bank financial institutions and instruments grow in importance.

In terms of foreign liabilities, the results reported in Table 20.4 suggest that there has been a tendency towards convergence among the banking systems of the EU and transition economies. It would appear that over time (during 1993–97) and across the 18 countries the banking systems have shifted towards convergence, if bank output is defined in terms of their foreign liabilities: the results bear the expected negative sign on the initial level of foreign liabilities (at 1993), tied down by variable q_0, with statistically significant estimates. The dynamics do seem to play a significant role; they bear statistically significant estimates. Overall, the results are consistent with our definition of convergence of bank output across the group of EU and transition economies, in terms of the growth rate of foreign liabilities versus the initial level at 1993. This suggests that the banking systems of the transition economies are converging on their EU counterparts. This process can be expected to continue as international capital flows become progressively freer.

Finally, it is debatable whether business-cycle swings have influenced the convergence of the banking systems in the EU and transition economies significantly. No attempt has therefore been made in this study to control for the separate cyclical swings in each country. Moreover, cycles affecting each country are far from being perfectly synchronized.

SUMMARY AND CONCLUSION

Following the participation of the EU member countries in the single market launched in January 1993, and the recent restructuring of banking systems in Central and Eastern Europe, the transition economies may expect convergence of their banking systems as a group as well as convergence of the banking systems of some progressive transition economies on the EU banking system. This chapter proposes and implements novel applications of econometric tests for convergence (hitherto popularized in the growth literature) to determine whether there has been a shift towards convergence of the banking systems first for a homogeneous group of Central and Eastern European transition economies, and second for a group of the transition economies and the EU. Models are specified for each of the main elements of the demand as well as the supply side of the banking sector, and are estimated and tested using data from the International Financial Statistics for the 1993–97 period.

The chapter uncovers a number of interesting findings. For the group of transition economies, convergence of the banking systems is found in terms of loans to government sectors as well as loans to the private sector, but not in terms of loans to public enterprises. These results emphasize the differences in the role of bank loans to public enterprises in some transition economies; possibly reflect different rates of progress with the resolution of bank bad-debt problems and privatization of state-owned enterprises. For the same group of transition economies, convergence of the banking systems is also found in terms of demand deposits and foreign liabilities, but not in terms of time and savings deposits. These results suggest that the banking systems of the transition economies have converged only in certain key aspects of their intermediated roles, but the overall convergence is yet to be achieved. This may reflect different rates of progress in developing alternative (to bank) savings instruments.

With respect to the larger group that encompasses the banking systems of transitional as well as EU countries, convergence of the banking systems is found only in terms of loans to the private sector, but not in terms of loans to government sectors. These results emphasize the differences in the role of bank loans to government in this group of countries; the banking systems have yet to achieve convergence in that respect, but this may reflect lack of progress with fiscal deficit reduction in transition economies relative to that achieved, post-Maastricht, in the EU and relative lack of progress with respect to developing domestic government bond markets as an alternative to bank finance. For the same group of EU and transition economies, convergence of the banking systems is also found in terms of foreign liabilities, but not in terms of demand deposits and time and savings deposits. This is likely to reflect the lack in developing non-bank financial intermediary and instruments in the transition, and some EU, economies. These results suggest that the banking systems of the transition economies have converged on the EU model only in certain key aspects of their intermediate roles, but that overall convergence is yet to be achieved especially in terms of bank loans to government as well as the mobilization of time and savings deposits. Convergence in these areas is likely to follow from further capital market developments in transition and some EU countries.

NOTES

1. This concept of convergence should not be confused with an alternative meaning of convergence in which the dispersion of bank output would tend to fall over time. In this chapter, we argue that even if absolute convergence holds in our sense, the dispersion of bank output growth rates does not decline over time.
2. The program DPD (dynamic panel data) has been used in the estimations (Arrelano and Bond 1988).
3. This is a group of transition economies, whose homogeneity derives from a broadly common heritage and some similarities in the transition process. However, the group includes clear candidates for joining the EU in the very short term as well as those whose prospects are long term.
4. This comprises a group of transition countries that are aspiring to join the EU in the near future: some of the countries (the Czech Republic, Poland, Estonia) in this group are regarded as having very good prospects of doing so, while others are candidates for a second wave of entry. Conformable data were not available on two expected first-wave entrants, Hungary and Slovenia.

REFERENCES

Ahn, Seung C. and Peter Schmidt (1997), 'Efficient estimation of dynamic panel data models: alternative assumptions and simplified estimation', *Journal of Econometrics*, **76** (1–2), 309–21.

Arrelano, M. and S. Bond (1988), 'Dynamic panel data estimation using DPD: a guide for users', Institute of Fiscal Studies Working Paper 88/15, London: IFS.

Arrelano, M. and S. Bond (1991), 'Some tests of specification for panel data: Monte Carlo evidence and an application to employment equations', *Review of Economic Studies*, **68**, 277–97.

Arrelano, M. and O. Bover (1995), 'Another look at the instrumental variables estimation of error-component models', *Journal of Econometrics*, **68**, 29–51.

Bahra, P., C.J. Green and V. Murinde (1997), 'Coping with financial reforms in transition economies: what have we learned?', in T. Kowalski (ed.), *Financial Reform in Emerging Market Economies*, Poznan: University of Poznan Press, pp. 11–39.

Barro, R.J. and X.X. Sala-i-Martin (1995), *Economic Growth*, New York: McGraw-Hill.

Baumol, W.J., R.R. Nelson and E.N. Wolff (1994), 'Introduction: the convergence of productivity, its significance and its varied connotations', in Baumol, Nelson and Wolff (eds), *Convergence of Productivity*, Oxford: Oxford University Press.

Bernard,A.B. and S.N. Durlauf (1996), 'Interpreting tests of the convergence hypothesis', *Journal of Econometrics*, **71**, 161–73.

Buch, C.M. (1996), *Creating Efficient Banking Systems: Theory and Evidence from Eastern Europe*, Tübingen: J.C.B Mohr (Paul Siebeck).

Doukas, J., V. Murinde and C. Wihlborg (1998), *Financial Sector Reform and Privatization in Transition Economies*, Amsterdam: North-Holland.

Mullineux, A.W. (1992), 'Introduction', in Mullineux (ed.), *European Banking*, Oxford: Basil Blackwell, pp. 1–11.

Mullineux, A.W. (1998), 'Banking sector restructuring in transition economies', in Doukas, Murinde and Wihlborg (eds), Ch. 2, pp. 21–33.

Murinde, V. (1992), 'Microeconomic policy in the banking industry: the implications of policy regime change involving financial restructuring', in D.P. Doessel (ed.), *Micro-economic Policy and Reform for International Competitiveness*, Brisbane: The Economic Society of Australia (Queensland), Inc, pp. 465–76.

Quah, D. (1993), 'Empirical cross-section dynamics in economic growth', *European Economic Review*, **37**, pp. 426–43.

Sala-i-Martin, X.X. (1996), 'Regional cohesion: evidence and theories of regional growth and convergence', *European Economic Review*, **40**, pp. 1325–52.

Walter, I. (1998), 'Design of financial systems and economic transformation', in Doukas, Murinde and Wihlborg (eds), Ch. 6, pp. 123–51.

Index